MIGRATION GOVERNANCE IN NORTH AMERICA

MCGILL-QUEEN'S REFUGEE AND FORCED MIGRATION STUDIES

Series editors: Megan Bradley and James Milner

Forced migration is a local, national, regional, and global challenge with profound political and social implications. Understanding the causes and consequences of, and possible responses to, forced migration requires careful analysis from a range of disciplinary perspectives, as well as interdisciplinary dialogue.

The purpose of the McGill-Queen's Refugee and Forced Migration Studies series is to advance in-depth examination of diverse forms, dimensions, and experiences of displacement, including in the context of conflict and violence, repression and persecution, and disasters and environmental change. The series will explore responses to refugees, internal displacement, and other forms of forced migration to illuminate the dynamics surrounding forced migration in global, national, and local contexts, including Canada, the perspectives of displaced individuals and communities, and the connections to broader patterns of human mobility. Featuring research from fields including politics, international relations, law, anthropology, sociology, geography, and history, the series highlights new and critical areas of enquiry within the field, especially conversations across disciplines and from the perspective of researchers in the global South, where the majority of forced migration unfolds. The series benefits from an international advisory board made up of leading scholars in refugee and forced migration studies.

8 Documenting Displacement
Questioning Methodological Boundaries in Forced Migration Research
Edited by Katarzyna Grabska and Christina R. Clark-Kazak

9 Voluntary and Forced Migration in Latin America
Law and Policy Reforms
Edited by Natalia Caicedo Camacho and Luisa Feline Freier

10 The Right to Research
Historical Narratives by Refugee and Global South Researchers
Edited by Kate Reed and Marcia C. Schenck

11 Kingdom of Barracks
Polish Displaced Persons in Allied-Occupied Germany and Austria
Katarzyna Nowak

12 Urban Refugees and Digital Technology
Reshaping Social, Political, and Economic Networks
Charles Martin-Shields

13 Migration Governance in North America
Policy, Politics, and Community
Edited by Kiran Banerjee and Craig Damian Smith

Migration Governance in North America

Policy, Politics, and Community

Edited by

Kiran Banerjee and Craig Damian Smith

McGill-Queen's University Press
Montreal & Kingston • London • Chicago

ISBN 978-0-2280-2047-9 (paper)
ISBN 978-0-2280-2048-6 (ePDF)
ISBN 978-0-2280-2049-3 (ePUB)
ISBN 978-0-2280-2050-9 (OA)

Legal deposit second quarter 2024
Bibliothèque nationale du Québec

Printed in Canada on acid-free paper that is 100% ancient forest free (100% post-consumer recycled), processed chlorine free

This book has been published with the help of a grant from the Canadian Federation for the Humanities and Social Sciences, through the Awards to Scholarly Publications Program, using funds provided by the Social Sciences and Humanities Research Council of Canada.

Funded by the Government of Canada | Financé par le gouvernement du Canada | Canada | Canada Council for the Arts | Conseil des arts du Canada

We acknowledge the support of the Canada Council for the Arts.
Nous remercions le Conseil des arts du Canada de son soutien.

McGill-Queen's University Press in Montreal is on land which long served as a site of meeting and exchange amongst Indigenous Peoples, including the Haudenosaunee and Anishinabeg nations. In Kingston it is situated on the territory of the Haudenosaunee and Anishinaabek. We acknowledge and thank the diverse Indigenous Peoples whose footsteps have marked these territories on which peoples of the world now gather.

Library and Archives Canada Cataloguing in Publication

Title: Migration governance in North America : policy, politics, and community / edited by Kiran Banerjee and Craig Damian Smith.
Names: Banerjee, Kiran, 1983– editor. | Smith, Craig Damian, author.
Series: McGill-Queen's refugee and forced migration studies ; 13.
Description: Series statement: McGill-Queen's refugee and forced migration studies ; 13 | Includes bibliographical references and index.
Identifiers: Canadiana (print) 20230577083 | Canadiana (ebook) 20230577113 | ISBN 9780228020479 (softcover) | ISBN 9780228020493 (ePUB) | ISBN 9780228020509 (OA) | ISBN 9780228020486 (ePDF)
Subjects: LCSH: Immigrants—Government policy—North America. | LCSH: Refugees—Government policy—North America. | LCSH: North America Emigration and immigration.
Classification: LCC JV6351.M54 2024 | DDC 304.87—dc23

This book was typeset in 10/13 Sabon.

This book is dedicated to the memory of Joseph Garcea.

Joseph was an original organizer of the initiative that informs this book and his contributions remain an indelible part of the project. Indeed, it was through innumerable discussions involving Joseph that the core ideas informing this volume began to take concrete form, with his direct involvement continuing until just the month before his passing in the fall of 2020.

Joseph was born in the town of Satriano, in the Calabria region of southern Italy. Although his subsequent scholarly and public policy contributions range across such areas as Canadian municipal policy, indigenous politics, refugee resettlement, multiculturalism, and theorizing the nature of citizenship and diversity in Canada, Joseph's abiding and intense engagement with migration remained a constant through his academic career. Indeed, there is a discernible line between Joseph's doctoral study on "Federal-Provincial Relations in Immigration," emphasizing the role of asymmetrical federalism, and his continued scholarship focused on understanding the complex, and increasingly transnational, dynamics of multileveled governance in migration policy – an important focal point of this project.

Joseph's first academic appointment, which he took up while completing his dissertation, was at the University of Saskatchewan; this was where he spent his entire career as a teacher and scholar. During his time at the University of Saskatchewan Joseph published prolifically, contributed his expertise to municipal, provincial, and federal governance, proved a paragon of university service, as well as mentored and supported both graduate students and early career faculty. His commitment to teaching – reflected by the graduate students he directly supervised and the additional thirty-seven committees he served on – was also marked by the multiple awards for teaching he received, including one of the highest honour the University of Saskatchewan offers to faculty, the Master Teaching Award.

Joseph was a remarkable human being who enriched the lives of many through his kindness, generosity, thoughtfulness, and insight. He is very much missed.

Contents

Figures and Tables

FIGURES

TABLES

Acknowledgments

We would like to thank everyone who has supported and advanced the development of this project and helped in the production of the edited volume.

First of all, we would like to thank the contributors for their many hours of hard work from our initial full-day workshop in February of 2021 to the many subsequent rounds of editorial feedback and exchange that followed. Their commitment to devote significant time and energy were integral to producing a collective intellectual endeavour that we are very proud to have out in the world.

Thanks is also due to Dalhousie University, Canada Excellence Research Chair in Migration and Integration Program at Toronto Metropolitan University, and the University of Saskatchewan for their institutional support at various key stages. We are also grateful to the Social Sciences and Humanities Research Council of Canada Connection Grants program, which provided essential funding for organizing the initial workshop on which this collection is based, as well as facilitating the publication of the volume.

We are particularly grateful for the work of Leah Simonot, who helped prepare the manuscript for the review process and publication, Shaanzéh Ataullahjan, who provided important assistance in planning and organizing the workshop, as well as to Adrian Aquino, who provided valuable research assistance to Joseph Garcea in the initial stages of this project. We would also like to thank Abha Agarwal for expertly copyediting the manuscript, Selin Kepenek for helping us map the major concepts across chapters, and Elena Gwynne for combining precision and speed when developing the index for the volume.

In addition, we would like to thank Emily Andrew, Jonathan Crago, and Kathleen Fraser for their guidance throughout the publication process, as well as all the staff at McGill-Queen's University Press who worked on the production of the volume. We are grateful for the initial encouragement and support provided by Megan Bradley and James Milner in their role as the series editors of McGill-Queen's Refugee and Forced Migration Studies series.

The editors would like to express our sincere gratitude to the anonymous reviewers for their insightful comments and constructive suggestions; their generous feedback enhanced and strengthened the book manuscript as a whole. Finally, we would like to thank David FitzGerald, Randall Hansen, Daniel Quinlan, and Anna Triandafyllidou for their advice and support at key stages of this project.

This book has been published with the help of a grant from the Federation for the Humanities and Social Sciences, through the Awards to Scholarly Publications Program, using funds provided by the Social Sciences and Humanities Research Council of Canada. We are grateful for the support this program has provided not only to our project, but to Canada's broader scholarly community.

Abbreviations

AASW	Alberta Assembly of Social Workers
ACA	Asylum Cooperative Agreement
ACCBP	Anti-Crime Capacity Building Program (Canada)
AFL-CIO	American Federation of Labor and Congress of Industrial Organizations
AIC	American Immigration Council
AMLO	Andrés Manuel López Obrador
API	Advance Passenger Information
APIS	Advance Passenger Information System (US)
BVOR	Blended Visa Office-Referred (Canada)
CARSI	Central America Regional Security Initiative
CBP	Customs and Border Protection (US)
CBSA	Canada Border Services Agency
CCINM	Consejo Consultivo del Instituto Nacional de Migración
CCPM	Consejo Consultivo de Política Migratoria
CEC	Canadian Experience Class
CEAS	Common European Asylum System
CEPAL/ECLAC	Comisión Económica para América Latina y el Caribe / Economic Commission for Latin America and the Caribbean
CIAIMM	Comisión Intersecretarial de Atención Integral en Materia Migratoria
CICR/ICRC	Comité Internacional de la Cruz Roja/International Committee of the Red Cross
CJEU	Court of Justice of the European Union
COMAR	Comisión Mexicana de Ayuda a Refugiados [Mexican Refugee Aid Commission]

CRRF	Comprehensive Refugee Response Framework
CSI	Container Security Initiative
CSO	Civil Society Organization
DAC	Development Assistance Committee
DACA	Deferred Action for Childhood Arrivals (US)
DCO	Designated country of origin
DED	Deferred Enforced Departure
DFN	Designated foreign national(s)
DHS	Department of Homeland Security (US)
DOF	Diario Oficial de la Federación (Mexico)
EASO	European Asylum Support Office; also, European Union Agency for Asylum (EUAA)
ECHR	European Court of Human Right
ECOWAS	Economic Community of West African States
EES	Entry-Exit System
ENI	European Neighbourhood Instrument
ENPI	European Neighbourhood and Partnership Instrument
ESTA	Electronic System for Travel Authorization
ETIAS	European Travel Information and Authorization System
EU	European Union
EUROJUST	European Union Agency for Criminal Justice Cooperation
EUROPOL	European Union Agency for Law Enforcement Cooperation
EUTF	European Union Emergency Trust Fund for Africa
FCC	Five Country Conference
FEMA	Federal Emergency Management Agency
FLACSO	Facultad Latinoamericana de Ciencias Sociales
FLQ	Front de libération du Québec
FSWP	Federal Skilled Worker Program (Canada)
G7	Group of Seven
GAM	Global Approach to Migration
GAMM	Global Approach to Migration and Mobility
GAR	Government-assisted refugee(s)
GCIM	Global Commission on International Migration
GCM	Global Compact for Safe, Orderly, and Regular Migration
GCR	Global Compact on Refugees
GDP	Gross domestic product
GFMD	Global Forum on Migration and Development
GMG	Global Migration Group

GNI	Gross national income
GTHA	Greater Toronto Hamilton Area
HLPF	United Nations High-Level Political Forum on Sustainable Development
IACHR	Inter-American Commission on Human Rights
IASC	United Nations Inter-Agency Standing Committee
IATA	International Air Transportation Agency
IBET	Integrated Border Enforcement Team
ICAO	International Civil Aviation Organization
ICE	Immigration and Customs Enforcement (US)
ICRMW	International Convention on the Protection of the Rights of All Migrant Workers and Members of Their Families
ICSS	Integrated Cargo Security Strategy
IDMC	Internal Displacement Monitoring Centre
IDP	Internally displaced person
IFRC	International Federation of Red Cross and Red Crescent Societies
IGC	Intergovernmental Consultations on Asylum and Immigration
IGO	Intergovernmental organization
IIRIRA	Illegal Immigration Reform and Immigrant Responsibility Act (US)
ILO	International Labour Organization
IMF	International Monetary Fund
IMP	International Mobility Program
IMRF	International Migration Review Forum
INA	Immigration and Nationality Act (US)
INM	Instituto Nacional de Migración (Mexico)
INS	Immigration and Naturalization Service (US)
IOM/OIM	International Organization for Migration / Organización Internacional para las Migraciones
IPCC	Intergovernmental Panel on Climate Change
IR	International Relations
IRB	Immigration and Refugee Board (Canada)
IRPA	Immigration and Refugee Protection Act (Canada)
JAP	Joint Action Plan
LAC	Latin America and the Caribbean
LIBE	Committee on Civil Liberties, Justice and Home Affairs (EU)
LMIA	Labour Market Impact Assessment
MCC	Millennium Challenge Corporation

MENA	Middle East and North Africa
MERCOSUR	Mercado Común del Sur / Southern Common Market
MIRPS	Marco Integral Regional para la Protección y Soluciones [Comprehensive Regional Protection and Solutions Framework]
MOU	Memorandum(s) of understanding
MPP	Migrant Protection Protocols
MTCR	Mexican Transit Control Regime
NAFTA	North American Free Trade Agreement
NDICI	Neighbourhood Development and International Cooperation Instrument
NGO	Nongovernmental organization
OAS	Organization of American States
OAU	Organization of African Unity
ODA	Official development assistance
OECD	Organisation for Economic Co-operation and Development
PDI	Plan de Desarrollo Integral para El Salvador-Guatemala-Honduras-México
PDTBS	Policy Dialogue on Transport and Border Security
PEM	Programa Especial de Migración 2014–18
PHARE	Pologne-Hongrie Actions pour la Reconversion Économique
PICMME	Provisional Intergovernmental Committee for the Movement of Migrants from Europe
PNP	Provincial Nominee Program (Canada)
PNR	Passenger name record
PPC	People's Party of Canada
PRM	Bureau of Population, Refugees, and Migration (US)
PSR	Private Sponsorship of Refugees / Privately sponsored refugee(s)
PTA	Protection Transfer Agreement
R4V	Inter-Agency Coordination Platform for Refugee and Migrants from Venezuela
RAD	Refugee Appeal Division
RCMP	Royal Canadian Mounted Police
RCP	Regional Consultative Process
RSD	Refugee status determination
SAB	Solidarity Across Borders
SADC	Southern African Development Community
SAH	Sponsorship Agreement Holder(s)

SAWP	Seasonal Agricultural Workers Program
SDG	UN Sustainable Development Goal(s)
SEGOB	Secretaría de Gobernación (Mexico)
SIDA	Swedish International Development Agency
SPP	Security and Prosperity Partnership
SRE	Secretaría de Relaciones Exteriores (Mexico)
STCA	US–Canada Safe Third Country Agreement / Canada–US Safe Third Country Agreement
TACIS	Technical Assistance to the Commonwealth of Independent States
TFW	Temporary foreign worker
TPD	Temporary Protection Directive
TPS	Temporary Protected Status
TRAC	Transactional Records Access Clearinghouse
TRIP	Traveler Redress Inquiry Program
TRP	Temporary resident permit
UN	United Nations
UNGA	UN General Assembly
UNHCR	United Nations High Commissioner for Refugees
UNRWA	United Nations Relief and Works Agency for Palestine Refugees in the Near East
UPM	Unidad de Política Migratoria (Mexico)
US-VISIT	United States Visitor Status Indicator Technology
USAID	US Agency for International Development
USCIS	United States Citizenship and Immigration Services
USMCA	United States-Mexico-Canada Agreement
USRAP	United States Refugee Admissions Program
WCO	World Customs Organization
WFP	World Food Programme
WHO	World Health Organization
WRMC	World Refugee and Migration Council

MIGRATION GOVERNANCE IN NORTH AMERICA

Continuity and Change in North American Migration Governance

Kiran Banerjee and Craig Damian Smith

Over five years have elapsed since the UN General Assembly affirmed the Global Compact on Refugees (GCR) and Global Compact for Safe, Orderly, and Regular Migration (GCM) in 2018. The development of this set of non-binding frameworks was undertaken partly as an international response to the growing perception of a series of intersecting global and regional migration and asylum crises – though calls for global governance regimes for migration have ebbed and flowed for decades (see Ghosh 2000, 2007; Sutherland 2017). While the proximate sources of political will for these efforts lay partly in the scale of displacement in war-torn regions of the world, the perception of crises was firmly rooted in the staggered, and then sudden, response of Global North states, particularly within Europe, to the effects of forced and mixed migration flows on their territory. Yet, far from mitigating crisis narratives and attendant policy responses, the intervening period has seen the unfolding of only widening discourses of uncontrolled migration across the Atlantic, which in turn have seen states adopt increasingly reactive policies. Migration and cross-border mobility more broadly have remained highly politicized and contested for some time, holding significant salience for interstate relations across the region. However, the issues of border security, immigration, asylum, and irregular arrivals have become only more prominent flashpoints in Canadian, American, and Mexican domestic politics, transborder relations, and regional dialogues.

Indeed, migration both within and to North America has witnessed significant changes over the past decade, which have increasingly placed transnational mobility at the forefront of politics across the continent. These developments include the emergence and seeming entrenchment of xenophobic populism in the US with troubling parallels already apparent in Canada; marked shifts in migration and security dynamics at the US-Mexico border; increased intercontinental mixed migration to and through Mexico; the replacement of the North American Free Trade Agreement (NAFTA) with a new trade and high-skilled worker mobility framework; emerging political implications and civil society mobilization around low-wage, temporary labour migration from Latin America and the Caribbean to the US and Canada; new forms of international cooperation to address displacement crises in Central and South America; unprecedented restrictions in American asylum and resettlement policy and subsequent moves to expand refugee settlement under the Biden administration; Canadian constitutional challenges to existing bilateral asylum coordination arrangements with the US; broader changes in forced displacement flows affecting North America as a whole, and conversely, the continent's effects on global responses to international displacement and demand for migration management. Most recently, the COVID-19 pandemic triggered unprecedented border shutdowns on a global scale, extending far further in scope and duration than the prior security-related border measures imposed by the United States in the immediate wake of 9/11 two decades earlier. The pandemic's ripple effects continue to be felt both across North America and globally at the time of writing, highlighting the deep interdependences between migration, transnational public health coordination, and the continent's broader political economy. Finally, the ongoing war in Ukraine has resulted in a set of new forced migration dynamics, where the welcome given to displaced Ukrainians in Europe and North America stands in stark contrast to widespread attempts to prevent asylum migration from the Global South – highlighting the potential for innovative approaches to displacement within the continent, while also illustrating the divergent treatment accorded to forced migrants from other parts of the world. Each of these developments comes with attendant political and policy implications at various levels of analysis.

This collection therefore comes at a pivotal moment of potential transformation, but also one defined by the retrenchment of established migration control dynamics and the adoption of policies that suggest a questionable commitment to upholding and respecting the rights of migrants of all categories. The confluence and impact of the aforementioned changes are yet to be addressed in a comprehensive volume – a lacuna which we intend to address in the interest of both contemporary analysis and informing future scholarship by drawing together an array of theoretical concepts, and by providing a series of deeper explorations into a range of topics around human mobility throughout the hemisphere. This book's goal is to advance our understanding of migration dynamics across North America, with a particular focus on intersecting policy frameworks operating in different issue areas. These include labour mobility, border security and controls, asylum and refugee policy, foreign policies of migration containment, forms of solidarity with precarious populations, and immigration and resettlement. Despite divergent imperatives, states, humanitarian groups, international organizations, and civil society recognize (at least in principle) that addressing complex migration dynamics within the region requires a higher degree of coherence and coordination that advances beyond existing multileveled migration policy frameworks. This modest consensus would appear to be informed by the two Global Compacts, as well as more nascent regional measures, including the creation of a private refugee sponsorship program in the US or the interregional development and migration plans evidenced in the June 2022 Los Angeles Declaration from the Summit of the Americas. Paralleling the relatively limited state of current policy across the continent is a need for new scholarship focused on emerging frameworks for managing migration in and to North America, as well as situating the continent within contemporary research on global governance and transnational migration flows.

To this end, this book offers an interdisciplinary and comparative approach to the study of mobilities in North America. As we elaborate below, the contributions that follow take a broad and holistic approach to conceptualizing regional migration governance in this volume, including contributions from political science, demography, geography, and sociology. While to date, scholarship on migration governance in North America has emphasized the continent's "lack of regionalism" in relation to other contexts including Europe, West Africa, or South America, it is nonetheless marked by deep regional interdependence, in addition to engagement with global migration governance, and has generated significant policy impacts on international mobility dynamics. In short, while often characterized by a dearth of formalized mobility arrangements from a comparative perspective, the region is defined by a high degree of cross-border movement, is a crucial destination for a range of categories of migrants, and includes a broad set of interactions between key state and substate actors which significantly influence both regional and international mobility dynamics.

As the editors of this book, our goal across the volume is to advance the understanding of migration governance within and between three North American countries – US, Canada, and Mexico – and their intersections at the global level. We hope that the interdisciplinary and cross-regional contributions that this initiative brings together will address some of the policy issues described earlier, and shed light on the more informal and often fragmented arrangements that constitute North American migration governance. The various analytic lenses and frameworks will be of interest to scholars and students from across different fields and disciplines. The contributors' focus on empirical case studies, analyzed from a rich field of theoretical insights, offers a new and coherent set of observations on North American migration governance, to both policymakers and academic readers alike, at a time that is crucial for continental and global mobility dynamics.

In the remainder of this introduction, we aim to accomplish two tasks. The first is to provide a general account of the state of cross-border mobilities in North America as well as broadly situate this volume's set of interventions within existing scholarship. This will serve to locate the subsequent chapters not only in the context of North America, but in the larger field of migration studies where increased attention has been devoted to grappling with the implications of various forms of regionalized governance. Given the inherently transnational and cross-disciplinary nature of migration studies, our overview has the modest objective of contextualizing the contributions in this volume relative to prior studies focused on North America, while aiming to act as a point of departure for framing future research in this context. The second purpose of the introduction is to problematize and flesh out the core concepts – *migration*, *governance*, and North America as a *region* – that inform the volume as a whole. Our aim here is to set the groundwork for advancing a nuanced perspective for approaching cross-border mobility across the continent by highlighting – and troubling – some of the key assumptions underlying these concepts. This in turn will offer a preliminary analytic frame for engaging with the wide range of disciplinary and theoretical perspectives taken up by the contributors to this volume.

NORTH AMERICAN MOBILITIES IN CONTEXT

North America is a crucial site for understanding the dynamics of contemporary mobility governance, with regard to both the region and beyond. Perhaps most significantly, the continent as a whole is a major destination for permanent immigration from around the globe – accounting for almost 20 per cent of the world's migrants (for a full picture, see Budiman 2020). As a regional, and indeed international, hegemon, the US is an exemplary "migration state" in the sense of Hollifield's (2004) compelling framing of the tensions implicit in contemporary forms of independency in the domain of cross-border mobility. The US has more immigrants than any country in the world, with over a quarter originally from Mexico; more than one million have arrived in the US per year over the last decade (Budiman 2020). During the same period, between 200 thousand and 300 thousand newcomers have come to Canada – which has until recently set targets of attracting up to 500,000 annually. If successfully implemented, this would amount to an official immigration intake rate well over one per cent of the 40 million threshold the country's population broke in June 2023 – largely due to the impact of immigration – further contributing to the already significant 21 per cent of the Canadian population being foreign-born. Mexico too has seen significant developments in its immigration patterns – shifting from a country of predominately outward emigration to the US, to seeing the rise of significant return migration over the past two decades (Masferrer and Roberts 2012). A key catalyst for this has been sustained economic development in Mexico; while arguably initially contributing to enabling outward migration, increased domestic opportunities combined with the long-term impacts of the 2007–08 economic crisis in the US had made Mexico a net receiver of immigration (Passel, Cohn, and González-Barrera 2012).

Overall, the number of migrants in North America has more than doubled over the last thirty years. These patterns of large-scale migration in the region, as well as more broadly, are tied to global demand for mobility in complex ways. According to international opinion-polling, the US and Canada are the top two desired destinations for the world's 750 million people with aspirations to emigrate – a demand which far exceeds the admittedly significant immigration goals that currently exist in North America (Esipova, Pugliese, and Ray 2018). Although not historically characterized as a country of immigration, Mexico's involvement in cross-border mobility has been both enduring and significant. The country remains the Western hemisphere's largest recipient of cash remittances, and is the third-largest recipient globally after China and India, receiving over USD 43 billion annually. The vast majority of those remittances come from family members in the US, and to a lesser degree Canada (McAuliffe and Triandafyllidou 2022). However, the scale of cross-border remittance flows has decreased in recent years, due in part to large-scale return migration from the US. More broadly, the past decade has seen a significant shift for Mexico from being defined – both domestically and internationally – as a country of emigration, to a newer regional role primarily as a country of destination and transit for migrants arriving from the southern hemisphere and beyond.

Likewise, together the US and Canada resettle the highest number of the world's refugees among the twenty-six states who consistently conduct resettlement. The drastic decline in resettlement under the Trump administration (which slashed resettlement from 100,000 to 15,000 annually over four years) pushed Canada into the top resettlement position in 2018. However, it remains a fact that together the two states continue to be crucial actors in the international communities' efforts at maintaining resettlement as a durable solution to forced displacement. The region is also the site of significant mixed migration and asylum flows, with increasingly global importance. Mexico has seen a shift in transit migration predominantly from Central and South America, to increasing intercontinental mixed migration en route to the US and Canada (Freier and Holloway 2019; Yates 2019). The country has more recently become a site of containment for hundreds of thousands of migrants as a result of the Trump administration's control policies, including Title 42 and the so-called Migrant Protection Protocols (more consistently and aptly referred to as "Remain in Mexico" policies). At the time of writing, the former were only recently rearticulated under the Biden administration after belated efforts to reverse these policies were blocked by the US federal courts, but then reinvigorated with new policies to curtail asylum migration, subtended by new resettlement pathways for displaced people from Cuba, Haiti, Nicaragua, and Venezuela. The resulting situation is one that starkly contradicts election campaign promises, as a result of domestic intransigence around comprehensive immigration reform at the federal level and tensions between federal and state policies, but also suggests the potential normalization of what were viewed as dramatic and controversial policy shifts in the US context.

Existing migration governance regimes in the Western hemisphere are functionally divided between North America, Central America, and South America. The North American Free Trade Agreement (NAFTA) and its successor are only weakly tied to Central America though a regional consultative mechanism (the Puebla Process), with insignificant levels of actual mobility resulting from it. Indeed, both NAFTA and the more recent USMCA (United States–Mexico–Canada Agreement) contain relatively marginal mobility arrangements, with these limited to narrow high-skilled labour migration streams. While there have been efforts to engage the Inter-American Commission on Human Rights (IACHR) of the Organization of American States (OAS) to address issues related to asylum access, these have had limit impacts on state practice to date. Moreover, while both the US and Canada rely on low-wage migration from Latin America and the Caribbean to fill crucial sectors of their economies including the agricultural, domestic care, and service industries, both countries increasingly focus on attracting high-skilled immigrants and eschew any binding regional agreements (Bloemraad 2014; Besco and Tolley 2019).

This means North America is something of a global outlier, since most of its formalized mobility arrangements are bilateral or regional (Hansen 2011; Hollifield and Wong 2015). Regional migration governance is often highly segmented between issue areas – thus high-skilled labour mobility, short-term temporary foreign worker schemes, asylum admissions, and coordination around displacement crises are the purview of different laws, norms, institutions, and practices. Robust migration governance frameworks are often an outgrowth of regional economic integration (as was the case with the development of the EU's Schengen regime) rather than a primary driver of regional integration (Lavenex 2019). Even though trade and economic integration are significant between Mexico, the US, and Canada, these states maintain a high degree of formal control and discretion over the movement of people in comparison to other transboundary flows. Under NAFTA and its recently renegotiated successor USMCA, mobility arrangements continue to focus on certain high-wage sectors with limited periods of residence tied to employment. However, some evidence suggests that the inclusion of the rights covered under the North American Agreement on Labour Cooperation has given rise to new forms of transnational solidarity and activism for vulnerable migrant workers in the US and Canada, particularly through the advocacy of trade unions in Mexico (Gabriel and Macdonald 2020). In the context of asylum and refugee policy, there is no fully regionalized coordination across the continent; nothing resembling the innovations of the Cartagena Declaration, the OAU (Organization of African Unity) Convention, or the EU's Common European Asylum System. The limited bilateral mechanisms that have emerged make no efforts to substantively expand international protection or harmonized standards for recognizing refugee status, but instead appear to be explicitly aimed at enhancing states' abilities to minimize their obligations toward asylum seekers.

However, this does not imply that no migration governance exists, rather that it is more analytically and politically complicated to unpack. Geddes (2021, 139) characterizes North America as a "region without regionalism," yet points out various levels of de facto governance repertoires. Hadj Abdou's (2019) concept of "double bilateralism," highlighting weak regionalism but strong borders as well as the role of power asymmetries, recognizes that both Mexico and Canada often defer to US interests, and are often put in the position of reacting to its policy preferences. Similarly, Lavenex (2019) describes North American migration governance as comprised of limited mobility rights, but with a strong and predominant focus on advancing control agendas in interactions with Latin America. Moreover, while linked in terms of trade through NAFTA and later USMCA, the goals of these modes of regional integration focus largely on the trade of goods and services, rather than on enabling the movement of people. Likewise, both Canada and Mexico are functionally integrated with US security and immigration authorities to facilitate the cross-border mobility of preferred travellers, but more often to control the movement of unwanted migration (Konrad and Nicol 2016). It is worth emphasizing the import of interstate power relations within the region. The US remains the undisputed economic and military hegemon in North America, with significant capacity to influence neighbours' policy decisions, both indirectly and directly. This has been perhaps most apparent in the context of American-Mexican relations; and, more recently, during the term of the Trump administration the

US has demonstrated an overt willingness to very publicly engage in coercive issue-linkage to force migration policy outcomes on Mexico. However, a more ecumenical field of study on regionalism helps us understand that migration governance can be analyzed both "from above," i.e., through state-led and international frameworks, and "from below," i.e., by looking at the role of migrant agency, civil society, and integration (Lavenex and Piper 2021).

To this end, this book draws from a broad field of scholarship that seeks to understand migration governance from several perspectives in order to offer readers a wide variety of insights, and to inform future research on migration governance in and from North America. Regional migration governance frameworks are diverse both in practice and in terms of their drivers (Lavenex et al. 2016). In North America, cooperation and interstate agreements are largely ad hoc and reactive. State sovereignty, combined with sustained US dominance of the region, largely defines the parameters and limitations of formal agreements. Yet it must also be recognized that even in the EU's Schengen area – the world's most developed space of free mobility – enforcement mechanisms for responsibility-sharing around forced displacement are profoundly politicized, prone to internal burden-shifting, and focused on externalized migration controls to keep asylum seekers at bay (Gottwald 2014; Greenhill 2016; Thielemann 2018).

Political discourse and the domestic framings that inform public perceptions of North American migration governance reflect contending dynamics which are most pronounced in the US and Canada. On the one hand, cross-border migration is often depoliticized when it comes to the majority of skilled workers or family-class immigrants arriving every year, while state-sanctioned cross-border mobilities related to business, tourisms, or personal travel, are usually even less central in public discourse. On the other hand, it remains a deeply contested area where cooperation and sovereign interests are both arrayed to harness immigration and emigration for economic benefit, but also to deter and deflect unwanted mobility, and mobilized at the domestic level for electoral gain – often by populist anti-immigrant parties and politicians. Carmel, Lenner, and Paul (2021) conceptualize the study of migration governance as encapsulating the practices of both governance and contestation against both formal and informal modes of controlling it. The plurality of topics and theories herein uncover and analyze multiple fields of governance. Such dynamics are often glossed over by positive analysis of North America as a site of significant immigration and refugee resettlement and thus providing improved life-chances for millions of people. Alternatively, in the more cautious and critical takes advanced by migration scholars, state sovereignty is viewed as the primary driver of policymaking, with consequent effects on managing migration organized to maximize economic and political gains, often at the expense of the rights of vulnerable people on the move.

In each of the chapters in this volume we have asked our authors to reflect not only on their particular site of analysis, but to explore the ways in which their findings advance our understanding of migration governance. These interventions are therefore meant to interrogate the nature of migration policies and practices in a continent defined by the lack of regionalism, but with deep and important ties to global mobility regimes. Likewise, the chapters recognize in different ways that despite the calls for safe, orderly, and well-managed migration at the global level, the most politically-salient migration dynamics are inherently "messy," and so is their governance (Triandafyllidou 2021). One key area not covered in the volume is the role of diaspora and immigrant communities, and how these communities affect and are affected by mobilities throughout the region. Here we point readers to excellent work on this subject, including Xóchitl Bada's *Mexican Hometown Associations in Chicagoacán* (2014), Alexandra Délano's *From Here and There: Diaspora Policies, Integration, and Social Rights Beyond Borders* (2018), and Adrián Félix's *Specters of Belonging: The Political Life Cycle of Mexican Migrants* (2019) to name but a few contemporary studies.

The interventions that inform this book not only coincide and engage with an increasingly rapid series of shifts in regional mobility, but also the coalescence of more long-term trends. To our knowledge, no contemporary collection addresses the study of mobility in North America from a regionalized and transnational perspective, despite the need for a critical approach toward the various and varied migration dynamics across the continent. This is not to say that earlier volumes have not engaged with migration in North America; we are beholden to, and attempt to build upon, the earlier work that has approached these dynamics through the broader prisms of regional integration, securitization, or bordering politics.

To take a few of the most prominent examples: written in the wake of 9/11, Andreas and Biersteker's collection, *The Rebordering of North America* (2003), offered an initial early assessment of changes to bilateral and trilateral relations across the continent, triggered by the new security environment and heightened US concerns. An important observation that runs through the volume is that, contrary to expectations of the time, border security and maintaining existing forms of integration across the region would prove compatible in the post-9/11 context. The emphasis of the volume brought together by Andreas and Biersteker is squarely on state actors, and much of the contributors' engagement accordingly takes up the economic and security dimensions of regional cooperation. Written some ten years later, the volume *North American Integration: An Institutional Void in Migration, Security and Development* (2013), edited by Mayer-Foulkes and Genna, engages with a broader set of domains for cross-border cooperation. Their work largely emphasizes the stalled nature of integration across the continent, due to the absence of further institutional development informed by a lack of political will.

From a very different – and far more recent – perspective, Bada and Gleeson's collection, *Accountability Across Borders: Migrant Rights in North America* (2019), gives much-needed attention to the role of civil society actors in shaping mobilities across the continent, even while acknowledging the powerful influence of state interests. Much like the other studies referred to above, Gleeson and Bada's volume offers an incisive analysis of cross-regional dynamics; however, their collection provides a more focused engagement with cross-border mobility and an importantly pluralistic view of the relevant nonstate actors and agents in the domain of migration. Finally, a more recent edited volume *Border and Migration: The Canadian Experience in Comparative Perspective* (Carpenter, Kelly, and Schmidtke 2023) offers important critical insights into Canadian policies and public discourses of Canada as a benevolent and attractive destination for immigrants. Contributions to the volume problematize a range of issues related to how Canadian policy interacts with hemispheric and global migration governance through temporary foreign worker schemes, refugee resettlement, and the digitization of border controls. We build upon these important insights in bringing together a broad array of perspectives that take up varying levels of analysis in their respective engagements with migration and mobility across North America.

By attending to a wide array of actors and overlapping structures of governance, the themes of the volume as a whole follow the lead of recent scholarship emphasizing the importance of multileveled and transnational aspects of migration policy (Caponio and Jones-Correa 2018; Geddes et al. 2019; Lavenex 2018). A focus on these interrelated areas promises to deepen our understanding of the variegated but interconnected governance frameworks, policy webs, and politics in North America. Equally important, various contributions highlight the interdependent and mutually reinforcing dimensions of effective domestic refugee resettlement, multilateral asylum policy, and the transnational dimensions of migration policy in the context of labour mobility and immigrant integration. This work compliments international relations (IR) scholarship on the complex relationships between migration policy and other emerging global governance frameworks impacting mobility, such as the global travel regime (Koslowski 2011). Many of the chapters also build upon existing literatures on regimes as sites for facilitating interstate coordination; while classically articulated by Krasner (1982) as an approach for conceptualizing interstate coordination more broadly, international regimes have proved especially salient in migration studies, offering analytic tools for looking at various dimensions of global migration, as well as connecting regional dynamics with those beyond the continent. In a similar vein, various contributions in the volume draw on analytic frameworks for explaining processes of transgovernmentalism (Keohane and Nye 1974; Slaughter 2005), practice theory (Reckwitz 2002; Schatzki, Knorr-Cetina, and von Savigny 2001), norm diffusion (Finnemore and Sikkink 1998) and localized policy implementation (Betts and Orchard 2014). These frameworks are taken up to explore recent shifts in how different institutional actors at varying levels of governance have responded to cross-border movements in North America. At the same time, a number of contributions offer case studies that complicate various dominant theoretical perspectives in migration studies. These interventions engage with dynamics informing existing forms of regional governance from the standpoint of migrants, displaced persons, as well as domestic publics, in order to draw attention to the variety of nonstate actors and agents that both shape and are impacted by existing institutional arrangements across the continent.

THEORIZING "MIGRATION" AND "GOVERNANCE" IN NORTH AMERICA AS A "REGION"

We acknowledge the delimited nature of our focus on migration governance *within* North America, given the region's extensive interconnections with cross-border mobilities that extend across the hemisphere and globally. Indeed, many of the chapters in this volume highlight the degree to which states identified as within the region impact, and are impacted by, global dynamics. Following earlier scholarship, we therefore explicitly recognize "regions" as contingent social constructions, while simultaneously acknowledging (as IR constructivists have long emphasized) the powerful and pervasive role such constructions can hold in shaping state behaviour. To be sure, regions are by no means uncontested categories and contemporary perceptions of North America are the product of complex historical processes; however, it seems undeniable that shared understandings of North America as a region significantly impact migration governance at multiple levels. This intersubjective dimension of regionalization is only heightened by the status of the US as a global hegemon, with considerable and enduring influence in reifying the terms and contours of regional arrangements in North America, but also by a great deal of historical cross-border engagement in terms of economic or ideational exchange. But equally important, this volume as a whole also takes an explicitly interdisciplinary approach that draws on insights from a range of fields. In doing so, the chapters that follow bring together scholars from across the continent, as well as engage with comparative research from beyond North America, recognizing the importance of an inclusive dialogue to explore regional dynamics.

While the volume focuses on "migration," the contributing chapters take a broad approach to human mobility, encompassing a broader set of phenomena that "official" definitions of global migration often elide or obscure – i.e., the distinction between international and internal migration, state-sanctioned mobilities vs. irregular migration, and forced vs. voluntary (predominantly economic) migration. We do so in order to decentre the state in our framing of the volume as a whole: "international migration" only makes sense against a statist background, but the chapters that follow explicitly engage with multiple levels of analysis. Adopting this stance requires complicating common assumptions about the state as a unitary actor – and integrating how bureaucratic-institutional factors inform particular policies and practices. Taking such an approach also requires expanding our scope of analysis to account for the agency of migrants, the role of civil society, and a broad array of sites of governance and politics operating both above and below, as well as across, the level of the state.

With the above considerations in mind, this volume adopts a capacious – and critical – approach to the concept of *governance*, building on theoretical perspectives from IR theory and more broadly, questioning the standard assumptions about who is governing whom – and to what ends – in the context of understanding North American mobilities. Conventionally, the idea of *government* evokes the central, and indeed sovereign, role of the state which, in Weberian terms, possesses the authority, legitimacy, and coercive means to steer or manage domestic policy and unilaterally determine the contours of interstate relations. Such standard assumptions are quickly upended by the essentially transnational nature of international migration, as well as the broader challenges posed by interdependencies between states that impact both cross-border and domestic mobilities. Here the notion of governance – in both international and global terms – has been deployed to theorize how coordination and cooperation between nominally sovereign states can take place. James Rosenau's (1995, 26) original conception of governance as a "set of norms, rules, arrangements and institutions meant to manage an issue-area in the absence of a central government" highlighted early on how the processes of governance *in* the world are not necessarily governance *of* it (for a full review of the global governance literature, see Domínguez and Flores 2018). A key and influential insight of Rosenau is that governance without government is a complex and often dynamic process that often requires moving beyond the state as the sole locus of analysis, given the important role played by regimes, international norms, and various forms of interdependencies that often engage a variety of nonstate actors.

From the standpoint of theorizing cross-border mobilities, the limitations of a state-centric approach to governance are manifestly obvious: indeed, international migration itself upends a number of assumptions that have long structured debates in the discipline of international relations (Banerjee and Smith 2020). This does not mean that the state – or the role of domestic politics – are unimportant for considering the dynamics of cross-border mobility in North America or more broadly. The domestic political salience of migration means that even in the face of evidence for the need for greater cooperation to manage it and secure the rights of migrants, and the fact that human mobility inherently involves interdependence, ceding sovereignty over borders and access to political community are the exception, rather than the rule. That is particularly the case both within North America and in its relations globally, given deep economic and power asymmetries (see Martin and Weerasinghe 2017).

From a legal perspective, all states in North America are parties to a range of international treaties protecting human rights *writ large* and ascribing particular duties to displaced people. In this sense to a certain extent the governance of migration, while not formally regionalized, is nested in overlapping legal frameworks. However, neither the US nor Canada (along with the majority of Global North states) have signed on to the 1990 International Convention on the Protection of the Rights of All Migrant Workers and Members of Their Families (UNGA 1990). It has long been recognized that despite the positive outcomes of cooperation, collective action around migration governance is remarkably rare (Ghosh 2000). Even when states share interest areas, for example in promoting circular migration, destination states tend to set policy and quotas without meaningful consultation with countries of origin (Lavenex and Piper 2021; Rudolph 2006).

ORGANIZATION OF THE BOOK

This book is divided into four parts that engage with North American migration from a set of different disciplinary and methodological perspectives. The chapters that follow offer a rich and diverse collection of research at various levels of analysis. Part I of the volume looks specifically at the politics and governance of migration in North America. Taking a broad regional approach focused on the policies of Canada, Mexico, and the United States, Elizabeth Ferris and Lea Matheson explore the role of global approaches and regionalized forms of cooperation for managing migration. Their analysis highlights how the three governments participated in negotiating the 2018 GCM alongside their policies toward Central American migrants, underscoring the degree to which divergences in national policies are shaped by both domestic and foreign policy considerations. Likewise, Luicy Pedroza and Isabel Gil-Everaert provide a compelling explanation of the myriad ways in which Trump administration's policy changes, and indeed policy coercion, upended and fundamentally undermined Mexican policy initiatives designed to promote a more humane and coherent approach to transit migration and asylum. Trade pressures and unilateral border control measures contributed to deep policy incoherence and stripped competences away from domestic policy actors who had advocated for and won important legislative and regulatory changes, placing them in the hands of actors concerned with external security and economic policy, ultimately pushing Mexico back into a space of migration containment and deportation.

Kiran Banerjee's contribution on the Canada-US Safe Third Country Agreement (STCA) takes up the framework as a key case of asylum coordination, both for the region and more broadly. He reconstructs the unique features that brought the agreement into being, in order to both explain why states have pursued these sorts of policies and shed light on why such frameworks often produced a host of unintended outcomes. While this volume generally agrees with broader scholarship that there is weak regionalization of migration governance in North America, it also identifies deep functional cooperation at several levels of analysis. In this vein, the chapter by Rey Koslowski and Geoff Leckey revitalizes theories of transgovernmental networks to investigate the modes by which civil servants and the bureaucratic networks they inhabit in the US and Canada collaborated to develop policies to manage transboundary mobility in the face of variations and political impasses around intergovernmental cooperation.

The chapters in Part II examine specific instances of North American migration governance through domestic, bilateral, and comparative perspectives, and some of their effects on global migration governance. In their contribution, Geoff Cameron and Shauna Labman compare the role of executive power in determining and delineating the scope of international refugee resettlement. Using long-term resettlement data and legislative analysis, they investigate how receiving states' domestic politics lead to policy volatility and contribute to the gap between international need and resettlement numbers. In a complementary vein, Alise Coen's contribution mobilizes theories around norm dynamics and internalization, coupled with an analysis of the deep rifts in American politics, to understand the changes in US refugee and asylum policy, and arrives at conclusions about how these have affected the international refugee regime.

Looking at the Canadian case, Triadafilos Triadafilopoulos and Zack Taylor's contribution unpacks the dialectic between well-managed migration for socioeconomic development and the inverse logic of controlling "unwanted" irregular flows to liberal democracies. Their chapter argues that this is ultimately an untenable balance – given the underlying moral costs entailed by managed migration regimes – which is likely to place significant stress on the normative commitments of liberal democratic states both in North America and more broadly. Finally, Bruno Dupeyron's contribution analyzes the weak governance mechanisms and knowledge production around climate-induced mobility in North America. His chapter offers a particular focus on state responses to climate-induced displacement, while also exploring how scholarship around climate mobility might contribute to its securitization.

Part III of the volume moves to a more societal, normative, and intersubjective set of cases, examining public opinion, migrant agency, and activism. Olga Odgers-Ortiz and Olga Olivas draw from in-depth ethnographic work with migrants who are trapped in Tijuana, Mexico, to illustrate how they respond to situations of *stranded*-ness. They illustrate that rather than being passive subjects, African migrants and migrant communities in Tijuana offer a paradigmatic case of responding to immobility by producing novel narratives of (im)mobility through religious beliefs, political engagement, and developing new and parallel life projects. Likewise, Eloy Rivas-Sánchez's chapter analyzes strategies of collective response from precarious, racialized immigrant communities to situations of increased vulnerability in the context of the COVID-19 pandemic. His contribution unpacks how responses from "below" have the potentiality to inform the development of larger, transnational, collective projects of mutual care, resilience, and renewal, upon which social life can flourish in the post-pandemic future. Scott Pruysers and Tobias Schminke provide novel empirical evidence on public attitudes to immigrants and refugees in North America. In particular, they show a clear role for populist attitudes in explaining anti-refugee sentiments in Canada, suggesting that populism can negatively affect public opinion on migration even in the absence of viable right-wing populist parties.

The collection of chapters in Part IV examine some of the more global dimensions of North American migration governance. Craig Damian Smith's chapter shows that, in contradiction to its role as a norm and policy entrepreneur around refugee protection and responsibility-sharing, Canada's orientation toward Latin America and the Caribbean is overwhelmingly focused on containing asylum seekers, while maintaining a dependent relationship on extracting mineral wealth and human capital through temporary foreign workers. In a similar vein, drawing lessons from Europe's use of development aid to forestall mixed migration to Europe, Nicholas Micinski, Kelsey Norman, and Ana Martín Gil show that migration management and development aid from the US to Latin America serve containment policies in the regions. They illustrate how foreign aid empowers local bureaucracies and security apparatuses to stop emigration and transit migration, rather than their purported purpose of addressing "root causes." Ruben Zaiotti explores how the puzzle of policy convergence around externalized migration controls between Europe and North America can be explained as instances of *practical learning* among policymakers by mimicking policies and repertoires of control. The chapter applies these insights through the study of policy convergence between Europe and North America around passenger name record (PNR) mobility screening systems, with insights for broader transatlantic policy convergence. Finally, and in a similar vein, Andrew Geddes's contribution illustrates how elite-level representations impact and condition responses to migration in Europe and North America. Drawing on the idea of distinct migration governance repertoires, his comparative intervention highlights the central role of perceptions and shared understandings in shaping the powerful effects of key actors in migration governance systems across these regions.

The volume concludes with an afterword by François Crépeau, who argues for a broad rethinking of the governance of human mobility as a whole. His intervention explicitly calls out the contradictory logics that inform today's predominantly state-centric approaches to migration while also putting forth an agenda for reforming current norms and practices. These recommendations have an undeniable salience when taken up in the context of the various contributions that inform this volume. Our hope is that this book will help inform not only scholarly discussion and debate, but also future policy developments impacting mobility in North America and beyond.

REFERENCES

Abdou, Leila Hadj. 2019. "North America: Weak Regionalism, Strong Borders." In *The Dynamics of Regional Migration Governance,* edited by Andrew Geddes, Marcia Vera Espinoza, Leila Hadj Abdou, and Leiza Brumat, 146–65. Northhampton: Edward Elgar Publishing.

Alonso, Alexandra Délano. 2018. *From Here and There: Diaspora Policies, Integration, and Social Rights Beyond Borders.* Oxford: Oxford University Press.

Andreas, Peter, and Thomas J. Biersteker, eds. 2003. *The Rebordering of North America: Integration and Exclusion in a New Security Context.* New York: Routledge.

Banerjee, Kiran, and Smith, Craig Damian. 2020. "International Relations and Migration: Mobility as Norm Rather Than Exception." In *Nomad-State Relationships in International Relations*, edited by Jamie Levin, 265–81. Cham: Palgrave Macmillan.

Bada, Xóchitl. 2014. *Mexican Hometown Associations in Chicagoacán: From Local to Transnational Civic Engagement.* New Brunswick, New Jersey: Rutgers University Press.

Bada, Xóchitl, and Shannon Gleeson, eds. 2019. *Accountability Across Borders: Migrant Rights in North America.* Austin: University of Texas Press.

Besco, Randy, and Erin Tolley. 2019. "Does Everyone Cheer? The Politics of Immigration and Multiculturalism in Canada." In *Federalism and the Welfare State in a Multicultural World*, edited by Elizabeth Goodyear-Grant, Richard Johnston, Will Kymlicka, and John Miles, 291–318. Montreal: McGill-Queen's University Press.

Betts, Alexander, and Phil Orchard, eds. 2014. *Implementation and World Politics: How International Norms Change Practice.* Oxford: Oxford University Press.

Bloemraad, Irene. 2014. "Commentary: A Restrictionist Shift That Matters." In *Controlling Immigration: A Global Perspective*, 3rd ed., edited by James Hollifield, Philip L. Martin, and Pia Orrenius, 117–21. Redwood City: Stanford University Press.

Budiman, Abby. 2020. *Key Finding about U.S. Immigrants.* Pew Research Centre. https://www.pewresearch.org/fact-tank/2020/08/20/key-findings-about-u-s-immigrants/. Accessed 1 June 2023.

Caponio, Tiziana, and Michael Jones-Correa. 2018. "Theorising Migration Policy in Multilevel States: The Multilevel Governance Perspective." *Journal of Ethnic and Migration Studies* 44 (12): 1995–2010.

Carmel, Emma, Katharina Lenner, and Regine Paul. 2021. "The Governance and Politics of Migration: A Conceptual-Analytical Map." In *Handbook on the Governance and Politics of Migration*, edited by Emma Carmel, Katharina Lenner, and Regine Paul, 1–23. Cheltenham: Edward Elgar Publishing.

Carpenter, Michael J., Melissa Kelly, and Oliver Schmidtke, eds. 2023. *Border and Migration: The Canadian Experience in Comparative Perspective.* Ottawa: University of Ottawa Press.

Domínguez, Roberto, and Rafael Velázquez Flores. 2018. "Global Governance." In *Oxford Research Encyclopedia of International Studies.* Oxford: Oxford University Press.

Esipova, Neli, Anita Pugliese, and Julie Ray. 2018. *More than 750 Million Worldwide Would Migrate if They Could.* Gallup World Survey. https://

news.gallup.com/poll/245255/750-million-worldwide-migrate.aspx. Accessed 1 June 2023.

Félix, Adrián. 2019. *Specters of Belonging: The Political Life Cycle of Mexican Migrants*. Oxford: Oxford University Press.

Finnemore, Martha, and Kathryn Sikkink. 1998. "International Norm Dynamics and Political Change." *International Organization* 52 (4): 887–917.

Freier, Luisa Feline, and Kyle Holloway. 2019. "The Impact of Tourist Visas on Intercontinental South-South Migration: Ecuador's Policy of "Open Doors" as a Quasi-Experiment." *International Migration Review* 53 (4): 1171–208.

Gabriel, Christina, and Laura Macdonald. 2020. "New Architectures for Migration Governance: NAFTA and Transnational Activism around Migrants' Rights." *Third World Quarterly* 42 (1): 68–85.

Geddes, Andrew, Marcia Vera Espinoza, Leila Hadj Abdou, and Leiza Brumat, eds. 2019. *The Dynamics of Regional Migration Governance*. Cheltenham: Edward Elgar Publishing.

Geddes, Andrew. 2021. *Governing Migration Beyond the State: Europe, North America, South America, and Southeast Asia in a Global Context*. Oxford: Oxford University Press.

Genna, Gaspare M., and David A. Mayer-Foulkes, eds. 2013. *North American Integration: An Institutional Void in Migration, Security and Development*. New York: Routledge.

Ghosh, Bimal, ed. 2000. *Managing Migration: Time for a New International Regime?* Oxford: Oxford University Press.

– 2007. "Managing Migration: Whither the Missing Regime? How Relevant is Trade Law to Such a Regime? *Proceedings of the American Society of International Law Annual Meeting* 101 (March): 303–6.

Gottwald, Martin. 2014. "Burden Sharing and Refugee Protection." In *The Oxford Handbook of Refugee and Forced Migration Studies*, edited by Elena Fiddian-Qasmiyeh, Gil Loescher, Katy Long, and Nando Sigona, 525–38. Oxford: Oxford University Press.

Greenhill, Kelly M. 2016. "Open Arms Behind Barred Doors: Fear, Hypocrisy and Policy Schizophrenia in the European Migration Crisis." *European Law Journal* 22 (3): 317–32.

Hansen, Randall. 2011. "Making Cooperation Work: Interests, Incentive, and Action." In *Migration, Nation States, and International Cooperation,* edited by Randall Hansen, Jobst Koehler, and Jeannette Money, 14–27. New York: Routledge.

Hollifield, James F. 2004. "The Emerging Migration State." *International Migration Review* 38 (3): 885–912.

Hollifield, James F., and Tom Wong. 2015. "The Politics of International Migration." In *Migration Theory: Talking Across Disciplines*, 3rd ed., edited by Caroline Brettell and James Hollifield. New York: Routledge.

Keohane, Robert O., and Joseph S. Nye. 1974. "Transgovernmental Relations and International Organizations." *World Politics* 27 (1): 39–62.

Koslowski, Rey. 2011. "Global Mobility Regimes: A Conceptual Framework." *In Global Mobility Regimes*, edited by Rey Koslowski, 1–25. New York: Palgrave Macmillan.

Konrad, Victor, and Heather Nicol. 2016. *Beyond Walls: Re-Inventing the Canada-United States Borderlands*. London: Routledge.

Krasner, Stephen D. 1982. "Structural Causes and Regime Consequences: Regimes as Intervening Variables." *International Organization* 36 (2): 185–205.

Lavenex, Sandra. 2018. "'Failing Forward' Towards which Europe? Organized Hypocrisy in the Common European Asylum System." *Journal of Common Market Studies* 56 (5): 1195–212.

– 2019. "Regional Migration Governance – Building Block of Global Initiatives?" *Journal of Ethnic and Migration Studies* 45 (8): 1275–93.

Lavenex, Sandra, Flavia Jurje, Terri E. Givens, and Ross Buchanan. 2016. "Regional Migration Governance." In *The Oxford Handbook on Comparative Regionalism*, edited by Tanja A. Börzel and Thomas Risse, 457–85. Oxford: Oxford University Press.

Lavenex, Sandra, and Nicola Piper. 2021. "Regions and Global Migration Governance: Perspectives 'from Above', 'from Below', and 'from Beyond.'" *Journal of Ethnic and Migration Studies* 48 (12): 2837–54. https://doi.org/10.1080/1369183X.2021.1972564.

Martin, Susan, and Sanjula Weerasinghe. 2017. "Global Migration Governance: Existing Architecture and Recent Developments." Chap. 5 in IOM *World Migration Report 2018*. Geneva: International Organization for Migration. https://publications.iom.int/system/files/pdf/wmr_2018_en_chapter5.pdf.

Masferrer, Claudia, and Bryan R. Roberts. 2012. "Going Back Home? Changing Demography and Geography of Mexican Return Migration." *Population Research and Policy Review* 31 (4): 465–96.

McAuliffe, Mary, and Anna Triandafyllidou, eds. 2022. *World Migration Report 2022*. Geneva: International Organization for Migration. https://publications.iom.int/books/world-migration-report-2022. Accessed 1 June 2023.

Passel, Jeffrey S., D'Vera Cohn, and Ana González-Barrera. 2012. *Net Migration from Mexico Falls to Zero—and Perhaps Less*. Washington: Pew Hispanic Center.

Reckwitz, Andreas. 2002. "Toward a Theory of Social Practices: A Development in Culturalist Theorizing." *European Journal of Social Theory* 5 (2): 243–63.

Rosenau, James N. 1995. "Governance in the Twenty-First Century." *Global Governance* 1 (1): 13–43.

Rudolph, Christopher. 2006. *National Security and Immigration: Policy Development in the United States and Western Europe since 1945*. Stanford: Stanford University Press.

Schatzki, Theodore R., Karin Knorr-Cetina, and Eike von Savigny, eds. 2001. *The Practice Turn in Contemporary Theory*. London: Routledge.

Slaughter, Anne-Marie. 2005. *A New World Order*. Princeton: Princeton University Press.

Sutherland, Donald. 2017. *Report of the Special Representative of the Secretary General on Migration*. UN General Assembly Report A/71/728. https://www.un.org/development/desa/pd/sites/www.un.org.development.desa.pd/files/unpd_cm15_201702_report_of_srsg_on_migration_-_a.71.728_advance_0.pdf. Accessed 1 June 2023.

Thielemann, Eiko. 2018. "Why Refugee Burden-Sharing Initiatives Fail: Public Goods, Free-Riding and Symbolic Solidarity in the EU." *Journal of Common Market Studies* 56 (1): 63–82.

Triandafyllidou, Anna. 2021. "The Global Governance of Migration: Towards a 'Messy' Approach." *International Migration* (special issue): 19–27.

UNGA (UN General Assembly). 1990. *International Convention on the Protection of the Rights of All Migrant Workers and Members of their Families*, A/RES/45/158. 18 December 1990. https://www.refworld.org/docid/3ae6b3980.html. Accessed 1 June 2023.

Yates, Caitlyn. 2019. "As More Migrants from Africa and Asia Arrive in Latin America, Governments Seek Orderly and Controlled Pathways." *Migration Information Source*. Washington, DC: Migration Policy Institute. https://www.migrationpolicy.org/article/extracontinental-migrants-latin-america. Accessed 1 June 2023.

PART ONE

Politics and Governance of Migration in North America

I

Divergent Paths? A Comparison of Canadian, Mexican, and US Multilateral Approaches to Managing Migration

Elizabeth Ferris and Lea Matheson

The three governments of North America – Canada, Mexico, and the United States – have different national interests with respect to migration which are reflected in their different approaches to global and regional multilateral cooperation on migration issues. This chapter explores the policies of the three North American governments with respect to: (a) global multilateral approaches to migration, specifically the Global Compact for Safe, Orderly, and Regular Migration (GCM), and (b) regional cooperation in managing migration from Central America. After a brief summary of the state of multilateral approaches to migration, the chapter provides capsule summaries of the ways that each government has approached both multilateralism and migration. The analysis then turns to the way these three governments participated in negotiating the 2018 GCM and their policies toward Central American migration. This comparative analysis illustrates how national migration policies are shaped by both domestic and foreign policy interests. The concluding section draws out the implications of this analysis for global and regional multilateral migration initiatives.

THE CONTEXT: AN EMERGING, IF MUCH DELAYED, GLOBAL MIGRATION REGIME

For the past seventy years, the global refugee regime has been grounded in a binding (though somewhat frayed) international convention and a single United Nations (UN) agency, the United Nations High Commissioner for Refugees (UNHCR) (Betts 2009; Betts and Milner 2019; Goodwin-Gill and McAdam 2007; van Riemsdijk, Marchand, and Heins 2021). While

Table 1.1 | Key dates: Development of global governance of migration

1950	Office of the United Nations High Commissioner for Refugees (UNHCR) established
1951	Convention on the Status of Refugees adopted
1951	Provisional Intergovernmental Committee for the Movement of Migrants from Europe (PICMME) created; became Intergovernmental Committee for Migration (ICM) in 1980 and International Organization for Migration (IOM) in 1989
1954	First United Nations World Population Conference held in Rome
1984	Cartagena Declaration adopted by the Colloquium on the International Protection of Refugees in Latin America, Mexico, and Panama
1985	Intergovernmental Consultations on Asylum and Immigration (IGC), first Regional Consultative Process (RCP)
1990	International Convention on the Protection of the Rights of All Migrant Workers and Members of Their Families (ICRMW) adopted
1994	The Cairo Conference on Population and Development
2000–02	UNHCR's Global Consultative Process
2001	IOM's International Dialogue on Migration Policy
2002	The Hague Declaration on the Future of Asylum and Migration Policy
2002	Secretary-General's Report: Strengthening the United Nations: An Agenda for Further Change (commonly known as the "Doyle Report")
2003–05	The Global Commission on International Migration (GCIM)
2003	Geneva Migration Group established
2004	Berne Initiative's publication on "Migration and International Legal Norms"
2004	Berne Initiative's "International Agenda for Migration Management"
2004	UN General Assembly adopts RES/58/208 calling for a High-level Dialogue on International Migration and Development
2004	Canada-US Safe Third Country Agreement (STCA)
2006	First High-level Dialogue on International Migration and Development, establishes the Global Forum on Migration and Development (GFMD)
2006	Transformation of the former Geneva Migration Group into the Global Migration Group (GMG)

Table 1.1 | *continued*

2013	Second High-level Dialogue on International Migration and Development, themed "Making Migration Work"
2015	Launch of the Agenda for Sustainable Development 2030
2015	UN launched process on the issue of migration
2016	First UN Summit on Addressing Large Movements of Refugees and Migrants
2016	New York Declaration for Refugees and Migrants adopted
2017	The San Pedro Sula Declaration adopted; the Comprehensive Regional Protection and Solutions Framework (MIRPS) established
2018	Global Compact for Safe, Orderly and Regular Migration (GCM) adopted by UN General Assembly
2018	Global Compact on Refugees adopted by UN General Assembly
2019	US-Mexico Safe Third Country Agreement
2019	Establishment of the UN Migration Network (replacing the Global Migration Group)
2019	First Global Refugee Forum
2022	First International Migration Review Forum
2022	Los Angeles Declaration on Migration and Protection (Summit of the Americas outcome)

global governance of refugees has been strong, regional mechanisms are weak. European efforts to develop a regional approach have been inconsistent and incomplete, Latin American initiatives have proliferated but implementation has been uneven, African efforts have remained aspirational, and regional approaches to refugees have been virtually nonexistent in Asia and the Middle East (Jubilut, Espinoza, and Maezzanoti 2021; Kneebone 2016; Sharpe 2018). National refugee policies are based on a relatively similar definition of refugees and, while approaches to refugee determination vary considerably, there is at least rhetorical commitment to international standards (Arnold-Fernandez 2019).

In contrast, the development and consolidation of a global migration regime has remained elusive (Betts 2011; Ferris and Donato 2019). There is no single, widely accepted international convention on migration.[1] Until 2016, when the International Organization for Migration (IOM) formally entered the UN system, no single UN agency was recognized as the lead on migration; instead there were various UN agencies and non-UN multilateral forums on migration, such as the Global Migration Group and the Global Forum on Migration and Development, which provided opportunities for discussion of migration issues (Betts and Kainz 2017). In contrast to the refugee regime, a hodgepodge of regional migration mechanisms emerged, mostly at the instigation of IOM (IOM n.d.).

The global migration regime has widely been considered fragmented with a variety of agreements and processes that cover different issues around the movement of people (Ferris and Donato 2019; Kainz and Betts 2021). Sometimes there are conflicts between the different regimes in play, most classically the interaction between the travel and the refugee regimes (Betts 2010). Overwhelmingly, current migration mechanisms focus on sharing information and occasionally best practices, rather than developing collaborative policies. True collaboration seems to happen mainly at the bilateral level through readmission agreements and memorandums of understanding (MOUs) to regulate the movement of labour migrants (ILO n.d.). Although there are international standards with respect to both recruitment and integration of migrants, national immigration policies are primarily developed in response to domestic factors, especially labour market needs. Decisions about migration, such as decisions about citizenship, are recognized as an expression of national sovereignty.

In 2016, the UN Global Summit on Refugees and Migrants adopted the New York Declaration which set out two very different processes for adopting two new global compacts – on refugees and migration (UN General Assembly 2016). This chapter focuses on the GCM, arguably the more ambitious and pathbreaking framework.

The GCM was endorsed by the UN General Assembly in 2018, resulting in the first global international migration framework firmly incorporating the issue of migration within the UN system. It is an international state-negotiated agreement that is nonbinding and recognizes state sovereignty (UN General Assembly 2019a). The GCM is a balanced compromise reflecting the issues and concerns of sending, transit, and receiving states based on common principles of cooperation, rule of law, human rights, people-centred approaches, and gender-responsive policies. The cooperative framework consists of twenty-three objectives calling for whole-of-government and whole-of-society approaches at the local, national, regional, and global levels. Overall, the objectives aim to harness the benefits of migration for states and protect migrants and communities from pre-departure to settlement.

The GCM also resulted in significant changes to the global migration architecture. In preparation for the GCM, IOM joined the UN system,

Table 1.2 | Basic migration data: Canada, Mexico, and the US

Country	Population (in millions)	Inflows of foreign population (in thousands), 2019	% of population that are migrants, 2020	Number of refugees/asylum seekers in 2020
Canada	38.01	341,000	21.3%	109,264
Mexico	128.9	39,000	0.9%	45,469
United States	329.5	1,031,000	15.3%	340,881

Sources: (1) Population: World Bank n.d. (2) Inflows of foreign population (in thousands): OECD n.d. (3) Per cent of population that are migrants: IOM n.d.a. (4) Number of refugees/asylum seekers in 2020 (Refugee population by country or territory of asylum): UNHCR n.d.a.

and subsequently the GCM recognized IOM's role as the coordinator and secretariat of the United Nations Network on Migration, the UN's coordination body on migration tasked with supporting the implementation of the GCM. Furthermore, the GCM established the International Migration Review Forum (IMRF) as the intergovernmental platform for states to discuss GCM implementation and guide the work of the UN. The IMRF is a formal and permanent platform within the UN system for states to discuss the implementation of the GCM at global, national, and local levels. Furthermore, it is linked to the UN's High Level Political Forum on Sustainable Development (HLPF). A Progress Declaration is an important part of the IMRF's outcomes: it will represent an action-oriented document highlighting the challenges and issues around the implementation of the GCM and, perhaps most importantly, recommending ways to strengthen international cooperation (UN General Assembly 2019b). These more formal structures and processes are likely to lead to both a more unified structure for global policy development and a pathway to formalization.

CANADA, MEXICO, AND THE US

Before turning to the ways in which the three countries approached the GCM, this section provides a capsule summary of Canadian, Mexican, and US perspectives on migration. The three countries have very different approaches to migration and very different experiences on the role of migration in their historical development. As will become apparent subsequently, these divergent domestic contexts are important to understanding the varying orientations that each state has taken toward the GCM and migration governance more broadly.

Canada

Immigration has been central to Canada's nation-building and identity. As a colonial nation, it was created by two founding settlers – the British and the French – as well as Indigenous peoples.[2] In efforts to expand and ward off encroachment from the south, Canada actively encouraged people – first from the British Isles and subsequently more broadly – to immigrate in order to populate the country. Today, given the combination of a low birth rate and aging population, immigration remains critical to ensure there are enough people within the labour market, paying taxes and spending money to sustain the economy. This reality has received increased political attention and is broadly reflected across Canadian public opinion, where significant support for continued immigration remains widespread (Wells 2022). In order to address the population shortage, Canada plans to welcome over 400,000 people annually over the course of the 2023–25 period (Government of Canada 2020).

Canada's immigration system has three broad categories: economic, family reunification, and humanitarian. Today, the majority of newcomers, approximately 60 per cent, are economic migrants whose entry is based on a points system around language, education, skills, and experience (Government of Canada 2022). Based on their points and current labour market needs, Canada then invites the individuals to apply for permanent status. Additionally, immigration is understood as an area of concurrent jurisdiction within the Canadian federation; accordingly, the provinces can nominate immigrants from the federal database based on their own provincial needs, except for Quebec, which selects its own skilled workers (Seidle 2010). Within its overall immigration strategy, Canada sets its refugee target which is approximately 15 per cent of the overall immigrant target. Canada resettles Convention refugees, persons in refugee-like situations, or those from vulnerable groups under refugee programs, including both government-assisted and private sponsorship. Refugees are granted permanent resident status on arrival in Canada allowing them to work and access government services, including education and health care.

Canada's immigration policy recognizes the importance of integration to the success of the migration process. Canada's history, building on three founding peoples, Indigenous, French, and British, is reflected in the

Canadian Multiculturalism Act which has been a foundation of Canada's identity. Multiculturalism policies have supported the participation of newcomers to the country with support from all levels of government and civil society. While not immune to the right-wing backlash around immigration, to date Canada has largely avoided this and there is widespread recognition that Canada's growth depends upon immigration.

As a western liberal democracy, Canada shares similar values with the US and, as close ally and geographic neighbour, Canada often takes similar foreign policy positions particularly around security. However, unlike the US's hegemonic power, as a middle power Canada places multilateralism at the centre of its foreign policy. In this regard, Canada did not engage in the 2003 Iraq conflict, was an active player in the Paris Climate Accord, is a member of the International Criminal Court, and spearheaded the International Land Mines Treaty.

Canada's only border is with the US and there are various bilateral agreements to oversee security, law enforcement, and the flow of people and goods. Since late 2004, the safe third country agreement (STCA) under the US-Canada Action Plan requires asylum seekers to request refugee protection in the first safe country they arrive in. Given the geographic barrier between Canada and Central America, Canada traditionally has not received high levels of migrants or asylum seekers from Central America; these movements have been even more limited with the STCA (see Banerjee in this volume). Canada does provide temporary visas for seasonal agricultural workers, largely intended for Central America and the Caribbean.

Mexico

Traditionally a country of emigration, Mexico is struggling with its relatively new reality of being both a transit and a destination country for Central American migrants. Until 1947, Mexico only allowed certain ethnic groups to immigrate; however, Mexico changed this policy in efforts to increase Mexico's cultural influence in Latin America and prioritized admission of foreigners with similar cultural and linguistic traits. Realistically, Mexico maintained its ability to systematically exclude certain groups much past 1947, prioritizing foreigners who were more able to "assimilate" (Fitzgerald 2005). In the 1960s and 1970s for example, Mexico provided refuge to thousands of exiles from South American dictatorships, especially from Argentina and Chile (Sharnak 2019). In the early 1980s through the mid-1990s, large numbers of Central Americans arrived in Mexico, fleeing civil conflict in their countries. Of the approximately 140,000 Guatemalan refugees (who were never recognized as such), around 50,000 remained in

Mexico and, in 1995, 22,000 Guatemalans were naturalized as Mexican citizens (Rodriguez de Ita 2008). Later, from the mid-1990s, large numbers of Central Americans began transiting Mexico in search of protection and economic security in the United States. In 2015, the Temporary Migration Regularization Program was established, which permitted those who entered Mexico between 2015 and 2017 without authorization to adjust their immigration status, provided they could produce various identifying documents. In addition, Mexico developed a bilateral labour migration program with Guatemala in 2014, which allowed the migration of some 10,000 people per year. While this program could have been renewed two years later, negotiations stalled and the program came to an end.

Other than those in transit, Mexico has historically received relatively few migrants and presently less than 1 per cent of Mexico's population are immigrants (Bautista Leon et al. 2021). Consequently, there has been very little support for migrant integration, although this may be changing as Mexico grapples with re-integrating Mexicans returning from the US (Masferrer and Pedroza 2022). Discussions of migration in Mexico, however, have largely centred on Mexican migration to the US, which has historically been very high; in fact, in the 2020s, around 25 per cent of all migrants in the US – around 11 million people – have been from Mexico (Israel and Batalova 2020). In recent years, Mexican migration to the US has declined significantly as a result of demographic change and more job opportunities in Mexico as well as more restrictive migration policies adopted by the US government (Congressional Research Service 2022; Durand and Massey 2019a, 2019b; Gramlich and Scheller 2021). While the US Border Patrol reported 1.6 million encounters with Mexicans on the southern border in 2000, by 2021, that figure had fallen to 608,000, surpassed by growing numbers of Central Americans and other nationalities (Gramlich and Scheller 2021).

Mexico's migration policies are inextricably linked with its relations with the US. In recent years, the US has pressured Mexico to adopt evermore stringent measures to prevent migrants from Central America from entering Mexico and continuing on to the United States (Congressional Research Service 2022). While Mexico's foreign policies are largely shaped by the United States – its largest trade partner, accounting for almost half of all exports and imports (World Bank n.d.b) – it has tried to assert independence from its powerful northern neighbour by becoming a leader on issues of concern to the Global South, such as the 2030 Agenda for Sustainable Development and migration (Jauberth et al. 2019; Pellicer Silva 2019). Like Canada, Mexico has a strong commitment to multilateralism and has tried to position itself as a champion of migrants rights, though many advocates stress the disparity between Mexico's rhetoric abroad and practice at home.

In this regard, of the three countries, Mexico is the only signatory to the International Convention on the Protection of the Rights of All Migrant Workers and Members of Their Families (ICRMW).[3] In 1980, Mexico presided over the Working Group tasked with drafting this convention. For many decades, the Mexican government has also played a key role in international efforts to strengthen asylum. In 1981, Mexico convened a five-day colloquium with the UNHCR which laid the groundwork for the Cartagena Declaration of 1984 – a regional framework which expanded the 1951 Refugee Convention to include those fleeing "generalized violence, foreign aggression, internal conflicts, massive violation of human rights or other circumstances which have seriously disturbed public order" (UNHCR 1984). Mexico was one of ten original signatories to this important declaration.

United States

Like Canada, the US considers itself to be a nation of immigrants, although its history has been an uneven one, with periods of relative openness to migrants interspersed with closed door policies (Martin 2021). As of 2018, about two-thirds of the 1 million immigrants entering the country annually are family reunification cases; the remaining one-third are on various labour visas (National Immigration Forum 2018). In addition, the US admits a significant number of refugees through refugee resettlement programs, although the number of refugees admitted has varied sharply in response to both humanitarian need and US domestic interests. The present refugee admissions ceiling is 125,000 – a dramatic increase from the target of 15,000 admissions in the last year of the Trump administration.[4]

Like Canada, the US has strong pro-immigration domestic constituencies and active diaspora groups, although it has also experienced much greater anti-immigrant sentiment and immigration issues in the US are much more politicized than in either Mexico or Canada. In contrast to other countries, including Canada, which have developed impressive support mechanisms for integration of refugees and migrants, the US does not provide much governmental support for integration; rather local governments and civil society groups try to fill the gap. The US was a leader in creating multilateral institutions from the end of World War II and, until fairly recently, supporting the establishment of UN agencies, international financial institutions, and regional organizations. And yet, as a hegemonic power, there were many times when the US acted unilaterally, particularly on security issues, and there has always been an "America First" component in US foreign policies (Council on Foreign Relations 2020; Jones,

Feltman, and Morehouse 2019). This tendency is evident even in the Biden administration, which has also taken important steps in reasserting the US's commitment to multilateral institutions. With respect to migration, however – perhaps because it is such a politically charged issue – the US has generally worked unilaterally or bilaterally rather than investing in a strong regional system. Presently the US seems blocked by domestic political pressures from adopting comprehensive immigration reform, leaving a patchwork of different policies and agencies responding in different ways to both new and long-term immigrants.

PERCEPTIONS AND RESPONSES IN NORTH AMERICA TO THE GCM

While the New York Declaration was negotiated under the Obama administration, the GCM process took place during Trump's presidency. Shortly before the negotiations were to start, the Trump administration announced it would not participate in the GCM, declaring the GCM process was inconsistent with US migration policies and that an international migration agreement would encroach on the sovereignty of the state (US Mission to the UN 2017). However, the US watched closely, with its officials from the US Mission to the UN quietly attending the negotiations even as the official US seat remained empty.

The absence of the US in the negotiations likely led to a more comprehensive GCM. Historically, the US has played a strong role in defining international migration governance, which was evident during the processes leading up to the New York Declaration in September 2016. However, the period surrounding the GCM process was also a time when the US was adopting more restrictive immigration policies, particularly with respect to the Central Americans arriving on its southern border. These restrictive policies intensified significantly after the inauguration of Donald Trump in January 2017. As evident by the US statement in the UN General Assembly when the GCM was endorsed, if the US had pressed these issues during the negotiating process, achieving consensus on the document would have been much more difficult (Veprek 2018).

In December 2021, the Biden administration reverted, at least in its initial months, to a more open position around migration and endorsed the GCM. Despite earlier claims, the US recognizes the GCM's foundation on the principle of state sovereignty and its nonbinding nature, yet also acknowledges that it reflects the values of the country toward migration (US, PRM 2021).

As a large migrant-receiving state, Canada plays a significant role within the international migration sphere and, until the GCM negotiations, took positions which were broadly similar to those of the US. The GCM negotiations also corresponded with the Canadian government's renewed multilateral engagement, including their bid for a UN Security Council seat. Reflecting these considerations, Canada played a constructive role within the GCM process by taking a balanced approach and often found commonalities with both traditional and non-traditional partners (Government of Canada 2018).

During the negotiations, Canada – like many other participating states – stressed the importance of national sovereignty and took positions that reflected its policies and commitments, including ensuring a gender-responsive approach and upholding the basic rights of migrants, Indigenous peoples, and children (Government of Canada 2018). Acknowledging that international migration was to become part of the UN system, Canada strongly advocated for IOM's leadership, in large part due to it being a state-centred organization. Albeit significantly smaller than the large movements of people in Europe and the US, Canada saw an increase of irregular migration between 2016 and 2019 (Leuprecht 2019). Since many migrants cross into Canada by land, there is often a narrative that links this increase in irregular crossings to Trump's policies around migration; however, the majority of people arrived in the US legally through tourist visas with the intention to enter Canada (Leuprecht 2019). Canada's engagement in the GCM did not capture much attention with the general public.[5]

As a migrant-sending, transit, and receiving country, Mexico has long been active in international migration discussions. The GCM negotiations were no exception, with Mexico playing a leading role throughout the process. Recognizing its strong diplomatic corps and its support of multilateral processes, the Mexican permanent representative to the United Nations, Ambassador Gómez-Camacho was appointed by the president of the General Assembly as one of the two co-facilitators to the GCM processes. With his deep knowledge on the workings of the UN and persuasive diplomatic skills, Gómez-Camacho stressed the comprehensive nature of the GCM, reassuring states that all interests were being addressed. Despite the political climate in which the GCM was negotiated, Mexico strategically guided discussions and drafted documents to reflect a balanced and comprehensive approach, accommodating concerns with both border management and migrants' rights.

Beyond facilitating the GCM, Mexico also negotiated during the process that informed the text of the compact by focusing on its long-standing positions. During the negotiations Mexico identified as a migrant-sending country, promoted recognition of migrants' rights and emphasized the positive contributions of migrants to countries of both origin and destination (Gobierno de México 2018). Mexico was forceful in calling for international migration to be permanently part of the UN system, which previously had remained a contentious point between receiving and sending countries.

The three countries' different experiences with migration at the domestic level and their views of multilateralism were reflected in their approaches to negotiating the GCM. By refusing to participate in the negotiations, the US rejected a multilateral approach to migration, in line with the current domestic political context and isolationist policies. Mexico and Canada, on the other hand, reinforced the importance of multilateralism. Mexico took a highly visible and positive leadership role which advanced international migration governance and the UN's role in addressing current global issues. Canada took a balanced approach and consolidated the perception that it is a constructive facilitator of global processes. It was also able to stake out a position independent of the US; however, Canada arguably lost an opportunity to take on a global leadership role.

CENTRAL AMERICA AND BROADER REGIONAL DYNAMICS OF MIGRATION

Since the region's civil wars of the 1980s and 1990s, Central Americans have moved in large numbers through Mexico to the United States, fleeing civil conflict, gang and domestic violence, poverty, and economic desperation. An average of 311,000 migrants left Northern Central America every year during 2014–20 (Congressional Research Service 2021). In 2014, the arrival of some 70,000 unaccompanied Central American children provoked the perception of a crisis for the US. During the Obama administration, the US focused on deporting unauthorized migrants, prioritizing those who had committed serious crimes, even as it increased the ceiling for refugee admissions through the US Resettlement Program. The Trump administration imposed draconian policies to deter Central Americans from arriving and seeking asylum, including the controversial "zero tolerance" policy which resulted in family separations and the Migrant Protection Protocols or the Remain in Mexico policy (Congressional Research Service 2019). The inauguration of President Joe Biden in January 2020 was followed almost immediately by a dramatic uptick in arrivals of Central Americans. Although the Biden administration had pledged to adopt a more humane border policy, to move on comprehensive immigration reform, and to undo many of the problematic policies of the Trump administration – including the Remain in Mexico policy – the administration, in fact, has not kept its campaign promises due in part to blockages by a series of judicial orders, mobilization of anti-immigrant sentiment, and a highly- politicized polity which has opposed most of the administration's priorities. Moreover, as a result of Title 42 – a public-health-related prohibition on entry, including for asylum seekers, issued by the Centers for Disease Control and Prevention in March 2020 and kept in place by the

Biden administration – some 1.7 million migrants were blocked from entry or expelled before Title 42 was rescinded in May 2023 (Montoya-Galvez 2022; Women's Refugee Commission 2022).

US policy has been clearly centred on preventing Central Americans from arriving on its borders through border control measures, detention of immigrants,[6] and more recently through a strategy to address the root causes for the migration (US National Security Council 2021). However, addressing the drivers of migration is a long-term endeavour and the Biden administration has followed in the footsteps of its predecessors in looking to Mexico as a more immediate means of preventing Central Americans from arriving at the US border. There is a long history of US financial support for Mexican efforts to fortify its border with Guatemala (Georgetown Law 2015). Since September 2014 – the end of the fiscal year for the federal budget – the US has provided over USD 100 million to the Mérida Initiative, intended to combat violence, drug trafficking, and other forms of organized crime. But funds have also gone toward purchasing non-intrusive inspection equipment, mobile kiosks, canine teams, and vehicles, and toward training Mexican officials in immigration enforcement, demonstrating how the migration issue was securitized well before Trump's accession to power (Congressional Research Service 2022; Zepeda and Fuentes-Carrera 2020). In June 2019, a US-Mexico Joint Declaration was issued in which Mexico agreed to "take unprecedented steps to increase enforcement to curb irregular migration, to include the deployment of its National Guard throughout Mexico, giving priority to its southern border" (US Department of State 2019). In compliance with the declaration, the López Obrador administration deployed 12,000 members of its then newly created National Guard to the southern border to "beef up immigration enforcement efforts" (Meyer and Isacson 2019). It also added more checkpoints on highways in the south and increased raids of *La Bestia*, the train many migrants use to travel through Mexico. With a greater focus on detaining and deporting migrants as quickly as possible, apprehensions of migrants at Mexico's southern border more than tripled since the implementation of the joint declaration (Fredrick 2019).

Connected to the above initiatives, the Trump administration also pressured Mexico to sign an STCA in 2019. This agreement would have paralleled those the US negotiated with Guatemala, El Salvador, and Honduras; although Mexico resisted, it agreed "on humanitarian grounds" to accept migrants returned to Mexico under the Migrant Protection Protocols (Guillén 2020). In February 2021, the US government terminated those agreements (Montoya-Galvez 2021).

In 2020, the then-US-president Trump threatened to apply tariffs on Mexican exports if Mexico refused to assist the US in controlling entry of

Table 1.3 | Central American migrant stock, 2000 and 2019

Country	Central American migrant stock, 2000	Central American migrant stock, 2019
Canada	73,045	97,520
Mexico	50,000	81,480
USA	2,069,629	3,741,824

Source: UN Migrant Stock by Origin and Destination 2019: https://www.un.org/development/desa/pd/content/international-migrant-stock.

Central Americans transiting through Mexico (Associated Press 2020; Kovic and Argüelles 2010; Meyer and Boggs 2016). Presently there seems to be an informal agreement between Mexico and the US that Mexico will do more to deter Central Americans from travelling through Mexico to the US border, including preventing their entry into Mexico at the Mexican-Guatemalan border (Aleazis 2021). As other nationalities began turning up at the US-Mexico border – particularly Venezuelans and Haitians – in January 2022, the Mexican government imposed a new visa requirement on Venezuelans seeking to enter Mexico, a move encouraged by the US (Chishti and Bush-Joseph 2022). In December 2021, the US and Mexico announced a new joint initiative, *Sembrando Oportunidades*, to address some of the pressures behind current Central American migration (Reuters 2021; USAID 2021; for further discussion of linkages between development and migration, see Gil, Micinski, and Norman in this volume). This initiative built on López Obrador's initial initiative Sembrando Vida – his ambitious comprehensive development plan which failed to secure international funding.

Mexico – once again – is caught in the difficult place between current Mexican president Andrés Manuel López Obrador's stated commitment to charting a foreign policy more independent of its northern neighbour and the reality of US pressure. At the same time, many Central Americans are applying for asylum to remain in Mexico; in fact, the number of asylum requests nearly tripled from 2020 to 2021, from around 41,000 to 123,000 (Al Jazeera 2021). But the Mexican asylum system is severely underfunded and underdeveloped, with staffing and infrastructure limitations (Kosten 2019). As a result, Mexico is currently dealing with asylum seekers and immigrants seeking to remain in

Mexico as well as with the tens of thousands of asylum seekers in transit and on their way to the US, many of whom will be told to return to Mexico to wait for their processing by the US. In addition, the US is deporting around 100,000 Mexicans every year back to Mexico, many of whom have lived for years in the US and who do not speak Spanish (Mattei 2022).

Although the US government has turned to Mexico to support its border policies – particularly to take measures to prevent Central Americans from entering and transiting through Mexico to the US – by and large its efforts to respond to the crisis at the border have been determined unilaterally. The issue of Central American migration is of high salience to the US government and increasingly important to Mexico. As table 1.3 indicates, there is a huge difference in the number of Central Americans living in the three countries.

In contrast to the US and Mexico, Canada has historically kept its distance from US policies toward Central American and Mexican migration. Canada has a long-standing relationship with Central American countries, including through multilateral organizations focusing on strengthening social, economic, and security issues, and bilaterally through labour agreements, such as the Guatemala Temporary Guest Worker Program since 2003. Canada has also provided humanitarian support to the region both bilaterally and multilaterally and has strengthened its economic ties as a way to promote sustainable growth (Government of Canada n.d.). Canada has established several free trade agreements and created opportunities for businesses around natural resources, most notably mining. Not without its downside, though, as Canada's role around mining and human rights abuses has been documented (see Smith in this volume).

The 1980s saw some of the largest numbers of Central Americans entering Canada. During the civil conflicts of the 1980s, Canada accepted the largest number of Central Americans, which also corresponded to an earlier Canadian bid for a UN Security Council seat (Anzueto 2018). However, unlike the US whose foreign policy focused on communist regimes, Canada's "middle power" perspectives were around democracy, peace, and poverty (Anzueto 2017). Additionally, in response to US immigration policy changes with the Immigration Reform and Control Act of 1986, there was a dramatic rise of Central Americans living in the US who requested asylum or entered Canada irregularly (Garcia 2006). While not explicitly targeting Central Americans, Canada passed new immigration policies targeting smugglers while also making it more difficult to immigrate.

Although Canada has long-standing bilateral labour migration agreements with Mexico and Guatemala (Clemens 2022), the number of Central Americans arriving on its borders or indeed Central American migrant stock in the country, has been quite low. Canada does not view Central

America as important to its foreign policy and has preferred to emphasize its strong refugee resettlement tradition than to take on the issue of Central America, seeing this as a product of US policies (Heilman 2018; Garcia 2006, 2018; Korducki 2019; Paperny 2021). The Roadmap for a Renewed US-Canada Partnership outlines Canada's approach toward Central America. In the roadmap, it is agreed that the two countries will expand support for capacity-building in Central America to address the sources of instability and irregular migration in the region (Government of Canada 2021). In this context Canada's focus is largely framed in terms of engaging with the "root causes of irregular migration and forced displacement in Central America" (Government of Canada, Immigration, Refugees and Citizenship Canada 2022).

However, in 2021, Lloyd Axworthy, former Canadian foreign minister, launched a new North American Task Force on Central American Migration as an initiative of the World Refugee and Migration Council, which he also initiated in 2017 (WRMC n.d.). The task force was based in large measure on a recognition that the issue of Central American migration was too much for any one country to address and that a regional approach is necessary. The task force completed its work in January 2022 and, among other things, proposed the creation of a new North American Council on Migration – built on the model of the Arctic Council, where Canada has played a leading role (WRMC 2022). In terms of Canadian foreign policy, this seems to represent an opportunity for Canada to demonstrate how it can continue to be helpful to the US in dealing with the difficult issue of Central American migrants. Canada was already taking steps to become more involved in Central American issues as evidenced by its leadership of the Comprehensive Regional Protection and Solutions Framework (MIRPS for its Spanish acronym) Support Platform in 2021 – an initiative developed to support the Global Compact on Refugees (GCR) (UNHCR n.d.a).

CONCLUSION

The three North American governments have different experiences with migration and face different domestic pressures on migration issues. Their policies toward the GCM and toward Central American migrants in particular reflect these realities.

With respect to the GCM, politics matters. This is most obvious in the case of the United States – as evidenced by the policy reversals among the Obama, Trump, and the Biden administrations. For both Canada and Mexico, supporting the GCM provided the opportunity to position themselves – both internationally and before their respective domestic audiences – as champions of migrants' rights, diplomacy, and multilateral approaches, while marking out foreign policies independent of the US. Given its long history as a migrant-sending nation, Mexico obviously has more interest in advocating for migrants' rights than either the US or Canada – neither of the two has signed the 1990 Migrant Workers' Convention, for example. Differences in support for the GCM are also due to different assessments of the importance of multilateralism by the three governments. While Mexico and Canada have historically supported multilateralism and the rule of law as a way of countering US hegemony, the US has consistently argued that migration is an issue best dealt with unilaterally and bilaterally. While there are opportunities for all three countries to work together in existing, and perhaps new, multilateral initiatives to respond to Central American migration – thus both strengthening regional multilateral instruments and perhaps finding more creative approaches to managing increasing flows – at the present time, it is uncertain whether this opportunity will be used. For the US, the domestic political pressures to avoid another crisis on its southern border – or at least the perception of a crisis – is likely to dominate its decision-making. In the leadup to US midterm elections in November 2022, the Republican party seemed eager to use the issue of unauthorized migration as a campaign issue while Democrats hoped to downplay its significance – even as the number of Central Americans arriving at the border was likely to increase. Mexico seems to perceive the issue of Central American migration as primarily a US issue rather than an urgent domestic priority. For example, it has yet to dedicate anywhere close to sufficient resources to its asylum office to process the growing number of asylum applications from Central Americans. In this context, Canada can be characterized as continuing to hold an arguably ambivalent position on these broader regional dynamics.

The issue of Central American migration is a huge domestic issue for the US, but is relatively unimportant for Canada. However, as the Axworthy initiative seems to suggest, recasting the issue of Central American migration as requiring a regional response – rather than a US unilateral one – could potentially pay off for Canada. If Canada is perceived as being helpful on this thorny issue for the US, there might be possibilities to leverage additional support from the US for issues of higher priority for Canada. Canada is seen in Central America and Mexico as a relatively impartial party to discussions of migration and thus could be well-placed to mediate tense discussions and to suggest creative solutions. Mexico has traditionally assisted US efforts to deter Central American migration to prevent the US imposition of punitive measures in other areas, such as tariffs. But the situation for Mexico is changing faster than its foreign policies would indicate. Mexico is becoming a migrant-receiving country but is largely acting as a migrant-sending country (in advocating for migrants' rights in the GCM, for example) and as a transit country (in bowing to US pressure in the case of Central American migrants). There is a gap between Mexico's championing of migrants' rights and its policies toward Central American and other migrants. Mexico is just beginning to adopt policies to support integration, for example. It will be interesting to see how those policies play out. Mexico wants to demonstrate that it is different from the US in its treatment of migrants but is concerned about being stuck with hundreds of thousands of Central Americans, the vast majority of whom really want to be in the US, and not in Mexico.

Examining the policies of these three North American countries toward both global multilateral initiatives and the present challenges posed by Central American migration shows fundamental differences in their approaches to migration – and to working together. This chapter has highlighted the role of domestic imperatives and transnational relations in framing each country's stance toward the processes surrounding the GCM, as well as how these considerations have informed their respective responses in the intervening time. The changing dynamics within each state, as well as the broader region, will continue to impact the prospects for broader coordination around migration across the continent.

NOTES

1 The 1990 UN Convention on the Rights of All Migrant Workers and their Families has not yet been ratified by governments of countries receiving migrants.

2 Migration has been the basis of Canada's development and identity. The first settlers to Canada were from European colonies. However, in line with the UN Declaration on the Rights of Indigenous Peoples and Canadian legislation, it must be recognized "First Nations, Inuit and the Métis Nation have, throughout history and to this day, lived in the lands that are now in Canada with their distinct identities, cultures and ways of life."

3 While part of its commitment to multilateralism, this is also in line with Mexico positioning itself as a migrant sending country reflecting the rights of Mexicans abroad.

4 Less than 12,000 refugees were resettled in fiscal year 2020 (Statista 2021). Note also that in fiscal year 2021, the US admitted some 75,000 Afghans to the country under its Humanitarian Parole program and in 2022, US President Biden offered to receive up to 100,000 Ukrainians – also as humanitarian parolees. These parolees are in addition to the ceiling on refugee admissions.

5 The increase of irregular migrants between 2016 and 2019 corresponded with both the GCM negotiations and the federal election in Canada. This created expectations of a focus on immigration during the campaign. However, there was little discussion except from the right-wing People's Party. For the most part, even though the opposition party expressed opposition to the GCM (Wright 2018) all political parties agreed on the importance of immigration (see Carbert 2019).

6 The number of immigrants in detention has increased by 55 per cent under the Biden administration and stands at 22,000 as of mid-January 2022. Particularly concerning are the high numbers of migrants testing positive for COVID-19 in these detention centres – where social distancing and PPE are in short supply (Women's Refugee Commission 2022, 15).

REFERENCES

Aleazis, Hamed. 2021. "Biden Wants Mexico to Do More to Stop Immigrants Trying to Cross the US Border." *Buzzfeed News*, 4 June 2021. https://www.buzzfeednews.com/article/hamedaleaziz/biden-mexico-migration-requests. Accessed 5 June 2023.

Al Jazeera. 2021. "Mexico Says Refugee Requests Tripled in 2021." *Al Jazeera*, 21 December 2021. https://www.aljazeera.com/news/2021/12/21/refugee-requests-in-mexico-triple-in-2021. Accessed 5 June 2023.

Anzueto, Marc-André. 2017. "Canadian Human Rights Policy toward Guatemala: The Two Faces of Janus?" *Latin American Perspectives* 44 (5): 74–90. https://doi.org/10.1177/0094582X17713746.

– 2018. "Canada's Approach toward Central American Migrants." *Policy Options*, 10 August 2018. https://policyoptions.irpp.org/magazines/august-2018/canadas-approach-toward-central-american-migrants/. Accessed 5 June 2023.

Arnold-Fernandez, Emily. 2019. "National Governance Frameworks in the Global Compact on Refugees: Dangers and Opportunities." *International Migration.* 57 (6): 188–207. https://onlinelibrary.wiley.com/toc/14682435/2019/57/6. Accessed 5 June 2023.

ASILE. n.d. "Global Asylum Governance and the European Union's Role." https://www.asileproject.eu/. Accessed 5 June 2023.

Associated Press. 2020. "Mexican President Defends Restrictive Immigration Policies." *Associated Press News*, 17 December 2020. https://apnews.com/article/international-news-mexico-coronavirus-pandemic-immigration-central-america-bfc07e78d2c5ca2b1fe2a72e0d37cf34. Accessed 5 June 2023.

Bautista Leon, Andrea, Maria Adela Angoa Perez, and Silvia Elena Giorguli Saucedo. 2021. "Integración Desigual en México: brechas y retos para la integración de inmigrantes centroamericanos en los inicios del siglo XXI" [Unequal integration in Mexico: gaps and challenges for the integraton of Central American migrants at the beginning of the 21st century]. World Refugee and Migration Council. https://wrmcouncil.org/spanish/integracion-desigual-en-mexico-brechas-y-retos-para-la-integracion-de-inmigrantes-centroamericanos-en-los-inicios-del-siglo-xxi/. Accessed 5 June 2023.

Betts, Alexander. 2009. *Protection by Persuasion: International Cooperation in the Refugee Regime*. Ithaca: Cornell University Press.

– 2010. "The Refugee Regime Complex." *Refugee Studies Quarterly* 29 (1): 12–37. https://academic.oup.com/rsq/article-abstract/29/1/12/1545224. Accessed 5 June 2023.

– 2011. *Global Migration Governance.* Oxford, UK: Oxford University Press.

Betts, Alexander, and Lina Kainz. 2017. "The History of Migration Governance." Refugee Studies Centre Working Paper Series 122. University of Oxford. https://www.rsc.ox.ac.uk/publications/the-history-of-global-migration-governance. Accessed 5 June 2023.

Betts, Alexander, and James Milner. 2019. "Governance of the Global Refugee Regime." World Refugee and Migration Council Research Paper no. 13. Centre for International Governance Innovation. https://wrmcouncil.org/publications/research-paper/governance-of-the-global-refugee-regime/. Accessed 5 June 2023.

Carbert, Michelle. 2019. "Federal Election 2019: Where do the Major Parties Stand on Immigration?" *Globe and Mail*, 23 September 2019. https://www.theglobeandmail.com/politics/article-federal-election-2019-where-do-the-major-parties-stand-on-immigration. Accessed 5 June 2023.

Chishti, Muzaffar, and Kathleen Bush-Joseph. 2022. "Amid Record Venezuelan Arrivals, Biden Administration Embraces Border Expulsions Policy." Article. Migration Policy Institute, Washington, DC, 27 October 2022. https://www.migrationpolicy.org/article/venezuelan-expulsions-policy-biden Accessed 5 June 2023.

Clemens, Michael A. 2022. "Pathways for Labour Migration from Northern Central America: Five Difficult but Necessary Proposals." World Refugee and Migration Council Research Paper Series. https://wrmcouncil.org/publications/research-paper/pathways-for-labour-migration-from-northern-central-america-five-difficult-but-necessary-proposals/. Accessed 5 June 2023.

Congressional Research Service. 2019. "The Trump Administration's 'Zero Tolerance' Immigration Enforcement Policy." https://trac.syr.edu/immigration/library/P15410.pdf. Accessed 5 June 2023.

– 2021. *Central American Migration: Root Causes and U.S. Policy*. IF11151, version 6. https://sgp.fas.org/crs/row/IF11151.pdf. Accessed 5 June 2023.

– 2022. *Mexico's Immigration Control Efforts*. https://fas.org/sgp/crs/row/IF10215.pdf Accessed 5 June 2023.

Council on Foreign Relations. 2020. *US Foreign Policy: Multilateralism or Unilateralism*. Council on Foreign Relations. https://modeldiplomacy.cfr.org/pop-up-cases/us-foreign-policy-multilateralism-or-unilateralism. Accessed 5 June 2023.

Durand, Jorge, and Douglas S. Massey. 2019a. "Debacles on the Border: Five Decades of Fact-Free Immigration Policy." *The Annals of the American Academy of Political and Social Science* 684 (1): 6–20.

– 2019b. "Evolution of the Mexico-U.S. Migration System: Insights from the Mexican Migration Project." *The Annals of the American Academy of Political and Social Science* 684: 21–42.

Ferris, Elizabeth, and Katharine Donato. 2019. *Global Governance of Refugees and Migration: Negotiating the Global Compacts*. London: Routledge.

Fitzgerald, David. 2005. "Nationality and Migration in Modern Mexico." *Journal of Ethnic and Migration Studies* 31 (1): 171–91. https://doi.org/10.1080/1369183042000305735.

Fredrick, James. 2019. "How Mexico Beefs Up Immigration Enforcement To Meet Trump's Terms." *National Public Radio*, 13 July 2019. www.npr.org/2019/07/13/740009105/how-mexico-beefs-up-immigration-enforcement-to-meet-trumps-terms. Accessed 5 June 2023.

Garcia, Maria Cristina. 2006. "Canada: A Northern Refuge for Central Americans." *Migration Policy Institute*, 1 April 2006. https://www.migrationpolicy.org/article/canada-northern-refuge-central-americans. Accessed 5 June 2023.

Georgetown Law Human Rights Institute Fact-Finding Project. 2015. *The Cost of Stemming the Tide: How Immigration Enforcement Practices in Southern Mexico Limit Migrant Children's Access to International Protection*. Washington, DC: Georgetown Law Human Rights Institute. https://www.law.georgetown.edu/human-rights-institute/wp-content/uploads/sites/7/2017/07/HRI-Fact-Finding-Report-Stemming-the-Tide-Web-PDF_English.pdf. Accessed 5 June 2023.

Gobierno de México. 2018. "UN General Assembly endorses Global Compact for Safe, Orderly and Regular Migration," press release #13, 19 December 2018. https://www.gob.mx/sre/prensa/un-general-assembly-endorses-global-compact-for-safe-orderly-and-regular-migration?idiom=en. Accessed 5 June 2023.

Goodwin-Gill, Guy S., and Jane McAdam. 2007. *The Refugee in International Law*. 3rd ed. New York: Oxford University Press.

Government of Canada. n.d. *Canada's Strategy for Engagement in the Americas*. https://www.international.gc.ca/americas-ameriques/assets/pdfs/strategy-eng.PDF. Accessed 5 June 2023.

– 2018a. "Global Compact for Safe, Orderly and Regular Migration." Government of Canada. National statement. 10 December 2018. Immigration, Refugees and Citizenship Canada. https://www.canada.ca/en/immigration-refugees-citizenship/news/2018/12/global-compact-for-safe-orderly-and-regular-migration.html. Accessed 5 June 2023.

– 2018b. *Government Response to the Report of the House of Commons Standing Committee on Citizenship and Immigration Entitled*. House of Commons https://www.ourcommons.ca/DocumentViewer/en/42-1/CIMM/report-23/response-8512-421-92. Accessed 5 June 2023.

– 2020. "Notice – Supplementary Information for the 2021-2023 Immigration Levels Plan." Ottawa. 30 October 2020. https://www.canada.ca/en/immigration-refugees-citizenship/news/notices/supplementary-immigration-levels-2021-2023.html. Accessed 5 June 2023.

– 2021. *Roadmap for a Renewed U.S.- Canada Partnership*. 23 February 2021. https://pm.gc.ca/en/news/statements/2021/02/23/roadmap-renewed-us-canada-partnership. Accessed 5 June 2023.

– 2022a. *Departmental Plan 2022-2023*. Immigration, Refugees and Citizenship Canada https://www.canada.ca/en/immigration-refugees-citizenship/corporate/publications-manuals/departmental-plan-2022-2023/departmental-plan.html. Accessed 5 June 2023.

– 2022b. "New Immigration Plan to Fill Labour Market Shortages and Grow Canada's Economy," press release, 14 February 2022. https://www.canada.ca/en/immigration-refugees-citizenship/news/2022/02/new-immigration-plan-to-fill-labour-market-shortages-and-grow-canadas-economy.html. Accessed 5 June 2023.

Government of the United States, Department of State Bureau of Population, Refugees, and Migration (US, PRM). 2021. "Global Compact for Safe, Orderly, and Regular Migration (GCM)." National statement. 17 December 2021. https://www.state.gov/global-compact-for-safe-orderly-and-regular-migration-gcm/. Accessed 5 June 2023.

Government of the United States, Department of State. 2019. Office of the Spokesperson. "U.S. - Mexico Joint Declaration." 7 June 2019. www.state.gov/u-s-mexico-joint-declaration/. Accessed 5 June 2023.

Government of the United States, National Security Council. 2021. *U.S. Strategy for Addressing the Root Causes of Migration in Central America*. https://www.whitehouse.gov/wp-content/uploads/2021/07/Root-Causes-Strategy.pdf. Accessed 5 June 2023.

Gramlich, John, and Alissa Scheller. 2021. *What's Happening at the US-Mexico Border in 7 Charts*. Pew Research Center. 9 November 2021.

https://www.pewresearch.org/fact-tank/2021/11/09/whats-happening-at-the-u-s-mexico-border-in-7-charts/. Accessed 5 June 2023.

Guillén, Tonatiuh. 2020. "Un paso adelante, tres atrás. La política migratoria en tiempos de AMLO y Trump" [One step forward, one step back. Migration policy in the times of AMLO and Trump]. In *Balance temprano. Desde la izquierda democrática*, edited by Ricardo Becerra and José Woldenberg, 111–28. Mexico City: Instituto de Estudios para la Transición Democrática.

Heilman, Jaymie. 2018. "Canada is Turning its back on Central American Refugees." *Policy Options*, 20 June 2018. https://policyoptions.irpp.org/magazines/june-2018/canada-is-turning-its-back-on-central-american-refugees/Accessed 5 June 2023.

Israel, Emma, and Jeanne Batalova. 2020. "Mexican Immigrants in the United States." *Migration Information Source*, 5 November 2020. Washington, DC: *Migration Policy Institute*. https://www.migrationpolicy.org/article/mexican-immigrants-united-states-2019. Accessed 5 June 2023.

ILO (International Labour Organization). n.d. "Bilateral Agreements and Regional Cooperation." International Labour Organization. https://www.ilo.org/asia/areas/labour-migration/WCMS_226300/lang--en/index.htm. Accessed 5 June 2023.

IOM (International Organization for Migration). n.d.a. "Immigration Data Portal." IOM. https://www.migrationdataportal.org/international-data?i=stock_abs_&t=2020. Accessed 5 June 2023.

– n.d.b. "Regional Consultative Processes on Migration." IOM. https://www.iom.int/regional-consultative-processes-migration Accessed 5 June 2023.

Jauberth, H. Rodrigo, Gilberto Castaneda, Jesus Hernández, and Pedo Vuskovic. 2019. *The Difficult Triangle: Mexico, Central America and the United States*. London: Routledge.

Jones, Bruce, Jeffrey Feltman, and Will Morehouse. 2019. *Competitive Multilateralism*. Washington, DC: Brookings Institution. https://www.brookings.edu/research/competitive-multilateralism/. Accessed 5 June 2023.

Jubilut, Liliana Lyra, Marcia Vera Espinoza, and Gabriela Maezzanoti, eds. 2021. *Latin America and Refugee Protection: Regimes, Logics and Challenges*. New York: Berghahn Books.

Kainz, Lena, and Alexander Betts. 2021. "Power and Proliferation: Explaining the Fragmentation of Global Migration Governance." *Migration Studies* 9 (1): 65–89. https://doi.org/10.1093/migration/mnaa015. Accessed 5 June 2023.

Kneebone, Susan. 2016. "Comparative Regional Protection Frameworks for Refugees: Norms and Norm Entrepreneurs." *International Journal of Human Rights* 20 (2): 153–72 https://doi.org/10.1080/13642987.2016.1141499.

Korducki, Kelli María. 2019. "A Blind Spot for Central America in Canada's Refugee Response." *Open Canada*, 22 July 2019. https://opencanada.org/blind-spot-central-america-canadas-refugee-response/. Accessed 5 June 2023.

Kosten, Dan. 2019. "Mexico's Asylum System Is Inadequate." National Immigration Forum. 29 October 2019. https://immigrationforum.org/article/mexicos-asylum-system-is-inadequate/. Accessed 5 June 2023.

Kovic, Christine, and Francisco Argüelles. 2010. "The Violence of Security: Central American Migrants Crossing Mexico's Southern Border." *Anthropology Now* 2 (1): 87–97. https://www.jstor.org/stable/41201225. Accessed 5 June 2023.

Leuprecht, Christian. 2019. "End of the (Roxham) Road: Seeking Coherence on Canada's Border-Migration Compact." (December) MacDonald-Laurier Institution Publication. https://macdonaldlaurier.ca/files/pdf/20191108_MLI_ROXHAM_ROAD_Leuprecht_PAPER_FWeb.pdf. Accessed 5 June 2023.

Martin, Susan F. 2021. *Nation of Immigrants*. Cambridge: Cambridge University Press.

Masferrer, Claudia, and Luicy Pedroza, eds. 2022. *The Intersection of Foreign Policy and Migration Policy in Mexico*. Colegio de Mexico. https://libros.colmex.mx/tienda/the-intersection-of-foreign-policy-and-migration-policy-in-mexico-today/. Accessed 5 June 2023.

Mattei, Léo. 2022. "On the Line: The Mexicans Deported from the US to a Homeland they Barely Know." *France* 24, 14 January 2022. https://www.france24.com/en/tv-shows/reporters/20220114-on-the-line-the-mexicans-deported-from-the-us-to-a-homeland-they-barely-know. Accessed 5 June 2023.

Meyer, Maureen, and Adam Isacson. 2019. *The Wall Before the Wall: Mexico's Crackdown on Migration at its Southern Border.* Washington, DC: The Washington Office on Latin America. www.wola.org/wp-content/uploads/2019/12/2019-FULL-Report-Mexicos-Southern-Border.pdf. Accessed 5 June 2023.

Meyer, Maureen, and Clay Boggs. 2016. "U.S. Support for Migration Enforcement in Mexico: A Humanitarian Perspective." *Georgetown Journal of International Affairs* 17 (1): 28–37. https://www.jstor.org/stable/26396150. Accessed 5 June 2023.

Montoya-Galvez, Camilo. 2021. "Division among Biden Appointees led U.S. to Embrace Trump-era Border Policies." *CBS News*, 3 November 2021. https://www.cbsnews.com/news/immigration-biden-border-policies-trump-era/. Accessed 5 June 2023.

– 2022. "What is Title 42, the COVID-19 Border Policy Set to End in Late May?" *CBS News*, 5 April 2022. https://www.cbsnews.com/news/title-42-immigration-border-biden-covid-19-cdc/. Accessed 5 June 2023.

National Immigration Forum. 2018. Fact Sheet: Family-based Immigration. https://immigrationforum.org/article/fact-sheet-family-based-immigration.

Paperny, Anna Mehler. 2021. "Canada could Take in Some Central American Migrants to Help U.S. – Minister." *Reuters*, 9 June 2021. https://www.reuters.com/world/americas/canada-could-take-some-central-american-migrants-help-us-minister-2021-06-09/. Accessed 5 June 2023.

Pellicer Silva, Olga. 2019. "México, el derrumbe de un régimen y la política exterior" [Mexico: the collapse of a regime and foreign policy]. *Foro Internacional* 59 (2–3): 579–607. https://forointernacional.colmex.mx/index.php/fi/article/view/2634. Accessed 5 June 2023.

Rodriguez de Ita, Guadalupe. 2008. "Un Mexico Protector … de asilados y refugiados durante la *guerra fría*. Entre la definición y la ambigüedad" [Mexico as protector of asylees and refugees during the cold war]. *Dimension Antropologica* 15 (43): 121–58. https://revistas.inah.gob.mx/index.php/dimension/article/view/1545/1489. Accessed 5 June 2023.

Seidle, Leslie F. 2010. "Intergovernmental Immigration Agreements and Public Accountability." *Policy Options*, 1 July 2010. https://policyoptions.irpp.org/magazines/immigration-jobs-and-canadas-futureintergovernmental-immigration-agreements-and-public-accountability/. Accessed 5 June 2023.

Sharnak, Debbie. 2019. "Why Mexico is a Haven for Political Exiles like Bolivia's Former President Evo Morales." *Washington Post*, 8 December is-haven-political-exiles-like-bolivias-former-president-evo-morales/. Accessed 5 June 2023.

Sharpe, Marina. 2018. *The Regional Law of Refugee Protection in Africa*. New York: Oxford University Press.

Statista. 2021. *Number of Refugees Admissions in the US from Fiscal Year 2009 to Fiscal Year 2021*. Statista. https://www.statista.com/statistics/200061/number-of-refugees-arriving-in-the-us/. Accessed 5 June 2023.

UN General Assembly. 2016. Resolution 71/1, *New York Declaration for Refugees and Migrants*, A/RES/71/1 (19 September 2016). https://www.un.org/en/development/desa/population/migration/generalassembly/docs/globalcompact/A_RES_71_1.pdf. Accessed 5 June 2023.

– 2019a. Resolution 73/195, *Global Compact for Safe, Orderly and Regular Migration*, A/RES/73/195 (11 January 2019). https://www.un.org/en/development/desa/population/migration/generalassembly/docs/globalcompact/A_RES_73_195.pdf. Accessed 5 June 2023.

– 2019b. Resolution 73/326, *Format and Organization Aspects of the International Migration Review Forums*, A/RES/73/326 (29 July 2019). https://documents-dds-ny.un.org/doc/UNDOC/GEN/N19/225/96/PDF/N1922596.pdf?OpenElement. Accessed 5 June 2023.

UNHCR (United Nations High Commissioner for Refugees). 1984. Declaración de Cartagena. UNHCR - Cartagena Declaration on Refugees, adopted by

the Colloquium on the International Protection of Refugees in Central America, Mexico and Panama, Cartagena de Indias, Colombia, 22 November 1984.
– n.d.a. "Comprehensive Regional Protection and Solutions Framework." United Nations High Commissioner for Refugees. https://globalcompactrefugees.org/mirps-en. Accessed 5 June 2023.
– n.d.b. Refugee Data Finder. https://www.unhcr.org/refugee-statistics/. Accessed 5 June 2023.
United States Department of State. 2021. "Revised National Statement of the United States of America on the Adoption of the Global Compact for Safe, Orderly and Regular Migration." 17 December 2021. https://www.state.gov/wp-content/uploads/2021/12/gcm-Accessible_12212021.pdf. Accessed 5 June 2023.
United States Mission to the United Nations. 2017. "United States Ends Participation in Global Compact on Migration," press release, 2 December 2017. https://usun.usmission.gov/united-states-ends-participation-in-global-compact-on-migration/. Accessed 5 June 2023.
United States National Security Council. 2021. *US Strategy for Addressing the Root Causes of Migration in Central America*. US Government: White House.
USAID (US Agency for International Development). 2021. "U.S.-Mexico Joint Statement on Sembrando Oportunidades," press release, 1 December 2021. https://www.usaid.gov/news-information/press-releases/dec-1-2021-us-mexico-joint-statement-sembrando-oportunidades. Accessed 5 June 2023.
van Riemsdijk, Micheline, Marianne H. Marchand, and Volker M. Heins, eds. 2021. "Special Issue: New Actors and Contested Architectures in Global Migration Governance." *Third World Quarterly* 42 (1). https://www.tandfonline.com/toc/ctwq20/42/1?nav=tocList Accessed 5 June 2023.
Veprek, Andrew. 2018. "Remarks to the UN General Assembly on the Global Compact for Migration Resolution," press release, 19 December 2018. https://usun.usmission.gov/remarks-to-the-un-general-assembly-on-the-global-compact-for-migration-resolution/. Accessed 5 June 2023.
Wells, Victoria. 2022. "Posthaste: Canadians Have Never Been so Supportive of Immigration, Survey Reveals." *Financial Post*, 26 October 2022. https://financialpost.com/executive/executive-summary/canadians-support-immigration. Accessed 5 June 2023.
Women's Refugee Commission. 2022. *The Biden Administration Falls Short on Asylum During Year One: A Call for Change in 2022*. New York: Women's Refugee Commission. https://www.womensrefugeecommission.org/research-resources/the-biden-administration-falls-short-on-asylum-during-year-one-a-call-for-change-in-2022/. Accessed 5 June 2023.

World Bank. n.d.a. Population data. World Bank. https://data.worldbank.org/indicator/SP.POP.TOTL. Accessed 5 June 2023.

– n.d.b. "Snapshot Mexico." World Integrated Trade Solution (WITS). https://wits.worldbank.org/CountrySnapshot/en/MEX. Accessed 5 June 2023.

WRMC (World Refugee and Migration Council). n.d. "North and Central American Task Force on Migration." World Refugee and Migration Council. https://wrmcouncil.org/north-and-central-american-task-force-on-migration/. Accessed 5 June 2023.

– 2022. *Summary Report of the North and Central American Task Force on Migration*. https://wrmcouncil.org/publications/task-force-summary-report-key-recommendations/. Accessed 5 June 2023.

Wright, Teresa. 2018. "Scheer Opposes Canada Signing UN Compact on Migrants, Liberals cry Foul." *National Post*, 4 December 2018. https://nationalpost.com/pmn/news-pmn/canada-news-pmn/scheer-opposes-canada-signing-un-compact-on-migrants-liberals-cry-foul. Accessed 5 June 2023.

Zepeda, Beatriz, and Julieta Fuentes-Carrera. 2020. "La frontera México-Guatemala y el perímetro de seguridad de Estados Unidos 2000-2020" [The Mexico-Guatemalan border and the US security perimeter 2000-2020]. In *Entre lo político y lo espacial: representaciones geopolíticas de la región transformazidora México-Guatemala* [Between the political and the spatial: geopolitical representations of the transforming Mexico-Guatemala region], edited by Julieta Fuentes-Carrea, 49–84. Mexico: Región Transfronteriza México Guatamala. https://www.researchgate.net/publication/348756157_La_frontera_Mexico-Guatemala_y_el_perimetro_de_seguridad_de_Estados_Unidos_2000-2020/link/600f61a2299bf14088c08169/download. Accessed 5 June 2023.

2

"Organized Hypocrisy" and the Impacts of US Burden-Shifting on Mexican and Regional Migration Governance

Luicy Pedroza and Isabel Gil-Everaert

This chapter adopts an interstate-level perspective to unpack and analyze the relationships between formal and informal migration policy changes in Mexico, between 2018 and 2021, as a response to dramatic shifts in United States asylum and refugee policies. We delineate the consequences for policy coherence in Mexico – which we define as regulatory contradictions and gaps among stated goals, actual policies, and new regulatory contradictions – particularly amid a challenging scenario of drastic increases in transit migration through Mexico for persons seeking protection in the US. Applying concepts from both public policy and international relations (IR), our larger argument advances a critical view of migration regimes and migration governance in instances of deep power asymmetry. In the case at hand, militarization, institutional displacement, loss of transparency, increasing normative incoherence, and the centralization of decision-making in all matters that touch on border control and the management of flows hamper the development of a regional approach to migration. The opaque position in which Mexican authorities must operate under US pressure further undermines the rule of law in Mexico, raising questions regarding its sovereignty over migration policy, most obviously, but also puts local communities at higher risk of falling prey to criminal organizations, and ultimately undermines accountability of Mexican authorities toward their citizenry.

One vehicle for and poignant illustration of these dynamics is the widespread presence of migrant and asylum seeker pushbacks and enforced immobility in border areas already wracked by endemic violence (see Odgers-Ortiz and Olivas-Hernández in this volume). These measures contradict the Mexican Constitution and its 2011 Migration Law, which promote freedom of movement in the territory and a human rights perspective on migration ostensibly centred on the goal of decriminalizing irregular migration. Yet, as we describe in detail below, and contrary to the Trump Administration's consistent framing, the US is not the only party to pay for and suffer from the situation of asylum migration at the US-Mexico border. In the cynical pursuit of burden-shifting under the name responsibility-sharing, or of chasing and detaining migrants under the guise of "securing" them (as used in Mexican legal parlance), migrants, international regimes, and effective and humane regional migration management suffer most.

We posit that the continued interstate practices delineate a hypocritically organized migration regime, in which the state security perspective is a fundamental feature of bilateral migration and border relations, and is not simply a byproduct of securitized practices – at the cost of migrant rights and international norms. We analyze the ongoing impacts of consistent agreements and patterns of behaviour in the realm of migration policy, echoing earlier theories from IR scholars including Kratochwil (1993) and Young (1983) that suggest regimes need not depend on the explicit agreement of parties or a process of negotiation around a set of constitutive norms, but can emerge out of policy imposition in situations of deep power asymmetry.

The first section of the chapter explores changes in Mexican mobility dynamics in the past decades, arguing that Mexico is consolidating into a space of mixed mobility flows, where expulsions coexist with its role as a state of transit, destination, and internal displacement. We show how the challenges posited by these mixed mobility dynamics have been met with changes in regional and national migratory policy in Mexico and the US which have undermined the refugee system, generated situations of entrapment, heightened risk and vulnerability for migrants, and resulted in a wide array of political and policy tensions at several levels.

The following section analyzes how the measures intended to contain US-bound migration in Mexico since 2019 resulted in a pattern of "intentional incoherence" (Boswell 2007) in migration policy. With this in mind, we analyze policy developments since 2010, starting with the important legislative changes of 2011, which amounted to a significant shift toward advancing a human rights approach toward migration. We then explain how an external policy shock, measures targeted at controlling transit migration, and decisions that weakened the interinstitutional framework to manage migration have foreclosed possibilities for coherently applying Mexico's own migration law.

The chapter's final section delves into a deeper analysis of the consequences of this failed attempt to address migratory challenges in Mexico. In this section, we explore institutional displacement, increasing normative incoherence, the erasure of civil society voices in migration policymaking, and the centralization of strategic decision-making in Mexico's foreign policy apparatus. We argue that the consequences of this migratory policy system are profound not only for migrants but also for a wide range of actors in the Mexican migration policy and local communities, and delineate a worrisome pattern for regional migration governance.

MEXICO'S CONTEMPORARY MIGRATION CHALLENGES

Mexico has witnessed significant changes in mobility dynamics since around 2010. For decades the country was, from a demographic and narrative standpoint, mainly a territory of expulsion and emigration (Asad and Garip 2019; Boruchoff 2019). Millions of Mexicans left their homes in search of jobs, higher wages, and better opportunities, primarily in the US (Durand 2016; Durand and Massey 2004; Massey, Durand, and Malone 2003). However, since the beginning of the XXIst century Mexico has transformed into a space of transit for hundreds of thousands of people fleeing their countries, mainly in Central America, seeking to reach the US for multiple and often overlapping reasons (FitzGerald and Arar 2018), including economic motivations, threats from political persecution, and rampant violence and insecurity.

Scholarly attention has increasingly shifted toward understanding the dangers and risks involved in transit migration, high costs of the journeys, impacts of intensified migration controls, border surveillance, and the gradual but steady strengthening of criminal networks that profit from smuggling, trafficking, and abuses perpetrated against migrants (Álvarez Velasco 2016; Anguiano Téllez, Hernández López, and Villafuerte Solís 2018; González, Zapata, and Anguiano Téllez 2017; Kuhner 2011; Martínez, Cobo, and Narváez 2015; Nájera Aguirre 2016; Torre Cantalapiedra and Yee-Quintero 2018; Willers 2016). A series of events have made this reality more broadly visible and engaged the attention of governments, civil society activists, and the public. Among these was the 2010 San Fernando massacre, where seventy-two migrants were murdered by a criminal group, which brought significantly greater attention to the threats faced by individuals navigating migration routes within Mexico. In 2014, what is now known as the "unaccompanied minors' crisis" triggered a series of public reactions in both the US and Mexico, mainly in terms of media coverage and subsequent policy changes. A few months after the arrival of close to 40,000 unaccompanied minors at the Mexico-US border (Ataiants et al. 2018; Ortíz de Zárate Béjar and Shubich 2018), the Mexican government announced the

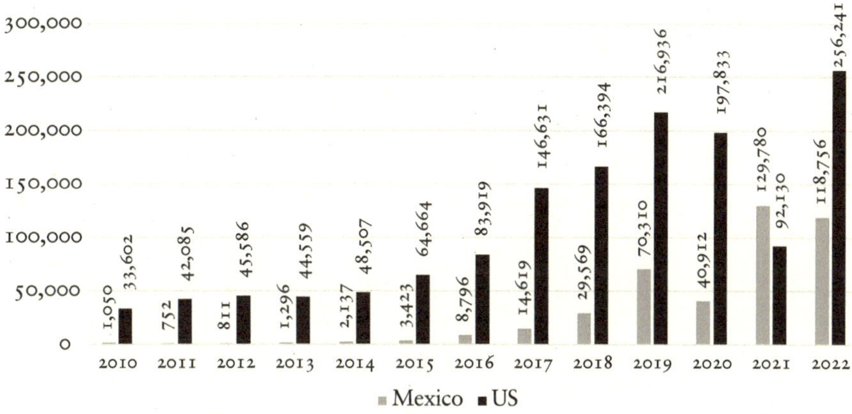

Figure 2.1 | Total number of asylum requests in Mexico and the United States, 2010–22

Source: Elaborated by authors with data from the COMAR Statistical bulletins and data from TRAC Immigration.

* Data for Mexico are reported by natural year and for the US by fiscal year.

implementation of the Southern Border Plan (Programa Frontera Sur). This plan was framed as a strategy to protect migrants' rights and it referred to the unaccompanied minors as the most vulnerable group in the context of transit migration. However, it also contained an extensive focus and devoted the majority of its budget to security, regulation, and migration control (Gil-Everaert 2020; Castillo García and Castañeda Sandoval 2009). It is no coincidence that these new migration controls occurred in the same year that Central Americans surpassed Mexicans in the number of border crossings to the US.[1] Removals of irregular migrants in Mexico spiked after the implementation of the Southern Border Plan (Knippen, Boggs, and Meyer 2015) and, in 2016, Mexico deported more Central American migrants than the United States (ICE 2016).

The Programa Frontera Sur marked the start of a process of consolidation of a new regional migration management system, which was largely dictated by the US and Mexican security and control interests. Despite efforts to halt northbound migration, the scale of flows continued to increase, along with a substantial expansion in the number of people fleeing their countries of origin to seek international protection in Mexico and the United States. Indeed, from 2014 onwards, asylum requests in Mexico started growing exponentially,

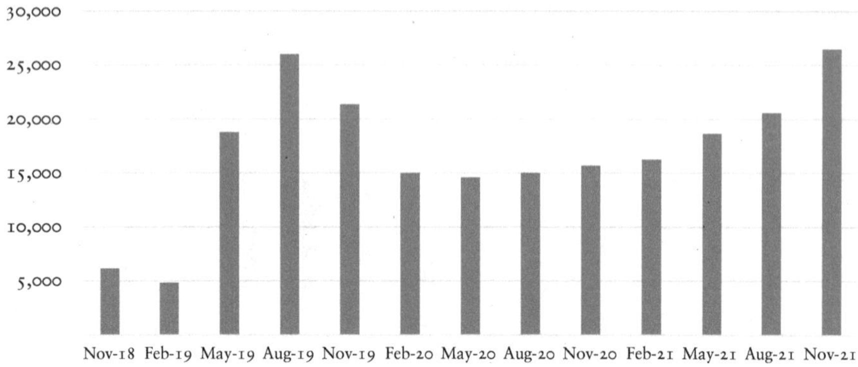

Figure 2.2 | Number of people on asylum waitlists at US-Mexico border, November 2018 to November 2021

Source: Authors' elaboration based on information from the Metering Updates published by the Strauss Center for International Security and Law at the University of Texas at Austin. Available at: https://www.strausscenter.org/campi-publications/.

more than doubling from one year to the next, as indicated in figure 2.1. By 2021, Mexico occupied third place globally in terms of the number of annual asylum requests (UNHCR 2023).

As described in figure 2.1, asylum requests in the US also increased over this period, reaching a peak of over 216,000 in 2019, followed by a downward trend and a new rise in 2022. While the 2020 decline (for both Mexico and the US) can be partly explained by pandemic-era mobility restrictions, it is also a result of cumulative shifts in asylum policies and procedures. As the number of asylum requests increased, the regional system that started with the implementation of the Programa Frontera Sur (initially focused on controlling unauthorized migration toward the US) soon expanded toward incorporating changes in refugee and asylum policies in both countries. These developments have mirrored global shifts toward the deterrence of refugees and creation of obstacles to accessing protection in what FitzGerald (2019) has termed an "architecture of repulsion."

In 2016, the US started the implementation of a "metering" policy to slow the arrival of asylum seekers along the Mexico-US border, which essentially meant registering for wait-lists before being allowed to cross the land border and start asylum procedures. Several waiting lists were implemented in different Mexican border cities, and by November 2021 more than 26,000 people were still waiting.

Despite these obstacles in the asylum process, people continued to transit through Mexico and arrive at the US border seeking protection. In 2018, the so-called migrant caravans started making their way north from places such as Honduras, Guatemala, and El Salvador with the objective of reaching the US. These groups of thousands of migrants and refugees moving together again triggered a series of restrictive and collaborative policy reactions, the most notorious and impactful of which was the Migrant Protection Protocols (MPP) program, more popularly known as the "Remain in Mexico" program. The protocols were a result of a series of bilateral negotiations between the Mexican and the US governments, achieved under the threat of imposing broad trade tariffs on Mexico. Since their implementation in early 2019, more than 78,000 asylum seekers were returned to Mexico to wait for their court date in US immigration courts.

Less than 1 per cent (742) of people who requested asylum under MPP were granted protection (TRAC Immigration 2021). Waiting times were significantly extended, partly due to the total closure of the US asylum system during the COVID-19 pandemic, but have continued up to the time of writing, when broader pandemic border restrictions have been lifted. In addition, in early 2020 the US implemented a policy known as Title 42 – ostensibly a public health measure which continued under the Biden administration and involves the expedited summary expulsion of anyone who attempts to cross the Mexico-US land border (see Coen in this volume). Title 42 is a section of the US Code of federal statutes that has existed since 1944, although 2020 was the first time it was used as an immigration control mechanism (García Cabezas 2022). Title 42 "empowers federal health authorities to prohibit migrants from entering the country if it is determined that doing so could prevent the spread of contagious diseases" (Gramlich 2022). In other words, under Title 42, all land border entries to the US (with the exception of US citizens and permanent residents) were prohibited.

Data show that the US expelled close to 2 million people under Title 42 between 2020 and 2022. However, it is important to note that one out of every three returns are of people who claim to be on at least their second attempt to cross the border (AIC 2022). Title 42 expulsions affected not only migrants but also asylum seekers, de facto impeding access to international protection. It has also generated a situation somewhat resembling a revolving door at Mexico's northern border, where thousands of people experience repeated returns. Since its implementation in March 2020, Title 42 has sparked a series of reactions ranging from public denunciation of how this policy violates the right and access to asylum, attempts from the

Table 2.1 | Total number of asylum seekers returned to Mexico under MPPs, January 2019 to March 2021

Mexican point of return	Men	Women	Total
El Chaparral	4,480	3,356	7,836
Mexicali	3,837	3,268	7,105
Nuevo Laredo	7,277	4,332	11,609
Matamoros	12,092	9,452	21,544
Ciudad Juárez	14,680	9,424	24,104
Piedras Negras	2,772	1,765	4,537
Nogales	634	682	1,316
Total	45,772	32,279	78,051

Source: Compiled by authors with data from the Mexican National Institute for Migration, provided through a request through the Freedom of Information Act.

Biden administration to lift the policy, and ensuing legal challenges which have kept it in place.[2]

A growing number of Mexican nationals who fled their homes due to situations of violence and insecurity among those waiting on metering lists, returned under MPP, and were kept in place by Title 42. The number of persons internally displaced due to violence and insecurity has increased significantly over the course of the so-called "war on drugs" in Mexico (Rodríguez 2022). According to the Internal Displacement Monitoring Center, 379,000 Mexicans were internally displaced between 2009 and 2021 (IDMC 2022). This trend is confirmed by the most recent Mexican Census data, which reveal that between 2015 and 2020 more than 250,000 Mexicans left their homes due to violence and insecurity (INEGI 2021). At least 10 per cent of those internally displaced in that period (2015–2020) are concentrated in northern border states.

This confluence of a rise in asylum requests and changes in the refugee regime have resulted in a series of significant developments for both migrants and policymakers. These include a record-level backlog of asylum requests both in the United States and Mexico, a substantial increase in waiting times for resolution of requests, as well as the emergence of diverse situations of immobility and entrapment of people seeking international protection across Mexico (see Odgers-Ortiz and Olivas-Hernández in this volume). Though space constraints limit multilevel analysis, it is important to note that jurisdictions along the border in both the US and Mexico (from municipalities to counties and states) have agency and influence on the broader bilateral and regional scenario. This is quite obvious on the US side, where governors of border states have not only their own takes on immigration enforcement but politicize migration in certain periods to grab the spotlight in the federal bipartisan divide – such as the legal battles around Title 42 (Puretz 2022).

MEXICAN INSTITUTIONAL ATTEMPTS TO MEET MIGRATION CHALLENGES

This policy constellation, which came to the fore during the 2016–20 Trump administration, created an external shock for Mexico, resulting in an overburdened Mexican asylum system, a humanitarian crisis on both Mexico's borders, extended delays in access to international protection, and heightened local tensions due to the entrapment of migrants in communities already troubled with insecurity and violence.

Far from being disjointed, the policy constellation of metering, the MPP, and Title 42 was purposefully designed to contain migration in Mexico and disincentivizing mobility. The policy shock provoked a paradigmatic change in Mexico, resulting in what Christina Boswell (2007) has compellingly described as "intentional incoherence" in migration policy. Boswell's concept of intentional incoherence applies to situations of migration policy dilemmas in which the state "solves" conflicting demands and requirements by resorting to nontransparent and uncontrolled policy responses (2007, 96). Such responses allow incoherence between norms and regulations and their implementation. In the next section, we clarify how Mexican authorities responded to external policy shocks by incoherently rearranging institutions (Migone and Howlett 2016, 1–87, 88). We contextualize by first recounting the trajectory of Mexican migration policy institutions leading up to this moment, unpack how that shock occurred, and then explore the reaction of Mexican institutional actors.

Mexico's Migration Policy Trajectory until 2018

In December 2018, Mexico's new foreign minister declared that Mexico was on track to become "a model for the implementation of the Global Compact" for a Safe, Regular and Orderly Migration (hereafter GCM) in

Marrakesh (Exteriores 2019). The process for the GCM's adoption had been led by Swiss and Mexican ambassadors, and the high-level visit strongly signalled the level of commitment to uphold a position that Mexico had provided considerable leadership on internationally (for further discussion of the role of North American states in the development of the GCM, see Ferris and Matheson in this volume). Indeed, through two different federal administrations over a course of twelve years, Mexico had developed a stronger legal and institutional framework to meet international commitments to manage migration comprehensively and coherently. The aforementioned San Fernando massacre of 2010 sparked an international outcry (particularly among Latin American countries that lost dozens of citizens as victims to organized crime). In its wake, activist groups, academics, migrant advocates, and civil society organizations (CSOs) found a window of opportunity to escalate pressure on successive federal governments and the legislature to bring Mexico's migration and refugee laws in line with international human rights norms. Their sustained work and interventions were necessary for the Migration Law of 2011. This work continued after the promulgation of the Law by tracking its implementation (or lack thereof) and identifying areas for improvement (Calderón Chelius 2012; Rojas and Hernández 2017).

The Migration Law of 2011 and the additional Refugee Law of 2011 fulfilled the expectations of activist coalitions, covering most aspects of relevance to the migration profile of Mexico at the time and mandated the application of the same normative principles to all migrant groups.[3] The only notable absences were a legal framework to address transit migration as well as vulnerable groups seeking humanitarian protection – particularly unaccompanied children, women, and a rising number of internally displaced persons (IDPs). Over time, the latter vulnerable groups would be covered by subsidiary laws; however, transit migration would continue to remain unaddressed. In hindsight, considering the developments reviewed at the outset of this chapter, the latter gap would prove pivotal.

In the years prior to 2018 and the inauguration of President Andrés Manuel López Obrador (AMLO), the government of Enrique Peña Nieto had overseen the development of the Programa Especial de Migración (Special Program for Migration, PEM). This policy strategy for migration management was based on adopting a coherent and comprehensive perspective that took account of the most important migrant groups at the time (INM 2018b) – emigrants, immigrants, transit migrants, and return migrants. In terms of institutional architecture, the leading political agency was the Unidad de Política Migratoria (Migration Policy Unit, UPM), under the Secretaría de Gobernación (Ministry of Interior, SEGOB), and the leading operational agency was the Instituto Nacional de Migración (National Migration Institute, INM), the agency in charge of migration control at large. Two different consultative bodies – the Consejo Consultivo de Política Migratoria de la Secretaría de Gobernación (CCPM), and the Consejo Ciudadano del Instituto Nacional de Migración (CCINM), consisting of a group of experts from academia and civil society assigned on a rotational basis – advised on the design and implementation of migration policy at the highest level. Although the migration management architecture and legal framework for migration policy as of 2018 still had weaknesses in terms of implementation, since 2011, it had taken on a position of overall political salience relative to the regulatory and institutional scenarios of other Latin American countries (Cantor, Freier, and Gauci 2015).

The election of the Trump administration provided an external shock that would fundamentally undermine progress toward a rights-based and coherent migration policy framework. Most notably, Mexico had resisted the pressure from the US to accept a safe third country agreement since Peña Nieto's government (Alianza Americas 2018; Senado de la República 2019). Mexican officials had provided a mixed response to migration flows – with a rhetorical emphasis on openness to legal migration and a practical increase in rejections and deportations. However, the Trump administration upset the status quo and framed the issue as a problem of Mexican unwillingness to control migration, and claimed that the Mexican government would pay political and economic costs for lack of policy compliance (these claims were often linked with plans for a "wall").

In November 2018, a few days after the first large "caravan" of migrants moved through Mexico with an accompanying outcry of Donald Trump (Fernández de la Reguera Ahedo et al. 2019), and a few days before the inauguration of the Mexican government elected in July 2018, a workshop convened by German foundations and think tanks brought together incoming politicians, CSOs, academics, and representatives of international organizations active in Mexican migration policy. The workshop's goal was to take stock of existing policies and outstanding challenges for the incoming government. Participants reached the conclusion that the most prominent policy problem was not regulatory; there were gaps between legal norms and their application, and a lack of coordination between agencies to that effect (Heinrich Böll Stiftung 2018). A document elaborated by the very agency in charge of migration policy, the UPM, confirmed this diagnosis of the exiting government (UPM 2018). The 2019 policy shock not only unsettled this diagnostic but set Mexico back several steps on the trajectory it had taken toward comprehensive migration management.

The State of Affairs at the Inauguration of President Andrés Manuel López Obrador

At the beginning of the AMLO administration in December 2018, not only did the foreign minister pledge to make Mexico a model for migration management, but also pledged solidarity and announced a new era of regional engagement. The main instrument for this would be the Plan de desarrollo integral El Salvador-Guatemala-Honduras-México, PDI (Comprehensive Development Plan El Salvador-Guatemala-Honduras-Mexico), by which the government of Mexico, with the backing of the Comisión Económica para América Latina y el Caribe / Economic Commission Office for Latin America and the Caribbean (CEPAL/ECLAC), would adopt a "human and not contentious perspective" on migration policy (United Nations ECLAC 2021). This new regional development plan would include investment to support the economic growth of southern Mexico, Guatemala, Honduras, and El Salvador and ostensibly contribute to stemming the outflow of migrants by promoting "a comprehensive management of the migratory cycle with human security, rights, and means of life, and person-centered security" (AMLO 2018; CEPAL 2018). Indeed, the AMLO government's first foreign policy act was to formalize this agreement under the auspices of the UN's ECLAC (elEconomista.es 2019). At the same time, the new government appointed an academic (rather than a politician), experienced in studying and observing different migrant groups, as the head of the corrupt and purge-resistant INM with a mandate to reform the agency from the inside (Eduardo 2011; Expansión Política 2019; Reuters 2020).

An initial demonstration of the new government's approach came in early 2019, when it responded to migrant caravans by issuing humanitarian documents allowing individuals to stay legally in Mexico for a year, and access employment, health, and education (INM 2018a). The Trump administration's reaction was immediate. Further talks between the US and Mexico governments about a possible safe third country agreement took place, with Mexico standing its ground in opposing such measures. Yet, as pressure mounted, the UPM became absent from these meetings (Durand Arp-Nisen 2019) and the Ministry of Foreign Affairs (Secretaría de Relaciones Exteriores, SRE) took over negotiations. US pressure increased as the number of migrants crossing through Mexico persisted, and reached a boiling point in May 2019, when the Trump administration threatened a blanket 5 per cent tariff on Mexican exports, which would increase by 5 per cent monthly until Mexico acceded (Mars, Sandoval, and Fariza 2019). As a response, the Mexican government deployed over 6,000 troops of the newly minted National Guard (a security body constituted overwhelmingly of military personnel who were offered incentives to transfer) on both borders, officially in support of the INM. Mexico agreed to the MPPs and thus acceded to taking back asylum seekers rejected at the US border.

The AMLO government in Mexico was left to justify its decision to accept what looked very much like a de facto safe third country agreement (although it bears important differences with other regional cases; see Banerjee in this volume) and to have granted the US government the competence to evaluate Mexican migration policy without formal commitments to share the costs for containment policies or to support Mexico's development plan in the South (Guillén 2020). The AMLO government argued that it had responded in a humanitarian manner to a unilateral US decision. Yet, this justification hardly managed to veil the fact that the decision was ultimately driven by foreign policy and trade concerns, given that 81 per cent of Mexican trade is concentrated with the US. In effect, considerations of advancing coherent and humane migration management were made subservient to coercion in the spheres of high politics.

Security deployments at Mexico's southern border proved effective in reducing transit migration of Central Americans reaching Mexico, which decreased by 36 per cent in only forty-five days (Nájera and Rojas 2019). However, it also meant that asylum requests in Mexico increased. Beyond the deployment of the National Guard, the crisis led to a major reallocation of policy mandates and operational roles. First, the aforementioned consultative councils ceased to meet (Pedroza 2021). Second, per decree, the president created the Comisión Intersecretarial de Atención Integral en Materia Migratoria (Intersecretarial Commission on Integral Attention to Migration, CIAIMM), a new interministerial body with members of sixteen government agencies under the lead of the SRE; civil society actors were present only by invitation to ad hoc meetings (González 2019). First informally and later formally (Martínez 2019; INM 2019), this commission obtained key functions in approving strategies to coordinate migration policy. Thus, it de facto displaced the legal functions of UPM under the Migration Law of 2011. Second, and most worryingly, the presidential decree that created the National Guard directed it to "support INM" in the "securing" of migrants (i.e., placing them in detention), and the guarding of migratory facilities (Secretaría de Gobernación 2019). A few days later, the head of INM resigned.

The Response to the Shock

The Mexican government reacted to the crisis in its bilateral relations by fragmenting institutional mandates and deviating from established command structures. In times of crisis, institutions are put to the test because their normal procedures become inapplicable and they must operate outside of their established routines (Boin and Lodge 2016). In the case at hand, mandate takeovers were very clearly a strong deviation (Masferrer and Pedroza 2021), with overlaps in competencies eventually leading to complete functional takeovers when the CIAIMM was legally mandated to set the goals of migration policy (DOF 2019). The upshot of this was that the oversight from civil society and academic experts was replaced by a new and murky framework in which agencies took over functions from other legally mandated actors for the sake of protecting economic and foreign policy interests at the expense of long-fought-for frameworks toward comprehensive and humane migration management.

Crises may potentially open spaces for radical change, yet can also result in regressive policies when new deviations are indefinitely prolonged, resulting in reduced responsiveness, transparency, legality, and coherence. More than just a temporary interministerial or interagency conflict, the impacts on Mexico shook the legal foundations of migration policy. This was perhaps most evident given that the National Guard came to act as a militarized arm of migration policies, and was de jure led by the Ministry of Interior but de facto led by the Ministry of Foreign Affairs in migration matters pertaining to the bilateral relationship to the US. The Constitutional commitments to freedom of movement of any person in Mexican territory (Art. 11 of the Constitution) and the human rights perspective on decriminalizing irregular migration (Migration Law of 2011) now stand in open contradiction with the new mandate of the National Guard to pursue and "secure" undocumented migrants. In a more general sense, Mexico has turned back from the inclusive and integrationist elements of its own migration and asylum regulations or, at the very least, tolerates that these elements coexist with migrants being chased, detained, and deported without due process.

Thus, administrative dysfunction has been formalized. The legal inconsistencies in the mandates among migration agencies have created a lack of responsivity over migration control authorities and facilities. The implications in this would soon become painfully clear. On 27 March 2023 a migrant detention center where migrants were kept locked, caught fire, leading to the death of 40 persons. This tragedy showed how the current dysfunctional and legally inconsistent scenario allows authorities de jure and de facto to evade responsibility and blame each other (Camhaji 2023). All of this affects the already overburdened Mexican asylum system. International organizations have been keen on supplementing the Mexican asylum system around human and financial resources where capacity was weakest (Roldán 2021; Gobernación 2021). However, the overall transfer of costs to Mexico and the requirement of asylum seekers to wait in Mexican territory sought to disincentivize asylum seekers from transiting to the US, thus undermining international protection norms in favour of economic and trade policy priorities.

BEYOND THE CRISIS: BILATERAL ORGANIZED HYPOCRISY

A degree of administrative dysfunction is perhaps to be expected, but is still worrisome (Chen and Shanks 2022; Bednar 2023). In the case at hand, institutional displacement, increasing normative incoherence, the erasure of civil society voices in migration policymaking, and centralization of decision-making on strategic matters have led to opacity in migration policy. This has adverse consequences for migrants, above all, but impacts a wide range of actors in the Mexican migration policy landscape who had invested years into advancing the development and clarification of mandates across agencies and the formation of representative councils to oversee their work. It would be shortsighted, however, to stop the analysis at the national frame. Just as the policy crisis was provoked by an external shock, its solution or lack thereof are part and parcel of a scenario with specific bilateral, but also global, features, all of which point to the emergence of a cynical global regime.

The AMLO government, which came to power with a strong mandate at its inauguration in December 2018, has seen its initial plans on migration policy both neglected and upended by US policy changes. The streamlined decision-making through the foreign policy sphere that the president chose to implement to (presumably) deal more efficiently with Trump administration's containment priorities lacks expertise to guide decisions in such a complex policy field. To some observers, the subordination of migration policy to foreign policy can be explained both by the lack of interest of President AMLO in migration policy as a whole (Délano 2018) and by the fact that the migration policy crisis endangered the AMLO administration's domestic political priorities by threatening to fundamentally undermine the well-being of the Mexican economy (Covarrubias 2021, 82). As a result, the foreign ministry focused the Mexican migration policy on controlling transit and asylum migration at borders and across the territory, and the agency charged with developing a comprehensive policy and rights approach was excluded in negotiations with the regional hegemon. One key result is that migrant integration, a key principle according to the Migration Law of 2011 (Preamble, Art. 15), has been lost as a priority amid the resulting institutional incoherence.

Migrants, institutional actors, and CSOs are not the only actors who have lost standing in the post-2019 context. The US holds responsibility for exerting its authority to maintain policies that condemn migrants to indefinite waiting periods in a place that they intended to only transit through. The Biden administration has not, despite its initial commitment to reverse the damage done by the Trump administration to the US asylum and refugee architecture, managed to change migration policies in a decisive direction that would include Mexico as an equal partner or allow it to shift back to its humane migration management policy agenda (see Coen in this volume). Despite some accomplishments regarding increasing refugee quotas and offering more work visas for Central American migrants, the MPPs and Title 42 remain in place due to injunctions in US domestic courts (Associated Press 2022; Eichensehr 2022). Amid US policy continuity – or rather, uncertainty about US policy stability – all integration policies in Mexico are thus set up to fail insofar as it is a territory where migrants have not chosen, but are legally obliged, to stay (Haas Pacuic, Sánchez-Montijano, and Zedillo Ortega 2021; París Pombo 2020).

Mexico's Failures upon Closer Inspection

At this point, it is important to observe that in the intergovernmental negotiations between Mexico and the US during the migration policy crisis, Mexico's negotiators largely failed to mitigate US policy influence. The point of reference here is the self-proclaimed vision of the government to advance its migration policy goals in such encounters. Initially, the AMLO government – backed by a supportive Congress – attempted to frame migration in bilateral relations with the US as an issue of "shared responsibility and a regional challenge that must be met collaboratively" and through "a vision that promotes investment and cooperation for development in Central America as the only real response to stop forced migration" (Senado de la República 2019, 4). Throughout the crisis, Mexican negotiators proved able to elicit only a mild expression of support from the US to the Mexican President's Comprehensive Development Plan, with no commitment of funds. Though Mexico has managed to resist signing a formal safe third country agreement, it has continuously accepted pushbacks of further groups of migrants seeking access to the US to claim asylum. Mexico has de facto become a barrier to the northbound mobility of migrants in the region, whatever be their country of origin or the underlying drivers of their migration decision-making. Mexico implements agreements made with the US in contravention of its own asylum and refugee laws, while also leaving migrants, activist organizations, and local communities vulnerable to being pressured or directly threatened by criminal groups. Turning Mexico into a 5,000 km borderland (Anguiano Téllez, Hernández López, and

Villafuerte Solís 2018; Anguiano Téllez and Trejo Peña 2007; González, Zapata, and Anguiano Téllez 2017) has resulted in, among other things, an excessive focus on border surveillance and restrictions on migration, leaving other complex dynamics, such as domestic criminal markets and institution-building efforts at the local level, out of the set of main priorities (Selee, Arnson, and Olson 2013). These policies had the knock-on effect of strengthening criminal organizations, especially the trafficking and smuggling networks. As migrants are faced with increased mobility restrictions, journeys become unsafer and costlier, benefiting the industry that profits on irregular migrants as sources of income, labour for exploitation, and trafficking (Andersson 2014; Gammeltoft-Hansen and Nyberg Sorensen 2013; Hernandez-Leon 2005). The strengthening of these organizations also trickles down to local communities, where levels of crime and violence have increased in the past years, leading to an increase in internal displacement due to violence and insecurity throughout the country (Rodríguez 2022; Rodríguez Chávez 2020).

However, there is no evidence that Mexico's foreign policy apparatus attributed much salience to the negative impacts on integration, the security of migrants, or Mexico's security situation in bilateral negotiations. This contrasts with the sustained discursive commitment of the Mexican government, over time, to advancing a comprehensive (in Spanish "integral") approach to migration management (Once Noticias 2021). The only mention of migrant's safety or Mexico's security situation is indirect, in the context of bilateral intelligence-sharing agreements to fight human trafficking and the infiltration of criminal organizations in migrant smuggling, both of which have been a strong focus of the US since the Biden administration's inauguration (Exteriores 2022; on intelligence-sharing, see also Koslowski and Leckey in this volume). The emphasis is however fully coherent with long-standing US priorities (regardless of the party in government) to deal with migration in Mexico and Central America through a securitized policy lens (Fernández-Kelly and Massey 2007; Menjívar 2014; Treviño Rangel 2016; Zepeda and Fuentes-Carrera 2020). Along the lines of what Krasner (1999) proposed of interstate dynamics in a highly asymmetric relation, Mexican sovereignty is undermined (and barely maintains its credibility) in accepting the externalization of migration policies that the US deems a priority. The emerging migration regime between the two counties is, in essence, structured on the basis of a new organized hypocrisy.

Against this backdrop, the evidence points to the two governments having different evaluations of the root causes of migration in the region (for one, violence and generalized insecurity; for the other, poverty), and thus of how to address them (for one, security, the fight against corruption, and the enhancement of the rule of law; for the other, socioeconomic development). However, there is convergence in seeing migration primarily as a problem that has to be solved and not a social reality that has to be acknowledged as a part of a socially and historically complex system that affects the region as a whole (Heredia Zubieta 2016; Selee and Ruiz Soto 2020). At the same time, neither government reflects on the impacts of their agreements on the global refugee regime – a weak, but nonetheless formal regime based on binding international treaties, of which the two states are party, sustained on the key principle of non-refoulement (for the effects of US policy on international protection norms, see Coen in this volume). Moreover, the control policies endorsed by both states entirely elide any consideration of the challenging task of integrating populations forced to remain in, or pushed back to, Mexico.

When observing all of Mexico's "failures" and apparently neglected policy priorities, a tentative conclusion crystallizes: the containment approach might also serve Mexican interests. A few years have passed since the 2019 policy shock, and while the institutional rearrangements and displacements that took place in that moment may have been unintended and made under duress, few agencies have been able to recover their functions.[4] The incoherent, opaque, and unaccountable institutional architecture of migration policy in Mexico endures. This is especially evident in the context of asylum and transit migration, suggesting that the two countries might share a quiet consensus that integration goals are better left abandoned, as the dire conditions of prolonged waiting continue to make Mexico an increasingly less attractive destination or transit state for migrants.

The absence of a systematic view of integration as a structuring principle of policy means that, in most places, the government only goes as far as to provide basic, short-term humanitarian assistance, if at all. Just as appeals to narratives of "crisis" are deployed to implement harsher migratory controls and obstacles to asylum, the conception of Mexico as a "space of transit" has consolidated narratives and policies that frame the current situation as an exception or emergency (Calhoun 2004, 2013; Fassin 2011; Ophir 2013). The discourse of exceptionality has, among other things, curtailed more sustainable efforts toward integration and more fundamental policy changes. Furthermore, the extremely unstable and opaque position in which Mexican authorities must operate under US pressure significantly limits their capacity to interact with other domestic and international actors in an accountable and transparent manner.

As described at the opening of the chapter, efforts to halt mobility and limit access to protection have generated prolonged waiting times, situations of entrapment, tensions with local populations, and made it impossible for migrants and asylum seekers to pursue integration, safety, and the advancement of life projects. These situations of precariousness and vulnerability are poignantly evident in border regions, which include some of the poorest and most violent spaces in the country. Unable to move due to legal constraints,[5] hundreds of thousands of asylum seekers remain trapped along Mexico's southern border for months, or even years, waiting for their asylum requests to be addressed by the Mexican government (Gil-Everaert 2021). Along the northern border, those returned under MPP, expelled under Title 42, or stranded due to the enforcement of metering lists, face situations of immobility and prolonged waiting as they attempt to seek asylum in the US (Gil-Everaert, Masferrer, and Rodríguez Chávez 2023).

In this context, local CSOs and religious organizations, as well as international NGOs and international organizations, notably the International Committee of the Red Cross and UNHCR, have filled the voids around integration and protection (CICR 2019). Some of this reflects a continuation of earlier trends where, for decades, CSOs have assumed protection responsibilities for migrants in Mexico. Most shelters and spaces of assistance are operated by religious groups or local organizations (Li Ng 2020; OIM 2018). Following bilateral agreements such as the MPP, where the Mexican government explicitly stated that it would assume the responsibility of attending to asylum seekers returned to Mexico, the federal government opened three centres for migrant integration (Centros Integradores para el Migrante) in cities near the northern border. However, these centres proved insufficient: full capacity was quickly reached, leaving many people looking for other shelter options; in other cities, these were inaugurated more than two years after the returns under MPP had started (Bienestar 2022). In Matamoros, Tamaulipas, the lack of action from the federal government and the tensions between federal and state officials gave rise to informal refugee camps where thousands of asylum seekers settled. These camps became places ridden with crime and poverty, where sanitary conditions quickly deteriorated and situations of heightened vulnerability placed thousands at risk (Human Rights First 2019; Jordan and Ferman 2019; Merchant 2019; PHR 2019).

CONCLUSION: A CYNICAL REGIME TAKING SHAPE?

The "Los Angeles Declaration on Migration and Protection" (The White House 2022), signed by the members of the Organization of American States (OAS), including Mexico and the US, declares these states' intent "to cooperate closely to facilitate safe, orderly, humane, and regular migration and, as appropriate, promote safe and dignified returns, consistent with national legislation, the principle of non-refoulement, and our respective obligations under international law." The declaration also proceeds with an acknowledgment that "addressing irregular international migration requires a regional approach." This chapter suggests that these goals will remain unachievable under the circumstances of burden-shifting created under the Trump administration and largely continued under the Biden administration. Quasi-formal agreements made under the coercive threat of sanctions have consolidated, while the principles and intentions stated in the Los Angeles Declaration are entirely nonbinding (Brumat 2022). Indeed, the declaration seeks to provide a framework for more robust and humane regional migration governance. However, having been signed by twenty out of thirty-five OAS members (notably not by Cuba and Venezuela, two of the countries currently with the largest regional emigration), it is likely to remain a contested mode of legitimating conditional bilateral agreements whereby Latin American countries must comply with information-sharing and border control measures in exchange for economic aid (Aguilera 2022).

This combination of hard power with "soft law" instruments is convenient for US policy priorities, but is not as easily accepted as legitimate in the region. It does not constitute a framework for enabling trustworthy cooperation, and falls far short of embodying a multilateral instrument agreed upon between parties to mediate between power and interests on the one hand, and expected results on the other, as the classic definition of an international regime would entail (Krasner 1982, 189). The mixture of burden-sharing rhetoric, against the backdrop of a burden-shifting reality imposed through coercion, has undercut the political momentum toward effective migration policy in Mexico and undermined the very institutions that would be required for any commitment to the regional management of migration to be credible and valid. Without respecting the domestic norms of other states and consideration of their legitimate interests in the realm of migration policy, the US has created barriers to the alleged goal of improved regional migration management and is responsible for propagating what we call a "cynical regime" of coerced cooperation across the region.

For international migration, the most encompassing international binding instruments have low rates of adoption and the most generally adopted instruments are nonbinding and often informal. These developments are illuminated by work on the constitutive elements of regimes beyond the notion of formal agreements. Kratochwil (1993) and Young (1983) offer a view of regimes as consistent practices or patterns of behaviour based on intersubjective understandings of a particular realm. This perspective emphasizes that regimes need not rest on the explicit agreement of parties or a process of negotiation around a set of constitutive principles and norms. In situations of deep power asymmetry, expectations may converge out of imposition. Following Rass and Wolff (2018, 19) and Parrenas (2021), we suggest that a de facto "migration regime" is taking shape through the practices of both strong and weak state actors that acquiesce to the externalization of protection obligations and to externalized border controls. Beyond what FitzGerald (2019) termed an "architecture of repulsion," we suggest that the policy crisis analyzed above resulted in a new and cynical regime, which mirrors long-standing practices generated in Europe under the guise of "mobility partnerships" and "readmission agreements" that respond to EU interests to reduce "illegal" migration (van Elsuwege and Vankova 2020, 180). For a growing number of countries in the Global North, a rhetorical convergence around the vacuous slogan of "safe, orderly and regular" migration hardly masks the proliferation of agreements to invert precisely the comprehensive and rights-based migration policy demands which were long fought for by migrants and migrant organizations across borders. Reflecting varying degrees of co-responsibility with countries of the Global South that accept these arrangements, the regime amounts to turning responsibility-sharing on its head, denying respect for migrants' mobility decisions, and neglecting social cohesion and integration as goals that communities which experience migration might legitimately pursue.

NOTES

1 According to the US State Department, during 2014, migratory authorities detained 211,184 people of Central American origin while during the same time period Mexican detentions were 172,560 (DHS 2014).

2 For a more detailed timeline on Title 42 from March 2020 until November 2022, visit: https://adamisacson.com/timeline-of-major-title-42-developments/ and https://www.wola.org/2022/12/weekly-u-s-mexico-border-update-if-title-42-ends-darien-gap-migration-slows mexico-asylum/.

3 The two relevant principles in the preamble of the Migration Law read: "Congruence, so that the Mexican State guarantees the rights that it demands for its nationals abroad for admission, entry, stay, transit, deportation and the assisted return of foreigners in its territory. An integral focus, in line with the complexity of international mobility of persons and the diverse expressions of migration in Mexico as a country of origin, transit, destination and return of migrants, considering their structural causes and their immediate and future consequences" (our translation).

4 The consultative councils with civil society presence have been the first to demand their reactivation (INM 2022).

5 According to Mexico's refugee law and bylaw, asylum seekers must remain in the state where they started their asylum request for the length of the process. If they move elsewhere, their asylum process is suspended.

REFERENCES

Aguilera, Jasmine. 2022. "New International Migration Agreement May Not Do Much." *Time*, 10 June 2022. https://time.com/6186209/declaration-migration-americas-summit/. Accessed 5 June 2023.

AIC (American Immigration Council). 2022. *A Guide to Title 42 Expulsions at the Border*. AIC. https://www.americanimmigrationcouncil.org/sites/default/files/research/title_42_expulsions_at_the_border_0.pdf. Accessed 5 June 2023.

Alianza Americas. 2018."México, ¿Tercer País seguro?" *Alianza Americas*. September 2018. https://www.alianzaamericas.org/blog-3/mexico-tercer-pais-seguro/. Accessed 5 June 2023.

Álvarez Velasco, Soledad. 2016. *Frontera Sur Chiapaneca. El muro humano de la violencia. Análisis de la normalización de la violencia hacia los migrantes indocumentados en tránsito*. Mexico City: Universidad Iberoamericana.

AMLO (Andrés Manuel López Obrador). 2018. "Avanzan trabajos sobre propuesta de AMLO rumbo al Plan de Desarrollo Integral para Centroamérica – AMLO." Lopezobdrador.org.mx. 23 November 2018. https://lopezobrador.org.mx/2018/11/23/avanzan-trabajos-sobre-propuesta-de-amlo-rumbo-al-plan-de-desarrollo-integral-para-centroamerica/. Accessed 5 June 2023.

Andersson, Ruben. 2014. *Illegality, Inc.* Oakland: University of California Press. http://www.ucpress.edu/book.php?isbn=9780520282520. Accessed 5 June 2023.

Anguiano Téllez, María Eugenia, and Alma Trejo Peña. 2007. "Políticas de Seguridad Fronteriza y Nuevas Rutas de Movilidad de Migrantes Mexicanos y Guatemaltecos." *LiminaR. Estudios Sociales y Humanísticos* 5 (2): 47–65. https://doi.org/10.29043/liminar.v5i2.250. Accessed 5 June 2023.

Anguiano Téllez, María Eugenia, Rafael Alonso Hernández López, and Daniel Villafuerte Solís, eds. 2018. *The World Through Borders: The Difficult Journey of Migrants in Transit*. Tijuana, Mexico: El Colegio de la Frontera Norte.

Asad, Asad L., and Filiz Garip. 2019. "Mexico-U.S. Migration in Time: From Economic to Social Mechanisms." *The ANNALS of the American Academy of Political and Social Science* 684 (1): 60–84. https://doi.org/10.1177/0002716219847148.

Associated Press. 2022. "US Supreme Court Rules against Biden in Key Immigration Case." *The Guardian*, 22 June 2022. https://www.theguardian.com/us-news/2022/jul/22/supreme-court-rules-against-biden-immigration-case. Accessed 5 June 2023.

Ataiants, Janna, Chari Cohen, Amy Henderson Riley, Jamile Tellez Lieberman, Mary Clare Reidy, and Mariana Chilton. 2018. "Unaccompanied Children at the United States Border, a Human Rights Crisis That Can Be Addressed with Policy Change." *Journal of Immigrant and Minority Health* 20 (4): 1000–10. https://doi.org/10.1007/s10903-017-0577-5.

Bednar, Nicholas. 2023. "The Public Administration of Justice." *Bednar Cardozo Law Review* 44. https://papers.ssrn.com/sol3/papers.cfm?abstract_id=4189963. Accessed 5 June 2023.

Boin, Arjen, and Martin Lodge. 2016. "Designing Resilient Institutions for Transboundary Crisis Management: A Time for Public Administration." *Public Administration* 94 (2): 289–98. https://doi.org/10.1111/padm.12264.

Boruchoff, Judith A. 2019. "Mexico-U.S. Migration and the Nation-State: A Transnational Perspective on Transformations since 1990." *The ANNALS of the American Academy of Political and Social Science* 684 (1): 43–59. https://doi.org/10.1177/0002716219856584.

Boswell, Christina. 2007. "Theorizing Migration Policy: Is There a Third Way?" *International Migration Review* 41 (1): 75–100.

Brumat, Leiza. 2022. "A US-Designed Migration Pact for the Americas?" EURAC Research. June 2022. https://www.eurac.edu/en/blogs/mobile-people-and-diverse-societies/a-us-designed-migration-pact-for-the-americas. Accessed 5 June 2023.

Calderón Chelius, Leticia. 2012. "Cambios en la agenda migratoria: entre el nuevo marco jurídico y las nuevas formas de migración en México." In *México ante los recientes desafíos de la migración internacional*, edited by Telésforo Ramírez García and Manuel Ángel Castillo, 19–50. Mexico City: Consejo Nacional de Población.

Calhoun, Craig. 2004. "A World of Emergencies: Fear, Intervention, and the Limits of Cosmopolitan Order." *Canadian Review of Sociology/Revue Canadienne de Sociologie* 41 (4): 373–95.

– 2013. "The Idea of Emergency: Humanitarian Action and Global (Dis) Order." In *Contemporary States of Emergency. The Politics of Military and Humanitarian Interventions*, edited by Didier Fassin and Mariella Pandolfi, 29–58. Brooklyn, NY: Zone Books.

Camhaji, E. 2023. Marcelo Ebrard y Adán Augusto López chocan por el reparto de responsabilidades tras la tragedia de Ciudad Juárez, *El País México*. Available at: https://elpais.com/mexico/2023-03-29/marcelo-ebrard-y-adan-augusto-lopez-chocan-por-el-reparto-de-responsabilidades-tras-la-tragedia-de-ciudad-juarez.html. Accessed 15 September 2023.

Cantor, David James, Luisa Feline Freier, and Jean-Pierre Gauci, eds. 2015. *A Liberal Tide? Immigration and Asylum Law and Policy in Latin America.* London: Institute of Latin American Studies, University of London.

Castillo García, Manuel Ángel, and Gilberto Castañeda Sandoval. 2009. Evaluación de la Política Migratoria hacia la Frontera Sur de México (2001–2006). El Colegio de México: Grupo Guatemala-México, Migración y Desarrollo. https://mexico-guatemala.colmex.mx/archivos/75/evaluacion-politica-migratoria-2001-1006.pdf. Accessed 5 June 2023.

CEPAL, México. 2018. "Cancilleres de El Salvador, Guatemala, Honduras y México presentaron Plan de Desarrollo Integral en el marco de la Conferencia para el Pacto Mundial sobre Migración." Comisión Económica para América Latina y el Caribe (CEPAL). 10 December 2018. https://www.cepal.org/es/comunicados/cancilleres-salvador-guatemala-honduras-mexico-presentaron-plan-desarrollo-integral. Accessed 5 June 2023.

Chen, Ming Hsu, and Daimeon Shanks. 2022. "The New Normal: Regulatory Dysfunction as Policymaking." Maryland Law Review 82: 300–64. https://papers.ssrn.com/abstract=3962594. Accessed 5 June 2023.

CICR (Comité Internacional de la Cruz Roja). 2019. "ACNUR y CICR construyen un albergue para personas migrantes, refugiadas y solicitantes de asilo en Coatzacoalcos." Press release, 18 February 2019. https://www.icrc.org/es/document/acnur-y-cicr-construyen-un-albergue-para-personas-migrantes-refugiadas-y-solicitantes-de. Accessed 5 June 2023.

Covarrubias, Ana. 2021. "Foreign Migration Policy." In *The Intersection of Migration Policy and Foreign Policy in Today's Mexico*, 81–7. Ciudad de México: El Colegio de México.

Délano, Alexandra. 2018. "Lo que no entienden los candidatos mexicanos sobre migración." *The New York Times*, 24 May 2018. https://www.nytimes.com/es/2018/05/24/espanol/opinion/opinion-delano-debate-elecciones-mexico-migracion.html. Accessed 5 June 2023.

DHS (Department of Homeland Security). 2014. "DHS Releases End of Year Statistics." 18 December 2014. https://www.ice.gov/news/releases/dhs-releases-end-year-statistics. Accessed 5 June 2023.

DOF (Diario Oficial de la Federación). 2019. *DECRETO por el que se crea la Comisión Intersecretarial de Atención Integral en Materia Migratoria.* https://www.dof.gob.mx/nota_detalle.php?codigo=5572790&fecha=19/09/2019. Accessed 5 June 2023.

Durand Arp-Nisen, Jorge. 2019. "Política migratoria: entre el discurso, la práctica y la coyuntura." *Foro Internacional* 59 (3–4): 1021–47. https://doi.org/10.24201/fi.v59i3-4.2650.

Durand, Jorge. 2016. *Historia mínima de la migración México - Estados Unidos*. Ciudad de México: El Colegio de México.

Durand, Jorge, and Douglas S. Massey, eds. 2004. *Crossing the Border. Research From the Mexican Migration Project*. New York: Russell Sage Foundation.

Eduardo, Lalo. 2011. "Segunda limpia en el INM; prevé despedir a 350 agentes." *Animal Político* (blog), 18 May 2011. https://www.animalpolitico.com/2011/05/segunda-limpia-en-el-inm-preve-despedir-a-350-agentes/. Accessed 5 June 2023.

Eichensehr, Kristen E., ed. 2022. "Biden Administration Continues Efforts to Change Immigration Policy Amidst Surges of Migrants and Court Losses." *American Journal of International Law* 116 (1): 197–205. https://doi.org/10.1017/ajil.2021.71.

elEconomista.es. 2019. "Cepal presenta el Plan de Desarrollo para el sur de México y Centroamérica." 20 May 2019. https://www.economiahoy.mx/economia-eAm-mexico/noticias/9889225/05/19/Cepal-presenta-el-Plan-de-Desarrollo-para-el-sur-de-Mexico-y-Centroamerica.html. Accessed 5 June 2023.

Expansión Política. 2019. "Tras depuración en el INM, se prevé contratar 825 nuevos elementos." *ADNPolítico*. 14 June 2019. https://politica.expansion.mx/mexico/2019/06/14/tras-depuracion-en-el-inm-se-preve-contratar-825-nuevos-elementos. Accessed 5 June 2023.

Fassin, Didier. 2011. *Humanitarian Reason: A Moral History of the Present*. Berkeley: University of California Press.

Fernández de la Reguera Ahedo, Alethia, Luciana Gandini, Eduardo Elías Gutiérrez López, and Juan Carlos Narváez Gutiérrez. 2019. *Caravanas migrantes: las respuestas de México*. Opiniones Técnicas sobre Temas de Relevancia Nacional, number 8. Ciudad de México: Universidad Nacional Autónoma de México. https://biblio.juridicas.unam.mx/bjv/id/5804. Accessed 5 June 2023.

Fernández-Kelly, Patricia, and Douglas S. Massey. 2007. "Borders for Whom? The Role of NAFTA in Mexico-U.S. Migration." *The ANNALS of the American Academy of Political and Social Science* 610 (1): 98–118. https://doi.org/10.1177/0002716206297449.

FitzGerald, David Scott. 2019. *Refuge beyond Reach: How Rich Democracies Repel Asylum Seekers*. New York: Oxford University Press.

FitzGerald, David Scott, and Rawan Arar. 2018. "The Sociology of Refugee Migration." *Annual Review of Sociology*" 44 (8): 1–20.

Gammeltoft-Hansen, Thomas, and Ninna Nyberg Sorensen, eds. 2013. *The Migration Industry and the Commercialization of International Migration*. London and New York: Routledge.

García Cabezas, Noemí. 2022. "¿Qué es el título 42?" Ayuda en Acción. 21 May 2021. https://ayudaenaccion.org/blog/derechos-humanos/titulo-42/. Accessed 5 June 2023.

Gil-Everaert, Isabel. 2020. "Migratory Timescapes: Experiences of Pausing, Waiting, and Inhabiting the Meanwhile of Migrants and Asylum Seekers in Mexico." PhD dissertation, City University of New York Graduate Center. https://academicworks.cuny.edu/gc_etds/4012. Accessed 5 June 2023.

– 2021. "Population Seeking International Protection." In *The Intersection of Foreign Policy and Migration Policy in Mexico Today*, edited by Claudia Masferrer and Luicy Pedroza, 47–54. Mexico City, Mexico: El Colegio de México.

Gil-Everaert, Isabel, Claudia Masferrer, and Óscar Rodríguez Chávez. 2023. "Concurrent Displacements: Return, Waiting for Asylum, and Internal Displacement in Northern Mexico." *Journal on Migration and Human Security* 11 (1): 125–48. https://doi.org/10.1177/23315024231158559.

González, Isabella. 2019. "Instala SRE comisión migratoria." *reforma.com*, 25 September 2019. https://www.reforma.com/instala-sre-comision-migratoria/ar1777269. Accessed 5 June 2023.

González, Jesús Eduardo, Rogelio Zapata, and María Eugenia Anguiano Téllez. 2017. "Migración centroamericana en tránsito por México." La situación demográfica en México 2016. Ciudad de México: Consejo Nacional de Población. https://www.gob.mx/cms/uploads/attachment/file/232085/10_Fagoaga_Zapata_Anguiano.pdf. Accessed 5 June 2023.

Gramlich, John. 2022. "Key Facts About Title 42, the Pandemic Policy that has Reshaped Immigration Enforcement at U.S.-Mexico Border." Pew Research Centre. 27 April 2022. https://www.pewresearch.orgfact-tank/2022/04/27/key-facts-about-title-42-the-pandemic-policy-that-has-reshaped-immigration-enforcement-at-u-s-mexico-border/. Accessed 5 June 2023.

Guillén, Tonatiuh López. 2020. "Un paso adelante, tres atrás. La política migratoria en tiempos de AMLO y Trump." In *Balance temprano. Desde la izquierda democrática*, edited by Ricardo Becerra and José Woldenberg, 111–328. Mexico City: Instituto de Estudios para la Transición Democrátia.

Haas Pacuic, Alexandra, Elena Sánchez-Montijano, and Roberto Zedillo Ortega. 2021. "Integración de migrantes en México: un llamado a la acción." *Nexos*, 24 February 2021. https://migracion.nexos.com.mx/2021/02/integracion-de-migrantes-en-mexico-un-llamado-a-la-accion/. Accessed 5 June 2023.

Heinrich Böll Stiftung. 2018. "Nuevos retos en materia de políticas migratorias en México." Heinrich Böll Stiftung. https://mx.boell.org/es/2018/10/31/nuevos-retos-en-materia-de-politicas-migratorias-en-mexico. Accessed 5 June 2023.

Heredia Zubieta, Carlos, ed. 2016. *El sistema migratorio mesoamericano*. Mexico City: COLEF and CIDE.

Hernandez-Leon, Ruben. 2005. "The Migration Industry in the Mexico-U.S. Migratory System." California Center for Population Research On-Line Working Paper Series. Los Angeles: University of California. https://escholarship.org/uc/item/3hg44330. Accessed 5 June 2023.

Human Rights First. 2019. *Trump Administration Delivers Asylum Seekers to Grave Danger in Mexico: 200+ Publicly Reported Cases of Rape, Kidnapping, and Assault Just the Tip of the Iceberg*. Human Rights First. https://www.humanrightsfirst.org/sites/default/files/MPP-One-Pager-September-2019.pdf. Accessed 5 June 2023.

ICE (Immigration and Customs Enforcement). 2016. "Fiscal Year 2016 ICE Enforcement and Removal Operations Report." ICE. https://www.ice.gov/sites/default/files/documents/Report/2016/removal-stats-2016.pdf. Accessed 5 June 2023.

IDMC (Internal Displacement Monitoring Centre). 2022. "Country Profile: Mexico." 18 May 2022. https://www.internal-displacement.org/countries/mexico. Accessed 5 June 2023.

INEGI (Instituto Nacional de Estadística y Geografía). 2021. "Censo de Población y Vivienda 2020." México: Instituto Nacional de Estadística y Geografía. https://www.inegi.org.mx/programas/ccpv/2020/#Tabulados. Accessed 5 June 2023.

INM (Instituto Nacional de Migración). 2018a. "El INAMI entrega Tarjetas de Visitante por Razones Humanitarias a miembros de la caravana migrante." Gobierno de Mexico, press release, 7 December 2018. http://www.gob.mx/inm/prensa/el-inami-entrega-tarjetas-de-visitante-por-razones-humanitarias-a-miembros-de-la-caravana-migrante?idiom=es. Accessed 5 June 2023.

– 2018b. "Programa Especial de Migración (PEM) 2014-2018." Gobierno de México. 4 January 2018. http://www.gob.mx/inm/documentos/programa-especial-de-migracion-pem-2014-2018-18281. Accessed June 5, 2023.

– 2019. "Se crea por Decreto Presidencial la Comisión Intersecretarial de Atención a Los Migrantes." Gobierno de México - Tema Migratorio. 19 September 2019. https://www.inm.gob.mx/gobmx/word/index.php/tema-migratorio-200919/. Accessed 5 June 2023.

– 2022. "Consejo Ciudadano del Instituto Nacional de Migración." Gobierno de México. 6 September 2022. http://www.gob.mx/inm/acciones-y-programas/consejo-ciudadano-del-instituto-nacional-de-migracion. Accessed 5 June 2023.

Jordan, Miriam, and Mitchell Ferman. 2019. "Stranded on Border, This Migrant Became the Camp Doctor." *New York Times*, 22 December 2019.

https://www.nytimes.com/2019/12/22/us/migrant-cuban-doctor-mexico.html. Accessed 5 June 2023.

Knippen, José, Clay Boggs, and Maureen Meyer. 2015. *Un camino incierto. Justicia para delitos y violaciones a los derechos humanos contra personas migrantes y refugiados en México*. WOLA. Advocacy for Human Rights in the Americas.

Krasner, Stephen D. 1982. "Structural Causes and Regime Consequences: Regimes as Intervening Variables." *International Organization* 36 (2): 185–205. http://www.jstor.org/stable/2706520. Accessed 5 June 2023.

– 1999. "Sovereignty: Organized Hypocrisy." Princeton, NJ: Princeton University Press. https://politicalscience.stanford.edu/publications/sovereignty-organized-hypocrisy. Accessed 5 June 2023.

Kratochwil, Friedrich. 1993. "Norms Versus Numbers: Multilateralism and the Rationalist and Reflexivist Approach to Institutions – A Unilateral Plea for Communicative Rationality." In *Multilateralism Matters. The Theory and Praxis of an Institutional Form*, edited by John Gerard Ruggie, 443–74. New York: Columbia University Press.

Kuhner, Gretchen. 2011. "La violencia contra las mujeres migrantes en tránsito por México." *Revista de derechos humanos*: 6 (June): 19–26.

Li Ng, Juan José. 2020. "Mapa 2020 de Casas Del Migrante, Albergues y Comedores Para Migrantes En México." BBVA Research. https://www.bbvaresearch.com/publicaciones/mapa-2020-de-casas-del-migrante-albergues-y-comedores-para-migrantes-en-mexico/?utm_source=twitter&utm_medium=social&utm_campaign=rrssresearch&utm_term=02032020. Accessed 5 June 2023.

Mars, Amanda, Pablo Ximénez de Sandoval, and Ignacio Fariza. 2019. "Trump anuncia un arancel general del 5% a México como castigo por la inmigración irregular." *El País*, 31 May 2019. https://elpais.com/internacional/2019/05/31/estados_unidos/1559256743_016777.html. Accessed 5 June 2023.

Martínez, César. 2019. "Dan a SRE rectoría en migración." *Reforma*, 19 September 2019. https://www.reforma.com/dan-a-sre-rectoria-en-migracion/ar1772642. Accessed 5 June 2023.

Martínez, Graciela, Salvador David Cobo, and Juan Carlos Narváez. 2015. "Trazando rutas de la migración de tránsito irregular o no documentada por México." *Perfiles Latinoamericanos* 23 (45): 127–55. https://doi.org/10.18504/pl2345-127-2015.

Masferrer, Claudia, and Luicy Pedroza, eds. 2021. *La intersección de la política exterior con política migratoria en México de hoy*. Mexico City: El Colegio de México. https://libros.colmex.mx/tienda/la-interseccion-de-la-politica-exterior-con-politica-migratoria-en-mexico-de-hoy/. Accessed 5 June 2023.

Massey, Douglas S., Jorge Durand, and Nolan J. Malone. 2003. *Beyond Smoke and Mirrors: Mexican Immigration in an Era of Economic Integration*. New York: Russell Sage Foundation.

Menjívar, Cecilia. 2014. "Immigration Law Beyond Borders: Externalizing and Internalizing Border Controls in an Era of Securitization." *Annual Review of Law and Social Science* 10 (1): 353–69. https://doi.org/10.1146/annurev-lawsocsci-110413-030842.

Merchant, Nomaan. 2019. "Tents, Stench, Smoke: Health Risks Are Gripping Migrant Camp." *Associated Press*, 14 November 2019. https://apnews.com/article/337b139ed4fa4d208b93d491364e04da. Accessed 5 June 2023.

Migone, Andrea, and Michael Howlett. 2016. "Charles E. Lindblom, 'The Science of Muddling Through.'" In *The Oxford Handbook of Classics in Public Policy and Administration*, edited by Martin Lodge, Edward C. Page, and Steven J. Balla, 80–95. Oxford: Oxford University Press. https://doi.org/10.1093/oxfordhb/9780199646135.013.33.

Nájera Aguirre, Jéssica Natalia. 2016. "El complejo estudio de la actual migración en tránsito por México: Actores, temáticas y circunstancias." *Migraciones Internacionales* 8 (3): 255–66.

Nájera, Alberto, and Ana Gabriela Rojas. 2019. "Cómo hizo AMLO para cumplir el acuerdo con Donald Trump que convirtió a México en 'sándwich migratorio.'" BBC *News Mundo*, 22 July 2019. https://www.bbc.com/mundo/noticias-america-latina-49055003. Accessed 5 June 2023.

OIM (Organización Internacional para las Migraciones). 2018. "Directorio de Casas y Albergues Para Personas Migrantes." OIM. https://mexico.iom.int/system/files/Publicaciones/Directorio%20de%20Casas%20y%20Albergues%20para%20personas%20migrantes%20digital_0.pdf. Accessed 5 June 2023.

Once Noticias. 2021. "Gobierno de México reafirmó compromiso con su política migratoria: SRE." *Once Noticias*, 8 April 2021. https://oncenoticias.digital/internacional/gobierno-de-mexico-reafirmo-compromiso-con-su-politica-migratoria-sre/23712/. Accessed 5 June 2023.

Ophir, Adir. 2013. "The Politics of Catastrophization: Emergency and Exception." In *Contemporary States of Emergency. The Politics of Military and Humanitarian Interventions*, edited by Didier Fassin and Mariella Pandolfi, 59–88. New York: Zone Books.

Ortíz de Zárate Béjar, Almendra, and Yoanna Shubich. 2018. "Humanitarian Crisis: Unaccompanied Migrant Minors from Central America to the US-Mexican Border." *The Copernicus Journal of Political Studies* 1 (7): 160–75. https://doi.org/10.12775/cjps.2015.01.11.

París Pombo, María Dolores. 2020. "¿Expulsar o integrar a las personas migrantes en México?" *Animal Político*, 18 February 2020. https://www.

animalpolitico.com/por-un-mundo-sin-fronteras/expulsar-o-integrar-a-las-personas-migrantes-en-mexico/. Accessed 5 June 2023.

Parrenas, Rhacel. 2021. "The Mobility Pathways of Migrant Domestic Workers." *Journal of Ethnic and Migration Studies* 47 (1): 3–24. https://doi.org/10.1080/1369183X.2020.1744837.

Pedroza, Luicy. 2021. "La silenciosa desaparición de los consejos consultivos en la gestión migratoria." *Nexos*, 9 June 2021. https://migracion.nexos.com.mx/2021/06/la-silenciosa-desaparicion-de-los-consejos-consultivos-en-la-gestion-migratoria/. Accessed 5 June 2023.

PHR (Physicians for Human Rights). 2019. "Unsafe, Unsanitary, Inhumane: PHR Medical Expert's Observations at the Matamoros Migrant Encampment." Press release, 26 September 2019. https://phr.org/news/phr-statement-on-migrant-protection-protocols/. Accessed 5 June 2023.

Puretz, Danielle. 2022. "Operation Lone Star: The Spectacle of Immigration Federalism." Capstone Project: City University of New York Graduate Center. https://academicworks.cuny.edu/gc_etds/5120.

Rass, Christoph, and Frank Wolff. 2018. "What Is in a Migration Regime? Genealogical Approach and Methodological Proposal." In *What Is a Migration Regime?*, edited by Andreas Pott, Christoph Rass, and Frank Wolff, 19–64. Migrationsgesellschaften. Wiesbaden: Springer Fachmedien. https://doi.org/10.1007/978-3-658-20532-4_2.

Reuters. 2020. "Instituto Nacional de Migración despide a 1,040 funcionarios por actos de corrupción." *El Economista*, 14 August 2020. https://www.eleconomista.com.mx/politica/Instituto-Nacional-de-Migracion-despide-a-1040-funcionarios-por-actos-de-corrupcion-20200814-0057.html. Accessed 5 June 2023.

Rodríguez, Oscar. 2022. "¿De dónde salieron y a dónde se fueron? Migración interna de regiones de alta violencia en México en las últimas dos décadas." *Revista EURE - Revista de Estudios Urbano Regionales* 48 (144): 1–23. https://doi.org/10.7764/EURE.48.144.12.

Rodríguez Chávez, Oscar. 2020. "Violencia, desplazamiento interno forzado y dinámica migratoria en México (1995-2015)." PhD thesis, Mexico City: El Colegio de México. https://colmex.userservices.exlibrisgroup.com/view/delivery/52COLMEX_INST/1211673186000271 6. Accessed 5 June 2023.

Rojas, Christian, and Gustavo Hernández, eds. 2017. "Informe alternativo sobre el cumplimiento de México de la Convención Internacional sobre la Protección de los derechos de todos los trabajadores migratorios y de sus familiares para el Comité de los Trabajadores Migratorios y de sus Familiares de Naciones Unidas (CMW)." Mexico City: REDODEM, GTPM, INILAB, Foro migraciones y otras.

Roldán, Johanna. 2021. "ACNUR En México." Presented at the Seminario

Perspectivas Internacionales Sobre Refugio y Asilo, El Colegio de México, Mexico City, 17 August 2021.

Secretaría de Bienestar, 2022. "Secretarías de Bienestar y del Trabajo inauguran Centro Integrador para el Migrante en Matamoros." gob.mx. 5 July 2022. http://www.gob.mx/bienestar/prensa/secretarias-de-bienestar-y-del-trabajo-inauguran-centro-integrador-para-el-migrante-en-matamoros-307248?idiom=es. Accessed 5 June 2023.

Secretaría de Gobernación. 2019. DECRETO *por el que se expide la Ley de La Guardia Nacional.* DOF 27/05/2019. https://www.dof.gob.mx/nota_detalle.php?codigo=5561285&fecha=27/05/2019. Accessed 5 June 2023.

– 2021. "Firman Comar y Acnur acuerdo a favor de personas refugiadas." gob.mx. http://www.gob.mx/segob/prensa/firman-comar-y-acnur-acuerdo-a-favor-de-personas-refugiadas?idiom=es. Accessed 17 December 2021.

Secretaría de Relaciones Exteriores. 2019. "El Canciller participó en la Conferencia Intergubernamental para la adopción del Pacto Mundial para una Migración Segura, Ordenada y Regular." gob.mx. http://www.gob.mx/sre/prensa/el-canciller-marcelo-ebrard-participo-la-conferencia-intergubernamental-para-la-adopcion-del-pacto-mundial-para-una-migracion-segura-ordenada-y-regular-en-marrakech-marruecos. Accessed 11 December 2019.

– 2022. "Plan de Acción 2022–2024 del Entendimiento Bicentenario: México y Estados Unidos enfrentan organizaciones criminales de manera conjunta." gob.mx. 31 January 2022. http://www.gob.mx/sre/prensa/plan-de-accion-2022-2024-del-entendimiento-bicentenario-mexico-y-estados-unidos-enfrentan-organizaciones-criminales-de-manera-conjunta?state=published. Accessed 5 June 2023.

Selee, Andrew, Cynthia Arnson, and Eric Olson. 2013. "Crime and Violence in Mexico and Central America: An Evolving but Incomplete U.S. Policy Response." Washington, DC: Migration Policy Institute. https://www.migrationpolicy.org/research/crime-and-violence-mexico-and-central-america-evolving-incomplete-us-policy-response. Accessed 5 June 2023.

Selee, Andrew, and Ariel G. Ruiz Soto. 2020. "Construcción de un nuevo sistema migratorio regional." Washington DC: Migration Policy Institute. https://www.migrationpolicy.org/sites/default/files/publications/rethinking-regional-relations-migration_esp_final.pdf. Accessed 5 June 2023.

Senado de la República. 2019. "Posicionamiento del Senado sobre el Acuerdo de Tercer País Seguro." Senado de la República LXIV Legislatura, Ciudad de México: Centro de Estudios Internacionales Gilberto Bosques.

Torre Cantalapiedra, Eduardo, and José-Carlos Yee-Quintero. 2018. "México ¿una frontera vertical? Políticas de control del tránsito migratorio irregular y sus resultados, 2007-2016." *LiminaR Estudios Sociales Y Humanísticos* 16 (2): 87–104.

Treviño Rangel, Javier. 2016. "Organizaciones de la sociedad civil y la 'securitización' de la migración internacional indocumentada en México." *Foro Internacional* (56) 2: 253–91. https://doi.org/10.24201/fi.v56i2.2316.

UNHCR (United Nations High Commissioner for Refugees). 2023. "Refugee Statistics." UNHCR. 2023. https://www.unhcr.org/refugee-statistics/. Accessed 5 June 2023.

UPM (Unidad de Política Migratoria). 2018. Informe de Evaluación del Programa Especial de Migración 2014-2018 (PEM). Ciudad de México: Secretaría de Gobernación. http://portales.segob.gob.mx/work/models/PoliticaMigratoria/CEM/UPM/PEM/Informe_Evaluaci%C3%B3n_PEM_Dic2018.pdf. Accessed 5 June 2023.

United Nations ECLAC (Economic Commission Office for Latin America and the Caribbean). 2021. Comprehensive Development Plan for El Salvador, Guatemala, Honduras and south-southeast Mexico: Summary. United Nations. LC/TS.2021/7. https://www.cepal.org/en/publications/47249-comprehensive-development-plan-salvador-guatemala-honduras-and-south-southeast. https://www.gob.mx/cms/uploads/attachment/file/462720/34.Hacia_un_nuevo_estilo_de_desarrollo___Plan_de_Desarrollo_Integral_El.pdf. Accessed 5 June 2023.

van Elsuwege, Peter, and Zvezda Vankova. 2020. "Migration and Mobility in the EU's Eastern Neighbourhood: Mapping out the Legal and Political Framework." In *Bilateral Relations in the Mediterranean: Prospects for Migration Issues*, edited by Francesca Ippolito, Gianluca Borzoni, and Federico Casolari, 160–84. Northampton, Mass.: Edward Elgar Publishing.

The White House. 2022. "Los Angeles Declaration on Migration and Protection." The White House. 10 June 2022. https://www.whitehouse.gov/briefing-room/statements-releases/2022/06/10/los-angeles-declaration-on-migration-and-protection/. Accessed 5 June 2023.

TRAC Immigration. 2022. "Details on MPP (Remain in Mexico) Deportation Proceedings." Transactional Records Access Clearinghouse (TRAC). https://trac.syr.edu/phptools/immigration/mpp4/. Accessed 5 June 2023.

Willers, Susanne. 2016. "Migración y violencia: Las experiencias de mujeres migrantes centroamericanas en tránsito por México." *Sociológica* 31 (89): 163–95.

Young, Oran. 1983. "Regime Dynamics: The Rise and Fall of International Regimes." In *International Regimes*. Ithaca, New York: Cornell University Press.

Zepeda, Beatriz, and Julieta Fuentes-Carrera. 2020. "La Frontera México-Guatemala y el perímetro de seguridad de Estados Unidos 2000–2020." In *Entre lo político y lo espacial: Representaciones geopolíticas de la región transfronteriza México-Guatemala,* edited by Julieta Fuentes-Carrera, 49–84. Mexico City: Centro de Investigación en Ciencias de Información Geoespacial.

3

Governance Breakdowns and Normative Deficits in Asylum "Coordination" in North America: The US-Canada Safe Third Country Agreement in Context

Kiran Banerjee

This chapter examines the provision of asylum in North America alongside the regional development of bilateral instruments for asylum coordination between signatories to the 1951 Convention Relating to the Status of Refugees (hereafter the 1951 Convention). It focuses on the emergence and subsequent impacts of the US-Canada Safe Third Country Agreement (STCA) since its creation over two decades ago, arguing that the endurance of the STCA reflects the widespread normalization of a once controversial practice – one initially viewed as potentially problematic by the United Nations High Commissioner for Refugees (UNHCR) and contrary to the fundamental norms of the refugee regime (UNHCR 1997, 1999).[1] The STCA also exemplifies a distinctly transnational tool by which states have come to exercise greater control over access to asylum. Unlike resettlement – which remains legally a matter of state discretion under the refugee regime – signatory states to the 1951 Convention are obligated to uphold rights intended to ensure access to due process for refugee status determination (RSD). The effects of "Safe Country" agreements on asylum, and the global refugee regime more broadly, have therefore taken on even greater salience given the narrowing of alternative pathways for refuge in the context of widespread and protracted international displacement.

The US-Canada STCA is among the earliest bilateral agreements directly addressing regional asylum policy and, at the time of its emergence, was concluded by two states widely viewed as global leaders in humanitarian assistance to refugees. More recently, the STCA has been the subject of increased media attention and contentious public debate in Canada, including criticisms regarding its unexpected role in incentivizing irregular migration from the United States and worries concerning the American government's ongoing commitment to refugee protection. The latter concerns have led to the resumption of legal challenges supported by civil society organizations (CSOs) in Canada regarding the lawfulness of the STCA on the grounds that it abrogates asylum seekers' rights under the Canadian Charter of Rights and Freedoms.

The analysis that follows proposes to look at the STCA from a transnational perspective in relation to the multilateral obligations of the 1951 Convention and the broader impacts of the agreement on asylum across the region. The chapter first briefly discusses the 1951 Convention and the subsequent 1967 Protocol Relating to the Status of Refugees (hereafter the 1967 Protocol) as the foundational instruments for the provision of international protection, particularly the treaty's ground norm of non-refoulement. On the basis of this engagement, the chapter then takes up the STCA, particularly its intended goal of facilitating bilateral asylum policy coordination. The aim of this analysis is to draw out some of the assumptions underlying the STCA's purported consistency with the 1951 Convention, including avoiding the possibility of indirect refoulment. The next section evaluates such compatibility, arguing that the assumption or "legal fiction" of equivalent protection across jurisdictions that underlies the STCA's claim to facilitate asylum coordination is proving impossible to sustain. The aim here is to offer a generic consideration of the implications of the STCA for states' parties, before turning to recent developments in cross-border asylum policy that suggest the STCA has contributed to a broader erosion of international protection.

The last section of the chapter addresses contemporary state practice regarding the increased use of bilateral agreements in the domain of refugee policy. While the STCA represented among the first frameworks aimed at bilaterally coordinating refugee reception and asylum access among signatory states to the 1951 Convention, the intervening period has seen a proliferation of similar interstate frameworks that has only heightened in recent years. Here I consider these developments by surveying recent agreements, focusing on those undertaken between the United States and other countries. The chapter concludes on a speculative note regarding the implications of the prior analysis for refugee protection within the broader region and beyond.

THE 1951 CONVENTION RELATING TO THE STATUS OF REFUGEES AND "TRANSNATIONAL" ASYLUM COORDINATION

The 1951 Convention emerged from the turmoil, violence, and mass displacement of World War II, unfolding against the backdrop of widespread state-based persecution and atrocities committed on civilian populations, including acts subsequently identified as crimes against humanity.[2] As the 1951 Convention's preamble makes clear, it was also developed in light of the growing recognition that responding to such levels of forced migration required a coordinated interstate approach, and that the humanitarian needs of refugees could only be effectively addressed through collective acts of international solidarity. These considerations can be taken to inform the 1951 Convention's object and purpose, which are aptly characterized as: "extending the protection of the international community to refugees" and assuring "the widest possible exercise of … fundamental rights and freedoms'" via the provision of international protection (Goodwin-Gill and McAdam 2007, 367).

Under this framework, access to international protection itself was underpinned by an implicit right to individual assessment under the 1951 Convention's five grounds for refugee status. The implication of this is made clear by what some have called the cornerstone of the treaty, Article 33, which articulates the contemporary refugee regime's ground norm of non-refoulement (UNHCR 1997). This is because, in this respect, the 1951 Convention explicitly qualifies and overrides states' parties right to exclude non-citizens by way of their usual powers under customary international law to control the movement of foreign nationals across their frontiers. Insofar as the substance of Article 33, as well as the provisions under Articles 31 and 32 (which, respectively, provide safeguards against the penalization of unlawful entry and summary expulsion), are understood to facilitate access to international protection, something resembling a requirement to recognize the right to *seek* asylum, though not a right to asylum itself, appears to be embedded in the 1951 Convention's central purpose.[3]

Following the creation of the Convention, the rapid spread and persistence of refugee situations, including those ensuing from decolonization and Cold-War era conflict, advanced the entrenchment of the UNHCR's institutional arrangements as well as the eventual introduction of additional legal instruments at both the regional and international levels. Chief among the latter was the 1967 Protocol, which addressed the temporal and geographic constraints of the 1951 Convention and thereby introduced a truly universal framework for the international refugee regime.[4] The 1967 Protocol's legal implications were complemented by the broader recognition of the international community that forced migration was indeed an enduring global concern. The subsequent growth in interstate uptake reflected this overall trend, with the 1951 Convention and 1967 Protocol gaining 146 and 147 signatories over the following half-century (UNHCR 2015).[5]

International consensus regarding the enduring importance of refugee protection would receive additional affirmation (although not much by way of further legal support) by way of the UN General Assembly's unanimous adoption of the 2016 New York Declaration for Refugees and Migrants, followed by the subsequent drafting of the 2018 Global Compact on Refugees (GCR), both of which emerged in the context of the current and still ongoing global refugee crisis (UNHCR 2018a). The latter instrument, while explicitly nonbinding, garnered the endorsement of 181 states when brought before the General Assembly and therefore could somewhat plausibly claim to express the "political will and ambition of the international community as a whole" (UN 2018). In so doing, the compact identified the 1951 Convention and its 1967 Protocol as the core of the global refugee protection regime while directly affirming the enduring importance of the "cardinal principle" of non-refoulement to the international community.

The above sketch of the normative contours of the refugee regime would appear to support a rather optimistic picture of the state of international protection. However, the current realities of enduring and widespread global displacement, reflected in the UNHCR's annual public reports of the past decade, paint a far different picture. Key causes of this progressively worsening situation (in the context of the UNHCR's official narrative) include both new and increasingly protracted conflicts, and with that only mounting displacement figures, as well as the ongoing difficulties in providing refugees access to "durable solutions" amid continued shortfalls in the organization's overall refugee assistance budget (UNHCR 2020, 4–13; 2021). The current humanitarian situation that the agency confronts is unprecedented: the UNHCR's most recent reports indicate there are more than 100 million persons of concern to the agency; moreover, many of those in need of international protection are effectively consigned to the near-permanent limbo of refugee camps with opportunities for third-country resettlement open only to a small fraction of the globe's displaced population (UNHCR 2022, 7–9). Less explicitly addressed by the UNHCR, but often emphasized by refugee studies scholars, has been the array of interdiction policies that states have introduced to deter the arrival of asylum seekers – policies which have sharply proliferated and spread since the end of the Cold War.[6]

Unilateral efforts to deflect asylum seekers have frequently relied upon an inherent weakness in the refugee regime's legal architecture, which largely limits states' positive obligations. Although the 1951 Convention emphasizes the enduring significance of international solidarity to enjoin states to support resettlement and humanitarian assistance, these are not framed as legally binding provisions.[7] A consequence of this is that financial contributions (beyond those reserved for the UNHCR's comparatively narrow core budget) as well as support for third-country resettlement are treated as discretionary initiatives and thereby subject to significant variation.[8] As a result, refugee assistance has increasingly devolved to a sort of "responsibility by proximity," with the onus disproportionately falling onto developing states acting as the first county of asylum in regions of origin (Doyle 2018). Conversely, states that are largely insulated from refugee flows by the accident of geographic distance (generally complemented by the deployment of interdiction policies such as pre-arrival visa requirements and carrier sanctions) have often found it easy to minimize their direct responsibility for providing international protection while still ostensibly upholding legal obligations. Notably, the 1951 Convention did not provide grounds for the formalization of harmonized standards for the adjudication of refugee status, leaving significant discretion in implementation.[9] While some states in the Global South have availed themselves of the UNHCR for conducting RSD, those in the Global North have largely guarded their domestic prerogative to determine asylum claims.[10]

Despite the proliferation of these tendencies among certain states, unilateral methods to managing or minimizing exposure to the binding obligations of the 1951 Convention are not without limitations. While a state may find it both convenient and permissible to apply immigration policies to block easy access to its territory to potential asylum seekers, the capacity to do so from the standpoint of international law must contend with the reality of a corresponding lack of authority over the immigration policies of other states. As is apparent in the context of migration more broadly, such considerations are always already transnational in form and defined by relations of interdependence between states. Moreover, given that the territorially triggered duties of the 1951 Convention remain legally binding for states parties, this situation may simply compel determined refugees in need of asylum to undertake transit through indirect and clandestine means, as well as considerably less safe migration routes.

The central lesson is that unilateral interdiction policies are likely to exacerbate – rather than resolve – the impact of displacement on receiving states, especially when enduring and high levels of protracted displacement lead to sudden increased arrivals of asylum seekers. The apparent solution to these dilemmas – from the standpoint of both states and asylum seekers – would lie in effective responsibility-sharing at a global level, given the normative demands implicit in the idea of international protection. However, the past two decades have seen an increased shift by states, particularly in the developing world, to agreements grounded in the concept of a "safe third country" of asylum alongside various forms of interdiction and externalization as a means to engage in "responsibility shifting" to reactively respond to only growing levels of global displacement.[11]

REGIONALIZING ASYLUM POLICY? THE US-CANADA SAFE THIRD COUNTRY AGREEMENT IN PRACTICE

The US-Canada STCA has been subject to a number of legal challenges in Canada, but has remained in force as a bilateral treaty impacting asylum access within the region. The normalization of this framework has informed subsequent dimensions of regional state practices effecting international protection, particularly in the context of the US. However, as will become apparent below, the STCA sits in a problematic and uneasy tension with the key multilateral legal instruments of the global refugee regime.

The STCA's origins can be traced to a series of bilateral negotiations concurrent with the development of the North American Free Trade Agreement (NAFTA).[12] Beginning in 1992, Canadian and American officials were in substantive discussions aimed at formalizing asylum coordination arrangements (Helton 1993, 737–8). Their ostensive aim was to conclude a memorandum of understanding (MOU), creating a framework for cooperation in the assessment of asylum claims to support the "effective identification and protection" of refugees by way of promoting the "fair and effective" operation of their respective asylum systems (Helton 1993, 748).[13] The more specific motivations of either state remain obscure in the context of the MOU; at the same time, both countries had respectively seen an increased politicization of asylum and refugee policy in public discourse, which may plausibly have influenced policy priorities. However, despite a presumed initial perception of shared interests, negotiations essentially came to an end in 1998, with the stalling of Canadian efforts to secure the MOU attributed to American indifference.[14]

Interest in bilateral asylum cooperation was renewed in the aftermath of 11 September 2001. Progress in the negotiations proved more rapid and the outcome more ambitious than earlier efforts. The groundwork for the STCA was advanced by the initial signing of the US-Canada Smart Border Declaration in 2001, which soon evolved into a 30-point action plan, with the latter's importance reflected in the high-profile meeting between President George W. Bush and Prime Minister Jean Chrétien the following year, to discuss and evaluate the development of the initiative (US 2009). Notably, the larger framework represented by the action plan linked the area of asylum coordination with the broader question of border security. These issues of border cooperation also had an important economic dimension, reflecting the need to balance perceived security concerns while maintaining critical trade relations (Parks 2004, 395–6). This was of no small import given that the countries in question share the longest international border, and, even in the wake of recent moments of escalation in American protectionism, still continue to affirm that they hold the world's most comprehensive trading relationship (US 2020). Thus, while the areas of asylum and refugee protection policy might seem distant from the domain of commerce, the larger action plan's framing of these issues under the rubric of border security may be taken as forging an issue-linkage between the areas, one which could have proved sufficient to overcoming prior constraints.[15]

The resulting negotiations culminated in both countries signing the STCA in 2002, which came into force at the end of 2004. The earlier action plan's references to asylum coordination explicitly invoked the issue of "forum shopping" – the allegedly problematic practice of refugees applying for asylum after previously transiting other states where they could have (at least in theory) lodged a comparable asylum claim – as a key concern.[16] In contrast, the text of the STCA does not directly mention or allude to "forum shopping" at any point; instead it opens with a preamble declaratively casting the bilateral agreement as expressing commitments to "enhancing" overall "cooperation and burden-sharing with respect to refugee status claimants," while explicitly reaffirming both countries' commitments to the 1951 Convention and 1967 Protocol, as well as the broader "principles of international solidarity that underpin the international refugee protection system" (Canada 2002).[17]

The STCA's content largely focuses on arrangements for circumscribing responsibility to the country of "last presence" for determining asylum claims. While the "last presence" designation originally applied between the US and Canada, it has been suggested that the STCA was modelled on the European Union's multilateral Dublin Convention which continues to require asylum seekers to seek protection in their first country of arrival as part of an EU-wide asylum framework (Macklin 2004, 370). Concurrent hearings in the US Congress indicate that the approach adopted by this aspect of the STCA was informed by the then nascent Dublin Convention, and apparent concerns regarding potential disputes in establishing the path of arrival of asylum claimants (US 2002, 13). Reflecting this parallel objective, the STCA's Article 4 may be read as the crux of the agreement by articulating provisions aimed at blocking individuals' capacity to claim asylum on arrival at a land border port of entry, in the event of having transited through either "safe" country where, presumably, a fair and effective asylum claim could have been lodged (Canada 2002, §§4–5). In addition to articulating a limited set of circumstances, allowing individuals meeting certain conditions (such as existing familial ties within either state party) to advance asylum claims, in exception to the broader requirements of the STCA, the treaty also includes provisions to facilitate the exchange of information to support the core goals of the agreement in relation to advancing bilateral asylum coordination, addresses a limited role for UNHCR to provide oversight of the framework, describes the dispute resolution mechanisms to resolved differences between the states parties, as well as provides conditions for the mutual modification or unilateral termination of the STCA (Canada 2002, §§7, 8, 10). In an apparent gesture toward the STCA's compatibility with responsibilities under the refugee regime, it also specifically requires both countries to not deport asylum seekers who were returned under the agreement to another state before RSD procedures were completed (Canada 2002, §3). The provision is clear in prohibiting the application of any future safe third country agreement or regulatory designation to supersede this safeguard, appearing to further emphasize the current STCA's consistency with the requirements of international refugee law.[18]

The STCA's basic framework remained unchanged for over two decades. In line with the agreement's provisions, subsequent to it coming into effect, the UNHCR issued at least one substantive monitoring report on the STCA in 2006 (UNHCR 2006). The appraisal regarding the practices of two major donor states that were party to the STCA was largely uncritical; however, the report raised concerns relating to the general implementation. The focal point of these concerns related to the "direct back policy" adopted by state parties under the framework, wherein Canada would generally return claimants from points of entry to wait in the US if Canadian border officials were unable to deal with the asylum claim at the time; although an opportunity to schedule a subsequent interview might be provided, the circumstances of claimants in the US might not subsequently allow this (UNHCR 2006, 6).[19] That said, the assessment may arguably have been shaped by the UNHCR's ongoing budgetary dependence on these countries for its humanitarian operations assisting the vast majority of the world's refugees, and the fact that the US at the time was the top country for resettlement.

While drawing little public attention in the United States, the STCA has undergone several court challenges in Canada during the intervening time. These began shortly after the STCA came into effect in 2004, with the mounting of a domestic legal challenge in 2007 supported by the Canadian

Council for Refugees, Amnesty International, and the Canadian Council of Churches.[20] The Federal Court's initial ruling found the STCA invalid on constitutional grounds, and "declared it to have no force and effect" insofar as the agreement "violated section 15 (equality) and section 7 (life, liberty, and security of the person) of the Canadian Charter of Rights and Freedoms" (Arbel 2013, 66). However, this decision was subsequently overturned by the Federal Court of Appeal in 2008, largely on technical grounds.[21]

Efforts at advancing the effective legal contestation of the STCA within Canada remained largely dormant for nearly a decade, recently resurfacing in a markedly different regional context. While the 2007 court challenge to the agreement had, in part, relied on highlighting the divergent standards of treatment provided to asylum seekers in the US and Canada, these differences had widened into a near chasm with the steady adoption of avowedly anti-immigrant and anti-refugee policies by the former US presidential administration of Donald Trump. Concurrent and related to the aforementioned changes in American policy, beginning in 2017 Canada witnessed a significant "uptick" in irregular border crossings from the US, resulting in a doubling in the number of asylum claims made in 2016 (Canada 2022). The STCA emerged as a source of intense controversy in Canadian public discourse, both among those dubious of the agreement's legitimacy in light of the increasingly doubtful status of the US as a "safe country," and others concerned with a so-called loophole for irregular border crossings that had come to light with the growing number of asylum seekers arriving in Canada (CBC 2018).

The latter situation was a result of the fact that, in addition to the STCA's formal references to the narrow grounds permitting individuals to gain exemption from the main provisions of the agreement, the overall framework only applied at official points of entry. This feature of the agreement allowed potential asylum seekers to eschew the STCA's constraints by avoiding official border crossings and proceeding to file inland claims for asylum once within Canada (Cowger 2017).[22] In between the agreement's unexpected tendency to incentivize irregular border movement, and amid significant growth in asylum seekers arriving from the US (characterized by increasingly hostile immigration policies), the issue of irregular migration had become highly politicized in Canada, leading the liberal government of Justin Trudeau to promise to "modernize" the framework (Macklin 2018). Within this context, the civil society groups that had played a role in supporting the earlier legal challenge to the STCA submitted a brief to the Government of Canada alleging that the American asylum system and immigration detention regime required Canada to withdraw from the agreement (Amnesty International and CCR 2017). That same year, faced with what they perceived as a lack of action on the part of the Trudeau government, these organizations filed a new federal court challenge (CCR 2017). While the focus of the case remained broadly similar to its precursor, the challenge included a number of individuals that were turned back by Canadian border officials under the STCA.

More recently, the COVID-19 pandemic witnessed significant changes in Canadian cross-border migration policy relative to the agreement, further complicating the status of the STCA. Amid the negotiations surrounding the then ostensibly temporary closure of the border between the US and Canada in April 2020, ambiguity remained in play with regard to the stance of Canada's liberal government toward the irregular border crossings that had become prominent flashpoints in public debate during the federal election the prior fall. Despite initial messaging indicating the contrary, the Canadian government imposed a border closure that made no allowances for individuals seeking asylum, at official ports of entry or otherwise.[23] The narrow exemption grounds from the STCA were eventually restored in late April 2020 (Connolly 2020). However, the broader policy of rejecting all other potential asylum claimants, regardless of the point of entry, was retained for significantly longer, thereby keeping the border closed to the vast majority of possible asylum claimants.[24]

The impact of the full border shutdown on asylum claimants may have initially been limited; there were relatively fewer border apprehensions or attempts to claim asylum, perhaps reflecting the broader slowdown of all travel during the early stages of the pandemic.[25] However, questions continued to be raised about whether the policy amounted to an abrogation of obligations to refugees, given valid worries about the US applying summary deportations to potential asylees.[26] Indeed, as Atak and Simeon (2018, 9) have noted, in the period leading up to the border closure, "almost 70 per cent of asylum claimants who illegally cross the US border into Canada were granted asylum," suggesting that the STCA directly impacted access to international protection.

These concerns received significant vindication some months later, with the release of the Federal Court of Canada's July 2020 ruling on the ongoing legal challenge to the STCA, which ruled in favour of the litigants and found the agreement in violation of sections 7 and 15 of the Charter of Rights and Freedoms. Notwithstanding this ruling, the Federal Court suspended its subsequent declaration of the invalidity of the STCA for a period of six months (Canada 2020b).[27] This was followed by the Federal Court of Appeal's decision, in October 2020, to further suspend the Federal Court's ruling pending appeal, on the basis of the liberal government's assertion that the voiding of the STCA would result in an "influx of refugee claimants" (Hill 2020); the Federal Court of Appeal subsequently ruled unanimously to uphold the constitutionality of the STCA in April 2021.

However, the legal outcome of the case remains pending at the time of writing: in December 2021, the Supreme Court of Canada granted leave to appeal the prior ruling, and, in October 2022, the court heard arguments from both federal government officials, as well as the Canadian Council for Refugees, Amnesty International, the Canadian Council of Churches, and a number of individual applicants. Over the course of the litigation, the STCA has remained in force, against the backdrop of the closure and subsequent reopening of US-Canada border crossings; the Supreme Court of Canada's final judgment regarding the legality of the framework will take place in a context reflecting important shifts in American asylum and immigration policy under the Biden administration.

These latter developments, however, do not necessarily resolve the broader questions regarding the legitimacy of the STCA. Indeed, the confluence of recent events further highlight the agreement's inability to address discrepancies in the domestic asylum and refugee policies of the states parties, which have been revealed to be highly susceptible to dramatic divergences. These considerations are unlikely to be addressed by the Canadian Government's efforts to "modernize" the agreement (Canada 2020d). Indeed, the announcement in late March 2023 that the US and Canada had concluded a protocol to the STCA caught both civil society groups and potential asylum seekers by surprise. The sudden release and application of the protocol immediately entailed extending the agreement to all cross-border movement (Canada 2023). This was far from accidental, given that the modifications to the STCA had been negotiated and finalized over a year prior and kept secret at Canada's request, purportedly to enable both governments time to implement necessary measures, while also intending to prevent a subsequent increase in irregular crossings (Walsh 2023).

However, the timing of the 2023 announcement unfolded against the backdrop of highly continuous decisions by the Biden administration to significantly transform the nature of asylum access at the southern US border. The ongoing appeal of the STCA's legal status had largely centered on its compatibility with section 7 of the Charter and it is probable the case will be decided on narrow, technical grounds, focused on the applicability of domestic law in a markedly transnational context. While the full implications of the Supreme Court of Canada's judgment are still pending at the time of writing, the court's ruling is not unlikely to result in the STCA remaining in effect given the scope of the appeal. However, further investigation of the bilateral agreement's normative status within the context of the refugee regime remains warranted, as does analysis of the STCA from the standpoint of its broader impacts on asylum policy and access to international protection both in the region and beyond.

NORMALIZING ASYLUM COORDINATION OR UNDERMINING REFUGEE PROTECTION?

In the previous section, we focused on the historical context of the unfolding of the STCA, as well as the more apparent domestic impacts of the agreement over the last two decades. Here, the remainder of the chapter shifts to a broader perspective, placing the STCA in the context of both comparative regional frameworks and more recent developments within North America. We begin by taking up a fundamental theoretical issue that underpins asylum coordination more broadly: the "legal fiction" of parallel protection standards which uniformly informs these approaches.

The 1951 Convention does not itself explicitly prohibit the general creation of "safe third country" frameworks which might purport to establish bilateral structures for coordinating asylum policies across signatory states (Lauterpacht and Bethlehem 2003, 122).[28] In this regard, it is silent on the matter to the same degree that it articulates no obligation on the part of refugees to seek asylum in any particular state (Settlage 2012).[29] However, for the former to be compatible with the fundamental purpose and core principles of the refugee regime, we must assume that these arrangements do not intrinsically undermine international protection. This in turn provides something of an immanent standard for assessing these approaches. In the absence of a de jure formal harmonization of asylum standards, states could rely upon what we might call a constitutive legal fiction of equivalent protection across relevant state jurisdictions.[30] However, when this fiction reveals itself to be a manifest falsehood that undermines access to international protection we can rightly call out practices of asylum coordination as contradicting the normative standards of the refugee regime.

Given these considerations, the compatibility of asylum coordination arrangements with the refugee regime should be assessed with regard to the overall object and purpose of the 1951 Convention, which, as noted above, is to enable the protection of refugees by the international community, and in doing so, assure refugees the widest possible exercise of fundamental rights and freedoms (Goodwin-Gill 2014, 367). The ultimate aim of securing international protection hinges most directly on realizing the refugee regime's ground-norm of non-refoulement, as well as related protections against the penalization of unlawful entry and summary expulsion.

Notably, the non-derogable prohibition on refoulment does not simply proscribe returning a refugee claimant to their country of origin. Rather, it is widely recognized to encompass "indirect" refoulment, thereby requiring states to refrain from returning refugees to any state where they may lack effective protection or be in danger of subsequent refoulement. This has not only been opined by scholars, but also unambiguously stated by UNHCR, whose interpretive guidance constitutes a crucial component of its overall supervisory role in relation to the 1951 Convention.[31] Indeed, in the absence of upholding such obligations, states parties' responses toward the arrival of refugees would be susceptible to dramatic and serious deviation from the object and purpose of the 1951 Convention. As Hathaway and Foster (2014, 46) indicate, "state parties have assumed obligations to refugees with whom they have a connection, in some cases based simply on their exercise of jurisdiction. If it were possible to circumvent the considerable range of obligations imposed on state parties by the simple expedient of transferring a refugee to another state, this would defeat the very raison d'être of the Convention."

In its most extreme unilateral form, a general lack of respect for the principle of non-refoulement, under which states viewed it as permissible to extinguish their obligations toward refugees by simply removing individuals from their jurisdiction, would resemble a situation not much different from the circumstances preceding the emergence of the global refugee regime. Although the 1951 Convention rightly emphasizes the importance of broader interstate coordination, the undermining of non-refoulement strikes at the very heart of international protection. Since state obligations relate directly to the presence of persons within their effective jurisdiction, it is the potential implications of the STCA for core norms of the 1951 Refugee Convention, and above all the principle of non-refoulement, that raises the central question about the legitimacy of interstate asylum coordination.

This is expressed in state practice through the widespread domestic institutionalization and implementation of RSD procedures, by which a person's claim to refugee status is properly assessed and recognized on an individual basis. The importance of states upholding their responsibilities to refugee claimants within their jurisdiction is especially salient with regard to fully respecting the principle of non-refoulement. As Lauterpacht and Bethlehem (2003, 118) note, "[t]he implementation of the principle of non-refoulement in general requires an examination of the facts of each individual case. In particular a denial of protection in the absence of a review of individual circumstances would be inconsistent with the prohibition of refoulement." The STCA intervenes in this process by effectively displacing responsibility for determining refugee status and the subsequent obligations related to the provision of international protection to the respective country of last transit, under the assumption that both state parties provide reasonably equivalent asylum procedures and therefore sufficient access to international protection.

As noted above, state obligations toward refugees cannot simply be extinguished by transferring individuals to another territory, and so any measures at asylum coordination would by extension require remaining consistent with those obligations. This latter assumption of guaranteeing at least approximately comparable procedures is explicitly presumed by the STCA itself. This is because the agreement appears to proscribe the removal of asylum seekers impacted by the framework prior to the adjudication of a refugee status claim "in order to ensure that refugee status claimants have access to a refugee status determination system" as well as the removal of individuals to "another country pursuant to any other safe third country agreement or regulatory designation" (Canada 2002, §3). Such provisions underscore the STCA's ostensive attempts to present itself as compatible with the normative principles underlying the global refugee regime.

At the same time, however, the agreement exhibits a number of structural features that render it incapable of fully maintaining the underlying international protection obligations of states parties. Although the STCA gestures toward the compatibility of both states parties' refugee policies with the 1951 Convention, it contains no provisions for harmonizing the respective domestic asylum policies between the two states, neither does it provide any convincing mechanism for assuring that fair RSD procedures are in fact available to individuals directly affected by the framework proximate to its application. As a result, the STCA appears to provide insufficient safeguards to avoid either direct or indirect refoulment, thereby facilitating breaches of core legal obligations undertaken by states party to the 1951 Convention.

This perhaps somewhat abstract discussion of the structure of the STCA can be further illuminated by a more concrete comparison. As indicated earlier, the European Union's Dublin Convention preceded the creation of the STCA and indeed may have functioned as an important model for North America. However, although the subsequent permutations of Dublin that have served to frame asylum coordination in Europe share some features – particularly with regard to fixing responsibility for claimants in the first country of asylum – there are some fundamental differences. Perhaps most crucially, the succession of Dublin Regulations that have emerged in Europe have always remained embedded within a larger supranational frame and the regional integration mechanisms that have structured the EU's development. In contrast, the STCA emerged against a backdrop of little to no substantive regionalism and represents a considerably more modest bilateral mechanism. This in turn informs some crucial divergences between the two frameworks which require attention.

First and foremost, Europe's common asylum system is premised – at least in principle – on a significant level of "harmonization" across EU member states. In essence, asylum coordination in the EU is linked to acceding to a high degree of shared standards, including both binding definitions of those entitled to international protection, which function as a "floor" for the domestic implementation of RSD, and common procedures for the treatment of asylum seekers. This in turn has opened space for a degree of normative evolution and consolidation in the context of the EU, where subsequent EU policies have led to the formalization of continent-wide standards for the recognition and reception of convention refugees, alongside the development of a "subsidiary protection regime" and temporary protection framework by way of the Common European Asylum System (McAdam 2005).[32] Although long dormant since its creation, the Temporary Protection Directive has been invoked for the first time as part of the EU's response to the crisis in Ukraine, and in this context has greatly facilitated the cross-border movement and reception of displaced persons across Europe. These innovations notably contrast with the divergent implementation of such measures across the US and Canada, with significant differences in asylum procedures and temporary protection provisions between the two countries. For instance, as Macklin (2003) has noted, even at the time the STCA came into force, US asylum policy imposed a one-year limit on making a claim to asylum for those already present within the US. While exceptions to the still-binding rule exist, there are well-grounded and persistent concerns "that the one-year filing deadline can, does and will arbitrarily disqualify persons who are in need of protection" (Macklin 2003, 15). The larger regionalization in which EU asylum coordination has emerged also provided a significant degree of transnational oversight; not only are Dublin regulatory requirements transposed into European law, but these are also more broadly embedded in quasi-judicial frameworks overseen by supranational bodies such as the Court of Justice of the European Union (CJEU) and European Court of Human Rights (ECHR).[33] In contrast, the STCA's model of bilateral asylum coordination lacks anything comparable to requiring common standards or offering oversight of state practices. This renders the North American situation far more overtly susceptible to political considerations impacting the reception and treatment of asylum seekers, as has been particularly evident in the context of the recent widening divergencies in US and Canadian RSD procedures.

This is not to gloss over important problems in the EU's asylum framework. For instance, the shared standards for protection coexist against a backdrop of divergent asylum recognition rates, given that member states continue to enjoy competency over the implementation of RSD. This has led to a situation where "recognition rates are alarmingly diverse" across EU member states (Guild et al. 2014, 40).[34] Scholarship on European refugee policy has also drawn important attention to how the integration dynamics of the EU can produce policy incoherencies in the common asylum system

(Lavenex 2018) or undermine reform in such areas as the development of responsibility-sharing among member states (Zaun 2018). Most importantly, the architecture of intra-European asylum coordination provides little to no attention to the agency of displaced persons, while arguably generating protection gaps in the reception of asylum seekers, given differing levels of state capacity. At the same time, however, the EU's framework can prove comparatively versatile in responding to protection needs when political will is present, while also opening up space for member states to "lead by example" in the context of relaxing the stringent application of the Dublin regulations in the face of a "mass influx" of asylum seekers.[35] In both cases, the larger backdrop of strong regional integration appears as a key factor – one which is markedly absent from the North American context.

THE STCA AND CURRENT STATE PRACTICE: AN EMERGING MODEL IN THE GLOBAL NORTH

While the US-Canada STCA once represented a uniquely bilateral innovation in transnational asylum coordination, there has been an increased upsurge in similar frameworks across a number of regions, with changes in the North American context largely driven by the initiative of the United States. These contemporaneous developments provide an important critical frame for assessing the STCA's potential impact in shaping interstate practice, suggesting that it may have paved the way for a far more radical set of approaches to asylum coordination that largely bypass the institutionalized norms of the refugee regime.

Overall, while the framework of the EU's common asylum system is a subject of considerable and compelling scholarly criticism, it does represent a very different regional approach to refugee protection, one that strongly contrasts with those that have predominated in North America. That said, more recent developments in Europe have suggested a turn to "bilateral" approaches that share important parallels with the STCA. Chief among these has been the EU-Turkey asylum statement of cooperation, based on the Joint Action Plan (JAP) between the EU and Turkey (Lehner 2019). Constructed in the wake of the "migration crisis" and the rapid rise of asylum seekers in Europe during 2015, the joint statement takes the form of a bilateral framework between the regional block and the Turkish government – one that is explicitly concerned with "ending irregular migration" from Turkey to the EU (EC 2016). The latter emphasis has led scholars and civil society groups to take a largely critical perspective on the EU-Turkey statement, insofar as its emphasis on maintaining access to asylum appears to largely represent window dressing for the otherwise overt extension of EU border externalization policies.

There is much to support this critical characterization, which casts the measure as a crude, but potentially effective, mechanism for addressing the challenges raised by the EU's migration crisis. However, even when bracketing the question of the underlying rationale of the EU-Turkey statement of cooperation, a number of striking divergences from prior EU asylum coordination efforts are apparent, with the bilateral architecture sharing important similarities with the STCA. This bilateral form is most apparent in the fact that the statement structures asylum coordination between the EU and a non-member state, and therefore places such arrangements largely outside the shared standards that characterize the EU's common asylum system constituted under the Dublin Regulations or the EU's judicial oversight mechanisms that allow for the application of the Dublin Regulations to be challenged in court. It therefore represents a significant departure from the EU's prior approach – one far more similar to the bilateral architecture that characterizes the STCA, which requires little by way of harmonized RSD procedures or indeed effective monitoring and oversight. Equally notable is the evident dispensing of the fiction of parallel safety available to asylum seekers across the respective parties' jurisdictions. This is apparent in both formal and substantive terms. In this regard it is worth noting that Turkey has acceded to the 1967 Protocol, but with continued reservations, thereby impacting the scope of its protection obligations to those displaced by events occurring in Europe. This means that not only is it untouched by the protection standards imposed by the Dublin Regulations, but that its formal obligations under the global refugee regime are considerably more limited. Indeed, because of the reservations that accompanied Turkey's accession to the 1967 Protocol, its commitments under international law remain constrained to the geographic limits that govern the 1951 Convention (Güler 2020).

This is far from inconsequential. The rights enjoyed by asylum seekers who would otherwise qualify as refugees in the EU are derived from the Turkish temporary protection regime, not international refugee law, indicating a far less stable status. Paralleling this, Turkey's 2014 legislation governing access to international protection solely recognizes "resettlement to a third country as the only durable solution available for non-European refugees compelled to flee their countries" (UNHCR 2014). Finally, from a more substantive perspective, advocacy organizations such as Amnesty International have questioned Turkey's credentials as a safe country, drawing attention to reports of forced repatriation (Amnesty 2016). Following the announcement of the framework, the broader context of the EU-Turkey agreement has been characterized by ongoing and increasingly overt tensions between the two partners. This period has also seen persistent doubts that "Turkey can be considered a safe country in which refugees and asylum seekers are given adequate care and protection from being sent back to Syria" (Terry 2021). The latter of course raises fundamental issues that strike at the core assumption of parallel safety underlying the entire framework as structured around asylum coordination in a manner consistent with the refugee regime. At the same time, however, the EU-Turkey framework has arguably "become a blueprint" for the EU's approach to externalized migration, with "resurgent interest" in having the pact renewed in the future (Terry 2021). Given the significant divergence from prior EU policy that the framework represents, these considerations point to a potential inflection point in European asylum policies.

Paralleling developments in the EU, the North American context has seen a similar uptake in bilateral arrangements, chiefly between the United States and other countries in the broader region. These agreements were initiated by the Trump administration in response to the growing numbers of asylum seekers from Central America, and advanced in tandem with increasingly punitive domestic measures directed at those crossing into the United States (Chishti and Bolter 2020). Resonances with the STCA are most apparent in the case of the Asylum Cooperative Agreements (ACAs) the US pursued with Guatemala, El Salvador, and Honduras. Although only the first of the agreements was fully implemented, prior to being dismantled under the Biden administration, all of these arrangements took an explicitly bilateral form and, while presented as asylum coordination frameworks, aimed at precluding individuals who had transited through these counties from applying for asylum in the US.

As Gil, Micinski, and Norman argue in this volume, the ACA between the US and Guatemala holds a number of striking parallels with the EU-Turkey deal. For our purposes it is worth highlighting the degree to which it also shares features with the STCA. Both agreements aimed primarily at displacing responsibility for asylum adjudication to another country, under the implicit assumption of equal access to protection, but without any oversight mechanisms or provisions pertaining to the harmonizing of asylum standards. The troubling implications of this in the case of the US-Guatemala ACA have been documented by human rights organizations, who contend that asylum seekers expelled while the agreement was in force were effectively denied access to international protection (HRW 2020). This arguably is directly a result of features common to both the ACA and STCA, which simply externalize responsibility for asylum without substantively requiring states parties to adhere to core norms of the refugee regime. In the case of the US-Guatemala ACA, this has led to significant gaps in protection for asylum seekers.

A parallel set of developments can be identified in the context of the Migrant Protection Protocols (MPP) introduced under the Trump administration to effectively block the arrival of asylum seekers into the US from its southern neighbour. More commonly known as the "Remain in Mexico" program, the MPP required potential asylum seekers to be removed to and made to wait within Mexico, pending the adjudication of their asylum claims; its direct impact could be observed in the immediate drop in irregular arrivals at the US-Mexico border (Soto 2020). Unlike the EU-Turkey agreement, which saw the EU mobilize positive inducements as part of securing Turkey's participation in the framework, the Trump administration pursued the MPP by way of coercive issue-linkage, using explicit threats of economic retaliation to motivate Mexico's compliance. Notably, the MPP fell short of formally accomplishing the full externalization of responsibility for asylum adjudication, when compared with either the ACA or the STCA; in principle, the agreement informing the MPP was limited to blocking admission pending a determination by US officials. However, this distinction arguably was more symbolic than practical: American promises to expedite asylum processing proved largely empty, with this period witnessing mounting immigration court backlogs (Chishti and Bolter 2021). Importantly in the context of this discussion, the MPP also appears to rely upon the presumption of safety and equivalent protection as a legal fiction to accomplish the transfer of significant legal responsibilities entailed under the 1951 Convention. Given the well-documented vulnerabilities facing individuals returned under the MPP, presenting waiting in Mexico as offering equivalent protection and safety is a manifest absurdity. However, the presumption of such fictions of safety as necessary to sustain the appearance of these arrangements as congruent with "protection" represents an important parallel between the MPP and the STCA.

CONCLUSION

The contemporary landscape of asylum coordination in both North America and Europe suggests that a troubling pattern of convergence may be underway, with particularly concerning consequences for access to international protection. Engaging with the potential undercurrents of "policy transfer" across the two regions remains well beyond the scope of this chapter (See Geddes, in this volume, for broader discussion of factors that impact migration policy transfer). However, the dynamics addressed above would suggest that key features of the STCA as a potential model of asylum coordination have emerged as predominant elements in both contexts. This chapter argued that a particularly problematic dimension of the architecture of the STCA as a framework for asylum coordination lies in its perverse deployment of the legal fiction of equivalent protection in the absence of any substantive institutional mechanisms that could ensure this claim. By dispensing with the pretense of upholding the core normative demands that form the backbone of international protection, the STCA represents a highly problematic model for regionalized asylum in the Global North, the proliferation of which may very well significantly contribute to undermining the effectiveness of the refugee regime.

By way of conclusion, it is worth acknowledging how the challenges raised by the SCTA and similar "safe country" agreements highlight a significant and enduring tension in the normative architecture of the 1951 Convention and the broader issues raised by forced displacement in a world of states. A relatively unique aspect of the 1951 Convention as a multilateral treaty is that it impacts the status and fundamental well-being of a particular class of individuals, who by definition lack the domestic protection afforded to citizens by their state of origin. In a very definitive sense, the situation of refugees is the result of the breakdown of the normative and legal link of individual persons to a state of nationality – one that is largely presupposed by international law and the larger framework of the interstate system.

Arguably a core purpose of the global refugee regime is to remedy this dilemma by way of implementing a multilateral framework for international protection. It does so by partially restoring what refugees have been denied via the immediate provision of protection afforded by refugee status and, ideally, through facilitating durable solutions to their displacement by promoting the integration of refugees into host societies via the mechanisms of resettlement and naturalization. Yet who or what should be taken to represent these individuals when the very basis of this remedial process is undermined or violated, and what concrete remedies are available to address the subsequent harms that refugees may face? The legal architecture of the refugee regime arguably provides no satisfying answer to this question, as evidenced by the endurance of the US-Canada STCA and the uptake of similar frameworks by states in the Global North. Within the currently existing framework of the regime there are no robust mechanisms for directly challenging the legality of state actions that compromise international protection and thereby mitigate the impact of such measures on refugees.[36] This suggests a clear need for further developments at the international level to bring about institutions and norms capable of advancing a more equitable refugee regime capable of effectively responding to the only growing levels of forced displacement (Banerjee 2017). However, contemporary developments, both in North America and beyond, suggest that for now many states are more than content to invest in the expedient of bilateral mechanisms which may directly contribute to undermining access to international protection.

NOTES

1 See UNHCR (1999) for a direct articulation of the organization's initial position: "The widespread misuse of the notion of "safe third country" has been another major concern for UNHCR. Due to an inappropriate application of this notion, asylum seekers have often been removed to territories where their safety cannot be ensured. This practice is clearly contrary to basic protection principles and may lead to violations of the principle of non-refoulement" (¶ 19).

2 For brief discussion of the latter, see Currie (2008, 74).

3 On the resistance of states to acceded to international instruments granting a right to asylum, see Hyndman (1986).

4 For the latter, see UNGA (1967, 267).

5 Delving further into the divergent patterns of accession to the 1951 Convention and 1967 Protocol is beyond the scope of this chapter. However, it is worth noting that many of the top hosting countries are conspicuously not signatories to both frameworks. Moreover, despite its important role in the global refugee regime, the United States has only signed the Protocol and not the Convention itself.

6 For two recent studies of these state practices of refugee deterrence, see Fitzgerald (2019) and Mountz (2020).

7 See the recommendations adopted by the Conference of Plenipotentiaries on the Status of Refugees and Stateless Persons as well as the 1951 Convention's preambulatory paragraphs; UNGA (1951, 144–52).

8 For a recent example, referenced in passing at the start of this chapter, consider the dramatic contraction in American refugee resettlement commitments, which plummeted during the course of the (now former) Trump presidential administration in the US. Worth noting in this regard is the fact that, while the US has remained a state party to the 1967 Protocol (and by extension, formally bound by the legal provisions of the 1951 Convention) this did not prevent the executive branch of government from reducing US support for refugee resettlement to historically unprecedented low figures (MPI 2020).

9 See Aleinikoff (1992), particularly 124–5, for an important and exceptionally compelling analysis of these considerations in the context of the 1951 Convention and the dynamics of contemporary refugee law.

10 For innovative discussion of the dynamics that have driven delegation to the UNHCR in some settings within the Global South, see Abdelaaty (2021). With regard to Global North countries, while the EU has seen substantial expansion in the harmonizing of asylum standards, RSD still

remain within the purview of individual states. The reality of substantial deviations in refugee recognition rates across countries of origins suggests the persistence of significant national discretion even in the context of the EU.

11 There is a long running literature on the "safe country" concept. See, for instance, Achermann and Gattiker (1995); Costello (2005); Moreno-Lax (2015). For earlier discussion by the UNHCR, see UNHCR (1999).

12 Although the bilateral origins of the STCA date from this time, it is worth acknowledging that the domestic groundwork for enabling such measures began significantly earlier. For instance, the 1988 amendments to the Immigration Act, 1976, first introduced a "safe third country" into Canadian law, a development that would inform the legal evolution of the first country of asylum in the context of the STCA. See Canada (2009).

13 See the appendix in Helton (1993) for the text of the draft MOU.

14 As the Canadian Council for Refugees suggests, "the United States, for whom the agreement would have few if any obvious advantages, was unwilling to pursue negotiations in the foreseeable future, and in February 1998, the Canadian Minister of Citizenship and Immigration announced that negotiations had been abandoned" (CCR 1998, 30).

15 The concept of issue-linkages plays a prominent role in the international relations literature on the formation of international regimes, as well as more bilateral forms of state cooperation. For discussion of the concept of issue-linkage in the refugee regime, see Betts (2011). For general discussion in the context of US-Canadian relations, see Bow (2009).

16 The much expressed concern of states with so-called forum shopping is itself arguably very much a product of the 1951 Convention having delegated the competency for RSD procedures to states themselves, which in turn have implemented the "Convention grounds" in sometimes significantly different ways through domestic legislation. In the context of Canada and the US (as well as other countries) this has led to marked divergencies in overall recognition rates across countries of origin. Arguably, if such a concern was indeed paramount, entrusting status determinations to the UNHCR or taking other means for formally harmonizing such standards would likely prove a more fair and effective mechanism.

17 For an assessment of the STCA's provisions relative to the various declarations in its preamble, see Macklin (2003).

18 At the same time, Article 9 stands out as anomalous against this background; the provision articulates an undefined enjoinment for state parties to assist each other with "the resettlement of persons determined

to require protection in appropriate circumstances" (Canada 2002, §9). Given the discretionary nature of third-country resettlement, a reasonable interpretation of this provision would seem to imply the outsourcing of states' respective responsibility for assisting convention refugees that have lodged effective asylum claims in their jurisdictions to the other country.

19 Notably, such practices and the concerns voiced by the UNHCR hold troubling parallels with dimensions of US migration policy in relation to its southern border discussed subsequently in this chapter. Relatedly, the UNHCR expressed concern regarding US detention policies, as well as the ability to appeal initial determinations under the STCA, especially "those who believe that the decision was not correct, and those to whom new information becomes available to support eligibility under an exception" (UNHCR 2006, 59).

20 See the discussion of Thompson (2010, 15–53), for an extensive account of the early role of Canadian civil society in contesting these measures.

21 These focused on the consideration that the litigant had not appeared at a border point of entry to request a determination of eligibility as well as the reversal of the public interest standing of the Canadian civil society groups that had supported the case. For further discussion, see Thompson (2010), Arbel (2013), and also: Canada (2009).

22 Despite the apparent surprise of many Canadian political leaders regarding the relation between the STCA and irregular border crossings, the outcome was largely anticipated by earlier scholars. See Macklin (2004, 419–23).

23 For the Canadian Government's account of the broader justifications for this policy, see: Canada (2020b).

24 For critical discussion of these policy decisions, see Mercier and Rehaag (2020). Notably, Canada only removed the temporary measures restricting asylum claims for persons seeking entry from the US between designated land ports of entry in November of 2021.

25 As CBC (2020b) reported, the number of individuals turned back from the border dropped by more than half relative to the year prior, falling from 663 in 2019 to 259 from the start of January to the end of September in 2020.

26 See CBC (2020a) and (2020b) for coverage of this in the Canadian Press.

27 For the legal ruling, see Canada (2020a). For the government's initial response, see Canada (2020c).

28 As UNHCR (2018b) has indicated more recently, "Refugees may be returned or transferred to a state where they had found, could have found

or, pursuant to a formal agreement, can find international protection. The 1951 Convention relating to the Status of Refugees and its 1967 Protocol do not prohibit such return or transfer."

29 As Settlage (2012, 150) rightly notes, "asylum seekers are not required by the UN Refugee Convention to apply for asylum in the first safe country to which they are able to travel" and that there are indeed "many legitimate reasons an asylum seeker might choose to apply for asylum in a country other than the one of first arrival, including the existence of support communities, extended family, or language affinity in the country of choice, or asylum laws that offer greater protection given her particular situation."

30 The idea of legal fiction employed here can be illustrated by a parallel found in general international law – the interstate system relies upon the constitutive "fiction" of sovereign equality between states. Of course, material differences in the power and capacity of states are an undeniable reality. However, the normative structure of the post-war interstate system fundamentally relies upon this assumption to frame the very idea of states as subjects under international law, as indicated in the codification of this principle in article 2(1) of the UN Charter. In much the same way, asylum coordination can be fruitfully assessed relative to the constitutive standards of international protection, if such interstate practices are to be understood as compatible with the global refugee regime.

31 As UNHCR (1997) has noted: "Whenever refugees – or asylum-seekers who may be refugees – are subjected, either directly or indirectly, to such measures of return, be it in the form of rejection, expulsion or otherwise, to territories where their life or freedom are threatened, the principle of non-refoulement has been violated." See also UNHCR's subsequent statement on this: "As a general rule, in order to give effect to their obligations under the 1951 Convention and/or 1967 Protocol, States will be required to grant individuals seeking international protection access to the territory and to fair and efficient asylum procedures" (UNHCR 2007, para. 8). Lauterpacht and Bethlehem (2003, 122) note that the prohibition on non-refoulement "also precludes the removal of a refugee or asylum seeker to a third State in circumstances in which there is a risk that he or she might be sent from there to a territory where he or she would be at risk."

32 A full discussion of the EU's common asylum system is beyond the scope of this chapter. However, it is worth noting some key elements of particular salience in the context of access to international protection: the Asylum Procedures Directive, the Reception Conditions Directive, and the Qualification Directive, together establish a framework of common standards for access to asylum procedures across member states, articulate how this should be carried out, how individuals seeking asylum should be

treated, and codify EU-wide definitions for Convention Refugees and those in need of subsidiary protection (i.e., persons with claims to international protection on other grounds).

33 For discussion of this context, see ECRE (2018), which takes up the impact of the landmark 2011 rulings of European Courts on the European Union's common asylum system; for instance, the ruling of the ECHR in *M.S.S. v. Belgium and Greece*, and the ruling of the CJEU in N.S./M.E. Both cases suggest a significant degree of oversight and constraint when compared to the North American context. More recently, the EU context has also the development of the European Union Agency for Asylum (EASO), now a fully-fledged EU asylum agency devoted to facilitating cooperation between EU member states on asylum and supporting the implementation of the Common European Asylum System (CEAS).

34 As a study for the European Parliament's Committee on Civil Liberties, Justice and Home Affairs (LIBE) summarized, "Recognition rates for those seeking international protection, however, reveal very significant differences even where countries of origin and profiles of asylum seekers are the same" (Guild et al. 2014, 24).

35 The former is evidenced by the strikingly unanimous adoption of the European Council's implementing decision regarding Temporary Protected Status (TPS) in the face of the high levels of displacement triggered by the ongoing conflict in Ukraine (EC 2022). Arguably Germany's unique response to the EU "migration crisis" furnishes an important example of the latter.

36 As Hathaway, North, and Pobjoy (2013, 323–6) rightly note: "In contrast to nearly every other major international human rights treaty, the Refugee Convention does not establish an interstate supervisory body to hold states accountable if and when they fail to meet their internationally defined protection obligations."

REFERENCES

Abdelaaty, Lamis Elmy. 2021. *Discrimination and Delegation: Explaining State Responses to Refugees*. New York: Oxford University Press.

Achermann, Alberto, and Mario Gattiker. 1995. "Safe Third Countries: European Developments." *International Journal of Refugee* Law 7 (1): 19–38.

Aleinikoff, T. Alexander. 1992. "State-centered Refugee Law: From Resettlement to Containment." *Michigan Journal of International Law* 14 (1): 120–38.

Amnesty International. 2016. "Turkey: No Safe Refuge: Asylum-Seekers and Refugees Denied Effective Protection in Turkey." https://www.amnesty.org/en/documents/eur44/3825/2016/en/. Accessed 5 June 2023.

Amnesty International and CCR (Canadian Council for Refugees). 2017. "Contesting the Designation of the US as a Safe Third Country." https://ccrweb.ca/sites/ccrweb.ca/files/stca-submission-2017.pdf. Accessed 5 June 2023.

Arbel, Efrat. 2013. "Shifting Borders and the Boundaries of Rights: Examining the Safe Third Country Agreement Between Canada and the United States." *International Journal of Refugee Law* 25 (1): 65–86.

Atak, Idil, and James C. Simeon. 2018. "Introduction." In *The Criminalization of Migration: Context and Consequences*, edited by Idil Atak and James C. Simeon, 3–33. Montreal and Kingston: McGill-Queen's University Press.

Banerjee, Kiran. 2017. "Rethinking the Global Governance of International Protection." *Columbia Journal of Transnational Law* 56 (2): 313–26.

Betts, Alexander. 2011. "The Refugee Regime and Issue-Linkage" In *Global Mobility Regimes*, edited by Rey Koslowski, 73–91. New York: Palgrave Macmillan.

Bow, Brian. 2009. *The Politics of Linkage: Power, Interdependence, and Ideas in Canada-US Relations*. Vancouver: UBC Press.

Canada. 2002. "Final Text of the Safe Third Country Agreement." Immigration, Refugees and Citizenship Canada. 5 December 2002. https://www.canada.ca/en/immigration-refugees-citizenship/corporate/mandate/policies-operational-instructions-agreements/agreements/safe-third-country-agreement/final-text.html. Accessed 5 June 2023.

– 2009. *Canadian Council for Refugees v. Canada*, 2008 FCA 229 (CanLII), [2009] 3 FCR 136. https://canlii.ca/t/1z69f. Accessed 5 June 2023.

– 2020a. *Canadian Council for Refugees v. Canada (Immigration, Refugees and Citizenship)*, 2020 FC770 (CanLII). https://canlii.ca/t/j8rd7. Accessed 5 June 2023.

– 2020b. "CIMM - Asylum Claimants and Border Restrictions (Orders in Council 10 and 14, STCA)." Immigration, Refugees and Citizenship Canada. 17 June 2020. https://www.canada.ca/en/immigration-refugees-citizenship/corporate/transparency/committees/cimm-june-17-2020/asylum-claimants-border-restrictions.html. Accessed 5 June 2023.

– 2020c. "Government of Canada to Appeal the Federal Court Decision on the Safe Third Country Agreement." 21 August 2020. *Public Safety Canada*. https://www.canada.ca/en/public-safety-canada/news/2020/08/government-of-canada-to-appeal-the-federal-court-decision-on-the-safe-third-country-agreement.html. Accessed 5 June 2023.

– 2020d. "Hot Issue Notes: Safe Third Country Agreement." *Public Safely Canada*. https://www.publicsafety.gc.ca/cnt/trnsprnc/brfng-mtrls/prlmntry-bndrs/20200621/028/index-en.aspx. Accessed 5 June 2023.
– 2022. "Asylum Claims by Year." Immigration, Refugees and Citizenship Canada. https://www.canada.ca/en/immigration-refugees-citizenship/services/refugees/asylum-claims.html. Accessed 5 June 2023.
– 2023. "Final text of the Additional Protocol to the Safe Third Country Agreement." Immigration, Refugees and Citizenship Canada. https://www.canada.ca/en/immigration-refugees-citizenship/corporate/mandate/policies-operational-instructions-agreements/agreements/safe-third-country-agreement/additional-protocol.html. Accessed 5 June 2023.
CCR (Canadian Council for Refugees). 1998. *Interdicting Refugees*. Canadian Council for Refugees. https://ccrweb.ca/sites/ccrweb.ca/files/interd.pdf. Accessed 5 June 2023.
– 2017. "Why the US is not Safe for Refugees: Challenging the Safe Third Country Agreement." Canadian Council for Refugees. https://ccrweb.ca/en/why-US-not-safe-challenging-STCA. Accessed 5 June 2023.
CBC (Canadian Broadcasting Corporation). 2018. "Would Scrapping Safe Third Country Agreement Lead to Influx of Asylum Seekers? Not Necessarily." *CBC News*, 26 June 2018. https://www.cbc.ca/news/canada/safe-third-country-agreement-trump-canadaasylum-refugee-1.4721151. Accessed 5 June 2023.
– 2020a. "Canada 'Urgently' Discussing Asylum Seeker Deportation Issue with U.S." *CBC News*, 27 March 2020. https://www.cbc.ca/news/politics/troops-trump-border-coronavirus-1.5512261. Accessed 5 June 2023.
– 2020b. "Canada has Turned Back 4,400 Asylum Seekers in 5 Years." *CBC News*, 24 November 2020. https://www.cbc.ca/news/politics/asylum-seekers-canada-us-trump-pandemic-1.5813211. Accessed 5 June 2023.
Chishti, Muzaffar, and Jessica Bolter. 2020. "Interlocking Set of Trump Administration Policies at the U.S.-Mexico Border Bars Virtually All from Asylum." Washington, DC: Migration Policy Institute. 20 February 2020. https://www.migrationpolicy.org/article/interlocking-set-policies-us-mexico-border-bars-virtually-all-asylum. Accessed 5 June 2023.
– 2021. "Court-Ordered Relaunch of Remain in Mexico Policy Tweaks Predecessor Program, but Faces Similar Challenges." Washington, DC: Migration Policy Institute. 2 December 2021. https://www.migrationpolicy.org/article/court-order-relaunch-remain-in-mexico. Accessed 5 June 2023.
Connolly, Amanda. 2020. "New Canada-U.S. Border Directive Restores Some Asylum Rules Suspended by Shutdown." *Global News*, 22 April 2020. https://globalnews.ca/news/6852591/canada-us-border-coronavirus-refugees/. Accessed 5 June 2023.

Costello, Cathryn. 2005. "The Asylum Procedures Directive and the Proliferation of Safe Country Practices: Deterrence, Deflection and the Dismantling of International Protection." *European Journal of Migration & Law* 7 (1): 35–70.

Cowger, Sela. 2017. "Uptick in Northern Border Crossings Places Canada-U.S. Safe Third Country Agreement under Pressure." Washington, DC: Migration Policy Institute. 26 April 2017. https://www.migrationpolicy.org/article/uptick-northern-border-crossings-places-canada-us-safe-third-country-agreement-under. Accessed 5 June 2023.

Currie, John H. 2008. *Public International Law*. Toronto: Irwin Law.

Doyle, Michael W. 2018. "Responsibility Sharing: From Principle to Policy." *International Journal of Refugee Law* 30 (4): 618-22.

EC (European Council). 2016. *EU-Turkey Statement*. European Council. https://www.consilium.europa.eu/en/press/press-releases/2016/03/18/eu-turkey-statement/. Accessed 5 June 2023.

– 2022. "Ukraine: Council Unanimously Introduces Temporary Protection for Persons Fleeing the War." European Council. https://www.consilium.europa.eu/en/press/press-releases/2022/03/04/ukraine-council-introduces-temporary-protection-for-persons-fleeing-the-war/. Accessed 5 June 2023.

ECRE (European Council on Refugees and Exiles). 2018. *Policy Note #16: To Dublin or Not to Dublin?* European Council on Refugees and Exiles. https://ecre.org/wp-content/uploads/2018/11/Policy-Note-16.pdf. Accessed 5 June 2023.

Fitzgerald, David. 2019. *Refuge Beyond Reach: How Rich Democracies Repel Asylum Seekers*. Oxford: Oxford University Press.

Goodwin-Gill, Guy S. 2014. "The International Law of Refugee Protection." In *The Oxford Handbook of Refugee and Forced Migration Studies*, edited by Elena Fiddian-Qasmiyeh, Gil Loescher, Katy Long, and Nando Sigona, 36–47. Oxford: Oxford University Press.

Goodwin-Gill, Guy S., and Jane McAdam. 2007. *The Refugee in International Law*. Oxford: Oxford University Press.

Guild, Elspeth, Cathryn Costello, Madeline Garlick, Violeta Moreno-Lax, Minos Mouzourakis, and Sergio Carrera. 2014. *New Approaches, Alternative Avenues and Means of Access to Asylum Procedures for Persons Seeking International Protection*. PE509.989. Brussels: European Parliament. https://www.europarl.europa.eu/RegData/etudes/STUD/2014/509989/IPOL_STU(2014)509989_EN.pdf. Accessed 5 June 2023.

Güler, Arzu. 2020. "Turkey's Geographical Limitation: The Legal Implications of an Eventual Lifting." *International Migration* 58 (5): 3–17.

Hathaway, James C., and Michelle Foster. 2014. *The Law of Refugee Status*. 2nd ed. Cambridge: Cambridge University Press.

Hathaway, James C., Anthony North, and Jason M. Pobjoy. 2013. "Supervising the Refugee Convention: Introduction." *Journal of Refugee Studies* 26 (3): 323–6.

Helton, Arthur C. 1993. "Toward Harmonized Asylum Procedures in North America: The Proposed United States-Canada Memorandum of Understanding for Cooperation in the Examination of Refugee Status Claims from Nationals of Third Countries." *Cornell International Law Journal* 26 (3): 737–52.

Hill, Brian. 2020. "Government Wins Court Challenge to Keep Safe Third Country Agreement in Place - For Now." *Global News*, 26 October 2020. https://globalnews.ca/news/7422641/government-wins-court-challenge-safe-third-country-agreement/. Accessed 5 June 2023.

HRW (Human Rights Watch). 2020. "Deportation with a Layover." Human Rights Watch. https://www.hrw.org/report/2020/05/19/deportation-layover/failure-protection-under-us-guatemala-asylum-cooperative. Accessed 5 June 2023.

Hyndman, Patricia. 1986. "Refugees Under International Law with a Reference to the Concept of Asylum." *Australian Law Journal* 60 (2): 148–55.

Lavenex, Sandra. 2018. "'Failing Forward' Towards which Europe? Organized Hypocrisy in the Common European Asylum System." *Journal of Common Market Studies* 56 (5): 1195–212.

Lauterpacht, Elihu, and Daniel Bethlehem. 2003. "The Scope and Content of the Principle of Non-Refoulement: Opinion." In *Refugee Protection in International Law: UNHCR's Global Consultations on International Protection*, edited by Erika Feller, Volker Türk, and Frances Nicholson, 87–177. Cambridge: Cambridge University Press.

Lehner, Roman. 2019. "The EU-Turkey-'Deal': Legal Challenges and Pitfalls." *International Migration* 57 (2): 176–85.

Macklin, Audrey. 2003. "The Value (s) of the Canada-US Safe Third Country Agreement." *Caledon Institute of Social Policy*: 1–23.

– 2004. "Disappearing Refugees: Reflections on the Canada-US Safe Third Country Agreement." *Columbia Human Rights Law Review* 36 (2): 365–426.

– 2018. "Citizenship, Non-Citizenship and the Rule of Law." *University of New Brunswick Law Journal* 69: 19–56.

McAdam, Jane. 2005. "The European Union Qualification Directive: The Creation of a Subsidiary Protection Regime." *International Journal of Refugee Law* 17 (3): 461–516.

Mercier, Elise, and Sean Rehaag. 2020. "The Right to Seek Asylum in Canada (During a Global Pandemic)." *Osgoode Hall Law Journal* 57 (3): 705–38.

Mountz, Alison. 2020. *The Death of Asylum: Hidden Geographies of the Enforcement Archipelago*. Minneapolis: University of Minnesota Press.

Moreno-Lax, Violeta. 2015. "The Legality of the "Safe Third Country" Notion Contested: Insights From the Law of Treaties." In *Migration and Refugee Protection in the 21st Century: Legal Aspects*, edited by Guy S. Goodwin-Gill and P. Weckel, 665–721. Hague Academy of International Law Centre for Research. Leiden and Boston: Martinus Nijhoff.

MPI (Migration Policy Institute). 2020. "U.S. Annual Refugee Resettlement Ceilings and Number of Refugees Admitted, 1980-Present." Washington, DC: Migration Policy Institute. http://migrationpolicy.org/programs/data-hub/charts/us-annual-refugee-resettlement-ceilings-and-number-refugees-admitted-united/. Accessed 31 May 2023.

Parks, Joseph. 2004. "The United States-Canada Smart Border Action Plan: Life in the Fast Lane." *Law and Business Review of the Americas.* 10 (2): 395–416.

Terry, Kyilah. 2021. "The EU-Turkey Deal, Five Years On: A Frayed and Controversial but Enduring Blueprint." Washington, DC: Migration Policy Institute. https://www.migrationpolicy.org/article/eu-turkey-deal-five-years-on. Accessed 5 June 2023.

Thompson, Andrew S. 2010. *In Defence of Principles: NGOs and Human Rights in Canada*. Vancouver: UBC Press.

Settlage, Rachel Gonzalez. 2012. "Indirect Refoulement: Challenging Canada's Participation in the Canada-United States Safe Third Country Agreement" *Wisconsin International Law Journal* 30 (1): 142–89.

Soto, Ariel. 2020. "One Year after the U.S.-Mexico Agreement: Reshaping Mexico's Migration Policies." Washington, DC: *Migration Policy Institute*. https://www.migrationpolicy.org/research/one-year-us-mexico-agreement. Accessed 5 June 2023.

UN (United Nations). 2018. "UN Affirms 'Historic' Global Compact to Support World's Refugees." 17 December 2018. https://news.un.org/en/story/2018/12/1028791. Accessed 5 June 2023.

UNGA (UN General Assembly). 1951. *Convention Relating to the Status of Refugees, 28 July 1951*, United Nations, Treaty Series, vol. 189. 1951. https://www.refworld.org/docid/3be01b964.html. Accessed5 June 2023.

– 1967. *Protocol Relating to the Status of Refugees, 31 January 1967*, United Nations, Treaty Series, vol. 606. https://www.refworld.org/docid/3ae6b3ae4.html. Accessed 5 June 2023.

UNHCR (United Nations High Commissioner for Refugees). 1997. *UNHCR Note on the Principle of Non-Refoulement.* https://www.refworld.org/docid/438c6d972.html. Accessed 5 June 2023.

– 1999. *Note on International Protection, 7 July 1999*. https://www.refworld.org/docid/3ae68d98b.html. Accessed 5 June 2023.

– 2006. *Monitoring Report: Canada-United States 'Safe Third Country' Agreement.* https://www.unhcr.org/home/protection/455b2cca4.pdf. Accessed 5 June 2023.

– 2007. *Advisory Opinion on the Extraterritorial Application of Non-Refoulement Obligations under the 1951 Convention relating to the Status of Refugees and its 1967 Protocol.* https://www.refworld.org/docid/45f17a1a4.html. Accessed 5 June 2023.
– 2014. *Submission by the United Nations High Commissioner for Refugees: For the Office of the High Commissioner for Human Rights' Compilation Report – Universal Periodic Review.* https://www.refworld.org/pdfid/5541e6694.pdf. Accessed 5 June 2023.
– 2015. *States Parties to the 1951 Convention relating to the Status of Refugees and the 1967 Protocol.* https://www.unhcr.org/protection/basic/3b73b0d63/states-parties-1951-convention-its-1967-protocol.html. Accessed 5 June 2023.
– 2018a. *Global Compact on Refugees.* https://www.unhcr.org/the-global-compact-on-refugees.html. Accessed 5 June 2023.
– 2018b. *Legal Considerations Regarding Access to Protection and a Connection Between the Refugee and the Third Country in the Context of Return or Transfer to Safe Third Countries.* https://www.refworld.org/docid/5acb33ad4.html. Accessed 5 June 2023.
– 2020. *Global Report.* https://www.unhcr.org/globalreport2019/.
– 2021. *Mid-Year Trends 2021.* https://www.unhcr.org/statistics/unhcrstats/618ae4694/mid-year-trends-2021.html. Accessed 5 June 2023.
– 2022. *Global Trends Report 2021.* https://www.unhcr.org/media/40152. Accessed 5 June 2023.
US (United States). 2002. "The U.S.-Canada Safe Third Country Agreement: Hearing on H.R. 5005 Before the House Committee on the Judiciary, Subcommittee on Immigration, Border Security, and Claims" 107th Congress. 16 October 2002. http://commdocs.house.gov/committees/judiciary/hju82363.000/hju82363_0.HTM. Accessed 5 June 2023.
– 2009. "U.S.-Canada Smart Border/30 Point Action Plan Update." US. Department of State. Office of Electronic Information, Bureau of Public Affairs. 6 December 2002. https://2001-2009.state.gov/p/wha/rls/fs/18128.htm. Accessed 5 June 2023.
– 2020. "U.S. Relations with Canada. Bilateral Relations Fact Sheet." US. Department of State. Bureau of Western Hemisphere Affairs. 16 July 2020. https://www.state.gov/u-s-relations-with-canada/. Accessed 5 June 2023.
Walsh, Marieke. 2023. "U.S., Canada kept migrant crossing deal a secret to avoid rush at the border." *Globe and Mail*, 26 March 2023. https://www.theglobeandmail.com/politics/article-roxham-road-deal-migrants/. Accessed 5 June 2023.
Zaun, Natascha. 2018. "States as Gatekeepers in EU Asylum Politics: Explaining the Non-Adoption of a Refugee Quota System." *Journal of Common Market Studies* 56 (1): 44–62.

4

Transgovernmental Cooperation and the Transformation of US and Canadian Border Security

Rey Koslowski and Geoff Leckey

Border control officials at ports and official border crossing points collect customs duties and enforce laws regulating the movement of goods, people, and conveyances. Border guards and coast guards stop people, conveyances, and the goods they carry from crossing borders between official crossing points, and channel these people and conveyances to official border crossings and ports where they can be properly inspected.

Given that Canada is the United States' largest export market and vice versa, border control authorities on both sides of the US-Canada border spend most of their time and energy inspecting goods and conveyances as well as stopping the smuggling of goods (e.g., untaxed cigarettes, illicit drugs, firearms, and cash). Despite often serving as subjects of intense public concern, illegal border crossings of prospective migrants have been relatively few compared to customs violations and the smuggling of contraband. Likewise, US-Canadian cooperation has been devoted much more to facilitating trade rather than stopping the unauthorized movement of people.

The US-Canada border was not of much concern to US and Canadian national security officials, and it was often said that the United States and Canada share "the world's longest undefended border." For example, in 2000, there were only 334 US Border Patrol agents (3.8 per cent of the 9,013 total) guarding the entire northern border (DOJ-OIG 2002) and half of the 126 official ports of entry into the US were left unguarded at night – orange cones were placed in the middle of the road indicating when crossings were closed (Flynn 2004, 187).

National security assessments of the border changed after the December 1999 arrest of "millennium bomber" Ahmed Ressam at the Port Angeles,

Washington, ferry crossing in a car full of explosives intended for an attack at Los Angeles LAX airport. International mobility, rather than migration, became the new security concern. Of the world's 271 million international migrants, defined by the UN as those who have lived outside of their country of nationality or birth for more than one year, only 0.4 per cent are either the 825,000 Canadians living in the US or the 270,000 Americans living in Canada (UN 2019). In contrast to the UN definition of migration, international (or global) mobility refers to movements of people across international borders for any length of time or purpose and is much greater in scale than international migration (see Koslowski 2011). For example, in 2022, over 29 million travellers were admitted into the US through official border crossing points along the US-Canada land border (US CBP 2023) and over 27 million travellers (including almost 5 million truck drivers) entered Canada over land border crossing points from the US (CBSA 2022). Finding potential terrorists within these travel flows became central to US-Canadian cooperation on border security.

Within months of the "millennium bomber" arrest, the al-Qaeda operatives who would pilot jetliners into the World Trade Center and the Pentagon began entering the US. The US government responded to the 11 September 2001 attacks (or 9/11 attacks) by implementing full screening of all cross-border travellers, partly motivated by several newspapers' mistaken reports that some of the hijackers entered the US from Canada (see, e.g., Brown and Connolly 2001). As cross-border movements of people virtually halted, trade stopped as well, but traveller screening was relaxed after US factories began closing for want of Canadian parts. Intensified border security measures taken since the 9/11 attacks have changed the meaning of the phrase "world's longest undefended border."

In the wake of the 9/11 attacks and the de facto self-imposed trade embargo, the US and Canada intensified cooperation on border security in order to restart and then maintain cross-border flows of goods and people. Interestingly, that cooperation has often been led by direct negotiations and collaboration between border security officials from the US Department of Homeland Security (DHS) and its Canadian counterpart, the Department of Public Safety and Emergency Preparedness, now known as Public Safety Canada, rather than foreign ministries and heads of state. Such cooperation is an example of what Robert Keohane and Joseph Nye Jr (1974, 43) referred to as "transgovernmental relations," which they defined as "sets of direct interactions among sub-units of different governments that are not controlled or closely guided by the policies of the cabinets or chief executives of those governments." Anne-Marie Slaughter (2005) subsequently built on this work by exploring networks of government officials who increasingly shaped the practice of world politics.

Contrary to the conceptualization of the state as unitary actor that is assumed in much International Relations (IR) scholarship, a significant share of interactions between the US and Canada have not been between heads of state or their foreign ministries but rather between government subunits, whether geographically delineated at the subnational level (states and provinces) or functionally delineated at the national level. This chapter argues that the prism of transgovernmental relations offers crucial insights to understanding the evolution of US-Canadian cooperation on the facilitation of cross-border movement of people and goods, and addressing unauthorized border crossers and the smuggling of contraband (on unauthorized border crossings, particularly clandestinely or between ports of entry to seek asylum under the 1951 Refugee Convention, see Banerjee in this volume). The theoretical prism of transgovernmental relations becomes even more useful when analysis of informal pragmatic cooperation within transgovernmental networks is paired with analysis of formal binational and multinational agreements that form a basis for further informal cooperation within transgovernmental networks. This interplay between transgovernmental networks and formal international agreements was evident in the evolution of US-Canadian cooperation from the announcement of the 2001 Smart Borders Accord to the 2005 Security and Prosperity Partnership (SPP), which replaced it, to the 2011 Beyond the Border agenda, which structured US-Canadian relations on border security up until the COVID-19 pandemic. Transgovernmental networks of DHS and Public Safety Canada officials, particularly from US Customs and Border Protection (CBP) and the Canada Border Services Agency (CBSA) respectively, enabled elected policymakers to succeed in achieving their objectives with respect to the Smart Border Accords and the Beyond the Border agenda. However, the SPP failed, largely due to policymakers' decision to adopt a more formal treaty-like structure with cumbersome bureaucratic processes aimed at an exceptionally wide range of objectives, while at the same time, lacking pre-existing trilateral transgovernmental networks to implement those objectives. The election of Donald Trump precipitated a decline in bilateral relations that led to the abandonment of the Beyond the Border agenda, while remaining transgovernmental cooperation faced the new challenge of dealing with the COVID-19 pandemic, which reframed cross-border security away from trying to stop potential terrorists to trying to stop the spread of infectious diseases. While trade flows continued, cooperation to facilitate travel effectively came to a halt when the border was closed to "nonessential" travel in March 2020, only lifting these restrictions over a year later – Canada in August 2021 and the US in November 2021.

We explain the value of transgovernmental relations in understanding US-Canadian cooperation on border security in three steps: first, we consider

IR and security studies perspectives on the cross-border movement of people and argue that a focus on transgovernmental relations offers a more useful conceptual approach. Second, we review the challenges of controlling the US-Canadian border and describe how transgovernmental relations furthered US-Canadian cooperation on border security, particularly after the Smart Borders Accord, as well as the limits of transgovernmental relations, as demonstrated with the SPP. Third, we use the prism of transgovernmental relations to evaluate the "Beyond the Border" initiative with particular attention paid to questions of sovereignty, resources, and trust, upon which successful negotiations and the implementation of resulting agreements often depend. We conclude with some thoughts on where transgovernmental relations stand in the wake of the COVID-19 pandemic.

INTERNATIONAL MIGRATION AND MOBILITY, SECURITY AND TRANSGOVERNMENTAL RELATIONS

International migration and mobility did not register as a significant factor in the post–World War II era IR scholarship largely due to the dominance of realism, with its preoccupation with military power and diplomacy among states. Neorealists privileged analysis of the international system structured by the distribution of states' military capabilities and largely ignored domestic politics, thus considering states as unitary actors (Waltz 1979). From a realist standpoint, the movement of unarmed refugees, immigrants, temporary workers, and tourists across international borders should not enter into security considerations because such cross-border movements had marginal impacts on the distribution of capabilities. While neoliberal institutionalists oppose neorealists' theoretical conclusions, they similarly understand world politics in terms of the interaction of rational "international actors," applied microeconomic models to understand international conflict and international cooperation (Keohane 1988), and similarly downplayed migration as a factor of international relations (Keohane and Milner 1996). The most prominent constructivist also adopted the state as unitary actor assumption (Wendt 1992) and, while some constructivists viewed migration as an issue that "could induce expansion in the conceptualization of security affairs" (Jepperson, Wendt, and Katzenstein 1996, 73), they generally shied away from analysis of "new security issues" such as migration in order to have their arguments taken seriously by mainstream neorealists and neoliberals (Katzenstein 1996, 7–11).

In contrast, Barry Buzan, Ole Waever, and other members of what became known as the Copenhagen School broadened the range of legitimate topics of security analysis to topics such as ethnicity, national identity, and migration as they developed the concept of "societal security" (Waever et al. 1993) and depicted the political usage of the linkage between international migration and security in the discourse of policymakers as the "securitization of migration." Their book became the first of many works on the "securitization of migration," which were critical of such linkage and implicitly, if not explicitly, critical of those policymakers who depict migration as a security issue.

Indeed, after the 11 September 2001 attacks, policymakers increasingly depicted migration as a security issue, but migrants were not the "new security threat." Rather it was the approximately two billion annual border crossings by tourists, students, business people, and commuters who travel internationally for stays of less than a year,[1] including the 9/11 hijackers, seventeen of whom entered the US on tourist visas, one on a business visa, and one on a student visa (The 9/11 Commission 2004, 215–41). From a border security standpoint, the increasing number of travellers is the main challenge for border control officials who attempt to identify small numbers of dangerous individuals within these growing flows.

Facing the prospect of terrorists crossing borders, border security officials worldwide tapped their transgovernmental networks to collectively combat terrorist travel. Often working through international organizations and international agencies including the UN Office on Drugs and Crime, the UN Counter-Terrorism Executive Directorate, the International Civil Aviation Organization, and INTERPOL, border security officials turned to international counterparts to jointly investigate human smuggling, develop hardened travel documents, and share biometric and biographical data of travellers.

International cooperation on securing international travel has increasingly relied on such transgovernmental networks of government officials who "increasingly exchange information and coordinate activity to combat global crime and address common problems on a global scale" (Slaughter 2005, 1). As Slaughter (1997, 184) put it, "the state is not disappearing; it is unbundling into its separate, functionally distinct parts" such as finance ministries, environment ministries, and even interior ministries. On this basis, we argue that rather than thinking of the world in terms of unitary states interacting through heads of state or foreign ministries, the state has become "disaggregated."

Nevertheless, we also agree with Slaughter's (2005, 19) position that the emerging "new world order of government networks will (not) replace the existing infrastructure of international institutions, but rather complement and strengthen them." As Kal Raustiala (2002) explains, adaptable and decentralized transnational networks constitute an ever greater share of international cooperation in relation to the "traditional liberal internationalist organization and treaty" but transgovernmental networks are "likely to bolster liberal internationalism" because "under some conditions networks should make treaties work better. Under other conditions networks perform a gap-filling role: where treaties are politically or economically precluded, networks provide an alternative mode of cooperation. In still other situations networks may smooth the negotiation of treaties" (Raustiala 2002, 6). Adopting an analytical focus on transgovernmental relations and viewing the state as "disaggregated" does not mean we believe that states, formal international agreements, and international organizations are somehow diminished but rather that interactions between states, bilaterally or within international organizations, are much more complex than unitary actor assumptions allow.

While transgovernmental border security networks exist on a global basis, they are much denser regionally, such as within the European Union (Geddes 2014), or bilaterally, such as between the US and Canada (Leuprecht et al. 2021). US-Canadian transgovernmental networks are themselves situated in transregional constellations of networks. For example, Andreas and Nadelmann (2008) argue that North America and the EU have developed a "nascent law enforcement alliance, held together by an increasingly dense set of transgovernmental policing networks and international agreements," while Bow and Zaiotti (2020) compare transgovernmental networks in the two regions and examine transatlantic security policy coordination, and Legrand (2015) explores transgovernmental policy networks in the Anglosphere of Australia, Canada, New Zealand, the United Kingdom, and the United States, including the Five Country Conference (FCC), "a forum for co-operation on migration and border security" with an "Information-Sharing Project" (DHS 2009). These bilateral, regional, and transregional networks often form the core groups that sponsor and support border security initiatives at the global level (see Koslowski 2011, 63–5; 2019). Hence, new border security programs initiated and/or technologies implemented by US-Canadian transgovernmental networks (e.g., extraterritorial preclearance, reciprocal inspection of containers on the other's territory, and machine-readable passports and passport readers) were subsequently adopted by other countries in widening circles of transgovernmental networks and international cooperation (Koslowski 2020).

Finally, of all the possible state dyads, viewing the US and Canada as unitary actors and focusing on interactions between heads of state and foreign ministries leads to an impoverished understanding of US-Canadian relations in general. As the US and Canada engaged each other in the years after World War II, the two governments mostly dealt with one another on the basis of unspoken, unwritten, and informal agreements that everyone understood and these "rules of the game" were "developed through … arguments about mutual obligation, and maintained through interpersonal contacts within the transgovernmental network that they defined" (Bow 2009, 2). Indeed, there is a long-standing analysis of transgovernmental relations between the US and Canada (Baker Fox, Hero, and Nye 1974; Holsti and Levy 1974) on issues ranging from energy (Greenwood 1974) to defence (Swanson 1974) to fisheries and pollution (Scott 1974) to combating international crime and smuggling (Legrand and Leuprecht 2021). In explaining the drivers behind transgovernmental cooperation, however, Bach and Newman (2014) noted that economic development and interdependence underpin demand for cross-border engagement. By corollary, then, should these no longer be viewed as desirable or a policy priority, the demands for cross-border engagement will wither. The same article argues that domestic political factors play a key role in driving transgovernmental network membership, and this has surely never been more true than in today's context.

THE CHALLENGES OF SECURITY ALONG THE US-CANADIAN BORDER AND THE EVOLUTION OF TRANSGOVERNMENTAL COOPERATION ON BORDER CONTROLS

Increased border inspections immediately after the 9/11 attacks led to traffic back-ups of up to fifteen hours at the border, which quickly became economically unsustainable. Up to ten million vehicles annually crossed the Ambassador Bridge between Windsor, Ontario, and Detroit, Michigan, along with approximately 25 per cent of US-Canadian merchandise trade, including automotive parts required for transborder just-in-time manufacturing. Within days of the attacks, Daimler-Chrysler announced that it would have to stop several US assembly lines for want of Canadian parts caught in the traffic back-ups at the border. Ford followed suit shortly thereafter.

In response to conflicting security and economic imperatives, various officials, such as US Ambassador to Canada Paul Cellucci (2001), and interest groups, such as the association of Canadian Manufacturers and Exporters (Canadian Newswire 2001), proposed to erect a "North American Security Perimeter" modelled after the European Union's Schengen Convention, whereby internal border controls are lifted as a common external border is established. Ten years later, the "Beyond the Border" declaration issued by the then US president Obama and the then Canadian prime minister Harper had as its subtitle: "A Shared Vision for Perimeter Security and Economic Competitiveness." For a variety of reasons, not the least of which is the lack of a customs union between the US and Canada (contrastingly established by the European Community in 1968), it is unlikely that such a North American Security Perimeter will come into being (Koslowski 2005b).

In contrast to the visions of ambassadors, presidents, and prime ministers, US and Canadian border control practitioners focused more on using technology and information-sharing. In the case of Canadian officials, two important things had already happened that made the fallout of 9/11 more manageable. First, Canada had already become used to writing down sets of rules governing its interactions with the US,[2] and second, Canadian officials (and border officials in particular) already knew what they wanted the next set of rules to be. As Stephen Clarkson (2003, 81) explains, "the Government of Canada actually set the bilateral agenda on these border issues because it had done its homework before 9/11 and because it was institutionally more nimble than the US government. For years Canada had been urging Washington to undertake joint measures that would improve border security and increase border efficiency." The near-closure of the border gave Canadian border officials an opportunity to revive existing proposals given the US attention to its northern border. The upshot was the Smart Border Declaration of 12 December 2001 and its thirty-point "Action Plan for Creating a Secure and Smart Border" (White House 2001), which subsequently became known as the Smart Border Accord. While some action plan points, such as "negotiate a safe third-country agreement to enhance the handling of refugee claims," encouraged US and Canadian diplomats to craft a bilateral treaty, which was signed the following year (see Banerjee in this volume), most points were rather technical and operational considerations that did not require treaty negotiations.

The action plan called for biometric identifiers in permanent resident cards and travel documents, sharing advance passenger information from the US Advance Passenger Information System (APIS) and its Canadian counterpart, developing compatible immigration databases, and expanding the NEXUS pre-approved passenger vehicle program as well as the NEXUS air pilot program. By the spring of 2003, significant strides were made in realizing many of the specific objectives of the action plan (Meyers 2003), and further progress was announced on 3 October 2003, highlighted by completed NEXUS implementations at nine of twenty-four land ports of entry for passenger vehicles.[3] As of December 2021, there were twenty-one land border crossings with NEXUS lanes going at least one way and over 1.65 million US and Canadian nationals enrolled in the program.[4]

The In-Transit Container Security Initiative between the US and Canada was a Smart Border Accord action item that deployed US Customs inspectors in Halifax, Vancouver, and Montreal, Canadian inspectors in Newark and Seattle, and became a model for a much broader Container Security Initiative (CSI) announced in January 2002 to pre-screen cargo containers at the world's twenty largest ports in terms of US-bound cargo shipments.

In a certain sense, the forward deployment of US Customs personnel with the CSI draws on a model of long-standing cooperation between the US and Canada on immigration. Ever since an agreement signed in 1894, US inspectors posted at Canadian ports of entry have inspected US-bound immigrants. Immigration inspectors were subsequently posted to Canadian airports to conduct "preclearance," inspections that essentially cleared US-bound passengers through US passport controls of flights from abroad connecting through Canadian airports.

Point 8 of the US-Canadian Smart Border Agreement outlines an agenda for cooperation on advance passenger data and point 17 deals with customs data. Soon thereafter, the US began requiring commercial airlines and ships to electronically submit passenger and crew manifests before arrival to the US,[5] and Canada began collecting Advance Passenger Information (API) and passenger name record (PNR) data by October 2002.[6] The following year, Canada and the US agreed to share passenger manifests and PNRs using automated data-sharing and a program that assesses risks of the passengers in question.[7]

The Smart Borders Agreement proposition to use advanced technology to track the entry and exit of individuals began to be realized with the establishment of a US biometric entry-exit program in 2002. Enrolment in the biometric entry-exit system was required of those travelling on a regular visa, those entering under the Visa Waiver Program, legal permanent residents, and several other categories of foreign nationals but not of US citizens or visa-exempt Canadian nationals entering the US through land border crossings.[8] The biggest challenge for implementing the entry-exit legislation has been collection of exit data, particularly biometric exit data and especially at land border crossings where the US maintains no physical infrastructure for collecting exit data (Koslowski 2005a). One could envision exit controls at all land border crossings that would mirror entry controls – with the construction of additional lanes and booths, the installation of biometric readers and workstations, and the hiring of inspectors to process departing foreigners and record exit data. In light of the tens of billions of dollars that such an undertaking would entail, the US Congress has not provided (nor have the Bush, Obama, Trump, and Biden administrations requested) such funding, but the physical limitations of entry-exit system implementation has been partially overcome by intensified US-Canadian cooperation, as is discussed in more detail ahead.

The US DHS, Public Safety Canada, and their counterpart interior ministries abroad are the key actors implementing international agreements negotiated by foreign ministries, but are also increasingly developing their own diplomatic capabilities and negotiating agreements governing visa policies and border controls. For example, the DHS established an international section of its Office of Policy and posted a DHS attaché at the US embassies in Ottawa, the EU, and Brussels. These DHS attachés supplemented CBP attachés posted to Ottawa and Brussels (as well as Mexico City) in 2003 – the first group of what has become twenty-three US CBP attaché offices in capitals around the world.[9] The Canada Border Services Agency did likewise.[10] Negotiations conducted by such attachés provide prime examples of transgovernmental relations within networks of government officials.

The sharing of ideas and direct negotiations between US and Canadian government officials within border control agencies of both countries have produced solutions to a variety of security problems in controlling the US-Canadian border, while at the same time maintaining flows of people, conveyances, and goods. These solutions then became incorporated into national policies and initiatives that border control agencies implement, often in a collaborative fashion.

An excellent concrete example of such organic growth is provided by Integrated Border Enforcement Teams (IBETs). Originally developed in 1996 as a local arrangement between agencies mandated to counter cross-border crime along land and marine borders between British Columbia and Washington State, IBETs were initially frowned upon by US and Canadian officials in Ottawa and Washington. After the 9/11 attacks, however, federal policymakers embraced IBET and touted their arrests of smugglers. These transgovernmental law enforcement teams now operate along all parts of the Canada-US border, and have been officially recognized by Ottawa and Washington as "valuable venues for the development of the concepts for the next generation of integrated law enforcement" (Public Safety Canada 2015, 12).

Transgovernmental cooperation between Canadian and US border control officials not only produced the 2002 Smart Border Accord, but the agreement embraced under-the-radar transgovernmental innovations such as IBET and helped institutionalize such transgovernmental relations. US and Canadian policymakers then built on the smart borders initiative by launching the SPP in 2005 and the Beyond the Border initiative in 2011. Many items of the Smart Borders Accord were implemented; for example, trusted traveller and trusted trader programs, mutual recognition of standards in airport security and container screening, and others (Goldfarb and Robson 2003, 27), which can largely be attributed to the preexistence of transgovernmental networks. However, even as transgovernmental relations facilitated the sharing of ideas and enabled the negotiation of policy initiatives, there have been implementation challenges that transgovernmental relations have not been overcome.

Indeed, by 2004, the pace of progress in implementing the Smart Border Accord slowed, largely due to a shift in US security efforts from its borders and relations with Canada and Mexico to the "Global War on Terrorism" primarily being waged in Afghanistan and the Middle East. Political focus returned, however, with the March 2005 launch of the SPP – much of which sought to build on the achievements of the Smart Borders Accord by attempting to trilateralize them. The underlying argument was that increasing cooperation on security, particularly border security, among Canada, the US, and Mexico would produce a more stable business environment, and a more prosperous economy would enable all three countries to better address security concerns (see Anderson and Sands 2007). The general consensus is that the SPP failed, or did not achieve a great deal in terms of concrete results. We have identified three reasons for this. All three have to do with the way the SPP was structured from the start, and two of the three relate to the operation of transgovernmental networks, or the lack thereof.

First, the SPP was too ambitious, heavy, and cumbersome. As Geoffrey Hale (quoted in Burney 2011, 50) observed, "The SPP died of analysis paralysis, administrative overload and the absence of political will". Colin Robertson (2011) put it more poetically: "Three hundred action items were generated and like Mao's thousand flowers enjoyed a brief bloom before they withered." Second, the SPP was a treaty-type organization, shackled with all the layers of process and oversight that go with it, rather than a transgovernmental one. Raustiala's (2002, 23–4) observation applies here: "Multilateral organisations are cumbersome and bogged down by procedural rules ... networks are, by contrast, flexible and adaptable." Third, the close and ubiquitous three-way transgovernmental networks, i.e. US-Canadian-Mexican, that would have been necessary did not exist. What was put in place instead was: "300 issues and a complex process, 20 trilateral working groups and the lack of a champion" (Robertson 2011). No amount of – artificially created – trilateral working groups can take the place of transgovernmental networks whose members are used to dealing with one another and getting things done.

The lack of transgovernmental border security networks was also partly structural. In contrast to Canada, Mexico does not conduct primary inspections of travellers crossing the land border from the US, only random customs inspections. There are no Mexican immigration inspectors across the border from US CBP officers at the US ports of entry. Therefore, there are no local Mexican immigration counterparts for local US CBP officials to discuss secure facilitation of cross-border travel through their mutual ports of entry – only customs officials (without a mandate to enforce immigration laws) and, in some cities, local consulate officials, who do not share the common experiences upon which border security networks are built. Moreover, three-way networks did not develop because, as an official well-placed to make the comment observes: "The dynamics of the northern border and the southern border are very different, and the US has two different sets of priorities when it views the northern and the southern borders. There is no three-way common cause."[11]

By 2010, SPP had clearly stalled, and so, acting on the perennial Canadian fear of increasing border controls with the economic consequences that entailed, Canadian Prime Minister Harper "pulled aside" President Obama at the G8 meeting in Canada and successfully urged reinvigoration of border security cooperation – though not in trilateral form. What Harper suggested was a return to bilateralism.

BEYOND THE BORDER

On 4 February 2011, President Obama and Prime Minister Harper issued a joint declaration, "Beyond the Border: A Shared Vision for Perimeter Security and Economic Competitiveness." In December of that year, they issued a corresponding action plan, with specific initiatives to address border threats, while expediting lawful trade and travel. The action plan also announced the launch of a Beyond the Border Working Group "composed of representatives from the appropriate departments and offices of our respective federal governments."[12] This is a classic example of transgovernmental networks at work. Using Anne-Marie Slaughter's (2005) terminology, Beyond the Border is an "institutionalized," "horizontal," "harmonization," and "mutual recognition" network of "executive regulators."

There are four key areas of cooperation,[13] and the action plan included a total of thirty-four items. Each action item was tagged with leading and supporting federal departments on either side of the border. There were to be annual joint reports, while in addition, each partner produced its own country report documenting how it had met (or otherwise) its set objectives for the year.

Based on the wording of the last available official document, the overall rate in achieving the thirty-four action items was quite high. Most were either completed or well on their way to completion and, while we have identified three that appear to be problematic, we have identified another three where success comes as something of a surprise. It is our contention that if overall there is a reasonable degree of realization of key outcomes, then it is due to the operation of transgovernmental networks.

Most of the officials on both sides knew one another; in many cases, they had close professional and sometimes personal relationships. Indeed, the officials had a large hand in selecting desirable goals that were both realistic and achievable. The stay-at-home officials are increasingly supplemented by liaison officers from relevant departments other than those of foreign affairs.[14] As Slaughter (2005, 39) noted: "Today readers of the popular press could be excused for thinking that diplomacy is conducted by everyone *but* the diplomats" (emphasis as per original). This trend has not abated since then. As of July 2016, 49 per cent of staff at the Canadian embassy in Washington, DC, were from Global Affairs Canada, and 51 per cent from other government departments.[15]

Slaughter (2005, 155) also noted that: "Where the negotiating states have failed to design and bring to life an implementing structure, national officials must fill the breach." In the case of Beyond the Border, however, it is not so much that the politicians "failed to design" a structure; rather, they knew they did not have to. And indeed, the networks of national officials are in fact the most efficient way to implement. If Beyond the Border had had a new superbureaucracy superimposed on it, it would surely have suffered the same fate as the SPP. In actual fact, oversight has been relatively light. Writing just before the anticipated declaration, Daniel Schwanen (2011, 141) proposed the adoption of "light joint mechanisms dedicated to making the vision a success," and the subsequent decision by both governments to take this approach is undoubtedly part of the reason for the overall effectiveness of the framework.

Although a preponderance of "low-hanging fruit" in the action plan may lead one to think that officials purposely set themselves up for what could not fail to be success, this is not the case. There have been some significant achievements in the face of what some officials and commentators feared might prove to be insurmountable obstacles. Given that the threats to successful negotiations tend to be "in one of three areas: sovereignty; resources; and trust,"[16] we examine each of our chosen three success cases, as well as the three cases that are stalled, looking for signs of the effect of these three issues. The following tough nuts ended up being cracked: the Entry-Exit Information System (Initiative 11); preclearance (Initiative 15); and enhanced national security information exchange (under Initiative 25, Pursuing National Security and Transnational Criminal Investigations).

First, despite the prediction that it would be difficult for Canadians to accept an entry-exit system, especially over the concerns of nationalists and civil liberties groups (Robertson 2011), implementation has proceeded smoothly. "Entry-Exit" refers to a joint Canadian-US program whereby the record of entry of an individual into one country becomes the record of exit of that individual from the other. The entry-exit program was deployed on 30 June 2013 to all automated common land border ports of entry for third-country nationals and permanent residents of Canada and the US (i.e., initially excluding the citizens of each country). By 2015, the two countries had shared 17.8 million entry records with no discernible impact on traveller experience (Public Safety Canada 2015). On 15 June 2016, legislation to enable the exchange of data on all travellers, including citizens, was introduced in the Canadian parliament, to which the public, despite strong concerns expressed by privacy and civil rights advocates, appeared largely indifferent. In July 2019, the joint US-Canadian entry-exit program expanded the exchange of data to include US and Canadian citizens (DHS 2019). Applying our template of "sovereignty, resources, and trust," this item started out with two out of three strikes against it: sovereignty and trust. Note that we are interpreting "sovereignty" to include areas where national legislation differs. In one case, it took a change in legislation to overcome the obstacle; while the other – public trust – turned out to be a non-issue.

Second, an extended preclearance agreement was reached in March 2015, including authorization for US officers to be armed in Canada – something which some had predicted would never happen. One of the three obstacles loomed large here – sovereignty – but was overcome once again by the introduction of new Canadian legislation. Similarly, the US Congress passed legislation in December 2016[17] to enable expansion of preclearance operations by ensuring that US personnel stationed in Canada can be held accountable for any criminal wrongdoing under US law (Johnson 2016).

Third, cooperation on the two countries' no-fly lists was agreed to. A joint redress working group was established to help those whose names are listed in error to have them removed. This meant sharing of more information on such travellers – but also on those whose names should remain, and the reasons why (the "derogatory information"). This is a breakthrough because precisely this information is among the most sensitive held, and jealously guarded, by intelligence agencies. The paramount obstacle here could easily have been trust; however, it would appear that the trust built up over the years between the US and Canadian intelligence and national security communities has been deep enough to carry the day.

We now look more closely at what is *not* working in the Beyond the Border process and examine the reasons why. Three of the thirty-four initiatives are clearly stalled. Therefore, even when an initiative is of manifest benefit, announced by governments, and meets with little or no resistance from the respective publics, the actual implementation can be so fraught with impediments that it is repeatedly delayed, eventually sidelined, and risks being ultimately quietly dropped. How can this happen, when the entire Beyond the Border program is an example of mandated "regulatory convergence," in which officials have received clear instructions from their political masters – and yet it has not come to pass?

Beyond the Border, then, is an example of the kind of structure described by Slaughter (2005, 49) in which the transgovernmental networks are told by the political level to go and get the job done, and the context is one of generally positive public attitudes. The examples of what has not worked are: domain awareness (Initiative 3); integrated cargo security (Initiative 5); and next-generation law enforcement (under Initiative 25, Pursuing National Security and Transnational Criminal Investigations). We again take as our premise that negotiations tend to break down around one of three areas: sovereignty, resources, and trust.

First, achieving domain awareness requires both governments to: "1) identify gaps and vulnerabilities in capabilities; 2) prioritize coverage of gaps; and, 3) establish a process to coordinate the joint procurement and deployment of technology along the border" (Public Safety Canada 2014). Progress first came in 2015, when, after three and a half years, a "first" gap analysis was conducted, covering ninety miles of the 5,525-mile border, to "develop a process" for similar analyses of the remaining 5,435 miles. By 2017 the US had completed its survey and shared its methodology with Canada (DHS 2017). The US DHS Northern Border Strategy (DHS 2018, 11) articulates Objective 2.1 as "Improve coordination, integration, and analysis across domestic and international domain surveillance and information-sharing systems" and notes that the "DHS utilizes a variety of surveillance, detection, and monitoring assets such as drones, ground sensors, and fixed towers to protect and secure the border." Post-2011, DHS's deployment of such assets along the US-Canadian border has been quite limited in the land and sea environment and has largely remained at the research and development stage with pilot project testing begun in 2021 and scheduled to continue into 2022 and more broadly to Air and Marine Operations sites in 2023 (DHS 2021a). While the DHS (2021b) describes its coordination with several US federal partners in the Air Domain Awareness program, there is no mention of coordination with Canadian agencies and no mention of "joint procurement and deployment of technology" (Public Safety Canada 2014). Therefore, out of the three initial Beyond the Border domain awareness objectives, one half of objective 1 has been completed, while progress on objectives 2 and 3 is nowhere to be found.

Since there is no indication of sovereignty concerns or lack of trust impeding progress, the issue must be one of resources. We interpret "resources" broadly to include setting overly ambitious targets. The two sets of officials appear to have been overwhelmed by the task, or were not the right ones to carry it out. This is an instructive instance of how transgovernmental networks simply cannot always accomplish everything they are asked to. In the words of an experienced senior official: "Negotiators have a mandate to cut a deal. The practicality of implementation is lost on those doing the negotiating."[18] Or, as Slaughter (2005, 57) puts it: "All the will and cooperation in the world cannot compensate for lack of capacity."

Second, the Integrated Cargo Security Strategy (ICSS) seeks to jointly address risks associated with shipments arriving from offshore as part of an ultimate perimeter security model in which containers would be "cleared once, accepted twice" by both countries. To test the concept, two binational pilots were conducted in British Columbia and Quebec. Interestingly, in looking at the plans at the outset, Robertson (2011) proclaimed: "The first test for the new deal will be in the pilots and practical implementation at ground level to create supply-chain security and efficiency by moving primary inspection to the perimeter." The 2015 joint implementation report (Public Safety Canada 2015, 4) explained: "While the pilots yielded positive results from a national security perspective, contraband risks could not be addressed at the perimeter due to various impediments, such as differences in legislative authorities and operational processes." There has been no movement toward implementation beyond this limited pilot stage.

The frank admissions here indicate sovereignty and, possibly, trust issues. We are again interpreting "sovereignty" to include areas where national legislation differs and neither country has been willing to amend its laws to converge with the other. The fact that "operational processes" do not require legislative change suggests that one or both countries have found something unacceptable in the other's risk mitigation measures. Such issues are specifically referenced as potential obstacles in the literature on transgovernmentalism. Rausitalia (2007, 57) warns that: "a basic but highly important issue of policy convergence is the requisite legal authority to cooperate meaningfully with foreign regulators" and furthermore notes that: "Differences in procedural rules … can be major impediments to regulatory cooperation." Slaughter (2005, 59), meanwhile, notes that: "A less demanding alternative to harmonization is mutual recognition by two countries of each other's regulatory standards and decisions," and the official report suggests that this alternative is what the two countries are now working toward.

Third, the Beyond the Border Action Plan calls for next-generation integrated law enforcement teams for criminal investigations and uniformed patrols at the land border, which would go beyond the coordinated actions of existing IBETs. The latest joint implementation report (Public Safety Canada 2015, 14) states, however: "more detailed scoping ... found that the existing legislative framework in both countries inhibits the implementation of 'Next Generation' as originally envisioned." Here the problem is addressed head-on: current legislative frameworks do not allow for the vision to be realized. We categorize this as a "sovereignty" issue: the laws of the two countries are not likely to be brought into convergence in the near future.

The above three cases provide some insight into what can derail transgovernmental networks from delivering on expectations: for example, concerns about sovereignty, resources, and trust. Of course, these can be exacerbated by other contextual factors that wax and wane over time but can also have a derailing or delaying impact; notably, the need for sustained political attention; bureaucratic inertia; and benign neglect of Canadian issues by the US. For example, lack of attention on the part of the US can lead to the same in Ottawa, as Canadian politicians cannot always muster the necessary political capital to keep Canadian issues at the top of the Washington agenda; and meagre political attention can be interpreted by all bureaucrats as meaning their efforts are less likely to be rewarded by results, hence dropping an issue to the bottom of their priorities. A former senior Canadian official makes two observations that are relevant here: first, you can run out of perseverance: "Too long a shelf life ... In these things, time is not your friend. Continuity of political support is needed."[19] And you can run out of political capital: "The signing of the document is not enough. The hard work comes after the fact. As each item is brought to Cabinet, you start to lose traction as right-wingers don't like this, left-wingers don't like that, and you find yourself spending a lot of political capital to keep it afloat."[20] By leveraging existing transgovernmental networks of border security officials as well as developing new ones, the US and Canada were able to achieve some of their shared border security objectives if not others.

When the then newly elected president Trump first met Prime Minister Trudeau on 13 February 2017, they issued a joint press release stating: "we are building a 21st century border through initiatives such as pre-clearance of people and integrated cross-border law enforcement operations" (White House 2017b), but actual progress in accomplishing the outstanding objectives stalled as the Trump administration imposed tariffs on softwood lumber and demanded renegotiation of the North American Free Trade Agreement (NAFTA). The prospect of a meeting between Trump and Trudeau dedicated to renewing the Beyond the Border Action Plan and giving another mandate to the Beyond the Border Working Group quickly became out of reach.

With little progress on remaining objectives, there was little to report. On 19 January 2017, the last day of the Obama administration, the DHS followed up on the September 2016 Beyond the Border Implementation Report with a fact sheet that outlined significant Beyond the Border accomplishments and future items for collaboration (DHS 2017), but the Trump administration never issued another Beyond the Border progress report. In contrast, Public Safety Canada issued a "close-out report" for the action plan in 2017 that provided an overview of the results achieved over the five-year period of the action plan (Public Safety Canada 2017). As the Northern Border Strategy (DHS 2018) issued by the DHS in June 2018 only included a passing reference to the Beyond the Border Action Plan, it became clear that the Trump and Trudeau administrations would not try to resuscitate it.

CONCLUSIONS

By territorially delineating states from one another, borders are constitutive of states as unitary actors, but border control is increasingly a function of international cooperation through transgovernmental networks. This dynamic is clearly evident in the international interactions between the US and Canada with respect to border security that defy unitary actor assumptions of much IR theory. Moreover, by analyzing interactions of these two disaggregated states in the area of border security, it becomes clear that US and Canadian politicians may envision a future of facilitated trade and travel across borders akin to that of the EU, but it is the transgovernmental networks that do the heavy lifting and ultimately determine how far the two governments can go. There are clear limitations to the extent that the vision articulated by heads of state in the Beyond the Border declaration has been realized through the work of transgovernmental networks, as our analysis of action plan completion indicates. Nevertheless, however one calculates Beyond the Border's success rate, it would have been much lower – in a sense, less *effective* – without the existence of the transgovernmental networks. However, it is worth noting the warning sounded by someone who has seen the operation of such networks up close: "Transgovernmental networks work best when there are forward-leaning, internationalist governments. They can only prosper if governments reward them and support them and they are seen as having legitimacy. When governments have little or no understanding of foreign relations, or show no foreign policy leadership, transgovernmental networks will not be encouraged and will wither."[21] Until the election of Donald Trump, cooperation to increase security along the US-Canadian border, while at the same time facilitating international travel and trade across it, seemed very likely to continue to gradually increase. Trump's inauguration, however, initiated a period of increasing US-Canadian conflict over trade policy and US immigration restrictions that spilled over into policies to secure international travel, including between the US and Canada.

Such increasing policy divergence between the US and Canada means an intentional shrinking, as a matter of policy, of the space within which transgovernmental networks can operate, through a combination of discouragement and tight circumscription. In such a situation, the individuals in that space are tugged in two directions: their room for manoeuvre is drastically reduced, while they remain aware that the continued existence and operation of the transgovernmental space remain important if further deterioration is to be counteracted and damage to both sides forestalled. The shrinking of the transgovernmental space takes us a long way from the heyday of US-Canada transgovernmental networks as described at the outset of this chapter: grievances become aired more openly, as opposed to behind closed doors; disagreements are not resolved solely on their technical merits; and linkages are made to other, unrelated issues.

Nevertheless, even as the divergence in immigration policies pursued by the Trudeau government and the Trump administration prompted several thousand asylum seekers to cross into Canada from the US (Forrest 2017), Canadian and US officials worked quietly and collegially to try to address this and other cross-border issues in a cooperative fashion (Reuters 2017). Initially, transgovernmentalism lived on, worked to "reduce friction" and "prevent shocks," and the DHS under Trump even issued a Northern Border Strategy that contains many of the same objectives found in the Beyond the Border Action Plan, stating that "DHS will engage with … Canadian partners to implement this Strategy" (DHS 2018, 8).

Policymakers' responses to the COVID-19 pandemic, however, strained the under-the-radar transgovernmental cooperation that might have been still operative during the Trump administration. For example, following Trump's 13 March 2020 executive order on COVID-19, the DHS submitted a request to the US Department of Defense on 19 March for "up to 1,000 personnel in support of CBP operations on the Northern Border … [and] to increase CBP's capacity to protect public health and prevent the spread of COVID-19" (DHS 2020). On 20 March 2020 the US and Canadian governments announced that they would both "temporarily" restrict all nonessential travel (recreational travel or tourism) through ports of entry on their land border.[22] Essentially, US and Canadian policymakers could be seen as largely engaging in symbolic politics, and treated the border as one more site of pandemic theatre.

Once community spread occurred in both countries, however, restrictions on nonessential travel were of limited public health value but they became politically difficult to lift. As long as COVID-19 infection rates were much higher in the US than in Canada, it was understandably difficult, from a political perspective, for Canadian policymakers to lift border controls. However, once Canadian provinces also endured their waves of case numbers greater than that of bordering US states, their reluctance to find a way to ease movements is harder to understand. And vice versa for US policymakers. During the beginning of the pandemic, while infection rates in the US were much higher than in Canada, the public health rationale for retaining restrictions, from the US perspective, on travellers from Canada seemed to diminish. At the same time, having Canadians travel to the pandemic's global epicentre and bring COVID-19 back home to Canada is something that Canadian policymakers would want to avoid. In this way, the mutual restrictions by both states enabled each state to stop their own citizens from bringing the disease home without imposing restrictions on the reentry of their own citizens, which is politically very difficult.

Even though these restrictions on nonessential travel across the US-Canada land border may have become politically convenient, there were many contradictions in both countries' public health response to cross-border travel. Visitors were denied entry in either direction but truck drivers could enter without being tested for COVID-19, as if they were immune by virtue of their "essential worker" status. Canadians could not drive across the land border but they could fly and gain entry to the US at airports. Despite decades of transgovernmental cooperation, the US and Canadian governments could not come up with a more nuanced and flexible set of policies and border control practices that could adjust to changing threat levels posed by differential rates of infection and movements of new variants. Robust transgovernmental cooperation between the DHS and Public Safety Canada should have led to more coordinated actions and the harmonization of rules as well as a more flexible policy implementation. Maybe dealing with a pandemic is just a bridge too far for US-Canadian transgovernmental cooperation on border security.

There is much more to this story of US and Canadian pandemic response and the demise of transgovernmental cooperation between the DHS and Public Safety Canada, as well as the Biden administration's continuation of travel restrictions and minimal outreach to Canada on border security matters well into President Biden's second year in office; however, such an exploration would require much more space than this chapter allows and will have to remain beyond the scope of our analysis, for now.

NOTES

This chapter is based on a paper originally prepared for and presented at the Homeland Defense and Security Education Summit, George Mason University, Arlington, VA, 23–24 March 2017. We thank the panel participants for feedback on the draft paper. We also thank Tom Reale for his research assistance with updating the manuscript. The analysis is primarily based on government documents, nongovernmental policy papers, and other open source materials, however, several current and former government officials were interviewed and responded to requests for information via email with the understanding that they could remain anonymous.

1 On annual international mobility statistics, see Koslowski (2011, 52–7).

2 Viewed through the lens of transgovernmentalism, these "sets of rules" in effect legitimize the respective transgovernmental networks and provide a guarantee of how they should behave towards one another.

3 *Smart Border Action Plan Status Report*, Office of Deputy Prime Minister Manley and DHS Press Office, 3 October 2003.

4 CBSA-ASFC Contact, e-mail message to author, 21 January 2022.

5 Section 402 of the Enhanced Border Security and Visa Entry Reform Act of 2002, Public Law 107–73, 14 May 2002.

6 "National Security in Canada-the 2001 Anti-Terrorism Initiative," Chapter 3 of the 2004 *Report of the Auditor General of Canada to the House of Commons*.

7 *Smart Border Action Plan Status Report*, Office of Deputy Prime Minister Manley and DHS Press Office, 3 October 2003.

8 Canadian nationals entering the United States for short stays are exempt from most visa requirements and if entering though land border crossings, they are also exempt from submitting biometrics upon entry; however, those who are entering the United States on a visa or by air or sea are required to submit biometrics.

9 CBP Attachés https://www.cbp.gov/border-security/international-initiatives/cbp-attaches.

10 CBSA-ASFC Contact, e-mail message to author, 21 January 2022.

11 Interview with former senior Canadian official, July 2016.

12 Both documents are posted at https://www.dhs.gov/action-plan.

13 "Addressing threats early"; "trade facilitation, economic growth, and jobs"; "cross-border law enforcement"; and "critical infrastructure and cyber security."

14 US: Department of State; Canada: Global Affairs Canada.

15 E-mail message to author from serving diplomat in Canadian Embassy in Washington, 10 July 2016.

16 Interview with a senior Canadian government lawyer, July 2016.

17 The Promoting Travel, Commerce and National Security Act of 2016, Public Law 114–316.

18 Interview with former senior Canadian official, July 2016.

19 Ibid.

20 Ibid.

21 Ibid.

22 "Joint Statement on US-Canada Joint Initiative: Temporary Restriction of Travelers Crossing the US-Canada Land Border for Non-Essential Purposes," DHS Press Release, 20 March 2020.

REFERENCES

Anderson, Greg, and Christopher Sands. 2007. *Negotiating North America: The Security and Prosperity Partnership*. Hudson Institute (Fall). https://www.hudson.org/content/researchattachments/attachment/680/hudson_negotiating_north_america_final.pdf. Accessed 10 February 2022.

Andreas, Peter, and Ethan Nadelmann. 2008. *Policing the Globe: Criminalization and Crime Control in International Relations*. New York: Oxford University Press.

Bach, David, and Abraham Newman. 2014. "The Domestic Drivers of Transgovernmental Regulatory Cooperation." *Regulation and Governance* 8 (4): 395–417.

Baker Fox, Annette, Alfred O. Hero, Jr, and Joseph S. Nye, Jr, eds. 1974. "Canada and the United States: Transnational and Transgovernmental Relations." *International Organization* 28 (4).

Bow, Brian. 2009. *The Politics of Linkage: Power, Interdependence, and Ideas in Canada-US Relations*. Vancouver: UBC Press.

Bow, Brian, and Ruben Zaiotti. 2020. "Transgovernmental Networks and Security Policy Coordination in North America and the European Union: A Framework for Transatlantic Comparative Research." *Journal of Transatlantic Studies* 18 (2): 177–89.

Brown, DeNeen L., and Ceci Connolly. 2001. "Suspects Entered Easily From Canada." *Washington Post*, 14 September 2001.

Burney, Derek H. 2011. "Boldly Bilateral: Thinking Big Again, Institute for Research on Public Policy." *Policy Options*, March 2011. http://irpp.org/wp-content/uploads/sites/2/assets/po/canada-us-conversations-and-relations/burney5.pdf. Accessed 10 February 2022.

Canadian Newswire. 2001. "Canada-U.S. Border Concerns Prompt Support for Perimeter Approach to North American Security." Canadian Newswire, 2 October 2001.

CBP (US Customs and Border Protection) 2023. "Traveler and Conveyance Statistics," 10 March 2023. https://www.cbp.gov/newsroom/stats/travel. Accessed 10 February 2022.

CBSA (Canada Border Services Agency). 2022. *2022 Year in Review: Accomplishments by the Numbers*. CBSA. https://www.cbsa-asfc.gc.ca/transparency-transparence/yir-aer-eng.html. Accessed 10 February 2022.

Cellucci, Paul. 2001. Remarks by Ambassador Paul Cellucci at the Canadian Club of Ottawa, 18 September.

Clarkson, Stephen. 2003. "The View From the Attic: Toward a Gated Continental Community?" In *The Rebordering of North America: Integration and Exclusion in a New Security Context*, edited by Peter Andreas and Thomas J. Biersteker, 68–89. New York: Routledge.

Department of Justice, Office of the Inspector General (DOJ-OIG). 2002. *Follow up Report on Border Patrol's Efforts to Improve Northern Border Security*. OIG Report No. I-2002-004.

Department of Homeland Security (DHS). 2009. Privacy Impact Assessment for the US-VISIT Five Country Joint Enrollment and Information-Sharing Project (FCC) November 2.

– 2017. *Beyond the Border U.S. Fact Sheet - January 2017*. https://www.dhs.gov/publication/beyond-border-us-fact-sheet-january-2017. Accessed 10 February 2022.

– 2018. *Department of Homeland Security Northern Border Strategy*, 12 June 2018.

– 2019. "U.S. and Canada Continue Commitment to Securing our Borders, Begin Phase III of the Entry/Exit Project Under the Beyond the Border Initiative," press release, 11 July 2019.

– 2020. "Request for Department of Defense (DoD) Assistance in support of U.S. Customs and Border Protection (CBP) on the Northern and Southwest Borders to Prevent the Spread of the Novel Coronavirus Disease (COVID-19) and Maintain Public Health," Memo from Juliana Blackwell, Executive Secretary (Acting), U.S. Department of Homeland Security, 19 March 2020.

– 2021a. *Air Domain Awareness and Protection of the National Airspace System Fact Sheet*, 20 April 2021.

– 2021b. "S&T Collaborates with Federal Partners to Improve Air Domain Awareness at the Northern Border." 4 February 2021. https://www.dhs.gov/science-and-technology/news/2021/02/04/feature-article-air-domain-awareness-northern-border. Accessed 10 February 2022.

Flynn, Stephen E. 2004. *America the Vulnerable*. New York: HarperCollins.

Forrest, Maura. 2017. "Number of Asylum-Seekers Crossing into Canada Declines in April, but Still Triple the Number Arrested in January." *National Post*, 15 May 2017.

Geddes, Andrew. 2014. "Migration in European Governance: The Constitution of a Transgovernmental Policy Field." In *Handbook of the International Political Economy of Governance*, edited by Anthony Payne and Nicola Phillips, 395–413. London: Edward Elgar.

Goldfarb, Danielle, and William B.P. Robson. 2003. *Risky Business: U.S. Border Security and the Threat to Canadian Exports*. CD Howe Institute Commentary 177, March. https://www.cdhowe.org/sites/default/files/attachments/research_papers/mixed/commentary_177.pdf. Accessed 10 February 2022.

Greenwood, Ted. 1974. "Canadian-American Trade in Energy Resources." *International Organization* 28 (4): 689–710.

Holsti, Kal J., and Thomas Allen Levy. 1974. "Bilateral Institutions and Transgovernmental Relations between Canada and the United States." *International Organization* 28 (4): 875–901.

Jepperson, Ronald L., Alexander Wendt, and Peter J. Katzenstein. 1996. "Norms, Identity, and Culture in National Security." In *The Culture of National Security: Norms and Identity in World Politics*, edited by Peter J. Katzenstein, 33–78. New York: Columbia University Press.

Johnson, Jeh. 2016. "Statement by Secretary Johnson on Congressional Support for Preclearance Expansion with Canada," press release, 19 December 2016. https://www.dhs.gov/news/2016/12/19/statement-secretary-johnson-congressional-support-preclearance-expansion-canada. Accessed 10 February 2022.

Katzenstein, Peter J. 1996. "Introduction: Alternative Perspectives on National Security." In *The Culture of National Security: Norms and Identity in World Politics*, edited by Peter J. Katzenstein, 1–32. New York: Columbia University Press.

Keohane, Robert O. 1988. "International Institutions: Two Approaches." *International Studies Quarterly* 32 (4): 379–96.

Keohane, Robert O., and Helen V. Milner. 1996. *Internationalization and Domestic Politics*. Cambridge, UK: Cambridge University Press.

Keohane, Robert O., and Joseph S. Nye, Jr. 1974. "Transgovernmental Relations and International Organizations." *World Politics* 27 (1): 39–62.

Koslowski, Rey. 2005a. *Real Challenges for Virtual Borders: The Implementation of US-VISIT*. Washington, DC: Migration Policy Institute.

– 2005b. "Smart Borders, Virtual Borders or No Borders: Homeland Security Choices for the United States and Canada." *Law and Business Review of the Americas* 11 (3–4): 527–50.

– 2011. *Global Mobility Regimes*. New York: Palgrave Macmillan.

– 2020. "The UN Global Compact for Migration and the Globalization of Border Controls," The Columbia University Human Rights Seminar, Columbia University, 3 February 2020.

Legrand, Tim. 2015. "Transgovernmental Policy Networks in the Anglosphere." *Public Administration* 93 (4): 973–91.

Legrand, Tim, and Christian Leuprecht. 2021. "Securing Cross-Border Collaboration: Transgovernmental Enforcement Networks, Organized Crime and Illicit International Political Economy." *Policy and Society* 40 (4): 565–86.

Leuprecht, Christian, Todd Hataley, Kelly Sundberg, Keith Cozine, and Emmanuel Brunet Jailly. 2021. "The United States–Canada Security Community: A Case Study in Mature Border Management." *Commonwealth and Comparative Politics* 59 (4): 376–98.

Meyers, Deborah Waller. 2003. "Does 'Smarter' Lead to Safer? An Assessment of the Border Accords With Canada and Mexico." MPI *Insight* June 2003, No. 2, Migration Policy Institute, Washington, DC.

Public Safety Canada. 2014. *2013–14 Report on the Beyond the Border Action Plan Horizontal Initiative*. https://www.publicsafety.gc.ca/cnt/rsrcs/pblctns/dprtmntl-prfrmnc-rprt-2014-15/btb/index-en.aspx. Accessed 10 February 2022.

– 2015. *2015 Beyond the Border Implementation Report*. https://www.publicsafety.gc.ca/cnt/rsrcs/pblctns/2015-bynd-brdr-mplmntn/index-en.aspx. Accessed 10 February 2022.

– 2017. *2016–17 Report on the Beyond the Border Action Plan Horizontal Initiative*. https://www.publicsafety.gc.ca/cnt/rsrcs/pblctns/2016-17-btbaphi/index-en.aspx. Accessed 10 February 2022.

Raustiala, Kal. 2002. "The Architecture of International Cooperation: Transgovernmental Networks and the Future of International Law." *Virginia Journal of International Law* 43 (1): 1–92.

Reuters. 2017. "Canada, U.S. to Tackle Border Crossing Asylum-Seekers." 1 March 2017. http://www.newsweek.com/canada-border-patrol-donald-trump-canadian-border-asylum-seekers-refugees-562635. Accessed 10 February 2022.

Robertson, Colin. 2011. "Taking the Canada-US partnership to the next level." *Policy Options*, 1 March 2011, Institute for Research on Public Policy. https://policyoptions.irpp.org/magazines/canada-us-conversations-and-relations/taking-the-canada-us-partnership-to-the-next-level/. Accessed 10 February 2022.

Schwanen, Daniel. 2011. *Beyond the Border and Back to the Future: Seizing the Opportunity to Enhance Canadian and US Economic Growth and Security*. C.D. Howe Institute Backgrounder, no. 141, August. https://www.cdhowe.org/sites/default/files/attachments/research_papers/mixed/Backgrounder_141.pdf. Accessed 10 February 2022.

Scott, Anthony. 1974. "Fisheries, Pollution, and Canadian-American Transnational Relations." *International Organization* 28 (4): 827–48.

Slaughter, Anne-Marie. 1997. "The Real New World Order." *Foreign Affairs* 76 (5): 183–97.

– 2005. *A New World Order*. Princeton, NJ: Princeton University Press.

Swanson, Roger Frank. 1974. "An Analytical Assessment of the United States-Canadian Defense Issue Area." *International Organization* 28 (4): 781–802.

The 9/11 Commission. 2004. *Final Report of the National Commission on Terrorist Attacks Upon the United States*. New York: W.W. Norton.

UN (United Nations). 2019. *International Migrant Stock 2019*. United Nations Department of Economic and Social Affairs, Population Division.

Wæver, Ole, Barry Buzan, Morten Kelstrup, and Pierre Lemaitre. 1993. *Identity, Migration and the New Security Agenda in Europe*. New York: St. Martin's Press.

Waltz, Kenneth N. 1979. *Theory of International Politics*. New York: Random House.

Wendt, Alexander. 1992. "Anarchy is What States Make of It: The Social Construction of Power Politics." *International Organization* 46 (2): 391–425.

White House. 2001. "Action Plan for Creating a Secure and Smart Border," press release, *White House, Office of Homeland Security*, 12 December 2001.

– 2017a. "Executive Order: Protecting the Nation from Foreign Terrorist Entry into The United States," *White House Press Release*, 27 January 2017.

– 2017b. Joint Statement from President Donald J. Trump and Prime Minister Justin Trudeau, White House Office of the Press Secretary, 13 February 2017.

PART TWO

North American Migration Governance in Comparative Perspective

5

The Dynamics and Divergences of Executive Discretion in Refugee Resettlement

Geoffrey Cameron and Shauna Labman

Refugee resettlement serves as an important element of global refugee policy even if it has never been presented as a solution for the vast majority of the world's refugees. Resettlement expands responsibility-sharing to states geographically removed from refugee crises and presents a durable solution for especially vulnerable refugee populations. Yet there is a persistent "resettlement gap" between the total number of populations identified by the United Nations High Commissioner for Refugees (UNHCR) that are prioritized for resettlement and the annual number of admissions in resettlement destination countries (Solf and Rehberg 2021). The dynamics of resettlement policymaking in destination countries presents a significant obstacle to closing the resettlement gap.

In this chapter, we examine the dynamics and divergencies of resettlement in North America, where the majority of the world's resettled refugees find permanent residence in Canada and the US. We argue that the entrenched role played by executive discretion in determining annual refugee resettlement numbers results in policy volatility, which, in turn, makes the goal of closing the resettlement gap largely elusive. This volatility and the role of executive discretion are most readily observable under the Trudeau-led Liberal government in Canada (2015–present) and the Trump administration in the US (2017–21), where executive discretion led to policy change in starkly diverging directions.

DYNAMICS AND DIVERGENCES IN CANADA AND THE US

Relatively removed geographically from refugee flows, both Canada and the US have been long-standing leaders in their resettlement programs and admissions. In 2018, Canada overtook the US as the world's leading country of refugee resettlement.[1] Yet, as recently as 2010, Canada accepted around 12,000 refugees – less than 20 per cent of the US admissions that year (about 73,000) (Falconer 2019). In the intervening years, Canada's numbers more than doubled on an annual basis while the US cut its commitment to the lowest levels since the passage of the 1980 Refugee Act. These diverging trajectories can be attributed to similar legal-structural features of both countries' resettlement programs, which vest authority over annual resettlement admissions within the office of the political executive. We contend that the kind of political insulation enjoyed by the executive in both countries creates an environment susceptible to policy volatility in relation to other areas of immigration policy, including the inland granting of asylum, making it susceptible to significant changes to total refugee admissions from one administration or government to the next.[2] In turn, these changes can have significant effects on global displacement dynamics and opportunities for durable solutions.

The US and Canadian refugee resettlement programs both trace their origins to policy responses to displaced people after World War II. The early involvement of religious voluntary groups in the implementation of refugee resettlement led to civil society groups becoming embedded in their programs and policy networks (Cameron 2021). The totality of the US resettlement program is implemented by a handful of voluntary groups who take on the role of settlement and integration policies after resettlement. The Canadian program is characterized by dual tracks of government-assisted and privately sponsored refugees (since 1979, the numbers of refugees admitted over each program have been comparable).[3] And while the close involvement of civil society groups in both countries' resettlement programs has at times enabled them to exert an expansionary influence on annual admission quotas, the significant and divergent changes between 2016 and 2020 reveal the extent to which resettlement policies are ultimately "anchored in the most politically insulated of arenas" – the executive office (Ellermann 2021, 362).

Shortly after forming government in November 2015, Prime Minister Justin Trudeau announced an accelerated expansion of refugee resettlement to admit 25,000 Syrian refugees to Canada. This program was accompanied by announced budget allocations of almost CAD 800 million over six years to support refugee processing and settlement and to contribute to the UNHCR budget (Gilmour 2018, 234). This contrasted with the previous Harper government's 2015 budget plan, which included no mention of refugees or support to Canada's refugee system. Furthermore, the Harper government targeted annual admissions of refugees from 2015–17 to be roughly 13,000 a year (Gilmour 2018, 235). Instead, under the Trudeau government, between November 2015 and January 2017, more than 40,000 Syrians were resettled in Canada alongside the continued resettlement of refugees from other parts of the world as well. Roughly 45 per cent of these Syrian refugees arrived under private sponsorship. The Prime Minister's personal engagement with every aspect of the Syrian program was evident, from Trudeau's appearance at Pearson Airport in Toronto to welcome a planeload of newcomers, to the #WelcomeRefugees branding displayed across the immigration and citizenship ministry website (Government of Canada 2020).

The legal basis for executive discretion in Canada can be traced at least as far as the 1910 Immigration Act, which granted cabinet authority to discriminate based on race and ethnicity and to block the admission of refugees (Cameron 2021, 44). As Kelley and Trebilcock (2010, 312) note in their history of Canadian immigration policy, "The mechanisms for setting policy, primarily through executive orders and Immigration Branch directives, enabled the Prime Minister, Cabinet, and bureaucrats within the Immigration Branch to shape immigration policy quickly and relatively easily in response to public and personal biases, in the absence of parliamentary scrutiny." Ellermann (2021, 40) finds that immigration policymaking in Canada is generally carried out with a high degree of political insulation from popular or interest group pressure. Although public engagement and debate have preceded some major changes to immigration law – such as the Green Paper process leading to the 1976 Immigration Act – the executive has retained uncontested authority over setting annual resettlement targets as part of its Annual Immigration Levels Plan. In other words, by both law and convention, the executive retains discretionary control over these annual numbers.

In the US, President Trump exercised the power of the presidency over annual resettlement admissions to drive the number of admitted refugees to historic postwar lows in 2020. Days after taking office in 2017, the president signed an executive order temporarily suspending admission of all resettled refugees and reducing the previous annual target of resettled refugees from 100,000 to 50,000 (Morello 2017). Most of these refugees arrived because they had already been ostensibly approved for resettlement. The number fell to 22,533 in 2018 and reached a low of 11,814 in 2020 (Migration Policy Institute 2023) (see figure 5.1). These policies had far-reaching consequences within a sector operated in cooperation with civil society groups that depend on per-refugee government subsidies, and as such "[decimated] the infrastructure designed to facilitate refugee resettlement in the U.S." (S. Martin 2020).

Presidential authority to augment or reduce annual refugee admissions without the approval of Congress has its origins in the implementation of the 1952 Immigration and Nationality Act (INA) and the passage

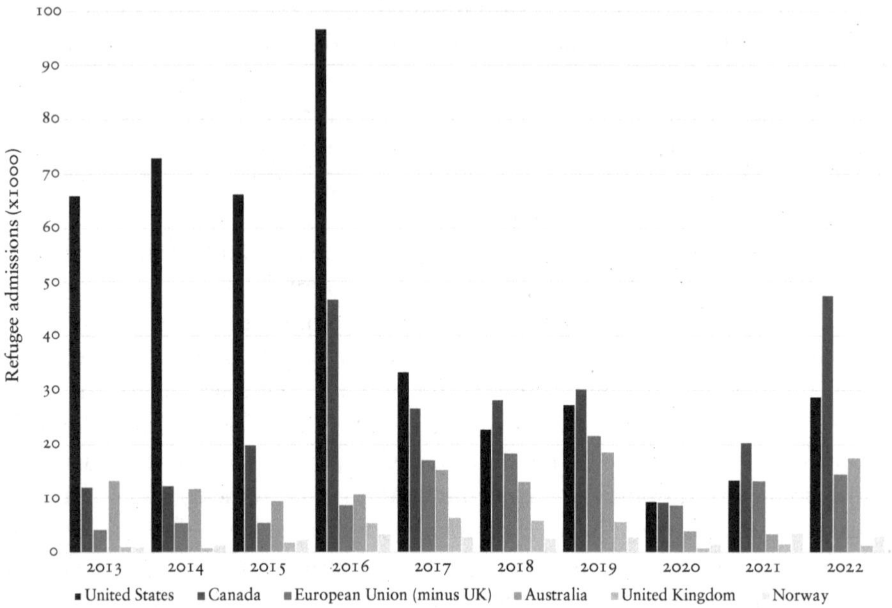

Figure 5.1 | Refugee admissions by destination, 2013–22

Source: Adapted from Falconer (2019, 3).

of the Refugee Act of 1980. The INA contained a provision allowing the attorney-general to temporarily "parole" (i.e., issue a visa to) any immigrant for reasons deemed strictly in the public interest. This statute was used by successive presidents, beginning with Eisenhower who admitted Cold-War refugees who would later be granted citizenship once it became clear they would be unable to return to their countries of origin (Cameron 2021). The repeated use of executive parole by presidents to admit refugees without congressional oversight eventually led to the passage of the 1980 Refugee Act (Leibowitz 1983), which empowers the president to set refugee admission limits through a formal proclamation at the start of each fiscal year, and sets no requirement for congressional approval (D.A. Martin 2020). While this framework is intended to permit flexibility in responding to emergency situations, it allowed President Trump to progressively lower refugee admissions to historic lows without any oversight by other branches of government.

LEGAL FRAMEWORKS

In this section, we narrate the development of legal frameworks for resettlement in Canada and the US. In Canada, resettlement was authorized by Cabinet through orders-in-council prior to the passage of the 1976 Immigration Act. Since that time, the minister of immigration has been required to consult with the provinces and others to present to Parliament each year the number of immigrants Canada intends to admit in future years. Nevertheless, Cabinet remains the ultimate authority over annual resettlement numbers. In the US, most refugees resettled before 1980 arrived via temporary parole, authorized by the attorney-general at the direction of the president. With the passage of the 1980 Refugee Act, Congress attempted to reassert itself into the setting of annual targets for the resettlement of refugees. However, the legislation requires only that certain congressional committees be consulted before setting these targets, and their approval remains in the control of the executive branch of government. While both countries have institutionalized resettlement programs through statutes, they continue to provide the executive branch of government with authority to determine annual admissions.

History and Legal Framework of Resettlement in Canada

Under Canada's constitution, responsibility for immigration is shared between the federal and provincial/territorial governments – although federal law prevails over provincial statutes. Canada's legal framework for refugee admissions is set out in the Immigration and Refugee Protection Act, 2001 (IRPA). The legislation requires the responsible minister to "consult with the governments of the provinces respecting the number of foreign nationals in each class who will become permanent residents each year" (IRPA, S.C. 2001, c. 27, s. 10(2)). An annual report is then prepared which includes "in respect of Canada, the number of foreign nationals who became permanent residents, and the number projected to become permanent residents in the following year" (IRPA s. 94(2)(B)). The Immigration Levels Plan is presented by the minister of immigration, refugees, and citizenship to Parliament each year, which includes setting out refugee resettlement targets.

It was the 1976 Immigration Act which first recognized the selection of refugees as a distinct class of immigrant admissions. The 1976 Immigration Act marked a shift in Canadian law replacing earlier "gatekeeper" immigration laws focused primarily on exclusion, as opposed to identifying classes for admission (Knowles 2007, 204). Canada had already moved from race-based admissions to a focus on economic skills and family reunification through regulatory changes in 1962 ("Order-in-Council PC 1962–86, 1962"). Canada acceded to the 1951 Convention Relating to the Status of Refugees and the 1967 Protocol Relating to the Status of Refugees in 1969. With the 1976 Immigration Act, Canada domestically affirmed these international commitments to refugee protection (Labman 2019, 39) although the government took a rather "myopic" view of asylum (Girard 2021, 5).

Canada had already been an active player in resettlement prior to the legislative recognition. More that 37,000 Hungarian refugees were resettled in Canada in 1956–57 and close to 12,000 refugees from Czechoslovakia were resettled in 1968–79. The arrival of nearly 8,000 Ugandan Asians between 1972–74 is hailed as Canada's first significant resettlement of refugees from outside of Europe ("The Ugandan Asian Refugees in Canada" n.d.) although these admissions sit in contrast to the more reluctant and limited admissions of Tibetan and Chilean refugees in the same period (Aiken 2001). These admissions relied on cabinet orders-in-council given the absence of an established legislative scheme (Knowles 2007).

In the years preceding the 1976 Immigration Act, the government's relative openness to refugee admissions was tied to the perception of public support for resettlement. A series of government research reports commissioned during the period of legislative consultation tabled before Cabinet as a green paper in 1974, as well as the report of Special Joint Committee of the Senate and House of Commons in 1975, following extensive public consultations, supported a continued commitment to refugee resettlement (Cameron 2021, 149–50). As the minister of manpower and immigration noted when introducing the law: "It is the willingness of communities to receive people and help them in tangible and intangible ways; to absorb the financial costs of a refugee movement … Governments can only legally – and sometimes perhaps they should do more – go as far and as fast as the people of the country are going to go along with" (Andras 1980, 8–9).

The 1976 Immigration Act required that the minister of immigration consult with the provinces and "such other persons, organizations and institutions as he deems appropriate" to present to Parliament each year "the number of immigrants that the Government of Canada deems it appropriate to admit during any specified period of time" (Immigration Act, 1976, 1976–77 (Can.), c. 52, s.7). The objective in setting immigration levels by the drafters of the 1976 Act was to establish attainable goals, as opposed to adhere to strict parameters (Dirks 1995, 32). Even with this intent it was initially suggested that refugee flows "were rather unpredictable and not at all amenable to projections and annual plans" (Dirks 1995, 33). The argument in favour of setting levels was that it "provides a flexible yet controlled response to refugee-producing situations as they evolve, and affords a means of reconciling perceived resettlement capacity with the actual extent of need abroad" (Hathaway 1988, 688). A legislative amendment in 1993 required the minister to submit an annual immigration plan to Parliament setting out both the total number of planned resettlement admissions and the admissions by class for the following year (S.C. 1992, c. 49, s. 3, adding s. 7(1), (2)).

Categories in Canada's resettlement admissions in the 1976 Act included convention refugees, private sponsorship, and expansion to designated classes of admissions "in accordance with Canada's humanitarian tradition with respect to the displaced and the persecuted," alongside the admission of other immigrant classes (Immigration Act, 1976, s. 6(3)). Family and humanitarian entrants were prioritized in processing (Green and Green 1999, 432). The structure of these admissions has been critiqued for "selective concern" rather than a need-based response whereby "a combination of ideological considerations and regard for domestic economic health restricts the program's purview to coincide with prevailing Canadian political and economic priorities" (Hathaway 1988, 688). This echoes earlier concerns over Canada's refugee admissions in the 1950s that while generous and second only to the US, were "carefully selected" and not dissimilar to other desired immigrants (Corbett 1957, 198). Admissions were also linked to border management. Matas (1991, 8) has shown how the designated classes for Latin America and subsequently the extended political prisoners and oppressed persons class offered a small route of legitimate admissions, while curtailing a surge of inland asylum claims through the introduction of visa requirements that "cut off the flow of spontaneous arrivals." Labman (2019, 127) has described this as a "politically discretionary settlement program with a label of refugee and humanitarian protection."

Canada's resettlement efforts surged in response to the Indochinese refugee crisis. Between 1975 and 1978, Canada admitted over 9,000 Southeast Asian refugees (Employment and Immigration Canada 1982, 8). By 1980, the admissions had reached 60,000, although this number has been credited to "twisting arms in Cabinet" by the ministers of external affairs and of employment and immigration, and numerically reflects the substantive contribution of the Canadian public through private refugee sponsorship (Knowles 2007, 217). While Canada's private sponsorship provisions preceded the crisis, the program enabled a proactive response by the Canadian public. As Freda Hawkins (1991, 79) has commented "It was a very timely plan."

Ellermann (2021, 194–5) notes how Canada shifted the predominance of its immigration attention from the family class to economic admissions in the mid-1980s to early 2000s, which "passed largely unnoticed by the Canadian public within the safety of the executive area in the form of regulatory reform" until the re-orientation crystallized with the IRPA in

2001. In the 1980s a ministerial program review recommended reducing humanitarian admissions to focus on admissions which would contribute to Canada's economy (Ellermann 2021, 221). Yet the 1985 Annual Report to Parliament still insisted "the increase in the economic stream must not ... be at the expense of the social and humanitarian streams" (Canada 1985). On the humanitarian front, however, inland asylum claims were taking a more prominent place in Canada's refugee policy. Inland claims increased in the 1980s (from ~1,600 at the beginning of the decade to over 60,000 cases in 1988) but so too did the debate on what constituted a fair and efficient system of refugee determination (Raska 2020). In 1985, the Supreme Court of Canada decided *Singh* v *Canada (Minister of Employment and Immigration)* [1985] 1 SCR 177, which held that refugee claimants were entitled to an oral hearing of their claim. As a result, the government established a new refugee determination system which commenced in 1989. By 1991, the shifting focus from refugee resettlement to processing asylum claims was clear. Canada's annual report to Parliament on immigration included a new section on inland refugee determinations and noted "Third country resettlement is considered only in exceptional circumstances" (Employment and Immigration Canada 1991, 7).

Canada did not however abandon its resettlement efforts. It did shift its approach, arguably influenced by, and aligning with, UNHCR's own reorientation, following an internal evaluation that articulated a need to efficiently see resettlement as a protection tool (Fredriksson and Mougne 1994) as well as internal pressure from advocates (Casasola 2001, 76; Garnier 2018, 124). While earlier critiques had accused Canada of "cherry-picking" the most desirable refugees for resettlement tied to their successful settlement potential (Dauvergne 2005, 93), by the late 1990s Canada was focused on the resettlement of vulnerable refugees – including women at risk, the elderly, and those with medical needs – as well as shifting from a focus on European refugees to other regions (Casasola 2001).

While Canadian resettlement numbers were high in the 1980s and early 1990s, the 1990s overall marked a significant drop. Canada struggled to meet its resettlement goals as countries navigated new realities of refugee flows at the end of the Cold War, and UNHCR took time to adapt its referral capacities (Fredriksson and Mougne 1994). Throughout the 1980s and 1990s, Canada's resettlement level plans projected three to five years in the future (Immigration, Refugees and Citizenship Canada 2020). In 1990, the government tabled an immigration plan for 1991–95 in its annual report to Parliament, based on comprehensive consultations (Employment and Immigration Canada 1991). When the governing political party in Canada flipped in the mid-2000s, this did not trigger a significant numeric shift in

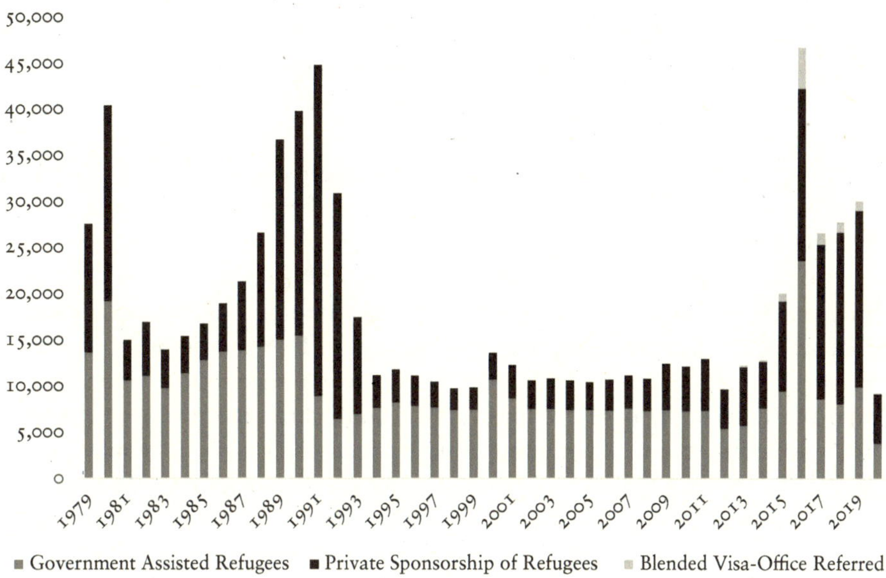

Figure 5.2 | Refugee admissions in Canada by program, 1979–2020

Sources: Data from Treviranus and Casasola (2003); Immigration, Refugees and Citizenship Canada (n.d., 2020a, 2021a).

resettlement admissions, demonstrating how policy, while vulnerable to volatility, can likewise hold static, thereby misrepresenting as stable.

The main lesson is that in the Canadian context, the federal government is conscious of public support for refugee resettlement, but the executive holds ultimate authority over resettlement numbers. As we show in the subsequent sections, in recent years this has aligned with a government drawn to resettlement as representative of their humanitarian identity and corresponding increases in admissions with a surge in 2016 admissions following the 2015 election. Within the existing legal framework, the party in power can determine annual resettlement numbers without any significant constraints, creating the potential for significant changes in total admissions from year to year (see figure 5.2).

History and Legal Framework of Resettlement in the US

Similar to Canada, US legislation gives the president significant powers to determine annual refugee admissions via resettlement. The Refugee Act of 1980 provides the legal framework for executive authority over annual refugee resettlement in the US. Signed into law by President Jimmy Carter, it has since ushered in the arrival of more than three million refugees. The act set the default annual refugee target at 50,000 per year, while authorizing the president to change the number from year to year following a consultation process with Congress, based on global displacement trends. This provision of the act continued an established practice of presidents setting annual resettlement numbers.

Prior to the passage of the Refugee Act, most refugees arrived via temporary parole. This was a feature of the 1952 Immigration and Nationality Act that was exploited by successive Republican and Democratic presidents to resettle refugees without obtaining congressional authorization. Under section 212(d)(5) of the 1952 act, the president could direct the attorney-general to "parole into the U.S. temporarily under such conditions as he may prescribe for emergent reasons or for reasons deemed strictly in the public interest any alien applying for admission to the U.S." In the context of a legal environment that restricted immigration by specific countries of origin, this provision was used by presidents to resettle refugees – often for reasons related to Cold-War foreign policy – outside of normal immigration channels. More than 38,000 Hungarian refugees arrived under executive parole starting in 1956 (almost identical to the numeric admissions of Hungarians to Canada at the same time), and more than 400,000 Indochinese refugees were paroled by the early 1980s (Bon Tempo 2008, 85, 151).

The parole statute gave presidents a free hand to admit as many refugees as they wanted, despite existing immigration law. Congress attempted to recapture authority over refugee resettlement with the Immigration Reform Act of 1965, which extended 17,400 "conditional entries" to refugees selected overseas – limiting these populations to refugees fleeing communist or Middle Eastern countries. While executive parole was maintained in the 1965 act, the Senate Judiciary Committee aimed to limit its use to "emergency, individual, and isolated situations" (Cameron 2021, 121). Nevertheless, in the year following the passage of the act, President Johnson proceeded to parole an additional 45,000 Cuban refugees for resettlement – explicitly rejecting the attempt to restrain executive authority.

The use of the executive parole authority would continue into the 1970s as a tool to resettle growing numbers of Czechoslovakians, Ugandan Asians, Soviet Jews, and refugees fleeing the Indochina War. The conflict between Congress and the White House over the repeated use of executive parole to resettle hundreds of thousands of refugees outside the quotas established by the 1965 act eventually propelled the legislative effort to pass the Refugee Act of 1980. By the late 1970s, Congress was seeking to reassert its voice in refugee policymaking (Bon Tempo 2008, 143). As Arnold Leibowitz

(1983, 64) observes, "It was the 1965 amendments to the Immigration and Nationality Act and the very broad use of executive parole authority that led to the Refugee Act of 1980."

The passage of the Refugee Act of 1980 marked the culmination of an evolving policy over the past several decades which had advanced through repeated negotiations between religious and voluntary groups and members of Congress and the White House. In his announcement of the legislation, Senator Ted Kennedy declared that it would ensure greater equity in the treatment of refugees, rationalize how the US responds to refugee emergencies, and assure "full and adequate federal support for the resettlement efforts of state, local, and voluntary agencies" (Cameron 2021, 147). The legislation accomplished several basic objectives: it redefined the term "refugee" along the more universal lines of the United Nations definition, increased the annual regular-refugee admission to 50,000 per year, and replaced the use of parole authority with new statutory language that ostensibly gave a role to Congress in determining refugee admissions. The law also established increased federal support for recognized voluntary agencies carrying out resettlement programs. It authorized the creation of a US coordinator for refugee affairs at the rank of ambassador. In addition, it finally divorced the definition of a refugee from that of an immigrant and clarified the distinction between a refugee (found outside the country) and an asylum seeker (present within it).

The role granted to Congress by the Refugee Act was, in fact, a minimal one. The president retained control over setting annual targets for the resettlement of refugees without needing to acquire congressional approval. Prior to setting the targets there are mandated cabinet-level consultations with certain congressional committees that are informed by extensive reporting requirements (D.A. Martin 1982, 96). However, these consultations are precursors to the creation of annual targets. Since the passage of the Refugee Act, the average resettlement target has been about 95,000 refugees per year (Refugee Council USA 2019). President Obama used his authority to set an admission target of 110,000 refugees for 2017, despite facing a Congress controlled by the Republican Party. Less than half this number would arrive that year, following a reversal by President Trump. The numbers fell even further in subsequent years, coming tragically close to the low quota numbers that preceded the passage of the 1980 Refugee Act.

The provisions of the 1980 Refugee Act reflect a pattern of path dependency that began with the use of the executive parole statute in the 1952 Immigration and Nationality Act. The restrictionist immigration policy at the time, which limited annual admissions according to country of origin, made it impossible for the US to admit refugees through normal immigration channels. Owing to a combination of domestic pressure and foreign policy, President Eisenhower and those who followed him made regular use of the parole power of the 1952 Act to target specific populations for resettlement in the US. The political dynamics of the Cold War significantly influenced the identification of these populations and provided much of the necessary stimulus to develop programs for their resettlement. The establishment of this customary power of the executive, while opposed at times by Congress, was finally formalized within the framework of the 1980 Act.

The 1980 Act provides the legislative framework for the contemporary US Refugee Admissions Program (USRAP), which has for most of its history received bipartisan support. Indeed, Republican presidents have proven to be just as active supporting refugee resettlement as their Democratic counterparts. President Reagan admitted more refugees than any other US president (Grossmann 2019). While resettlement declined briefly after the 11 September 2001 attacks, numbers soon moved back above 70,000 per year under President George W. Bush. The more recent decline of resettlement under President Trump has been an historic anomaly, even for Republican presidents. Nevertheless, these dynamics illustrate the power possessed by US presidents to determine annual refugee admissions via resettlement. The consequences of these executive powers in the US and Canada for the volatility of refugee resettlement are discussed in the following section.

DYNAMICS AND DIVERGENCES

Here we examine the dynamics of refugee resettlement in Canada and the US during a similar timeframe, comparing the Trudeau government in Canada (2015–present) and the Trump administration in the US (2017–21). In Canada, refugee admissions via resettlement have become a prominent theme in political campaigns. The Trudeau-led Liberal government advanced an accelerated program of resettlement for Syrian refugees soon after forming government in 2015. It also fundamentally shifted the proportional relationship between government resettlement and private sponsorship. In the US, on the other hand, the Trump administration used its power to influence refugee admissions in the opposite direction. Refugee resettlement numbers fell to historic lows because of halted resettlement, blocked arrivals from specific countries, and the introduction of new vetting measures. The implications of these changes in resettlement have included a dramatic loss in capacity within voluntary groups and their affiliated organizations which implement the bulk of the US resettlement program. The US and Canada present diverging policy directions, yet both are the result of high levels of executive discretion over annual resettlement admissions.

Expansion of Resettlement under the Trudeau Government

Catherine Dauvergne (2005, 46) has argued that humanitarianism is central to a liberal theory of migration even when not at the forefront of actual admissions. While Canada creates its own narrative as a "humanitarian nation," there are particular moments when the country's humanitarian efforts have been externally recognized. In 1986, the UNHCR awarded the Nansen Refugee Award to "the people of Canada" for the resettlement of Indochinese refugees.[4] In 2015, Canada's swift resettlement of 25,000 Syrian refugees was similarly met with international accolades. Filippo Grandi, the commissioner at UNHCR, praised Canada, stating: "I urge other countries to follow Canada's lead" (UNHCR 2015).

What was exceptional in Canada's Syrian resettlement began with the fact that resettlement admissions became an election issue in 2015 (Lenard 2021). National media noted that "swathes of Canadians of all political stripes will now urge the next government to show generosity of spirit" (Ivison 2015). While the Liberal Party made their promise to admit 25,000 Syrians, the New Democratic Party made the lesser but still significant statement to admit 10,000 more Syrians, and the Conservative Party battling to maintain power was pressured to speed up its admissions process and shifted from a promise to resettle 10,000 Syrians over three years to promising these admissions within one year. Some suggest resettlement admissions were the "biggest" election issue in 2015 (Ivison 2015). Public awareness and concern were heightened due to the escalating crisis in Syria, but also the "individualized" and "overwhelming focus" of media on the Kurdi family (Tyyskä et al. 2017). While the tragic image of Alan Kurdi who drowned alongside his mother and older brother on a Turkish beach reverberated around the world, and his name stood to represent the anonymous drowning deaths of far too many children and other asylum seekers, the Canadian connection was particularly evident. The photograph appeared amid Canada's 2015 election campaign and the Kurdi family had relatives in Canada.

The Liberal Party of Canada won the election and assumed power on 4 November 2015, immediately commencing action on their resettlement commitments. On 12 November, Prime Minister Trudeau set out in his mandate letter to the newly appointed minister of immigration, refugees, and citizenship as a first priority to "Lead government-wide efforts to resettle 25,000 refugees from Syria in the coming months" (Trudeau 2015). In just over 100 days, Canada resettled 26,172 Syrian refugees (Kiziltan 2020, xiv). As of October 2020, Canada had welcomed almost 45,000 Syrian refugees – over 21,000 through government support and almost 19,000

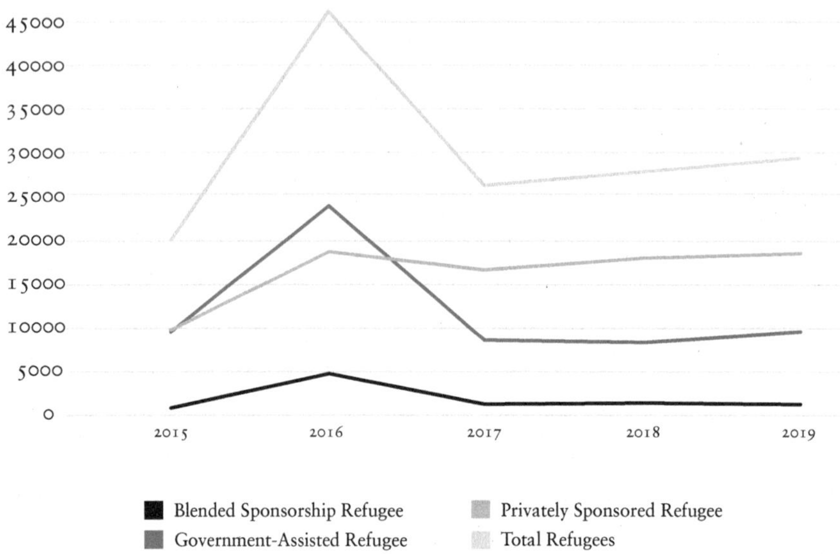

Figure 5.3 | Refugee admissions in Canada by program, 2015–19

Source: "Refugees," in Immigration, Refugees and Citizenship Canada (2021a).

through private sponsorship, with the remainder coming through a blended program that combines government assistance and private sponsorship support (Government of Canada 2020). The messaging on resettlement was overt in Operation Syrian Refugees where the government labelled its own website tracking Syrian Resettlement progress as "#WelcomeRefugees" (Government of Canada 2020). While Canada has a consistent history of generous yearly resettlement, the Syrian initiative is most comparable to the initiative almost four decades earlier when 60,000 Indochinese arrived in 1979–80 (Molloy et al. 2017).

The Canadian public responded to the Syrian crisis in a manner similar to their actions in the Indochinese crisis. A new cohort of Canadians engaged in sponsorship outside of the long-standing and repeat sponsorship community, and initially unimpacted by echo-effect considerations, these new sponsors embraced a sponsorship of strangers. Absent the need to name those they wished to sponsor, this uptake also benefited from the new Blended Visa Office-Referred stream introduced in 2013 (Labman and

Hyndman 2019). Recognizing the numeric benefit of sponsorship support to their Syrian initiative, in September 2016, the Canadian government announced at the UN Summit for Refugees and Migrants a joint project with the UNHCR and the Open Society Foundations to export the Canadian sponsorship model to interested states. The Global Refugee Sponsorship Initiative was then formally launched in Ottawa, Canada, in December 2016. In the Global Compact on Refugees (GCR) affirmed by the United Nations General Assembly in 2018 "community sponsorship" is included as a complementary pathway for admission.

While government and private sponsorship set a point of numeric equivalency to each other when the Trudeau government came to power, resettlement through private sponsorship has surged past government admissions in the intervening years overtaking government numbers in 2017 (see figure 5.3).

The Trudeau-led Liberal government was not the first to embrace refugee sponsorship. Increasing reliance on and allotment to private sponsors was evident during the years of the Harper-led Conservative government during 2006–15, although overall numbers of admissions did not change significantly (Labman 2016, 71). While governments increasingly lean on sponsors through their continual contributions and keenness to sponsor refugees, the strength of the sponsorship voice in Canada maintains the pressure on the government to act. In 2021, there were 130 Sponsorship Agreement Holders across Canada representing a diversity of religious, ethnocultural, and other groups (Immigration, Refugees and Citizenship Canada 2021b).[5] Sponsorship comes with a community of advocacy. In 1994, an NGO/government committee was established, followed by the Refugee Sponsorship Training Program in 1998 and the Sponsorship Agreement Holders Association was incorporated in 2011 ("History of the Association" n.d.). Sponsors maintain pressure on the Canadian government both to enable increased sponsorship and also to maintain complementary government resettlement numbers.

The Canadian government's incentive to maintain resettlement numbers can also be contrasted to its response to asylum claims. Despite the name change to focus on refugee protection in the law in 2001, the IRPA brought in limitations to asylum access. In introducing this legislation, the minister of immigration was unequivocal: "Closing the back door to those who would abuse the system allows us to ensure that the front door will remain open" (CBC News 2000). Canada had only "reluctantly" (Dirks 1995, 62) begun to see itself as a country of first asylum in the late 1980s and, by the year 2000, was pushing against this identity. Michael Casasola (2001, 79), reviewing the proposed changes in the new law, noted astutely: "the resettlement initiatives became an important part of selling the bill to the Canadian public ... Resettled refugees were presented as part of the refugees using the front door."

While some of the most overt obstacles to asylum introduced in the IRPA by the Conservative government were later retracted by the governing Liberal party (Immigration, Refugees and Citizenship Canada 2019b), the Liberal government also quietly created new obstacles to asylum. In April 2019, while publicly acknowledging the fortieth anniversary of Canada's private sponsorship program with the minister of immigration noting: "We can all take pride in the example Canadians set for the world" (Immigration, Refugees and Citizenship Canada 2019a), the government almost simultaneously tabled an omnibus bill which included a provision, now s. 101(1)(c.1) of IRPA, introducing a new ground of ineligibility for refugee protection. The 2019 mandate letter to the minister of immigration following the October election included less ambitious resettlement directions to "Ensure the effective implementation of Canada's increased annual Immigration Levels Plan for 2020-22" and "Introduce a dedicated refugee stream to provide safe haven for human rights advocates, journalists and humanitarian workers at risk, with a target of helping resettle as many as 250 people a year" (Trudeau 2019).

The takeover of Afghanistan by the Taliban played out in August 2021 as Canada once again prepared for a federal election. Two days prior to calling the election, the Liberal government committed to resettling 20,000 Afghan refugees. During the campaign, the Conservative Party of Canada committed to match this number (Levitz 2021). However, the Conservative Party of Canada's election platform included a proposal to "Replace public, government-assisted refugee places with more private and joint sponsorship places" (Conservative Party of Canada 2021, 129). Overall, and despite the hope of some advocates, the Afghan resettlement initiative did not however play out as a key election issue in the way the Syrian resettlement promises had.

Following the election, the Liberal government doubled their commitment to resettle 40,000 Afghan refugees (Department of Finance Canada 2021, 14). Demonstrating executive discretion in strong support of Afghan resettlement, the prime minister's mandate letter addressed to the Minister of Immigration in December 2021 focused on facilitating the continued Afghan resettlement and increasing the levels to 40,000 as well as expanding resettlement opportunities (Trudeau 2021). The efforts to resettle Afghans focused both on those still in the country and on those who had crossed into other countries thereby triggering the need for special immigration measures. Minister of Immigration Sean Fraser acknowledged that he did not think "permanent, ordinary refugee resettlement programs are particularly well designed to respond to crises as they occur in real time" (House of Commons 2022).

Canada's executive discretion has enabled the swift introduction of significant increases in resettlement while also fundamentally shifting the proportional relationship between government resettlement and private sponsorship. While the COVID-19 pandemic limited and shifted migration and travel since 2020, Canada announced its Immigration Levels Plan for 2022–24 on 14 February 2022.[6] This was the first plan since October 2020, at which point the government had announced significant increases to its annual admissions, raising the intended overall yearly numbers to 400,000. The ability of the prime minister and Cabinet to adjust resettlement numbers swiftly has enabled Canada to respond quickly to emerging crises, while also placing growing expectations on a voluntary sector that implements a significant proportion of the Canadian resettlement program.

Attenuation of Resettlement under the Trump Administration

The expansion of resettlement in Canada was accompanied by the attenuation of resettlement in the US (see figure 5.4). Between 2016 and 2020, refugee resettlement numbers fell to historic lows because of executive orders by President Trump to temporarily halt resettlement, block arrivals from specific countries, and implement new vetting measures. In addition to the reduction of resettlement in general, there was also a significant shift in the religious composition of arriving refugees: non-Christian refugees went from being the majority of resettled refugees to less than a quarter. The implications of these changes in resettlement were keenly felt by the handful of voluntary groups and their affiliated organizations, which provided much of the infrastructure for refugee resettlement, constituting part of the "administrative deconstruction" pursued by the Trump administration to diminish institutional capacity as a means of policy disruption (Beers 2020).

The first measure to reduce refugee resettlement was in the context of what quickly became known as "the Muslim ban." Executive Order 13769 was issued on 27 January 2017, which included prohibiting entry by citizens of Iraq, Iran, Libya, Somalia, Sudan, Syria, and Yemen; barring admission of Syrian refugees; suspending resettlement for 120 days; and mandating that all provisions take effect immediately. Subsequent legal challenges led to the issuance of a second legal order on 6 March 2017 (Executive Order 13780), which repeated the temporary suspension of the resettlement program and announced that the annual refugee resettlement cap would be reduced by half. A third version of a similar order was finally appealed to the Supreme

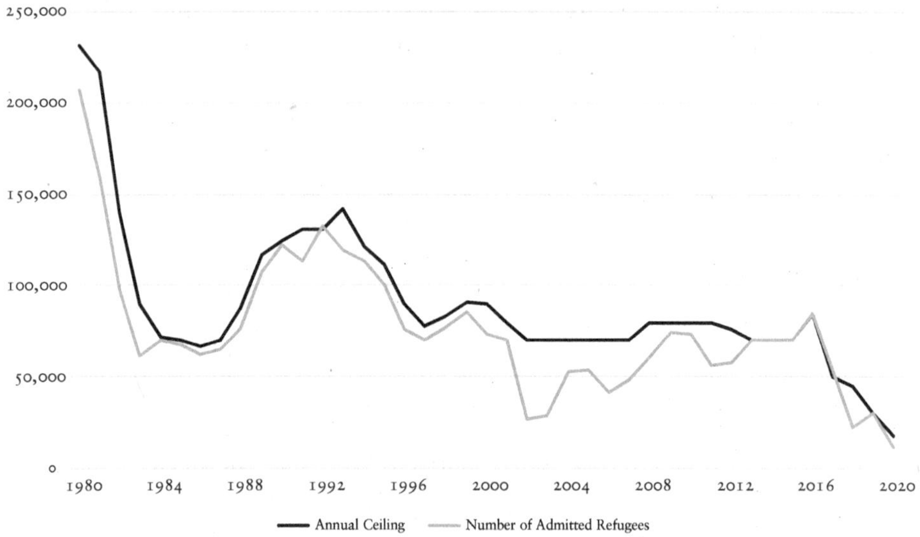

Figure 5.4 | Annual US refugee admissions, 1980–2020

Note: Includes Amerasian immigrants except in FY 1980 to 1988. Data from the Department of State Worldwide Refugee Admissions Processing System (WRAPS) on refugee arrivals differ slightly from the Department of Homeland Security's Yearbook of Immigration Statistics due to a different data collection approach.

Source: Migration Policy Institute (MPI) tabulation of WRAPS data from the Department of State's Bureau of Population, Refugees, and Migration, available at www.wrapsnet.org/admissions-and-arrivals/.

Court, which in turn upheld the executive action and affirmed the broad discretionary power of the presidency over the admission of foreigners. It referred to the Immigration and Nationality Act, which empowers the president to "suspend the entry of all aliens or any class of aliens" if he "finds" that entry "would be detrimental to the interests of the U.S." (Hurd and Schwartz 2018). While expressing some disapproval of the president's public remarks that fall short of "the principles of religious freedom and tolerance on which the Nation was founded," the court decided that the matter of limiting immigration and reducing refugee resettlement was "within the core of executive responsibility" (Hurd and Schwartz 2018).

The wider implications of reducing refugee resettlement from Muslim-majority countries included a pronounced shift in the religious composition

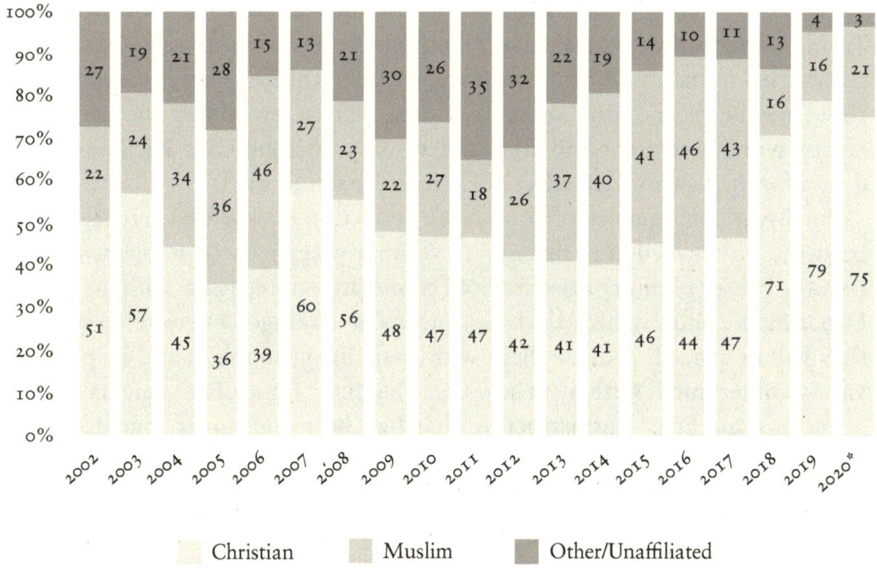

Figure 5.5 | Religious affiliation of refugees admitted to the US, 2002–20

Source: Beers (2020, 8).

of those resettled (see figure 5.5). Muslim refugees were nearly half of all admitted refugees in 2016, but less than a quarter in 2020. More than 12,000 Syrian refugees were admitted in 2016; whereas only 481 arrived in 2020 (International Refugee Assistance Project 2021, 4). By comparison, Christian refugees rose as a percentage of the overall numbers, as high as 79 per cent in 2019. Nevertheless, the total number of Christian refugees resettled in the US dropped. World Relief and Open Doors USA reported in 2020 that the combined number of Christians from the countries where they face the most persecution that were admitted to the US in President Trump's first three years in office was lower than that of 2016 alone (Morello 2020).

Another policy lever used by the Trump administration to reduce refugee resettlement was the introduction of "extreme vetting measures," which significantly slowed the arrival of refugees under USRAP – with disproportionate implications for Muslim refugees (International Refugee Assistance Project 2021, 4). The introduction of new vetting techniques prior to the Trump administration already resulted in delayed arrivals and discretionary denials for refugees from countries such as Syria, Iraq, and Somalia. However, the Trump administration's directive to introduce new security-related vetting reforms led to increased data collection, expanded security checks, expanded social media vetting, and other measures that overwhelmed the agencies tasked with these responsibilities and resulted in significant backlogs and delays for those who were selected for resettlement to the US.

Finally, a consequence of the overall reduction of resettled refugees has been the diminished capacity of the voluntary agencies to implement the USRAP. These voluntary agencies hold cooperative agreements with the State Department, under which they agree to receive refugees, determine where they will be placed, provide them with basic living supplies, and help with various other initial settlement services. The CEO of one of the nine national agencies remarked: "Infrastructure that had been built over four decades was ultimately decimated in four years … The Trump administration … tried to disassemble the entire resettlement infrastructure" (Finnegan and Gittleson 2021, para. 4–6). The reduction in the total numbers of refugees meant that voluntary agencies lost a key source of government revenue, and operational systems built to settle refugees had to be temporarily disassembled. The Trump administration also added further challenges to the work of these agencies. One executive order directed that states and localities had to give written approval of the resettlement of refugees in their jurisdictions before voluntary agencies could assign them to those locations (S. Martin 2020). While forty-two governors proactively welcomed refugees to their states, and the order was eventually stayed by a federal judge; it nevertheless added further obstacles to the resettlement of refugees in the US.

With relative insulation from countervailing pressure, the Trump administration used a series of executive orders to significantly alter the US refugee resettlement program. The annual number of admissions dropped because of actions taken to temporarily suspend admissions and block entry to the US from Muslim-majority countries that had been significant sources of refugees. Furthermore, the development of "extreme vetting" procedures significantly stalled or blocked the arrival of refugees (International Refugee Assistance Project 2021). This overall reduction of arrivals was directed by the White House, and the exercise of executive power was largely upheld by the courts.

CONCLUSION

This chapter has analyzed the development of executive discretion over refugee resettlement in North America and examined its recent consequences under the Trudeau-led Liberal government in Canada (2015–present) and the Trump administration in the US (2017–21). These consequences include policy volatility, albeit in opposite directions. While policy volatility can generate positive outcomes, such as the rapid increase of resettlement spots in Canada, it also characterizes the rapid declines witnessed under the Trump administration. The implications of policy volatility can be significant, especially on the downside. It requires the mobilization of significant resources to increase or rebuild state capacity to resettle significantly more refugees. Furthermore, because resettlement programs rely upon extensive cooperation between state agencies and the voluntary sector of religious and civil society groups, these groups are not always able to immediately augment organizational infrastructure in response to changing demands from the government. Policy volatility can erode state and civil society capacity to sustain long-standing refugee resettlement programs that are key elements of the global refugee regime, and necessary ingredients for closing the "resettlement gap."

These implications are particularly relevant at a time when a growing number of countries are participating in refugee resettlement, and many are working in close collaboration with religious and voluntary groups to implement their programs. Where resettlement programs develop or expand through the incorporation of community or private sponsorship, the dynamics of policy volatility can significantly affect the future sustainability of such programs. In countries with nascent or growing resettlement programs, they need to develop capacity for the work of settlement and socioeconomic integration. Dramatic changes in admissions from one year to the next places pressures on both the bureaucratic apparatus of the state and on the infrastructure of nonprofit organizations who often bear significant responsibility for implementation.

Because Canada and the US are international leaders when it comes to refugee resettlement numbers, they are also – whether tacitly or intentionally – policy leaders for other country participants in resettlement. Their demonstrated ability to project, and meet, multiyear annual targets for resettlement has the potential to establish a best practice to be emulated by other states. In the longer term, an international legal regime of responsibility-sharing – according to which destination countries make binding commitments to resettle a fixed percentage of refugees in need of resettlement annually – is a goal toward which refugee advocates can continue to advance.

NOTES

This chapter benefited from the research assistance of Kaila Ladd, joint master's student in peace and conflict studies at the universities of Winnipeg and Manitoba. It also benefited from the research and expertise of Robert Falconer, who supplied the original data for figures 5.1 and 5.2.

1 Though it must be noted that its ascendance was largely the result of a drastic decline in US resettlement spots, and less of a significant increase in Canadian resettlement quotas.
2 Ellermann (2021) makes a similar argument.
3 From 1979 to 2019, 401,516 refugees were resettled under the government-assisted program and 359,720 arrived via private refugee sponsorship (van Haren 2021).
4 Since 1954, the UNHCR has recognized individuals, groups, and organizations with the Nansen Refugee Award on a yearly basis to recognize exceptional efforts in protecting refugees.
5 Sponsorship Agreement Holders are organizations that have a formal agreement with the Canadian government to sponsor refugees.
6 While as noted, the Immigration Levels Plan is to occur by 1 November each year, the 2021 plan was delayed by the Federal election followed by the holiday break. The legislation stipulates that "The Minister must, on or before November 1 of each year or, if a House of Parliament is not then sitting, within the next 30 days on which that House is sitting after that date, table in each House of Parliament a report on the operation of this Act in the preceding calendar year" (IRPA, s. 94(1)). A plan for 2023–25 was released on 1 November 2022. On 1 November 2023, the 2024–26 plan was released.

REFERENCES

Aiken, Sharryn J. 2001. "Of Gods and Monsters: National Security and Canadian Refugee Policy." *Revue Québécoise de Droit International* 14 (2): 1–51.

Andras, Robert. 1980. "An Historical Sketch of Canadian Immigration and Refugee Policy." In *The Indochinese Refugee Movement: The Canadian Experience*, edited by Howard Adelman, 3–9. Toronto: Operation Lifeline.

Beers, Daniel J. 2020. "The End of Resettlement? U.S. Refugee Policy in the Age of Trump." *Social Sciences* 9 (8): 129–73.

Bon Tempo, Carl Joseph. 2008. *Americans at the Gate: The United States and Refugees During the Cold War*. Politics and Society in Twentieth-Century America. Princeton: Princeton University Press.

Cameron, Geoffrey. 2021. *Send Them Here: Religion, Politics, and Refugee Resettlement in North America*. Montreal: McGill-Queen's University Press.

Canada. 1985. *Annual Report to Parliament on Future Immigration Levels*. Ottawa: Supply and Services Canada.

Casasola, Michael. 2001. "Current Trends and New Challenges for Canada's Resettlement Program." *Refuge: Canada's Journal on Refugees* 19 (4): 76–83.

CBC News. 2000. "Ottawa Gets Tough on Immigrant Smuggling." *CBC News*, 8 April 2000. https://www.cbc.ca/news/canada/ottawa-gets-tough-on-immigrant-smuggling-1.242380. Accessed 5 June 2023.

Conservative Party of Canada. 2021. "Canada's Recovery Plan, 2021." The Conservatives. https://cpcassets.conservative.ca/wp-content/uploads/2021/08/25132033/5ea53c19b2e3597.pdf. Accessed 5 June 2023.

Corbett, David. 1957. *Canada's Immigration Policy: A Critique*. Toronto: University of Toronto Press.

Dauvergne, Catherine. 2005. *Humanitarianism, Identity, and Nation: Migration Laws of Australia and Canada*. Law and Society. Vancouver: University of British Columbia Press.

Department of Finance Canada. 2021. "Economic and Fiscal Update, 2021" Catalogue no. F1-52E/F1-85S-PDF. https://www.budget.gc.ca/efumeb/2021/report-rapport/EFU-MEB-2021-EN.pdf. Accessed 5 June 2023.

Dirks, Gerald E. 1995. *Controversy and Complexity: Canadian Immigration Policy During the 1980s*. Montreal: McGill-Queen's University Press.

Ellermann, Antje. 2021. *The Comparative Politics of Immigration: Policy Choices in Germany, Canada, Switzerland, and the U.S.* Cambridge: Cambridge University Press.

Employment and Immigration Canada. 1982. "Indochinese Refugees: The Canadian Response, 1979 and 1980." The Government of Canada Catalogue no. MP23-60/1982E-PDF. https://cihs-shic.ca/wp-content/uploads/2015/03/Indochinese-Refugees-Cdn-Response-report-ENG.pdf. Accessed 5 June 2023.

– 1991. *Annual Report to Parliament: Immigration Plan for 1991-1995 Year Two*. Canada.

Falconer, Robert. 2019. "Slamming the Golden Door: Canada-U.S. Migration Policy and Refugee Resettlement." *The School of Public Policy Publications* 12 (October): 13. https://doi.org/10.11575/sppp.v12i0.69152.

Finnegan, Conor, and Ben Gittleson. 2021. "Trump 'Decimated' Refugee Program Hampering Biden's Historic Goal: Advocates." *ABC News*, 18 February 2021. https://abcnews.go.com/Politics/trump-decimated-refugee-program-hampering-bidens-historic-goal/story?id=75911102. Accessed 5 June 2023.

Fredriksson, John, and Christine Mougne. 1994. "Resettlement in the 1990s: A Review of Policy and Practice." UNHCR, December 1994. https://www.unhcr.org/3ae6bcfd4.pdf. Accessed 5 June 2023.

Garnier, Adèle. 2018. "Resettled Refugees and Work in Canada and Quebec: Humanitarianism and the Challenge of Mainstream Socioeconomic Participation." In *Refugee Resettlement: Power, Politics, and Humanitarian Governance*, edited by Adèle Garnier, Liliana Lyra Jubilut, and Kristin

Bergtora Sandvik, 118–38. Studies in Forced Migration. New York: Berghahn Books.

Gilmour, Julie F. 2018. "The Trudeau Government, Refugee Policy, and Echoes of the Past." In *Justin Trudeau and Canadian Foreign Policy*, edited by Norman Hillmer and Philippe Lagassé, 233–46. Canada and International Affairs. New York: Springer International Publishing. https://dx.doi.org/10.1007/978-3-319-73860-4_12.

Girard, Raphael. 2021. "Effects of Postwar Immigration Selection Policy on Ethnocultural Diversity in Canada." *The Canadian Immigration Historical Society Bulletin* 96 (March): 24.

Government of Canada. 2020. "#WelcomeRefugees: Canada Resettled Syrian Refugees." 9 December 2020. https://www.canada.ca/en/immigration-refugees-citizenship/services/refugees/welcome-syrian-refugees.html. Accessed 5 June 2023.

Green, Alan G., and David A. Green. 1999. "The Economic Goals of Canada's Immigration Policy: Past and Present." *Canadian Public Policy* 25 (4): 425–51. https://doi.org/10.2307/3552422.

Grossmann, Matt. 2019. "How Trump Politicized Refugees - Niskanen Center." Podcast transcript. The Science of Politics. https://www.niskancenter.org/how-trump-politicized-refugees/. Accessed 4 January 2022.

Hathaway, James. 1988. "Selective Concern: An Overview of Refugee Law in Canada." *McGill Law Journal* 33 (4): 676–715.

Hawkins, Freda. 1991. *Critical Years in Immigration: Canada and Australia Compared*. 2nd ed. McGill-Queen's Studies in Ethnic History. Montreal: McGill-Queen's University Press.

"History of the Association." n.d. The Canadian Refugee Sponsorship Agreement Holders Association. https://www.sahassociation.com/about/history/. Accessed 5 June 2023.

House of Commons. 2022. "Honouring Canada's Legacy in Afghanistan: Responding to the Humanitarian Crisis and Helping People Reach Safety" Report of the Special Committee on Afghanistan. 44th Parliament, 1st Session.

Hurd, Hilary, and Yishai Schwartz. 2018. "The Supreme Court Travel Ban Ruling: A Summary." *Lawfare Blog* (blog). 26 June 2018. https://www.lawfareblog.com/supreme-court-travel-ban-ruling-summary. Accessed 5 June 2023.

Immigration Act, 1976, 1976–77 (Can.), c. 52.

IRPA (Immigration and Refugee Protection Act). 2001. Immigration and Refugee Protection Act (IRPA) S.C. 2001, c. 27. https://laws.justice.gc.ca/eng/acts/i-2.5/.

Immigration, Refugees and Citizenship Canada. n.d. Specialized Dataset "Canada - Admissions of Permanent Residents by Immigration Category,

1980 - Q2 2016." https://open.canada.ca/data/en/dataset/ad975a26-df23-456a-8ada-756191a23695.
– 2019a. "Canada Celebrates 40 Years of the Refugee Sponsorship Program." News release. 9 April 2019. https://www.canada.ca/en/immigration-refugees-citizenship/news/2019/04/canada-celebrates-40-years-of-the-refugee-sponsorship-program.html. Accessed 5 June 2023.
– 2019b. "Canada Ends the Designated Country of Origin Practice." News release. 17 May 2019. https://www.canada.ca/en/immigration-refugees-citizenship/news/2019/05/canada-ends-the-designated-country-of-origin-practice.html. Accessed 5 June 2023.
– 2020a. *2020 Annual Report to Parliament on Immigration.* https://www.canada.ca/en/immigration-refugees-citizenship/corporate/publications-manuals/annual-report-parliament-immigration-2020.html#permanent. Accessed 5 June 2023.
– 2020b. "CIMM - Immigration Levels Plan 2020-2022." Government of Canada. March 2020. https://www.canada.ca/en/immigration-refugees-citizenship/corporate/transparency/committees/march-12-2020/immigration-levels-plan.html. Accessed 5 June 2023.
– 2021a. *2021 Annual Report to Parliament on Immigration.* https://www.canada.ca/en/immigration-refugees-citizenship/corporate/publications-manuals/annual-report-parliament-immigration-2021.html. Accessed 5 June 2023.
– 2021b. "Private Sponsorship of Refugees Program – Sponsorship Agreement Holders." Service initiation. Government of Canada. October 2021. https://www.canada.ca/en/immigration-refugees-citizenship/services/refugees/help-outside-canada/private-sponsorship-program/agreement-holders/holders-list.html. Accessed 5 June 2023.
International Refugee Assistance Project. 2021. "Debunking 'Extreme Vetting': Recommendations to Build Back the U.S. Refugee Admissions Program (June 2021) | International Refugee Assistance Project." June 2021. https://refugeerights.org/news-resources/debunking-extreme-vetting-recommendations-to-build-back-the-u-s-refugee-admissions-program. Accessed 5 June 2023.
Ivison, John. 2015. "Migrant Crisis Suddenly the Biggest Issue in the Election Campaign — and Harper's on the High Wire." *National Post*, 3 September 2015. https://nationalpost.com/news/canada/john-ivison-migrant-crisis-suddenly-the-biggest-issue-in-the-election-campaign-and-harpers-on-the-high-wire. Accessed 5 June 2023.
Kelley, Ninette, and Michael J. Trebilcock. 2010. *The Making of the Mosaic: A History of Canadian Immigration Policy.* 2nd ed. Toronto: University of Toronto Press.

Kiziltan, Ümit. 2020. "A National Project: Syrian Refugee Resettlement in Canada." In *A National Project: Syrian Refugee Resettlement in Canada*, edited by Margaret Walton-Roberts, Luisa Veronis, and Leah K. Hamilton. Toronto: McGill-Queen's University Press.

Knowles, Valerie. 2007. *Strangers at Our Gates: Canadian Immigration and Immigration Policy, 1540–2006*. Revised. Toronto: Dundurn.

Labman, Shauna. 2016. "Private Sponsorship: Complementary or Conflicting Interests?" *Refuge: Canada's Journal on Refugees* 32 (2): 67–80.

– 2019. *Crossing Law's Border: Canada's Refugee Resettlement Program*. Vancouver: University of British Columbia Press.

Labman, Shauna, and Jennifer Hyndman. 2019. "BVOR Briefing Note." Centre for Refugee Studies, York University. 1 May 2019. https://crs.info.yorku.ca/files/2019/04/BVOR-Briefing-2019-May. Accessed 5 June 2023.

Leibowitz, Arnold H. 1983. "The Refugee Act of 1980: Problems and Congressional Concerns." *Annals of the American Academy of Political and Social Science* 467 (1): 163–71.

Lenard, Patti Tamara. 2021. "How Exceptional? Welcoming Refugees the Canadian Way." *American Review of Canadian Studies* 51 (1): 78–94. https://doi.org/10.1080/02722011.2021.1874230.

Levitz, Stephanie. 2021. "Conservatives Would Match Liberal Commitment to Resettle at Least 20,000 Afghans, Erin O'Toole Says." *The Toronto Star*, 18 August 2021. https://www.thestar.com/politics/federal-election/2021/08/18/conservatives-would-match-liberal-commitment-to-resettle-at-least-20000-afghans-erin-otoole-says.html. Accessed 5 June 2023.

Martin, David A. 1982. "The Refugee Act of 1980: Its Past and Future." *Michigan Journal of International Law* 3 (1).

– 2020. "The Refugee Act of 1980: A Forlorn Anniversary." Lawfare Blog. 19 March 2020. https://www.lawfareblog.com/refugee-act-1980-forlorn-anniversary. Accessed 5 June 2023.

Martin, Susan. 2020. "Rebuilding the U.S. Refugee Resettlement Program." The Center for Migration Studies. 26 August 2020. https://cmsny.org/publications/rebuilding-the-U.S.-refugee-resettlement-program/. Accessed 5 June 2023.

Matas, David. 1991. "Political Prisoners and Oppressed Persons Class and the Soviet Union." *Refuge* 10 (3): 5–8. https://doi.org/10.25071/1920-7336.21614.

Migration Policy Institute. 2023. "U.S. Annual Refugee Resettlement Ceilings and Number of Refugees Admitted, 1980-Present." Migration Policy Institute, Washington, DC, 11 February 2023. https://www.migrationpolicy.org/programs/data-hub/charts/U.S.-annual-refugee-resettlement-ceilings-and-number-refugees-admitted-united. Accessed 5 June 2023.

Molloy, Michael J., Peter Duschinsky, Kurt F. Jensen, and Robert J. Shalka. 2017. *Running on Empty: Canada and the Indochinese Refugees, 1975–1980*. McGill-Queen's Studies in Ethnic History. Montreal: McGill-Queen's University Press.

Morello, Carol. 2017. "Trump Signs Order Temporarily Halting Admission of Refugees, Promises Priority for Christians." *The Washington Post*, 27 January 2017. https://www.washingtonpost.com/world/national-security/trump-approves-extreme-vetting-of-refugees-promises-priority-for-christians/2017/01/27/007021a2-e4c7-11e6-a547-5fb9411d332c_story.html. Accessed 5 June 2023.

– 2020. "Trump Administration Admitting Fewer Persecuted Christian Refugees." *The Washington Post*, 10 July 2020. https://www.washingtonpost.com/national-security/trump-administration-admitting-fewer-persecuted-christian-refugees/2020/07/10/889953a-c2dd-11ea-864a-0dd31b9d6917_story.html. Accessed 5 June 2023.

Raska, Jan. 2020. "Canada's Refugee Determination System." Canadian Museum of Immigration at Pier 21. https://pier21.ca/research/immigration-history/canadas-refugee-determination-system. Accessed 5 June 2023.

Refugee Council USA. 2019. "Where Are the Refugees? Drastic Cuts to Refugee Resettlement Harming Refugees, Communities, and American Leadership." Refugee Council USA, 29.

Solf, Benedicta, and Katherine Rehberg. 2021. "The Resettlement Gap: A Record Number of Global Refugees, but Few Are Resettled." Migration Policy Institute Feature (October), Washington, DC. https://www.migrationpolicy.org/article/refugee-resettlement-gap. Accessed 5 June 2023.

Treviranus, Barbara, and Michael Casasola. 2003. "Canada's Private Sponsorship of Refugees Program: A Practitioner's Perspective of its Past and Future." *Journal of International Migration and Integration/Revue de l'integration et de la migration internationale*, 4(2): 177–202.

Trudeau, Justin. 2015. "Minister of Immigration, Refugees and Citizenship Mandate Letter." Office of the Prime Minister. 12 November 2015. https://pm.gc.ca/en/mandate-letters/2015/11/12/archived-minister-immigration-refugees-and-citizenship-mandate-letter. Accessed 5 June 2023.

– 2019. "Minister of Immigration, Refugees, and Citizenship Mandate Letter." Office of the Prime Minister. 13 December 2019. https://pm.gc.ca/en/mandate-letters/2019/12/13/archived-minister-immigration-refugees-and-citizenship-mandate-letter. Accessed 5 June 2023.

– 2021. "Minister of Immigration, Refugees and Citizenship Mandate Letter."

Office of the Prime Minister. 16 December 2021. https://pm.gc.ca/en/mandate-letters/2021/12/16/minister-immigration-refugees-and-citizenship-mandate-letter. Accessed 5 June 2023.

Tyyskä, Vappu, Jenna Blower, Samantha DeBoer, Shunya Kawai, and Ashley Walcott. 2017. "Syrian Refugee Crisis in Canadian Media. RCIS Working Paper, 2017/3." Ryerson Centre for Immigration and Settlement, April.

"The Ugandan Asian Refugees in Canada." n.d. Carleton University Library Archives and Special Collections, Uganda Collection. https://carleton.ca/uganda-collection/the-ugandan-asian-refugees-in-canada/. Accessed 5 June 2023.

United Nations High Commissioner for Refugees. 2015. "UNHCR Hails Canada's Pledge to Take Another 25,000 Syria Refugees." UNHCR, 10 November 2015. https://www.unhcr.org/news/press/2015/11/5641dec16/unhcr-hails-canadas-pledge-25000-syria-refugees.html. Accessed 5 June 2023.

– 2023. UNHCR Refugee Data Finder. https://www.unhcr.org/refugee-statistics/download/?url=2bxU2f. Accessed 5 June 2023.

van Haren, Ian. 2021. "Canada's Private Sponsorship Model Represents a Complementary Pathway for Refugee Resettlement." Migration Policy Institute Feature (July), Washington, DC. https://www.migrationpolicy.org/article/canada-private-sponsorship-model-refugee-resettlement. Accessed 5 June 2023.

6

Trump, Biden, and the US Role in the International Refugee Regime

Alise Coen

As the hegemon within both global and regional North American migration and refugee governance, the United States represents a crucial case for scrutinizing the domestic implementation of refugee and asylum protection standards and their effects on the international refugee regime. While historically considered a leader in refugee responsibility-sharing, dramatic shifts in its policies and discourse after the 2016 election of Donald Trump called attention to the US role in delegitimizing refugee protection and a rules-based international order (Barnett 2021, 137; Benhabib 2020, 77; Carayannis and Weiss 2021, 5; Coen 2018, 1270). During the Trump presidency, the US subverted a series of refugee protection principles and norms, including non-refoulement, non-detention, non-penalization, non-discrimination, and responsibility-sharing. The confluence of US policies undermining these principles represented an unparalleled departure from the normative architecture of the refugee regime.

This chapter explores two interrelated questions surrounding the US role in the refugee regime: first, how have ideological and partisan forces mediated the domestic internalization and implementation of refugee protection norms and principles? Second, how have those domestic dynamics impacted refugee protection at the international level? In pursuing the first question, the chapter sheds light on the role of political polarization in generating fluctuations within migration governance and helps clarify the conditions under which states might be more (or less) inclined to fear reputational costs associated with violations of refugee rights. With the second question, the chapter explores the global effects of uneven domestic norm internalization and implementation.

Together, these two queries advance our understanding of a crucial moment in North American migration governance wherein the hegemon of the refugee regime antagonized and contested refugee protection norms to an unprecedented degree. The chapter shows how US policies during the Trump administration were facilitated by partisan polarization and *America First* ideological precepts, which generated regional and global consequences. The chapter also offers insights for anticipating future shifts and continuities in refugee governance. As domestic ideational forces fashion uneven constraints on the US role within the refugee regime, trends toward and away from refugee protection are likely in areas that governments perceive as more "controllable" – such as the resettlement of overseas refugees and humanitarian parolees and the allocation of funding to international refugee-serving institutions.

To begin, I introduce the chapter's conceptual approach and its focus on refugee protection norms. Next, I offer an overview of the US position within the refugee regime and a brief history of bipartisan trends around refugee protection to contextualize Trump-era policy changes. I then examine how domestic political polarization has shaped uneven refugee protection, particularly in the realms of responsibility-sharing and non-discrimination. I also discuss intensifications of US norm violations vis-à-vis non-detention, non-penalization, and non-refoulement. In addressing the chapter's two interconnected questions, I foreground how the domestic dynamics of ideology and partisanship drove US defections from the global refugee regime and triggered wider international effects, particularly emboldening other governments to subvert refugee protection norms. Finally, I assess shifts and continuities in refugee protection during the first two years of the Biden presidency. I conclude with implications for trajectories of migration governance and the refugee regime.

NORMS, IDEOLOGY, AND THE REFUGEE REGIME

Within International Relations (IR), theoretical approaches attuned to the role of ideas and discourse in global politics highlight the importance of norms, defined as standards of appropriate behaviour based on collective understandings and moral assessments (Coen 2021, 342; Katzenstein 1996, 5; Legro 1997, 33). Norms help determine what is considered right, good, and acceptable (Risse 2017). The global refugee regime encompasses a bundle of normative principles regarding how states ought to behave in their treatment of refugees and asylum seekers. These principles are codified in the 1951 Refugee Convention and its 1967 Protocol, and have been reinforced through a number of international legal instruments.[1] Refugee protection norms include prohibitions on the return of refugees to territories where they might face irreparable harm, torture, or other serious human rights violations (non-refoulement); prohibitions on restricting refugees' freedom of movement (non-detention); prohibitions on penalizing refugees for irregular entry through criminal prosecution, fines, or imprisonment (non-penalization); prohibitions on denial of protection based on race, religion, or national origin (non-discrimination); and expectations to participate in international "burden-sharing" (responsibility-sharing).[2]

One of the most prominent theories of norms in IR proposes a three-stage model in which norms emerge, cascade, and then become *internalized*, in that they acquire a "taken-for-granted quality" and are no longer contested (Finnemore and Sikkink 1998, 895). Critiques of this model have pointed out that norms are often contested and interpreted differently within processes of *implementation* – that is, the processes through which commitments to international standards manifest in the domestic practices and discourses of local actors (Betts and Orchard 2014, 7). In the realm of refugee protection, there is a need to better understand the conditions under which global treaty norms vary in their domestic implementation (Betts 2014, 33). Wealthy and powerful states clearly have the capacity to exploit gaps in international law to evade their obligations toward refugees and asylum seekers (Coen 2021; FitzGerald 2019; Ghezelbash 2020), yet it remains unclear why they do not always do so uniformly. This puzzle is related to the need to better understand how and why refugee protection principles experience dissimilar levels of *internalization* – that is, how and why their acceptance among domestic policy actors varies. The departures of the Trump administration from refugee protection norms and the attendant effects of those departures across global migration dynamics heighten questions around how ideology and partisanship intervene in refugee governance and mediate the extent to which refugee protection principles are valued and prioritized locally.

The chapter's exploration of ideational forces around norm internalization and implementation[3] complements Cameron and Labman's focus in this volume on institutional forces around executive power. Domestic institutions and ideas are interdependent, and decision-making procedures are constituted and shaped by norms (Risse 2017). Executive interpretations regarding which refugee policies are appropriate and desirable are influenced by the ideologies and discourse of political elites beyond the executive branch, including those of co-partisans who have the potential to shore up or impede the president's agenda. Executive discretion in US refugee and asylum policymaking arguably amplifies the power of particular ideologies, which can be more rapidly implemented with relatively few institutional constraints and with significant effects on the global refugee regime. Previous work has demonstrated that Democrats tend to be more ideologically liberal and emphasize norms around fairness and compassion, for example, while Republicans tend be more ideologically conservative and elevate values related to loyalty and tradition (Federico et al. 2013; Haidt and Joseph 2007; Haidt, Graham, and Joseph 2009; Weinschenk and Dawes 2019). More attention is needed regarding how these orientations interact and evolve in the implementation of refugee protection.

US HEGEMONY AND BIPARTISAN TRENDS IN REFUGEE PROTECTION

The United States has been described as "the global hegemon within the refugee regime" (Loescher and Milner 2011, 202) and a "world leader on refugee and humanitarian issues" (Ferris and Donato 2020, 2). The US government has historically contributed around one-third of the UN refugee agency's (United Nations High Commissioner for Refugees or UNHCR) annual budget and served as the largest provider of annual refugee resettlement quotas worldwide (Suhrke and Garnier 2018, 247). The United States is also a regional hegemon within North American migration governance (Abdou 2019; Ayres and Macdonald 2015), with hemispheric cooperation around asylum seekers and irregular migration understood as "mirroring U.S. interests" and "deferring to U.S. goals" (Lavenex 2019, 1283; Slack and Heyman 2020, 337). Governments in the region and around the world often emulate and cite US approaches in devising and justifying their refugee and immigration policies (Adamson 2006, 186; Ghezelbash 2018; Goldenziel 2018; Whitaker 2008, 253). In Mexico and Guatemala, migrant detention practices have been heavily influenced by the United States (Castillo 2016; Flynn 2014), connecting with what Lavenex (2006) describes as the "shifting up and out" of border control policies to repress undesired migration (see also Gil, Micinski, and Norman in this volume on the use of foreign aid to contain asylum seekers).

While the refugee regime lacks coercive enforcement mechanisms for norm compliance, the extent to which governments adhere to refugee protection principles through a sense of obligation or reputation rather than compulsion bolsters the normative authority of global refugee governance (Lake 2010) and the legitimacy of the refugee regime. In the decades prior to 2017, the United States carved out a "singularly important" role in the refugee regime through voluntary contributions to responsibility-sharing (Suhrke and Garnier 2018, 247). Bipartisan support for resettlement among policymakers from the two major political parties in the US system – Republicans and Democrats[4] – signalled refugee protection standards possessed some level of normative power even in the absence of coercion. Official party platforms are crafted by party elites to articulate the core values of their group and offer valuable insights into how Republican and Democratic priorities transform over time (Azari 2016). Reaching back to 1956, the Republican Party Platform endorsed US provisions of "asylum for thousands of refugees, expellees and displaced persons" as part of "our responsibility for world leadership." The platform aligned refugee protection with national identity, linking ideas of America as "a haven for oppressed peoples" with its heritage and "traditions" (The American Presidency Project 1956). Such frameworks enabled US refugee responsibility-sharing to be understood as mutually supportive of more ideologically liberal concerns about caring for vulnerable and oppressed groups (Haidt and Joseph 2007), as well as more ideologically conservative emphases on maintaining American traditions (Federico et al. 2013, 591) – themes that I discuss in further detail in the subsequent sections.

Throughout the Cold War, Democrats harmonized refugee resettlement efforts with liberal ideological focuses on fairness and compassion (Gries 2014, 79), supporting the admission of "our fair share of refugees" as part of US contributions "to alleviate suffering" (The American Presidency Project 1960). Republicans similarly constructed their party as a caretaker of "suffering people," particularly those harmed by "the brutal acts of Communist Vietnam" (The American Presidency Project 1980). Alongside the geostrategic and ideational context of anticommunism, bipartisan support for responsibility-sharing reflected lower levels of domestic political polarization vis-à-vis refugee protection. Protection norms were more evenly internalized across the spectrum of Democratic and Republican political elites, which, at the time, included "conservative Democrats" and "liberal Republicans" (Abramowitz 2010, 36).

The lack of polarization over refugee policy enabled the 1980 Refugee Act to pass through Congress with bipartisan support, codifying key principles of the Refugee Convention into US law.[5] This incorporation of international treaty standards into domestic statute signalled an important level of norm internalization among political elites. However, it also formalized a legal basis for separating *refugees* (who typically apply for protection outside the borders of the US, undergo multiagency screening procedures, and already have legal status upon entry) from *asylum seekers* (who submit applications for asylum on US territory or upon arriving at a US port of entry). In doing so, it paved the way for a particular kind of bipartisan consensus wherein refugee responsibility-sharing via highly selective and controlled overseas resettlement efforts could be supported, while refugee protection principles regarding spontaneous arrivals of asylum seekers were evaded and violated.

In the decades following the passage of the Refugee Act, both Democrats and Republicans largely upheld this consensus. Lawmakers and presidents of both parties associated asylum seekers arriving at the US southern border with unauthorized entry and racialized notions of an "illegal immigration" problem (Hamlin 2012, 38; Hing 2019; Nayak 2015), while linking overseas refugee and parolee admissions with US foreign policy and humanitarian hegemony. Throughout the 1990s and 2000s, Republicans and Democrats emphasized the unlawful status of asylum seekers from Mexico, Central America, and Haiti to evade non-refoulement, non-detention, and non-penalization – devising policies contrary to the underlying spirit and purpose of these principles while claiming technical compliance with their legal requirements (Búzás 2017; Coen 2021). Examples include the introduction of "expedited removal" and expansion of mandatory detention measures as part of the 1996 Illegal Immigration Reform and Immigrant Responsibility Act (IIRIRA) – signed into law by Democratic president Bill Clinton and supported by many Democrats within Congress (Kerwin 2018). Both Republican and Democratic administrations also sustained the interdiction and detention of Haitian asylum seekers at the Guantánamo Bay naval base (Paik 2016).

At the same time, lawmakers and presidents of both parties generally supported international "burden-sharing" norms through refugee resettlement, and the global regime became dependent on US contributions. Increases in refugee admissions ceilings in the 1990s and the establishment of a national "Refugee Day" unfolded during the conservative Republican presidency of George H.W. Bush, who shored up bipartisan "pride in our leading efforts to assist refugees" (The American Presidency Project 1990). When annual refugee admissions declined in the wake of the 9/11 attacks, Republican lawmakers joined with Democrats to establish the Bipartisan Congressional Refugee Caucus and worked across party lines to pressure the conservative administration of George W. Bush toward increasing resettlement slots (Lawyers Committee for Human Rights 2003, 45). Republican Party Platforms throughout the 2000s committed to responsibility-sharing as a means of preserving "America's longstanding practice of aiding the innocent victims of political repression, conflict, famine, and natural disasters" (The American Presidency Project 2000) and protecting "refugees from troubled lands … who stood with America in dangerous times" (The American Presidency Project 2008) – aligning refugee protection with conservative ideological emphases on tradition and loyalty (Haidt, Graham, and Joseph 2009). Amid the 2012 elections, Republican political elites continued to affirm US contributions to refugee resettlement as part of the "country's historic tradition of welcoming refugees" (The American Presidency Project 2012).

While US admissions fluctuated and favoured certain groups in these decades, the United States typically resettled more refugees per year than all other member states of the Organisation for Economic Cooperation and Development (OECD) combined (Brown and Scribner 2014, 102). At the international level, it was increasingly recognized that US support in funding and resettlement had "profound" consequences on the ability of global regime actors such as UNHCR to effectively function and fulfill refugee protection missions (Loescher 1994, 356, 377). With the rise of political polarization in US domestic politics (Grossman and Hopkins 2016; Mason 2018), however, the ideational bases of cross-party support for refugee responsibility-sharing began to shift. The 2016 election cycle foregrounded the increasingly asymmetrical internalization of refugee protection norms along ideology and partisan identity, amplifying the extent to which the global refugee regime could no longer count on bipartisan elite support for US voluntary contributions.

POLARIZED DISRUPTION: RESPONSIBILITY-SHARING AND NON-DISCRIMINATION

The 2016 elections reflected a new level of elite polarization over refugee responsibility-sharing and uneven levels of norm internalization around the applicability of international protection. As Democrats elevated commitments to multilateralism, multicultural diversity, and the protection of vulnerable groups, including refugees and asylum seekers, conservatives and Republicans moved toward America First logics wherein international obligations toward refugees were understood as antagonistic to national interests and identity. These domestic dynamics had important effects on the global refugee regime. Guided by the America First ideology, Trump and a cohort of Republican lawmakers appealed to conservative emphases on "toughness," masculinity, resistance to racial pluralism, and skepticism toward international organizations (Aggestam and True 2021; Gries 2014, 10–11; Quaraishi 2020, 108–9) to antagonize refugee protection principles in unprecedented ways. Following the 2016 elections, interrelated challenges to refugee responsibility-sharing and non-discrimination norms manifested in dramatic cuts to resettlement, halts in funding to the United Nations Relief and Works Agency for Palestine Refugees (UNRWA), and policies discriminating against Muslim refugees.

As US contributions to global resettlement slots fell by roughly 85 per cent – from nearly 85,000 refugee admissions in FY 2016 to less than 12,000 by FY 2020 – many Republican and conservative lawmakers made sense of the cuts through America First interpretations of national interests and identity. Rep. Jeff Duncan (R-SC), for instance, cast the suspension of the refugee program as evidence that Trump was "making the safety & security of the American people his top priority," while Sen. Steve Daines (R-MT) justified pausing refugee admissions on the basis that "we are at war with Islamic extremists … the safety of U.S. citizens must be our number one priority" (Blake 2017). In contrast, within liberal visions, responsibility-sharing was defended as aligning with America's "foundational values" and "our humanitarian duty of providing those escaping persecution the opportunity to seek protection" (Menendez 2018). Democratic senators urged the administration to recognize that refugee resettlement provided "a tool to advance U.S. foreign policy interests" through maintaining "critical alliances" and "U.S. leadership" (US Senate Committee on Foreign Relations 2018). Resistance from liberal lawmakers condemning Trump's retreats from responsibility-sharing as "abandoning the persecuted" (Markey 2018) and "assaulting those that are most vulnerable" (Veasey 2019) highlighted the asymmetrical internalization of refugee protection principles among political elites and fed into cycles of "pernicious polarization," reinforcing Republican desires to anger and attack partisan rivals (McCoy and Somer 2019). Alongside appealing to Trump supporters, anti-refugee policies provided opportunities for Republican officials to display hostility toward the partisan outgroup – an increasingly important motivation and deliberate electoral strategy in US politics (Tappin and McKay 2019).

How did such domestic dynamics impact refugee protection at the international level? US retreats from responsibility-sharing echoed across global resettlement chains and significantly impacted countries of first asylum (Fee and Arar 2019; Suhrke and Garnier 2018). In Africa, which has the highest resettlement needs worldwide, historic lows in US contributions to resettlement increased pressures on host countries and drove higher numbers of refugees in the region to pursue dangerous and irregular migration routes (Mbiyozo 2021). Trump-era admissions cuts also impacted regional refugee governance, intensifying refugee status determination (RSD) backlogs and destabilizing asylum dynamics across North and South America (Ardalan 2020; Brito 2020; Kocher 2021; Smith 2020). America First contestations of international "burden-sharing" prompted a nearly 50 per cent decline in worldwide resettlement slots, with the International Rescue Committee (2019) lamenting that while US leadership had "previously spurred a race to the top in meeting humanitarian obligations … today it leads a race to the bottom." UNHCR (2019) underscored the dependence of the global regime on US voluntary contributions, explaining that the cuts "constrain UNHCR's ability to deliver on its refugee protection mandate."

US departures from responsibility-sharing also manifested in the removal of financial support for Palestinian refugees. Beginning in 2018, the Trump administration halted funding for millions of Palestinian refugees in Jordan, Lebanon, Syria, Gaza, and the West Bank by defunding UNRWA. This move represented a break with all previous administrations, which had sustained contributions regardless of party or ideology such that the US was the agency's primary financial supporter (Loescher 2021, 6). Within liberal and Democratic communities, the defunding was understood as a "moral outrage" and a "callous" move which would exacerbate Palestinian "suffering" (Brunnstrom 2018). Liberal emphases on protecting vulnerable groups were harmonized with concerns about "public health in the refugee population" (Warner 2018). In contrast, Republican and conservative frameworks made sense of the policy change by linking UNRWA with Palestinian and Islamic "extremism" (Schaefer and Phillips 2018), aligning the defunding with heightened suspicions of Palestinians and Muslims among conservatives (Gries 2014, 200). The withholding of support to a UN agency also resonated with conservative interpretations of the United Nations as the purveyor of a "new globalism" endangering traditional Christian values (Henley 2017).

At the international level, US defection from responsibility-sharing in this realm exacerbated one of the major protection gaps of the refugee regime – its bifurcation of Palestinians from other refugee populations[6] and perpetuation of their "invisibilization."[7] UNHCR's statute does not extend to Palestinian refugees, and they are often excluded from definitions of refugeehood which would grant them access to "durable solutions" (Akram 2014). As a result, over five million Palestinians remain reliant on UNRWA's humanitarian relief programs (al Husseini 2010). The US defunding prompted reductions in staffing, health, education, and food assistance (Farrell and al-Mughrabi 2020), intensifying the already precarious conditions in which Palestinian refugees live and worsening the "layers of crisis" around food insecurity, overcrowding in camps, and lack of access to essential services (UNRWA 2021). The US halt in funding also emboldened governments in the United Kingdom and Gulf countries to reduce their multiyear commitments to the agency (Wintour 2021).

The Trump administration's disruption of responsibility-sharing vis-à-vis Palestinian refugees was related to its subversion of non-discrimination and targeting of Muslim refugees. The travel ban[8] and use of "enhanced vetting"[9] to restrict admissions from Muslim-majority countries (see further discussion by Cameron and Labman in this volume) enabled the administration to reduce Muslim refugee admissions by roughly 87 per cent (Chishti and Pierce 2020). These policies aligned with nativist ideological components of America First, seeking to defend the nation from outsiders and "foreign cultural influences" (Powers, Reifler, and Scotto 2021, 5). Public opinion data showed that while over 80 per cent of self-identified Democrats opposed the travel ban, over 80 per cent of self-identified Republicans favoured the policy (Pew 2017; CNN-ORC 2017). Conservative and Republican interpretations made sense of the restrictions as safeguarding "the American people" and "the West" from terrorism and "radical Islam" (Blake 2017; Dumain 2017). Rep. Louie Gohmert (R-TX), for instance, countered non-discrimination principles in the case of "so-called Syrian refugees" through logics in which "it is okay to discriminate" against someone who "wants to destroy our way of life, bring down our government, destroy Western civilization … bring down our Constitution and have it submissive to sharia law" (Gohmert 2016). Rep. Peter King (R-NY) defended the ban on the basis that non-discrimination principles were only relevant for American citizens and did not apply to migrants and refugees as "people coming in from outside the country" (Blake 2017).

At the international level, the discriminatory policies contributed to delays and denials in resettlement, disproportionately impacting Muslim refugees from three countries – Syria, Iraq, and Somalia (Greenberg, Gelatt, and Holovnia 2019). Populations in all three of these countries faced mass atrocity crimes, including war crimes and crimes against humanity (Global Centre for the Responsibility to Protect 2016, 2018). The denial of safe haven to civilians attempting to flee such circumstances undermined the fundamental purposes of the refugee regime and breached its prohibitions on withholding protection on the grounds of nationality or religion. Both the travel ban and "enhanced vetting" measures established group-based denials of protection on the grounds of national origin. When contextualized within Trump's calls for a "total and complete shutdown" of Muslims entering the United States and other anti-Muslim statements (Hassan 2017), these policies also challenged religious non-discrimination.

Encouraged by US policies and presidential discourse, political leaders and candidates in European countries elevated platforms opposing Muslim immigration (Marko 2019, 251). Governments in Poland and Hungary echoed the Trump administration's conflation of Syrian refugees with threats of terrorist infiltration and foreign invasion (Narkowicz 2018; Tharoor 2016). Trump's America First approach and its attendant breaches of non-discrimination additionally bolstered nativist approaches in India (De Souza and Hussain 2021), fuelling migration and citizenship policies targeting the Rohingya and other Muslim asylum seekers (BBC 2019; OHCHR 2018). Such examples foreground how hegemonic challenges to non-discrimination embolden other governments to adopt analogous approaches.

INTENSIFIED CONTESTATION: NON-DETENTION, NON-PENALIZATION, AND NON-REFOULEMENT

As previously mentioned, the US approach to migration governance vis-à-vis asylum seekers spontaneously arriving on or approaching its territory has long been animated by norm violation and evasion. Trump-era policies intensified contestations of non-detention, non-penalization, and non-refoulement. The administration launched the "Remain in Mexico" program, removing roughly 70,000 asylum seekers to Mexico – where they were often at risk of violence and refoulement (Ghezelbash 2020; Margulies 2021). Additionally, under its "zero-tolerance" policy, the Department of Justice pursued federal criminal prosecution for *all* irregular entries, including individuals expressing fear of returning to their home countries (Kandel 2018). The strict enforcement of prosecution increased the detention and separation of families, many of whom were asylum seekers fleeing El Salvador, Honduras, and Guatemala (Garrett 2020).

Human rights and refugee advocacy groups called attention to the policy's violation of international norms, citing the Refugee Convention's provisions against treating those fleeing persecution punitively (Refugees International 2018; WOLA 2018). Such critiques resonated unevenly among political elites, with Democratic legislators strongly condemning the zero-tolerance approach as "cruel," "sickening," "barbaric," and "inhumane,"[10] while Trump officials defended the policy in terms of "law enforcement," "orderly and lawful processes," and ending "lawlessness" (Fox News 2018; Fritze 2018). The justificatory focus on law and order resonated among conservative audiences, for whom immigrant threats to "order" are often bound up with cultural threats to whiteness and protestant Christian values (Gries 2016, 42).

Visibility around the separation of families aspect of the policy contradicted the conservative ideological emphases on family values (Haidt, Graham, and Joseph 2009), prompting several prominent Republicans to condemn that component (Watkins 2018). Amid this intraparty pressure, Trump signed an executive order to "maintain family unity." The order perpetuated violations of non-detention, instructing that such unity could be achieved "by detaining alien families together where appropriate" as cases of improper entry made their way through immigration courts (Federal Register 2018).

Echoes of the zero-tolerance approach emerged both regionally and globally. Shortly after the Trump administration defended US breaches of non-detention and non-penalization, the Australian government drew attention for intensifying its practices of separating refugee families (UNHCR 2018). In North America, the Mexican government shifted its efforts toward increasingly detaining Central American asylum seekers as Trump pressured the AMLO (Andrés Manuel López Obrador) administration to align its practices with the US approach (Meyer and Isacson 2019). The highly visible and unapologetic subversion of non-detention norms by the hegemon within the refugee regime reinforced transnational trends toward increased restrictions on freedom of movement for asylum seekers (Hungarian Helsinki Committee 2019), signalling that such practices would not only go unpunished but were largely acceptable within collective understandings of appropriate behaviour among the Global North countries.

The onset of the COVID-19 pandemic in 2020 exacerbated US violations of non-detention and non-refoulement. The Trump administration rapidly expelled over 200,000 people across the US-Mexico border – including thousands of unaccompanied migrant children who were removed without asylum screenings (Barnes and Makinda 2021; Montoya-Galvez 2020). Officials also refused to accept asylum applications at ports of entry and physically blocked individuals with claims of persecution from stepping onto US territory (Slack and Heyman, 335). To justify these practices, the Trump administration invoked Title 42, a public health ordinance established during the 1940s, which allows the Surgeon General to prohibit the entry of individuals when "there is serious danger of the introduction of [communicable] disease" (Government Publishing Office 1944). Scientists at the Centers for Disease Control and Prevention initially refused to obey the administration's directives, arguing there was no evidence that border closures and expulsions would slow the coronavirus. Trump officials intervened to "force" the agency to comply (Dearen and Bruke 2020).

The detention and refoulement of thousands of people with asylum claims not only challenged refugee protection norms but also worsened the conditions for disease spread (Bonfiglio et al. 2020; Slack and Heyman 2020). Human rights organizations warned that the administration was flouting domestic and international obligations to process asylum seekers and avoid returning them to countries where they faced harm, cautioning that the use of the public health ordinance "essentially eliminated asylum at the US-Mexico border" (Human Rights First 2020). Democratic lawmakers pushed back on Title 42 expulsions by calling attention to US obligations under the Refugee Convention and the Convention against Torture (Leahy 2020). While liberal interpretations conceived of Trump's policies as reversing "40 years of proud U.S. leadership in providing safe haven" (Feinstein 2020), Trump defended his approach as that of "a wartime president" and framed border closures as necessary to "win this war" and "defeat this enemy" (White House Archives 2020). Such logics envisioned the coronavirus as an external rather than internal threat and encouraged conservative audiences to link southern border crossers with dangers to public health. Public opinion studies subsequently found Republicans far more supportive than Democrats of restricting movement across the US-Mexico border as an appropriate response to the COVID-19 pandemic (Gadarian, Goodman, and Pepinsky 2021).

At the international level, non-refoulement is considered the most strongly institutionalized and clearly codified refugee protection norm (Betts 2015; Loescher and Milner 2011, 192; Orchard 2017). While the relationship between non-refoulement and a positive right to be granted asylum remains debated (Goodwin-Gill 2011, 445; Grover 2018; Moran 2021), the refugee regime is premised on "access to asylum" (Betts 2011b, 76). Repeated US violations of non-refoulement and denials of access to asylum using the pretext of the pandemic expanded space for governments around the world to follow suit and adopt similar policies. Australia, Canada, and a multitude of European countries, for example, blocked access to asylum through parallel public health "emergency" measures (European Migration Network 2021; Ghezelbash and Tan 2020). US policies restricting and violating the rights of asylum seekers perpetuated an international diffusion process wherein the governments of other countries "borrow" and "transfer" similar tactics (Ghezelbash 2018).

RECOMMITTING TO THE REFUGEE REGIME?

The transition from Trump to Biden spotlighted shifting ideological interpretations of national interests and identity. Democratic officials interpreted Americanness in prisms of tolerance and inclusion that more closely aligned with international non-discrimination principles, rejecting the travel ban as xenophobic and "un-American" (The American Presidency Project 2020). Biden's inauguration in 2021 reoriented several US policies away from the America First vision and toward a more multilateralist approach supportive of international responsibility-sharing. "Cooperation," "collective strength," and "multilateral institutions" were elevated as legitimate means of responding to global challenges (The White House 2021b). The newly elected administration revoked Trump's executive actions targeting Muslim refugees and restored funding to UNRWA – policy changes which were constructed by Biden officials as aligning with "U.S. interests and values" (BBC 2021). In issuing an executive proclamation on "Ending Discriminatory Bans on Entry to the United States," Biden described the previous administration's breach of non-discrimination as "contravening our values," "jeopardizing our global network of alliances," and "inconsistent with our history of welcoming people of all faiths" (The Federal Register 2021a). Such frames appealed to liberal ideological inclinations regarding diversity and inclusion ("people of all faiths") and multilateralism ("global alliances"), rendering violations of non-discrimination contrary to American identity ("our values").

IR scholars suggest global norms become better internalized and implemented when political leaders render them compelling in domestic discourses (Betts and Orchard 2014; Winanti and Hanif 2020, 271). By intertwining "our values" with "international obligations" toward refugees (The Federal Register 2021b), Biden officials helped legitimize refugee protection and responsibility-sharing – but primarily among liberal domestic audiences. Biden's promise to raise refugee admissions as part of the restoration of America's "moral leadership" and identity as a "safe haven" (The White House 2021a) were largely geared toward Democratic voters. Public opinion data suggest that these frames resonated unevenly across partisan communities, with self-identified Democrats roughly twice as likely as Republicans to believe "sheltering refugees is part of America's heritage and principles" and to affirm that the United States has "a moral obligation to accept refugees facing persecution" (NPR/Ipsos 2021).

Despite raising annual refugee admissions ceilings during the first two years of its term, the Biden administration fell short of pledges to rebuild refugee resettlement.[11] In implementing the Doha Agreement that was negotiated under Trump, the administration oversaw a calamitous withdrawal from Afghanistan in late 2021, which triggered a humanitarian crisis and intensified threats of Taliban persecution for hundreds of thousands of Afghans. Responsibility-sharing commitments by the United States, Canada, and coalition partners in Europe were relatively weak and failed to meet the resettlement targets promised in the immediate aftermath of the withdrawal (Alhmidi 2022; European Council on Refugees and Exiles 2022). Deficiencies in responsibility-sharing impacted regional migration dynamics in the Middle East and Central Asia and worsened conditions for Afghan asylum seekers in countries such as Turkey, Iran, and Pakistan (Chohan, Majidi, and Sadat 2022) – where deportations and violations of non-refoulement increased (Latifi 2022; Sinha 2022). Domestic ideological forces intervened in US responsibility-sharing, as a cohort of Republican lawmakers reiterated America First logics to slow momentum around Afghan resettlement and turn local attention toward the potential cultural and security threats posed by Afghan refugees (Coen 2022).

Through Operation Allies Welcome, the Biden administration resettled roughly 88,500 Afghan nationals via humanitarian parole in the year following the withdrawal (US Department of Homeland Security 2022). US officials intertwined justifications for protecting Afghan "refugees" with logics emphasizing special duties of care owed to Afghan "allies" who aided US and NATO military operations during the twenty-year war in Afghanistan. Most Afghans deemed deserving of resettlement were expected to prove their service to those missions in some way (Coen 2022). In addition to the limited scope by which Afghans received protection through resettlement, the nature of that protection was also limited by the temporary legal status afforded to parolees – positioning many resettled Afghans in a precarious protection window set to expire after two years. Attempts to normalize their status and facilitate access to permanent residency through the 2022 Afghan Adjustment Act were overwhelmingly supported by Democrats but were blocked by a small group of Republican senators in Congress (Gypson 2022).

Domestic polarization and uneven norm internalization manifested most prominently in the Biden administration's attempts to change course toward overseas refugees and parolees. Biden officials pointed to the emergency resettlement initiatives for Afghans and Ukrainians[12] as testaments to the administration's recommitment to refugee responsibility-sharing (The White House 2022a), liberal visions of "who we are as a country" (The White House 2021c), and aspirations to "lead the world in responding to the needs of refugees" (The White House 2022b). In the context of US policies toward asylum seekers arriving in less "controlled" processes along the southern border shared with Mexico, however, the first two years of Biden's term reflected more continuity than change. Biden officials rescinded the zero-tolerance approach and attempted (unsuccessfully) to suspend the Remain in Mexico program,[13] yet sustained Title 42 expulsions throughout 2021. By the time the Biden administration announced plans to lift the public health order in March 2022, nongovernmental organizations (NGOs) had tracked thousands of kidnappings and violent assaults against individuals blocked at US ports of entry or removed to Mexico as a result of the policy (Human Rights First 2021b).

The administration's efforts to terminate Title 42 were stalled amid Republican-led lawsuits and court orders, keeping the policy in place. At the same time that the administration challenged the legality of Title 42 in federal courts, it also expanded its use as an immigration restriction tool. Biden officials developed a limited humanitarian parole program for Venezuelans with financial sponsors in the United States, for example, but invoked Title 42 to immediately expel Venezuelans arriving without documentation (Chishti and Bush-Joseph 2022). This approach was widened at the end of 2022 to encompass Cubans, Nicaraguans, and Haitians. At the international level, the administration's extension of Title 42 accentuated the US role in decades-long processes solidifying a global system of containment and "remote control" toward asylum seekers approaching or arriving irregularly at territorial borders (FitzGerald 2019). The continuity in US breaches of refugee protection principles using the pretext of the pandemic bolstered the persistence of similar policies worldwide (UNHCR 2022). The window of exception to Title 42 granted for Ukrainian nationals in the weeks following Russia's 2022 invasion – which enabled roughly 20,000 Ukrainians to enter the United States through its southern border with Mexico while asylum seekers of other nationalities were turned away (Rodriguez and Batalova 2022) – also contributed to a global erosion of non-discrimination norms vis-à-vis the differential treatment of white European migrants.

While Biden's perpetuation of policies violating refugee protection norms reinforced the lack of accountability and enforcement mechanisms within the refugee regime, his approach entailed significant domestic costs in terms of intraparty backlash. Liberal coalitions shamed the continued practices "undermining refugee protections" and the use of the pandemic to circumvent "refugee laws and treaties" (Human Rights First 2021a). Two high-level officials resigned, condemning the Biden administration's "inhumane, counterproductive decision to deport thousands of Haitian refugees" and use of Title 42 to "violate our legal obligation not to expel or return ('refouler') individuals who fear persecution, death, or torture" (Ramji-Nogales 2021). Democratic political elites pressed against failures to offer Haitian migrants a "meaningful opportunity to seek asylum" and called attention to the "inhumane treatment" they received (Broadwater and Sullivan 2021). These pressures from liberal allies triggered an investigation into misconduct among border patrol agents and enabled promises to allow some Haitian asylum seekers to remain in the US as they applied for humanitarian protection (Gramer 2021).

Lawmakers such as Rep. Raúl Grijalva (D-AZ) – former co-chair of the Congressional Progressive Caucus – also called attention to the administration's racialized "dual standard" at the southern border with Mexico regarding the relatively favorable treatment of Ukrainian asylum seekers and their exemption from Title 42 while migrants and asylum seekers of other nationalities were blocked from entry (Beitsch 2022). Liberal Democratic members of Congress pressed Biden officials to "treat Black and Latino immigrants, including Haitians, Mexicans, and Central Americans fleeing dire situations, with the same dignity" as Ukrainian migrants (García 2022) and scrutinized the exceptions made for Ukrainians while "too many Black and Brown migrants in our hemisphere have been denied the opportunity to seek humanitarian protection" (US Senate Committee on Foreign Relations 2022). The administration's decision to end the Title 42 exemption window for Ukrainians in April 2022 was shaped in part by these growing critiques around non-discrimination violations from within the Democratic Party.

CONCLUSION

This chapter has highlighted the central place of North American migration governance in the norms and institutions underpinning the international refugee regime. The United States is a hegemon not only within the region, but also within the refugee regime's global architecture. During the Trump administration, North America became a site of unprecedented challenges to the principles governing the protection of refugees and asylum seekers. In a landscape of growing political polarization, Trump and a cohort of Republican lawmakers disrupted US contributions to refugee resettlement and financial support for UNRWA, justifying those disruptions and the discriminatory new measures targeting Muslim refugees through appeals to America First ideas and discourse. The Trump administration also appealed to conservative ideological principles and identities in intensifying US contestations of non-detention, non-penalization, and non-refoulement. As demonstrated throughout the chapter, these policy moves impacted both regional and global migration dynamics.

Repeated failures to uphold international standards erode the legitimacy of the refugee regime (Coen 2018, 1284; Reichel 2019, 203; Whitaker 2008, 255), and can become de-stigmatized over time such that they are perceived as "normal" and cease to generate meaningful sanctions or shaming responses. The unparalleled level of Trump-era defections from the refugee regime generated no meaningful sanctions on US behaviour, though shaming responses were prevalent among international NGOs and human rights groups, whose resistance efforts "kept the norms, principles and laws of the refugee regime alive" (Barnes and Makinda 2021, 1688). Although the governments of other countries criticized the travel ban, defunding of UNRWA, and separation of asylum-seeking families at times, they remained largely muted in the wake of the dramatic cuts to refugee resettlement and the use of Title 42 to rapidly expel migrants and block access to asylum. Condemnations from UNHCR were relatively reserved, typically manifesting as expressions of "concern" over US policy moves. The absence of a more forceful UNHCR response underscores the agency's dependence on voluntary contributions from the US – a dependence which endures US abuses of its hegemonic status.

Through its scrutiny of US hegemony within global and North American refugee governance, the chapter reminds us that state interests are neither fixed nor constant in the realm of migration (Banerjee and Smith 2020, 276; Betts 2011a, 22). Ideological and partisan dynamics have mediated the internalization and implementation of refugee protection principles. As distinct political communities interpret and encounter (de)legitimizations of refugee protection differently, trends toward and away from refugee protection implementation fluctuate. When the Biden administration transitioned into power in 2021 and moved away from America First frameworks, the US ended the discriminatory travel ban, restored funding to UNRWA, and began to redevelop humanitarian migration pathways. The effects of Trump-era departures from the regime lingered, however, slowing progress on rebuilding the domestic resettlement infrastructure needed to follow through on increased pledges of refugee resettlement. During the first two years of its term, the Biden administration relied primarily on temporary humanitarian parole programs to implement responsibility-sharing. Continuity in the US approach toward migrants arriving irregularly at the southern border with Mexico recalled previous decades of bipartisan infringements on non-refoulement, non-detention, and non-penalization vis-à-vis the treatment of asylum seekers denied the conferral of "refugee" status.

Still, intraparty backlashes to anti-asylum measures were more forceful among Democrats than Republicans. Pressures from liberal coalitions narrowed the parameters of policy options available to Biden officials in ways that were unlikely to have restrained Republican officials during the same period. Polling data from 2021, for example, found self-identified Republicans were twice as likely as Democrats to believe that migrants crossing the southern border were "responsible for much of the spread of the coronavirus in the U.S." (NPR/Ipsos 2021). Efforts by the Biden administration to reverse some of the measures used by the Trump administration to limit access to asylum (Sullivan 2022) were geared toward addressing criticisms from liberal political elites and progressive coalitions – criticisms which likely would have been embraced by a Republican administration focused on attacking partisan opponents and appealing to America First worldviews. Indeed, Republican officials repeatedly organized lawsuits to keep Trump-era migration policies in place.

Better attention to the role of ideology and partisanship in migration governance can help account for changes in the degree to which states "apply universal and humanity-embracing standards" or turn toward more "exclusionary" notions of national sovereignty (Goldin, Cameron, and Balarajan 2011, 267). With the intensification of political polarization, liberals and Democrats are more likely than conservatives and Republicans to construct national identity and interests as congruent with refugee protection principles and orient US policies toward strengthening rather than retreating from the global refugee regime. Given the greater focus on multilateralism and restorations of US "moral leadership" within liberal ideological prisms, Democrats also appear more inclined than Republicans to fear reputational costs associated with violations of refugee rights. At the same time, the endurance of US violations and evasions of refugee protection norms vis-à-vis asylum seekers raises questions about the kinds of refugee policies that are more (or less) resistant to ideological and partisan pressures.

Greater fluctuations in norm implementation can be anticipated in areas of refugee protection that governments perceive as more controllable, such as the admission and resettlement of overseas refugees and humanitarian parolees and the allocation of funding to international refugee-serving institutions. In the arena of spontaneous arrivals of asylum claimants – an arena long constituted by political elites from both major political parties of the United States as "disorderly" and bound with unlawful entry – the influence of ideological forces will likely remain somewhat blunted and require more vocal and organized efforts at intraparty pressure (particularly among liberals seeking to curtail the norm violations of Democratic presidencies). At both the regional and international levels, these trajectories point toward a deepening of the limitations of the refugee regime in reserving protection for those who are deemed most easily managed and "controlled," reinforcing genealogies of inequitable and colonial dynamics (Achiume 2015; Chimni 1998; Krause 2021; Mayblin 2014) in migration governance.

NOTES

1 Examples include the International Covenant on Civil and Political Rights, the Convention against Torture, the European Convention on Human Rights, the Cartagena Declaration on Refugees, the Organization of African Unity Refugee Convention, UN resolutions, and the UNHCR Executive Committee conclusions.

2 It is important to note that levels of precision and codification across these norms vary (see Smith in this volume regarding responsibility-sharing norms), and there is disagreement over which practices constitute violations and whether protections apply only to recognized *refugees* or also to *asylum seekers* whose claims have not yet been decided (Coen 2021; Costello, Foster, and McAdam 2021; Dowd 2010).

3 For more detailed discussion of the extensive literature on norms in International Relations and concepts like norm internalization, implementation, and contestation, see Acharya (2004), Wiener (2009, 2014), and Wolff and Zimmermann (2016). For further discussion on how these concepts relate to refugee protection, see Betts and Durieux (2007), Betts and Orchard (2014), Coen (2021, 2022), and Hall (2019).

4 Throughout the chapter, the affiliations of elected officials are identified by D for Democrat and R for Republican, and by location using US state abbreviations.

5 The law adopts the Convention's definition of *refugee*, for example, and incorporates aspects of non-refoulement and non-discrimination (Government Publishing Office 1980).

6 Article 1D of the Refugee Convention (UNHCR 1951) states that it "shall not apply" to persons receiving assistance from UN agencies other than UNHCR, creating a foundation for excluding Palestinians assisted by UNRWA from the Convention's benefits.

7 Migration governance scholarship has also contributed to this invisibilization by excluding UNRWA from analyses of the international refugee regime (Abu-Laban 2021).

8 Executive Order 13769, "Protecting the Nation from Foreign Terrorist Entry into the United States" (commonly referred to as the travel ban), indefinitely blocked Syrian refugees from entry, declared the US refugee admissions program suspended for 120 days, and restricted migrants from seven Middle Eastern and North African countries (Federal Register 2017a; Waslin 2020).

9 See "Proclamation 9645 of 24 September 2017 - Enhancing Vetting Capabilities and Processes for Detecting Attempted Entry into the United States by Terrorists or Other Public-Safety Threats" (Federal Register 2017b).

10 See, for example, statements by Speaker of the House Nancy Pelosi (D-CA), Rep. Pramila Jayapal (D-WA), and Sen. Michael Bennet (D-CO) (Lambert and Brice 2018; Jayapal 2018).

11 Formal refugee admissions in 2021 and 2022 remained very low as domestic resettlement agencies – which were significantly downsized and defunded under Trump – began to restore staffing and operations but prioritized accommodating humanitarian parolees from Afghanistan and Ukraine (US Department of State 2022).

12 In the months following Russia's 2022 invasion of Ukraine, over 82,000 Ukrainian nationals were admitted into the United States as part of the Biden administration's Uniting for Ukraine program (USCIS 2022).

13 Lawsuits from Republicans in Texas and Missouri challenged the administration's efforts to terminate the program (Chishti and Bolter 2021).

REFERENCES

Abdou, Leila Hadj. 2019. "North America: Weak Regionalism, Strong Borders." In *The Dynamics of Regional Migration Governance*, edited by Andrew Geddes, Marcia Vera Espinoza, Leila Hadj Abdou, and Leiza Brumat, 146–65. Northampton, MA: Edward Elgar.

Abramowitz, Alan I. 2010. *The Disappearing Center: Engaged Citizens, Polarization, and American Democracy*. New Haven: Yale University Press.

Abu-Laban, Yasmeen. 2021. "Re-Defining the International Refugee Regime: UNHCR, UNRWA, and the Challenge of Multigenerational Protracted Refugee Situations." In *Research Handbook on the Law and Politics of Migration*, edited by Catherine Dauvergne, 310–22. Northampton, MA: Edward Elgar.

Acharya, Amitav. 2004. "How Ideas Spread: Whose Norms Matter? Norm Localization and Institutional Change in Asian Regionalism." *International Organization* 58 (2): 239–75.

Achiume, E. Tendayi. 2015. "Syria, Cost-Sharing, and the Responsibility to Protect Refugees." *Minnesota Law Review* 100 (2): 687–761.

Adamson, Fiona B. 2006. "Crossing Borders: International Migration and National Security." *International Security* 31 (1): 165–99.

Aggestam, Karin, and Jacqui True. 2021. "Political Leadership and Gendered Multilevel Games in Foreign Policy." *International Affairs* 97 (2): 385–404.

Akram, Susan. 2014. "UNRWA and Palestinian Refugees." In *The Oxford Handbook of Refugee and Forced Migration Studies*, edited by Elena Fiddian-Qasmiyeh et al., 227–40. New York: Oxford University Press.

Alhmidi, Maan. 2022. "'My Heart is Crying:' Afghan Refugees Wait on Family Members to Join Them in Canada." CTV *News*, 22 December 2022. https://www.ctvnews.ca/canada/my-heart-is-crying-afghan-refugees-wait-on-family-members-to-join-them-in-canada-1.6205883. Accessed 14 February 2023.

al Husseini, Jalal. 2010. "UNRWA and the Refugees: A Difficult but Lasting Marriage." *Journal of Palestine Studies* 40 (1): 6–26.

The American Presidency Project. 1956. "Republican Party Platform of 1956." 20 August 1956. https://www.presidency.ucsb.edu/documents/republican-party-platform-1956. Accessed 14 February 2023.

– 1960. "1960 Democratic Party Platform." 11 July 1960. https://www.presidency.ucsb.edu/documents/1960-democratic-party-platform. Accessed 14 February 2023.

– 1980. "Republican Party Platform of 1980." 15 July 1980. https://www.presidency.ucsb.edu/documents/republican-party-platform-1980. Accessed 14 February 2023.

– 1990. "Proclamation 6219—Refugee Day, 1990." 30 October 1990. http://www.presidency.ucsb.edu/ws/index.php?pid=1924. Accessed 14 February 2023.

– 2000. "2000 Republican Party Platform." 31 July 2000. https://www.presidency.ucsb.edu/documents/2000-republican-party-platform. Accessed 14 February 2023.

– 2008. "2008 Republican Party Platform." 1 September 2008. https://www.presidency.ucsb.edu/documents/2008-republican-party-platform. Accessed 14 February 2023.

– 2012. "2012 Republican Party Platform." 27 August 2012. https://www.presidency.ucsb.edu/documents/2012-republican-party-platform. Accessed 14 February 2023.

– 2020. "2020 Democratic Party Platform." 17 August 2020. https://www.presidency.ucsb.edu/documents/2020-democratic-party-platform. Accessed 14 February 2023.

Ardalan, Sabrineh. 2020. "The Trump Administration, COVID-19, and the Continuing Assault on the Rights of Asylum Seekers and Refugees." *International Journal of Refugee Law* 32 (4): 685–9.

Ayres, Jeffrey, and Laura Macdonald. 2015. "Is North America Unravelling? Transformations of Regionalism in North America." In *Limits to Regional Integration*, edited by Søren Dosenrode, 179–98. New York: Routledge.

Azari, Julia. 2016. "The Platforms Are a Window into the Future of the Parties." *FiveThirtyEight*, 19 July 2016. https://fivethirtyeight.com/features/the-platforms-are-a-window-into-the-future-of-the-parties/. Accessed 14 February 2023.

Banerjee, Kiran, and Craig Damian Smith. 2020. "International Relations and Migration: Mobility as Norm Rather Than Exception." In *Nomad-State Relationships in International Relations: Before and After Borders*, edited by Jamie Levin, 265–81. Cham, Switzerland: Palgrave Macmillan.

Barnes, Jamal, and Samuel M. Makinda. 2021. "A Threat to Cosmopolitan Duties? How COVID-19 Has Been Used as a Tool to Undermine Refugee Rights." *International Affairs* 97 (6): 1671–89.

Barnett, Michael. 2021. "Change in or of Global Governance?" *International Theory* 13 (1): 131–43.

BBC. 2019. "Citizenship Amendment Bill: India's New 'Anti-Muslim' Law Explained." 11 December 2019. https://www.bbc.com/news/world-asia-india-50670393. Accessed 14 February 2023.

– 2021. "Biden Administration to Restore $235 Million in U.S. Aid to Palestinians." 7 April 2021. https://www.bbc.com/news/world-middle-east-56665199. Accessed 14 February 2023.

Beitsch, Rebecca. 2022. "Critics Decry Double Standard on Migrants Amid Ukraine Crisis." *The Hill*, 31 March 2022. https://thehill.com/policy/national-security/600440-critics-decry-double-standard-on-refugees-amid-ukraine-crisis/. Accessed 14 February 2023.

Benhabib, Seyla. 2020. "The End of the 1951 Refugee Convention? Dilemmas of Sovereignty, Territoriality, and Human Rights." *Jus Cogens* 2 (1): 75–100.

Betts, Alexander. 2011a. "Introduction: Global Migration Governance." In *Global Migration Governance*, edited by Alexander Betts, 1–33. New York: Oxford University Press.

– 2011b. "The Refugee Regime and Issue-Linkage." In *Global Mobility Regimes*, edited by Rey Koslowski, 73–91. New York: Palgrave Macmillan.

– 2014. "From Persecution to Deprivation: How Refugee Norms Adapt at Implementation." In *Implementation and World Politics*, edited by Alexander Betts and Phil Orchard, 29–49. New York: Oxford University Press.

– 2015. "The Normative Terrain of the Global Refugee Regime." *Ethics & International Affairs* 29 (4): 363–75.

Betts, Alexander, and Jean-Francois Durieux. 2007. "Convention Plus as a Norm-Setting Exercise." *Journal of Refugee Studies* 20 (3): 509–35.

Betts, Alexander, and Phil Orchard. 2014. *Implementation and World Politics: How International Norms Change Practice*. New York: Oxford University Press.

Blake, Aaron. 2017. "Whip Count: Here's where Republicans Stand on Trump's Controversial Travel Ban." *Washington Post*, 31 January 2017. https://www.washingtonpost.com/news/the-fix/wp/2017/01/29/heres-where-republicans-stand-on-president-trumps-controversial-travel-ban/. Accessed 14 February 2023.

Bonfiglio, Genna, Kaylin Rosal, Andrés Henao-Martínez, Carlos Franco-Paredes, Eric M. Poeschla, Jamie Moo-Young, Trina Seefeldt, Hillary Dunlevy, Michelle Haas, and Janine Young. 2020. "The Long Journey Inside Immigration Detention Centers in the USA." *Journal of Travel Medicine* 27 (7): 1–3.

Brito, Maximo O. 2020. "COVID-19 in the Americas: Who's Looking After Refugees and Migrants?" *Annals of Global Health* 86 (1): 69.

Broadwater, Luke, and Eileen Sullivan. 2021. "House Democrats Demand Answers by Friday about the Border Patrol's Treatment of Haitian Migrants." *The New York Times*, 22 September 2021. https://www.nytimes.com/2021/09/22/us/politics/house-democrats-haitian-migrants.html. Accessed 14 February 2023.

Brown, Anastasia, and Todd Scribner. 2014. "Unfulfilled Promises, Future Possibilities: The Refugee Resettlement System in the United States." *Journal on Migration and Human Security* 2 (2): 101–20.

Brunnstrom, David. 2018. "Trump Cuts More than $200 Million in U.S. Aid to Palestinians." *Reuters*, 24 August 2018. https://www.reuters.com/article/us-usa-palestinians/trump-cuts-more-than-200-million-in-u-s-aid-to-palestinians-idUSKCN1L923C. Accessed 14 February 2023.

Búzás, Zoltán I. 2017. "Evading International Law: How Agents Comply with the Letter of the Law but Violate its Purpose." *European Journal of International Relations* 23 (4): 857–83.

Carayannis, Tatiana, and Thomas G. Weiss. 2021. "The 'Third' UN: Imagining Post-COVID-19 Multilateralism." *Global Policy* 12 (1): 5–14.

Castillo, Alejandro. 2016. "The Mexican Government's Frontera Sur Program: An Inconsistent Immigration Policy." *Council on Hemispheric Affairs*, 26 October 2016.

CNN-ORC. 2017. "CNN-ORC Poll." 3 February 2017. http://i2.cdn.turner.com/cnn/2017/images/02/03/rel2a.-.trump.pdf Accessed 14 February 2023.

Coen, Alise. 2018. "International Order, the Rule of Law, and U.S. Departures from Refugee Protection." *The International Journal of Human Rights* 22 (10): 1269–84.

– 2021. "Can't Be Held Responsible: Weak Norms and Refugee Protection Evasion." *International Relations* 35 (2): 341–62.

– 2022. "Localizing Refugeehood: Norms and the U.S. Resettlement of Afghan Allies." *International Affairs* 98 (6): 2021–38.

Costello, Cathryn, Michelle Foster, and Jane McAdam. 2021. *The Oxford Handbook of International Refugee Law*, New York: Oxford University Press.

Chimni, B.S. 1998. "The Geopolitics of Refugee Studies: A View from the South." *Journal of Refugee Studies* 11 (4): 350–74.

Chishti, Muzaffar, and Sarah Pierce. 2020. "Despite Trump Invitation to Stop Taking Refugees, Red and Blue States Alike Endorse Resettlement." Migration Policy Institute, Washington, DC, 29 January 2020. https://www.migrationpolicy.org/article/despite-trump-invitation-stop-taking-refugees-red-and-blue-states-alike-endorse-resettlement. Accessed 14 February 2023.

Chishti, Muzaffar, and Jessica Bolter. 2021. "Court-Ordered Relaunch of Remain in Mexico Policy Tweaks Predecessor Program, but Faces Similar Challenges." Migration Policy Institute, Washington, DC, 2 December 2021. https://www.migrationpolicy.org/article/court-order-relaunch-remain-in-mexico. Accessed 14 February 2023.

Chishti, Muzaffar, and Kathleen Bush-Joseph. 2022. "Amid Record Venezuelan Arrivals, Biden Administration Embraces Border Expulsions Policy." Migration Policy Institute, Washington, DC, 27 October 2022. https://www.migrationpolicy.org/article/venezuelan-expulsions-policy-biden. Accessed 14 February 2023.

Chohan, Naima, Nassim Majidi, and Fahim Sadat. 2022. "One Year On: The Situation for At-Risk Afghans in Afghanistan and Abroad" [Webinar]. Migration Policy Institute, Washington, DC, 10 August 2022. https://www.migrationpolicy.org/events/one-year-situation-afghanistan. Accessed 14 February 2023.

Dearen, Jason, and Garance Burke. 2020. "Pence Ordered Borders Closed after CDC Experts Refused." *AP News*, 3 October 2020. https://apnews.com/article/virus-outbreak-pandemics-public-health-new-york-health-4ef0c6c5263815a26f8aa17f6ea490ae. Accessed 14 February 2023.

De Souza, Rebecca, and Syed Ali Hussain. 2021. "'Howdy Modi!': Mediatization, Hindutva, and Long Distance Ethnonationalism." *Journal of International and Intercultural Communication* 16 (2): 138–61. https://doi.org/10.1080/17513057.2021.1987505.

Dowd, Rebecca. 2010. "Dissecting Discrimination in Refugee Law: An Analysis of its Meaning and its Cumulative Effect." *International Journal of Refugee Law* 23 (1): 28–53.

Dumain, Emma. 2017. "S.C. Rep. Jeff Duncan Uses Provocative Image to Underscore Threat of 'Radical Islamic Terrorism.'" *The Post and Courier*, 17 June 2017. https://www.postandcourier.com/news/s-c-rep-jeff-duncan-uses-provocative-image-to-underscore-threat-of-radical-islamic-terrorism/article_06e687f6-4b9c-11e7-a957-67d919c35808.html. Accessed 14 February 2023.

European Council on Refugees and Exiles. 2022. "Joint Statement: One Year After the Country's Takeover by the Taliban – How Did Europe Welcome Afghans in Need of Protection?" 9 September 2022. https://ecre.org/joint-statement-one-year-after-the-countrys-takeover-by-the-taliban-how-did-europe-welcome-afghans-in-need-of-protection/. Accessed 14 February 2023.

European Migration Network. 2021. "The Impact of COVID-19 in the Migration Area in EU and OECD Countries." April 2021. https://www.oecd.org/migration/mig/00-eu-emn-covid19-umbrella-inform-en.pdf. Accessed 14 February 2023.

Farrell, Stephen and Nidal al-Mughrabi. 2020. "U.N. Refugee Agency for Palestinians Appeals for Money to Pay Salaries." *Reuters*, 9 November 2020. https://www.reuters.com/article/israel-palestinians-unrwa-int/u-n-refugee-agency-for-palestinians-appeals-for-money-to-pay-salaries-idUSKBN27P22W. Accessed 14 February 2023.

Federal Register. 2017a. "Executive Order 13769 of January 27, 2017." 1 February 2017.

– 2017b. "Proclamation 9645 of September 24, 2017 - Enhancing Vetting Capabilities and Processes for Detecting Attempted Entry into the United States by Terrorists or Other Public-Safety Threats." 27 September 2017.

– 2018. "Executive Order 13841 of June 20, 2018 - Affording Congress and Opportunity to Address Family Separation." 25 June 2018.
– 2021a. "Proclamation 10141 of January 20, 2021 - Ending Discriminatory Bans on Entry to the United States." 25 January 2021.
– 2021b. "Executive Order 14013 of February 4, 2021." 9 February 2021.
Federico, Christopher M., Christopher R. Weber, Damla Ergun, and Corrie Hunt. 2013. "Mapping the Connections Between Politics and Morality." *Political Psychology* 34 (4): 589–610.
Fee, Molly and Rawan Arar. 2019. "What Happens When the United States Stops Taking in Refugees?" *Context* 18 (2): 18–23.
Feinstein, Dianne. 2020. "Congressional Democrats Call on Administration to Reverse Policies Targeting Asylum Seekers." 19 June 2020. https://www.feinstein.senate.gov/public/index.cfm/2020/6/congressional-democrats-call-on-administration-to-reverse-policies-targeting-asylum-seekers. Accessed 14 February 2023.
Ferris, Elizabeth G., and Katharine M. Donato. 2020. *Refugees, Migration and Global Governance*. New York: Routledge.
Finnemore, Martha and Kathryn Sikkink. 1998. "International Norm Dynamics and Political Change." *International Organization* 52 (4): 887–917.
FitzGerald, David S. 2019. *Refuge Beyond Reach: How Rich Democracies Repel Asylum Seekers*. New York: Oxford University Press.
Flynn, Michael. 2014. "There and Back Again: On the Diffusion of Immigration Detention." *Journal on Migration and Human Security* 2 (3): 165–97.
Fox News. 2018. "Sessions Defends Zero Tolerance Immigration Policy." 18 June 2018. https://www.foxnews.com/transcript/sessions-defends-zero-tolerance-immigration-policy. Accessed 14 February 2023.
Fritze, John. 2018. "Citing Bible, Trump Administration Digs in on 'Zero Tolerance' Immigration Policy.'" *USA Today*, 14 June 2018. https://www.usatoday.com/story/news/politics/2018/06/14/jeff-sessions-sarah-sanders-defend-zero-tolerance-immigration-policy/703664002/. Accessed 14 February 2023.
Gadarian, Shana Kushner, Sara Wallace Goodman, and Thomas B. Pepinsky. 2021. "Partisanship, Health Behavior, and Policy Attitudes in the Early Stages of the COVID-19 Pandemic." *PLoS One* 16 (4). https://doi.org/10.1371/journal.pone.0249596.
García, Jesús. 2022. "Biden, Democrats Must End Title 42 Now." *Latino Rebels*, 25 April 2022. https://www.latinorebels.com/2022/04/25/chuytitle42/. Accessed 14 February 2023.
Garrett, Terence Michael. 2020. "The Security Apparatus, Federal Magistrate Courts, and Detention Centers as Simulacra: The Effects of Trump's Zero

Tolerance Policy on Migrants and Refugees in the Rio Grande Valley." *Politics & Policy* 48 (2): 372–97.
Ghezelbash, Daniel. 2018. *Refuge Lost: Asylum Law in an Interdependent World.* New York: Cambridge University Press.
– 2020. "Hyper-Legalism and Obfuscation: How States Evade Their International Obligations Towards Refugees." *The American Journal of Comparative Law* 68 (3): 479–516.
Ghezelbash, Daniel, and Nikolas Feith Tan. 2020. "The End of the Right to Seek Asylum? COVID-19 and the Future of Refugee Protection." *International Journal of Refugee Law* 32 (4): 668–79.
Global Centre for the Responsibility to Protect. 2016. "R2P Monitor: Issue 30." 15 November 2016. https://www.globalr2p.org/publications/r2p-monitor-issue-30-15-november-2016/. Accessed 14 February 2023.
– 2018. "Atrocity Alert No. 131: Myanmar (Burma), Iraq and Somalia." 14 November 2018. https://www.globalr2p.org/publications/atrocity-alert-no-131-myanmar-burma-iraq-and-somalia/. Accessed 14 February 2023.
Goldenziel, Jill I. 2018. "When Law Migrates: Refugees in Comparative International Law." In *Comparative International Law,* edited by Anthea Roberts, Paul B. Stephan, Pierre-Hugues Verdier, and Mila Versteeg, 397–418. New York: Oxford University Press.
Gohmert, Louie. 2016. *The Congressional Record*, 16 June 2016, H3959-H3960.
Goldin, Ian, Geoffrey Cameron, and Meera Balarajan. 2011. *Exceptional People: How Migration Shaped Our World and Will Define Our Future.* Princeton, NJ: Princeton University Press.
Goodwin-Gill, Guy S. 2011. "The Right to Seek Asylum: Interception at Sea and the Principle of Non-Refoulement." *International Journal of Refugee Law* 23 (3): 443–57.
Government Publishing Office. 1944. 42 U.S. Code § 265 – Suspension of Entries and Imports from Designated Places to Prevent Spread of Communicable Diseases. 1 July 1944. https://www.govinfo.gov/content/pkg/USCODE-2010-title42/pdf/USCODE-2010-title42-chap6A-subchapII-partG-sec265.pdf. Accessed 14 February 2023.
– 1980. Public Law 96-212 – Refugee Act of 1980. 17 March 1980. https://www.govinfo.gov/content/pkg/STATUTE-94/pdf/STATUTE-94-Pg102.pdf. Accessed 14 February 2023.
Gramer, Robbie. 2021. "Democrats See Broken Promises in Biden's Haiti Policies." *Foreign Policy*, 8 October 2021. https://foreignpolicy.com/2021/10/08/biden-haiti-migration-refugee-democrats-backlash-state-department/. Accessed 14 February 2023.
Greenberg, Mark, Julia Gelatt, and Amy Holovnia. 2019. "As the United

States Resettles Fewer Refugees, Some Countries and Religions Face Bigger Hits than Others." Migration Policy Institute, Washington, DC, 19 September 2019. https://www.migrationpolicy.org/news/united-states-refugee-resettlement-some-countries-religions-face-bigger-hits. Accessed 14 February 2023.

Gries, Peter Hays. 2014. *The Politics of American Foreign Policy: How Ideology Divides Liberals and Conservatives over Foreign Affairs*. Stanford, CA: Stanford University Press.

– 2016. "Liberals, Conservatives, and Latin America: How Ideology Divides Americans Over Immigration and Foreign Aid." *Latin American Research Review* 51 (3): 23–46.

Grossman, Matt, and David A. Hopkins. 2016. *Asymmetric Politics: Ideological Republicans and Group Interest Democrats*. New York: Oxford University Press.

Grover, Sonja C. 2018. "In Defense of Non-Refoulement." In *Child Refugee Asylum as a Basic Human Right*, edited by Sonja C. Grover, 225–37. New York: Springer.

Gypson, Katherine. 2022. "U.S. Lawmakers Fail to Pass Afghan Adjustment Act by Year's End." VOA, 20 December 2022. https://www.voanews.com/a/us-lawmakers-fail-to-pass-afghan-adjustment-act-by-year-s-end/6884480.html. Accessed 14 February 2023.

Haidt, Jonathan, Jesse Graham, and Craig Joseph. 2009. "Above and Below Left-Right: Ideological Narratives and Moral Foundations." *Psychological Inquiry* 20 (2–3): 110–19.

Haidt, Jonathan and Craig Joseph. 2007. "The Moral Mind." In *The Innate Mind*, Volume 3, edited by Peter Carruthers, Stephen Laurence, and Stephen Stich, 367–92. New York: Oxford University Press.

Hall, Nina. 2019. "Norm Contestation in the Digital Era: Campaigning for Refugee Rights." *International Affairs* 95 (3): 575–95.

Hamlin, Rebecca. 2012. "Illegal Refugees: Competing Policy Ideas and the Rise of the Regime of Deterrence in American Asylum Politics." *Refugee Survey Quarterly* 31 (2): 33–53.

Hassan, Oz. 2017. "Trump, Islamophobia and U.S.-Middle East Relations." *Critical Studies on Security* 5 (2): 187–91.

Henley, Wallace. 2017. "Immigration, the United Nations and the New Globalism." *The Daily Citizen*, 8 January 2017. https://dailycitizen.focusonthefamily.com/immigration-the-united-nations-and-the-new-globalism/. Accessed 14 February 2023.

Hing, Bill Ong. 2019. *American Presidents, Deportations, and Human Rights Violations: From Carter to Trump*. New York: Cambridge University Press.

Human Rights First. 2020. "Pandemic as Pretext: Trump Administration Exploits COVID-19, Expels Asylum Seekers and Children to Escalating Danger." 13 May 2020. https://www.humanrightsfirst.org/resource/pandemic-pretext-trump-administration-exploits-covid-19-expels-asylum-seekers-and-children. Accessed 14 February 2023.

– 2021a. "178 Groups Denounce Biden Administration's Continued Violation of Refugee Protections." 6 August 2021. https://www.hrw.org/news/2021/08/06/178-groups-denounce-biden-administrations-continued-violation-refugee-protections#. Accessed 14 February 2023.

– 2021b. "Illegal and Inhumane." October 2021. https://www.humanrightsfirst.org/sites/default/files/IllegalandInhumane.pdf. Accessed 14 February 2023.

Hungarian Helsinki Committee. 2019. "Crossing a Red Line: How EU Countries Undermine the Right to Liberty by Expanding the Use of Detention of Asylum Seekers upon Entry." https://www.globaldetentionproject.org/wp-content/uploads/2019/02/crossing_a_red_line_REPORT.pdf. Accessed 14 February 2023.

International Rescue Committee. 2019. "New IRC Analysis of U.S. Refugee Resettlement." 18 June 2019. https://www.rescue.org/press-release/new-irc-analysis-us-refugee-resettlement-shows-vastly-reduced-arrivals-time-record. Accessed 14 February 2023.

Jayapal, Pramila. 2018. "Jayapal Goes Inside Federal Detention Center to Meet with Asylum-Seeking Women." 9 June 2018. https://jayapal.house.gov/2018/06/09/jayapal-goes-inside-federal-detention-center-meet-asylum-seeking-women-0/. Accessed 14 February 2023.

Kandel, William A. 2018. "The Trump Administration's 'Zero Tolerance' Immigration Enforcement Policy." *Congressional Research Service*, 20 July 2018. https://trac.syr.edu/immigration/library/P14693.pdf. Accessed 14 February 2023.

Katzenstein, Peter. 1996. *The Culture of National Security: Norms and Identity in World Politics*. New York: Columbia University Press.

Kerwin, Donald. 2018. "From IIRIRA to Trump: Connecting the Dots to the Current US Immigration Policy Crisis." *Journal on Migration and Human Security* 6 (3): 192–204.

Kocher, Austin. 2021. "Migrant Protection Protocols and the Death of Asylum." *Journal of Latin American Geography* 20 (1): 249–58.

Krause, Ulrike. 2021. "Colonial Roots of the 1951 Refugee Convention and its Effects on the Global Refugee Regime." *Journal of International Relations and Development* 24 (3): 599–626.

Lake, David. 2010. "Rightful Rules: Authority, Order, and the Foundations of Global Governance." *International Studies Quarterly* 54 (3): 587–613.

Latifi, Ali M. 2022. "Over 240,000 Afghan Refugees Deported from Iran and Turkey." *Middle East Eye*, 15 November 2022. https://www.middleeasteye.net/news/iran-turkey-afghan-refugees-deported. Accessed 14 February 2023.

Lavenex, Sandra. 2006. "Shifting Up and Out: The Foreign Policy of European Immigration Control." *West European Politics* 29 (2): 329–50.

– 2019. "Regional Migration Governance – Building Block of Global Initiatives?" *Journal of Ethnic and Migration Studies* 45 (8): 1275-293.

Lambert, Lisa and Makini Brice. 2018. "White House Defends Immigration Policy as Outrage Grows Over Children." *Reuters*, 18 June 2018. https://www.reuters.com/article/us-usa-immigration-trump/white-house-defends-immigration-policy-as-outrage-grows-over-children-idUSKBN1JE1L5. Accessed 14 February 2023.

Lawyers Committee for Human Rights. 2003. "Assessing the New Normal: Liberty and Security for the Post-September 11 United States." https://www.humanrightsfirst.org/sites/default/files/AssessingtheNewNormal.pdf. Accessed 14 February 2023.

Leahy, Patrick. 2020. "Leahy Leads Judiciary Committee Democrats in Demanding Answers about DHS' Newly Claimed Authorities to Override Federal Laws at Southern Border." 7 April 2020. https://www.leahy.senate.gov/press/leahy-leads-judiciary-committee-democrats-in-demanding-answers_about-dhs-newly-claimed-authorities-to-override-federal-laws-at-southern-border. Accessed 14 February 2023.

Legro, Jeffrey. 1997. "Which Norms Matter? Revisiting the 'Failure' of Internationalism." *International Organization* 51 (1): 31–63.

Loescher, Gil. 1994. "The International Refugee Regime: Stretched to the Limit?" *Journal of International Affairs* 47 (2): 351–77.

– 2021. *Refugees: A Very Short Introduction.* New York: Oxford University Press.

Loescher, Gil, and James Milner. 2011. "UNHCR and the Global Governance of Refugees." In Betts, *Global Migration Governance,* edited by Alexander Betts, 189–209. New York: Oxford University Press.

Markey, Ed (@SenMarkey). 2018. "The Trump administration is proposing to slash refugee admissions before the legally-mandated consultation with Congress. At every turn, we must resist this administration's efforts to isolate America and abandon the persecuted." Twitter, 17 September 2018. https://twitter.com/senmarkey/status/1041835389789581313. Accessed 14 February 2023.

Margulies, Peter. 2021. "The Courts Restore the 'Remain in Mexico' Program: An End to Judicial Deference?" *Lawfare*, 3 September 2021. https://www.lawfareblog.com/courts-restore-remain-mexico-program-end-judicial-deference. Accessed 14 February 2023.

Marko, David Everett. 2019. "Nevertheless, They Persist: American and European Muslim Immigrants in the Era of Trump." *Journal of Muslim Minority Affairs* 39 (2): 246–58.

Mason, Lilliana. 2018. *Uncivil Agreement: How Politics Became Our Identity.* Chicago: The University of Chicago Press.

Mayblin, Lucy. 2014. "Colonialism, Decolonization, and the Right to be Human: Britain and the 1951 Geneva Convention on the Status of Refugees." *Journal of Historical Sociology* 27 (3) 423–41.

Mbiyozo, Aimée-Noël. 2021. "Refugee Pressure Rises as Funding Dwindles." *Institute for Security Studies*, 11 February 2021. https://issafrica.org/iss-today/refugee-pressure-rises-as-funding-dwindles. Accessed 14 February 2023.

McCoy, Jennifer and Murat Somer. 2019. "Toward a Theory of Pernicious Polarization and How it Harms Democracies." *The Annals of the American Academy of Political and Social Science* 681 (1): 234–71.

Menendez, Bob (@SenatorMenendez). 2018. "1. Truly repugnant to see the Trump Administration double down on rejecting our foundational values & drastically decrease the number of refugees we accept. This rejects our humanitarian duty of providing those escaping persecution the opportunity to seek protection & safe haven." Twitter, 18 September 2018. https://twitter.com/senatormenendez/status/1042166727675731970. Accessed 14 February 2023.

Meyer, Maureen, and Adam Isacson. 2019. "The 'Wall' Before the Wall: Mexico's Crackdown on Migration at its Southern Border." WOLA, 17 December 2019. https://www.wola.org/analysis/mexico-southern-border-report/. Accessed 14 February 2023.

Montoya-Galvez, Camilo. 2020. "How Trump Officials Used COVID-19 to Shut U.S. Borders to Migrant Children." *CBS News*, 2 November 2020. https://www.cbsnews.com/news/trump-administration-closed-borders-migrant-children-covid-19/. Accessed 14 February 2023.

Moran, Clare Frances. 2021. "Strengthening the Principle of Non-Refoulement." *The International Journal of Human Rights* 25 (6): 1032–52.

Narkowicz, Kasia. 2018. "'Refugees Not Welcome Here:' State, Church and Civil Society Responses to the Refugee Crisis in Poland." *International Journal of Politics, Culture, and Society* 31 (4): 357–73.

Nayak, Meghana. 2015. *Who Is Worthy of Protection? Gender-Based Asylum and U.S. Immigration Politics.* New York: Oxford University Press.

NPR/Ipsos. "Over Two-Thirds of Americans Support Resettling Afghan Allies in the United States." 9 September 2021. https://www.ipsos.com/en-us/news_and_polls/over-two-thirds-americans-support-resettling-afghan-allies-united-states-09092021. Accessed 14 February 2023.

OHCHR (Office of the High Commissioner for Human Rights). 2018. "UN Human Rights Experts Alarmed by India Move to Deport Rohingya Men." 2 October 2018. https://www.ohchr.org/en/NewsEvents/Pages/DisplayNews.aspx?NewsID=23674&LangID=E. Accessed 14 February 2023.

Orchard, Phil. 2017. "The Dawn of International Refugee Protection: States, Tacit Cooperation and Non-Extradition." *Journal of Refugee Studies* 30 (2): 282–300.

Paik, A. Naomi. 2016. *Rightlessness: Testimony and Redress in U.S. Prison Camps since World War II*. Chapel Hill: University of North Carolina Press.

Pew Research Center. 2017. "Views of Trump's Executive Order on Travel Restrictions." 16 February 2017. https://www.pewresearch.org/politics/2017/02/16/2-views-of-trumps-executive-order-on-travel-restrictions/. Accessed 14 February 2023.

Powers, Kathleen E., Jason Reifler, and Thomas J. Scotto. 2021. "Going Nativist: How Nativism and Economic Ideology Interact to Shape Beliefs about Global Trade." *Foreign Policy Analysis* 17 (3): 1–23.

Quraishi, Uzma. 2020. *Redefining the Immigrant South: Indian and Pakistani Immigration to Houston During the Cold War*. Chapel Hill: University of North Carolina Press.

Ramji-Nogales, Jaya. 2021. "How an Internal State Department Memo Exposes 'Title 42' Expulsions of Refugees as Violations of Law." Just Security, 5 October 2021. https://www.justsecurity.org/78476/how-an-internal-state-department-memo-exposes-title-42-expulsions-of-refugees-as-violations-of-law/. Accessed 14 February 2023.

Refugees International. 2018. "The Trump Zero Tolerance Policy: A Cruel Approach with Humane and Viable Alternatives." 31 July 2018. https://www.refugeesinternational.org/reports/2018/7/31/trump-zero-tolerance-policy. Accessed 14 February 2023.

Reichel, Ellen. 2019. "Navigating between Refugee Protection and State Sovereignty." In *International Organizations Under Pressure: Legitimating Global Governance in Challenging Times*, edited by Klaus Dingwerth, Antonia Witt, Ina Lehmann, Ellen Reichel, and Tobias Weise, 195–231. New York: Oxford University Press.

Risse, Thomas. 2017. *Domestic Politics and Norm Diffusion in International Relations: Ideas Do Not Float Freely*. New York: Routledge.

Rodriguez, Joshua, and Jeanne Batalova. 2022. "Ukrainian Immigrants in the United States." Migration Policy Institute, Washington, DC, 20 June 2022. https://www.migrationpolicy.org/article/ukrainian-immigrants-united-states. Accessed 14 February 2023.

Schaefer, Brett D., and James Phillips. 2018. "Why Trump Was Right to End Funding for the UN Palestinian Aid Organization." *The Heritage Foundation*, 6 September 2018. https://www.heritage.org/middle-east/commentary/why-trump-was-right-end-funding-the-un-palestinian-aid-organization. Accessed 14 February 2023.

Sinha, Rhea. 2022. "No Place to Call Home: The Plight of Afghans." *Observer Research Foundation*, 9 June 2022. https://www.orfonline.org/expert-speak/no-place-to-call-home-the-plight-of-afghans/. Accessed 14 February 2023.

Slack, Jeremy, and Josiah Heyman. 2020. "Asylum and Mass Detention at the U.S. Mexico Border during Covid-19." *Journal of Latin American Geography* 19 (3): 334–39.

Smith, Craig Damian. 2020. "Extraction, Dependence, and Responsibility-Sharing: Taking Stock of Canada's Role in Western Hemispheric Migration Governance." *Ryerson Centre for Immigration and Settlement (RCIS) Working Paper* No. *2020/16*, 1–31.

Suhrke, Astri, and Adèle Garnier. 2018. "The Moral Economy of the Resettlement Regime." In *Refugee Resettlement: Power, Politics, and Humanitarian Governance*, edited by Adèle Garnier, Liliana Lyra Jubilut, and Kristin Bergtora Sandvik, 244–52. New York: Berghahn Books.

Sullivan, Eileen. 2022. "Biden Administration Prepares Sweeping Change to Asylum Process." *The New York Times*, 24 March 2022. https://www.nytimes.com/2022/03/24/us/politics/us-asylum-changes.html. Accessed 14 February 2023.

Tappin, Ben M., and Ryan T. McKay. 2019. "Moral Polarization and Out-Party Hostility in the U.S. Political Context." *Journal of Social and Political Psychology* 7 (1): 213–45.

Tharoor, Ishaan. 2016. "Hungary Mimics Trump, Repeats Message that London and Other European Cities are 'No-Go Zones.'" *The Washington Post*, 21 September 2016. https://www.washingtonpost.com/news/worldviews/wp/2016/09/21/hungary-mimics-trump-repeats-message-that-london-and-other-european-cities-are-no-go-zones/. Accessed 14 February 2023.

UNHCR (United Nations High Commissioner for Refugees). 1951. The Refugee Convention, 1951. https://www.unhcr.org/4ca34be29.pdf. Accessed 14 February 2023.

– 2018. "UNHCR Urges Australia to End Separation of Refugee Families." 17 July 2018. https://www.unhcr.org/en-us/news/briefing/2018/7/5b-4daf354/unhcr-urges-australia-end-separation-refugee-families.html. Accessed 14 February 2023.

– 2019. "UNHCR Troubled by Latest U.S. Refugee Resettlement Cut." 2 November 2019. https://www.unhcr.org/en-us/news/press/2019/11/5dbd87337/unhcr-troubled-latest-refugee-resettlement-cut.html. Accessed 14 February 2023.

– 2022. "COVID-19 Platform: Temporary Measures and Impact on Protection." Updated 7 January 2022. https://data2.unhcr.org/en/dataviz/127. Accessed 14 February 2023.

UNRWA (United Nations Relief and Works Agency for Palestine Refugees). 2021. "UNRWA Raises Alarm on the Situation of Palestine Refugees in Lebanon." 1 April 2021. https://www.unrwa.org/newsroom/press-releases/unrwa-raises-alarm-situation-palestine-refugees-lebanon. Accessed 14 February 2023.

USCIS (United States Citizenship and Immigration Services). 2022. "Fiscal Year 2022 Progress Report." December 2022. https://www.uscis.gov/sites/default/files/document/reports/OPA_ProgressReport.pdf. Accessed 14 February 2023.

US Department of Homeland Security. 2022. "Operation Allies Welcome Announces Departure of All Afghan Nationals from the National Conference Center Safe Haven in Leesburg, VA." 27 September 2022. https://www.dhs.gov/news/2022/09/27/operation-allies-welcome-announces-departure-all-afghan-nationals-national. Accessed 14 February 2023.

US Department of State. 2022. "Report to Congress on Proposed Refugee Admissions for Fiscal Year 2023." 8 September 2022. https://www.state.gov/report-to-congress-on-proposed-refugee-admissions-for-fiscal-year-2023/. Accessed 14 February 2023.

US Senate Committee on Foreign Relations. 2018. "Menendez Leads Democrats in Urging Secretary Pompeo Improve Refugee Admissions as Key Foreign Policy Priority." 1 May 2018. https://www.foreign.senate.gov/press/ranking/release/menendez-leads-democrats-in-urging-secretary-pompeo-improve-refugee-admissions-as-key-foreign-policy-priority. Accessed 14 February 2023.

– 2022. "Chairman Menendez on New 'Uniting for Ukraine' Parole Program for Ukrainian Refugees." 21 April 2022. https://www.foreign.senate.gov/press/dem/release/chairman-menendez-on-new-uniting-for-ukraine-parole-program-for-ukrainian-refugees. Accessed 14 February 2023.

Veasey, Mark (@RepVeasey). 2019. "Today's action by this administration is part of their continued assault on those that are most vulnerable. This is utterly shameful and goes against our American values." Twitter, 26 September 2019. https://twitter.com/repveasey/status/11773510980147978 24. Accessed 14 February 2023.

Warner, Mark R. 2018. "Warner Joins Letter Strongly Opposing Cuts to Aid to Palestinian People." 21 September 2018. https://www.warner.senate.gov/public/index.cfm/2018/9/warner-joins-letter-strongly-opposing-cuts-to-aid-to-palestinian-people. Accessed 14 February 2023.

Waslin, Michele. 2020. "The Use of Executive Orders and Proclamations to Create Immigration Policy: Trump in Historical Perspective." *Journal on Migration and Human Security* 8 (1): 54–67.

Watkins, Eli. 2018. "These Republicans Have Criticized Trump's 'Zero Tolerance' Immigration Policy." CNN, 18 June 2018. https://www.cnn.com/2018/06/18/politics/republican-party-family-separation/index.html. Accessed 14 February 2023.

Weinschenk, Aaron, and Christopher T. Dawes. 2019. "Moral Foundations, System Justification, and Support for Trump in the 2016 Presidential Election." *The Forum* 17 (2): 195–208.

Whitaker, Beth Elise. 2008. "Funding the International Refugee Regime: Implications for Protection." *Global Governance* 14 (2): 241–58.

White House Archives. 2020. "Remarks by President Trump, Vice President Pence, and Members of the Coronavirus Task Force in Press Briefing." 18 March 2020. https://trumpwhitehouse.archives.gov/briefings-statements/remarks-president-trump-vice-president-pence-members-coronavirus-task-force-press-briefing-5/. Accessed 14 February 2023.

The White House. 2021a. "Remarks by President Biden on America's Place in the World." 4 February 2021. https://www.whitehouse.gov/briefing-room/speeches-remarks/2021/02/04/remarks-by-president-biden-on-americas-place-in-the-world/. Accessed 14 February 2023.

– 2021b. "Remarks by President Biden before the 76th Session of the United Nations General Assembly." 21 September 2021. https://www.whitehouse.gov/briefing-room/speeches-remarks/2021/09/21/remarks-by-president-biden-before-the-76th-session-of-the-united-nations-general-assembly/. Accessed 14 February 2023.

– 2021c. "On-the-Record Press Call with the Regional Reporters Association by White House Coordinator for Operation Allies Welcome Jack Markell and Secretary of Homeland Security Alejandro Mayorkas on Operation Allies Welcome." 24 September 2021. https://www.whitehouse.gov/briefing-room/press-briefings/2021/09/24/on-the-record-press-call-with-the-regional-reporters-association-by-white-house-coordinator-for-operation-allies-welcome-jack-markell-and-secretary-of-homeland-security-alejandro-mayorkas-on-operation/. Accessed 14 February 2023.

– 2022a. "Remarks by President Biden Providing an Update on Russia and Ukraine." 21 April 2022. https://www.whitehouse.gov/briefing-room/

speeches-remarks/2022/04/21/remarks-by-president-biden-providing-an-update-on-russia-and-ukraine-3/. Accessed 14 February 2023.

– 2022b. "Statement by President Joseph R. Biden, Jr. on World Refugee Day 2022." 30 June 2022. https://www.whitehouse.gov/briefing-room/statements-releases/2022/06/20/statement-by-president-joseph-r-biden-jr-on-world-refugee-day-2022/. Accessed 14 February 2023.

Wiener, Antje. 2009. "Enacting Meaning-in-use: Qualitative Research on Norms and International Relations." *Review of International Studies* 35 (1): 175–93.

– 2014. *A Theory of Contestation*. New York: Springer.

Winanti, Poppy Sulistyaning, and Hasrul Hanif. 2020. "When Global Norms Meet Local Politics: Localizing Transparency in Extractive Industries Governance." *Environmental Policy and Governance* 30 (5): 263–75.

Wintour, Patrick. 2021. "UN Palestine Refugee Agency 'Close to Collapse' after Funding Cuts." *Guardian*, 5 November 2021. https://www.theguardian.com/world/2021/nov/05/un-palestine-aid-agency-is-close-to-collapse-after-funding-cuts. Accessed 14 February 2023.

WOLA (Washington Office on Latin America). 2018. "WOLA Report: The Zero Tolerance Policy." 16 July 2018. https://www.wola.org/analysis/wola-report-zero-tolerance-policy/. Accessed 14 February 2023.

Wolff, Jonas, and Lisbeth Zimmermann. 2016. "Between Banyans and Battle Scenes: Liberal Norms, Contestation, and the Limits of Critique." *Review of International Studies* 42 (3): 513–34.

7

The Changing Contours of Migration Governance in Canada

Triadafilos Triadafilopoulos and Zack Taylor

States across the Global North invest significant resources into the management of migration. At the core of these efforts is selectivity. Advanced industrialized democracies increasingly admit immigrants based primarily on their likelihood of contributing to the economy and perceived ability to successfully integrate into the society of the receiving state. Where migration is required to meet regional or sector-specific demands for labour, carefully administered temporary foreign worker (TFW) programs, often organized through bilateral agreements between migrant-sending and migrant-receiving states, are the instrument of choice. The quest for "appropriate" immigrants has also led to the expansion of pathways to permanent residency for international students who earn their degrees in many receiving countries' post-secondary institutions. Even refugee resettlement schemes rely on selectivity, to demonstrate that receiving states are meeting their humanitarian obligations and responding to the needs of the "truly" persecuted. The strict deterrence of irregular migration represents the apex of selectivity. Thus, the borders of nation-states are *selectively permeable*, letting in some while excluding others.

Official rhetoric regarding "successfully managed migration" in advanced industrialized democracies often points to positive-sum outcomes across both sending and destination states, as well as for migrants themselves. Highly skilled immigrants with a pathway to citizenship pursue social mobility for themselves and their children, while TFWs earn higher wages and sending states reap the benefits of remittances, fuelling economic development. Receiving societies supplement their shrinking populations with new cohorts of well-educated and skilled prospective citizens, while providing succour to bona fide refugees, and benefiting from the infusion of sector- and region-specific labour provided by guest workers. This official narrative of "win-win" outcomes for states and migrants of course provides a very partial – and indeed misleading – picture of the realities of contemporary migration policies.

Any system of well-managed migration requires the efficient exclusion of unwanted migrants. This is especially true of uninvited migrants who exercise their agency by choosing their destinations and seeking access to them through various means, including irregular entry, sometimes with the aid of increasingly sophisticated networks of smugglers. The overall scale of the challenge for receiving states is, for the most part, relatively unimportant. However, irregular modes of access – via small boats and/or dangerous land crossings – tend to evoke more intense media attention and, hence, more scrutiny from democratic publics. From the standpoint of political leaders and policymakers, what is important is providing these publics with evidence that unwanted, unselected, and unauthorized migration is being met by effective countermeasures.

The dialectical interplay of openness and closure that is at the heart of managed migration has led to a two-sided trend in migration governance. More and more countries have opened themselves to migration, implementing various measures to admit highly skilled immigrants, with substantial rights and access to permanent residency. There has also been a parallel uptake in measures centred on lower-skilled TFWs, with more circumscribed rights and limited access to permanent residency (Ruhs 2013). This shift toward greater openness to some classes of economic migrants has coincided with a ratcheting up of coercive measures aimed at restricting access to unselected and unwanted migrants, including asylum seekers (de Haas, Natter, and Vezzoli 2018). In a world in which more and more people are willing and able to cross international borders, control measures undertaken to demonstrate successful stewardship of borders are an essential component of managed migration policy regimes.

The contending logics of managed migration are especially evident in Canada. Since the late 1980s, successive Canadian governments have expanded access to economic migrants, while limiting access to less desirable family class immigrants and asylum seekers (Ellermann 2021). Control over unwanted migration has helped build popular support for expansive migration policies. Indeed, Canada is noteworthy for not only demonstrating consistently high levels of public support for immigration, but for the apparent cross-party consensus on the need for economic migration. Refugee resettlement programs, which are also selective, have been expanded by Canadian governments in part to demonstrate that Canada is meeting its humanitarian obligations.

The Canadian case also demonstrates the changing nature of migration governance. Up until the mid-2000s, the federal government was responsible for almost all immigrant selection (with an important exception for Quebec, which gained significant control over this area in the 1990s). Under this immigration regime, admission policy aimed at recruiting highly skilled immigrants vetted by the "points system" through the Federal Skilled Worker Program (FSWP). However, this centralized, top-down approach was found wanting for several reasons:

1 highly skilled immigrants lacked Canadian credentials and work experience and therefore fared poorly in the labour market;
2 most immigrants settled in only a few parts of the country – principally in southern Ontario, in the Greater Toronto and Hamilton Area (GTHA) – so that most provinces received relatively few immigrants; and
3 employers complained that immigration policy did little to address their needs for workers, especially in lower-skilled occupations and in regions outside of southern Ontario, the Lower Mainland of British Columbia, and in the Greater Montreal Area.

Over the past two decades, Canadian governments have responded by reinventing Canada's immigration policy, making it more responsive to the needs of employers, provinces, and other stakeholders, such as colleges and universities. Canada now admits more TFWs than immigrants and the proportion of lower-skilled guest workers has increased significantly, through both TFW programs and the International Mobility Program (IMP), which is subject to limited oversight (Lange, Skuterud, and Worswick 2022; O'Donnell and Skuterud 2022). Provincial Nominee Programs (PNP) have been expanded, granting provinces more say in admissions, while the number of international students attending Canadian colleges and universities has expanded massively, in part because rules regulating international graduates' access to the Canadian labour market have been liberalized through the Canadian Experience Class (CEC) scheme (Schinnerl 2021). The PNP and CEC have engendered the significant expansion of two-step migration, whereby migrants who arrive on a temporary visa (for example through the IMP or on a study permit) apply for permanent residency. In the field of refugee resettlement, the private sponsorship program expanded significantly between 2016 and 2019, while the number of government-sponsored refugees has remained relatively stable, with the exception of 2016, the year of large-scale Syrian refugee settlement.

The federal government now oversees an immigration program that grants greater authority to a broad array of public and private actors. This approach to migration governance addresses some of the problems associated with the more centralized framework that emerged from the late 1980s to the mid-2000s. However, Canada's current approach has spawned its own set of concerns and demands, including requests for an expansion of two-step migration to include lower-skilled TFWs, many of whom were deemed "essential workers" during the government-mandated shutdowns associated with the COVID-19 pandemic. Some observers worry that the merits of the previous centralized model, which privileged highly skilled and adaptable immigrants, have been lost in the rush to establish a loosely structured system based on short-term demands (Lange, Skuterud, and Worswick 2022). Critics have also pointed out that TFWs and international students have been subject to abuse, in part because newer programs are so loosely regulated (Hune-Brown 2021).

Our chapter begins by looking at the broad dynamics that have come to increasingly define migration policy across advanced industrialized democracies. After elaborating our argument concerning managed migration and the selective permeability of national borders, we turn to the Canadian case, noting that from the late 1980s to the early 2000s, governments consciously built popular support for a robust system of managed migration by targeting highly skilled economic immigrants, curtailing family class immigration, and narrowing access to asylum seekers. The result was the first iteration of what some refer to as the Canadian "model" of immigration governance. While the aim of enforcing strict control over unwanted, irregular migration has been maintained, and new measures have been introduced to this end, other elements of the Canadian model have given way to a more decentralized and fragmented approach that has more in common with countries such as the United States and Germany, which also rely on two-step migration. As such, Canada represents a premier example of the emerging mode of migration governance among industrialized democracies in North America and beyond. The degree to which a governance model that combines selectivity (buttressed by illiberal restrictions on unwanted migrants) and dispersed authority in admissions is ultimately workable remains to be seen, however. We conclude by discussing potential future tensions in Canada's emerging migration governance model, tensions which remain especially salient given the marked interest across other states in emulating elements of the Canadian migration regime.

MANAGED MIGRATION AND SELECTIVE PERMEABILITY

Over the course of the 1990s, 2000s, and 2010s, advanced industrialized democracies have increasingly adopted managed migration policies. Typically, these emerging policy regimes include some means of selecting permanent, economic immigrants, usually well-educated and highly skilled individuals with knowledge of the receiving state's official language(s) and work-related skills. Formal ranking or "points" systems have grown in popularity, based on their promise of measuring prospective immigrants' "human capital." Depending on the precise nature of a given state's admissions regime, an offer of employment may also be taken into consideration. In some cases (e.g., Germany), the turn to selective immigration policies targeting highly skilled workers has led to the fashioning of an official state narrative of "welcome" that features positive declarations of the benefits of cultural diversity (Triadafilopoulos 2019). New countries of managed migration have also made it much easier for international students who earn their degrees at their post-secondary institutions to find paid work and apply for permanent residency, which in most cases puts them on a path toward citizenship via naturalization (Baas 2019).

The targeting of skilled workers and well-educated university and college graduates is meant to satisfy demands for "knowledge workers" and provide some assurance to democratic publics that these prospective permanent residents and potential citizens will be successfully integrated. The policy narratives that typically accompany highly skilled immigration tend to highlight the benefits of such flows for the receiving society. Highly skilled immigrants are deemed to provide the much-needed skilled labour that advanced industrialized states require and contribute to both the economic and social-political development of the receiving society. Within these narratives, selective immigration policies that focus on the recruitment of the world's "best and brightest" make immigration "safe" for the nation-state (Winter 2021).

Growing recognition of regional and sector-specific labour market needs have led to the return of guest-worker migration in advanced industrialized democracies. Unlike policies targeting the highly skilled, TFW programs operate in the shadows and frequently lack an accompanying policy narrative. Nevertheless, they account for growing numbers of migrants in advanced industrialized democracies. Contemporary managed migration systems typically combine immigration policies offering permanent residency to highly skilled workers with TFW programs that offer a much more constrained set of rights and little to no access to permanent residency to lower-skilled workers. The increased uptake of these policies across advanced industrialized democracies signals that the old distinction between labour-importing "guest workers countries" and "settler nations" no longer holds (Dauvergne 2016).

While all states party to the Refugee Convention must consider asylum seekers' claims to refugee status, there has also been growing interest and experimentation with refugee resettlement policies, patterned after those pioneered by Canada and the United States (Smith 2020). Resettlement programs enable states to fulfill their humanitarian obligations under international law, while also responding the demands of domestic humanitarian interest groups and maintaining a degree of selectivity (exercised by governments and private groups that sponsor refugees). Crucially, refugee resettlement initiatives are inherently discretionary in the context of the refugee regime; resettlement is therefore highly consistent with the broader priorities underlying managed migration and is perceived by both policymakers and the publics as explicitly state controlled. The narrative around resettlement frequently features appeals to meeting the needs of the "truly" persecuted and dispossessed. Conversely, asylum seekers are often accused of exploiting the Refugee Convention to access countries otherwise closed to them.

The proliferation of instruments of openness – points systems, TFW programs, and refugee resettlement schemes – has coincided with the simultaneous expansion of "global regimes of closure," which feature their own array of policy instruments including, but not limited to, expansive visa controls, carrier sanctions, safe third country agreements (STCAs), border fortifications, detentions, and offshore processing of asylum claims (FitzGerald 2019). As noted, this is no coincidence. To be successful politically, governments must demonstrate to voters that they are in control of their borders and immigration is being administered to advance the national interest (Ruhs 2013). Unselected and uninvited migrants that arrive through irregular means usually catalyze strong reactions, regardless of their number. It is the irregularity of unplanned entries that generates a rhetoric of "crisis" amplified by the media and critics of immigration, most notably extreme right-wing populist parties (Krzyżanowski 2020). The need to impose effective border control, in the name of maintaining public support for managed migration, leads governments to search for new methods, often borrowing innovations pioneered by other jurisdictions. The democratically derived demand for control also leads to innovations in the global governance of migration, with rich receiving countries working with authoritarian sending and transit states to restrict flows of irregular migrants.

To sum up, contemporary managed migration schemes seek to square the contending logics of economically desirable openness with democratically required closure. These trends therefore represent something of an intensification of what Hollifield (2004) earlier identified as the "emerging migration state" – one that balances the extension of rights with the imperatives of maintaining security and promoting economic development. Evolving forms of migration governance allow for the admission of some classes of migrants while pursuing the strict control and exclusion of others, in the name of upholding public support for managed migration. While greater openness marks the liberalization of mobility in the twenty-first century, the evermore novel modes of exclusion require the illiberal application of coercive state power, to limit the rights of TFWs and deter unplanned flows of uninvited migrants to the greatest extent possible.

Control over unwanted migrants is exercised by central governments, often through cooperation with other states, but the responsibility for the selection of economic migrants is dispersed to a range of public and private actors, including substate governments, employers, and post-secondary educational institutions. Canada serves as an excellent case for demonstrating this shift toward more fragmented forms of selective permeability.

MANAGED MIGRATION AND SELECTIVE PERMEABILITY IN CANADA: TOWARD THE "CANADIAN MODEL"

Managed migration has long been key to Canada's economic and political development, with the selection process reflecting prevailing occupational and racial preferences (FitzGerald and Cook-Martín 2014; Triadafilopoulos 2012). The National Policy, introduced by Canada's federal government in 1878, called for the promotion of immigration to facilitate the settlement of the then newly established western provinces, stimulate domestic demand for goods and services, and meet the labour needs of a nascent manufacturing sector (Kelley and Trebilcock 2010, 62–3). Farmers were granted preference in admissions, along with "white" Europeans and North Americans. Racialized groups, such as "Asiatics" were strictly excluded through a panoply of laws and regulations. Selection based on occupational and racial distinctions was a crucial tool in Canada's efforts to settle its western territories while preserving its identity as a "white man's country" (Triadafilopoulos 2012, 35–6).

World War II catalyzed a gradual shift away from racially discriminatory immigration policies, both in Canada and across other advanced industrialized democracies (FitzGerald and Cook-Martín 2014; Joppke 2005; Triadafilopoulos 2012). The discrediting of scientific racism, emergence of a global human rights regime, and acceleration of the decolonization movement contributed to the questioning of the legitimacy of Canada's racialized admissions system. Domestic reformers, foreign governments, and international organizations leveraged this shift in normative contexts to vigorously challenge Canada's discriminatory immigration policies (Triadafilopoulos 2012). Changes to immigration policy in the 1950s granted some access to previously excluded groups (Elrick 2022). Immigrants demonstrating "exceptional merit" were exempted from racially restrictive controls, to assuage criticism of Canadian policy while adapting immigration to meet the needs of an urbanizing, knowledge-based economy and middle-class society (Elrick 2022).

In 1962, the Diefenbaker government publicly announced that Canada would no longer refer to race in its admissions decisions. The introduction of the "points system" in 1967 reinforced this trend by formally introducing an immigration system that excluded considerations of race as a basis for admission. The points system drew on the experiments of the 1950s and the early 1960s, making human capital the principal means of weighing prospective immigrants' suitability, universalizing immigrant admissions, and aligning immigration policy with Canada's transformation into an increasingly urban, industrialized society. It also signalled to critics that Canadian governments were serious about moving away from race as a criterion for selection.

The changes to immigration policy introduced through the 1950s and the 1960s were entrenched in the Immigration Act of 1976. The fundamental principles and objectives of Canadian immigration policy set out in the 1976 Immigration Act endure to this day. They include:

1 promotion of economic, social, demographic, and cultural goals;
2 endorsement of family reunification; and
3 fulfillment of Canada's international obligations under the United Nations 1951 Convention and 1967 Protocol Relating to Refugees (Knowles 2007, 169).

The Immigration Act defined three classes of immigrants: the economic class, selected through the points system; the family class, recruited through sponsorship by Canadian citizens and permanent residents; and the humanitarian class, which included individuals resettled by the Canadian state and authorized private sponsors, and individuals claiming asylum after arriving in Canada ("inland" claimants/asylum seekers). As with previous immigration acts, the detailed operation of Canada's immigration system would be determined by regulations, with an important role for ministerial discretion.

By the mid-1980s, the human capital orientation of Canada's immigration system was challenged by shifts in overall admissions. The share of family

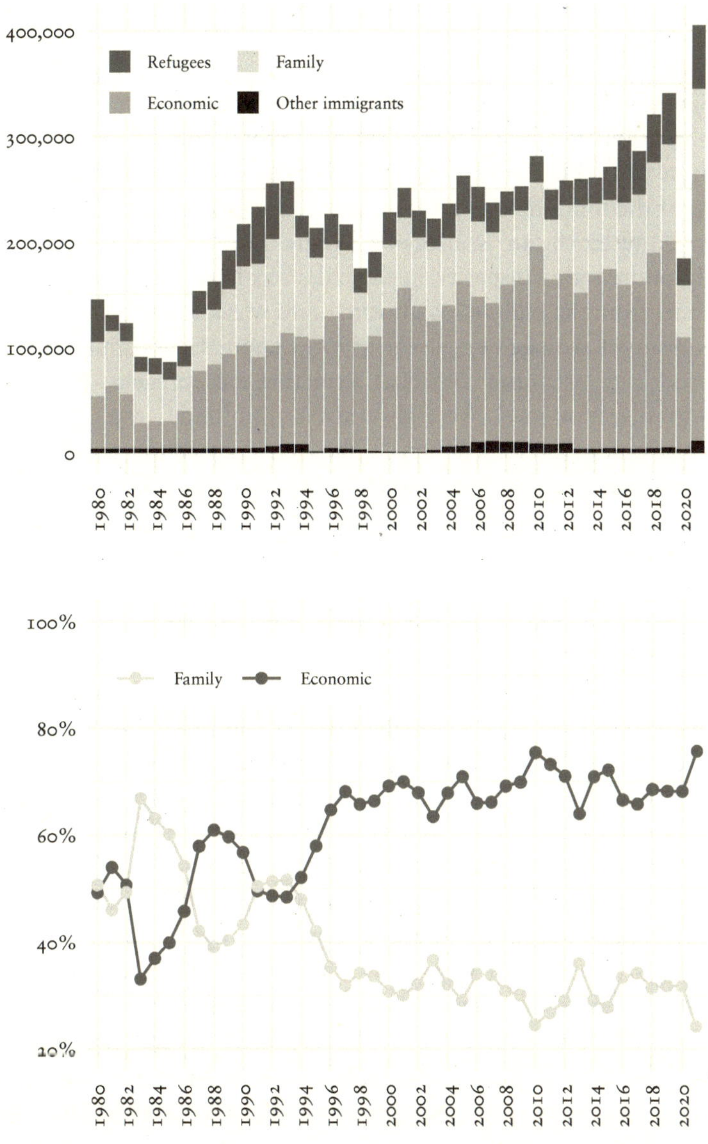

Figure 7.1 | Permanent resident admissions by Canada by class, 1980–2021

Note: The overall volume of permanent resident admissions has increased considerably since the early 1980s (top panel). Since the mid-1990s, policy has favoured economic class migrants selected on the basis of education, skills, and official language competence over family reunification (bottom panel). Total immigration was lower in 2020 due to COVID-19 pandemic-related border restrictions.

Source: Immigration, Refugees, and Citizenship Canada (2016, 2022b).

class immigrants, which accounted for 35 per cent of the total immigration intake in 1975, rose to 55 per cent in 1983, while the share of economic class immigrants fell from 73 per cent of the total admissions in 1971 to 31 per cent in 1983 (Ellerman 2021, 217). Family class admissions exceeded 60 per cent of the total immigration intake from 1983 to 1985 (see figure 7.1).

Prime Minister Brian Mulroney's Progressive Conservative government began to address this disparity in the balance of economic and family class immigrants from the mid-1980s onward. This was accomplished by dropping a prerequisite of arranged employment for economic class applicants in 1986 and introducing programs aimed at attracting entrepreneurs and investors. Annual immigration levels were also raised, from under 100,000 in 1985 to over 200,000 in 1990 (see figure 7.1). These changes led to a tripling of admissions of economic immigrants between 1985 and 1989 (Ellermann 2021, 222).

The Mulroney Conservative government tabled a five-year plan in 1990, calling for immigration to continue to rise to an annual intake of 250,000 individuals by 1995. Future immigration levels would remain at 250,000 per year, regardless of prevailing economic conditions. This marked an end to Canada's traditional "tap-on/tap-off" approach, which tied economic immigration to the state of the economy. A 1992 report, *Managing Immigration: A Framework for the 1990s*, justified the decision to increase immigration levels independently of labour market conditions by pointing to Canada's transition to a "globalized, highly competitive, knowledge-based economy" (Simmons 2010, 82–3). The report also called for further reductions to family class immigration. As Ellermann (2021, 224) notes, "[b]y 1995 ... the per centage of family immigrants had dropped from 50 per cent in 1984, when Mulroney took office, to 36 per cent" (see figure 7.1).

This transformation of Canadian immigration policies would prove to be enduring, setting the stage for an emerging cross-party consensus on the importance of economic migration. The Liberal governments of prime ministers Jean Chrétien and Paul Martin completed the Mulroney Conservatives' efforts to shift Canada's immigration policy toward attracting large numbers of highly skilled economic immigrants. By the late 1990s, political parties, civil servants, and key stakeholders – most notably employers – agreed on the need for Canada's immigration system to complement a labour market that prized flexibility.

The move toward a more economically driven approach was influenced by a combination of neoliberal ideas (Joppke 2021) and, perhaps more importantly, claims that Canada's prevailing policies failed to advance the national interest. During the late 1980s and the 1990s, the populist Reform Party and other critics pointed to the size of family class admissions, arguing that sponsored immigrants, who were not vetted by the points system, typically lacked the tools needed to succeed in a knowledge-based economy (Abu-Laban 1998). Elderly parents and grandparents were singled out as especially unproductive – and costly – consumers of welfare benefits. The Canadian public shared many of these concerns and support for immigration was tepid through the 1980s and early-to-mid-1990s. The shift to an immigration program focused on the recruitment of highly skilled immigrants, who would serve the national interest, sought to defuse these criticisms, and generate more public support for Canada's immigration policies.

The late 1980s and the early 1990s were also marked by increasingly contentious debates over asylum seekers (Kelley and Trebilcock 2010). As a signatory to the 1951 Refugee Convention and its 1967 Protocol, Canada was required to consider all applications for asylum made on Canadian territory. This obligation was reinforced by the 1976 Immigration Act's acknowledgement that Canada would fulfill its "international legal obligations with respect to refugees and … uphold its humanitarian tradition with respect to the displaced and persecuted" (Labman 2019, 40). As Shauna Labman (2019, 44) has argued, there is an important distinction contained in this statement. Whereas Canada's legal obligations under the Refugee Convention pertained to its treatment of asylum seekers who made a refugee claim upon landing in Canada, the invocation of Canada's "humanitarian tradition" referred to a history of resettling refugees through discretionary acts of kindness, typically exercised in an ad hoc manner, and based on a high degree of self-interest.

Changes in the dynamics of international migration in the late 1980s and the 1990s forced Canadian policymakers to significantly reconsider their approach toward refugees. Asylum claims rose steadily in the 1980s and precipitously in the 1990s. The arrival of asylum seekers by boat, often with the assistance of human smugglers, generated intense media coverage and led to heightened concerns about the integrity of Canada's system of border control. In this context the Reform Party "raised the spectre of 'illegal immigration' and 'bogus refugees' to further demonstrate [its] contention that Canadian immigration policy and immigration regulations were too lax" (Abu-Laban and Gabriel 2002, 64). This broader context also witnessed the growing politicization of asylum policy in public debate.

As was true of their efforts to tamp down family class admissions, Canadian governments responded to these criticisms with legislation to discourage asylum seeking. After 173 asylum seekers arrived by boat off the coast of Nova Scotia in July 1987, the Mulroney government amended the Immigration Act to "deter refugee claimants, impose more stringent detention provisions, and expand inadmissibility provisions" (Kelley and Trebilcock 2010, 406). It also passed Bill C-86 in 1992 to prohibit refugee claimants from "seeking employment until a final determination of their claim" had been made (Kelley and Trebilcock 2010, 408). When four ships containing some 600 migrants from China arrived on Canada's shores in the summer of 1999, many of the immigrants, including children, were detained until their identities could be confirmed. Most of these individuals were returned to China, and only about 5 per cent of those who claimed refugee status were granted asylum or allowed to remain on a Minister's Permit (Kelley and Trebilcock 2010, 422).

By the end of the 1990s, the basic parameters and priorities of the Canadian model of immigration and refugee policy were in place, exemplifying what Joppke (2021) characterizes as "courting the top" while "fending off the bottom." Immigration aimed first and foremost at meeting Canada's economic needs through the recruitment of well-educated and highly skilled immigrants. While family class immigration would continue to be an important part of Canada's immigration program, its standing as compared to economic migration was decidedly inferior. Although Canada was obliged to consider claims for asylum by uninvited migrants that managed to gain a foothold in Canadian territory, measures would be taken to reduce their numbers and streamline the status determination process. As we point out ahead, refugee policy would emphasize resettlement, which was also based on selection.

The entrenchment of these core principles of Canada's immigration policy were clear in the Immigration and Refugee Protection Act (IRPA) of 2001. The minister of immigration and citizenship, Elinor Caplan, described it as a "tough bill" designed to enable the government to close "the back door to those who would abuse the system" to ensure "that the front door will remain open … to genuine refugees and to the immigrants our country will need to grow and prosper in the years ahead" (cited in Kelley and Trebilcock 2010, 425). The IRPA's "skeletal" structure established a broad framework for immigration policymaking, "leaving the details to the executive to design and implement through regulation, with minimal parliamentary scrutiny" (Kelley and Trebilcock 2010, 425). This regulatory framework would, when combined with considerable ministerial discretion, provide the basis for subsequent evolution of the Canadian immigration regime.

TOWARD FRAGMENTATION: A NEW MODEL OF MIGRATION GOVERNANCE

As Canadian decision-makers intended, annual admissions since the early 2000s have skewed heavily toward economic immigrants. The FSWP favoured the admission of immigrants with advanced degrees, professional designations, and extensive foreign work experience. However, by the mid-

2000s, academics and other analysts noted that these well-qualified immigrants experienced worrying rates of unemployment and falling earnings relative to native-born Canadians and previous immigrant cohorts, despite having satisfied the more stringent admission requirements (Boyd 2013; Reitz, Curtis, and Elrick 2014). The FSWP, which traditionally operated on a first-come-first-served basis, was also beset by backlogs, with applicants typically waiting several years to have their cases decided.

The Conservative government of Prime Minister Stephen Harper sought to address these problems through several reforms which shifted authority away from the federal government to employers, provinces, and other actors, while simultaneously allowing far more dynamic and fine-grained shifts in admissions. The introduction of the Express Entry system, which parallels the FSWP, marks an important and fundamental component of this shift (Hiebert 2019). Applicants submit a "preliminary expression of interest" which is screened by the federal government through a new – and considerably more complex – comprehensive ranking system that scores education, skills, work experience, language ability, and other measures of human capital. Would-be immigrants receive additional points if they have a job offer from an employer or have been nominated by a provincial or territorial government. Applicants who exceed the points threshold are invited to apply in periodic "draws" from the pool. Unlike in the past, applicants do not need to apply from outside Canada; they may hold visas as TFWs or foreign students and receive extra points for Canadian work experience. Selecting from a pool of applicants already in Canada is meant to improve immigrants' economic and social integration, thereby addressing one of the principal shortcomings of the preceding Canadian model. The Express Entry system is also designed to avoid the backlogs that impacted the original "points system." However, at the time of writing, Canada's immigration system is beset by unprecedented backlogs in processing applications across all programs: for permanent residency, citizenship, and all manner of visas (Dayal 2022).

Express Entry is part of a more general trend toward "two-step" immigration, through which TFWs and international students can convert their temporary status to permanent residency. Two-step pathways have grown in importance as the number of migrants admitted under low- and high-skill TFW schemes and as students has dramatically increased. The number of international study permit holders grew from 122,665 in 2000 to 617,250 in 2021. Over the same period, the number of TFWs, including those under the IMP, grew from 66,625 to 519,880.[1] While the TFW program requires employers to prove, through a Labour Market Impact Assessment (LMIA) that temporary workers are required to fill labour

Table 7.1 | Region of citizenship of permit holders by year permit issued by Canada, 2022

Region	Temporary Foreign Worker	International Mobility Program	International Student
Africa	4%	5%	9%
Caribbean	10%	1%	1%
Central Asia	0%	0%	1%
East Asia	12%	13%	25%
Europe	6%	31%	9%
Latin America	49%	6%	6%
Middle East	1%	3%	4%
North America	1%	4%	2%
Oceania	0%	2%	0%
South Asia	14%	34%	38%
Southeast Asia	2%	1%	4%
Stateless	0%	0%	0%
TOTAL	129,015	428,510	621,565

Note: Top three sources in each stream are highlighted in black and grey, respectively. Data are for January to November 2022 (most recent available).
Source: Immigration, Refugees, and Citizenship Canada (2022d).

market gaps, the IMP, which includes employees of multinational corporations transferring location, post-graduate employees, and spouses of skilled workers and students, does not. Although controversy has led to new restrictions on the TFW program, the IMP has expanded dramatically in recent years (O'Donnell and Skuterud 2022; Vosko 2022).

While Canada has long since abandoned racial or country-of-origin criteria, these programs predominantly draw from countries whose populations are de facto racialized groups in Canada (see Chartrand and Vosko 2021; Vosko 2022). A majority of low-skilled TFWs work either in the agricultural or care sectors; most of the former come from Central America (especially Mexico and Guatemala), while most of the latter come from the Philippines and Caribbean countries. Half of higher-skilled IMP visa holders come from South Asia, China and East Asia, and the Middle East. A majority of international students are from South and East Asia – principally India and China (see table 7.1). Arguably, the selection outcomes that have come to predominate these programs appear to reproduce racialized patterns of immigration.

The CEC allows international students who earn post-secondary degrees in Canada to apply to have their status changed to permanent residents. As the number of international students has grown, they have become a lucrative source of revenue for colleges and universities, who lobbied successfully for the liberalization of policies regulating international graduates' access to the Canadian labour market (Schinnerl 2021). Many post-secondary institutions have formed relationships with international recruitment agents to which they pay as much as CAD 5,000 per student (Hune-Brown 2021). Journalists have reported on the unscrupulous behaviour of some of these agents as well as the exploitation of foreign students by landlords and private vocational colleges (Bascaramurty, Bhatt, and Rana 2021; Kahlon 2022).

Selection for these pathways increasingly involve subnational governments. The PNP, introduced by the Liberals in 1995, is meant to assist low-immigrant provinces and territories by enabling them to select a limited number of economic migrants, including low-skilled TFWs, in accordance with their demographic and labour market needs. By 2007, all the provinces (except Quebec, which already been granted extensive power to select immigrants through the Canada-Quebec Accord, 1991) and two of Canada's three northern territories had enacted PNP agreements (Banting 2012). PNP began modestly; however, by 2019 this migration stream constituted over a third of total economic immigration. A new municipal nomination program, launched in 2021, may play a growing role in the future.

These policy changes amount to the fragmentation and decentralization of the previously highly centralized system of migrant selection based on human capital characteristics. They also vindicate Pierson's dictum that policy begets politics, as the feedback effects of the CEC and PNP have supercharged the lobbying efforts of universities and colleges and the provinces (Pierson 1993). Today, a significant proportion of migrants are effectively selected by employers and university and college recruiters and registrars, with the provinces playing an important intermediary role. The result is a departure from the commonly held image of the "Canadian model" in which economic immigrants are selected according to uniform criteria – the traditional "points system" introduced in 1976. As Banting (2012, 104) puts it, Canada has moved "from a world in which one government was clearly responsible for immigration to one in which everyone and no one is in charge and accountable." This represents a significant – and arguably fundamental – transformation of the Canadian approach to managed migration.

DIFFERENTIAL ACCESS: REGULATING ASYLUM SEEKERS AND REFUGEES

Less visible to Canadians, at least most of the time, is the admission of refugees and asylum seekers. In some countries, these categories are conflated with "immigration" more broadly. In Canada, there is a firm distinction between selective (economic) immigration, the planned resettlement of refugees per international obligations, and the management of unplanned flows of irregular asylum seekers. The federal government has continued to maintain tight control over the regulation of irregular migration through its policies on asylum seeking. However, responsibility for refugee resettlement has increasingly been delegated to private sponsors, in keeping with the more general trend toward fragmentation discussed earlier.

The organization of Canada's refugee system has enabled this trend. The system features two distinct parts: the In-Canada Asylum Program and the Refugee and Humanitarian Resettlement Program. The asylum program provides protection to people in Canada unable or unwilling to return to their home country because they have a well-founded fear of persecution (as per the Refugee Convention) or are at risk of torture, or cruel or unusual punishment (as per the United Nations Convention Against Torture and Other Cruel, Inhuman or Degrading Treatment or Punishment). Successful claimants receive convention refugee status or are deemed a "person in need of protection" (in cases that fall under the UN Convention on Torture) and are eligible to apply for permanent residency. Failed claimants receive a conditional removal order and must leave Canada within thirty days of the decision. However, rejected claimants may seek a stay of removal and apply for leave for judicial review, a temporary resident permit, a pre-removal risk assessment, or permanent residency on humanitarian and compassionate grounds; appeal their decision to the Refugee Appeal Division (RAD); or seek judicial review through the Federal Court. Many of these procedural protections have become increasingly entrenched in Canadian asylum policy since the 1980s, and notably predate the changes in the dynamics of international migration and growing politicization of asylum discussed earlier.

Asylum Seekers

Asylum policy has always been controversial. Public dissatisfaction has increased when asylum seekers have landed in Canada, usually by boat, without prearranged authorization. These events have raised public concern that economic migrants, who would not otherwise qualify for admission to Canada, are using rules designed to protect the rights of refugees to enter the country (Lawlor and Tolley 2017). Irvine (2011, 186) finds that immigration officials share these concerns. Some of his interviewees stated that "an overly fair refugee determination system, too many opportunities to appeal decisions, and long delays in processing claims [made] the Canadian system more susceptible to abuse." Officials have also remained sensitive to the impacts of these perceptions on broader Canadian support for sustained immigration (Paquet 2021).

Governments have responded to public concern by recalibrating criteria and procedures. Less than nine months after a ship carrying Tamil migrants landed off the coast of British Columbia, the Harper government passed Bill C-11, the Balanced Refugee Reform Act, in June 2010. In August of that year, a second ship carrying Tamil migrants landed in British Columbia. Before the ship reached the port, a Citizenship and Immigration Canada spokesman announced that the government was committed to "cracking down on bogus refugees, while providing protection to those that truly need our help" (cited in Labman 2019, 48). Two months later, the government introduced Bill C-49, the Preventing Human Smugglers from Abusing Canada's Immigration System Act. The bill, which died on the order paper when the 2011 election was called, was reintroduced after the Conservatives won a majority government. Bill C-31, the Protecting Canada's Immigration System Act, came into effect on 28 June 2012.

According to the new rules, asylum seekers arriving from "designated countries of origin" (DCOs) that generally do not produce refugees have their applications decided on a fast-track basis, with the intent to expedite their removals. Refugees who arrive in a group of two or more fall under the "irregular arrivals" category and are termed "designated foreign nationals" (DFNs) (Labman 2019, 49). They may be detained while their applications are considered and cannot appeal if their claims are rejected. Even when they receive convention refugee status, DFNs face a "five-year suspension before being eligible to apply for permanent residency, temporary residency, or permanent residency on humanitarian and compassionate grounds" (Labman 2019, 50).

Perhaps as a result of these policy changes, asylum claims fell between 2012 and 2016. They rose sharply in 2017 and 2018, due to changes to American immigration and refugee policies. The Trump administration adopted a more hostile and punitive approach to irregular migration, especially at the United States' southern border with Mexico. Seeking more favourable treatment, many asylum seekers residing in the United States crossed the Canada-US land border irregularly, bypassing official points of entry to avoid being sent back under the terms of the 2002 Canada-US Safe Third Country Agreement (which holds that asylum seekers must make their claim in the country of first arrival; see Banerjee in this volume for further discussion). This drew significant press attention, raising concerns regarding the Canadian government's ability to control its borders (Boyd and Ly 2021).

The Liberal government of Prime Minister Justin Trudeau introduced legislation to check the flow of asylum seekers in its 2019 omnibus budget bill. Changes included an amendment to the IRPA, "denying refugee claimants the right to a hearing if they ever sought asylum in any country 'holding information-sharing agreements' with Canada" (Boyd and Ly 2021). The budget also included "substantial funding for enhanced law enforcement" and a "comprehensive Border Enforcement Strategy to 'better detect and intercept individuals who cross Canadian borders irregularly and *who try to exploit Canada's immigration system*'" (Boyd and Ly 2021, emphasis in the original). The Trudeau government's stance on asylum seekers in 2019 demonstrates that the hardening of policies toward asylum seekers is based on a durable and long-standing consensus between the federal Liberal and Conservative parties. Strict control of irregular migration, overseen by the federal government, remains a critical part of Canada's otherwise transformed immigration system.

Refugee Resettlement

Although asylum seekers select Canada as a potential site of refuge, Canada's Refugee and Humanitarian Resettlement Program endows the Canadian state and authorized private sponsors with the power to decide who merits sanctuary. Government-assisted refugees (GARs) are referred by the United Nations High Commissioner for Refugees (UNHCR) and already meet the conditions of the Refugee Convention. The Government of Canada conducts additional vetting, facilitates their travel to Canada, grants them permanent residency upon arrival, and covers the costs of their resettlement for one year. GARs are entitled to services such as orientation sessions and life skills training through the Resettlement Assistance Program. After their first year in Canada, all resettled refugees are eligible for means-tested government social programs, including income-support programs for the unemployed, seniors, and the disabled.

Privately sponsored refugees (PSRs) are sponsored by groups of private individuals in Canada (Martani 2021). Private Sponsorship Agreement Holders (SAHs) are organizations that have a signed agreement with the Canadian government to sponsor a refugee or refugees, or to assist other sponsoring "constituent groups" with their applications. Faith-based organizations account for 75 per cent of SAHs (Hyndman, Payne, and Jiminez 2017, 58).

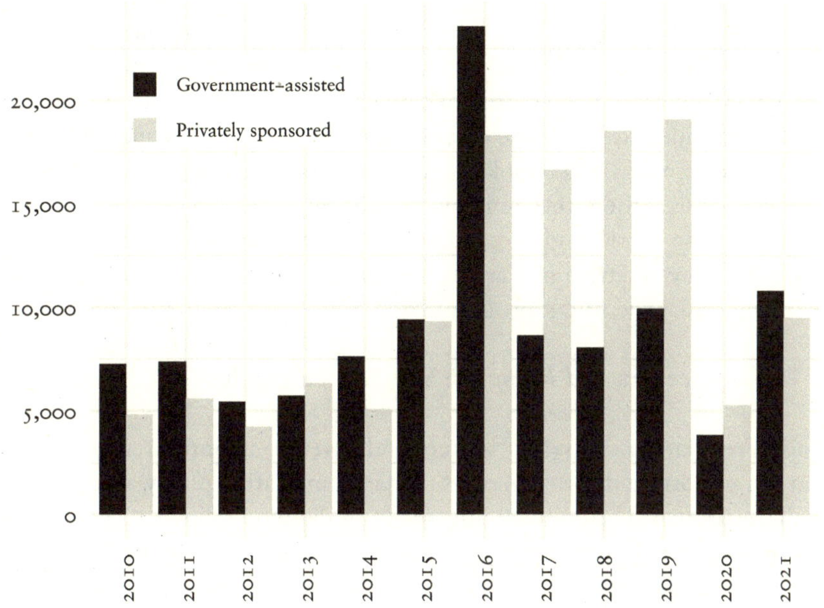

Figure 7.2 | Flows of government-assisted and privately sponsored refugees in Canada, 2010–21

Source: Immigration, Refugees, and Citizenship Canada (2016, 2022b).

Refugees can also be sponsored by "Groups of Five," through which five or more Canadian citizens and/or permanent residents, having demonstrated their financial means and sponsorship ability, enter into an agreement to support a refugee or refugees. Private sponsors are obliged to provide financial support to the refugees under their care for one year.

The overall size of Canada's refugee resettlement program remained relatively stable between 2000 and 2014, averaging about 11,500 per year, before more or less doubling between 2015 and 2019 – mostly as a result of the Syrian refugee emergency. A significant share of responsibility for refugee resettlement, like economic immigration, has been shifted to private actors, diminishing the federal government's role. In its 2012 budget, the Harper government shifted 1,000 refugees from the GAR program to private sponsorship and created the Blended Visa Office-Referred (BVOR) program. The latter matches convention refugees identified by the UNHCR with private sponsors in Canada, splitting settlement costs over one year between the government and private sponsors.

The share of resettled refugees falling under private sponsorship increased significantly between 2017 and 2019, eclipsing the GAR program after 2017 (see figure 7.2). The volume of refugees resettled declined during the COVID-19 pandemic. While the balance of refugees settled through the GAR and PSR programs in 2021 looks much the same as in 2015 – i.e., before the refugee crisis – the future remains unclear given the emergence of crises elsewhere in the world and the ongoing effects of the pandemic. In 2021, 9,505 PSRs were resettled in Canada, as against 10,805 GARs and 55 refugees falling under the BVOR program.

Asylum Seekers and Refugees: Selective Permeability in Action

Canada's regulation of asylum seekers and UNHCR-anointed refugees represents an important dimension of its managed migration policy, one that is, overall, restrictive. The political imperative of demonstrating that Canada's borders are secure has, in the past two decades, led to the hardening of the border toward asylum seekers, alongside the broader framing of irregular migrants as queue-jumpers and exploiters of Canadians' goodwill (Lawlor and Tolley 2017; Molnar Diop 2013).

Our evaluation of Canada's refugee resettlement system is equivocal. On the one hand, Canada has emerged as the world's top resettlement country (in terms of refugee numbers), surpassing the United States in 2018 (see Cameron and Labman in this volume for comparative discussion of these two cases). Canada's unique system of private sponsorship has also been applauded and efforts are underway to "export" it (Smith 2020). Canadian governments refer to their records in resettlement to demonstrate that they consistently meet their humanitarian obligations to refugees. On the other hand, Canada's substantive contribution to meeting the needs of the world's refugees is limited. Refugees have always accounted for the lowest share of annual immigration admissions. Even in 2016, which witnessed a one-time expansion of Canada's resettlement program to fulfill a Liberal Party election pledge to resettle 25,000 Syrian refugees, the admission of refugees accounted for less than 16 per cent of Canada's total immigration intake. Worth emphasizing in this context is the convergence of resettlement with the broader imperatives of Canada's migration management regime: unlike asylum seekers, resettled refugees are explicitly admitted under the discretion of the Canadian state. Of the 58,435 refugees admitted to Canada in 2016, 79.3 per cent came through resettlement programs; barely one-fifth came through the asylum program (Immigration, Refugees and Citizenship Canada 2017). Even if Canada's commitment to settling 30,000 refugees per year places it atop the world's refugee resettlement rankings, it is a modest gesture in a world in which the UNHCR designates approximately one million refugees in urgent need of resettlement (Lenard 2021). Nevertheless, Canadian governments regularly cast their refugee resettlement policies as evidence of Canada's efforts to solve the global refugee crisis.

CONCLUSION

Since the 1980s, successive Canadian governments have consistently geared Canada's migration policy regime to admitting economic immigrants and limiting access to family immigrants and asylum seekers. The Canadian public has voiced its support for this policy choice. Banting and Soroka (2020) have noted that public opinion on immigration has grown steadily more positive since Canada focused its efforts squarely on attracting economic immigrants and limiting unwanted migration. The Environics Institute for Survey Research's (2020) "Focus Canada" survey found that "strong and increasing majorities of Canadians express comfort with current immigration levels, see immigrants as good for the Canadian economy ... and believe that immigration is essential to building the country's population ... By a five-to-one margin, the public believes immigration makes Canada a better country." Public support has been reinforced by Canadian governments' success in presenting their policies through an effective governance narrative. As Daniel Hiebert (2016, 5) has noted, "framing immigration in economic terms and presenting it as a solution to the nation's problems has led to a mutually reinforcing set of outcomes: Canadians expect immigration to be coordinated with economic need and, as a result, they have typically supported immigration mainly when it is aligned with economic concerns." Going one step further, we would suggest that continued popular support for immigration more broadly is contingent on the Canadian state being perceived as an effective agent of migration management by voting publics. The dramatic expansion of IMP, international student admissions with limited oversight, and the emergence of "two-step" pathways to permanent residency with substantial involvement of subnational governments, universities, and colleges, complicates the public image of Canada having a centralized, points-based immigration and citizenship regime.

Support for immigration extends beyond public opinion to include the media, business and labour organizations, and civil society more broadly. Most remarkably, all three of Canada's major political parties agree on the fundamental features of Canada's immigration system (Taylor 2021). Anti-immigrant campaigns are rare. The People's Party of Canada's attempt to politicize immigration in the 2019 federal election ended with the party polling under 2 per cent and its leader, Maxime Bernier, losing his seat in the

House of Commons (Ling 2019). Bernier's party fared only slightly better in the 2021 federal election, with increased support coming from its opposition to the federal government's COVID-19 mandates and not immigration (Chown Oved 2021).

Canada's success in dampening anti-immigrant politics and managing an expansive immigration system geared toward admitting economic migrants has attracted the attention and earned the approval of foreign observers. The Organisation for Economic Co-operation and Development (OECD), the UNHCR, and other actors hold Canada up as a model worthy of emulation. Even former American president Donald Trump, the world's most infamous nativist, spoke favourably of Canada's selective immigration policies (Porter 2017).

Canada's emerging approach to migration governance is in line with a more general trend among industrialized democracies. Unwanted flows of unselected migrants are dealt with quickly, often through the rights-restrictive measures, such as the United Kingdom's move to "offshore" its asylum system, the radical cuts to refugee admissions in the United States, and ongoing efforts in Europe to strictly police asylum through an array of rights-restrictive initiatives. Interventions along these lines are defended with reference to enabling the efficient administration of immigration systems and maintaining the political support of voters wary of uncontrolled migration.

The Canadian case also reveals that successful managed migration policies generate significant costs that are mostly borne by migrants. Canada's byzantine system of TFW programs have created a large and growing cohort of precarious workers, many of them racialized, whose rights are necessarily limited. The vast majority of low-skill TFWs are "wanted" for their labour, but "not welcome" as prospective permanent residents and citizens (Zolberg 1987). Indeed, with few exceptions, the Canadian state has effectively implemented guest-worker programs that are designed to render the presence of TFW's permanently temporary. This dynamic is rooted in the core logic of all guest-worker systems, which are designed to treat human beings as economic inputs, purposefully obscuring their status as persons and severely liming their access to fundamental human rights (such as the right to mobility).

Even more clearly, Canada's steady narrowing of access to asylum seekers has helped build support for managed migration among the Canadian public but downgraded the status and rights of refugees. While there is no gainsaying that other countries have implemented even more egregiously illiberal policies to stem flows of unwanted migrants, including asylum seekers, Canada is very much part of this trend – the trajectory of which points toward continuing closure. The degree to which illiberal policies of closure, premised on political considerations rooted in deference to the will of voting publics, are compatible with the premises of liberal democracy is an open question. This question will only become more salient as climate change, political instability, and desperation borne out of economic decline in many parts of the world generate increasing flows of irregular migration.

The steady fragmentation of Canada's system of migration governance also raises questions concerning its long-term sustainability. Ongoing efforts by the Bank of Canada to reduce runaway inflation by raising interest rates have the Canadian economy, at the time of writing, poised to drift into recession (Lundy 2022a). Nevertheless, provinces and employers continue to demand increases to all forms of economic migration to meet acute demands for labour, including lower-skilled TFWs (Lundy 2022b). For their part, universities and colleges have grown increasingly dependent on the revenues generated by international students, and inflows of international students will remain high for the foreseeable future (Keung 2022). While the degree to which study permit holders take on low-skilled jobs during the course of their studies is unknown, there is mounting evidence suggesting that their contributions are significant (Crossman et al. 2021).

The Trudeau government has largely acceded to the demands of employers and provinces by raising its annual immigration targets and loosening restrictions on the TFW and IMP streams (Osman 2022; Subramaniam and Lundy 2022). There is no sign of a serious reconsideration of the steps taken to entrench two-step migration since the mid-2000s or revisit the consequences of moving away from a focus on skilled immigration to a system increasingly geared toward temporary flows of lower-skilled workers to fill labour market gaps. Moreover, the responsible federal minister announced in November 2022 the intention to increase the number of permanent resident admissions to 500,000 annually by 2025, even as it considers waiving eligibility requirements for 450,000 applicants in order to clear a massive, multiyear review backlog (Al Mallees 2023; Lundy 2023). If, or when, economic conditions deteriorate and acute labour demand shifts to increasing unemployment, the merits of Canada's fragmented system of migration governance will be put to the test. As an important forerunner in the development of novel approaches to migration control, both in the context of economic immigration and refugee resettlement, Canadian policies have already become important in the context of discussions of managed migration across advanced industrialized economies, in North America and more broadly. The lessons learned will therefore be of interest to policymakers in Canada and beyond.

NOTE

1 Total number of valid permits as of 31 December (Immigration, Refugees and Citizenship Canada 2022a, 2022c).

REFERENCES

Abu-Laban, Yasmeen. 1998. "Welcome/Stay Out. The Contradiction of Canadian Integration and Immigration Policies at the Millennium (1)." *Canadian Ethnic Studies Journal* 30 (3): 190–213.

Abu-Laban, Yasmeen, and Christina Gabriel. 2002. *Selling Diversity: Immigration Multiculturalism, Employment Equity, and Globalization.* Toronto: University of Toronto Press.

Al Mallees, Nojoud. 2023. "Immigration Minister Says Canada Needs More Mewcomers as Targets get Mixed Reviews." *Globe and Mail*, 13 January 2023. https://www.theglobeandmail.com/politics/article-liberal-minister-says-canada-needs-more-immigration-as-targets-get/. Accessed 14 January 2023.

Banting, Keith. 2012. "Canada." In *Immigrant Integration in Federal Countries*, edited by Christian Joppke and F. Leslie Seidle, 79–112. Montreal and Kingston: McGill-Queen's University Press.

Banting, Keith, and Stuart Soroka. 2020. "A Distinctive Culture? The Sources of Public Support for Immigration in Canada, 1980–2019." *Canadian Journal of Political Science* 53 (4): 821–38.

Baas, Michiel. 2019. "The Education-Migration Industry: International Students, Migration Policy and the Question of Skills." *International Migration* 57 (3): 222–34.

Bascaramurty, Dakshana, Neha Bhatt, and Uday Rana. 2021. "Canada's International Student Recruiting Machine Is Broken." *Globe and Mail*, 4 November 2021. https://www.theglobeandmail.com/canada/article-india-canada-international-student-recruitment/. Accessed 5 November 2021.

Boyd, Monica. 2013. "Accreditation and the Labour Market Integration of Internationally Trained Engineers and Physicians in Canada." In *Wanted and Welcome? Policies for Highly Skilled Immigrants in Comparative Perspective*, edited by Triadafilos Triadafilopoulos, 165–97. New York: Springer New York.

Boyd, Monica, and Nathan T.B. Ly. 2021. "Unwanted and Uninvited: Canadian Exceptionalism in Migration and the 2017–2020 Irregular Border Crossings." *American Review of Canadian Studies* 51 (1): 95–121. https://doi.org/10.1080/02722011.2021.1899743.

Chartrand, Tyler, and Leah F. Vosko. 2021. "Canada's Temporary Foreign Worker and International Mobility Programs: Charting Change and Continuity Among Source Countries." *International Migration* 59 (2): 89–109. https://doi.org/10.1111/imig.12762.

Chown Oved, Marco. 2021. "Maxime Bernier and the People's Party of Canada Fail to Win any Seats." *Toronto Star*, 20 September 2021. https://www.thestar.com/politics/federal/2021/09/20/maxime-bernier-and-the-peoples-party-of-canada-fail-to-win-any-seats.html. Accessed 5 January 2022.

Crossman, Eden, Youjin Choi, and Feng Hou. 2021. "International Students as a Source of Labour Supply: Engagement in the Labour Market During the Period of Study." Statistics Canada. https://www150.statcan.gc.ca/n1/pub/36-28-0001/2021011/article/00001-eng.htm. Accessed 5 January 2022.

Dauvergne, Catherine. 2016. *The New Politics of Immigration and the End of Settler Societies*. Cambridge: Cambridge University Press.

Dayal, Pratyush. 2022. "With More Than 2.4M Immigration Applications in Canada's Backlog, Many Here and Overseas Feel Lost." CBC *News*, 28 July 2022. http://www.cbc.ca/news/canada/saskatoon/more-than-2-4-million-immigration-applications-in-backlog-1.6529154. Accessed 5 August 2022.

de Haas, Hein, Katharina Natter, and Simona Vezzoli. 2018. "Growing Restrictiveness or Changing Selection? The Nature and Evolution of Migration Policies." *International Migration Review* 52 (2): 324–67.

Ellermann, Antje. 2021. *The Comparative Politics of Immigration: Policy Choices in Germany, Canada, Switzerland, and the United States*. New York: Cambridge University Press.

Elrick, Jennifer. 2022. *Making Middle-Class Multiculturalism: Immigration Bureaucrats and Policymaking in Postwar Canada*. Toronto: University of Toronto Press.

Environics Institute for Survey Research. 2020. *Focus Canada – Fall 2020 Canadian Public Opinion About Immigration and Refugees*. Environics Institute for Survey Research. 7 October 2020. https://www.environicsinstitute.org/docs/default-source/project-documents/fc-fall-2020---immigration/focus-canada-fall-2020---public-opinion-on-immigration-refugees---final-report.pdf?sfvrsn=bd51588f_2. Accessed 15 January 2022.

FitzGerald, David Scott. 2019. *Refuge Beyond Reach: How Rich Democracies Repel Asylum Seekers*. Oxford: Oxford University Press.

FitzGerald, David Scott, and David Cook-Martín. 2014. *Culling the Masses: The Democratic Origins of Racist Immigration Policy in the Americas*. Cambridge, MA: Harvard University Press.

Hiebert, Daniel. 2016. *What Is so Special about Canada? Understanding the Resilience of Immigration and Multiculturalism*. Washington, DC:

Migration Policy Institute. https://www.migrationpolicy.org/research/whats-so-special-about-canada-understanding-resilienceimmigration-and-multiculturalism. Accessed 17 August 2022.

– 2019. "The Canadian Express Entry System for Selecting Economic Immigrants: Progress and Persistent Challenges." Migration Policy Institute, Washington, DC. https://www.migrationpolicy.org/research/canadian-express-entry-system-selecting-economic-immigrants, access on 17 August 2022.

Hollifield, James F. 2004. "The Emerging Migration State." *International Migration Review* 38 (3): 885–912.

Hune-Brown, Nicholas. 2021. "The Shadowy Business of International Education." *The Walrus*, 18 August 2021. https://thewalrus.ca/the-shadowy-business-of-international-education/. Accessed 14 February 2022.

Hyndman, Jennifer, William Payne, and Shauna Jiminez. 2017. "Private Refugee Sponsorship in Canada." *Forced Migration Review* (54): 56–9.

Immigration, Refugees and Citizenship Canada. 2016. "Canada - Admissions of Permanent Residents by Immigration Category, 1980–Q2 2016." https://www.cic.gc.ca/opendata-donneesouvertes/data/IRCC_PRadmiss_0002_E.xls. Accessed 14 August 2022.

– 2017. 2017 *Annual Report to Parliament on Immigration*. https://www.canada.ca/en/immigration-refugees-citizenship/corporate/publications-manuals/annual-report-parliament-immigration-2017.htl#sec1_1. Accessed 15 December 2022.

– 2022a. "International Mobility Program work permit holders on December 31st by province/territory of intended destination and program." https://www.cic.gc.ca/opendata-donneesouvertes/data/EN_ODP_annual-TR-work-IMP_PT_program_year_end.xlsx. Accessed 15 December 2022.

– 2022b. "Permanent Residents – Monthly IRCC Updates – Canada – Admissions of permanent resident by province/territory of intended destination and immigration category." https://www.cic.gc.ca/opendata-donneesouvertes/data/IRCC_M_PRadmiss_0001_E.xlsx. Accessed 15 December 2022.

– 2022c. "Temporary Foreign Worker Program work permit holders on December 31st by province/territory of intended destination and program." https://www.cic.gc.ca/opendata-donneesouvertes/data/EN_ODP_annual-TR-work-TFW_PT_program_year_end.xlsx. Accessed 15 December 2022.

– 2022d. "Temporary Residents: Temporary Foreign Worker Program (TFWP) and International Mobility Program (IMP) Work Permit Holders – Monthly IRCC Updates." https://open.canada.ca/data/en/dataset/360024f2-17e9-4558-bfc1-3616485d65b9. Accessed 15 December 2022.

Irvine, Sandy. 2011. "Canadian Refugee Policy: Understanding the Role of International Bureaucratic Networks in Domestic Paradigm Change." In *Policy Paradigms, Transnationalism, and Domestic Politics*, edited by Grace Skogstad, 171–201. Toronto: University of Toronto Press.

Joppke, Christian. 2005. *Selecting by Origin: Ethnic Migration in the Liberal State*. Cambridge, MA: Harvard University Press.

– 2021. *Neoliberal Nationalism: Immigration and the Rise of the Populist Right*. Cambridge, UK: Cambridge University Press.

Kelley, Ninette, and Michael Trebilcock. 2010. *The Making of the Mosaic: A History of Canadian Immigration Policy*. Toronto: University of Toronto Press.

Kahlon, Balraj S. 2022. "Canada's Exploitation of Punjabi International Students is History Repeating Itself." *Toronto Star*, 1 June 2022. https://www.thestar.com/opinion/contributors/2022/06/01/canadas-exploitation-of-punjabi-international-students-is-history-repeating-itself.html. Accessed 15 August 2022.

Keung, Nicholas. 2022. "Canada Rolls out Measures to Help International Students Stay – and Work – in this Country." *Toronto Star*, 2 August 2022. https://www.thestar.com/news/canada/2022/08/02/canada-rolls-out-measures-to-help-international-students-stay-and-work-in-this-country.html. Accessed 15 August 2022.

Knowles, Valerie. 2007. *Strangers at Our Gates: Canada, Immigration and Immigration Policy, 1540–2006*. Toronto: Dundurn Press.

Krzyżanowski, Michał. 2020. "Discursive Shifts and the Normalisation of Racism: Imaginaries of Immigration, Moral Panics and the Discourse of Contemporary Right-Wing Populism." *Social Semiotics* 30 (4): 503–27.

Labman, Shauna. 2019. *Crossing Law's Border: Canada's Refugee Resettlement Program*. Vancouver: University of British Columbia Press.

Lange, Fabian, Mikal Skuterud, and Christopher Worswick. 2022. "The Economic Case Against Low-Wage Temporary Foreign Workers." Institute for Research on Public Policy. Last modified 27 April 2022. https://policyoptions.irpp.org/magazines/april-2022/temporary-foreign-workers-wages/. Accessed 15 August 2022.

Lawlor, Andrea, and Erin Tolley. 2017. "Deciding who's Legitimate: News Media Framing of Immigrants and Refugees." *International Journal of Communication* 11: 967-91.

Lenard, Patti Tamara. 2021. "How Exceptional? Welcoming Refugees the Canadian Way." *American Review of Canadian Studies* 51 (1): 78–94.

Ling, Justin. 2019. "How Maxime Bernier Lost his Seat. Canada's Nationalist People's Party Has Run a Familiar Populist Playbook – and Ended up a Joke." *Foreign Policy*, 20 October 2019. https://foreign

policy.com/2019/10/20/canada-maxime-bernier-populism-peoples-party/. Accessed 21 August 2022.

Lundy, Matt. 2022a. "Canada to Enter 'Moderate and Short-lived' Recession in 2023, RBC Economists Warn." *Globe and Mail*, 7 July 2022. https://www.theglobeandmail.com/business/article-canada-to-enter-moderate-and-short-lived-recession-in-2023-warns-rbc/. Accessed 15 August 2022.

– 2022b. "Canadian Employers are Ramping up their Search for Temporary Foreign Workers Amid Labour Crunch." *Globe and Mail*, 11 August 2022. https://www.theglobeandmail.com/business/article-canadian-employers-are-ramping-up-their-search-for-temporaryforeign/. Accessed 15 August 2022.

– 2023. "Ottawa Eyes 'Aggressive Measures' to Clear Immigration Backlog, Memo Reveals." *Globe and Mail*, Last modified 17 January 2023, accessed 31 January 2023. https://www.theglobeandmail.com/business/article-immigration-backlog-visitor-visas-canada/.

Martani, Ervis. 2021. "Canada's Private Sponsorship Program: Success, Shortcomings, and Policy Solutions." Working Paper No. 2021/6. Ryerson Centre for Immigration and Settlement, Canada Research Excellence Chair in Migration and Integration.

Molnar Diop, Petra. 2013. "The 'Bogus' Refugee: Roma Asylum Claimants and Discourses of Fraud in Canada's Bill C-31." *Refuge: Canada's Journal on Refugees* 30 (1): 67–80.

O'Donnell, Ian, and Mikal Skuterud. 2022. "The Transformation of Canada's Temporary Foreign Worker Program." *Canadian Public Policy* 48 (4): 518-38. https://doi.org/10.3138/cpp.2021-093.

Osman, Laura. 2022. "Canada Sets Ambitious Immigration Targets for Post-pandemic Recovery." *Globe and Mail*, 14 February 2022. https://www.theglobeandmail.com/canada/article-canada-sets-ambitious-immigration-targets-for-post-pandemic-recovery-2/. Accessed 15 August 2022.

Paquet, Mireille. 2021. "Researching, Monitoring, and Managing: Immigration Policy Work in Canada." *American Review of Canadian Studies* 51 (1): 62–77.

Pierson, Paul. 1993. "When Effect Becomes Cause: Policy Feedback and Political Change." *World Politics* 45 (4): 595–628.

Porter, Catherine. 2017. "Canada's Immigration System, Lauded by Trump, Is More Complex Than Advertised." *New York Times*, 2 March 2017. https://www.nytimes.com/2017/03/02/world/canada/immigration-trump.html. Accessed 12 April 2022.

Reitz, Jeffrey G., Josh Curtis, and Jennifer Elrick. 2014. "Immigrant Skill Utilization: Trends and Policy Issues." *Journal of International Migration and Integration* 15 (1): 1–26.

Ruhs, Martin. 2013. *The Price of Rights*. Princeton, NJ: Princeton University Press.

Schinnerl, Sandra. 2021. "The Influence of Higher Education on Immigration Policy in Canada." PhD diss., Interdisciplinary Studies, University of British Columbia.

Simmons, Alan B. 2010. *Immigration and Canada: Global and Transnational Perspectives*. Toronto: Canadian Scholars' Press.

Smith, Craig. 2020. "A Model for the World? Policy Transfer Theory and the Challenges to Exporting' Private Sponsorship to Europe. In *Strangers to Neighbours Refugee Sponsorship in Context*, edited by Shauna Labman and Geoffrey Cameron, 286–302. Montreal and Kingston: McGill-Queen's University Press.

Subramaniam, Vanmala, and Matt Lundy. 2022. "Ottawa Expands Access to Temporary Foreign Workers to Ease Labour Crunch." *Globe and Mail*, 4 April 2022. https://www.theglobeandmail.com/business/article-ottawa-loosens-restrictions-on-temporary-foreign-workers/. Accessed 12 April 2022.

Taylor, Zack. 2021. "The Political Geography of Immigration: Party Competition for Immigrants' Votes in Canada, 1997–2019." *American Review of Canadian Studies* 51 (1): 18–40. https://doi.org/10.1080/02722011.2021.1874732.

Triadafilopoulos, Triadafilos. 2012. *Becoming Multicultural: Immigration and the Politics of Membership in Canada and Germany*. Vancouver: University of British Columbia Press.

– 2019. "Germany's Post-2015 Immigration Dilemmas." *Current History* 118 (806): 108–113.

Vosko, Leah F. 2022. "Temporary Labour Migration by any Other Name: Differential Inclusion Under Canada's 'New' International Mobility Regime." *Journal of Ethnic and Migration Studies* 48 (1): 129–52. https://doi.org/10.1080/1369183X.2020.1834839.

Winter, Elke. 2021. "Multicultural Citizenship for the Highly Skilled? Naturalization, Human Capital, and the Boundaries of Belonging in Canada's Middle-class Nation-building." *Ethnicities* 21 (2): 289–310.

Zolberg, Aristide R. 1987. "Wanted But Not Welcome: Alien Labour in Western Development." In *Population in an Interacting World*, edited by William Alonso, 36–73. Cambridge, MA: Harvard University Press.

8

The Regulation of North American Climate Mobilities

Bruno Dupeyron

In North America, the impact of climate change is felt most acutely when populations are suddenly forced to leave their homes and to relocate, either temporarily or permanently. Climate change has also impacted transnational migration to North America, with evidence suggesting that ecological degradation and droughts influence asylum migration to Mexico, the United States, and Canada. In Central America's dry corridor, which includes Guatemala, El Salvador, Honduras, and Nicaragua, droughts have been more frequent and intense since the 1980s. In 2019, the area was entering its fifth consecutive drought year. In 2020, two-thirds of the 10.5 million people who live in the dry corridor were in impoverished smallholder farmer communities. In this context, droughts had affected agricultural production, income, and food security, consequently generating internal displacements and migrations (Depsky and Pons 2020), not only in the region, but also within Mexico, Costa Rica, and the United States. In the 2010s, emigration from the dry corridor increased dramatically: between 2010 and 2015 outward migration multiplied by fivefold (WFP 2020). In the second half of the decade, migrant movements to the United States also spiked, with a total amount of apprehensions and expulsions by the US Customs and Border Patrol for the dry corridor of 165,816 in 2017, 228,909 in 2018, 623,148 in 2019, and 107,089 in 2020 (US Customs and Border Protection 2021).

In late 2018, media framing of Central American caravans was influenced by the Trump administration's racialized and securitized view of US border control (Fleuriet and Castellano 2020). In this political context, Western mainstream media used two core narrative frames that not only ignored Central American migrants' agency, but also dismissed socioeconomic and political migration drivers. On one hand, media representations employed a Western ethnocentric perspective to analyze these mobilities to the United

States; rather than providing a more expansive engagement, which would require attending to overlapping political and ecological migration drivers, media coverage dramatized these events and focused on their spectacular nature. On the other hand, some media coverage tried to engage with understanding the "root causes" of the Central American migration crisis, but generally did so narrowly, with emphasis on domestic violence and gang-based violence alongside related governance considerations, and relatively marginal attention to climate issues (Chattopadhyay 2019).

In this context, the perspective of the media to understand these "root causes" can be attributed to broader changes in migration patterns. In contrast to cross-border movements over previous years, family units, women, and children outpaced previous arrivals of single men, and mainstream media commentators consequently became more attentive to the consequences of the climate crisis, in addition to drivers such as gang violence or poverty. In doing so, media coverage intersected with a growing body of scholarship focused on the intersection of climate change with a wider array of causes of forced migration. Although climate change may certainly be analyzed as one of the drivers of internal and international migration, other factors are also emphasized in the literature – for instance environmental degradation, economic and social inequalities, and conflict (Piguet, Kaenzig, and Guélat 2018). The long-standing and pervasive role of US foreign policies across Central America should also be considered: systemic issues, such as support for dictatorships, responses to political and social movements, resource extractivism and the consequent ecological destruction; rampant poverty; and food insecurity triggered by the imposition of neoliberal reforms also significantly aggravate climate change events (Copeland 2020). While the US as a hegemon plays an outsized role in many of these dynamics, the role of Canadian mining corporations in Latin America should not be omitted (Imai, Gardner, and Weinberger 2017; see also Smith in this volume).

In the continental example of the dry corridor – centred on Central America, Mexico, and the United States – environmental factors are not the only drivers of migration, but one of many (Hoffmann et al. 2020). The Intergovernmental Panel on Climate Change (IPCC) agrees that the relationship between climate events and involuntary displacements remain complex and somewhat overdetermined (IPCC 2022 AR6 WGII). Yet, our murky understanding of the environmental migration paradigm is further biased by the predominance of state and international perspectives, which are resistant to applying the "refugee" label to people displaced from climate change, since this designation implies protection obligations on part of the receiving states.[1] Instead, climate change is often framed as a security issue, rather than a humanitarian policy concern. In addition, most climate events and processes displace people internally, and thus are often not framed within a security versus humanitarian paradigm.

Natural disasters and extreme weather events, such as heatwaves, heavy rain, drought and associated wildfires, and coastal flooding, have occurred with greater intensity and frequency across Canada, the United States, and Mexico over the past decades (IPCC 2022 AR6 WGII). The most recent IPCC (2022 AR6 WGII) report lists three main categories for how climate change impacts human systems: (i) water scarcity and food production (e.g., agriculture / crop production, animal and livestock health and productivity, fisheries yields and aquaculture production); (ii) health and well-being (e.g., infectious diseases, heat, malnutrition, mental health, displacement); and (iii) cities, settlements, and infrastructure (e.g., inland flooding, flood / storm induced damages in coastal areas, damages to infrastructures, and damages to key economic sectors). These impacts may trigger internal and/or international displacements. For instance, wildfires in the Canadian boreal forest will continue to be more frequent, due to the decrease in fuel moisture[2] in several areas, which will, in turn, stress fire management agencies and affect population displacement and public health (Coogan et al. 2021; Dodd et al. 2018; Palinkas 2020a). In the United States, hurricanes Katrina and Rita affected 1.5 million people; many of them had to relocate after 2005 from New Orleans to Atlanta and Houston (Palinkas 2020b), which impacted not only their income (Do Yun and Waldorf 2016), but also their mental health (Raker et al. 2019). Finally, Central American migrants have also been impacted by climate change events that have triggered displacement. These populations use Mexico as a country of transit and a destination; this is particularly challenging for undocumented migrants, as similar climate issues also destabilize regions of Mexico, which is only compounded by the pressures from sustained internal migration trends and the emergence of domestic anti-immigrant sentiments (Casillas 2020).

Thus, a series of intersecting climate change events and processes are inducing increased levels of displacement, whether domestic, international, or both. Yet, state policy responses have largely been confined to frameworks defined by either national security or humanitarianism. Despite the apparent differences in terms of framing and policy implications, both perspectives are resistant to the nuances and complexities presented by climate-driven migration, as they embed fundamental assumptions regarding threats to either states or the human security of affected populations. Moreover, both approaches arguably have only offered narrow and short-term policy responses to climate-induced displacements. In addition, neither national security nor humanitarianism addresses the intersecting causes of displacement in a manner that fully acknowledges the complex dynamics that drive forced migration within North America or more broadly. This is salient because focusing on those intersecting factors may prove essential to offering long-term policy solutions to climate-induced displacement in North America. Finally, the prisms offered by the imperatives of national security and humanitarianism force us to adopt alternatively limited perspectives, whether framed in domestic or international terms. However, recognizing the essentially contextual and transnational nature of these issues for North America indicates that we should consider them from an explicitly regional perspective, and to develop regionalized policy responses.

In sum, the complex landscapes of internal and international climate mobility in North America are often reduced to an opposition between securitization and humanitarian policies, practices, and framings not only among practitioners, but also among scholars. Such binaries are not only analytically problematic, but also forestall the development of effective policy responses to the ongoing challenges of climate-induced migration across the continent. This chapter argues that it is not only possible, but necessary, to go beyond the security-humanitarian dichotomy in order to critically examine the regional regulation of climate mobility. In doing so, the chapter also contends that adopting new policy frames and responses must be based on the adoption of new theoretical lenses.

From a theoretical perspective, I employ a political sociology framework that borrows several concepts from Bourdieu's (1977, 1984, 1998; Bourdieu and Wacquant 1992) sociology of practice and Wacquant's (2005, 2012a, 2012b, 2014) critical sociology of the neoliberal state. Wacquant's approach essentially examines the domestic aspects of neoliberalism, which this chapter deploys to analyze internal displacements. In developing my analysis, I focus on one event of internal displacement, partly related to forced climate mobility within Canada: the case of the diverted flood to Lake St Martin First Nation and the imposed relocations implemented by the Canadian state. There are two interrelated reasons to focus on this case study: first, McAdam (2020) notes that, although evacuations are a form of displacement, especially when explicitly orchestrated by the state, they are mostly ignored in the forced migration literature. She considers several factors that may explain this research gap: for instance, the blurred lines between pre-emptive evacuations and forced displacements, and concludes that evacuations would benefit from further conceptual and empirical analysis. Second, and due to this research gap, I demonstrate that Wacquant's conceptual framework helps to decentre the debate from the security-humanitarian paradigm. Using this framework, the chapter focuses on three main factors – the role of state, market, and citizenship – to make sense of this forced displacement event in the province of Manitoba. To develop this analysis, the chapter relies on primary and secondary sources, specifically scholarly, government, intergovernmental organizations' (IGO), and non-governmental organizations' (NGO) documents.

The chapter's first section critically engages with a selection of the scientific literature on the intersections of climate and mobility, and shows how the security-humanitarian paradigm is unsatisfactory because it neglects the root causes that it purports to address. In the second section, I explain how both theoretical frameworks – Bourdieu's and Wacquant's – contribute to analyzing climate mobility and its regulation, with a focus on the role of neoliberal states in processes of domestic and international displacement. In the third and fourth sections, I focus on Canada to apply this dual framework, beginning with Canada's international and regional role in migration management, before turning to the chapter's central case study to examine internal displacements in the domestic context. My conclusion considers how this multilayered analytical framework is able to provide important traction and insight for addressing broader research challenges related to understanding displacement in the North American context.

THE REGULATION OF CLIMATE MOBILITY IN NORTH AMERICA: QUESTIONING THE SECURITY-HUMANITARIAN PARADIGM

Burzyński et al. (2021) have shown that the literature studying the link between climate change and migration is extremely heterogeneous, reflecting a myriad of research questions, methodological approaches, and a general lack of consistent findings. The IPCC has not been absent in this debate concerning climate change and migration (IPCC WGII and WGIII 2022). The IPCC was established in 1988 as an intergovernmental body of the United Nations and has emerged as one of the main authoritative voices in international anthropogenic climate change science. The IPCC undertakes a systematic review of the existing scientific literature and publishes an assessment report every five to six years; the first of these reports was issued in 1990 and the latest (sixth) was issued in 2021–22. Assessment reports include a compressed synthesis of the main natural, political, and socioeconomic impacts and risks due to climate change, along with a selection of policy responses to address these challenges. The IPCC's general approach suggests a broadly apolitical orientation to the subject of climate change, putting itself forward as a neutral, technical advisory body. However, Beck and Mahony (2018) argue that the IPCC is a "boundary organization" between science and politics that produces "boundary objects," such as temperature targets like 2°C or 1.5°C. It also generates, within and around itself, some forms of "boundary work" that has three main features: the IPCC's boundary work is meant to legitimize its scientific autonomy, despite its influence on social and political issues; it serves to determine who is allowed to speak; and it is continually negotiated in practice (Beck and Mahony 2018). Thus, the IPCC exerts substantial power in global climate politics, and determines in every report what the impacts, risks, and policy options are for a broader international audience. For instance, carbon capture and storage have not been mentioned systematically in the latest reports; in the same vein, the intersection between climate change and displacement seems to be tenuous and debatable in the latest IPCC assessment reports, with varying exaggerated predictions.

Although this scientific literature on the intersection of climate change and migration is difficult to synthesize – mainly due to its multidisciplinary nature – a fairly constant analytical boundary divides it into two strands of research. The first strand focuses on the security policy aspects of climate-induced migrations, while the second strand examines its humanitarian policy facets. Boas and colleagues (2019), along with others (for instance, Gemenne 2011; McLeman 2019), interrogate this distinction when they argue that the link between climate change and migration is inaccurately presented by academia and policy actors as an increased international security risk. They suggest that the main policy issue of climate change and migration is not its supposed security consequences, but how it has been constructed, instrumentalized, and legitimized by security actors. Piguet (2022, 10) alludes to a similar concern when he concludes, after reviewing the existing literature and proposing new research questions, that "[it] remains a challenge … to frame appropriate mobility policies that do not simply force people to either stay in place or migrate. This is perhaps one of the central works in progress over the next 10 years." Questioning security policies and the corresponding security narrative of climate migration is not a neutral task, as it reframes the issue in explicitly humanitarian terms. Finally, Kita and Raleigh (2018) show that conceptual and empirical evidence to substantiate the link between environmental migration and insecurity is lacking: in fact, there is no compelling evidence that migrants generate violence, since migrants are often preoccupied with their integration in their place of destination.

Boas and colleagues (2019, 901–2) challenge the predominant security narrative by providing key examples of problematic research deployed in the service of the Global North's securitization agenda. However, they do not show where this narrative is specifically situated, nor how this narrative is supported and articulated among and within several fields of power. Despite this omission, they propose six research priorities in order to challenge the dominant securitization perspective. These are addressed briefly ahead, interspersed with additional sources from the literature. However, the first priority is to interrogate the notion that climate change generates mass human migration, instead of simplistically assuming that there is causal link or correlation between the two. Boas et al. suggest, along with Gemenne, that it is extremely difficult to identify or predict a plausible figure for the total number of persons impacted by climate-induced migration, due to the multicausal nature of displacement and the lack of a clear distinction between voluntary and forced migration (Gemenne 2011, 6). Kita and Raleigh (2018) argue that the linkages between environmental change, migration, and security are relatively weak and unconvincing, and, for this reason, anxieties surrounding hypothetical conflicts and instabilities due to climate migrations should be toned down. Likewise, Gregory White (2011) has shown that state anxieties around climate-induced migrations have triggered early analyses and state narratives by security and intelligence communities in order to intensify and externalize border security regimes.

The second dominant priority for the scholarly literature is to question the notion of migration in the context of climate change, and eventually replace it with a more neutral term – e.g., climate mobility. In fact, the use of the concept of migration implicitly suggests that people not only move permanently, but also over long distances. However, in the context of climate change, displacements (and the absence of displacements) are much more complex and nuanced, suggesting that the climate-displacement nexus can be better captured and analyzed through the agnostic notion of "mobility." With this mobility approach, it is also possible to reposition and question the normalized mobilities of the Global North – e.g., tourism and business trips – that affect climate change and impact specific sites. The use of more neutral notions, such as mobility, is certainly welcomed as a basis to both depoliticize and, conversely, repoliticize dominant state and mainstream media narratives as well as open up analytic space for people's agency in their mobility representations and practices.

The third research priority in the literature calls for a broader approach to human mobility in the context of climate change, and the subsequent rights and duties of states. Instead of a narrow perspective that assumes climate change causes human mobility, scholars propose to examine how climate change may affect current and future human mobility. In a complementary vein, McAdam (2012, 2019) has more broadly interrogated the political and legal aspects of displacement caused by climate change. McAdam's work asks whether this requires us to revisit traditional international protection, or if it is it necessary to create new institutional and policy instruments to respond to these challenges.

The fourth priority of the scientific literature addresses the trap of simplistic interpretations by media and policy fields, which in turn promote narratives of crisis, mass migration, and political demands for border securitization. Boas and colleagues (2019) argue that policy should rely on research that offers a more neutral perspective. However, here the authors propose a normative statement that appears to border on wishful thinking. In fact, the instrumentalization of research by other fields (and vice versa) illustrates how research is dependent on policy (e.g., governments, international organizations, research funding agencies that offer funding with predetermined research objectives, and think tanks), as well as other fields (e.g., news media, social media). Indeed, the IPCC's "boundary work" offers a compelling example that Boas and colleagues do not fully consider, even though this boundary work is constructed and reproduced by academic actors (Beck and Mahony 2018).

The fifth priority is to directly involve populations who are affected by climate mobilities in research initiatives. The suggestion that, with appropriate funding, representative Indigenous actors can lead or co-lead research projects focusing on the impact of climate change is quite stimulating. The salience of this priority is particularly compelling for Canada following the work of the Truth and Reconciliation Commission in emphasizing the historical and ongoing injustices experienced by First Nations and other Indigenous communities. This is because Indigenous peoples in Canada have been historically subjected to forced migrations, while rural and remote Indigenous communities continue to be more substantially exposed to evacuations due to climate events than the general population (Coogan et al. 2019).[3]

Lastly, research on climate mobilities should avoid biases arising from studying areas that are sensitive to climate change and suspected as sources of onward migrations to the Global North. Work in this area should also analyze how destination areas construct "others" in responding to mobility, regulate global migrations through unequal border policies, and shape political responses to perceived migrations. However, this shift in research from sending to destination areas should be made cautiously, since border securitization is increasingly externalized (Zaiotti 2016). The European Border and Coast Guard Agency, also known as Frontex, is an example of this externalization of border security. Frontex conducts operations to support increasingly militarized approaches to European border control. This results in an intensification of the securitization of migration in the European Union (Léonard and Konert 2022), which in turn is linked to the increased deaths of migrants at the gates of Europe (Clochard 2017). Reflecting the growing convergence of externalization and securitization, later, in 2022, Frontex was likely to send, for the first time in its history, armed forces beyond Europe, with an initial contingent going to Senegal (EUobserver 2022; Frontex 2021). This example about Frontex, far from EU's external borders, suggests that Frontex global mobilities, along with the mobilities of other organizations and agencies, will also need to be scrutinized by researchers focusing on state and international organization responses to climate change mobility.[4]

Together, these strands of research provide helpful guidance for addressing existing limitations in common approaches to climate mobilities, both in scholarship and broader public discourse. However, at the same time, these interventions illustrate the difficulty of effectively interrogating the predominate security perspective without also questioning the humanitarian approach. For instance, Jakobsson (2021, 21) notes that the United Nations Inter-Agency Standing Committee (IASC) task force, created in 2008 to work on climate change migration and displacement, included the International Federation of Red Cross and Red Crescent Societies (IFRC), International Organization for Migration (IOM), and United Nations High Commissioner for Refugees (UNHCR). The policy entrepreneurs across these agencies worked in order to legitimize climate-induced migration issues, with the aim of enabling future recognition of this issue area. In the context of his analysis, Jakobsson characterizes these humanitarian actors in contrast to security actors (including the IOM in the category "humanitarian actors"). The lack of qualification in this context is surprising as the IOM has a past track record as a migration and border securitization entrepreneur (Geiger and Pécoud 2020) since it often serves (Global North) states' interests in the field of migration and border control. In the last decade, however, the IOM has increasingly adopted the migration narratives of NGOs in order to balance border security and humanitarianism. For instance, counting migrants' deaths in Europe was a counter-narrative practice developed by NGOs in the 1990s to criticize deadly European policies. Notably, since 2013, the IOM has appropriated this practice, and has also been counting migrant deaths, and in this way trying to balance border security with considerations of migrant human security and rights (Heller and Pécoud 2020).

In this context it is apparent that the scholarly dichotomy between security and humanitarian policies limits analysis of how climate mobility is regulated in North America. As this discussion has suggested, there is considerable overlap between security and humanitarian perspectives within the setting of global policy development around migration. This in turn suggests the possibility of similar dynamics at the regional level. In the next section, I propose an alternative analytical model that focuses mainly on the notions of state, market, and citizenship.

ANALYZING CLIMATE MOBILITY THROUGH THE LENS OF RACIAL CAPITALISM AND THE PRISM OF STATE, MARKET, AND CITIZENSHIP

Given the considerations discussed in the previous section, the main task of this chapter is to provide resources to attempt to move beyond this security-humanitarian impasse. To do so, I take up a dual-layered analytical framework, drawing on the conceptual work of scholars of racial capitalism, complemented by a political-sociology approach, specifically Loïc Wacquant's historical anthropology of neoliberalism.

Go (2021) notes that the study of racial capitalism as a distinct phenomenon emerged in the 1970s in the context of Marxist analyses of South African apartheid. Racial capitalism has subsequently become a central concept to historians who have studied the connection between slavery and capitalism (Johnson 2020; Robinson 2000; it has also been taken up in other disciplines – for instance, in law, political science, and sociology (Gill 2021; Leong 2013; Virdee 2019). Although the study of racial capitalism continues to manifest itself as a loose, multidisciplinary literature that examines and interrogates the relationship between racial inequalities and capitalism, it can be helpful to briefly consider three of its main facets. First, work on racial capitalism shows – through both historical case studies and contemporary analysis – how racial stratifications and capitalist economies are interdependent. Secondly, scholars of racial capitalism emphasize the need to analyze capitalism in its global context, rather than a national one. Finally, the research agenda that has emerged around racial capitalism often has explicitly political ambitions, as it seeks to link anti-racist and anti-capitalist struggles (Go 2020). In the context of North American climate mobilities, using the lens of racial capitalism draws analytic attention to how international and domestic regulations of mobility impose an exorbitant burden on racialized communities. Within such a framework, climate change is viewed as "a logical consequence of an economic system based on extraction, accumulation through dispossession, and white supremacy" (Gonzalez 2020, 1). Quijano (2014) and Grosfoguel (2016) show how persistent Eurocentric hierarchies of power, such as the nation-state and colonialism, are integral to maintaining socioeconomic inequalities and inherently racist practices globally, including bordering and migratory policies. However, the global perspective of racial capitalism may prove limited insofar as it may follow a US ethnocentric logic, by which the notion of race, constructed in the American context, is diffused to other jurisdictions where it loses its analytical pertinence. This challenge is captured by what Bourdieu and Wacquant (1999) have called "the cunning of imperialist reason," where even genuinely critically oriented scholarship may risk universalizing aspects of a particular historical tradition and context. Although their critique cannot be levelled against all work on racial capitalism, it provides a needed caution against this analytic trap which informs my own engagement. In addition, we should consider that the US scholarship on racial capitalism is not uniform, since racial capitalism is rooted in Marxist analyses of South African apartheid that can trigger methodological and ideological dissents. Besides, in contrast to what Bourdieu and Wacquant suggest, the most recent scholarship of racial capitalism in the United States appears to be quite nuanced and reflexive (Jenkins and Leroy 2021).

The second layer of analysis I draw on complements racial capitalism, as it preserves some of its key facets, but focuses on the national level, without ignoring international dynamics. This approach is borrowed from Loïc Wacquant, whose conceptual framework helps us understand how even an ostensibly humanitarian perspective is instrumentalized by security actors. This uptake can be understood as an attempt to make climate mobility approaches and policies apparently more compassionate and palatable to distant Western publics, even while policies arrayed against displaced people are effectively maintained.

My claim is that punitive and protective approaches to climate migration must not be seen as opposites. Instead, they should be interpreted in light of the concept of "bureaucratic field" (Bourdieu 1994), for which Bourdieu uses the analogy of "two hands": the right one that is both economic and penal, and the left one that is historically social and protective. With the advent of neoliberal policies and reforms, the left hand is increasingly emptied of its social and protective substance so as to become a second right hand, one that is punitive and restrictive toward the subaltern. In this context, neoliberalism is understood as "the reengineering and redeployment of the state as the core agency that sets the rules and fabricates the subjectivities, social relations and collective representations suited to realizing markets," or more simply as "an articulation of state, market and citizenship that harnesses the first to impose the stamp of the second onto the third" (Wacquant 2012a, 66, 71). In other words, the purpose of neoliberalism is to profoundly transform the state so that the success of markets is the main policy priority, anchored by state rules and norms. In turn, these rules and norms are oriented in order to conform individuals to market imperatives. Thus, the objective of neoliberalism is to create a virtuous circle in which the state is one of three core components.

These conceptual frames reinject into the analysis of climate mobilities several institutional dynamics that forefront processes of "market-conforming state crafting" (Wacquant 2012a, 71). The ideology of neoliberalism is often predicated on a supposed opposition between states and "free" markets. However, Peck (2010, 9) reminds us that neoliberalism requires the control and regular use of the state "in the interests of shaping a pro-corporate, free-trading 'market order.'" The institutional instruments that allow for these forms of neoliberal state-building and corresponding market orders involve, for instance, the regulation of workers and consumers' mobility – whether this mobility is national or international – often along class and racial lines. The current construction of "climate refugees" as a category is certainly amplified by security and humanitarian narratives; however, this dual narrative contributes to the control and deployment of the state in the service of market interests. Bringing this to the fore helps us analyze contemporary forms of climate displacement through a more critical lens.

Wacquant (2012b, 71) suggests conceiving of neoliberalism as defined by "market-conforming state crafting," wherein the fundamental feature of neoliberalism is "an articulation of state, market and citizenship." He therefore proposes a "thick" sociological conception of neoliberalism that has three dimensions. The first dimension contends that neoliberalism isn't fundamentally an economic project; rather, it is a political project implemented not by restricting and delimiting the scope of government, but by "reengineering the state." The second dimension of Wacquant's account underscores how neoliberalism shifts the "bureaucratic field" (Bourdieu 1994) toward the economic and penal hand of the state: the left hand of the state is transformed into a second right hand that is disciplinary and abusive toward those at the bottom of the class structure. This shift consequently orients the state toward two main sets of policies. The first set of priorities has been analyzed under the concept of "workfare" or disciplinary social policies by Peck (2010). The second set of priorities has been analyzed by building on Peck's conceptual framework to propose the related notion of "prisonfare" (Wacquant 2010, 2012a). For Wacquant, the implementation of the latter program of interventions contributes to the expansion and glorification of the penal wing of the state in contemporary social policy.

Wacquant's approach suggests that the penal apparatus is one of the core features of the neoliberal state as it must deal with the consequences of its own neoliberal policies generating socioeconomic inequality, social instability, and ethno-racial anxiety. Climate mobility may arguably be seen as one of the emerging and increasingly predominate consequences of the pro-market/pro-capitalist policies that continue to threaten and destroy ecosystems and livelihoods. By extension, applying Wacquant's perspective on the neoliberal state and its policies helps reveal how North American states classify and stratify climate mobility, domestically and internationally, often with an immediate or looming "penal response" toward unwanted individuals. What is at play here is not only the state's responses to climate migration, but also state preparedness (or lack thereof) relative to climate events, whether domestic, regional, or international.

At the beginning of this chapter, I used the example of the dry corridor countries. Now, if we change scales and take an overarching view from a broad regional perspective, we can observe that US refugee and asylum policy is extremely restrictive for Latin Americans. Between 2010 and 2020, US refugee admissions from Latin American countries have been consistently low: only 4 per cent of all asylum seekers who were granted refugee status to the US were from Latin America and the Caribbean (Monin, Batalova, and Lai 2021). During the same period, the majority of Latin American refugees (75 per cent) were from Cuba. Yet only 15 per cent of those Latin American refugees were from the dry corridor (Monin, Batalova, and Lai 2021). Efforts to limit the arrival of forcibly displaced persons from the southern hemisphere have only increased in recent years. In 2019, Mexico and the US signed an agreement creating the Migrant Protection Protocols (MPPs, also known as the "Remain in Mexico" program), which allowed the US administration to send asylum seekers back to Mexico while their asylum application is processed (Kocher 2021). As a direct result of this policy, between January 2019 and March 2020, nearly 70,000 people were sent back to Mexico, often to manifestly unsafe conditions. While the US and Canada only admit a limited number of refugees from Latin America, their influence on Latin America often exacerbates the situation of populations across the region. This is because global capitalism does little to reduce deep inequalities that worsen current vulnerabilities to climate crises, international development initiatives are minimal, and extractivism both negatively impacts local economies and damages ecosystems (Artiga-Purcell and Alejandro 2022).

The recent research synthesis from the IPCC shows that the most socioeconomically unequal countries are also those that are most exposed to the impacts of climate change, making them in turn susceptible to more inequalities and challenges related to climate change. By drawing on Wacquant's analysis we can observe that the main political option in Canada, the United States, and Mexico is a very short-term and individualistic approach – one which leans toward sacrificing the most vulnerable to climate events and processes. The divergent responses to the impact of hurricane Katrina in 2005 (impacting essentially Louisiana and Mississippi) and hurricane Sandy in 2012 (which mostly affected the east coast of the US) significantly reflect Wacquant's framework: race and class played a major role in state policy. While Katrina's impact included the permanent displacement of people, the Federal Emergency Management Agency (FEMA)'s approach in black and poor neighbourhoods (Hartman and Squires 2006), characterized by Crowley (2006, 129) as a "disaster of a disaster response," alongside the enduring impact of racial discriminatory policies and practices made the return to New Orleans more difficult for African Americans than White people (Green, Kouassi, and Mambo 2013). The broader context also underscored how decades of punitive policies against the most vulnerable populations in these areas made them much more exposed to natural disasters.

In contrast, as hurricane Sandy affected the New York Metropolitan Area, the emergency response was less heavy-handed, though the most affected in flooded areas were poor African Americans, poor Latinos, and poor whites over the age of sixty-five (Faber 2015). The international response to hurricane Katrina was impressive: within one month, 133 governments and twelve international organizations offered aid to the US, including Canada and Mexico. However, the US reaction to this offer of global assistance was inconsistent. On one hand, the US government acknowledged theses expressions of international support and sympathy, but it did not confirm whether it intended to accept or reject this aid (with the exception of offers from Cuba, Iran, and Venezuela that were left apparently unanswered). On the other hand, the sudden realization that the US could be in a position to be a recipient of aid was apparently a surprise, as no plan to receive and manage international aid existed (Kelman 2007).

Despite numerous policy suggestions (e.g., Andrasko 2022; Yayboke et al. 2020), states have yet to agree on an international framework to regulate climate mobility. National governments remain the main actors empowered to unilaterally implement relevant measures, based on their specific interests. For instance, people forcibly displaced by natural and environmental events are not considered for refugee protection under the 1951 Refugee Convention. However, other legal mechanisms have been used to provide temporary protection, such as for individuals from regions impacted by natural disasters. In the North American context, those forcibly displaced due to environmental events can be granted assistance though certain mechanisms, especially if they are already on American soil and cannot return due to specific conditions, e.g., the Temporary Protected Status (TPS), or the Deferred Enforced Departure (DED)[5] in the US, or in the Canadian context the temporary resident permit (TRP) for individuals already within Canada (Yayboke et al. 2020, 8). In the US, granting TPS provides access to the job market and contributes to supporting increased remittances to affected countries, which can positively impact post-disaster recovery efforts. However, TPS provides no path to permanent residency and offers no right to family reunification (Miyares et al. 2019). In contrast, the Canadian immigration system is more flexible and allows, under several conditions, for TRP holders to apply for permanent residence (IRCC 2015). Notably, in the US TPS can be both extended and terminated by the executive branch (National Immigration Forum 2021; see also Cameron and Labman, and Coen in this volume on the role of executive discretion in US refugee policy), while the Canadian TRP is subject to specific administrative conditions.

Support within the region for emerging migration governance initiatives has proved markedly uneven. In 2018, Canada and Mexico voted in favour of the nonbinding Global Compacts, while the United States withheld support of these frameworks (See Ferris and Matheson in this volume for further discussion). One of Canada and Mexico's ostensive obligations under the Global Compacts is to create pathways and policies for displaced people who are forced to leave their country because of both sudden-onset natural disasters and slow-onset degradation. More specifically, Objective 5 of the Global Compact for Safe, Orderly and Regular Migration (GCM) is to "enhance availability and flexibility of pathways for regular migration," and paragraph 21(g) requires signatories to "develop or build on existing national and regional practices for admission and stay of appropriate duration based on compassionate, humanitarian or other considerations" (Canadian Association of Refugee Lawyers 2021). Yet, Canada has an ambiguous international role given the broader lack of climate mobility regulation in North America. In addition, contemporary state responses to climate mobility within Canada show a discriminatory approach, in particular toward Indigenous peoples.

THE AMBIGUOUS INTERNATIONAL ROLE OF CANADA IN THE ABSENCE OF REGIONALIZED CLIMATE MOBILITY REGULATION IN NORTH AMERICA

Since there is no fully regionalized mobility regime in North America, Canada has largely used multilateral forums (e.g., UNHCR, IOM) and bilateral agreements to promote its immigration policy interests. On one hand, Canada's liberal public discourse showcases its refugee resettlement programs and the country's leading role in forging international declarations, such as the Global Compacts, which are used to promote a progressive image of the country, domestically and overseas. On the other hand, Canada is engaged in border security and immigration management policy initiatives that are meant to externalize migration issues, for instance to Mexico and Central America (see Triadafilopoulos and Taylor in this volume on Canada's migration management dualism). Climate mobility is barely mentioned in the Canadian policy discourse, and seems to fall into this externalization approach: people forcibly displaced by climate events will remain in their country or in neighbouring countries. Yet, how are we to make sense of this paradoxical humanitarian-security policy approach? Wacquant's framework shows that Canada's immigration policy is not contradictory if we consider that humanitarian principles and policies are increasingly subordinated to selecting specific categories of migrants and displaced people.

The two-year negotiations of the Global Compact on Refugees (GCR) reveal that Canada had a leading role in this process – formally as chair of the Executive Committee of the UNHCR and informally during the discussions. Canada gained legitimacy as "a norm entrepreneur and leader on issues of gender inclusion, accountability, and inclusive and participatory mechanisms" (Milner 2021, 42). It also facilitated conversations among several stakeholders, using its "history of refuge" (IRCC 2020), and its policy track record of welcoming refugees through innovative policy programs. Regarding climate mobility, Canada was not opposed to several paragraphs of the GCR that mention the existence of both "sudden-onset natural disasters and environmental degradation" (para. 12), and recognize "the reality of increasing displacement in the context of disasters, environmental degradation and climate change" (UNHCR n.d.). As both Global Compacts are nonbinding and do not require ratification instruments, they serve to distill incentives and ideas regarding internal and international mobilities; for instance, the notion of "shared responsibilities" (see para. 11 and 12 of the GCM) that was supported by the IOM, and several of its members states, including Canada (House of Commons of Canada 2018), along with the framing of the GCM in the context of a "safe, orderly and regular migration." In sum, Canada's "migration diplomacy" (Adamson and Tsourapas 2019) has been largely diffused into both Global Compacts.

Despite this ostensive norm entrepreneurship, Canada's immigration department has increasingly adopted measures focused on controlling and deterring "unwanted" migration. This has been particularly apparent in the context of Canada's refugee system, where regulatory and legislative changes implemented over the past decade have imposed disproportionately harsh measures on asylum seekers (Atak, Hudson, and Nakache 2018). Commenting on more recent developments, undertaken concurrently with Canada's involvement in the Global Compacts, Atak and Nakache (2021) have drawn attention to Canadian efforts to discourage irregular migration that undermine the rights of migrants and forcibly displaced people, emphasizing the lack of safeguards for protecting undocumented persons in the context of increasingly externalized migration controls. An important example they highlight in their discussion is the Canadian Anti-Crime Capacity Building Program (ACCBP), which offers assistance to tackle migrant smuggling and train law enforcement and border officials across various states, including Mexico. The support of policing and border security efforts in Mexico is a form of externalization of Canada's border security management within North America (Young 2018). In other words, such policies seek to reduce arrivals of irregular migrants and other undesirable categories of people by outsourcing interdiction efforts to Mexico. This approach holds striking similarities with elements of US border policy toward Mexico, or the EU's common border policy with African countries, both of which have become increasingly securitized and externalized for certain types of migrants and displaced people, who are simultaneously criminalized by states and forced to use criminal organizations to migrate (Zaiotti 2016).

In addition, Canada has progressively developed a select interstate network for information-sharing. The first main agreement of this kind, the US-Canada Smart Border Declaration, was concluded with the American government in 2001, in the aftermath of the 9/11 terrorist attacks. The Smart Border Declaration included, for instance, the identification of common biometric data, additional levels of security screening within refugee and asylum processing, and the exchange of information between the two countries (US Department of State 2002). In 2003, under the same pretense of security, the Asylum Annex allowed the automated and systematic sharing of information about asylum seekers. Additional bilateral agreements – for instance, the 2011 Beyond the Border accord – have expanded the use of information-sharing via asylum systems' databases, which can be accessed with a mere biometric query (IRCC 2012). In 2009, Canada sought to expand its information-sharing policy with the United Kingdom, Australia, and New Zealand. After being deemed successful, deeper agreements were signed with those three countries in 2015 and 2016, to enable automatic data exchanges, in particular on refugee claimants. The Five Eyes countries (Australia, Canada, New Zealand, the United Kingdom, and the United States) use this automated and systematic sharing of information in order to identify and exclude unwanted migrants, including refugee claimants. However, scholars have increasingly raised concerns regarding these measures by pointing to examples of how countries included in these initiatives are potentially in breach of their responsibilities under international refugee law, or have introduced policies that erode the effectiveness of international protection (Atak, Ellis, and Abu Alrob 2021).

Canada's dualistic approach to migration can be interpreted through racial capitalism lenses and Wacquant's framework: the "extreme selectivity of penalization" is based on the "class position, ethnic membership or civic status, and place of residence" and is used to manage poverty with an iron hand (Wacquant 2014, 14). Wacquant (2014) notes that "penality [is] an operator of *negative sociodicy*," by which he means that a number of institutions – paradigmatically the criminal justice system – inscribe sanctions that hamper the lives of people at the bottom of the social pyramid. A classic example is the criminal record that affects employment chances, housing opportunities, mobility, etc., and serves to legitimize and reinforce the individual's undesirable position in the society. The salience of this example has only taken on greater relevance for migration policy, given the growing entwinement of criminal penalties with immigration control and increased criminalization of unwanted cross-border movements, both in Canada and more broadly (Atak and Simeon 2018). Conversely, a *positive sociodicy* (Wacquant 2014, 14) reflects, for instance, how upper-class individuals' cultural capital justifies a greater economic capital, and, in the context of migration, how different types of ideational and material capital impact varying forms of mobility both within and between states.

A DISCRIMINATORY APPROACH TO CLIMATE MOBILITY WITHIN CANADA: THE CASE OF THE GOVERNMENT-DIVERTED FLOOD TO LAKE ST MARTIN FIRST NATION

Racial capitalism and Wacquant's framework presented in the previous section allow us to analyze climate mobility in North America without simply assuming an opposition between security and humanitarian efforts. On the contrary, the dichotomy between security and humanitarianism becomes less stable when we consider the objective of "market-conforming state crafting" that requires people, domestically and internationally, to follow market injunctions imposed by the iron hand of the state, according to Wacquant. This is particularly the case for those at the bottom of society whose circumstances are overdetermined by a number of factors – e.g., race, class, and citizenship. The case study of the diverted flood to Lake St. Martin provides a domestic example of forced displacement for Canada, caused due to climate events and government decisions. By studying this case, our analysis will focus on the role of government policies, before, during, and after the 2012 flood. This case must be located in the broader Canadian context of colonialism, one that is arguably mitigated by the resurgence of Indigenous communities and contemporary advancement of reconciliation practices (Asch, Tully, and Borrows 2018). At the same time, the Truth and Reconciliation Commission calls to action have been implemented slowly and selectively (Jewell and Mosby 2021) and much of Canada's ongoing climate policy ignores Indigenous rights (Deranger 2021; Indigenous Climate Action 2021). With these considerations in mind, applying Wacquant's framework is still useful for advancing beyond the narrow security-humanitarian debate. Additionally, engaging with racial capitalism and Wacquant's framework in the context of this specific case study shows how the class-race axis in this neoliberal moment of Canadian colonization can be critically examined.[6] As the case illustrates, when a flood threatened a number of rural communities, the government and market actors in Canada decided to selectively target Indigenous peoples' communities and preferentially displace them. It also shows how the forced displacement of Indigenous communities is undertaken and managed by government structures and policies that continue to penalize and racialize Indigenous persons in urban contexts, and how these communities respond to these measures and maintain their unity.

So how did the event unfold? In 2011, a "super flood" hit parts of the province of Manitoba in Canada. In order to protect private properties and business interests, the provincial government chose to divert water to Lake St. Martin and First Nation land. Consequently, Lake St Martin First Nation and Little Saskatchewan First Nation members experienced this "human-made flood" in the form of a state-directed natural disaster (Ballard, Coughlin, and Martin 2020). Under government evacuation orders, members of these Indigenous communities were forced to leave their land and reside for seven years in precarious conditions, often housed in urban hotels and temporary residences. Thompson, Ballard, and Martin (2014) interviewed a number of community members who had been displaced and found that racism and jurisdictional issues represented major obstacles to relocating permanently. Reflecting these enduring challenges, it was only in 2018 that community members were able to effectively resettle, with this outcome becoming possible largely as a result of a controversial legal settlement that was reached in 2017 (Thompson 2018).

Indigenous reserve lands in Canada generally face high flood risks. Indigenous people living on reserve therefore face a disproportionate risk of flooding, which is aggravated by limited information and resources to conduct flood risk assessments (Thistlethwaite et al. 2020). In the case at hand, forced mobility was indirectly caused by environmental factors, but directly produced by government officials who decided to sacrifice two First Nation communities. Those displaced felt like "refugees" within the Canadian state, and were denied the proper support they needed, under circumstances that were engineered by governmental officials in order to preserve non-Indigenous private interests and infrastructures. Racial capitalism and Wacquant's perspective are useful to make sense of this theoretical and policy outcome, which demonstrates the active role of the state in creating forms of internal displacement within Canada.

Lake St Martin First Nation and Little Saskatchewan First Nation members conform to three differential criteria (class, ethnicity, and residence) that determine and were implicitly used to orient the decision of the provincial government. Arguably, the official economic calculus underlying this decision inherently reflects a logic of penalization; far from simply reflecting a natural event, those guiding policy were given the opportunity to select who should be targeted by the flood. Without government intervention, the flood would have impacted white settlers' farms and residences, which were apparently seen as more deserving and valuable than Indigenous communities. The far-from-neutral categorization made by the provincial government determined who became the victims of the Canadian state's politico-administrative decision. This course of action and the subsequent "racist backlash from non-Indigenous people" that these displaced communities confronted was further legitimized by years of judicial inaction that confined community members within insecure housing, while simultaneously disconnecting them from the land (Thompson 2018).

This case study also illustrates the notion of liberal-paternalism in the context of state responses to climate displacement, or to use Wacquant's concept, the role of the *Centaur-state* in contemporary neoliberalism, liberal for those at the top and paternalistic for those at the bottom. This is perhaps most apparent in the experiences of members of the Lake St Martin First Nation and Little Saskatchewan First Nation communities following their "initial" displacement and the extended precarity they were made to endure following their evacuation. While those who hold economic and cultural capital at the top of the social structure can be trusted with the market principle of *laissez-faire et laissez passer* ("let them do and let them pass"), those at the bottom of the social structure, devoid of similar resources, are met with suspicion and fierce control (Wacquant 2014, 13). Being relocated to urban settings for eight years (sometimes relocated more than ten times) meant that First Nation members were unable to access and afford healthy food options, to have stability and security, and were forced to face intensified racism and discrimination (Ballard, Coughlin, and Martin 2020). This manufactured vulnerability was directly informed by government policies, which not only produced the initial circumstances of displacement, but were arguably responsible for perpetuating and extending the situation of precariousness confronted by members of these communities.

Finally, this case study shows that North American climate mobility is not only an international matter, but is also symptomatic of internal displacements within Canada itself. In the domestic context, the security-humanitarian paradigm, normally constructed for the global or international stage, becomes irrelevant. It is even absurd to use it, when we know that one of the main causes of forced displacement originates from government intervention, and that the subsequent absence of government action for several years aggravated Indigenous people's welfare. However, the concept of racial capitalism and Wacquant's approach provide pertinent lenses to analyze the forced internal displacement of Indigenous peoples, as they highlight the interplay and interdependence of race and capitalism in the domestic Canadian context.

CONCLUSION

The regulation of climate mobility in North America requires us to adopt critical lenses in order to move beyond a dominant security-humanitarianism paradigm. I borrowed those advanced by Wacquant and have aimed to show how this regulation operates in the climate-displacement context by following the triad of state-market-citizenship in my analysis. This critical framing helps draw attention to the ambiguous role of Canada, internationally and regionally – enlightened and tolerant with domestic and foreign audiences, but engaged in the criminalization of migrants and displaced people of the Global South.[7] The main case study taken up by the chapter builds on this critical framing. In doing so, the case of the 2011 government-diverted flood to Lake St Marin First Nation illustrates how "market-conforming state craft" operates domestically in the context of forced internal displacement. In unpacking the case, the chapter has aimed to emphasize and articulate how climate events have disparate effects, due to factors related to race, class, and citizenship.

By way of conclusion, two questions may be taken up as possible avenues for further work at the intersection of climate change and mobility. First, what is the role of researchers in the climate migration debate – as well as broader climate crisis – and how should this role be connected to other areas of society? Second, how should we, as researchers, convey scientific findings and debates from specialized disciplines to broader publics in deeply divided polities? Here it is crucial to emphasize and interrogate the varying ways researchers of climate mobility see their role: as researchers sensu stricto? As researchers who also serve the interests of their government? As researchers who also have a broader sociopolitical or social justice role? The evolving perspective that research participants need to be more involved in the research process and be considered co-researchers contributes to this redefinition of roles and exchange of knowledge. In this context, more progressive approaches to knowledge mobilization may help shape knowledge into instruments of potential action (Krause and von Denkowski 2020), though a central question persists: who will benefit from this knowledge and tools? How can displaced people, with limited economic and social capitals, benefit from them, while policy and humanitarian decision-makers are traditionally the ones who are research funders and research interlocutors? We return here to a key concern of racial capitalism that explicitly recognizes in its scope the need for political objectives and activism. Moreover, it is important to ask how climate mobility scholars can forge research networks that challenge the academic ethnocentrism of the Global North. Addressing this should not only be taken up geographically, but also with an acknowledgement of the different ways of knowing and different ways of practice that exist among subaltern and historically marginalized communities (Baldwin, Frölich, and Rothe 2019). Here, the issue of developing a more pluralistic and inclusive approach to the relationship of climate change and human mobility is related to questioning our limited, though dominant, view of Western science. This in turn may require scholars to substantively engage with other, non-Western, scientific approaches, including from Indigenous people, to productively inform ongoing climate mobility research (Whyte, Talley, and Gibson 2019). This could potentially, for instance, be articulated through the recognition of co-authorship for research contributors who are not affiliated with universities and would otherwise be seen as mere research participants.

NOTES

1 Notably, recently scholarship has increasingly connected climate change to paradigmatic cases of contemporary forced migration, including those which the Global North states recognize as claims to refugee status. See for instance Abel et al. (2019).

2 Fuel moisture is a useful concept in wildfire management: "the moisture content of live and dead vegetation is not in itself a weather element. It is a product, however, of the cumulative effects of past and present weather events and must be considered in evaluating the effects of current or future weather on fire potential. Fuel moisture content limits fire propagation. When moisture content is high, fires are difficult to ignite, and burn poorly if at all. With little moisture in the fuel, fires start easily, and wind and other driving forces may cause rapid and intense fire spread. Successful fire-control operations depend upon accurate information on current fuel moisture and reliable prediction of its changes" (National Wildfire Coordinating Group 2021). In addition, Ellis and colleagues (2022) tell us that wildfire activity is increasingly driven by climate change, and that "fuel moisture provides a powerful means of detecting changing fire potential."

3 In this context researchers have multiple obligations. For instance: the body of research about Indigenous issues, often accumulated without respecting Indigenous rights and Aboriginal traditional knowledge (ATK), must be critically reexamined (AFN n.d., 15); the fundamentally different epistemologies and political economies of Aboriginal knowledge and Western science require that researchers, trained in Western scientific knowledge, accept the principles of an Aboriginal knowledge protocol, which are often materialized by an agreement between researchers and knowledge-providing communities (AFN n.d., 16); working with Indigenous research partners – not research subjects – requires that "Aboriginal [peoples's] distinctive perspectives and understandings, deriving from their cultures and histories and embodied in Aboriginal languages" must be reflected in the research (AFN n.d., 15).

4 As a sidenote, as the authorship of the paper is largely centred on the Global North, it is important to recall how academic capitalism reinforces "power relations and contextuality" (Paasi 2005, 2015). This may imply that researchers studying mobilities might consider having international teams with a fair representation of researchers and students from both the Global South and the Global North.

5 The DED (formerly Extended Voluntary Departure) allows certain individuals from designated countries and regions facing political or civic conflict or natural disaster to stay in the United States (Immigration National Forum 2021).

6 Arguably, much of the vulnerability and adaptation literature does not directly confront the state structures and policies that contribute to generating climate mobility. See, e.g., Adger, de Campos, and Mortreux (2018); Timmer et al. (2021).

7 Although beyond the scope of this chapter, Wacquant's conceptual framework could also be mobilized to analyze regional and international mobilities that are partially induced by climate issues. For instance, US border security policies could also be scrutinized in order to understand how persons from Latin America, including those forcibly displaced by environmental events, are predominantly rejected by US authorities. See Jones (2021, 2022) for discussion of recent dynamics within the US.

REFERENCES

Abel, Guy J., Michael Brottrager, Jesus Crespo Cuaresma, and Raya Muttarak. 2019. "Climate, conflict and forced migration." *Global Environmental Change* 54: 239–49.

Adamson, Fiona B., and Gerasimos Tsourapas. 2019. "Migration Diplomacy in World Politics." *International Studies Perspectives* 20 (2): 113–28. https://doi.org/10.1093/isp/eky015.

Adger, W. Neil, Ricardo Safra de Campos, and Colette Mortreux. 2018. "Mobility, Displacement and Migration, and Their Interactions with Vulnerability and Adaptation to Environmental Risks." In *Routledge Handbook of Environmental Displacement and Migration*, edited by Robert McLeman and François Gemenne, 29–41. London and New York: Routledge.

Andrasko, Becca. 2022. "Looking Ahead: A Human Security Perspective to Tackling the Potential for Widespread Environmental Migration in Latin America." In *The Climate-Conflict-Displacement Nexus from a Human Security Perspective*, edited by Mohamed Behnassi, Himangana Gupta, Fred Kruidbos, and Anita Parlow, 71–110. Cham: Springer International Publishing. https://doi.org/10.1007/978-3-030-94144-4_5.

Artiga-Purcell, James Alejandro. 2022. "Variegated Extractivism: Rescaling El Salvador's Anti-Metal Mining and pro-Extractive Politics." *The Extractive Industries and Society* 9: 101035. https://doi.org/10.1016/j.exis.2021.101035.

Asch, Michael, James Tully, and John Borrows, eds. 2018. *Resurgence and Reconciliation: Indigenous-Settler Relations and Earth Teachings*. Toronto, Buffalo, and London: University of Toronto Press.

AFN (Assembly of First Nations). n.d. "First Nations Ethics Guide on Research and Aboriginal Traditional Knowledge." https://www.afn.ca/uploads/files/fn_ethics_guide_on_research_and_atk.pdf.

Atak, Idil, and James C. Simeon, eds. 2018. *The Criminalization of Migration: Context and Consequences*. Montreal: McGill-Queen's University Press.

Atak, Idil, Graham Hudson, and Delphine Nakache. 2018. "The Securitisation of Canada's Refugee System: Reviewing the Unintended Consequences of the 2012 Reform." *Refugee Survey Quarterly* 37 (1): 1–24.

Atak, Idil, Claire Ellis, and Zainab Abu Alrob. 2021. "Refugee System as a Bordering Site: Security, Surveillance, and the Rights of Asylum Seekers in Canada." In *Migration, Security, and Resistance: Global and Local Perspectives*, edited by Graham Hudson and Idil Atak, 25–46. London and New York: Routledge.

Atak, Idil, and Delphine Nakache. 2021. "A Critical Look at Canada's Implementation of the Global Compact for Migration." *Refugee Law Initiative Blog*, 1 February 2021. https://rli.blogs.sas.ac.uk/2021/02/01/a-critical-look-at-canadas-implementation-of-the-global-compact-for-migration/. Accessed 1 March 2023.

Baldwin, Andrew, Christiane Fröhlich, and Delf Rothe. 2019. "From Climate Migration to Anthropocene Mobilities: Shifting the Debate." *Mobilities* 14 (3): 289–97. https://doi.org/10.1080/17450101.2019.1620510.

Beck, Silke, and Martin Mahony. 2018. "The IPCC and the New Map of Science and Politics." *Wiley Interdisciplinary Reviews. Climate Change* 9 (6): e547. https://doi.org/10.1002/wcc.547.

Ballard, Myrle, Juliana Coughlin, and Donna Martin. 2020. "Reconciling with Minoaywin: First Nations Elders' Advice to Promote Healing from Forced Displacement." *Canadian Journal on Aging / La Revue Canadienne Du Vieillissement* 39 (2): 169–77. https://doi.org/10.1017/S0714980819000412.

Boas, Ingrid, Carol Farbotko, Helen Adams, Harald Sterly, Simon Bush, Kees van der Geest, Hanne Wiegel, Hasan Ashraf, Andrew Baldwin, et al. 2019. "Climate Migration Myths." *Nature Climate Change* 9 (12): 901–3. https://doi.org/10.1038/s41558-019-0633-3.

Bourdieu, Pierre. 1977. *Outline of a Theory of Practice*. Translated by Richard Nice. Cambridge Studies in Social and Cultural Anthropology. Cambridge: Cambridge University Press. https://doi.org/10.1017/CBO9780511812507.

– 1984. *Distinction: A Social Critique of the Judgement of Taste*. Cambridge: Harvard University Press.

– 1994. "Rethinking the State: On the Genesis and Structure of the Bureaucratic Field." *Sociological Theory* 12 (1): 1–19.

– 1998. *Practical Reason: On the Theory of Action*. Stanford, CA: Stanford University Press.

Bourdieu, Pierre, and Loïc J.D. Wacquant. 1992. *An Invitation to Reflexive Sociology*. Chicago: University of Chicago Press.

– 1999. "On the Cunning of Imperialist Reason." *Theory, Culture & Society* 16 (1): 41–58.

Burzyński, Michał, Christoph Deuster, Frédéric Docquier, and Jaime de Melo. 2021. "Climate Change, Inequality, and Human Migration." *Journal of the European Economic Association* (20) 3: 1145–97. https://doi.org/10.1093/jeea/jvab054.

Canadian Association of Refugee Lawyers. 2021. "Report on Climate Migrants." https://carl-acaadr.ca/wp-content/uploads/2021/11/CARL-Climate-Migration-Report-FINAL.pdf. Accessed 2 March 2023.

Casillas, Rodolfo. 2020. "Migración internacional y cambio climático: conexiones y desconexiones entre México y Centroamérica." *URVIO Revista Latinoamericana de Estudios de Seguridad* 26 (April): 73–92. https://doi.org/10.17141/urvio.26.2020.4038.

Chattopadhyay, Sumana. 2019. "Invited Article: 'You Are Not Welcome Here!' Understanding News Coverage of Central American Migrant

Families in Trump's America." *Journal of Family Communication* 19 (3): 177–90. https://doi.org/10.1080/15267431.2019.1632866.

Clochard, Olivier, ed. 2017. *Atlas des migrants en Europe. Approches critiques des politiques migratoires*. Paris: Dunod.

Coogan, Sean C.P., François-Nicolas Robinne, Piyush Jain, and Mike D. Flannigan. 2019. "Scientists' Warning on Wildfire – a Canadian Perspective." *Canadian Journal of Forest Research* 49 (9): 1015–23. https://doi.org/10.1139/cjfr-2019-0094.

Coogan, Sean C.P., Lori D. Daniels, Den Boychuk, Philip J. Burton, Mike D. Flannigan, Sylvie Gauthier, Victor Kafka, Jane S. Park, and B. Mike Wotton. 2021. "Fifty Years of Wildland Fire Science in Canada." *Canadian Journal of Forest Research* 51 (2): 283–302. https://doi.org/10.1139/cjfr-2020-0314.

Copeland, Nicholas. 2020. "A New Deal for Central America." *NACLA Report on the Americas* 52 (1): 67–76. https://doi.org/10.1080/10714839.2020.1733234.

Crowley, Sheila. 2006. "Where is Home?" In *There Is No Such Thing as a Natural Disaster: Race, Class, and Hurricane Katrina*, edited by Chester W. Hartman, and Gregory D. Squires, 121–66. New York: Routledge.

Depsky, Nicholas, and Diego Pons. 2020. "Meteorological Droughts Are Projected to Worsen in Central America's Dry Corridor throughout the 21st Century." *Environmental Research Letters* 16 (1): 1–14. https://doi.org/10.1088/1748-9326/abc5e2.

Deranger, Eriel. 2021. "The Climate Emergency & the Colonial Response." Toronto: Yellowhead Institute. https://yellowheadinstitute.org/2021/07/02/climate-emergency-colonial-response/. Accessed 1 March 2023.

Do Yun, Seong, and Brigitte S. Waldorf. 2016. "The Day After the Disaster: Forced Migration and Income Loss After Hurricanes Katrina and Rita." *Journal of Regional Science* 56 (3): 420–41. https://doi.org/10.1111/jors.12250.

Dodd, Warren, Patrick Scott, Courtney Howard, Craig Scott, Caren Rose, Ashlee Cunsolo, and James Orbinski. 2018. "Lived Experience of a Record Wildfire Season in the Northwest Territories, Canada." *Canadian Journal of Public Health* 109 (3): 327–37. https://doi.org/10.17269/s41997-018-0070-5.

Ellis, Todd M., David M.J.S. Bowman, Piyush Jain, Mike D. Flannigan, and Grant J. Williamson. 2022. "Global Increase in Wildfire Risk Due to Climate-Driven Declines in Fuel Moisture." *Global Change Biology* 28 (4): 1544–59. https://doi.org/10.1111/gcb.16006.

EUobserver. 2022. "Frontex Plan to Deploy to Africa Gets Initial 'Green Light.'" EUobserver. 2022. https://euobserver.com/migration/154357.

Faber, Jacob William. 2015. "Superstorm Sandy and the Demographics of Flood Risk in New York City." *Human Ecology* 43 (3): 363–78.

Fleuriet, K. Jill, and Mari Castellano. 2020. "Media, Place-Making, and Concept-Metaphors: The US-Mexico Border during the Rise of Donald Trump." *Media, Culture & Society* 42 (6): 880–97. https://doi.org/10.1177/0163443719890539.

Frontex. 2021. "Africa-Frontex Intelligence Community Meets in Senegal." 2021. https://frontex.europa.eu/media-centre/news/news-release/africafrontex-intelligence-community-meets-in-senegal-sRP1tC. Accessed 1 March 2023.

Geiger, Martin, and Antoine Pécoud, eds. 2020. *The International Organization for Migration: The New 'UN Migration Agency' in Critical Perspective*. Palgrave MacMillan.

Gemenne, François. 2011. "How they Became the Human Face of Climate Change. Research and Policy Interactions in the Birth of the 'Environmental Migration' Concept." In *Migration and Climate Change*, edited by Étienne Piguet, Antoine Pécoud, and Paul De Guchteneire, 225–59. Cambridge: Cambridge University Press.

Gill, Bikrum Singh. 2021. "A World in Reverse: The Political Ecology of Racial Capitalism." *Politics*, 1–16. https://doi.org/10.1177/0263395721994439.

Go, Julian. 2021. "Three Tensions in the Theory of Racial Capitalism." *Sociological Theory* 39 (1): 38–47. https://doi.org/10.1177/0735275120979822.

Gonzalez, Carmen. 2020. "Climate Change, Race, and Migration." *Journal of Law and Political Economy* 1 (1): 109–46. https://doi.org/10.5070/LP61146501.

Green, Rodney D., Marie Kouassi, and Belinda Mambo. 2013. "Housing, Race, and Recovery from Hurricane Katrina." *The Review of Black Political Economy* 40 (2): 145–63. https://doi.org/10.1007/s12114-011-9116-0.

Grosfoguel, Ramón. 2016. "What is Racism?" *Journal of World-Systems Research* 22(1): 9–15. https://doi.org/10.5195/jwsr.2016.609.

Hartman, Chester W., and Gregory D. Squires, eds. 2006. *There Is No Such Thing as a Natural Disaster: Race, Class, and Hurricane Katrina*. New York: Routledge.

Heller, Charles, and Antoine Pécoud. 2020. "Counting Migrants' Deaths at the Border: From Civil Society Counterstatistics to (Inter)Governmental Recuperation." *American Behavioral Scientist* 64 (4): 480–500. https://doi.org/10.1177/0002764219882996.

Hoffmann, Roman, Anna Dimitrova, Raya Muttarak, Jesus Crespo Cuaresma, and Jonas Peisker. 2020. "A Meta-Analysis of Country-Level Studies on Environmental Change and Migration." *Nature Climate Change* 10 (10): 904–12. https://doi.org/10.1038/s41558-020-0898-6.

House of Commons of Canada. 2018. "New Tools for the 21st Century - The Global Compact for Safe, Orderly and Regular Migration and The Global Compact for Refugees: An Interim Report." Standing Committee on Citizenship and Immigration. Ottawa: House of Commons of Canada. https://www.ourcommons.ca/DocumentViewer/en/42-1/CIMM/report-23. Accessed 5 March 2023.

Imai, Shin, Leah Gardner, and Sarah Weinberger. 2017. "The 'Canada Brand': Violence and Canadian Mining Companies in Latin America." SSRN Scholarly Paper 2886584. Rochester, NY: Social Science Research Network. https://doi.org/10.2139/ssrn.2886584.

IRCC (Immigration, Refugees and Citizenship Canada). 2012. "Implementing Arrangement between the Department of Citizenship and Immigration of Canada and the Canada Border Services Agency, on the One Side, and the Department of State and the Department of Homeland Security of the United States of America, on the Other Side, concerning Biometric Visa and Immigration Information Sharing." Ottawa: Government of Canada. https://www.canada.ca/en/immigration-refugees-citizenship/corporate/mandate/policies-operational-instructions-agreements/agreements/implementing-arrangement-canada-united-states-america-biometric-information-sharing.html. Accessed 5 March 2023.

– 2015. "Temporary Resident Permits: Applying for Permanent Residence." Program Descriptions. 2015. https://www.canada.ca/en/immigration-refugees-citizenship/corporate/publications-manuals/operational bulletins-manuals/permanent-residence/non-economic-classes/permits.html. Accessed 5 March 2023.

– 2020. "Canada: A History of Refuge." Education and Awareness. 24 August 2020. https://www.canada.ca/en/immigration-refugees-citizenship/services/refugees/history.html. Accessed 5 March 2023.

Indigenous Climate Action. 2021. "Decolonizing Climate Policy in Canada." Ottawa: Indigenous Climate Action. https://static1.squarespace.com/static/5e8e4b5ae8628564ab4bc44c/t/6061cb5926611066ba64a953/1617021791071/pcf_critique_FINAL.pdf. Accessed 3 March 2023.

Jakobsson, Elin. 2021. "How Climate-Induced Migration Entered the UN Policy Agenda in 2007–2010: A Multiple Streams Assessment." *Politics and Governance* 9 (4): 16–26. https://doi.org/10.17645/pag.v9i4.4519.

Jenkins, Destin, and Justin Leroy, eds. 2021. *Histories of Racial Capitalism*. New York: Columbia University Press.

Jewell, Eva, and Ian Mosby. 2021. "Calls to Action Accountability: A 2021 Status Update on Reconciliation." Toronto: Yellowhead Institute.

Johnson, Walter. 2020. *The Broken Heart of America: St. Louis and the Violent History of the United States*. New York: Basic Books.

Jones, Reece. 2021. *White Borders: The History of Race and Immigration in the United States from Chinese Exclusion to the Border Wall*. Boston, MA: Beacon Press.
– 2022. *Nobody Is Protected: How the Border Patrol Became the Most Dangerous Police Force in the United States*. First Hardcover Edition. Berkeley, CA: Counterpoint Press.
Kelman, Ilan. 2007. "Hurricane Katrina Disaster Diplomacy." *Disasters* 31 (3): 288–309. https://doi.org/10.1111/j.1467-7717.2007.01010.x.
Kita, Stern Mwakalimi, and Clionadh Raleigh. 2018. "Environmental Migration and International Political Security: Rhetoric, Reality and Questions." In *Routledge Handbook of Environmental Displacement and Migration*, edited by Robert McLeman and François Gemenne, 356–69. London and New York: Routledge.
Kocher, Austin. 2021. "Migrant Protection Protocols and the Death of Asylum." *Journal of Latin American Geography* 20 (1): 249–58. https://doi.org/10.1353/lag.2021.0010.
Krause, Ulrike, and Cordula von Denkowski. 2020. "Transfer of Knowledge for and with Whom? Ethical Reflections on Participatory Research with Displaced People." In *Wissensmobilisierung Und Transfer in Der Fluchtforschung – Kommunikation, Beratung Und Gemeinsames Forschungshandeln*, edited by Monika Gonser, Karin Zimmer, Nikola Mühlhäußer, and Danielle Gluns, 137–49. Muenster, NY: Waxmann.
Léonard, Sarah, and Christian Kaunert. 2022. "The Securitisation of Migration in the European Union: Frontex and Its Evolving Security Practices." *Journal of Ethnic and Migration Studies* 48 (6): 1417–29. https://doi.org/10.1080/1369183X.2020.1851469.
Leong, Nancy. 2013. "Racial Capitalism." *Harvard Law Review* 126 (8): 2151–226.
McAdam, Jane. 2012. *Climate Change, Forced Migration, and International Law*. Oxford: Oxford University Press.
– 2019. "Global Compact for Safe, Orderly and Regular Migration." *International Legal Materials* 58 (1): 160–94. https://doi.org/10.1017/ilm.2019.6.
– 2020. "Displacing Evacuations: A Blind Spot in Disaster Displacement Research." *Refugee Survey Quarterly* 39 (4): 583–90. https://doi.org/10.1093/rsq/hdaa017.
McLeman, Robert. 2019. "International Migration and Climate Adaptation in an Era of Hardening Borders." *Nature Climate Change* 9 (12): 911–18. https://doi.org/10.1038/s41558-019-0634-2.
Milner, James. 2021. "Canada and the UN Global Compact on Refugees: A Case Study of Influence in the Global Refugee Regime." In *International*

Affairs and Canadian Migration Policy, edited by Yiagadeesen Samy and Howard Duncan, 41–63. Canada and International Affairs. Cham: Springer International Publishing. https://doi.org/10.1007/978-3-030-46754-8_3.

Miyares, Ines, Richard Wright, Alison Mountz, and Adrian Bailey. 2019. "Truncated Transnationalism, the Tenuousness of Temporary Protected Status, and Trump." *Journal of Latin American Geography* 18 (1): 210–16. https://doi.org/10.1353/lag.2019.0011.

Monin, Kira, Jeanne Batalova, and Tianjian Lai. 2021. "Refugees and Asylees in the United States." Migrationpolicy.org. 12 May 2021. https://www.migrationpolicy.org/article/refugees-and-asylees-united-states-2021. Accessed 5 March 2023.

National Immigration Forum. 2021. "Fact Sheet: Temporary Protected Status (TPS)." National Immigration Forum. 2021. https://immigrationforum.org/article/fact-sheet-temporary-protected-status/. Accessed 5 March 2023.

National Wildfire Coordinating Group. 2021. "Weather and Fuel Moisture." 2021. https://www.nwcg.gov/publications/pms425-1/weather-and-fuel-moisture. Accessed 5 March 2023.

Palinkas, Lawrence A. 2020a. *Global Climate Change, Population Displacement, and Public Health: The Next Wave of Migration*. Cham: Springer International Publishing. https://doi.org/10.1007/978-3-030-41890-8.

– 2020b. "Hurricane Katrina and New Orleans." In *Global Climate Change, Population Displacement, and Public Health: The Next Wave of Migration*, edited by Lawrence A. Palinkas, 17–33. Cham: Springer International Publishing. https://doi.org/10.1007/978-3-030-41890-8_2.

Paasi, Anssi. 2005. "Globalisation, Academic Capitalism, and the Uneven Geographies of International Journal Publishing Spaces." *Environment and Planning A* 37 (5): 769–89. https://doi.org/10.1068/a3769.

– 2015. "Academic Capitalism and the Geopolitics of Knowledge." In *The Wiley Blackwell Companion to Political Geography*, edited by John Agnew, Virginie Mamadouh, Anna J. Secor, and Joanne Sharp, 507–23. New Jersey: Wiley-Blackwell. https://doi.org/10.1002/9781118725771.ch37.

Peck, Jamie. 2010. *Constructions of Neoliberal Reason*. New York: Oxford University Press.

Piguet, Etienne. 2022. "Linking Climate Change, Environmental Degradation, and Migration: An Update after 10 Years." *WIREs Climate Change* 13 (1): e746. https://doi.org/10.1002/wcc.746.

Piguet, Étienne, Raoul Kaenzig, and Jérémie Guélat. 2018. "The Uneven Geography of Research on 'Environmental Migration.'" *Population and Environment* 39 (4): 357–83.

Quijano, Aníbal. 2014. *Cuestiones y Horizontes: De la Dependencia Histórico-Estructural a la Colonialidad/Descolonialidad del Poder*. Buenos Aires: CLACSO. http://biblioteca.clacso.edu.ar/clacso/se/20140424014720/Cuestionesyhorizontes.pdf. Accessed 5 March 2023.

Raker, Ethan J., Sarah R. Lowe, Mariana C. Arcaya, Sydney T. Johnson, Jean Rhodes, and Mary C. Waters. 2019. "Twelve Years Later: The Long-Term Mental Health Consequences of Hurricane Katrina." *Social Science & Medicine* 242 (December): 112610. https://doi.org/10.1016/j.socscimed.2019.112610.

Robinson Cedric. 2000. *Black Marxism: The Making of the Black Radical Tradition*. Chapel Hill: University of North Carolina Press.

Thistlethwaite, Jason, Andrea Minano, Daniel Henstra, and Daniel Scott. 2020. "Indigenous Reserve Lands in Canada Face High Flood Risk." Centre for International Governance Innovation. https://www.jstor.org/stable/resrep24941. Accessed 1 March 2023.

Thompson, Shirley. 2018. "Take Three: Filming Three Participatory Videos with Displaced Indigenous People from Little Saskatchewan First Nation and Lake St. Martin First Nation." *International Journal of Humanities, Arts and Social Sciences* 4 (4): 168–78. https://dx.doi.org/10.20469/ijhss.4.10002-4.

Thomspon, Shirley, Myrle Ballard, and Donna Martin. 2014. "Lake St. Martin First Nation Community Members' Experiences of Induced Displacement: 'We're like Refugees.'" *Refuge* 29 (2): 75–86.

Timmer, Alexandra, Moritz Baumgärtel, Louis Kotzé, and Lieneke Slingenberg. 2021. "The Potential and Pitfalls of the Vulnerability Concept for Human Rights." *Netherlands Quarterly of Human Rights* 39 (3): 190–7. https://doi.org/10.1177/09240519211048009.

UNHCR (United Nations High Commissioner for Refugees). n.d. "Climate Change and Disaster Displacement in the Global Compact on Refugees." https://www.unhcr.org/5c9e13297.pdf. Accessed 5 March 2023.

US Customs and Border Protection. 2021. "Stats and Summaries." https://www.cbp.gov/newsroom/media-resources/stats; see in particular: https://www.cbp.gov/sites/default/files/assets/documents/2021-Aug/USBORD~3.PDF. Accessed 2 March 2023.

US Department of State. 2002. *U.S. - Canada Smart Border/30 Point Action Plan Update*. Washington, DC: The White House. 6 December 2002. https://2001-2009.state.gov/p/wha/rls/fs/18128.htm. Accessed 2 March 2023.

Virdee, Satnam. 2019. "Racialized Capitalism: An Account of Its Contested Origins and Consolidation." *Sociological Review* 67 (1): 3–27.

Wacquant, Loïc. 2005. "'Enemies of the Wholesome Part of the Nation':

Postcolonial Migrants in the Prisons of Europe." *Sociologie* 1 (1): 31–51.
– 2010. "Crafting the Neoliberal State: Workfare, Prisonfare, and Social Insecurity." *Sociological Forum* 25 (2): 197–220. https://doi.org/10.1111/j.1573-7861.2010.01173.x.
– 2012a. "Three Steps to a Historical Anthropology of Actually Existing Neoliberalism." *Social Anthropology* 20 (1): 66–79. https://doi.org/10.1111/j.1469-8676.2011.00189.x.
– 2012b. "The Wedding of Workfare and Prisonfare in the 21st Century." *Journal of Poverty* 16 (3): 236–49. https://doi.org/10.1080/10875549.2012.695540.
– 2014. "Marginality, Ethnicity and Penality in the Neoliberal City: An Analytic Cartography." *Ethnic and Racial Studies* 37 (10): 1686. https://doi.org/10.1080/01419870.2014.931996.
White, Gregory. 2011. *Climate Change and Migration: Security and Borders in a Warming World*. USA: New York: Oxford University Press.
Whyte, Kyle, Jared L. Talley, and Julia D. Gibson. 2019. "Indigenous Mobility Traditions, Colonialism, and the Anthropocene." *Mobilities* 14 (3): 319–35. https://doi.org/10.1080/17450101.2019.1611015.
WFP (The World Food Program USA). 2020. "The Dry Corridor in Central America." WFP. https://www.wfpusa.org/emergencies/dry-corridor/. Accessed 5 March 2023.
Yayboke, Erol, Trevor Houser, Janina Staguhn, and Tani Salma. 2020. "A New Framework for U.S. Leadership on Climate Migration." Center for Strategic and International Studies (CSIS). https://www.jstor.org/stable/resrep27039.
Young, Julie E.E. 2018. "The Mexico-Canada Border: Extraterritorial Border Control and the Production of 'Economic Refugees.'" *International Journal of Migration and Border Studies* 4 (1–2): 35–50. https://doi.org/10.1504/IJMBS.2018.091225.
Zaiotti, Ruben, ed. 2016. *Externalizing Migration Management: Europe, North America and the Spread of "Remote Control" Practices*. London: Routledge. https://doi.org/10.4324/9781315650852.

PART THREE

Migration Norms, Values, and Narratives across Canada, Mexico, and the US

9

Waiting as Mobility Control: Coping Practices of African Migrants in Mexico

Olga Odgers-Ortiz and Olga Olivas-Hernández

Migrants and asylum seekers across the globe confront increasingly significant wait times while navigating through different migration systems. Migratory flows through Mexican territory, far from being an exception to this trend, seem to constitute a paradigmatic case in which the Mexican state imposes bureaucratic requirements that seek to prevent, or at least delay, migrants' mobility from its southern border with Guatemala to the United States (Arriola 2021). The obstacles that migrants must face to cross Mexico, what Campos-Delgado (2021) calls the "Mexican Transit Control Regime," (MTCR) or a form of migratory "probation" (Vianelli, Gill, and Hoellerer 2021). When coupled with more recent migration policies implemented by the United States, including the Migrant Protection Protocols (MPPs) and Title 42,[1] (see Pedroza and Gil-Everaert in this volume) Mexican territory, particularly its northern border with the United States, has become a place of waiting for thousands of migrants from around the world (Vidal and Musset 2016).

Thousands of migrants remain stranded for indeterminate periods in Mexico in their transit to the United States and Canada. Therefore, by its geopolitical position, Mexico has become a container or buffer zone for mixed migration within the migratory landscape of the Americas. Entrapment in Mexico becomes a critical obstacle to fulfilling migration projects intended to end in North American destinations. Yet those who find themselves immersed in it also develop strategies of resistance in the face of uncertainty (Gil-Everaert 2020).

Our goal in this chapter is to move beyond understanding analysis bureaucratic and legal structuring of entrapment in the border area to observe ways in which migrants and asylum seekers cope with it. To put our argument succinctly, we draw on ethnographic fieldwork with African migrants in Tijuana to show that *strandedness* does not entail passivity, and coping strategies are paramount features of migratory systems. We employ the term "strandedness" to denote the condition experienced by individuals or families who left their places of origin or residence with a project in mind, but were forced to stop in a non-chosen location and forced to wait for an uncertain period. We find it necessary to analyze strandedness, not only because it is a key feature for understanding mobility in North America, but also because entrapment produces uncertainty, which undermines the well-being of migrants (Phillimore and Cheung 2021; Sagbakken, Bregård, and Varvin 2020).

Our main argument in this chapter is that far from being passive victims, stranded migrants engage in practices of resistance (Gil-Everaert 2020) and coping strategies to give meaning to extended waiting periods. If understanding mobility control policies is crucial to understanding how migration systems work, understanding how coping strategies are produced and applied is equally relevant. Accordingly, this chapter aims to offer an account of life while waiting as part of analyzing the governance of migration in North America. In other words, we consider it essential to understand how the consequences of strandedness are experienced in the daily lives of migrants and refugees to understand the functioning of a migration policy that is "[g]etting farther away from, not closer to, comprehensive and humane migration policy" (Pedroza and Gil-Everaert, in this volume).

Therefore, we consider that analyzing how migrants face strandedness in crucial locations of migratory entrapment is critical to understanding the governance of migration in North America. We focus our analysis on Tijuana, located on Mexico's northern border, not only because we identify this area as a critical case of migrant entrapment, but also because of its geopolitical position: Mexico has become a container or buffer zone for mixed migration flows, particularly at these strategic and large-scale border crossings.

In other words, instead of explaining broader policy changes, this chapter drills down to how specific policies that extend waiting times affect the lives of people on the move. Moreover, although the specific processes by which entrapment occurs may vary from one context to another, in all cases, waiting involves increasing financial and emotional investment, which must be borne by those trying to reach their migratory destination – in this sense, analyzing the experience of being stranded at the US-Mexico border contributes to understanding what it means to be a migrant in the Americas.

In addition, it is important to remember that migration throughout the Americas has diversified to include increasingly large groups of extracontinental migrants, predominantly from Africa, South Asia, and Europe. In this chapter we analyze the narratives of African migrants stranded in Tijuana, Mexico, to understand how they understand and experience waiting. Through extensive fieldwork, we identify three main coping strategies through religious beliefs, political engagement, and developing future-oriented parallel projects (Acharya and Northcott 2007; Khawaja et al. 2008; Zbidat et al. 2020). Analyzing these coping strategies allows us to contribute to the understanding of how the policies of containment impact migrants' lives and the ways in which migrants manage these adverse circumstances.

These coping strategies are particularly important among African migrants, since, in contrast to those coming from Latin American countries, people from Africa have significant and unique vulnerabilities. The distance from their place of origin, their poor proficiency in the Spanish language, the fragility of their migratory networks, the scarcity of economic resources, cultural distance, and racialized status (by which they are labelled as foreigners) intersect to place them in a position of extreme vulnerability. Thus, the focus on African migrants offers a unique object of analysis, in contrast with the prevalent media and academic focus on people from Latin America, not only because of the increased vulnerability of this population but also because the extent – and duration – of their trajectories allows them to narrate their entrapment in Tijuana within a broad spatial and temporal perspective. Currently, studies on African migration in this context are extremely scarce.

In order to present our analysis of coping strategies developed by stranded African migrants in Mexico's northern border, this chapter is organized in five sections. We start with a literature review about migration trends, policies of containment, and forced immobility during migratory journeys. Then, following a brief discussion about strandedness, uncertainty, and coping strategies to frame our approach to the situation of African migrants in Mexico, we argue that strandedness produces uncertainty and undermines the well-being of African migrants, requiring the production of coping strategies. The third section describes our methodological perspective. The fourth section is focused on our interlocutors' narratives to describe the migratory routes, entrapment times, and processes experienced by African migrants stranded in Tijuana. In the fifth section, based on the analyzed ethnographic material, we describe three coping strategies: producing new narratives through religious beliefs, political engagement, and raising parallel life projects. Finally, we discuss these results.

MIGRATION TRENDS, POLICIES OF CONTAINMENT, AND FORCED IMMOBILITY

During the last decade, the migratory profile of those arriving in Tijuana, seeking to reach the US, has changed significantly. Before 2016, most migrants arriving in this border region were Mexicans searching for the "American Dream." They were joined by many Central Americans, who generally followed the same routes, trying to be indistinguishable from them. To a lesser extent, Latin Americans of various other nationalities joined these flows.

However, by 2016 a significant flow of Haitian migrants coming from temporary stays in South America (Brazil and Chile mainly) changed the migration physiognomy in the region. Some African migrants who were co-workers with the Haitian population in South America also travelled in this period (Alarcón and Ortiz 2017; Yee-Quintero 2017). Although the number of African migrants was still minimal as of 2016,[2] media reports suggested a higher number given that Haitian migrants often presented themselves as Congolese upon arriving at Mexico's southern border, assuming that this would decrease their chances at immediate deportation. Regardless, there has been a significant increase in African migration beyond the initial misunderstanding since that time.

Although there has been a growing interest in African migration to Mexico, specialized publications on this topic remain relatively scarce. Several authors (Chan-Pech 2019; FLACSO 2011; Jiménez-Martínez and Martínez Cruz 2021; Ray and Leyva Flores 2020) agree that African migrants arrive in Mexico primarily by land, from the south of the continent, on established mixed migration routes. These new dynamics are implicated in broader dynamics. As Yates and Bolter (2021) and Smith (2022) point out, the increase in African migration to Latin America is due to the intensification of control of mobility in Europe – in transit and destination countries – causing some Latin American countries to be perceived as alternative destinations (Brazil, Chile, Argentina) or as the beginning of new transit routes to the US or Canada (Marcelino and Cerutti 2012).

FLACSO (2011) identifies two main means of entry: maritime (via Cuba, Corn Island, and Little Corn Island in Nicaragua and San Andres Island in Colombia) and air (Argentina, Brazil, Venezuela, Ecuador, Panama, and Nicaragua). Others (IOM 2013; Yates and Bolter 2021) point to Ecuador and Brazil as main entries. Access through Ecuador would be related to migratory facilities associated with "a policy of universal citizenship, adopted by the Ecuadorian State in 2008" (Echeverri and Acevedo 2018, 107). The importance of Brazil lies in a more significant historical link, reflected in that "it is the Latin American country with the most embassies and consulates in Africa" (Yates and Bolter 2021, 1). Ménard Marleau (2018) points to Brazil and Ecuador as main entries for Senegalese migrants heading to Argentina, but insists that their mobility is "non-continuous, non-linear and non-unidirectional" (Ménard Marleau 2018, 36). Similarly, Zubrzycki (2021, 258) suggests that Senegalese migration to Argentina is considered as fragmented migration, given the constant reevaluation of opportunities driving toward unplanned trajectories.

In 2016, Gattari (2016, 42) pointed out some settlement processes associated with the difficulty of continuing the northward journey and the lengthening of waiting times. In particular, she mentions the formation of families with Argentine women, as African migrants mainly were young, single men. For Yates and Bolter (2021), the main route across the American continent starts in Peru, passes to Brazil – where there are usually extended sojourns – and continues through Ecuador and Colombia whether the borders are crossed in a documented or clandestine manner. Once in Colombia, migrants face one of the most dangerous steps – the Darien Gap – to reach Panama. In Panama, migrants are often detained by the authorities and taken to the border with Costa Rica. From Costa Rica, they continue overland through Nicaragua, Honduras, and Guatemala to reach Mexico, mainly through the city of Tapachula.

Migrants face diverse obstacles along the route from their places of origin to Mexico, which force them to make unwanted and unforeseen stops for indefinite periods. These include the difficulty in obtaining the economic resources for onward travel, the lack of documents to cross borders which forces them onto more dangerous irregular routes, and the imposition of extended waiting times for administrative procedures that allow them to continue their journey legally. These three types of obstacles are related. For instance, the cost of asylum and migration procedures and the consequent waiting times drain the resources migrants could have gathered or received from their relatives abroad. The other option, crossing the US border clandestinely, is both more expensive and dangerous, with greater risk of physical assault and/or being robbed of resources. We are most interested in the effects of state policies on waiting times because unlike the other two factors (economic difficulties and lack of documents), the latter is part of the MTCR (Campos-Delgado 2021) and is used as a deterrent to migration (Gammeltoft-Hansen and Tan 2017; Kent, Norman, and Tennis 2020). State-imposed protracted waiting constitutes an example of how migration governance regimes significantly impact the rights and well-being of migrants.

In the last decade, there has been growing interest in understanding periods of immobility or entrapment occurring in migratory journeys. On the one hand, several authors have questioned the validity of the category "migration in transit" due to the complexity of waiting times, which can lead to transformations in migration projects (Collyer 2010; Duvell 2012; Hess 2012; Shum 2020; Wyss 2019). Among other alternatives, "mixed migration," "fragmented journeys" (Collyer 2010), "onward migration" (Shum 2020), or "fluid (im)mobility" (Arriola 2021) have been proposed, although, so far, there is no consensus about how to designate these forms of mobility. On the other hand, there has been growing interest in understanding what waiting means for stranded migrants, as well as in analyzing how they cope with this situation (Gil 2020; Odgers, Olivas, and Bojorquez 2023). While stranded, migrants and asylum seekers are in a highly vulnerable situation, where uncertainty, precarity, and insecurity are paramount. Thus, recent literature identifies extended waiting times as a deterrent to mobility (Campos-Delgado 2021; Gammeltoft-Hansen and Tan, 2017; Kent, Norman, and Tennis 2020). This chapter engages with that literature and aims to analyze the consequences of lengthy waiting times for migrants and asylum seekers.

STRANDEDNESS, UNCERTAINTY, AND COPING STRATEGIES

From a structural or systemic perspective, we can consider that the condition of strandedness is produced by the combined effect of different states' migration policies, which configure what Michel Agier (2008) calls the (transnational) management of undesirables. In essence, "undesirable" populations are pressured to leave certain territories and arrive in other countries where effective mechanisms to implement their reception are nonexistent. It produces places of strandedness, which become visible with the appearance of refugee camps or overcrowded detention centres for immigrants. Following Gammeltoft-Hansen and Tan (2017) and Campos-Delgado (2021), we argue that the increase in waiting times is not an unintended effect of current migration policies. It is a control and deterrence strategy over migration. Therefore, migrants are "stranded within their mobility" rather than "in waiting," which means that official and extraofficial devices force them to remain for uncertain and extended periods in places they did not choose.

As described before, there are some hot spots for migration strandedness in Mexico, including at its northern and southern borders. We consider that understanding the devices that produce strandedness is essential, but it is not enough. In addition to analyzing the structural dimension that immobilizes populations within their migration trajectories, it is necessary to add a phenomenological analysis that understands the experience of strandedness from asylum seekers' and migrants' perspectives. Strandedness implies a tension between the desire to move forward and the need to integrate into an unchosen place. However, more profoundly, strandedness produces a tension between putting life on hold for months or years on the one hand, and life that continues moving forward despite everything on the other. These tensions affect migrants' well-being, so they must develop strategies to cope in order to manage the effects on their well-being.

Coping strategies are often used by migrants globally to help improve their immediate well-being during indefinite waiting periods. Mathews and Izquierdo (2010, 5) propose that "wellbeing is an optimal state for an individual, community, society, and the world as a whole. It is conceived of, expressed, and experienced in different ways by different individuals and within the cultural contexts of different societies." Philimore and Cheung (2021) argue that the uncertainty caused by entrapment is a form of violence undermining the mental health of refugees. However, migrants and asylum seekers do not remain passive in the face of this form of violence. In this sense, our chapter builds on several recent studies that have identified similar trends globally. Gil-Everaert (2020, 1) analyzes how asylum seekers "reconcile long-term future projects with immediate future during moments of waiting," developing tactics to *inhabit the meanwhile* while not giving up on their projects, and "interactively inhabit the meanwhile and actively construct meaning in suspension, belonging in exclusion, home in homelessness and routine in temporal uncertainty" (Gil-Everaert 2020, 14). In their study of Syrian refugees in Germany, Zbidat et al. (2020) identify six coping strategies: activity, cognitive coping, social coping, religious coping, avoidance, and emotional coping. Using the case of Sudanese refugees in Brisbane, Khawaja et al. (2008) similarly find four coping strategies: reliance on religious beliefs, cognitive strategies such as reframing the situation, relying on inner resources, and focusing on future wishes and aspirations.

To approach the relationship between places of strandedness and well-being experiences, we consider it important to understand the social meaning these places have. Not only as a "context in which well-being as an outcome emerges" (Atkinson, Fuller, and Painter 2016), but as places that are "inherently relational in both its production and its influence" (Atkinson, Fuller, and Painter 2016, 3; Schwanen and Atkinson 2015). In this sense, it is important for us to understand the role played by the places where strandedness occurs in affecting migrant experiences of pursuing well-being through different coping strategies, producing new narratives about their conditions. It is important to recall that – unlike the situations observed by Zbidat et al. (2020) and Khawaja et al. (2008) in other locations where migrants are in a place of potential permanence and cope with bureaucratic and other barriers to integration – strandedness is crucial for understanding the uncertainty experienced by refugees in Mexico's northern border.

METHODS

This chapter is based on ethnographic fieldwork conducted in migrant and refugee shelters, including a community centre in Tijuana, Mexico. As part of the fieldwork, we participated in several activities coordinated by various shelters and community centres for migrants from 2018 to 2021. Before March 2020, activities were held in person. We also collaborated in Spanish language lessons organized by the community centre, which allowed us to contact migrants from Cameroon, Ghana, Burkina Faso, Guinea Conakry, and Togo. Members of the African population seldom go to shelters, preferring to rent accommodations independently, even if that requires them to live in precarious and crowded apartments. Spanish lessons continued online after the COVID-19 pandemic outbreak.

Our fieldwork allowed us to gather a wide range of data, including everyday routines, emotional and health concerns, fears, and projects for the future. Per the refugees' request, we assisted them in various immigration and asylum-seeking procedures, such as translating regulations and instructions, completing official forms, requesting appointments at the Mexican Refugee Aid Commission (Comisión Mexicana de Ayuda Refugiados [COMAR])[3] or Mexican embassies, and support in family reunification procedures for those who had obtained refugee status in Mexico. This engagement allowed us to learn "from below" about the obstacles and waiting times involved in these processes, the emotions experienced, and strategies developed by the refugees and asylum seekers. We also accompanied the participants in several activities, including medical appointments, administrative procedures (e.g., obtaining a driver's licence, registering for taxes, signing up for a phone line), and political demonstrations. While our project initially focused on the experience of migrants of all nationalities who find themselves trapped in mobility, we later decided to concentrate our attention on people from Africa, due to the accumulation of vulnerabilities present in their experience. Our qualitative and ethnographic approach focuses on gaining empirical data on the individual life experiences of our collaborators. It is not representative of all migrants in this situation but gives us a closer approach to this population's conditions in the city.

After developing relations of confidence, we invited six persons to participate in in-depth interviews. We carried out follow-up interviews several months apart in most of the cases, allowing us to gather data about changing circumstances. The interviews delved into past and present experiences, including the reasons and circumstances of the departure from their places of origin, the journey, their current legal and emotional situations, and their immediate and long-term plans. The interviews also addressed strategies for dealing with obstacles in the journey, immigration procedures, and coping with the emotional difficulties of waiting and travel. We also used social networks (Facebook and WhatsApp) to follow up with participants who had crossed the border to the US during the study.

Participants are from various countries; the youngest is eighteen years old, while the oldest is over fifty. Some are of rural origin and have little formal education, while others have had access to university studies. Despite this diversity, they all have in common that they entered Mexico's southern border after a long and exhausting journey, and passed through Brazil, Chile, or Ecuador in highly precarious conditions. All of them received refugee status in Mexico, without having applied for it, and their initial intentions were to reach the US or Canada.[4] All were stranded in Mexico and faced the dilemma of either attempting family reunification in Mexico based on their refugee status or continuing to try to move north as asylum seekers in the US or Canada.

Being granted refugee status in Mexico was not expected by most of our collaborators. It affected how they envisioned their migration projects, especially after learning of the limitations and extended waiting periods for requesting asylum in the United States, or the lack of information and feasibility for requesting asylum in Canada from Mexico. These situations contributed to the strandedness conditions and impacted how this population redefined their strategies to move forward with a migration project. Moving forward could include illegal border crossings and family reunification in Mexico. In some cases, they continued with the plan of reaching the US in the future while accessing their rights as refugees in Mexico. The mobility process became exhausting, with administrative procedures creating a distinct sense of protracted uncertainty, undermining their well-being.

More broadly, our interviews and engagement showed that African migrants dealt with political, social, material, and cultural difficulties in the journey from their places of origin to northern Mexico. However, these frustrations and exhaustion did not mean that research collaborators were merely passive subjects in their strandedness. On the contrary, they undertook coping mechanisms which allowed for greater personal agency – a dynamic which is often overshadowed in studies examining overall trends in regional mobility.

Under these circumstances, African migrants actively developed coping strategies as part of a meaning-making process allowing them to deal with difficulties they lived in the past, handle challenges they were facing in the present, and envision desirable futures. We identified three main strategies related to religious orientations, political engagement, and redefinition of the migratory project based on the development of parallel life projects.

We found that research participants either turned to religious practices or reinterpreted their situations from a religious/spiritual stance, allowing them to give meaning to their adversity and cultivate hope. This strategy was mainly based on personal resources and had an individual orientation. They were often not related to a religious community in Tijuana, and turning to this strategy was related to the individuals' religious trajectories.

On the other hand, political engagement relied on community support and demonstrated an active stance to pursue social and political change in favour of their communities. Turning to this strategy was, in most cases, the result of civil society organizations (CSOs) supporting migrants on a day-to-day basis but also advocating for their rights, including encouraging communities to have an active role in the process.

Finally, some participants redefined their migration projects by developing parallel life projects, including settling in Mexico and at the same time planning to continue journeys to the US. Through this strategy, migrants widened their future possibilities and opportunities. Redefining migratory projects was often facilitated by access to material, social, cultural, and personal resources, since it involved the investment of all these resources without certainty of achieving migratory goals.

All participant names were replaced by pseudonyms, except when participants explicitly asked for their real names to be used. All respondents signed an informed consent form. From an interpretive (Glaser and Strauss 1967) narrative (Andrews 2002) approach, the data analysis aims to reconstruct migratory trajectories, identifying strategies developed to cope with uncertainty during waiting periods. All the study procedures were reviewed and approved by the Ethics Committee of El Colegio de la Frontera Norte and adhered to the principles of the Helsinki Declaration and other guidelines for the protection of human subjects. All participants were informed of the aims and procedures of the research project, their rights as participants, and the risks and benefits their participation entailed. Before being interviewed, they read and signed an informed consent letter in their preferred language (Spanish or French).

MIGRATORY ROUTES, ENTRAPMENT PROCESSES, AND "WAITING TIMES" EXPERIENCED BY AFRICAN MIGRANTS STRANDED IN TIJUANA

In what follows, we describe the individual narratives, trajectories, and experiences of four research collaborators: Aziz, Carvel, Jade, and Joy. We describe the difficulties and limitations they experienced in their journeys from their places of origin to Mexico, and the administrative procedures and different challenges that shaped their condition of strandedness.

Fleeing from the violence in her place of origin, where she was a torture victim, in 2019, Jade[5] managed to cross 100 kilometres clandestinely until she left her country and reached Nigeria. She had no money to pay for her lodging when she arrived, but she trusted that her relatives would provide her with the essentials to continue her journey. However, the hotel owner where she was staying withheld her phone and passport, forcing her into prostitution because she had not paid the rent for her room (and knowing that she would not be able to do so if her phone was not returned).

After several months, she escaped when a client decided to help her, for superstitious reasons.[6] Jade managed to get a new phone to communicate with her relatives, get money, and leave Nigeria for Ecuador. She breathed a sigh of relief on the flight to Ecuador as she imagined that the trip from Quito to the US would be short and easy. However, in Quito, Jade was unable to find employment due to her lack of Spanish proficiency and the employers' racist hiring criteria.[7] As a result, she had to stay there for months, sometimes sleeping on the streets, and eating food found in garbage cans. Some fellow countrymen who met her by chance helped her, and only then did she manage to leave Ecuador and continue the journey toward the US.

From Ecuador to Mexico, each border imposed unwanted waiting times on her journey, which varied from days to months, and were marked by precarity and uncertainty. Sometimes the trip was delayed because of geographical obstacles, including jungles or river crossings, or overall travel costs.[8] Waiting times in Mexico were the longest because of mobility control policies that were unclear to her. At Mexico's southern border, she had to wait for months for her migratory regularization before continuing to the northern border.[9] When she finally arrived in Tijuana, more than a year had passed since she began her journey. She was tired and her body worn out by the experiences of torture in her place of origin, jungle crossings, and the inhumane living conditions.

Her attempt to file an asylum application in the US faced a long bureaucratic waiting period in Tijuana.[10] In addition, due to the outbreak of the COVID-19 pandemic, the border remained closed for nearly a year, leaving

Jade, along with an increasing number of African migrants, stranded in their attempt to reach the US. More than two years passed since her arrival in Tijuana, and more than three since her departure from her hometown. At the time of writing, Jade was still waiting to reach the US or Canada.

In the narratives gathered in our fieldwork, a recurring bottleneck was found in Tapachula, at the southern Mexican border. The case of Carvel, a migrant from Cameroon, helps us understand some of the conditions that migrants face in southern Mexico. Arriving in Tapachula, Carvel did not know why he was detained at the Migration Station, where he stayed for weeks, while Central Americans who arrived at the same time were released much earlier. After being interviewed by COMAR, he did not understand why he was allowed to leave the Migration Station but could not leave Tapachula. Moreover, he did not understand why Mexico finally granted him refugee status as a stateless person when his goal was to cross Mexico to apply for asylum in the US. He presented his Cameroon passport to the migratory authorities and did not identify himself as a stateless person. The resolution of this unsolicited process took a little over three months. The waiting was marked by the lack of knowledge of the administrative procedures and uncertainty about possible outcomes. However, the longest waiting time began with his arrival in Tijuana to request asylum in the US.

Even before March 2020 (when the pandemic began), waiting times to initiate the asylum request in the US were longer than one year (Odgers and Olivas 2019). Nonetheless, this situation became worse once the pandemic began, as Joy's case illustrates. Joy had fled from violence in Cameroon, leaving behind five children. When Joy arrived in Tijuana in January 2020, she desperately sought to initiate her asylum application. However, shortly after the outbreak of the COVID-19 pandemic in March 2020, the border was closed, and the US suspended asylum applications indefinitely. Desperate, far from her children, and in a city that she did not know and where a language she did not understand was spoken, she tried to cross the border clandestinely, aiming to turn herself into the immigration authorities and ask for asylum. Nevertheless, a few hours after being detained, she was returned to Tijuana under Title 42. After the border reopened in November 2021, information regarding new asylum procedures remained confusing and constantly changing.

In some cases, finding themselves in an indefinite wait with unexpected refugee status leads migrants to redefine their strategy and initiate a family reunification process in Mexico since being recognized as a refugee confers permanent resident status, which gives them the right to family reunification. Family reunification procedures, however, are longer and more costly than migrants usually imagine at the beginning of their application. As described ahead, initiating the unification process does not imply that the project of applying for asylum in the US has been abandoned. On the contrary, the strategy of developing parallel migration projects is often triggered once migrants become aware of delays to asylum applications in the US.

Mamadou fled for his life, leaving his wife and five children in Togo, his home country. He is in his early fifties, has a university education, and before migrating had a white-collar job. Now that he is a refugee in Mexico, he works in a metal recycling plant. He has begun the process of family reunification. Following the current legislation, which grants every permanent resident the right to family reunification, Mamadou went to the National Institute of Migration (INM) offices to start his application. However, he was told that unlike other permanent residents, refugees must first obtain the extension of the refugee status to their families, and only then initiate the process.

He went to COMAR to file his application; however, COMAR in Tijuana is only a representative office, which meant his file had to be sent to Mexico City. He was told that he had to wait at least three months before getting a response. In the meantime, he began legalizing his children's birth certificates, which would be requested by the INM, and must be notarized at a Mexican consulate. However, Mexico does not have a consulate in Togo; therefore, the documents had to be legalized at the Mexican consulate in Nigeria. Mamadou had to pay an acquaintance to do the paperwork in Nigeria, as it would be extremely costly and dangerous for his family to go.

The Mexican embassy's online appointment forms repeatedly malfunctioned, forcing Mamadou to try day after day to obtain the appointment. The embassy stated that the documents had to first be legalized by the Nigerian government, despite the fact that they were issued by Togo, followed by a costly translation from French to English. The procedural costs drained Mamadou's savings of three months of work. The English translation only served this stage because, after the Mexican embassy in Nigeria legalized the documents, Mamadou had to pay for their translation into Spanish. Mamadou was aware that the reunification process would be long and expensive, but every time a new unforeseen obstacle presented itself, he became more depressed and distressed at the thought of his family in danger. He questioned why family reunification procedures for refugees are longer and more expensive than for other permanent residents, when Mexico has already acknowledged the dangerous situations prevailing in the refugees' countries of origin.

While it is not only African migrants who face administrative absurdities which prolong strandedness, it is also true that they have additional vulnerabilities compared to Latin American migrants since they must face more protracted, expensive, and dangerous journeys; do not speak Spanish; face a more significant cultural distance; suffer more racism; lack consolidated social networks; and have less knowledge about migration procedures and their rights. For all these reasons, the experience of being trapped is full of uncertainty and undermines their emotional well-being. The following section discusses the relationship between strandedness, uncertainty, and coping strategies. As previously stated, strandedness should be considered as part of a transcontinental migratory system. As shown above, this system delays and filters migrants through their vulnerabilities. Thus, for those who do not have the possibility of returning to their places of origin, the entrapment deteriorates and lengthens their waiting processes, without changing their migratory objectives. This situation forces them to develop coping strategies that allow migrants trapped in mobility to construct a sense of waiting.

MAKING MEANING: RELIGION, POLITICAL ENGAGEMENT, AND FACING THE FUTURE THROUGH PARALLEL PROJECTS

We have argued that strandedness negatively affects migrants' well-being due to the uncertainty and indeterminacy it produces in different aspects of their lives, both present and future. We have also stated that to pursue well-being under these adverse circumstances, African migrants develop coping strategies to make meaning of their situations through new narratives, where hope can emerge in the places and times of strandedness. Strategies for making sense of strandedness are diverse, fluctuating, and often fragmentary. This section discusses those that appear most frequently in the narratives and conversations collected during our fieldwork. However, it is worth mentioning that far from being a stable and finished process, the search for meaning never ends and may involve changing strategies.

Waiting as Part of God's Plan

Mamadou is a Muslim and tries to follow the precepts of his faith rigorously. He faced difficulties in attending the only mosque in Tijuana due to its great distance from his home and place of work. However, he respects dietary restrictions, performs five daily prayers (although he must adjust his schedule to his work breaks), and fasts during Ramadan. During the long process of applying for family reunification described before, Mamadou experienced several moments of depression and anxiety, and stated that only prayer helped him regain his calm at such times. He thanks God for enabling him to leave his country alive and for the fact that a country he had never thought of before offered him a refuge that he did not request.

Joy, who now works at a migrant shelter, goes even further. She maintains that she can be empathetic and better understand the suffering of the people who arrive at the shelter asking for help in her work because she also suffered on her way to Tijuana. That is why, she argues, God keeps her in Tijuana: her suffering makes sense only while stranded.

Turning to religious practices to cope with adversities while being stranded also shapes the meaning that the experience of waiting has for asylum seekers and refugees. As in the cases mentioned earlier, the religious orientation of the migrants impacts how they reinterpret life experiences at different temporalities. For instance, past events in Mamadou's case (fleeing his home country as an opportunity to continue alive), present situations in Joy's case (being stranded as God's will, to provide support to others in need), and future possibilities (with God's support, their situations could improve).

Political Engagement

Shortly after arriving in Tijuana, Jade participated in the marches for International Women's Day on 8 March. Although she does not speak Spanish, she joined the contingent to shout slogans at the top of her lungs. As a woman who was a victim of torture and sexual aggression, Jade said it was a liberating experience. It was also the beginning of her involvement with various transborder political associations with which she now actively participates. She thinks that perhaps, while she is stuck in Tijuana, she will contribute so that girls can aspire to a better life than the one she has had.

Jade's active role in shaping the social meaning of the place she inhabits, while she remains stranded, results from her interaction with a community with whom she shares the meaning of well-being. Through political engagement, the place of strandedness is also experienced as a social, cultural, and political place where her voice and claims can be heard, and it is possible to fight against injustices.

Coping through Parallel Projects

When Carvel arrived in Tapachula, he did not understand Spanish, knew nothing about Mexico other than that it shared a border with the US, and his only goal was to cross the northern border to seek asylum. While he was being held at the Migratory Station, he thought he would get a safe conduct to get to the northern border. He was surprised when he received refugee status in Mexico as a stateless person. Being recognized as a refugee, at first, did not transform his plans. He travelled to Tijuana with his permanent resident card as a refugee, intending to apply for asylum in the US. However, the border had been closed indefinitely due to the COVID-19 outbreak by that time. Carvel was distressed and depressed due to feeling stuck in an unfamiliar country whose language he did not speak and where he knew no one. However, in his stranded situation, another African who had obtained refugee status explained that this status gave him the right to family reunification. If he made the appropriate arrangements, his family could come to Tijuana legally, by plane, comfortably, and without having to face the suffering and dangers he had faced. The idea of being reunited with his family, even if it was in Tijuana, was appealing. Furthermore, it seemed like a dream that his family could arrive, with visas in hand, all the way to the US border. That is why, without giving up on filing his asylum application in the US, he began the lengthy and costly process of family reunification. Working hard in Tijuana to pay for paperwork and plane tickets had clear meaning.

At the age of eighteen, Aziz had already made the undocumented journey from his home country of Ghana to the US-Mexico border twice. The first time he was deported to Mexico, while still a minor. Now, while he waits for the opportunity to apply for asylum, he works in the parking lot of a supermarket, where he spends his time making plans while working. One day Aziz dreams of bringing a wife from Ghana that his family would choose for him; another day he thinks about revalidating his school diplomas to continue studying in Tijuana and attend university in the future, and sometimes he also plans to enlist in the Mexican army to secure a livelihood. At the same time as he longs for all these dreams, in which he invests energy and emotions, he knows he could suspend these plans if he gets authorization to cross the border to seek asylum in the US.

Both cases show different modalities of developing parallel migration projects that serve as coping strategies. The first one shows a mobilization of material, social, and emotional resources to pursue two different migration projects, which are not exclusive if they remain uncertain or at a certain point could become complementary. Therefore, the efforts while being stranded are worth pursuing as leading toward a potential (in some cases also desirable) and feasible future. The second case shows an investment of emotions and thoughts delving into dreams of possible futures. Even though material and social resources are not invested, imagining future possibilities of well-being also acts as a coping strategy to face the hopelessness that could be experienced while stranded.

CONCLUSION

This chapter aimed to show how the lengthening of waiting times, produced by prolonged and sometimes absurd administrative procedures, is part of the MTCR, acting as a deterrent to mobility. We also sought to show the relationship between the lengthening of the waiting period, uncertainty, and the degradation of emotional well-being. Finally, we demonstrated some migrants' and asylum seekers' coping strategies to face uncertainty during extended periods.

The strategy of turning to faith is probably the most frequently mentioned. However, participants professing a minority religion must pursue this resource almost exclusively individually due to the absence of a community of believers in the city.

Political engagement as an asylum seeker or refugee is less commonly referred to. However, it shows us a vital process that this population could experience, leading them to a sense of social integration while being stranded. The capacity of agency that asylum seekers and refugees could experience through political engagement also nurtures a sense of well-being in pursuing a deserved future.

The construction of parallel projects is challenging to achieve. In some cases, it requires financial resources; a short-, medium-, and/or long-term vision of the future; and significant emotional maturity. When it is not achieved, instead of allowing parallel plans, it can lead to the construction of consecutive projects, which dizzyingly replace each other, while also producing frustration and anxiety. However, even in those cases, dreaming of possible futures and possible escapes from migratory entrapment remains a coping strategy and an act of resistance.

However, it is vital to insist on the fragility of these processes, which do not prevent suffering or allow for a full regaining of emotional well-being. Undoubtedly, at times migrants trapped in the mobility process manage to give meaning to the wait. However, this does not happen all the time, and the precarious balance is lost every time a new obstacle arises or a new administrative deadline is enforced.

Considering that the externalization of border processes has a low probability of ending, it is worth thinking that places of strandedness will continue to emerge and the entrapment times will lengthen more. Therefore, the waiting conditions could get worse. Currently, these three processes – a proliferation of strandedness places, prolonging of entrapment, and worsening of waiting conditions – constitute a central aspect of the mobility control mechanisms defining the migratory systems.

Nonetheless, as we have shown in this chapter, to understand the way migration occurs in North America, it is equally necessary to comprehend how migrants stranded within their mobility process face their entrapment. This way, without undervaluing the entrapment's impact on their emotional well-being, we argue that it is crucial to identify their coping strategies. In the case of the African population stranded on the Mexico-US border, we have identified at least three main coping strategies. However, new ones will emerge under even longer protracted waiting times. Finally, it is worth reminding ourselves that migrants stranded within their mobility are part of the population in the Americas. In that way, migratory entrapment is becoming a distinctive feature of our contemporary societies.

NOTES

1 Following Title 42, on 21 March 2020, President Donald Trump determined, "To help prevent the introduction of COVID-19 into border facilities and into the U.S., persons subject to the order will not be held in congregate areas for processing and instead will immediately be expelled to their country of last transit" (US CBP 2021).

2 The National Migration Institute in Mexico reports that in 2016, the number of people from countries in African detained at Migration Stations (detention centres for undocumented migrants traveling through the country) due to the lack of regular documentation to travel through Mexico was 3,910. The highest annual number was registered in 2019, with 7,065 persons. There was a decrease once the pandemic began, to 590 and 2,034 in 2020 and 2021, respectively (UPMRIP 2022). Another piece of data that shows an increase in this population in Mexico is related to the humanitarian visas granted in the country. In 2016, twenty-one people from Africa were given this document, and 1,575 in 2021. Other relevant data concern the number of people from Africa registered as permanent residents related to refugee status; sixteen such persons were granted permanent residency in 2016, and ninety-three in 2021 (UPMRIP 2022). Nonetheless, we should look this data carefully because the African migrant community in Mexico continues to be less visible in terms of statistical data, and there is a lack of sociodemographic information about this population in the country (Serra Mingot and Gonález Zepeda 2022).

3 COMAR (Comisión Mexicana de Ayuda a Refugiados) is the only agency authorized to grant refugee status in Mexico. It is governed by the "Law on Refugees, Complementary Protection and Political Asylum" and international agreements signed by Mexico. COMAR receives refugee

applications and issues an "Initiation of the refugee process" certificate. During the study of his/her case, the applicant must remain in the state where he/she filed the application.

Suppose that, at the end of the analysis, COMAR approves the application. In that case, it issues a letter recognizing refugee status, with which the applicant may receive a resident card from the National Migration Institute. Or suppose that, once COMAR concludes the analysis, it determines that the applicant does not meet the conditions to be admitted as a refugee. In that case, it issues an exit order that establishes the term within which the applicant must leave the national territory.

4 In fact, due to their lack of understanding of Spanish and their lack of knowledge of immigration and asylum legislation, African migrants verbally request a safe conduct permit to reach the northern border upon arriving in Mexico. This document does not exist, so the authorities redirect them to request asylum. All the migrants interviewed by us indicated that they did not realize that they were being redirected to request asylum, so they were bewildered when they received refugee status.

5 To maintain her confidentiality, we have redacted Jade's sociodemographic information (place of origin, age, and occupation). This is not the case for the other collaborators we introduce in the chapter.

6 Jade explains that her Nigerian client practiced witchcraft in which evil spirits possessed him. To free himself from them, he had to perform sexual intercourse so that the evil spirits would pass on to his sexual partner. He experienced no guilt in transferring evil spirits to a woman he considered unworthy, as he assumed that Jade engaged in prostitution by choice. However, upon discovering that she was a prisoner in the brothel, he felt guilty for having transmitted malevolent spirits to her and feared punishment. To free himself from that danger, he decided to help Jade escape.

It is important to note that Jade, who identifies as a Christian, believes in witchcraft and evil spirits. Consequently, she feared that evil spirits might invade her unless she strongly preserved her faith in Christ.

7 Some of our interlocutors stated that they were discriminated against in Ecuador based on their phenotypic characteristics and lack of Spanish proficiency, making it very hard to navigate the country's economic, social, and cultural systems.

8 Even though there is a lack of general information about the travel costs and times it takes to migrate from Africa to Mexico, some of our interlocutors shared that moving from Brazil to Mexico took them from eight to eleven months. Regarding the travel costs, some of them spent thousands of American dollars. In other cases, it was hard to calculate because they were working for food, transportation, or a place to live

during their journey, meaning they were not receiving money in exchange for their work but the resources they needed.

9 In fact, upon crossing the border, Jade and the group of African migrants with whom she traveled the last leg of the journey were stopped by agents of the National Migration Institute (the equivalent of the immigration police). Subsequently, they were taken to Tapachula, to the Migration Station, the detention centre for migrants in an irregular situation. At the immigration station, Jade presented her passport and requested safe conduct to reach the northern border. However, in this process, she was not assisted by an interpreter and had to make herself understood in English – which is not her mother tongue, and she has a limited command of the language.

She remained at the Migration Station for more than a month until she received a "certificate of initiation of processing" of her refugee application. Under current legislation, Jade had to remain in Tapachula while COMAR analyzed her refugee application. It was not until more than two months later, when the refugee status was granted, that she could continue – legally – her journey to the northern border.

10 When Jade arrived in Tijuana the year before the pandemic, people wanting to request asylum in the US had to register themselves in a "notebook" in Tijuana and wait for their turn to start the asylum application. In some cases, it could take months or a year to begin the application process. In Jade's case, she could never start the process because the US administration suspended asylum requests for almost two years during the pandemic.

REFERENCES

Acharya, Manju P., and Northcott, Herbert. C. 2007. "Mental Distress and the Coping Strategies of Elderly Indian Immigrant Women." *Transcultural Psychiatry* 44 (4): 614–36.

Agier, Michel. 2008. *Gérer les Indésirables: Des camps de réfugiés au gouvernement humanitaire*. Paris: Éditions Flammarion.

Alarcón, Rafael, and Cecilia Ortiz. 2017. "Los haitianos solicitantes de asilo a Estados Unidos en su paso por Tijuana." *Frontera Norte* 29 (51). http://www.scielo.org.mx/scielo.php?script=sci_arttext&pid=S0187-73722017000200171.

Andrews, Molly. 2002. "Narrative and Life History." In *Lines of Narrative: Psychosocial Perspectives*, edited by Molly Andrews, Shelley Day Sclater, Corinne Squire, and Amal Treacher, 75-127. London: Routledge.

Arriola, Luis Alfredo. 2021. "Central American Asylum Seekers in Southern Mexico: Fluid (Im)mobility in Protracted Migration Trajectories." *Journal of Immigrant & Refugee Studies* 19 (4): 1–15.

Atkinson, Sarah, Sara Fuller, and Joe Painter. 2016. "Wellbeing and Place." In *Wellbeing and Place*, edited by Sarah Atkinson, Sara Fuller, and Joe Painter, 1–14. New York: Routledge.

Campos-Delgado, Amalia. 2021. "Bordering through Exemption: Extracontinental Migration Flows in Mexico." *International Journal for Crime, Justice and Social Democracy* 10 (3): 30–40.

Chan-Pech, Candido. 2019. "Flujos migratorios en el sur de Chiapas: una narrativa local del impacto de las caravanas migrantes y los grupos africanos." *Revista Política, Globalidad y Ciudadanía* 5 (10): 43–62.

Collyer, Michael. 2010. "Stranded Migrants and the Fragmented Journey." *Journal of Refugee Studies* 23 (3): 273–93.

Duvell, Franck. 2012. "Transit Migration: A Blurred and Politicised Concept." *Population, Space and Place* 18 (4): 415–27. https://doi.org/10.1002/psp.631.

Echeverri Zuluaga, Jonathan, and Liza Acevedo Sáenz. 2018. "Pensando a través de la errancia: travesías y esperas de viajeros africanos en Quito y Dakar." *Antípoda: revista de antropología y arqueología* 32 (July): 105–23.

FLACSO (Facultad Latinoamericana de Ciencias Sociales). 2011. "Diagnóstico sobre la situación actual, tendencias y necesidades de protección y asistencia de las personas migrantes y refugiadas extracontinentales en México y América Central." Facultad Latinoamericana de Ciencias Sociales San Jose.

Gammeltoft-Hansen, Thomas, and Nikolas F. Tan. 2017. "The End of the Deterrence Paradigm? Future Directions for Global Refugee Policy." *Journal on Migration and Human Security* 5 (1): 28–56.

Gattari, María de Los Angeles. 2016. "Nueva migración africana hacia Argentina: Los jóvenes africanos en la ciudad de Rosario." *Contexto Internacional* 14: 39–45.

Gil-Everaert, Isabel. 2020. "Inhabiting the Meanwhile: Rebuilding Home and Restoring Predictability in a Space of Waiting." *Journal of Ethnic and Migration Studies* 47 (19): 4327–43.

Glaser, Barney, and Anselm Strauss. 1967. *The Discovery of Grounded Theory: Strategies for Qualitative Research*. New Brunswick, NJ: Aldine.

Hess, Sabine. 2012. "De-naturalising Transit Migration. Theory and Methods of an Ethnographic Regime Analysis." *Population, Space and Place* 18 (4): 428–40.

IOM (International Organization for Migration). 2013. "Migrantes extracontinentales en América del Sur: Estudio de casos." *Organización Internacional para las Migraciones.*

Jiménez-Martínez, Lucett Guadalupe, and Jessica Martínez Cruz. 2021. "Los derechos humanos de los migrantes africanos en México: ¿realidad o retórica?" *Revista IUS* 15 (47): 293–324.

Kent, Jonathan, Kelsey P. Norman, and Katherine H. Tennis. 2020. "Changing Motivations or Capabilities? Migration Deterrence in the Global Context." *International Studies Review* 22 (4): 853–78.

Khawaja, Nigar G., Katherine M. White, Robert Schweitzer, and Jaimi Greenslade. 2008. "Difficulties and Coping Strategies of Sudanese Refugees: A Qualitative Approach." *Transcultural Psychiatry* 45 (3): 489–512.

Marcelino, Pedro F., and Marcela S. Cerrutti. 2012. "Recent African Immigration to South America: The Cases of Argentina and Brazil in the Regional Context." In *Development, Institutional and Policy Aspects of International Migration Between Africa, Europe and Latin America and the Caribbean*, edited by Jorge Martínez Pizarro and Leandro Reboiras Finardi, 107–45. LC/W 461. Santiago: United Nations Economic Commission for Latin America and the Caribbean. https://repositorio.cepal.org/bitstream/handle/11362/3963/S1200080_en.pdf?sequence=1&isAllowed=y.

Mathews, Gordon, and Carolina Izquierdo. 2010. "Introduction: Anthropology, Happiness, and Well-Being." In *Pursuits of Happiness: Well-Being in Anthropological Perspective*, edited by Gordon Mathews and Carolina Izquierdo, 1–20. NED-New ed. New York: Berghahn Books. http://www.jstor.org/stable/j.ctt9qd4gh.6.

Ménard Marleau, Andrée. 2008. "¿Irse o quedarse? Las formas y dinámicas de movilidad de los migrantes senegaleses en América del Sur (2007–2016)." Master's Thesis, Quito, Ecuador: FLACSO Ecuador.

Odgers, Olga, and Olga Olivas. 2019. "Les «caravanes de migrants» : figées dans la mobilité." *La Lettre de l'IHEAL-CREDA*, 27 (March).

Odgers, Olga, Olga Olivas, and Ietza Bojorquez. 2023. "Waiting in Motion. Migrants' Involvement in Civil Society Organizations while Pursuing a Migration Project Under *Strandedness*." *Journal of Immigrant and Refugee Studies*. https://doi.org/10.1080/15562948.2022.2155335.

Phillimore, Jenny, and Sin Yi Cheung. 2021. "The Violence of Uncertainty: Empirical Evidence on how Asylum Waiting Time Undermines Refugee Health." *Social Science & Medicine* 282 (August): 114154.

Ray, Madeline, and René Leyva Flores. 2020. "Migración Irregular Africana En México: Implicaciones Para La Salud Pública." *Frontera Norte* 32 (June): 1–10. https://doi.org/10.33679/rfn.v1i1.2058.

Sagbakken, Mette, Ida M. Bregård, and Sverre Varvin. 2020. "The Past, the Present, and the Future: A Qualitative Study Exploring How Refugees' Experience of Time Influences Their Mental Health and Well-Being." *Frontiers in Sociology* 5 (46): 1–16.

Schwanen, Tim, and Sarah Atkinson. 2015. "Geographies of Wellbeing: An Introduction." *The Geographical Journal* 181 (2): 98–101.

Serra Mingot, Ester, and Carlos Alberto Gonález Zepeda. "Transnational Social Protection Infrastructures: African Migrants in Mexico." *International Migration* (May): 1–13. https://doi.org/10.1111/imig.13029.

Shum, Terence Chun Tat. 2020. "Stuck in Transit: Asylum-seeking Habitus and Onward Migration Aspirations of Sri Lankan Tamil Asylum-seekers in Bangkok." *Migration and Development*: 1–20.

Smith, Craig Damian. 2022. "Visa Policies, Migration Controls, and Migrant Aspirations." *Yale Journal of International Law*, Symposium: Managing Mixed Migration, April 2022, 22–33. https://cpb-us-w2.wpmucdn.com/campuspress.yale.edu/dist/8/1581/files/2022/04/3-Smith_Visa-Policies-Migration-Controls-and-Mobility-Aspirations__YJIL-ONLINE.pdf.

US CBP (US Customs and Border Protection). 2021. "Nationwide Enforcement Encounters: Title 8 Enforcement Actions and Title 42 Expulsions 2022." US Customs and Border Protection. https://www.cbp.gov/newsroom/stats/cbp-enforcement-statistics/title-8-and-title-42-statistics.

UPMRIP (Unidad de Política Migratoria, Registro e Identidad de Personas). 2022. *Boletínes Estadísticos*. Centro de Estudios Migratorios de la Unidad de Política Migratoria, Registro e identidad de Personas de la Secretaría de Gobernación. http://www.politicamigratoria.gob.mx/es//PoliticaMigratoria/Boletines_Estadisticos.

Vianelli, Lorenzo, Nick Gill, and Nicole Hoellerer. 2021. "Waiting as Probation: Selecting Self-Disciplining Asylum Seekers." *Journal of Ethnic and Migration Studies* 48 (5), 1–20.

Vidal, Laurent, and Alain Musset. 2016. *Waiting Territories in the Americas: Life in the Intervals of Migration and Urban Transit*. Newcastle-upon-Tyne, England: Cambridge Scholars Publishing.

Wyss, Anna. 2019. "Stuck in Mobility? Interrupted Journeys of Migrants with Precarious Legal Status in Europe." *Journal of Immigrant & Refugee Studies* 17 (1): 77–93. https://doi.org/10.1080/15562948.2018.1514091.

Yates, Caitlyn, and Jessica Bolter. 2021. "Migración africana a través del continente americano: Impulsores, rutas y respuestas normativas." Washington, DC: *Migration Policy Institute*. https://www. migrationpolicy.org/sites/default/files/publications/mpi-african-migration-americas-esp_final.pdf.

Yee-Quintero, José-Carlos. 2017. "Caracterizando a los solicitantes de asilo a Estados Unidos: el caso de los haitianos en 2016." In *Vidas en vilo. Historias y testimonios de migrantes internacionales*, edited by Patrick Murphy, Rafael Alarcón, Marie-Laure Coubes, José-Carlos Yee, and Macrina Cárdenas, 53–81.

Zbidat, Ali, Ekaterini Georgiadou, Andrea Borho, Yesim Erim, and Eva Morawa. 2020. "The Perceptions of Trauma, Complaints, Somatization, and Coping Strategies among Syrian Refugees in Germany—A Qualitative Study of an at-risk Population." *International Journal of Environmental Research and Public Health* 17 (3): 693.

Zubrzycki, Bernarda. 2021. "Migraciones fragmentadas. Contextualizando la migración senegalesa en Argentina y Brasil." *Diarios del terruño* (July–December) 12: 258–73.

10

Unruly Political Uprisings: Migrant Justice Activism in Canada and the United States

Eloy Rivas-Sánchez

Several years of work with migrants of precarious status who have crossed borders "irregularly" and with migrant justice activists working in Latin America, has left me with the deep conviction that Canada and the US, the richest countries of the Americas and two of the world's wealthiest, are hostile and restrictive when it comes to addressing the needs and fundamental human rights of undocumented migrants. This is in sharp contrast to policies in some Latin American countries, such as Peru, Uruguay, Argentina, Ecuador, Mexico, Colombia, and Brazil where, notwithstanding several forms of repression and control, undocumented migrants and those crossing the border irregularly are offered access to health services, education, and often regularization programs (see Vera Espinoza et al. 2021). Although the Trump administration's infamous policies on detentions, deportations, and border security were the most grotesque example of this North American trend, they have long precedents in the US, and do not occur in isolation within the context of North American migration governance. The Canadian state, which sells itself globally as a champion of human rights and an immigrant-welcoming country, has developed a similar (although more subtle) architecture of excluding undocumented migrants and controlling entry. The COVID-19 pandemic was deeply instructive in this regard. Undocumented migrants and failed refugee claimants were the only segment of the population that was denied access to governmental relief funds, ignoring dozens of emergency rallies and cries from civil society demanding a humanitarian response (Wells 2020). Canada was one of the very few wealthy countries in the world which continued immigrant detention and deportation throughout the pandemic, except for four months in 2021. In fact, the highest number of deportations, including of refugee claimants who provided essential services, occurred in 2021 in the middle of the pandemic (Christoff 2021; Paperni, 2021).

Critical literature on North American migration governance, principally on seasonal agricultural workers and refugee claimants, engages with the question of how migrant precarity is produced and reproduced through state practices (e.g., Gabriel and Macdonald 2018; Gurung, Amburgey, and Craig 2021; Ilcan, Rygiel, and Baban 2018; Jackson and Bauder 2014; Parreñas et al. 2021; Reid-Musson 2014). This chapter contributes to the literature by using the concept of "multiplication of borders" to engage with the question of how those policies are contested on the ground. It draws upon a multisited ethnographic work conducted with precarious status immigrants in Canadian urban centres since 2015, which included working for two years as a factory worker with undocumented populations and organizing with Solidarity Across Borders (SAB), a Montreal-based civil society group. The chapter also draws on comparative research I conducted in New York City (NYC) in situ, while attending political protests and training at the Institute for the Radical Imagination and the People's Forum in NYC.

The discussion focuses on Montreal, Canada, but provides points of comparison with the dynamics in the US, specifically in NYC. Rather than offering a causal argument, the chapter explores how undocumented migrants' precarity has been shaped and contested on both sides of the border during the COVID-19 crisis and shares some insights that may help to explain outcomes of political activism. Despite shared experiences of precarity, migrant activism showed significant variation in types of mobilization and policy outcomes. In Montreal, Canada, undocumented migrants' activism has taken the form of unruly, intermittent, and hybrid insurgencies, combining online and street mobilizing tactics – perhaps a reflection of the material conditions in which undocumented migrants in urban Canada live: in a floating, nomadic form. In New York City, migrant justice activism takes more pragmatic forms, focused on legislative change through mass mobilization – perhaps a reflection of the material conditions of abundant social infrastructure, long histories of labour union engagement and organizing, dense social networks, and expanded mobilizing structures.

In Montreal, migrant justice activism has been based on a combination of mutual aid and "oppositional" repertoires of protest, opposing detentions, deportations, and demanding "status for all," while, in New York City, a combination of oppositional protest, including hunger strikes, mutual aid, and legislative change, has been more popular and effective. The Montreal and, more broadly, the Canadian ways of doing migrant justice activism have attained few substantial legislative or regulatory victories. The major gain has been contributing to the formation of a dense network of individuals both in rural and urban centres engaged in solidarity and mutual aid practices and also to the shaping a new migrant political insurgency – which I call "nomadic, hybrid activism" – meaningfully engaged in unruly radical politics and political insurgencies, despite migrants' precarious and nomadic existence.

The chapter is divided into three parts. First, it succinctly discusses the concept of "multiplication of borders" and how this concept can help explain the shaping of migrant legal precarity in the North American context. Second, it discusses how migrant precarity, including undocumented precarity, expanded in the context of the COVID-19 crisis. It then discusses ways in which this state-induced precarity has been contested through grassroots politics and provides some insights on which factors may explain why those struggles and demands have had differing levels of success.

THE PROLIFERATION OF BORDERS IN NORTH AMERICA

The "proliferation of borders" is a concept coined by Sandro Mezzadra and Brett Neilson (2013; see also Mezzadra 2016), and refers to the process by which barriers created by policies regulating migrant workers' labour, stay, membership, and participation in host societies become expanded and multiplied. Those barriers are produced through social forces that simultaneously include migrant workers as labour commodities while excluding them from meaningful social relations, belonging, and participation in the host societies. This "differential inclusion" (Mezzadra and Neilson 2012, 69) is shaped by the incorporation of "foreign" labour in the receiving countries' labour markets through multiple hiring schemas, assigning migrants different positions in the local societies according to the conditions specified by labour contracts (when there are contracts) and temporary migration policies (Mezzadra 2016). Migrant labour becomes "multiple" (fragmented) because of migrants' different status within the labour market, labour process within receiving societies, and social relations mediated through differences in legal status, temporality, income, and ethnicity. For example, migrant workers in Canada are barred from labour organizing, and face reprisals and deportations if they complain about abuse or dangerous work conditions.

Multiple borders separate migrant workers both from one another and the society in which they live and work. The proliferation of borders in advanced capitalist societies thus work as an "apparatus" in the Foucauldian sense; that is, they work as an assemblage of institutions, rules, and regimes of subjectification that, as any other technology of power, is purposely managed to tame, govern, subordinate, control, or orient subjects' behaviours and thoughts in favour of a certain model of social order (Foucault 2007,

1–7; Agamben 2009, 3–6). Driven by corporate needs, the North American "apparatus" or "regime" of labour mobility governance comprises an assemblage of laws and regulations that reproduce a social order that historically sustains itself upon the subsumption, appropriation, and exploitation of indentured labour provided by "inferiorized" subjects (e.g., Indigenous, Black, Mexican, Chinese) and selective settlement processes based on racial criteria (Binford and Preibisch 2021; Porter 1970, 61–8).

Evidence produced by social scientists on both sides of the border suggests that the multiplication of borders through state-induced multiplication of barriers separating precarious migrants from each other and excluding them from meaningful participation in host societies, work as a mechanism through which migrant precarity, migrant "illegality," or undocumented-ness are produced (Bacon 2008; Basok, Bélanger, and Rivas 2014; Calavita 2010; Dauvergne 2017; De Genova 2004; Goldring, Berinstein, and Bernhard 2009; Luibhéid 2013). In Canada, for example, the pioneer theorization on the production of migrant precarity developed by Goldring, Berinstein, and Bernhard (2009) has scrutinized the social and institutional processes by which immigrants become "illegals," or gradually descend into different degrees of legal precarity. In their work, the legal and institutional mechanisms through which the Canadian state incorporates immigrants into the Canadian society are the main determinants of the gradual precarization of their legal statuses. The fact that the Canadian state assigns newcomers with different rights and privileges according to the categories or legal conditions under which they were incorporated into Canadian society (i.e., as temporary foreign workers, international students, refugee claimants, and other legally precarious categories) creates forms of stratification which locates some of them outside of fundamental social rights. This situation, along with the fact that some of the legal and institutional channels available for immigrants to remain legally in the country do not work properly, make some immigrants lose their legal status and remain in the country under conditions of legal and social precarity.

Similarly, in the United States, the foundational works by De Genova (2002, 2004, 2014), Calavita (1982, 2010), and Ngai (2004) have examined the processes by which the regulation of labour and human mobility across US and Mexican borders (a border which remained unregulated since its inception through the US intervention in Mexican territory in 1848 until 1920) through the formation of the US Border Patrol in 1924, the Bracero Program in 1942, and the reforms to immigration laws in 1965, made possible the production of "illegal" and deportable immigrants along with the formation and expansion of architectures of border control in the United States, all of which De Genova (2004) calls "the social production of migrant illegality."

Inspired by the works mentioned, a robust body of knowledge in Canada and the US have amassed evidence showing how state practices (Chomsky 2014), narratives of national security (Dauvergne 2017; Diop 2013), binational agreements seeking "smart border security" (Atak and Crépeau 2013; Mountz 2020), and the expansion of highly restrictive temporary guest workers programs (Foster 2012) on both sides of the North American border have made external and internal borders proliferate to keep undesirable migrants under control, or "out," even when they live "inside" national boundaries (Binford 2019; Goldring 2010). Reduced to the status of labour commodities and divided by skills, salary scales, ethnicities, temporalities, legal status, and hierarchical access to rights, migrant workers (even when they live as refugee claimants or undocumented) live and work in the North American context as denizens or precarious status immigrants (Goldring, Berinstein, and Bernhard 2009) with limited or no access to the rights associated with permanent residency or citizenship, in conditions of deportability (Basok, Bélanger, and Rivas 2014; Vosko 2016, 2018), labour precarity (Fudge and MacPhail 2009; Goldring and Landolt 2013), racial subordination and disposability (Stasiulis 2020), food and housing insecurity (Weiler, McLaughlin, and Cole 2017), and highly restricted mobility (Polanco 2019; Sharma 2012).

THE INTENSIFICATION OF BORDERS AND CRISIS OF SOCIAL REPRODUCTION UNDER THE COVID-19 CRISIS

The COVID-19 pandemic meant that borders were further multiplied and migrant precarity became amplified. Geographical borders became even more hermetic and selective. In Canada, during spring 2020, the number of seasonal agricultural migrant workers shrank, which created a labour shortage both in the agricultural sector and in the food industry more broadly (Sheldon 2020). Asylum seekers arriving by land through entry points from the US were not allowed to submit applications (Canadian Council for Refugees 2020). Interprovincial human mobility reduced significantly.

Similarly, "internal borders" multiplied in the pandemic context. In Canada, an important number of the undocumented population lost employment, or their working days were drastically reduced. In Montreal, many lost their ability to pay monthly bills, buy food, pay rents, and send remittances to relatives. Two periods of curfew, one in 2019 and the other in 2021–22, further affected the ability to work, as many worked night shifts. The presence of police in the public sphere surveilling people to respect curfews and social distancing, and the fact that detention and deportation continued to be practised and indeed rose in 2020 to the highest number since 2015 (Christoff 2021) all increased fears of deportation and social isolation. *Deportability*, understood as the objective and subjective experience shaped by fears of being detained and forcibly removed (De Genova 2002), intensified in the pandemic context. This also dissuaded people with precarious immigration status, mainly undocumented, from attending hospitals to get COVID-19 tests and vaccines (Rivas-Sánchez 2021).

Because they had no access to employment insurance and emergency support as avenues such as the Canada Emergency Response Benefit (CERB) were unavailable to them, undocumented workers struggled to meet their most basic needs. All this created a crisis of social reproduction – that is, a general difficulty to satisfy basic needs as social and biological beings due to radical shortage of resources (Federici and Jones 2020; Vosko and Spring 2021). Although federal and provincial governments announced routes for fast-tracked regularization programs which would create opportunities for permanent residency and eventually citizenship, particularly targeting those labelled as "essential workers" such as those working in residential and long-term care centres, those routes had a limited coverage.

The situation in the US was similar. Migration scholars and organizations working with undocumented populations reported job losses in great numbers, disproportionate COVID-19 infections, and psychological stress among members of this population (Borjas and Cassidy 2021; Garcini et al. 2021; Noe-Bustamante 2021). Loss of income greatly affected food and housing security, at home and abroad, and their exclusion from social benefits and emergency relief during the pandemic enacted through the Coronavirus Aid, Relief, and Economic Security Act (CARES Act) (US Department of the Treasury 2020), increased their precarious situation. Moreover, despite the evidence of disproportionate health inequality, precarious migrants were excluded from the Congressional decision to initiate a waiver for coronavirus responses that allowed health providers to bill for telemedicine through the Coronavirus Preparedness and Supplemental Appropriations Act. On 24 February 2020, the Trump administration decided to put the public charge rule into effect. This allowed the Department of Homeland Security (DHS) to consider immigrants' access to federal health programs as grounds for denying citizenship applications (HSD 2019) and discouraged undocumented immigrants from seeking health services.

In addition to being affected by the COVID-19 crisis in terms of health and income, housing, and food insecurity, immigrants with precarious legal status in the US were targets of stigmatization and social intolerance, as the government and certain sectors of the American population regarded them as vectors of the COVID-19 infection (Mukumbang 2021). In addition, there was a surge in deportations of anyone detained at border stations without regard to fair asylum procedures (Miroff 2020a, 2020b; Perez 2020). In effect, on 20 March 2020, the Trump administration enacted a public health order, benignly called Title 42, to immediately turn back asylum seekers at the border, citing risks from the rapid transmission of COVID-19 (CDC 2020). All these factors put undocumented workers in the US in a crisis of social reproduction, as defined earlier.

RESPONDING TO THE MULTIPLICATION OF BORDERS: MULTIPLICATION OF PRECARITIES PROLIFERATION OF STRUGGLES

The proliferation of borders does not operate without resistance, particularly from labour and grassroots solidarity. Migrant labour's circulation within global capitalism does not occur as mere labour commodity. Migrant workers also circulate within global markets in the form of a creative force driven by a desire to satisfy fundamental human needs and enact ways to contest their conditions (Chironi and Tomasello 2017). Although the proliferation of borders imposes obstacles to a free and dignified presence in host societies, their influence in receiving societies can be profound (Bauder 2006; Villegas 2020). Creative acts of contestation, passive forms of resistance, and political participation and solidarity (with or without the support of unions and organized labour) open "cracks in the borders" and modes of reclaiming freedom (Rivas-Sánchez 2021).

A key social force opposing the multiplication of borders and migrant precarity in North America comes from historical solidarity movements in urban and rural settings. Sanctuary Cities (or cities of refuge) and Solidarity Cities (Bauder and Gonzalez 2018), which were originally propelled by secular and faith-based revolutionary sectors of society during the second half of the twentieth century (Ridgley 2008), and which expanded to Canadian cities in the first decade of the twenty-first century (Moffette and Ridgley 2018), constitute important solidarity countermovements. Sanctuary Cities may have limitations, such as the reproduction of conservative discourses reinforcing "heteronormative familism" and the reproduction of problematic classifications separating "deserving vs undeserving" immigrants (see: Atak and Hudson 2022; Jeffries and Ridgley 2020). However, they provide access to municipal services, information, basic legal protections (Paquet et al. 2021) and other social infrastructures upon which excluded migrants can find access to education, health care, social services, and other basic grounds for survival. These cities also help provide the foundations upon which forms of community-building and political participation operate at the margins and from below (Bauder 2016).

Montreal and NYC are both sanctuary cities. Historically, these are "young" sanctuary cities – NYC and Montreal – as both declared their sanctuary status in 2017. However, they provide access to some basic services and infrastructures of protection that can serve as grounds of survival for unauthorized residents. In NYC, sanctuary policies are more robust, with municipal authorities issuing IDs that provide membership and access to municipal services; private, faith-based institutions – which provide shelter, food, clothing, and other basic material means of survival to residents regardless of migratory status; and community organizations – which organize unauthorized residents politically and provide them with information and material/moral support.

In Montreal, sanctuary policies are more limited (Agyeman and Duprey 2020), and are provided mainly through churches and community organizations, with little and even contradictory engagement from the municipal authorities. For example, the City of Montreal has been addressing the right to membership and access to municipal services to unauthorized residents by issuing them municipal ID cards (McKenna 2022), while at the same time allowing the police to actively search, arrest, and hand over unauthorized residents to federal police (Moffette 2021).

Perhaps more important than the sanctuary status, is the fact that they are also *rebel cities* (Harvey 2013), which host a history of struggles carried out to resist the reorganization of space and social life at the service of capital accumulation. Those histories of struggle are more evident in the case of NYC where, for generations, migrants have been playing a key role in building both the city and a migrant labour movement that contests social exclusion of migrants (see Finesurrey 2023). In Montreal, migrants' political struggles have received weaker support from civil society because the Quebecoise society and many of its mainstream political forces tend to see migrants (principally non-white, racialized immigrants) as a threat to their language, heritage, and values (Rioux 2005). Nevertheless, over the last three decades, organizations such as SAB, No One Is Illegal, and the Center for Immigrant Workers have carried out advocacy, outreach, rallies, and everyday support work, specifically targeting racialized immigrants and unauthorized workers, creating social spaces for a rich assemblage of organizing (Rivas-Sánchez 2023).

Those infrastructures of dissent, to invoke Alan Sears' (2006) concept, shaped some of the ways in which civil society on both sides of the border responded to deepening precarity throughout the COVID-19 pandemic. In effect, a number of organizations and individuals engaged in grassroots, day-to-day, spontaneous gestures of solidarity and mutual aid aimed at providing care to the most vulnerable. Some political protests were led by unauthorized migrants themselves with the support of local organizations, including the Status for All campaign in Canada, while other protests were more spontaneous.

Mutual Aid and Solidarity: The Politics of Radical Love

The pandemic created both a crisis of health and a crisis of labour, which, in Canada, disproportionately affected racialized workers employed in key sectors of the economy, particularly services and food production (Bryant, Aquanno, and Raphael 2020; Rocha, Shingler, and Montpetit 2020). Precarious migrant workers were disproportionately affected (Vosko and Spring 2021, 1775). In urban centres, unauthorized workers faced unemployment, food insecurity, anxiety, and isolation, as deportability persisted (Rivas-Sánchez 2021). The health of temporary migrant workers was disproportionately affected in rural areas, particularly on farms (Haley et al. 2020; Vosko and Spring 2021). Considered economically "essential," these workers continued to be "imported" and employed in Canadian agricultural sectors.

In the Canadian cities, principally in Montreal, Toronto, and Vancouver, local migrant justice organizations responded by collecting and distributing food, money, and other essentials. Likewise, in rural communities in Alberta, British Columbia, Ontario, and Quebec, organizations linked to SAB, No One is Illegal, Justice 4 Migrant Workers, Migrant Rights Network (MRN), Lynden Friends of Migrant Farmworkers, and Migrante, among others, allied with neighbourhood organizations and professional networks, mostly health and social workers associations to mobilize students, academics, activists, and the general public to create support communities offering temporary refuge and basic necessities (Alcaraz et al. 2022).[1] In some Southern Ontario rural communities, for example, networks led by educators, religious ministers, psychologists, and social workers, created "*paquetes de apoyo*" (solidarity kits), which included food and cash, but also offered moral and spiritual support to temporary migrant workers, undocumented workers, and refugee claimants (Rivas-Sánchez 2021). Some local farmers donated food, which was delivered weekly to those who lost jobs and faced food insecurity. Such support packages included not only food, but also cash, and also offered psychological support (delivered through teleconferencing), legal support, and visits to provide mealtime company in open spaces to help them overcome challenges generated by isolation.

In Montreal, SAB engaged in a variety of struggles in order to facilitate, cultivate, and practice what they call "*solidarité sans frontieres*." The notion of "Solidarity without borders," or "across borders" in the political grammar of this anti-systemic network, refers to acts of mutual aid and solidarity aimed at making sure that migrants with precarious legal status can access essential public services and support from which they are legally excluded. Throughout the COVID-19 crisis, SAB coordinated campaigns to issue municipal IDs to unauthorized workers and fundraised to collect and redistribute food and funds. It also provided information to guide precarious immigrants to access health and other social services without the need to provide personal information or documents. Mutual Aid weekly meetings coordinated through teleconferencing made possible the development of common spaces facilitating personal/social connections/interactions through which people could help each other, despite social distancing. This work allowed thousands of migrants to access health care, including mental health services, legal counselling, vaccines, money, food, clothing, computers to have access to the internet, and other essentials.

In parallel to the acts of mutual aid and solidarity, organizations also engaged in direct political action. In Montreal and Toronto, MRN and SAB – the two migrant justice organizations with the most presence across Canada – developed, with the assistance of digital technologies, hybrid methods of political organizing, to challenge exclusion and deportability at the local levels. One of the very first campaigns was carried out in Montreal between April and May 2020, when SAB organized the *#FreeThemAll #HungerStrikeLaval* campaign. This campaign consisted in organizing "Freedom Caravans" protesting for undocumented migrants being held in federal detention centres and supporting a one-week hunger strike led by migrants detained in the *Centre de surveillance de l'immigration de Laval* (Solidarity Across Borders 2020). This campaign resulted in the release of thirty-six undocumented immigrants from detention. Members of this network provided ex-prisoners with housing, food, and financial support while legal campaigns were launched to prevent their deportations.

In summer of 2021, the Status for All Caravan was planned and coordinated by more than thirty migrant justice organizations across Canada. Roughly a thousand people from rural and urban centres, undocumented migrants and failed refugee claimants, temporary foreign workers, migrant justice organizers, students, Indigenous organizations, educators, intellectual workers, sex workers, union militants, religious organizations, and other activists walked hundreds of kilometres from Montreal and from Toronto to Ottawa. In the culminating rally at the entrance of the Canadian parliament, activists demanded the Government of Canada implement a "full and comprehensive regularization program that allows those persons living without status in the country legal paths to permanent residency and eventually citizenship" which is the main demand of the pan-Canadian coalition of the MRN (MRN 2021). Likewise, in High River, Alberta, a network of social workers, in coordination with social justice organizations, worked in collaboration with the Alberta Assembly of Social Workers (AASW) and the grassroots organization, Migrante, to provide support to migrant workers infected by COVID-19 while working in the local meatpacking company (the Cargill meatpacking plant).

These and other struggles have been expressed in both negative and positive forms. In their negative form, they are expressed through campaigns against deportations (No One is Illegal; No border, No Nations, Stop the Deportations); rallies rejecting deportation centres (Centres de surveillance de l'immigration); rallies refusing borders ("Les frontieres tuent" or "Borders Kill"), and campaigns against abuse and exploitation in the workplace. In their positive form, those struggles are expressed through rallies in solidarity with those who are incarcerated in the Centres de Surveillance de l'immigration (Solidarité avec les sans papiers; solidarity with those without status), and the campaign Status for All, perhaps one of the most popular among the immigrant communities in Canada.

The mobilizations carried out in this context, demanding status for all, articulated alliances among very distinct sectors of the Canadian public. Organizations working with refugees, international students, queer activists, temporary foreign workers (TFWs) dismissed during the pandemic, undocumented workers, the student movement, feminists, unions, anti-racist organizations, educators, and health workers have worked together to make sure that those who were left behind in the context of the pandemic, receive the support they need while pushing their main demand of "status for all."

This type of activism has been successful at cultivating forms of social belonging and political participation among those marginalized by the Canadian immigration system. They have been successful at empowering migrants with precarious status to practice mutual aid and solidarity, which have had the effect of helping those negated to come to "life," to a public existence, not as subjects of charity and compassion, but as political subjects who gain their place as legitimate members of the local and global community.

MIGRANT JUSTICE ACTIVISM IN CANADA AND THE US: DIFFERENCES, REPERTOIRES, OUTCOMES

However important be the gains produced by solidarity, Canadian migrant justice campaigns have not yet achieved their objectives of status for all, stopping deportations, or abolishing immigrant detention. During the pandemic, and up to the time of writing, the Canadian state has continued to detain and remove migrants at rates exceeding pre-pandemic numbers and has continued to negate access to fundamental social services and benefits to undocumented workers. In what follows, I offer some reflections on these dynamics by briefly comparing migrant justice activism and outcomes between New York City and Montreal.

Universal Principles vs Pragmatic Demands

Migrant justice campaigns in Canada seem to have framed their demands mostly based on a combination of general principles of universal justice and abolitionism expressed through political slogans such as "Status for All" and "No Prisons, No Borders, No Nations, Stop the Deportations," often with less emphasis on specific demands. In contrast, in the US, while the demand "status for all" and the abolitionist demands "no prisons, no borders, no nations" guide the values of solidarity movements, their activism, at least during the pandemic, included more specific and practical demands. For example, in New York, the migrant justice coalition Making the Road New York launched in March 2020 the campaign #FundExcludedWorkers. This campaign used a variety of repertoires of protest, including street protests, blockades, and a hunger strike targeting the state governor and legislators with a specific demand: to allocate in the budget a special fund for workers who were not eligible for federal or other forms of financial aid. Massive protests blocking main streets in NYC and a nine-day hunger strike pressured the State of New York to release USD 2.1 billion in April 2021 for those purposes (Henney 2021). This achievement benefited 130 thousand undocumented workers in the New York State, as well as other "non-traditional workers," including rideshare drivers and street vendors among others, who were originally denied relief funds. Each individual received a one-time maximum payment of USD 15,600, which is equivalent to six months of traditional pandemic unemployment benefits (Gabbatt 2021).

Therefore, if we compare how demands were framed during the pandemic on both sides of the US-Canada border, demands in Canada were framed around broader terms, while in the US they were more focused on specific issues without (or with less) reference to political slogans and universal demands. Moreover, despite the radicality in framing, Canadian organizations' demands remain governed by the duality of citizenship/non-citizenship, in effect recognizing that it is only through state recognition that social belonging, rights, benefits, and freedoms are granted. Behind the "status for all" demand in the pandemic context displayed by Canadian networks is the idea that rights and belonging are attained only through the legal achievement of Canadian citizenship. This demand also assumes that legal status is the central mechanism by which people can access benefits, protections, and exercise their rights. In NYC, in contrast, although those concerns are not set aside (the demand for a "legalization program" is persistent across the migrant justice movements in the US), migrant justice organizing did not set legal status as a necessary condition by which they would have access to relief funds. They acted politically with the basic assumption of their right to be socially supported, by virtue of their presence as people and of contributions to the society where they live. This vision of rights transcends citizenship. This political demand seems to be invoking the principle of *jus domicile* as a premise for citizenship that Canadian scholars have theorized in detail (Bauder 2012). It seems that pragmatic demands among US migrant rights movements, in combination with mass mobilizations, were important to attain those victories.

Hybrid, Unruly Political Uprisings vs Mass Mobilization

While Canadian migrant justice activism has been based in hybrid forms of protest, those in the US included a great deal of mass mobilization. Both forms of contentious politics have important political outcomes. Mass mobilization in the US, particularly in NYC, attained important victories that provide protection to those most vulnerable, including but not limited to undocumented people. Although migrant justice activism in Canada has attained less prominent gains, it has produced a type of activism that is original, revolutionary, and innovative within its own context.

Throughout the COVID-19 pandemic, migrant justice activism in Canada mobilized precarious migrants using digital technologies. SAB, for example, created an autonomous, decentralized virtual network where migrant justice activists, migrants including non-status migrants, refugee claimants, and activists of all kinds, met regularly to exchange ideas and experiences and plan political actions. To ensure that people with precarious status can participate in the virtual meetings, the network also distributed computers among non-status immigrant activists who belong to the organizing network.

Having people "connected" brought many benefits. Precarious status immigrants, who often face social isolation in Canada, could participate, attend meetings, exchange experiences, provide and receive help, ideas, and coordinate collective efforts aimed at providing collectivized mutual aid in a moment of crisis of social reproduction (food and money collection and redistribution, medicines, tips to survive difficulties in life, etc.).

Many applications and technologies are used in this collective work to get interconnected and run this virtual meeting point. But, among all of them, teleconferencing has proved to be a crucial "mobilizing structure." Teleconferencing has led to the shaping of hybrid communities of resistance across space and time. Combining online communication and "on the ground" organizing seems to be shaping the development of a form of political activism that is in unruly, sporadic, and nomadic, and a form of political subjectivity that is difficult to be governed and disciplined by the apparatus of exclusion shaped by the proliferation of borders.

The flexibility in organizing facilitated by digital technologies has made it possible that precarious status immigrants could attend meetings more easily. As precarious status immigrants, including non-status immigrants, are subsumed by the Canadian labour markets whether through highly constraining conditions (when working with temporary visas) or through precarious and unstable conditions, their belongingness to Canadian society is unstable, and their lived existence is characterized by impermanent employment and housing. Many thus lack social networks, have unstable and often changing housing and family arrangements, and face continuous changes in work and life schedules. These conditions often constrain attendance to in-person meetings, as that format requires them to move through the city, with the concomitant physical effort, emotional energy, and risk that this requires. The opportunity to attend meetings via teleconferencing changed this situation, and provided these nomadic activists with more autonomy and control over their own involvement in organizing and political participation.

The former situation of expanded engagement has given rise to a new form of migrant justice activism that I would like to call "nomadic hybrid activism." This uneven and unruly political engagement through digitally-assisted technologies allows for contestation or transgression of the confinements created by precarious labour and deportability which often reduces the body and mind of the migrant to unprotection and isolation. Even more, this intermittent participation has also given rise to a type of contestation that is also unruly and intermittent. As local migrant justice activists in Canada are often also part of the "precariat" with impermanent, unstable, and unpredictable work, their activism couples with the nomadic and intermittent character of the precarious status migrant workers. Therefore, the struggles in which both migrant workers and activists engage happens often in the form of an unruly and intermittent political protest.

This unruly political activism has certainly not resulted in the fundamental changes Canadian migrant justice activism envisions. But it has made possible the emergence of this new political engagement. Mutual aid, solidarity, and learning local politics for the undocumented have been made possible. Along the way, or through this kind of political practice, this style of engagement has shaped a new form of political subjectivity, characterized by its ungovernable character. Unlike the undocumented worker from the previous in-person-only activism, who was "forced" to choose between attending an assembly or work in a factory or farm (which prevented them from accessing those networks, learning languages, receiving support, finding friends or love, and experiences offered by the new "homeland") the hybrid, nomadic activist can keep in regular contact with allies, search for help, follow up on events, and have a more meaningful life in the local society. This situation makes the migrant rebel nomad a person with more choices and opportunities to do something more than simply work for a living, all of which may help her/him/them to eventually escape exploitation and to intermittently overcome fears produced by deportability. These new forms of life are perhaps the most positive outcomes I have witnessed in the Canadian migrant rights context.

To sum up, while in the Canadian context the positive outcomes are more qualitative and produced in the acts of engaging in political struggles, in the US context the outcomes can be measure in quantitative terms. The reason for this success and for the mass character of this mobilization could be related to several factors, but it seems that the density of this demographic matters. Precarious immigrants, including undocumented workers, are significant in number. It is calculated that in cities such as NYC and Los Angeles, one in ten workers is undocumented. In the State of New York there are 835,000 undocumented workers (Migration Policy Institute 2019), and 80 per cent of them have lived there between five and thirty years (Passel and Cohn 2019). The State of New York hosts one of the oldest and most expansive social infrastructure providing services, advocacy, support, and sanctuary to undocumented and other precarious status immigrants. Perhaps paradoxically, services provided by the state can also work as important vehicles that, as an intended consequence, sustain vibrant, connected, and less isolated and oppressed communities. Additionally, the rights to own a home, to have a driver's licence, and to access health care are obtained through several venues in cities such as New York, and also play an important part in the production and reproduction of more connected and less isolated migrant communities. Those demographic facts, resources, freedoms, access to support and advocacy, it can be argued, have served as vehicles or "mobilizing structures" as defined by Doug McAdam (1999).

In Montreal, unlike NYC, although the city proclaimed itself a sanctuary city in 2017 (Eleftheriou-Smith 2017), there is no historical tradition of offering city services to the undocumented migrant population. The City of Montreal only recently offered IDs to access city pools, libraries, and other services, but the police continue to keep these migrants under surveillance and the threat of detention. In 2019, the Montreal police contacted the Canadian Border Services Agency 2,500 times to inquire about the immigration status of persons stopped in the city (Moffette 2021; Pouliot 2020). Furthermore, the precarious status population in Montreal tend to be subsumed in exploitative, time-demanding, and strenuous jobs that often keep them alienated from socialization outside of their work, which estranges them from society and prevents them from developing meaningful social bonds (Rivas-Sánchez 2019). Perhaps this is what explains the success of activism based less on mass mobilization, and more in a nomadic, intermittent, and unruly engagement.

The role of labour unions needs to be considered as well when talking about the difference of outcomes. In the United States, unions have played an important role in strengthening undocumented workers' political organizing through resources and political training as mobilizing structures. The history of the Industrial Workers of The World (IWW) organizing precarious migrant workers at the beginning of the twentieth century is telling in itself. But more recently, since the beginning of the twenty-first century, in response to a dramatic growth of undocumented labour in several sectors of US industry, the American Federation of Labor and Congress of Industrial Organizations (AFL-CIO) has been organizing with migrant workers, including undocumented migrant workers, has been the first to reject the 1986 immigration laws that imposed sanctions against employers hiring undocumented labour, and, more recently, has been growing campaigns to improve working conditions and attaining better wages (Ness 2011, 15). In sharp contrast, Canadian unions have historically passed from sustaining openly racist and exclusionary views against "foreign" workers, sometimes even encouraging deportation and social exclusion (Goutor 2007), to a more friendly position, although remaining divergent and ambiguous (Foster, Taylor, and Kahn 2015). Today, the work of unions supporting or organizing with undocumented migrant workers is virtually nonexistent, although many of their members, most prominently academics and other intellectual workers from Canadian colleges and universities, constitute an important component of the migrant justice activism.

FINAL REFLECTIONS

By comparing the dynamics in Canada and the US, I argue that in the United States, longer traditions of migrant activism, a greater number of precarious status immigrants, more organizing infrastructure, and a larger population engaged in struggles have produced a type of activism that is pragmatic, massive, and effective.[1] Important victories during the COVID-19 pandemic occurred because of this combination of approach and established social conditions. Seen from a long historical view, migrant justice activism in the United States has moved far past the central strategy and cross-national coordination that, building upon migrant's rich social networks, militant/fighting disposition, interethnic and intraethnic solidarity, and workplace militancy, led to the historical 2006 migrant uprisings across the US (Ness 2006). The Excluded Workers movement, seen from that historical point of view, was more fragmented and discontinuous (often a material reflection of the fragmented social life that migrants live in late-capitalist North America) than the migrant rights movement was in 2006. However, the effects of that political work, even with its limitations, speak for themselves in that the goal of access to the CARES Act was achieved.

In Canada, activism that is more inclined to frame demands through principles of universal justice with fewer pragmatic demands, and a smaller cohort of precarious status migrants engaged in those struggles, have been less successful if judged in pragmatic and quantitative terms. However, the production of a nomadic, unruly political subject engaged with hybrid forms of contentious politics that are proving to be capable of liberating migrants from detention centres while discursively keeping alive the idea that "no one is illegal," and that all humans deserve to be recognized with a legal status regardless of their social origin, is worth attention, particularly in the historical context in which xenophobia is increasing. The unruly political insurgent produced in the light of migrant justice struggles in Montreal remains embryonic, but may have important impacts on migration governance in North America in the future.

NOTES

1 Solidarité sans frontières | Solidarity Across Borders | Solidaridad sin fronteras (referred hereafter as SAB) is a migrant justice organization based in Montreal, Quebec. Its main work consists in confronting "an unjust immigration and refugee determination system" through popular education, political protests, and support for undocumented immigrants. Composed by dozens of social justice organizations and SAB is recognized by Canadian organizers as one of the most copious and politically influential organizations on migrant justice issues not only in Quebec, but in several Canadian provinces, as its work is caried out through networks and alliances with organizations across Canada. For more details about SAB's principles, actions, and demands, visit: https://www.solidarityacrossborders.org/en/a-propos/our-principles.

Migrant Rights Network (MRN) is a pan-Canadian alliance formed by migrant justice individuals and organizations dedicated to mobilizing and supporting local and national struggles in defense of migrants' rights. Because of its composition, MRN has a presence across Canada. For more details about MRN's goals, history, actions and demands, visit: https://migrantrights.ca/about/.

2 The emphasis in this chapter has been on understanding why some of these struggles have been successful (or not) from a comparative perspective. Although beyond the scope of the chapter, further research in this area might consider the role of national governance systems and how these dynamics impact to what degree these struggles' political goals are achieved.

REFERENCES

Agamben, Giorgio. 2009. "What is an Apparatus?" In *What is an Apparatus? and Other Essays*, translated by David Kishik and Stefan Pedatella. Stanford: Stanford University Press.

Agyeman, Julian, and Alexandra Duprey. 2020. "Are you really a Sanctuary City?" *Agriculture and Human Values* 37(3): 611–12.

Alcaraz, Nellie, Liza Lorenzetti, Sarah Thomas, and Rita Dhungel. 2022. "Breaking Isolation: Social Work in Solidarity with Migrant Workers through and beyond COVID-19." *Social Work* 67 (1): 48–57.

Atak, Idil, and François Crépeau. 2013. "The Securitization of Asylum and Human Rights in Canada and the European Union." In *Contemporary Issues in Refugee Law*, edited by Satvinder Singh Juss and Colin Harvey, 227–57. Cheltenham: Edward Elgar Publishing.

Atak, Idil, and Graham Hudson. 2022. "Montreal's Sanctuary Policy for Non-Status Migrants: Opportunity and Obstacles." *Canada's Journal on Refugees* 38 (2): 1–13.

Bacon, David. 2008. *Illegal People: How Globalization Creates Migration and Criminalizes Immigrants*. Boston: Beacon Press.

Basok, Tanya, Danièle Bélanger, and Eloy Rivas. 2014. "Reproducing Deportability: Migrant Agricultural Workers in South-Western Ontario." *Journal of Ethnic and Migration Studies* 40 (9): 1394–413.

Bauder, Harald. 2006. *Labor Movement: How Migration Regulates Labor Markets*. New York: Oxford University Press.

– 2012. "Jus Domicile: In Pursuit of a Citizenship of Equality and Social Justice." *Journal of International Political Theory* 8 (1–2): 184–96.

– 2016. "From 'dysfunctionality' to solidarity." *Dialogues in Human Geography* 6 (1): 69–72.

Bauder, Harald, and Dayana A. Gonzalez. 2018. "Municipal responses to 'illegality': Urban sanctuary across national contexts." *Social Inclusion* 6 (1): 124–34.
Binford, Leigh. 2019. "Assessing Temporary Foreign Worker Programs through the Prism of Canada's Seasonal Agricultural Worker Program: Can They be Reformed or Should They be Eliminated?" *Dialectical Anthropology* 43 (4): 347–66.
Binford, Leigh, and Kerry Preibisch. 2021. "Interrogating Racialized Global Labor Supply: Caribbean and Mexican Workers in Canada's SAWP." In *Tomorrow We're All Going to the Harvest*, edited by Leigh Binford, 93–115. Austin: University of Texas Press.
Borjas, George J., and Hugh Cassidy. 2022. "The Fall and Rise of Immigrant Employment during the COVID-19 Pandemic." Harvard University Working Paper. https://scholar.harvard.edu/files/gborjas/files/rle2022.pdf. Accessed 9 June 2023.
Bryant, Toba, Scott Aquanno, and Dennis Raphael. 2020. "Unequal Impact of COVID-19: Emergency Neoliberalism and Welfare Policy in Canada." *Critical Studies: An International and Interdisciplinary Journal* 15 (1): 22–39.
Calavita, Kitty. 1982. "California's 'Employer Sanctions': The Case of the Disappearing Law." *Research Report Series* # 39. University of California.
– 2010. *Inside the State: The Bracero Program, Immigration, and the I.N.S.* New Orleans: Quid Pro Books.
Canadian Council for Refugees. 2020. "COVID-19 Q&A. Questions Relating to Refugee Claims." http://www.ccrweb.ca/en/covid-19-qa. Accessed 9 June 2023.
CDC (Centers for Disease Control and Prevention). 2020. *Order Suspending Introduction of Certain Persons from Countries where a Communicable Disease Exists.* www.cdc.gov/quarantine/pdf/CDC-Order-Prohibiting-Introduction-of-Persons_Final_3-20-20_3-p.pdf. Accessed 9 June 2023.
Chomsky, Aviva. 2014. *Undocumented: How Immigration Became Illegal.* Boston: Beacon Press.
Christoff, Stefan. 2021. "Canada is Deporting its 'Guardian Angels.'" *Aljazeera*, 23 July 2021. https://www.aljazeera.com/opinions/2021/7/23/trudeaus-canada-is-deporting-its-guardian-angels. Accessed 9 June 2023.
Chironi, Daniela, and Federico Tomasello. 2017. "Living Labour and Social Movements: A Dialogue with Antonio Negri." *Anthropological Theory* 17 (4): 518–25.
De Genova, Nicholas P. 2002. "Migrant 'Illegality' and Deportability in Everyday Life." *Annual Review of Anthropology* 31 (1): 419–47.
– 2004. "The Legal Production of Mexican/Migrant 'Illegality.'" *Latino Studies* 2 (2): 160–85.

– 2014. “Immigration Reform and the Production of Migrant Illegality.” In *Constructing Immigrant “Illegality”: Critiques, Experiences, and Responses*, edited by Cecilia Menjívar and Daniel Kanstroom, 37–62. New York: Cambridge University Press.

Dauvergne, Catherine. 2017. “Making People Illegal.” In *Migrants and Rights*, edited by Mary Crock, 77–94. Abingdon: Routledge.

DHS (Department of Homeland Security). 2019. *Inadmissibility on Public Charge Grounds Rule*. 2019-17142. https://www.federalregister.gov/documents/2019/08/14/2019-17142/inadmissibility-on-public-charge-grounds. Accessed 9 June 2023.

Diop, Petra Molnar. 2013. “The ‘Bogus’ Refugee: Roma Asylum Claimants and Discourses of Fraud in Canada’s Bill C-31.” *Refuge* 30 (1): 67–80.

Eleftheriou-Smith, Loulla-Mae. 2017. “Montreal Becomes ‘Sanctuary City’ for Undocumented Immigrants.” *The Independent*, 21 February 2017. https://www.independent.co.uk/news/world/americas/montreal-sanctuary-city-undocumented-immigrants-canada-quebec-ontario-toronto-london-hamilton-mayor-denis-coderre-a7591266.html. Accessed 9 June 2023.

Federici, Silvia, and Campbell Jones. 2020. “Counterplanning in the Crisis of Social Reproduction.” *South Atlantic Quarterly* 119 (1): 153–65.

Finesurrey, Samuel. 2023. “A People’s History of New York City.” *CUNY Academic Commons*, 12 February 2023. https://historynyc.commons.gc.cuny.edu/immigrant-nyc/. Accessed 9 June 2023.

Foster, Jason, Alison Taylor, and Candy Khan. 2015. “The Dynamics of Union Responses to Migrant Workers in Canada.” *Work, Employment and Society* 29 (3): 409–26.

Foster, Jason. 2012. “Making Temporary Permanent: The Silent Transformation of the Temporary Foreign Worker Program.” *Just Labour: A Canadian Journal of Work and Society* 19 (Autumn): 22–46.

Foucault, Michel. 2007. *Security, Territory, Population: Lectures at the Collège de France 1977–1978*. Translated by Graham Burchell. Basingstoke: Palgrave Macmillan.

Fudge, Judy, and Fiona MacPhail. 2009. “The Temporary Foreign Worker Program in Canada: Low-Skilled Workers as an Extreme form of Flexible Labor.” *Immigration and Nationality Law Review* 30 (1) 843–86.

Gabbatt, Adam. 2021. “New York to Give up to $15,600 to Undocumented Migrants hit by COVID.” *The Guardian*, 8 April 2021. https://www.theguardian.com/us-news/2021/apr/08/new-york-undocumented-migrants-covid-cash. Accessed 9 June 2023.

Gabriel, Christina, and Laura Macdonald. 2018. “After the International Organization for Migration: Recruitment of Guatemalan Temporary

Agricultural Workers to Canada." *Journal of Ethnic and Migration Studies* 44 (10): 1706–24.

Garcini, Luz M., Ryan Daly, Nellie Chen, Justin Mehl, Tommy Pham, Thuy Phan, Brittany Hansen, and Aishwarya Kothare. 2021. "Undocumented Immigrants and Mental Health: A Systematic Review of Recent Methodology and Findings in the US." *Journal of Migration and Health* 4: 100058.

Goldring, Luin. 2010. "Temporary Worker Programs as Precarious Status." *Canadian Issues/Thèmes canadiens* (Spring): 50–4.

Goldring, Luin, Carolina Berinstein, and Judith K. Bernhard. 2009. "Institutionalizing Precarious Migratory Status in Canada." *Citizenship Studies* 13 (3): 239–65.

Goldring, Luin, and Patricia Landolt. 2013. "The Social Production of Non-citizenship: The Consequences of Intersecting Trajectories of Precarious Legal Status and Precarious Work." In *Producing and Negotiating Non-citizenship: Precarious Legal Status in Canada*, edited by Luin Goldring and Patricia Landolt, 154–74. Toronto: University of Toronto Press.

Gurung, Tashi W., Emily Amburgey, and Sienna R. Craig. 2021. "Unsettling the American Dream: Mobility, Migration and Precarity among Translocal Himalayan Communities during COVID-19." *Development and Change* 52 (6): 1277–300.

Goutor, David. 2007. *Guarding the Gates: The Canadian Labour Movement and Immigration, 1872–1934*. Vancouver: University of British Columbia Press.

Haley, Ella, Susana Caxaj, Glynis George, Jenna Hennebry, Eliseo Martell, and Janet McLaughlin. 2020. "Migrant Farmworkers Face Heightened Vulnerabilities During COVID-19." *Journal of Agriculture, Food Systems, and Community Development* 9 (3): 35–9.

Harvey, David. 2013. *Rebel Cities: From the Rights to the City to the Urban Revolution*. London: Verso.

Henney, Megan. 2021. "NY Creates $2B Fund to Provide Illegal Immigrants with COVID Relief Fund to Offer One-Time Payments of up to $15,600." *Fox Business*, 8 April 2021. https://www.foxbusiness.com/politics/new-york-fund-coronavirus-aid-undocumented-immigrants.

Ilcan, Suzan, Kim Rygiel, and Feyzi Baban. 2018. "The Ambiguous Architecture of Precarity: Temporary Protection, Everyday Living and Migrant Journeys of Syrian Refugees." *International Journal of Migration and Border Studies* 4 (1–2): 51–70.

Jackson, Samantha, and Harald Bauder. 2014. "Neither Temporary, nor Permanent: The Precarious Employment Experiences of Refugee Claimants in Canada." *Journal of Refugee Studies* 27 (3): 360–81.

Jeffries, Fiona, and Jennifer Ridgley. 2020. "Building the sanctuary city from the ground up: Abolitionist solidarity and transformative reform." *Citizenship Studies* 24(4): 548–567.

Luibhéid, Eithne. 2013. *Pregnant on Arrival: Making the Illegal Immigrant*. Minneapolis: University of Minnesota Press.

McAdam, Doug. 1999. *Political Process and the Development of Black Insurgency, 1930–1970*. 2nd ed. Chicago and London: University of Chicago Press.

McKenna, Kate. 2022. "Montreal Renews Program Offering Municipal ID to Undocumented Immigrants." CBC *News*, 22 February 2022. https://www.cbc.ca/news/canada/montreal/municipal-montreal-id-1.6360290.

Mezzadra, Sandro. 2016. "MLC 2015 Keynote: What's at Stake in the Mobility of Labour? Borders, Migration, Contemporary Capitalism." *Migration, Mobility, and Displacement* 2 (1): 31–43.

Mezzadra, Sandro, and Brett Neilson. 2012. "Between Inclusion and Exclusion: On the Topology of Global Space and Borders." *Theory, Culture and Society* 29 (4–5): 58–75.

– 2013. *Border as Method, or, the Multiplication of Labor*. Durham and London: Duke University Press.

Migration Policy Institute. 2019. *Profile of the Unauthorized Population: New York*. Washington, DC: Migration Policy Institute. https://www.migrationpolicy.org/data/unauthorized-immigrant-population/state/NY. Accessed 9 June 2023.

Miroff, Nick. 2020a. "Trump Administration has Expelled 10,000 Migrants at the Border During Coronavirus Outbreak, Just 100 in CBP Custody." *The Washington Post*, 9 April 2020. https://www.washingtonpost.com/national/trump-administration-has-expelled-10000-migrants-at-the-border-during-coronavirus-outbreak/2020/04/09/b177c534-7a7b-11ea-8cec-530b4044a458_story.html. Accessed 9 June 2023.

– 2020b. "Under Trump Border Rules, US has Granted Refuge to Just two People since Late March, Records Show." *Washington Post*, 13 May 2020. https://www.washingtonpost.com/immigration/border-refuge-trump-records/2020/05/13/93ea9ed6-951c-11ea-8107-acde2f7a8d6e_story.html. Accessed 9 June 2023.

Moffette, David. 2021. "Municipal Immigration Policing and Resistance to Internal Bordering in Canada." In *Migration, Security, and Resistance*, edited by Graham Hudson and Idil Atak, 161–82. Abingdon: Routledge.

Moffette, David, and Ridgley, Jennifer. 2018. "Sanctuary City Organizing in Canada From Hospitality to Solidarity." *Migration and Society* 1 (1): 147–55.

Mountz, Alison. 2020. *The Death of Asylum: Hidden Geographies of the Enforcement Archipelago*. Minneapolis: University of Minnesota Press.

MRN (Migrant Rights Network). 2021. *Hundreds of Migrants Make Pre-Election Demands in Ottawa.* https://migrantrights.ca/hundreds-of-migrants-make-pre-election-demands-in-ottawa/. Accessed 9 June 2023.

Mukumbang, Ferdinand C. 2021. "Pervasive Systemic Drivers Underpin COVID-19 Vulnerabilities in Migrants." *International Journal for Equity in Health* 20 (1): 1–7.

Ness, Immanuel. 2006. "The Rise of Migrant Militancy: Militant Organizing by Immigrants in New York City Could Show the Way for a Revitalized Labor Movement." *Dollars & Sense Annual Labor Issue: The New Militancy* 267 (September and October).

– 2011. *Guest Workers and Resistance to U.S. Corporate Despotism.* Urbana and Springfield: University of Illinois Press.

Ngai, Mae. 2004. *Impossible Subjects: Illegal Aliens and the Making of Modern America.* Princeton: Princeton University Press.

Noe-Bustamante, Luis, Jens Manuel Krogstad, and Mark Hugo Lopez. 2021. "For U.S. Latinos, COVID-19 Has Taken a Personal and Financial Toll." Pew Research Center. https://www.pewresearch.org/race-ethnicity/2021/07/15/for-u-s-latinos-covid-19-has-taken-a-personal-and-financial-toll/.

Paperny, Anna Mehler. 2021. "Canada Deporting Thousands even as Pandemic Rages." *Reuters*, 22 January 2021. https://www.reuters.com/article/us-health-coronavirus-canada-deportation-idUSKBN29R1EL.

Paquet, Mireille, Noémie Benoit, Idil Atak, Meghan Joy, Graham Hudson, and John Shields. 2022. "Sanctuary cities and Covid-19: The Case of Canada." In *Migration and Pandemics*, edited by Anna Triandafyllidou, 85–102. Bern: Springer.

Parreñas, Rhacel, Patricia Landolt, Luin Goldring, Tanya Golash-Boza, and Rachel Silvey. 2021. "Mechanisms of Migrant Exclusion: Temporary Labour, Precarious Noncitizenship, and Technologies of Detention." *Population, Space and Place* 27 (5): 1–6.

Perez, Sonia D. 2020. "Guatemala Says U.S. Deportations are Driving a Spike in Coronavirus Cases." *Time,* 14 April 2020. Accessed 9 June 2023.

Passel, Jeffrey S., and D'Vera Cohn. 2019. "20 Metro Areas are Home to Six-in-Ten Unauthorized Immigrants in U.S." Pew Research Center. https://www.pewresearch.org/fact-tank/2019/03/11/us-metro-areas-unauthorized-immigrants/. Accessed 9 June 2023.

Polanco, Geraldina. 2019. "Migration Regimes and the Production of (Labor) Unfreedom." *Journal of Asian American Studies* 22 (1): 11–30.

Porter, John. 1970. *The Vertical Mosaic. An Analysis of Social Class in Canada.* Toronto: University of Toronto Press.

Pouliot, Gaétan. 2020. "Les policiers de Montréal ne pourront plus appeler directement les agents frontaliers." *Radio Canada*, 8 October 2020. https://ici.radio-canada.ca/nouvelle/1723427/spvm-policiers-montreal-sans-papier-agents-frontaliers. Accessed 9 June 2023.

Reid-Musson, E. 2014. "Historicizing Precarity: A Labour Geography of 'Transient' Migrant Workers in Ontario Tobacco." *Geoforum* 56: 161–71.

Ridgley, Jennifer. 2008. "Cities of Refuge: Immigration Enforcement, Police, and the Insurgent Genealogies of Citizenship in US Sanctuary Cities." *Urban Geography* 29 (1): 53–77.

Rioux, Christian. 2005. "L'énigme québécoise." *In Les nationalismes québécois face à la diversité ethnoculturelle*, edited by Labelle Micheline, Antonius Rachad, and Toussaint Pierre, 256–67. Montreal: Éditions de L'Institut d'Études Internationales de Montréal.

Rivas-Sánchez, Eloy. 2019. "Travail abstrait, socialisation et social (dés) intégration des sans papiers au Canada." In *Travail, mobilités, subjectivités et formes d'assujettissement dans les Amériques*, edited by Alexis Martig and Jorge Pantaleón, 201–28. Quebec: Presses de l'Université Laval-Collection Nord/Sud.

– 2021. "Cracks in the Borders: Migrant Insurgencies in Canada, Solidarity, Refuge, and Protection of Life in the Times of COVID-19 [In Spanish]." *Revista de Sociología* 33 (2021): 95–121.

– 2023. "Global Citizenship from Below: Nomadic Proletariat, Digital Technologies, and the Grass Roots Making of Global Citizenship." In *L'épicentre: Démocratie, Éco*Citoyenneté mondiale et Éducation transformatoire* [*The Epicenter: Democracy, Eco*Global Citizenship and Transformative Education*], edited by Paul R. Carr, Gina Thésée, and Eloy Rivas-Sánchez. New York: Dio Press.

Rocha, Roberto, Benjamin Shingler, and Jonathan Montpetit. 2020. "Montreal's Poorest and Most Racially Diverse Neighbourhoods Hit Hardest by COVID-19, Data Analysis Shows." *CBC News*, 11 June 2020. https://www.cbc.ca/news/canada/montreal/race-covid-19-montreal-data-census-1.5607123. Accessed 9 June 2023.

Sears, Alan. 2006. "Creating and Sustaining Communities of Struggle: The Infrastructure of Dissent." *New Socialist*: 32–3.

Sharma, Nandita. 2012. "The 'Difference' that Borders Make: 'Temporary Foreign Workers' and the Social Organization of Unfreedom in Canada." In *Legislated Inequality: Temporary Labour Migration in Canada*, edited by Patti Tamara Lenard and Christine Straehle, 26–47. Montreal: Mc-Gill Queen's University Press.

Sheldon, Mia. 2020. "We Need All Hands on Deck': Canadian Farmers Struggle with Labour Shortfall Due to COVID-19." *CBC News*, 20 April

2020. https://www.cbc.ca/news/canada/farm-labour-foreign-workers-covid-19-1.5535727. Accessed 9 June 2023.

Solidarity Across Borders. 2020. *#HungerStrikeLaval Teach in – The Struggle Continues*. Solidary Across Borders, 8 April 2020. https://www.solidarityacrossborders.org/en/hungerstrikelaval-teach-in-the-struggle-continues. Accessed 9 June 2023.

Stasiulis, Daiva. 2020. "Elimi(nation): Canada's 'Post-Settler' Embrace of Disposable Migrant Labour." *Studies in Social Justice* 14 (1): 22–54.

US Department of the Treasury. 2020. *About the CARES Act and the Consolidated Appropriations Act*. https://home.treasury.gov/policy-issues/coronavirus/about-the-cares-act. Accessed 9 June 2023.

Vera Espinoza, Marcia, Victòria Prieto Rosas, Gisela P. Zapata, Luciana Gandini, Alethia Fernández de la Reguera, Gioconda Herrera, Stephanie López Villamil et al. 2021. "Towards a Typology of Social Protection for Migrants and Refugees in Latin America During the COVID-19 Pandemic." *Comparative Migration Studies* 9 (52): 4–28.

Villegas, Paloma E. 2020. *North of El Norte: Illegalized Mexican Migrants in Canada*. Vancouver: University of British Columbia Press.

Vosko, Leah F. 2016. "Blacklisting as a Modality of Deportability: Mexico's Response to Circular Migrant Agricultural Workers' Pursuit of Collective Bargaining Rights in British Columbia, Canada." *Journal of Ethnic and Migration Studies* 42 (8): 1371–87.

– 2018. "Legal but Deportable: Institutionalized Deportability and the Limits of Collective Bargaining Among Participants in Canada's Seasonal Agricultural Workers Program." *Industrial and Labor Relations Review* 71 (4): 882–907.

Vosko, Leah F., and Cynthia Spring. 2021. "COVID-19 Outbreaks in Canada and the Crisis of Migrant Farmworkers' Social Reproduction: Transnational Labour and the Need for Greater Accountability among Receiving States." *Journal of International Migration and Integration* 23 (4): 1765–91.

Weiler, Anelyse M., Janet McLaughlin, and Donald C. Cole. 2017. "Food Security at whose Expense? A Critique of the Canadian Temporary Farm Labour Migration Regime and Proposals for Change." *International Migration* 55 (4): 48–63.

Wells, Nick. 2020. "Advocacy Group says Undocumented Migrants Need Access to Government Benefits." *The Canadian Press*, 16 April 2020. https://www.cbc.ca/news/canada/british-columbia/undocumented-workers-1.5535344. Accessed 9 June 2023.

11

Prejudicial Populists? Evidence from Canada

Scott Pruysers and Tobias Gerhard Schminke

Narendra Modi's election as India's prime minister in 2014, Donald Trump's victory in the 2016 US presidential election, the UK's Brexit referendum, and Jair Bolsonaro's success in the 2019 Brazilian election – these are just a few of the examples that made the 2010s a decade of populist triumphs. However, even though the dominant electoral successes were on the political right, one should not underestimate the scope and number of victories of the populist left and centre. For example, in the wake of the Great Recession of 2008–09, the public debt crises propelled the Greek Syriza, the Spanish Podemos, and the Italian Five Star Movement into government. In recent years, personalized or celebrity populism of the political centre has strengthened its foothold in Eastern Europe. Of these, the election of Ukrainian president Volodymyr Zelensky in 2019 (Wilson et al. 2020, 71) or the victory of "There Is Such a People" in the Bulgarian national parliament election in July 2021 (Yovcheva 2020) are some of the more prominent examples.[1] Simply put, populists span the ideological spectrum as much as they do the globe.

Due to the electoral success of populists around the world, a growing literature has begun to explore the political consequences of populism (such as, Houle and Kenny 2016). One of the more fruitful avenues of this research has been understanding the relationship between populism, specifically its manifestation on the right of the political spectrum, and prejudicial rhetoric and policies directed at a variety of outgroups such as immigrants and refugees. Indeed, a compelling body of evidence now links right-wing populist parties and governments to restrictive immigration policies, racist and xenophobic campaign messaging, and attacks on multiculturalism and pluralism more generally (Hogan and Haltinner 2015; Joppke 2020; Krzyżanowski 2020; McKeever 2020; Santi Amantini 2021; Shehaj, Shin, and Inglehart 2019). Importantly, research suggests that even when locked out of government, populist parties have managed to have an outsized influence on immigration policy through indirect means (Akkerman 2018; McKeever 2020). As Mudde (2004, 563) explains: "When explicitly populist outsider groups gain prominence, parts of the establishment will react by a combined strategy of exclusion and inclusion; while trying to exclude the populist actor(s) from political power, they will include populist themes and rhetoric to try and fight off the challenge."

As indicated earlier, much of the comparative research on populism and immigration has focused on the radical right. Far less attention, by contrast, has been devoted to the underlying philosophy that unifies populists across the ideological spectrum – a "thin" ideology that tends to vilify elites and praise ordinary people (Mudde 2004). McKeever (2020, 2), for instance, notes that "for right-wing populists, the enemy of the people is not just elites but also 'others', including immigrants, Muslims, and regional minorities." An important question, however, is whether these negative attitudes toward immigrant outgroups extend to populists in general. In other words, *once populism is stripped of its left-right ideological trappings, do populists still express prejudicial attitudes?* We suggest that prejudicial sentiments are symptomatic of the underlying populist philosophy and are therefore not restricted to the right. As an ideology that inherently separates society into "in" and "out" groups, we hypothesize that the populist ideology broadly – not just right-wing variants specifically – provides the groundwork for exclusionary attitudes and preferences. To that end, we explore the extent to which populist ideology and prejudicial attitudes are related to one another. In doing so we ask the following question: are Canadians who support the underlying populist philosophy more likely to also express anti-refugee sentiments?[2]

We consider attitudes toward refugees rather than (im)migrants more generally for at least three reasons. First, it is undeniable that we are in the midst of an ongoing global refugee crisis. According to the United Nations, there were nearly 26.6 million refugees as of mid-2021 – a figure that rises to more than 84 million if we include other groups of forcefully displaced peoples (UNHCR 2021). Understanding attitudes toward refugees is therefore a critical aspect of developing and implementing policy solutions to the crisis. Second, refugees and their resettlement have been politicized in recent years, and Canada is no exception (see, for example, Gagnon and Larios 2021). The 2015 Canadian election, for instance, saw the major parties address the Syrian refugee crisis and adopt differing stands on the issue. Finally, because refugees are forcefully displaced, individuals may have more empathy toward refugees than other migrants – a notion that is supported by the fact that people around the world tend to be more supportive of refugees than immigrants (Rasmussen and Poushter 2019). By focusing our analysis on refugees, we provide a harder test for our hypothesis that populist attitudes are related to prejudicial sentiments.

To explore the relationship between general populist attitudes and anti-refugee sentiments, this chapter draws on an original survey of more than 2,500 voting-age Canadians. Canada serves as a useful case to study this question as it is a country with a long history with refugee resettlement, has recently begun to resettle more refugees than any other, and has seen the issue of refugee resettlement become highly politicized during recent elections (Pruysers 2020). We are especially interested in whether the broad philosophical outlook of populism is related to prejudicial attitudes and whether this holds even when controlling for left-right political ideology.

Our results reveal a number of important findings. First, the bivariate data reveal that a considerable proportion of the Canadian population (roughly 30 per cent) express anti-refugee sentiments. This underscores that, despite their portrayal as open and accepting, many Canadians hold somewhat negative views about refugees. Second, our multivariate analysis reveals a clear role for populist attitudes in explaining anti-refugee sentiments even after controlling for standard factors such as gender, age, and employment status. Third, and importantly, populist sentiments continue to exert explanatory power even when controlling for the left-right ideology of the respondent. Given the electoral context in Canada, our results suggest that populism can negatively affect public opinion regarding refugees and resettlement even in the absence of truly viable right-wing populist parties. This in turn has important consequences for understanding Canadian policy toward refugees given the presumptive responsiveness of elected government officials toward their voting publics.

REFUGEE RESETTLEMENT IN CANADA: A BRIEF HISTORY

Canada is often quick to claim that it is "a global leader in protecting those who need it most." The Government of Canada website, for instance, boasts that the country "welcomed nearly half of all refugees resettled around the world in 2020" (Government of Canada 2021). In 2018, after right-wing populist president Donald Trump reduced the United States refugee intake to the lowest number possible via executive prerogative (see Cameron and Labman in this volume), no other country resettled more refugees per year than Canada (Radford and Connor 2020). Overall, the country welcomed more than a million refugees between 1980 and 2018 (UNHCR Canada 2019). In addition to government initiatives, the Private Sponsorship of Refugees Program (PSR) offers individuals and private organizations the ability to voluntarily assist in resettling refugees (Labman 2016). The Government of Canada (2020) reports that two million Canadians have been involved in resettling Syrian refugees and that, at a broader level, the PSR program has admitted more than 300,000 refugees since 1979 (nearly 8,000 per year).

Beyond quantity, the United Nations High Commissioner for Refugees (UNHCR Canada 2019) has emphasized the successful integration of resettled refugees into Canadian society: 95 per cent of refugees report a strong sense of belonging to Canada – which is even higher than what is reported among the Canadian-born population, where 91 per cent describe that they have the same feeling. In addition, refugees in Canada appear to be relatively economically successful. Wilkinson and Garcea (2017), for instance, note that the employment status and income levels of refugees "catch up to those of native-born Canadians over time."[3]

Canada's relative success in this area represents a decades-long experiment with refugee resettlement. Since World War II, Canada's refugee policy has gradually become more refined and less restrictive. The oversupply of labour during the Great Depression and World War II, and the security concerns around Soviet spies had reduced Canada's immigration department to a minuscule administrative unit within the Department of Mines and Resources in the 1950s. The reduction of immigration services came after the country had, at its peak, seen around one million immigrants in just three years at the beginning of the century (Molloy and Madokoro 2017, 53–4). With the creation of the International Refugee Organization under the United Nations umbrella, Canada once again became more active in resettling refugees amid labour shortages in 1947 (Molloy and Madokoro 2017, 53). Several refugee resettlement initiatives followed, moving from an ad hoc admission system to a legally enshrined standardized approach. Some of the most notable resettlement programs have included refugees from Hungary in 1956, Tibet in 1971–75 (Raska 2016), Uganda in 1972–73 (Howard 1981), Chile in 1973 (Diab 2015, 51), South-East Asia in 1975, and Syria in 2015–16 (Garcea and Kikulwe 2019).[4]

In 1976, the Immigration Act provided detailed provisions for refugee status, defining Canada's role in terms of fulfilling "international legal obligations to refugees and to uphold its humanitarian traditions concerning the displaced and the persecuted" (Molloy and Madokoro 2017, 57). In addition, the Canadian Charter of Rights and Freedoms 1982 provided a formal framework for multiculturalism and a constitutional space for new immigrants (Laselva 2019, 13). Immigration and refugee laws remained, relatively speaking, accommodating. Beyond the legal framework, there is a somewhat consistent and persistent, at least rhetorical, commitment by the political elite to multiculturalism in Canada. Prime Minister Justin Trudeau, for example, expressed these sentiments during the Syrian refugee crisis: "This is not just about welcoming 25,000 Syrian refugees, it's welcoming 25,000 new Canadians" (CBC 2015a).[5] In addition to elite support, the Canadian population has generally been portrayed as being open and accepting as well. When asked if immigrants are negative or positive for their country, Canadians had, out of eighteen countries sampled, the most positive attitudes toward foreign newcomers (Gonzalez-Barrera and Connor 2019). For more on the dynamics of refugee resettlement in Canada see Cameron and Labman (this volume).

Despite its international reputation and (comparatively) supportive policies and attitudes, a large minority of Canadians are nonetheless unhappy with the current immigration and refugee resettlement regime. A 2020 Environics Institute poll, for instance, finds considerable dissatisfaction among voting-age Canadians (Neuman 2020). The poll, conducted in September 2020, reveals that more than a quarter (27 per cent) of Canadians feel that there is "too much immigration to Canada." Likewise, the same report finds that more than a third of Canadians (35 per cent) feel that many people claiming to be refugees are "not real refugees," and more than four in ten (44 per cent) believe that too many immigrants do not adopt core "Canadian values."[6] Such feelings are beginning to be reflected in the party system as well. Reflecting this reality, the People's Party of Canada (PPC) has called for reduced immigration in recent elections. The party's platform, for instance, promises to "substantially lower the total number of immigrants and refugees Canada accepts every year" and pledges to take "every measure necessary ... to stop the flow of illegal migrants" (PPC 2021).

POPULISM AND PREJUDICE?

What accounts for negative or prejudicial attitudes toward outgroups such as immigrants and refugees? Gravelle (2018, 449) notes that there is "no shortage of studies" seeking to explain why some individuals are open and accepting toward "outsiders" such as immigrants and refugees while others express more restrictionist attitudes. Among other factors, the literature has identified political orientation (Banting 2010; Brooks, Manza, and Cohen 2016 Chandler and Tsai 2001; Gravelle 2016; Wilkes, Guppy, and Farris 2008), individual differences in personality (Hodson, Hogg, and MacInnis 2009; Pruysers 2020; Sibley and Duckitt 2008), varying levels of intergroup contact (Gravelle 2018; Pettigrew and Tropp 2006), and sociodemographic factors such as age, gender, and income (Ceobanu and Escandell 2010) as correlates of anti-immigrant and anti-refugee sentiments. One possible factor that has received less attention, however, is that general populist attitudes may be related to anti-refugee sentiments (see Martinez, van Prooijen, Van Lange 2023). Medeiros (2021) and Pruysers (2021) both find that populist attitudes are present in Canada even in the absence of strong supply-side factors (i.e., electorally viable populist parties). To what extent do populist attitudes help explain anti-refugee sentiments?

In approaching this question, a definitional jungle welcomes those who dare to dive deeper into the populism literature. Part of the difficulty in defining populism is that populists around the world vary, often quite considerably, from one another. There are populists on the right of the political spectrum and there are populists on the left and centre too. Bakker, Rooduijn, and Schumacher (2016, 302) write about the diverging policy preferences of populists: "some are pro-gay marriage, while others abhor it. Some worship the invisible hand of the market, but others sanctify the universal welfare state." Despite these ideological and programmatic differences, a growing literature highlights an underlying (and unifying) populist philosophy – what Mudde (2004) calls the thin ideology of populism.

Freeden (1998, 750–1) explains that a "full ideology," such as liberalism or socialism, offers "a full morphology, containing particular interpretations and configurations of all the major political concepts attached to a general plan of public policy that a specific society requires. That fullness exists either by design or by default as a reaction to ideological rivals." A thin-centred ideology, by contrast, "severs itself from wider ideational contexts, by the deliberative removal and replacement of concepts. The consequence is a structural inability to offer complex ranges of argument because many chains of ideas one would normally expect to find stretch from the general and abstract to the concrete and practical" (Freeden 1998, 750–1). Hence, populism struggles to exist without a full-fledged host ideology, a fact that helps to explain why populist movements can span the ideological spectrum (see also Stanley 2008).

What, then, is this populist ideology that unifies populists? According to Mudde (2004, 543), the populist ideology is one "that considers society to be ultimately separated into two homogeneous and antagonistic groups, "the pure people" versus "the corrupt elite," and which argues that politics should be an expression of the volonté générale (general will) of the people." Spruyt, Keppens, and Van Droogenbroeck (2016, 336), for instance, summarize the ideational understanding of the populist ideology as having four central components: "(1) the existence of two homogeneous groups, that is, 'the people' and 'the established elite'; (2) between which an antagonistic relationship exists; (3) whereby 'the people' are portrayed as virtuous, and the elite are denigrated; and (4) the will of the people is considered the ultimate source of legitimacy (popular sovereignty)." Pruysers (2020, 4) notes that although populism generally portrays the elite as being out of touch and ignoring the interests of ordinary people, the argument often goes further, suggesting that elites also actively work *against* the interests of the citizenry. Who exactly comprises the "people" and the "elite" in the populist ideology varies based on national context, time, and the left-right ideology of the host party.

Right-wing populists generally see the "elite" as comprising elected members of the state, its supporting bureaucracy, and its highly professional liberal supporters in civil society – individuals such as academics and journalists (Erisen et al. 2021). When combined with the extreme right, right-wing populists often accuse minorities (immigrants, refugees, etc.) of cooperation and collusion with the elite for their own benefit. As such, minorities are often carved out from this general pool of "the people" (Bonikoswski 2016, 10). This allows right-wing populists to hold on to the elite vs people dichotomy while expressing xenophobic and nativist policies, as they do not consider various minority outgroups to be part of the virtuous people.

The "elite" in left-wing populism, by contrast, commonly refers to forces outside of governments, such as wealthy capital, the international regimes managing commercial and financial relations, such as the International Monetary Fund (IMF) or the World Bank, and other supranational organizations that exert influence over domestic politics. In this regard, left-wing populists are often portrayed as being less nativist and more open to embracing the inclusion of ethnic, linguistic, sexual, and other disenfranchised minorities. In this sense, "the people" tends to be more inclusive among left-wing populists.

While the literature typically finds that xenophobic and nativist policies and attitudes are indeed more prevalent among right-wing populists (Akkerman 2018; McKeever 2020; Santi Amantini 2021), there is some evidence that these same prejudicial attitudes can manifest among left-wing populists too (Ghodsee 2008; Ruzza 2019). Kopyciok and Silver (2021), for example, demonstrate in the European context that voters of left-wing populist political parties are not immune to xenophobic attitudes. They show that far-left populist voters, even when controlling for demographic factors and attitudinal differences, still hold xenophobic attitudes – even though they emphasize that the level is lower than among voters of the far-right populists. Building on Goodhart (2004), Kopyciok and Silver (2021, 3) describe the "progressive dilemma" that results from the left's marriage of progressive professionals (who emphasize diversity) and the working class (who emphasize solidarity). As they note: "Whichever way they go, left parties may alienate some of their once loyal supporters. They can appeal either to privileged liberal egalitarian voters, who eschew ethnic nationalism and support cultural diversity, or to working-class voters, who benefit from redistributive policies and feel threatened by globalization and immigrant competition for jobs or benefits" (Kopyciok and Silver 2021, 3). When diversity and solidarity collide, it opens the possibility for anti-immigrant and more nativist sentiments to take hold within left-wing populist movements. In this sense, while the path and theoretical reasoning are different, both left and right-wing populists *can* come to the same conclusion: outsiders, which could include immigrants and refugees, are not part of the virtuous people that their populism seeks to emphasize and protect.

Perhaps, however, there is more to this. Is there something inherent in the populist outlook that encourages prejudicial sentiments? As an ideology that inherently separates society into ingroups (the people) and outgroups (the elite), it would not be entirely surprising to find prejudicial attitudes among populists: their underlying philosophy is already in the business of division. Using this logic, for example, Singh (2021, 250) connects populism and nationalism, noting that both ideologies have a "shared claim to represent an 'us' as distinct from a 'them.'"[7] Is it possible that individuals who express support for the underlying populist philosophy (regardless of left-right ideology) are more prejudicial in their overall outlook? In the remainder of the chapter, we explore this possibility and test a single hypothesis – namely, that *individuals who agree with the underlying populist ideology will hold more prejudicial attitudes and therefore express more negative views about refugees.*

DATA AND METHODS

To study the relationship between populist sentiments and anti-refugee attitudes, we draw upon a large sample of more than 2,500 voting-age Canadians. Respondents completed a twenty-five-minute survey that included a variety of questions regarding their basic demographics (age, gender, income, etc.), political behaviours (turnout, trust, ideology, etc.), policy attitudes, and personality traits. Consistent with recent Canadian election studies (i.e., Stephenson et al. 2020), participants were recruited from a nationally representative survey panel maintained by Qualtrics. Additionally, recruitment for this project included a number of different sampling targets to ensure a sample that was reflective of broader Canadian society. This included targets for respondent gender (i.e., 50 per cent men and 50 per cent women) as well as age (i.e., 45 per cent of respondents being under 44). The final sample includes 2,551 Canadians of voting age (M_{age} = 47.2, SD = 16.4) with a very slight majority of participants being men (50 per cent male; 49 per cent female; 1 per cent non-binary gender). Twenty-two per cent of the sample self-identified as a visible minority or persons of Indigenous heritage. Moreover, 17 per cent reported being born outside of Canada. Consistent with actual demographic patterns, a majority of our sample reside in Ontario and Quebec (57 per cent).

The sample is highly reflective of the Canadian population in other ways as well. Take education as an example. According to the 2016 Canadian census, 22 per cent of Canadians had a community college diploma and 29 per cent had a university degree (total college and university = 51 per cent; Statistics Canada 2017). Our data are remarkably similar with 26 per cent having a university degree and 31 per cent having a college diploma (57 per cent combined). Despite the potential limitations of online non-probability samples, therefore, we believe the findings remain robust and illuminating in the context of the case at hand.[8] Data were collected online via the Qualtrics survey platform between 14 August and 12 September 2019.

The data we draw upon include multiple questions regarding attitudes toward refugees in Canada. Using a number of distinct items, we are able to construct an additive scale of (anti-)refugee attitudes as the outcome variable of interest for this chapter (see also Pruysers 2020). The scale comprises four items and a Cronbach's Alpha of 0.75 suggests a good degree of internal consistency among the items, allowing them to be combined into a single variable for analysis. The items used to create the final dependent variable asked respondents: "To what extent do you agree or disagree with the following statements," where each statement was measured on a five-point scale (strongly agree to strongly disagree). These statements were: "Most people claiming to be refugees are not real refugees"; "Canada should do more to help refugees" [reverse coded]; "People coming to Canada claiming to be refugees are imposing a severe strain on our welfare system"; "Being a refugee is a choice – a person's circumstances aren't to blame." The scale therefore ranges from 4 to 20 with a mean value of 11.8 and a standard deviation of 3.8.[9] Higher values on the four-item additive scale represent more negative attitudes toward refugees.

Table 11.1 includes the distribution of responses to the individual survey items. Immediately obvious from this data is that a non-insignificant minority – approximately a third of all respondents – express attitudes that are not especially supportive of refugees or their circumstances. Thirty-four per cent of respondents, for instance, agreed (strongly or somewhat) that most people claiming to be refugees are not "real" refugees. Likewise, half of all respondents feel that refugees are imposing a "severe" strain on the Canadian welfare system. What's more, only a third (32 per cent) agree that Canada should "do more" to help refugees. This parallels our earlier point that, despite its international reputation, many Canadians hold negative

Table 11.1 | Attitudes toward refugees among Canadians

	Strongly disagree	Somewhat disagree	Neither disagree nor agree	Somewhat agree	Strongly agree	N
Most people claiming to be refugees are not real refugees.	16% (400)	20% (512)	30% (772)	22% (571)	12% (294)	2,549
Canada should do more to help refugees.	16% (400)	20% (508)	32% (822)	22% (556)	10% (262)	2,548
People coming to Canada claiming to be refugees are imposing a severe strain on our welfare system.	10% (262)	15% (389)	25% (628)	27% (690)	23% (577)	2,546
Being a refugee is a choice – a person's circumstances aren't to blame.	31% (799)	23% (577)	26% (659)	13% (318)	8% (195)	2,548

attitudes about refugees. Our data are remarkably consistent with a 2020 Environics Institute poll (Neuman 2020). Though some of the questions differ, the pattern of responses is highly consistent. This, of course, provides additional confidence in the data.

To capture acceptance of the populist philosophy, we draw upon eight items that capture the "thin" populist ideology (see Akkerman, Mudde, and Zaslove 2014; see also Spruyt, Keppens, and Van Droogenbroeck 2016; Mudde 2004; Pruysers 2021). Consistent with the construction of our refugee measure, each item is weighted the same, and a Cronbach's

Table 11.2 | Populist sentiments among Canadians

	Strongly disagree	Somewhat disagree	Neither disagree nor agree	Somewhat agree	Strongly agree	N
The politicians in the Canadian parliament need to follow the will of the people.	2% (52)	4% (103)	14% (368)	45% (1140)	35% (886)	2,549
The people, and not politicians, should make our most important policy decisions.	3% (86)	12% (315)	27% (688)	36% (905)	22% (553)	2,547
The political differences between the elite and people are larger than the differences among the people.	3% (67)	6% (149)	33% (834)	36% (917)	23% (579)	2,546
I would rather be represented by a citizen than by a specialized politician.	4% (91)	11% (281)	32% (816)	34% (855)	20% (502)	2,545
Elected officials talk too much and take too little action.	2% (45)	6% (157)	20% (499)	37% (931)	36% (916)	2,548
Politics is ultimately a struggle between good and evil.	10% (247)	14% (365)	35% (881)	26% (663)	15% (390)	2,546
What people call "compromise" in politics is really just selling out on one's principles.	5% (131)	15% (370)	32% (818)	33% (840	15% (385	2,544
Interest groups have too much influence over political decisions.	2% (60)	7% (174)	27% (675)	35% (895)	29% (743)	2,547

Alpha of 0.804 suggests a good degree of internal consistency among the items, allowing them to be combined into a single variable for analysis.[10] The items asked respondents, "To what extent do you agree or disagree with the following statements," where each statement was measured on a five-point agree-disagree scale. These statements were: "The politicians in the Canadian parliament need to follow the will of the people"; "The people, and not politicians, should make our most important policy decisions"; "The political differences between the elite and the people are larger than the differences among the people"; "I would rather be represented by a citizen than by a specialized politician"; "Elected officials talk too much and take too little action"; "Politics is ultimately a struggle between good and evil"; "What people call 'compromise' in politics is really just selling out on one's principles"; and "Interest groups have too much influence over political decisions."[11] The scale, therefore, ranges from 8 to 40 with a mean value of 29.3 and a standard deviation of 5.3.[12] Higher values on the eight-item additive scale represent higher levels of populist sentiment.

Table 11.2 includes the distribution of responses to the individual items. High levels of agreement with the various items reveal that there is considerable support for general populist sentiments in Canada.[13] More than half (58 per cent) of the sample, for instance, believe that "the people" and not "politicians" should be in charge of important policy decisions. Similarly, 54 per cent reported that they would rather be represented by a citizen than a politician.

In addition to populist sentiments, our analysis controls for a variety of other potential explanatory factors that have been identified in the broader literature relating to attitudes toward immigrants and immigration more generally (Banting 2010; Ceobanu and Escandell 2010; Gravelle 2016; Harell et al. 2012). This includes sociodemographic characteristics such as age, gender, visible minority status, education, employment status, household income, and a variable which captures whether a respondent was born outside of Canada. Additionally, we include a number of politically oriented variables. This includes a measure of respondent ideology which uses self-placement on the left-right political spectrum (where 0 is left and 10 is right), satisfaction with democracy, and political interest.

RESULTS

From a simple bivariate perspective, populist attitudes and anti-refugee sentiments are strongly correlated with one another ($p < .001$). How does this relationship hold when accounting for other explanatory factors? Table 11.3 explores this relationship in a multivariate analysis and reports the

Table 11.3 | Multivariate results

Criteria	Model 1		Model 2		Model 3		Model 4	
	B	S.E.	B	S.E.	B	S.E.	B	S.E.
Age	.024**	.005					.022**	.004
Gender	.539**	.149					.402**	.136
Under-employed	.056	.181					.124**	.163
Foreign born	.501*	.217					.240	.195
Visible minority	.105	.205					.340	.185
Education	–.386**	.071					–.197**	.065
Income	.024	.037					.017	.033
Left-right			.577**	.030			.523**	.030
Satisfaction with democracy			–1.594**	.149			–1.286**	.149
Political interest			–.193**	.022			–.217**	.022
Populism scale					.175**	.014	.137**	.013
Constant	11.491**	3.74	11.093**	.203	6.679**	.407	6.455**	.526
R2	0.027		.172		.061		.226	

*p < .05; **p < .01.

results of four different model specifications. In model 1, we include our standard sociodemographic variables. This includes age, gender, employment, foreign-born, visible minority, education, and income. Model 2, by contrast, contains a number of politically oriented controls, including left-right ideology, satisfaction with democracy, and political interest. Model 3 contains a single variable, our populism scale. Finally, model 4 presents the results of the full model with the variables from models 1 to 3 in a single multivariate analysis.

Beginning with model 1, we see that a number of our demographic controls are significantly related to anti-refugee sentiments. Men, older respondents, and those born abroad are all more likely to hold negative attitudes toward refugees in the Canadian case. Those individuals with higher levels of education, by contrast, tend to hold more positive views of refugees. Turning to model 2, we see that all three political variables are statistically significant. Those who express greater satisfaction with democracy and those who have higher levels of political interest are more likely to hold positive views of refugees. This is consistent with the politicization of refugees in contemporary politics. Those on the right of the political spectrum, by contrast, are more likely to hold negative views. Model 3 replicates the bivariate results and shows that populist attitudes are indeed related to anti-refugee sentiments: individuals who express greater agreement with the populist items tend to hold more negative views about refugees.

Model 4, when combining the variables from the previous models, provides a consistent set of results that follows expected patterns. Only two variables are different than previous models. First, the coefficient for our foreign-born variable loses its significance once the political variables are entered into the analysis. Conversely, our employment variable (underemployed) was not significant in model 1 but is in model 4. Besides these minor differences, the final model reproduces the earlier three sets of results. Importantly for the purpose of this chapter, the relationship between populist attitudes and negative perceptions of refugees is confirmed even when accounting for a variety of other explanatory factors like ideology. The importance of populist attitudes in understanding anti-refugee sentiments can be seen in the general model performance statistics as well. Whereas demographic variables account for less than 3 per cent of the total variance (see model 1), populist attitudes account for some 6 per cent (see model 3). With that said, the politically oriented variables, specifically ideology, appear to be driving the explanatory power of the overall model. This should not be particularly surprising, as the relationship between more right-wing ideology/partisanship and negative attitudes toward migrants has been well-documented in the literature (Banting 2010; Gravelle 2016).[14]

CONCLUSIONS

While much of the literature focuses on the xenophobic and nativist tendencies and rhetoric of right-wing populists (McKeever 2020; Stockemer 2017; Stockemer and Barisione 2017), this chapter explored the relationship between the thin populist ideology (i.e., emphasis on the people; anti-elitism, etc.) and prejudicial attitudes in the form of anti-refugee sentiments. Drawing on a large, representative sample of voting aged Canadians, we hypothesized that individuals who expressed greater support for the underlying populist ideology would hold more negative attitudes toward outgroups, specifically refugees. Controlling for a variety of other possible explanatory factors – such as age, gender, income, education, employment status, and political interest – we find that support for populist ideals is indeed related to more negative views about refugees in the Canadian context. Importantly, this relationship holds even when accounting for ideological placement on the left-right spectrum.

Consistent with Medeiros (2021) and Pruysers (2021), we find compelling evidence for the presence of populist attitudes in Canada despite the lack of truly viable populist parties and public figures.[15] Nearly six out of ten respondents, for instance, agreed (somewhat or strongly) with the assertion that "the people, and not politicians, should make our most important policy decisions." This populist bent, combined with the fact that a considerable minority of Canadians hold negative attitudes toward migrants, suggests that if properly mobilized, anti-migrant attitudes could be politicized into becoming a salient election issue and could have a contagion effect on other parties (McKeever 2020). Though requiring further study, the protests and blockades of 2022 associated with the so-called Freedom Convoy in Canada (Proudfoot 2023) revealed many potential linkages between populist ideals and prejudicial attitudes. While potential implications regarding party politics or policy contagion remain unclear, the evidence provided here suggest that a sizeable portion of the Canadian electorate hold both populist and anti-refugee attitudes, and that these two sets of attitudes are indeed related to one another. Overall, data reveal that populism can negatively affect public opinion regarding refugees and resettlement even in the absence of viable right-wing populist parties. Such a finding helps us better understand why public sentiments toward outgroups like refugees remain mixed in Canada, even when political elites and government policies are relatively supportive.

While this chapter has focused on the Canadian case, the implications are much broader. The general populist ideology can be found across the North American continent – in Canada (Medeiros 2021; Pruysers 2021), the United States (Bakker, Rooduijn, and Schumacher 2016; Pied 2019), and Mexico (Dussauge-Laguna 2022; Puente 2020) – much like it is in Europe and South America. In some cases, the politicization of anti-migrant sentiments via populist discourse is already under way. In the United States, for example, populist appeals have already been linked to a number of restrictive immigration policies and proposals debated and enacted under the Trump administration (Joppke 2020; Nagel 2019). And as we noted earlier, the emergence of fringe parties such as the PPC, as well movements such as the Freedom Convoy, highlight this linkage in Canada too. This chapter, however, reveals that this dynamic is not only limited to the political right: we find that populism broadly (not the right-wing variant specifically) is related to anti-refugee sentiments. Such a finding may hold important implications for the Mexican case, where left-wing populist political figures with anti-liberal tendencies, such as President Andrés Manuel López Obrador, have been electorally successful in recent years. While further replication and study is warranted, the findings presented here raise a number of important questions regarding the formation of anti-refugee attitudes in the North American context and beyond.

NOTES

1 See Poguntke and Webb (2018) for a discussion of personalization, presidentialization, and populism.

2 Understanding specific populist movements and parties is important. However, individual-level populist attitudes have been less studied. As Ditto and Rodriguez (2021, 24) suggest, the key to understanding populist political movements "is the psychology that underlines them."

3 Likewise, other evidence suggests that refugees tend to pay more in income tax than they receive in public benefits and services (UNHCR Canada 2019), again suggesting a level of economic success.

4 Note, however, that excessive enthusiasm at the elite level has not always been immediate. For example, Prime Minister Pierre Trudeau delayed the intake of Chilean refugees in the 1970s. Diab (2015, 55–6) explains this inaction with security concerns relating to the connections between the Chilean left-wing opposition members and the militant Quebec independence movement, such as the Front de libération du Québec (FLQ). The author explains the eventual acceptance of the refugees with civil society lobbying (Diab 2015, 59). This case highlights the fact that different groups (civil society, political elites, etc.) can be at odds with one another on refugee policy.

5 In the context of the Syrian resettlement question, Kymlicka (2021) concludes that the electorate was generally unresponsive to an extreme

anti-multicultural discourse initiated by the Conservative Party during the 2015 general election. Kymlicka goes on to describe this as a "reaffirmation of Canadian exceptionalism."

6 These proportions are even higher when "Don't know" and "Neither agree nor disagree" responses are removed from the data.

7 Note that the literature has often warned against conflating populist with other related concepts such as nationalism, and especially nativism. Roodujin (2019), for instance, explains the difference as follows: "Where populism concerns the vertical relationship between 'the people' and 'the elite', nativism is about the horizontal antagonism between 'the nation' and 'dangerous others.'" Likewise, drawing on data from the 2015 Canadian Election Study (CES), Medeiros (2021) provides evidence that nativist and populist attitudes are distributed very differently – at least in the Canadian population – suggesting that the two concepts are indeed distinct. Furthermore, despite highlighting their similarities, Singh (2021, 252) ultimately concludes that populism and nationalism are "overlapping but analytically distinct phenomena."

8 While online non-probability samples have a number of potential limitations (including concerns about sample representativeness, respondent fatigue, and data quality), a number of recent studies (Breton et al. 2017; Stephenson and Crête 2011) highlight the benefits of online surveys and suggest that some concerns may be overstated.

9 Though not included, a histogram of the anti-refugee variable reveals a clear normal distribution.

10 Factor analysis on both the refugee and populism scales confirm this as well. Factor analysis for the four refugee items confirms that there is indeed only one underlying factor (eigenvalue of 2.32 which explains 58 per cent of the total variance). Likewise, factor analysis on the eight items tapping into populism reveal one primary factor (eigenvalue 3.43 which accounts for 43 per cent of the total variance).

11 Besides altering these items for a Canadian sample (i.e., changing wording from "Dutch" to "Canadian"), these eight items are identical to those found in Akkerman, Mudde, and Zaslove (2014).

12 Like our anti-refugee attitudes variable, populist attitudes are normally distributed.

13 See Medeiros (2021) for a discussion of the presence of populist attitudes in Canada despite the absence of salient supply-side factors (i.e., successful populist parties).

14 This is reflected in elite/party sentiments as well. During the 2015 general election, for example, the Liberals promised to resettle more than double the amount of Syrian refugees (CBC 2015b).

15 While some may point to Maxime Bernier and the People's Party of Canada (PPC), the party's electoral showing in both 2019 and 2021 reveal the narrow support the party enjoys. In 2019, for example, the party captured just 1.6 per cent of the total vote. Even in 2021, during the height of the global pandemic, the party won less than 5 per cent.

REFERENCES

Akkerman, Agnes, Cas Mudde, and Andrej Zaslove. 2014. "How Populist Are the People? Measuring Populist Attitudes in Voters." *Comparative Political Studies* 47 (9): 1324–53. https://doi.org/10.1177/0010414013512600.

Akkerman, Tjitske. Rep. 2018. *The Impact of Populist Radical-Right Parties on Immigration Policy Agendas: A Look at the Netherlands*. Washington, DC: Migration Policy Institute.

Bakker, Bert N., Maathijs Rooduijn, and Gijs Schumacher. 2016. "The Psychological Roots of Populist Voting: Evidence from the United States, the Netherlands and Germany." *European Journal of Political Research* 55 (2): 302–20. https://doi.org/10.1111/1475-6765.12121.

Banting, Keith G. 2010. "Is There a Progressive's Dilemma in Canada? Immigration, Multiculturalism and the Welfare State, Presidential Address to the Canadian Political Science Association, Montreal, June 2, 2010." *Canadian Journal of Political Science / Revue Canadienne de Science Politique* 43 (4): 797–820. http://www.jstor.org/stable/40983555.

Bonikowski, Bart. 2016. "Three Lessons of Contemporary Populism in Europe and the United States." *Brown Journal of World Affairs* 23 (1): 9–24.

Breton, Charles, Fred Cutler, Sarah Lachance, and Alex Mierke-Zatwarnicki. 2017. "Telephone versus Online Survey Modes for Election Studies: Comparing Canadian Public Opinion and Vote Choice in the 2015 Federal Election." *Canadian Journal of Political Science* 50 (4): 1005–36. https://doi.org/10.1017/s0008423917000610.

Brooks, Clem, Jeff Manza, and Emma D. Cohen. 2016. "Political Ideology and Immigrant Acceptance." *Socius: Sociological Research for a Dynamic World* 2: 1–12. https://doi.org/10.1177/2378023116668881.

CBC News. 2015a. "7 Memorable Quotes from Metro Morning's Interview with Justin Trudeau." *CBC/Radio Canada*, 24 November 2015. https://www.cbc.ca/news/canada/toronto/programs/metromorning/justin-trudeau-on-metro-morning-top-7-quotes-from-the-interview-1.3334393. Accessed 25 August 2022.

– 2015b. "Ottawa Moves to Speed up Syrian Refugee Resettlement with New Measures." *CBC/Radio Canada*, 20 September 2015. https://www.cbc.ca/news/politics/canada-election-2015-chris-alexander-refugees-1.3235415. Accessed 25 August 2022.

Ceobanu, Alin M., and Xavier Escandell. 2010. "Comparative Analyses of Public Attitudes toward Immigrants and Immigration Using Multinational Survey Data: A Review of Theories and Research." *Annual Review of Sociology* 36 (1): 309–28. https://doi.org/10.1146/annurev.soc.012809.102651.

Chandler, Charles R., and Yung-mei Tsai. 2001. "Social Factors Influencing Immigration Attitudes: An Analysis of Data from the General Social Survey." *The Social Science Journal* 38 (2): 177–88. https://doi.org/10.1016/s0362-3319(01)00106-9.

Diab, Suha. 2015. "Fear and (in)Security: The Canadian Government's Response to the Chilean Refugees." *Refuge: Canada's Journal on Refugees* 31 (2): 51–62. https://doi.org/10.25071/1920-7336.40309.

Ditto, Peter H., and Cristian G. Rodriguez. 2021. "Populism and the Social Psychology of Grievance." In *The Psychology of Populism: The Tribal Challenge to Liberal Democracy*, edited by Joseph P. Forgas, William D. Crano, and Klaus Fiedler, 23–41. New York: Routledge.

Dussauge-Laguna, Mauricio I. 2022. "The Promises and Perils of Populism for Democratic Policymaking: The Case of Mexico" *Policy Sci* 55: 777–803. https://doi.org/10.1007/s11077-022-09469-z.

Erisen, Cengiz, Mattia Guidi, Sergio Martini, Selin Toprakkiran, Pierangelo Isernia, and Levente Littvay. 2021. "Psychological Correlates of Populist Attitudes." *Political Psychology* 42 (S1) (December 2021): 149–71. https://doi.org/10.1111/pops.12768.

Freeden, Michael. 1998. "Is Nationalism a Distinct Ideology?" *Political Studies* 46 (4): 748–65. https://doi.org/10.1111/1467-9248.00165.

Gagnon, Audrey, and Lindsay Larios. 2021. "The Politicization of Immigration and Integration at the Subnational Level: Electoral Campaigns in Ontario and Quebec." *Canadian Journal of Political Science* 54 (3): 696–716. https://doi.org/10.1017/s0008423921000469.

Garcea, Joseph, and Daniel Kikulwe. 2019. "The Liberal Plan for Resettling Syrian Refugees in Canada: The Justificatory Narrative and Counter-Narrative." *Canadian Ethnic Studies* 51 (2): 87–106. https://doi.org/10.1353/ces.2019.0012.

Ghodsee, Kristen. 2008. "Left Wing, Right Wing, Everything: Xenophobia, Neototalitarianism, and Populist Politics in Bulgaria." *Problems of Post-Communism* 55 (3): 26–39.

Gonzalez-Barrera, Anna, and Phillip Connor. 2019. "Around the World, More Say Immigrants are a Strength than a Burden." Pew Research Center. 14 March 2019. https://www.pewresearch.org/global/wp-content/uploads/sites/2/2019/05/Pew-Research-Center_Global-Views-of-Immigrants_2019-03-14_Updated-2019-05-02.pdf. Accessed 25 August 2022.

Goodhart, David. 2004. "Too Diverse?" *Prospect Magazine* 95: 30–7. https://www.prospectmagazine.co.uk/magazine/too-diverse-david-goodhart-multculturalism-britain-immigration-globalisation. Accessed 25 August 2022.

Government of Canada. 2020. "By the Numbers – 40 Years of Canada's Private Sponsorship of Refugees Program." Government of Canada. 21 July 2020. https://www.canada.ca/en/immigration-refugees-citizenship/news/2019/04/by-the-numbers--40-years-of-canadas-private-sponsorship-of-refugees-program.html. Accessed 25 August 2022.

– 2021. "Canada Announces 3 New Initiatives to Welcome and Support More Refugees." Government of Canada. 30 June 2021. https://www.canada.ca/en/immigration-refugees-citizenship/news/2021/06/canada-announces-3-new-initiatives-to-welcome-and-support-more-refugees.html. Accessed 25 August 2022.

Gravelle, Timothy B. 2016. "Party Identification, Contact, Contexts, and Public Attitudes toward Illegal Immigration." *Public Opinion Quarterly* 80 (1): 1–25. https://doi.org/10.1093/poq/nfv054.

– 2018. "Partisanship, Local Context, Group Threat, and Canadian Attitudes towards Immigration and Refugee Policy." *Migration Studies* 6 (3): 448–67. https://doi.org/10.1093/migration/mnx058.

Harell, Allison, Stuart Soroka, Shanto Iyengar, and Nicholas Valentino. 2012. "The Impact of Economic and Cultural Cues on Support for Immigration in Canada and the United States." *Canadian Journal of Political Science* 45 (3): 499–530. https://doi.org/10.1017/s0008423912000698.

Hodson, Gordon, Sarah M. Hogg, and Cara C. MacInnis. 2009. "The Role of 'Dark Personalities' (Narcissism, Machiavellianism, Psychopathy), Big Five Personality Factors, and Ideology in Explaining Prejudice." *Journal of Research in Personality* 43 (4): 686–90. https://doi.org/10.1016/j.jrp.2009.02.005.

Hogan, Jackie, and Kristin Haltinner. (2015). "Floods, Invaders, and Parasites: Immigration Threat Narratives and Right-Wing Populism in the USA, UK and Australia." *Journal of Intercultural Studies* 36 (5): 520–43. https://doi.org/10.1080/07256868.2015.1072907.

Houle, Christian, and Paul D. Kenny. 2016. "The Political and Economic Consequences of Populist Rule in Latin America." *Government and Opposition* 53 (2): 256–87. https://doi.org/10.1017/gov.2016.25.

Howard, Rhoda. 1981. "The Canadian Government Response to Africa's Refugee Problem." *Canadian Journal of African Studies / Revue Canadienne des Études Africaines* 15 (1): 95–116. https://doi.org/10.2307/485134.

Joppke, Christian. 2020. "Immigration in the Populist Crucible: Comparing Brexit and Trump." *Comparative Migration Studies* 8 (49): 1–18. https://doi.org/10.1186/s40878-020-00208-y.

Kopyciok, Svenja, and Hilary Silver. 2021. "Left-Wing Xenophobia in Europe." *Frontiers in Sociology* 6: 1–17. https://doi.org/10.3389/fsoc.2021.666717.

Kymlicka, Will. 2021. "The Precarious Resilience of Multiculturalism in Canada." *American Review of Canadian Studies* 51 (1): 122–42. https://doi.org/10.1080/02722011.2021.1878544.

Krzyżanowski, Michał. 2020. "Discursive Shifts and the Normalisation of Racism: Imaginaries of Immigration, Moral Panics and the Discourse of Contemporary Right-Wing Populism." *Social Semiotics* 30 (4): 503–27. https://doi.org/10.1080/10350330.2020.1766199.

Labman, Shauna. 2016. "Private Sponsorship: Complementary or Conflicting Interests?" *Refuge: Canada's Journal on Refugees* 32 (2): 67–80. https://doi.org/10.25071/1920-7336.40266.

Laselva, Samuel V. 2019. "Understanding Canada's Origins: Federalism, Multiculturalism, and the Will to Live Together." In *Canadian Politics*, edited by James Bickerton and Alain Gagnon, 7th ed., 3–20. Toronto: University of Toronto Press.

Martínez, Cristhian A., Jan-Willem van Prooijen, Paul A.M. Van Lange. 2023. "The Hateful People: Populist Attitudes Predict Interpersonal and Intergroup Hate." *Social Psychological and Personality Science* 14 (6): 698–707. https://doi.org/10.1177/19485506221127491.

McKeever, Anna. 2020. *Immigration Policy and Right-Wing Populism in Western Europe*. Basingstoke, UK: Palgrave Macmillan.

Medeiros, Mike. 2021. "Demand without Supply: Populist Attitudes without Salient Supply-Side Factors of Populism." *Canadian Journal of Political Science* 54 (4): 918–38. https://doi.org/10.1017/s0008423921000779.

Molloy, Michael J., and Laura Madokoro. 2017. "Effecting Change: Civil Servants and Refugee Policy in 1970s Canada." *Refuge: Canada's Journal on Refugees* 33 (1): 52–61. https://doi.org/10.25071/1920-7336.40448.

Mudde, Cas. 2004. "The Populist Zeitgeist." *Government and Opposition* 39 (4): 41–63. http://www.jstor.org/stable/44483088.

Nagel, Caroline. 2019. "Populism, immigration and the Trump phenomenon in the U.S." *Environment and Planning C: Politics and Space* 37 (1): 12–16. https://doi.org/10.1177/0263774X18811923c.

Neuman, Keith. 2020. "Canadian Public Opinion about Immigration and Refugees." Environics Institute for Survey Research. 7 October 2020. https://www.environicsinstitute.org/projects/project-details/canadian-public-opinion-about-immigration-and-refugees. Accessed 25 August 2022.

Pettigrew, Thomas F., and Linda R. Tropp. 2006. "A Meta-Analytic Test of Intergroup Contact Theory." *Journal of Personality and Social Psychology* 90 (5): 751–83. https://doi.org/10.1037/0022-3514.90.5.751.

Pied, Claudine M. 2019. "Ethnography and the Making of "The People": Uncovering Conservative Populist Politics in the United States" *The American Journal of Economics and Sociology* 78 (3): 761–86. https://doi.org/10.1111/ajes.12280.

Poguntke, Thomas, and Paul Webb. 2018. "Personalization and Presidentialization Reconsidered." In *The Personalization of Democratic Politics and the Challenge for Political Parties*, edited by William Cross, Richard Katz, and Scott Pruysers, 181–97. Lanham, MD: Rowman and Littlefield.

PPC (People's Party of Canada). 2021 "Immigration." People's Party of Canada. https://www.peoplespartyofcanada.ca/immigration. Accessed 25 August 2022.

Proudfoot, Shannon. 2023. "One Year Later. What the Convoys Left Behind." *Globe and Mail*, 26 January 2023. https://www.theglobeandmail.com/politics/article-ottawa-convoy-protests-supporters. Accessed 25 May 2023.

Pruysers, Scott. 2020. "Personality and Attitudes towards Refugees: Evidence from Canada." *Journal of Elections, Public Opinion and Parties*: 1–21. https://doi.org/10.1080/17457289.2020.1824187.

– 2021. "A Psychological Predisposition towards Populism? Evidence from Canada." *Contemporary Politics* 27 (1): 105–24. https://doi.org/10.1080/13569775.2020.1851930.

Puente, Khemvirg. 2020. "Mexico: The Rise of Presidential Populism and the Decline of Congress." In *Legislative Decline in the 21st Century*, edited by Irina Khmelko, Rick Stapenhurst, Michael L. Mezey, 158–69. New York: Routledge.

Radford, Jynnah, and Phillip Connor. 2020. "Canada Now Leads the World in Refugee Resettlement, Surpassing the US." Pew Research Center. 20 August 2020. https://www.pewresearch.org/fact-tank/2019/06/19/canada-now-leads-the-world-in-refugee-resettlement-surpassing-the-u-s/. Accessed 25 August 2022.

Raska, Jan. 2016. "Humanitarian Gesture: Canada and the Tibetan Resettlement Program, 1971–5." *Canadian Historical Review* 97 (4): 546–75. https://doi.org/10.3138/chr.raska.

Rasmussen, Raea, and Jacob Poushter. "People around the World Express More Support for Taking in Refugees than Immigrants." Pew Research Center. 9 August 2019. https://www.pewresearch.org/fact-tank/2019/08/09/people-around-the-world-express-more-support-for-taking-in-refugees-than-immigrants/. Accessed 25 August 2022.

Rooduijn, Matthijs. 2019. "State of the Field: How to Study Populism and Adjacent Topics? A Plea for Both More and Less Focus." *European Journal of Political Research* 58 (1): 362–72.

Ruzza, Carlo. 2019. "Populism, Migration, and Xenophobia in Europe." In *Routledge Handbook of Global Populism*, edited by Carlos de la Torre, 201–16. London: Routledge.

Santi Amantini, Laura. 2021. "Populist Anti-Immigrant Sentiments Taken Seriously: A Realistic Approach." *Res Publica* 28 (1): 1–21. https://doi.org/10.1007/s11158-021-09516-1.

Shehaj, Albana, Adrian J. Shin, and Ronald Inglehart. 2019. "Immigration and Right-Wing Populism: An Origin Story." *Party Politics* 27 (2): 282–93. https://doi.org/10.1177/1354068819849888.

Sibley, Chris G., and John Duckitt. 2008. "Personality and Prejudice: A Meta-Analysis and Theoretical Review." *Personality and Social Psychology Review* 12 (3): 248–79. https://doi.org/10.1177/1088868308319226.

Singh, Prerna. 2021. "Populism, Nationalism, and Nationalist Populism." *Studies in Comparative International Development* 56 (2): 250–69. https://doi.org/10.1007/s12116-021-09337-6.

Spruyt, Bram, Gil Keppens, and Filip Van Droogenbroeck. 2016. "Who Supports Populism and What Attracts People to It?" *Political Research Quarterly* 69 (2): 335–46. https://doi.org/10.1177/1065912916639138.

Stanley, Ben. 2008. "The Thin Ideology of Populism." *Journal of Political Ideologies* 13 (1): 95–110. https://doi.org/10.1080/13569310701822289.

Statistics Canada. 2017. "Education Highlight Tables, 2016 Census." Statistics Canada. 23 November 2017. https://www12.statcan.gc.ca/census-recensement/2016/dp-pd/hlt-fst/edu-sco/Table.cfm?Lang=E&T=11&Geo=00&View=2&Age=2. Accessed 25 August 2022.

Stephenson, Laura. B., and Jean Crete. 2011. "Studying Political Behavior: A Comparison of Internet and Telephone Surveys." *International Journal of Public Opinion Research* 23 (1): 24–55. https://doi.org/10.1093/ijpor/edq025.

Stephenson, Laura B., Allison Harell, Daniel Rubenson, Peter John Loewen. 2020. "2019 Canadian Election Study (CES) - Online Survey." *Havard Dataverse, V1*. https://doi.org/10.7910/DVN/DUS88V.

Stockemer, Daniel. 2017. *The Front National in France Continuity and Change under Jean-Marie Le Pen and Marine Le Pen*. Cham, Switzerland: Springer International Publishing.

Stockemer, Daniel, and Mauro Barisione. 2017. "The 'New' Discourse of the Front National under Marine Le Pen: A Slight Change with a Big Impact." *European Journal of Communication* 32 (2): 100–15. https://doi.org/10.1177/0267323116680132.

UNHCR Canada (United Nations High Commissioner for Refugees, Canada). 2019. *Are Refugees Good for Canada? A Look at Canadian Refugee*

Integration. Ottawa: UNHCR Canada. https://www.unhcr.ca/wp-content/uploads/2019/11/Are-Refugees-Good-for-Canada-A-Look-at-Canadian-Refugee-Integration-November-2019.pdf. Accessed 25 August 2022.

UNHCR (United Nations High Commissioner for Refugees). 2021. "Refugee Statistics." UNHCR. 10 November 2021. https://www.unhcr.org/refugee-statistics/. Accessed 25 August 2022.

Yovcheva, Teodora. 2020. "The Many Forms of Celebrity Populism in Eastern Europe." Europe Elects. 25 July 2020. https://europeelects.eu/2020/07/25/the-many-forms-of-celebrity-populism-in-eastern-europe/. Accessed 25 August 2022.

Wilkes, Rima, Neil Guppy, and Lily Farris. 2008. "'No Thanks, We're Full': Individual Characteristics, National Context, and Changing Attitudes toward Immigration." *International Migration Review* 42 (2): 302–29. https://doi.org/10.1111/j.1747-7379.2008.00126.x.

Wilkinson, Lori, and Joseph Garcea. 2017. *The Economic Integration of Refugees in Canada: A Mixed Record?*. Washington, DC: Migration Policy Institute.

Wilson, Andrew, Marcin Kaczmarski, Janis Kluge, András Rácz, and Tatiana Stanovaya. 2020. "Russia and its Post-soviet 'Frenemies': Breaking Free from the Post-Soviet Time Loop?" *In Russian Futures 2030: The Shape of Things to Come*, edited by Sinikukka Saari and Stanislav Secrieru. European Union Institute for Security Studies (EUISS). http://www.jstor.org/stable/resrep26053.9.

PART FOUR

Global Dimensions of Migration in North America

12

Extraction, Dependence, Containment: Questioning Canada's Role as Immigration and Refugee Norm Entrepreneur

Craig Damian Smith

Canada is often framed as a middle power, with relatively weak global economic and security influence, but strong normative power and authority in multilateral institutions. Significant aspects of its status are associated with success in attracting and integrating immigrants, role as a top country for refugee resettlement, and position as a policy and norm entrepreneur around international responsibility-sharing. Canada's foreign policy is thus often framed through status-seeking, rather than geostrategic behaviour.

This chapter complicates that picture by examining Canada's responses to forced migration in Latin America and the Caribbean (LAC). I begin with the observation that Canada has engaged in limited responsibility-sharing for growing and complex displacement in the region, in contrast with its attention to other regions. Latin America is undergoing two major displacement crises – with almost six million displaced in the region from Venezuela and over 500,000 displaced from the North of Central America (El Salvador, Guatemala, and Honduras) since 2017. Together these crises match the scale of displacement from Syria or Ukraine. In contrast to those crises, Canada's response to displacement in LAC is primarily through financial contributions to emergency appeals and bolstering asylum capacity in host and transit states. International resettlement, a major pillar of Canada's humanitarian foreign policy, is virtually absent. Only 1 per cent of refugees resettled to Canada come from the LAC region.

This is puzzling because Canada's global practices show a clear commitment to responsibility-sharing norms. Its refugee resettlement program is the cornerstone of that commitment and part of its international identity. I explain this puzzle through two factors. First, Canada's economic dependence on resource extraction from the region predate and prevail over its turn to norm entrepreneurship around responsibility-sharing. Second, migrants from the region represent one of the largest groups of asylum seekers in Canada. Geographical proximity means that Canadian policy is focused on containing migrants in order to forestall large-scale chain migration, which it can largely control through strict visa regimes for regions from which it resettles refugees. In sum, while Canada shows a normative commitment to resettlement at the global level, its regional policy is driven by strategic logics.

I begin the chapter by describing Canada's extractive and dependent relationship with LAC. Vast portions of the Canadian economy are bound up in foreign mining, with a particular focus on Latin America. Those extractive relationships extend to human capital given that Canada's agri-food sector and food security depend on temporary foreign workers (TFWs) from the region. I then outline Canada's place in institutionalized mobility frameworks in the Western hemisphere, which are limited to facilitating small-scale business travel with free trade partners and partnering with the US to stop asylum seekers from arriving in Canada. I also explain Canada's global role as a policy and norms entrepreneur around humanitarianism and refugee resettlement in order to illustrate its weak responsibility-sharing in the LAC region. I then explain the puzzle of the lack of refugee settlement from LAC by suggesting that Canada's regional selection criteria is based on domestic political and economic interests. My conclusion reflects on how these tensions impact analysis of Canada's place in North American migration governance.

CANADA'S EXTRACTIVE AND DEPENDENT RELATIONSHIP WITH LATIN AMERICA

Canada's foreign policy toward Latin America has been described as "frustratingly hot and cold" (McKenna 2018, 20). It was largely influenced by Cold-War politics until the late 1980s, with varying support for right-wing regimes or engagement with socialist governments. Canada developed its first coherent regional policy in 1989 under the Conservative Mulroney government, the same year it joined the Organization for American States (OAS) as a full member. The Harper government's 2007 "Americas Strategy" sought to move away from humanitarian and development aid in Africa, and renew focus on instrumentalizing aid and diplomacy to serve Canada's economic and trade interests in the Western hemisphere (Brown 2016). While it included language on democracy promotion, economic development, regional security, and poverty reduction, its major focus was signing bilateral free trade deals and opening the door for Canadian extractive capital (McKenna 2018; Shamsie and Grinspun 2010). In turn, subsequent Liberal governments shifted to focus on development and humanitarian assistance further abroad (Macdonald 2019). Regardless, Canada's extractive focus with LAC has persisted and deepened over time.

Canadian engagement with the LAC region is intimately tied to mining. More than 70 per cent of the world's mining firms are domiciled in Canada given permissive laws and tax breaks for extractive industries. Commodities companies make up over 40 per cent of the Toronto Stock Exchange – one of the most important indicators of Canada's economic well-being. Canadian firms are involved in 60 to 70 per cent of all mining operations in LAC, and are supported by Canadian diplomacy through Export Development Canada and Global Affairs Canada (and its precursors). The 2007 "Americas Strategy" effectively re-tasked Canadian diplomacy to facilitate market access, particularly for mining firms (Blackwood and Stewart 2012). In 2015 the OAS (2015, 46) specifically singled out Canada, recognizing that "Canadian embassies are directly involved in procuring [mining concessions], labeled *economic diplomacy*, thereby deepening the necessary state connections for a framework of foreign state accountability" (emphasis as per original). Governments in the region have become increasingly reliant on proceeds from concessions to Canadian mining companies, which in turn lends an outsized influence on state-society relationships (Grigera 2017; Grinspun and Mills 2015).

Canadian mining operations often come at significant social cost, and are implicated in human rights abuses, environmental degradation, water scarcity, and fracturing local communities (Birn, Shipton, and Schrecker 2018). While quantitative analysis suggests that Canadian firms have slightly better human rights records than other foreign firms, they perform worse than local firms (Haslam, Tanimoune, and Razeq 2018), and are often strongly associated with violence in the region (Imai, Gardner, and Weiberger 2017). Local subsidiaries of Canadian firms have been implicated in state capture and the direct payment to national police and militaries for enforced evictions, targeted sexual violence, and assassinations, particularly in indigenous regions (Binks-Collier 2020). The Working Group on Mining and Human Rights in Latin America's (2014) submission to the OAS's Inter-American Commission on Human Rights provided evidence that Canadian mining operations are directly responsible for displacing local communities, that many "relocation" schemes for Indigenous communities did not meet the benchmark for prior informed consent, and that Canadian mining operations are linked to both internal and international displacement (OAS 2015).

Canadian companies and their local subsidiaries have been directly implicated in cases of targeted killings of community members who oppose mining operations (see Imai, Gardner, and Weiberger 2017). Indeed, Latin America is the site of the most targeted killings of local communities and solidarity groups organizing to resist ecological damage and displacement (Global Witness 2019). Rather than working toward comprehensive reform and oversight, over the past decade, Canadian companies have filed for international arbitration against Latin American countries when resistance from local communities has affected the value of their assets (Moore and Perez Rocha 2019). The Liberal Trudeau government, which has led Canada's rebranding as a refugee and rights norms entrepreneur, has done little to broaden Canadian engagement beyond this extractive agenda or to help safeguard local communities, despite direct calls from victims or the stated good governance and rights protections in its Feminist Foreign Assistance policy (Garcia 2016).

The extractive agenda and dependence on the LAC region extend to human capital. Canadian agriculture – another major sector of the economy – is increasingly dependent on TFWs from LAC countries (see Rivas-Sánchez in this volume). The first cohort of the Seasonal Agricultural Workers Program (SAWP) recruited 266 workers from Jamaica to Ontario in 1966, and has grown yearly in the intervening fifty-five years, making the SAWP one of the world's most enduring programs of its type globally (Binford 2017; Budworth, Rose, and Mann 2017). In 1974, the SAWP was expanded to include workers from Mexico and other Caribbean states. The sector's reliance on foreign workers has major implications for production levels and food security (Falconer 2020a).

SAWP visas allow migrants to work in Canada for a maximum of eight continuous months, though they can return to Canada for work without limit for subsequent work permits. The proportion of TFWs in the sector increased by 52 per cent from 2015 to 2019. In 2019, approximately 55,000 people arrived in Canada under the program (Falconer 2020b). More than 50 per cent are recruited from Mexico, followed by Guatemala and Jamaica, with the remainder drawn from other LAC countries. They amount to 20 per cent of Canada's food production workforce. Their earnings contribute to remittances – a higher and more stable source of foreign currency inflows than either foreign direct investment or development assistance for middle-income countries (Wells et al. 2014; World Bank 2019). Remittances are crucial since they often go directly to households and communities. While data are not available for overall remittances from the SAWP workers, LAC countries are some of the world's most reliant as a proportion of GDP (see table 12.1). In 2017 (latest available data), USD 1.24 billion in remittances flowed directly from Canada to the region.

Table 12.1 | Remittances from Canada to Latin America and the Caribbean, 2019

Country	% of GDP	Total (billions USD)	From Canada (millions USD) (2017)
Haiti	37.1	3.2	133
Honduras	22	5.4	38
El Salvador	21	5.6	157
Jamaica	16.4	2.5	315
Nicaragua	13.2	1.6	25
Guatemala	13.1	10.6	142
Dominican Republic	8.1	7.2	34
Mexico	3.2	38.5	156
Ecuador	3.1	3.2	39
Colombia	2.1	6.8	113
Peru	1.5	3.3	57
Brazil	0.2	3.3	31

Source: World Bank "Migration & Remittances Data (April 2020); "Bilateral Remittances Matrix (2017)". https://www.worldbank.org/en/topic/migration remittancesdiasporaissues/brief/migration-remittances-data.

Unlike the majority of immigrant categories, most SAWP labourers are explicitly barred from a path to permanent residency in Canada (see Triadafilopoulos in this volume on Canada's objectives to manage international migration through regulatory categories). Activists and civil society organizations (CSOs) have called on governments to offer more (and basic) rights for seasonal migrant workers and equivalent paths to citizenship as enjoyed by other immigrant classes (see UFCW 2020).[1] Migrant farm workers in Canada are largely tied to a single employer and are structurally vulnerable to unsafe working conditions, employer abuse, wage theft, and, in some cases, human trafficking. They are susceptible to retributive actions from employers, including being refused work for failing to meet production quotas, deportation if they lose their employment, and being blacklisted for advocacy (Silverman and Hari 2016; for similar dynamics in the US see Golash-Boza's 2015 "neoliberal cycle" of migration and deportation of Latin American migrant workers). They are largely barred from the right to collective bargaining that most other workers in Canada enjoy. While unsafe working conditions have been documented for at least two decades, the COVID-19 pandemic brought their outsized precarious status to the attention of the international media (see Beaumont 2020; Porter 2020; Triandafyllidou and Nalbanian 2020).

Canada's dependence on migrant workers for a viable agrifood sector (and migrants' dependence on remittances) is wrought with inherent normative and political trade-offs. As noted in other cases, particularly the relationships between Europe and its peripheries or South-South migration from Asia to Gulf States, migration interdependence necessarily entails significant power differentials and strategic interests (see Malit and Tsourapas 2021; Tsourapas 2018). The program's endurance is predicated on maintaining migrants' temporary status (see Fudge 2012). To draw one comparative example, European domestic court decisions on guest-workers' rights to citizenship had long-term implications for European capacities to meet labour market needs and for migrants' to access work and crucial remittances (see Castles 2006; Martin 2015). These dynamics can be understood through what Ruhs and Martin (2008) described as the "rights/numbers trade-off." Demand for temporary workers is dictated almost entirely by industry, rather than by the overall domestic labour supply or permanent immigration schemes. Higher numbers of temporary workers (and thus a greater flow of remittances to home countries) are correlated with employers offering fewer rights. The provision of more rights, higher wages, and better labour standards in European states resulted in less demand from industry, upsetting the often-touted "triple win" from migration for receiving countries, migrants, and source countries (see Castles and Ozkul 2014; Consterdine and Samuk 2018; Joppke 2003; Hollifield 2004).

Admittedly, the comparison to historical guest-worker schemes is not precisely analogous to Canada's SAWP. It is more readily comparable to contemporary temporary migration to the EU through the 2014 Seasonal Workers Directive for third country nationals (which came into force in 2017) allowing for nine-month residence for the purposes of "low-skilled" seasonal work in most EU member states (see Guild 2017; Zoetweij-Turhan 2017). The directive (and state agreement to it) is based on positive incentives for leaving within the given period of employment and thus avoiding unintended policy outcomes of incentivizing large-scale visa-overstaying. The directive is thus a partial recognition that the radical curtailing of labour immigration in the 1980s severed more organic circular migration systems and contributed to massive increase in irregular migration and asylum in the 1990s. In turn, the asylum crises of the 1990s facilitated the rise of anti-immigrant parties in Western Europe, shifted the political centre to the right on immigration issues, and contributed to the continent's decades-long immigration and asylum policy morass (see Bade 2003; Moch 2003). While perhaps not ethically justifiable (see Carens 2008; Wright, Groutsis, and van den Broek 2017), the SAWP fundamentally implies trade-offs between Canada's interests in extracting labour with few rights provisions, in return for migrants' interests in working for higher wages than they would earn at home (see Ruhs 2013).

MIGRATION GOVERNANCE, RESPONSIBILITY-SHARING, AND CANADA'S GLOBAL STATUS-SEEKING

Turning attention back to the macro level: definitions of migration governance centre on norms, institutions, laws, and practices for facilitating or controlling human mobility, and ensuring the rights of migrants (see Awad 2017; Betts and Kainz 2017; Martin and Weerasinghe 2017). Migration governance can include bilateral, multilateral, or supranational consultative processes, treaties, and institutions, and a range of actors including states, CSOs, international financial institutions, regional bodies, and UN institutions. Migration governance encapsulates broad and often overlapping frameworks and actors (see Betts 2010; Hansen, Koehler, and Money 2011).

With the exception of treaties and laws around refugees and asylum, most formalized mobility arrangements are bilateral or regional (Hollifield and Wong 2022). Regional migration governance is often highly fragmented between subregions and issues areas. High-skilled labour migration, TFW schemes, asylum admissions, and coordination around displacement are the purview of different laws, norms, institutions, and practices. Robust migration governance frameworks are often an outgrowth of regional economic integration rather than being a primary driver (Lavenex 2019). Even where trade and economic integration are significant, states maintain a high degree of control over the movement of people in comparison to other transboundary flows, and burden-shifting around displacement is a perennial issue (Gottwald 2014; Greenhill 2016; Thielemann 2018).

In North America, formalized migration governance has been limited to trade-related mobility through Chapter 16 of the North America Free Trade Agreement (NAFTA) – which offered short-term visas for business and investment travel, longer-term intercompany transfers, and mutual recognition of professional credentials. It was monitored by a side agreement on North American Agreement on Labour Cooperation (see Lavenex et al. 2016). NAFTA fostered localized circular migration between Canada and the US, and the US and Mexico, rather than any substantial regional integration (Duina 2016). NAFTA's mobility mechanisms were included as Chapter 16 of the new United States-Mexico-Canada Agreement, which entered into force on 1 July 2020, under "Temporary Entry for Business Persons." In effect, it carried over the provisions for business-related travel from NAFTA.[2]

South and North American migration governance are geographically separated by Central America, where Canada is part of the Puebla Process (or the Regional Conference on Migration) along with the US, Mexico, and several Central American states. The process is predominantly consultative, with no binding responsibility-sharing. It does not include clauses for facilitating mobility from the region to Canada or vice versa. Further South, Canada has no meaningful connections with MERCOSUR (the Southern Common Market) – the most comprehensive and robust regional arrangement in the hemisphere.[3]

Despite the absence of binding frameworks, state behaviour is nonetheless informed and often driven by international norms, by which I mean expected behaviour from actors with a given identity (Finnemore and Sikkink 1998; Katzenstein 1996; see also Coen in this volume on the role of norms in the international refugee regime). Practices, institutions, laws, and political culture all inform state identity and behaviour. For example, Canada's international reputation and political culture are profoundly intertwined with large-scale immigration, including well-established practices around international refugee resettlement and supporting multilateral humanitarian and development efforts for displaced people. Canada has engaged in relatively broad and consistent refugee resettlement as a mode of responsibility-sharing, despite the fact that resettlement is not a binding obligation under international law.

Indeed, in recent decades, Canada has acted as a consistent norm and policy entrepreneur for increased resettlement. It helped lead the 2001 United Nations High Commissioner for Refugees (UNHCR) Convention Plus Framework, and subsequent Working Group on Resettlement in 2003, which developed the notion of the "Strategic Use of Resettlement" to maximize benefits not only to refugees, but to host and receiving states given the scarcity of available resources and resettlement spaces (van Selm 2018). Canada also authored the 2004 Multilateral Framework of Understandings on Resettlement, which called for increased responsibility-sharing and a focus on resettlement from refugee hosting regions (Labman 2019, 58–9).

In 2018 Canada became the world's top country of resettlement after the Trump administration slashed US refugee quotas from 100,000 to 15,000 over four years (see Radford and Connor 2019; Cameron and Labman; Coen in this volume). Resettlement moved from a primarily domestic issue to a central plank of foreign policy as Canada sought to export its refugee resettlement programs through the Global Refugee Sponsorship initiative, which it lobbied to have included in the 2018 Global Compact on Refugees (GCR; Smith 2020). Canada's identity, and thus its expected behaviour, is significantly influenced by its practices supporting international efforts for responsibility-sharing through resettlement.

Responsibility-sharing is a core norm of the refugee regime (despite its obvious weakness in terms of addressing overall global resettlement needs). It assumes that states share a common but differentiated responsibility to address forced displacement (Dowd and McAdam 2017). However, responsibility-sharing has no clear benchmarks or binding oversight mechanisms, and states see little risk other than reputational costs for not accepting responsibilities for displacement. Regardless, states have self-interested reasons for addressing displacement crises (Betts 2011; Loescher, Betts, and Milner 2008). Support for host states can help ensure local and regional stability and ameliorate chances for protracted refugee situations and conflict spillovers (see Greenhill 2010; Salehyan and Gleditsch 2006). Providing early solutions to displacement, including safe mobility pathways, might also help forestall irregular migration – though rich states are hesitant to embark on bold experiments to test these policies (see Triandafyllidou, Bartolini, and Guidi 2019; Zimmerman 2009). Conversely, limiting access to asylum and short-term visas contribute to increased irregular migration – a point I return to in the further sections – in terms of asylum seekers from LAC arriving in Canada (Czaika and Hobolth 2016).

Canada's most robust and institutionalized mode of asylum governance is arguably through the bilateral Canada-US Safe Third Country Agreement (STCA), the original purpose of which was to keep refugee claimants from LAC states out of Canada (see Banerjee; Koslowski and Leckey in this volume), rather than to protect the rights of migrants or facilitate orderly mobility. The STCA was negotiated in the wake of the events of 11 September 2001, signed in 2002, and came into force on the last day of 2004. It was originally conceived to stop the so-called border rush of Central American asylum seekers from entering Canada in the mid-to-late 1990s (Garcia 2006). Though framed in terms of mutual responsibility, the vast majority of asylum seekers crossing the border historically moved north to Canada, where the provision of asylum and rights for asylum seekers are far more liberal.

While often overlooked in academic and advocacy literature, the STCA is predicated on the norm of responsibility-sharing for international protection. The preamble to the STCA recognizes "both countries' traditions of assistance to refugees and displaced persons abroad, consistent with the principles of international solidarity that underpin the international refugee protection system, and committed to the notion that cooperation and burden-sharing with respect to refugee status claimants can be enhanced."[4] Importantly, until 2023, the agreement only applied to official ports of entry on the land border, meaning that people who arrived at airports or crossed between ports of entry were eligible to claim asylum, which, as described ahead, includes an increasing number of asylum seekers from the LAC states. However, in the spring of 2023, the Trudeau and Biden administrations announced a deal to extend the STCA to the entirety of the border, in exchange for a non-binding commitment to resettle a small number of people (up to 15,000 annually) from Latin America – largely ignoring the fact that the majority using the route were from Africa, the Middle East and North Africa (MENA) region, and South Asia.

CANADA'S RESPONSE TO HEMISPHERIC DISPLACEMENT

Roughly 10 per cent of the world's displaced people reside in the Western hemisphere. To date, Canada's efforts at responsibility-sharing in the region have predominantly taken the form of modest financial support and political activism, which stand in stark contrast to its engagement with other crises. As of October 2021, the UNHCR recorded 5.9 million Venezuelan refugees and migrants living outside the country, 4.9 million of whom were still in Latin America (UNHCR 2022). The scale of displacement from Venezuela thus mirrors the displacement from the Syrian Civil War, to which Canada responded by significantly increasing international resettlement, and Russia's invasion of Ukraine, to which Canada responded by waiving visa requirements and offering long-term residency permits to all Ukrainians. The Canadian government explicitly ruled out any special resettlement initiatives for Venezuelan refugees (Government of Canada 2020).

Regional host states have taken differentiated approaches to the influx, with some instances of backlash from host populations and citizens around border regions, and a cooling response to local integration as the Venezuelan crisis wears on (see Selee and Bolter 2020). By and large, however, neighbours have kept borders open and worked to regularize status and access to social welfare, employment, and education (see Chaves-González and

Echeverría-Estrada 2020; Freier and Parent 2019). MERCOSUR states have established mechanisms for responsibility-sharing and local integration (see Cantor, Freier, and Gauci 2015).

Closer to home, states in the North of Central America (NCA) are characterized by endemic poverty, corruption, criminality, generalized violence, lack of access to education and services, gender and sexual-identity-based violence and discrimination, and weak or repressive states. Violence in the region is staggering. The LAC region accounts for only 8 per cent of the world's population, but 33 per cent of global homicides (Muggah and Tobón 2018). Violence is particularly acute in cities (see Chioda 2017). The homicide rate for young men is ten times higher than for women, at an average of 94 in 100,000. Coupled with the effects of political repression, economic decline, climate change, ecological degradation, and natural disasters, the situation has given rise to a major displacement crisis with regional and international impacts.

At the end of 2021 there were over 500,000 refugees and asylum seekers from NCA states worldwide, most hosted in neighbouring states. Almost 322,000 asylum claims from these countries were lodged between 2014 and 2019, an increase of 632 per cent from the previous five-year period. An additional 98,000 people were forced to flee from Nicaragua since 2018. Internal displacement is likewise significant. The Internal Displacement Monitoring Centre estimates at least 714,000 internally displaced persons (IDPs) in the NCA countries. Secondary displacement is common, with refugees and IDPs displaced twice on average (Norwegian Refugee Council 2017). As of July 2020, Canada had contributed USD 3.9 million to the UNHCR's humanitarian operations in the region, which are currently only 33 per cent funded (UNHCR 2020).

Canada and Regional Response Frameworks

The international community has recognized that traditional humanitarian "care and maintenance" approaches to displacement are failing displaced and host populations alike. Return to countries of origin and international resettlement is exceedingly unlikely. In September 2016 all UN member states signed the New York Declaration for Refugees and Migrants, leading to the two Global Compacts. Signed in 2018, the compacts reflect various elements of the UN's Agenda 2030 Sustainable Development Goals (SDGs) around inclusive and sustainable development, and safe, orderly, and productive migration management. The GCR is framed around the goals of "predictable and equitable burden and responsibility-sharing" and "collective outcomes and progress" toward easing pressure on host states, enhancing refugee self-reliance, expanding access to third country solutions (i.e., resettlement), and supporting conditions for return to countries of origin.

Tools for effective responsibility-sharing are encapsulated in GCR's Comprehensive Refugee Response Framework (CRRF), which calls for collaboration between humanitarian and development actors through what is referred to as the "Humanitarian-Development Nexus." It proposes novel international finance and development mechanisms to support host states, livelihoods, educational programs, and inclusion of refugees and migrants in social systems to foster self-reliance rather than short-term humanitarian assistance. Linking humanitarian and development assistance is necessary given that the majority of the world's refugees will spend decades displaced close to countries of origin. It is also particularly important given that most of the world's displaced people live alongside host populations. Latin America has the world's most urbanized displaced population, with roughly 95 per cent living in urban areas, making traditional humanitarian assistance challenging (Devictor 2017). Importantly, the CRRF calls for the creation of *new, and additional* funding mechanisms "over and above regular development assistance." While calls to link humanitarian and development are not new, the CRRF offers a novel avenue for responsibility-sharing for displaced people at a unique historical moment.[5]

Six countries in Central America have signed on to a regional implementation of the CRRF. The Brazil Declaration and Plan of Action, signed in December 2014 by twenty-eight countries and three territories, included "Solidarity with the NTCA [Northern Triangle of Central America] in Seeking and Implementing Durable Solutions." The Comprehensive Regional Protection and Solutions Framework is implemented as a regional cooperation agreement in Central America, known by its Spanish acronym MIRPS (Marco Integral Regional de Protección y Soluciones). Canada has yet to meaningfully contribute, or promise to contribute to any unique funding or responsibility-sharing through MIRPS. Canadian development projects included in official MIRPS documents are merely existing programming repackaged as "root causes" interventions rather than new or additional support (see Micinski, Norman, and Gil in this volume for a comparative explanation of root causes approaches in Latin American and Europe).[6]

Canada's responsibility-sharing through financial support is complicated by rather paltry official development assistance (ODA) to LAC. This is partly due to the fact that most countries in the region are considered middle-income states, and thus not considered a high priority for Canadian assistance (see Macdonald 2019). The North and Central America subregion accounts for a total of 7 per cent of Canadian ODA. Canada's global development assistance will remain stagnant at 0.26 per cent of GNI (a significant decrease from 0.31 per cent from the 2012 assessment), and thus is set to decrease in real dollar terms against inflation and economic growth (CCIC 2018). The Organisation for Economic Co-operation and Development's (OECD's) 2018 ODA peer review (OECD 2018) ranks Canada seventeenth out of thirty-seven member states, despite the fact that Canada's economic performance is far above average. Canada contributed CAD 2.2 million in emergency humanitarian relief for Latin America from 2017 to 2019. In 2019, it pledged CAD 52.9 million in longer-term support to regional responses, including humanitarian and development aid, with an additional CAD 27 million promised in May 2020 to assist host states during the COVID-19 pandemic, for a total contribution of CAD 80 million. The regional response framework has a current funding gap of over USD 1.1 billion.[7]

Canada takes part in the Inter-Agency Coordination Platform for Refugee and Migrants from Venezuela (R4V), and a regional interagency platform, comprising states, intergovernmental organizations (IGOs), nongovernmental organizations (NGOs), and CSOs. From a more political standpoint, in 2017, Canada took a lead role in the Lima Group – a group of fourteen states allied in their calls for regime change in Venezuela, which recognized the opposition politician Juan Guaidó's claim as the country's leader. The Lima Group was predominantly made up of right-wing governments with poor records on human rights, good governance, and rule of law, in addition to often brutal persecution of indigenous peoples and repression of opposition politicians, civil society groups, and protestors (see Amnesty International 2019; Freedom House 2020; Kimber and Kirk 2019).

The Absence of Resettlement from Latin America

Given the scale of displacement in Latin America and Canada's well-established norms and practices, it might be assumed that Canada would play a lead role in facilitating resettlement from the region in the absence of meaningful commitments to financial responsibility-sharing. From January 2015 to November 2021, Canada resettled a total of 175,390 people from around the world. Of those resettled during this period, 101,615 were from MENA, 52,735 from sub-Saharan Africa, and 18,270 from the Asia-Pacific region. Only 1,285 were resettled from the Western hemisphere, amounting to under 1 per cent of resettlement over the six-year period. Of those, 965 were resettled from Colombia, with the remainder distributed across the whole of the continent (figure 12.1). While complicated by the fact that private refugee sponsorship now outpaces the resettlement of government-assisted refugees (GARs) nominated by the UNHCR,

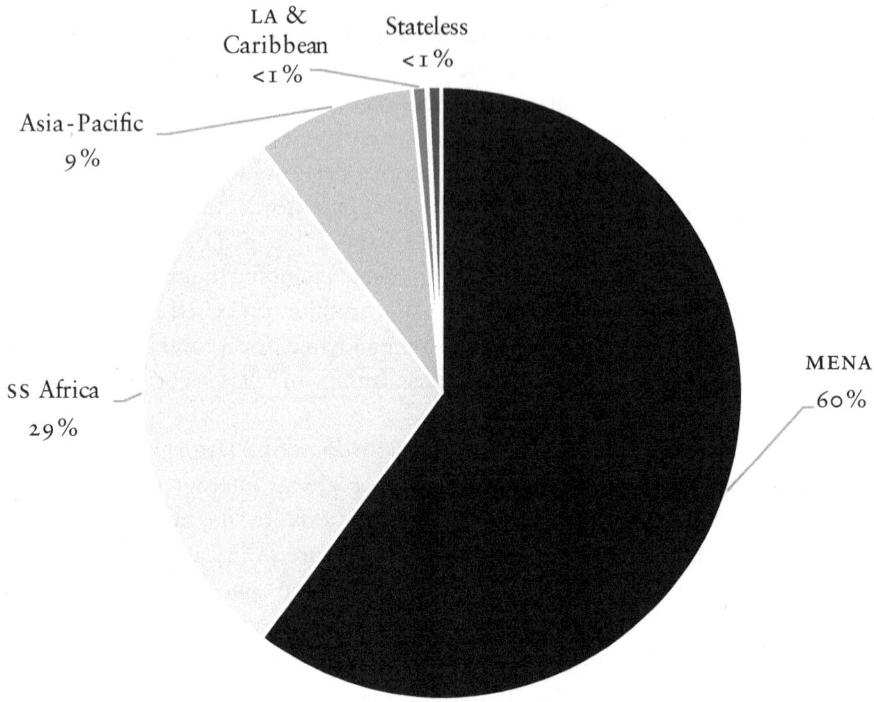

Figure 12.1 | Refugee resettlement to Canada by region of origin: January 2015 to November 2021

Source: Govt. of Canada / IRCC. "Admissions of Resettled Refugees by Country of Citizenship and Immigration Category". https://open.canada.ca/data/en/dataset/4a1b260a-7ac4-4985-80a0-603bfe4aec11.

the overall figures illustrate that Canada all but ignores resettlement from LAC states.

While resettlement from LAC is hampered by limited capacity to identify and register refugees with the UNHCR or the host states, UNHCR's planning figures for 2021 projected a total of 674,000 registered refugees and 2.8 million asylum seekers in Latin America, in addition to the 4.3 million displaced from Venezuela, as part of an overall total of 18.3 million people of concern or in refugee-like situations in the Americas (UNHCR 2021). The region's displaced population are therefore not out of reach for governments considering resettlement as part of their responsibility-sharing agendas.

Canada, however, has largely ignored new resettlement programs under the MIRPS process. The Protection Transfer Arrangement (PTA) – an agreement for increased responsibility-sharing between the UNHCR, the IOM, and the host state governments in the NCA states – was designed to resettle people identified as particularly vulnerable (see UNHCR 2018). UNHCR recommended 785 people for resettlement in 2016 – the first year of the program – 150 of whom were resettled to the United States. Since then, 3,100 people have been identified as requiring immediate resettlement. Canada accepted eleven people in 2017, zero in 2018, and zero in 2019. In 2020, Canada ended its engagement with the PTA, and ignored appeals from UNHCR in Mexico to resettle vulnerable people trapped there, particularly LGBTQIA+ asylum seekers (see Blanchfield 2019). In 2022 Canada signed on to the nonbinding OAS Los Angeles Declaration, which aimed at greater responsibility-sharing in the region. However, it predicated its commitment to resettle up to 15,000 refugees from LAC annually on extending the STCA to the entirety of the US-Canada border, connecting stricter border policies and truncating asylum access on a small and as-of-yet untested resettlement mechanism.

One of Canada's more original and singular engagements with displacement from the region is through the through Immigration and Refugee Board (IRB) twinning projects to increase protection and refugee status determination (RSD) capacity in Mexico, by sending senior decision-makers to advise COMAR (Mexico's asylum agency). The IRB's 2019 budget listed CAD 60,000 for the project. In addition, Canada is cooperating with the UNHCR's Regional Asylum Capacity Support Group, which is geared toward US and Canadian support for COMAR. They began meeting in June 2019 after a two-year hiatus. The idea is to support COMAR through country-of-origin information, translating IRB country-of-origin profiles to Spanish, and developing institutional plans to increase COMAR capacity. Marginally increasing Mexican asylum capacity pales in comparison to the scale of the problem. More to the point, Mexico is far from a safe country for migrants, and the country systematically deports vulnerable people (see Odgers-Ortiz and Olivas in this volume).

ASYLUM CLAIMS AS AN INDICATOR OF NEED?

While minor in comparison to displacement in the region, asylum seekers from LAC states represent a significant and growing proportion of asylum claims in Canada. Just over 280,000 people claimed asylum in Canada from 2013 to 2021. Disaggregated by region of origin, LAC asylum seekers composed the second largest regional group overall, slightly more than from

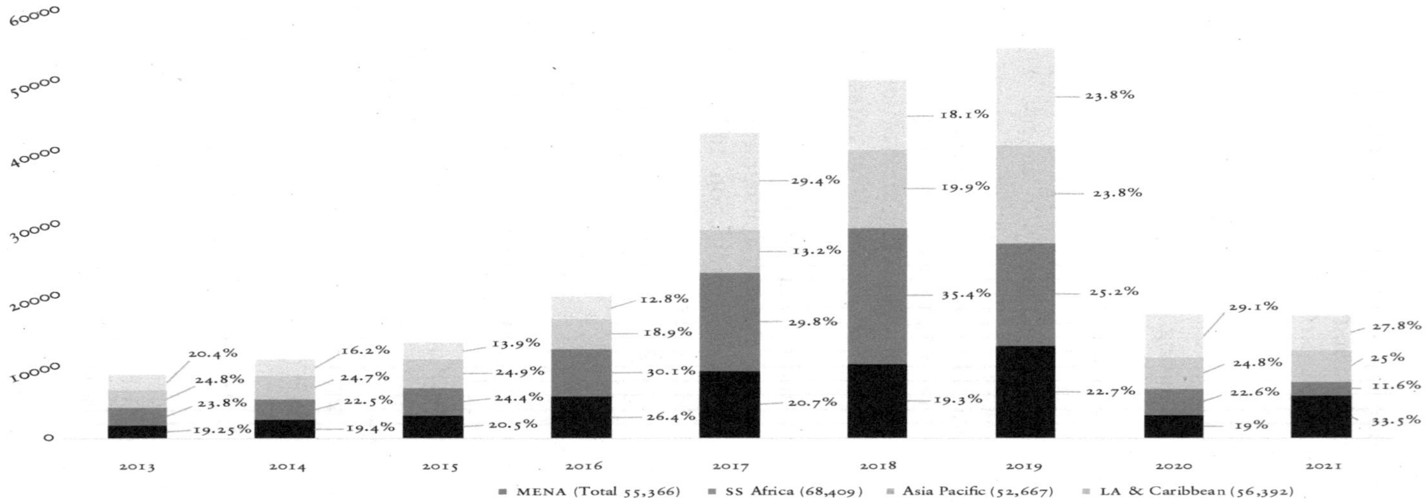

Figure 12.2 | Asylum claims in Canada by region of origin: January 2013 to September 2021

Sources: "Refugee claims by year" in Immigration, Refugees, and Citizenship Canada, "Refugees and asylum," Government of Canada, 2021. http://www.canada.ca/en/immigration-refugees-citizenship/services/refugees/asylum-claims.html.

Table 12.2 | Mexican asylum statistics in Canada, January 2013 to September 2021

	Referred	Accepted	Rejected	Rate	Abandoned / Withdrawn	Backlog
2013	128	16	39	29%	24	53
2014	86	28	43	39.5%	9	58
2015	111	40	39	50%	12	78
2016	250	29	53	35%	46	200
2017	1,459	111	221	33.5%	99	1,221
2018	3,157	190	363	34%	295	3,525
2019	5,634	602	1,045	36.5%	672	6,829
2020	2,088	757	1,119	40%	448	6,607
2021 (Sept)	1,948	922	1,309	38%	313	6,015

Source: Immigration & Refugee Board of Canada, "New System Refugee Claim Statistics," https://irb-cisr.gc.ca/en/statistics/protection/Pages/index.aspx.

MENA, but less than sub-Saharan Africa. Their proportion has grown consistently in recent years, representing almost 30 per cent of asylum claims in fiscal years 2017, 2020, and 2021. The region has accounted for 56,392 out of 252,255, or 22.4 per cent of all asylum claims in Canada since 2013 (see figure 12.2).

While the increase in asylum claims from Latin America and the Caribbean are a rough indicator of a growing need and the sense that Canada represents a viable option for asylum, the situation is somewhat complicated by the relationship between Canadian visa policies and asylum claims. The removal of visa requirement for Mexico in 2016 as part of trade and tourism negotiations was followed by an immediate spike in asylum claims. Mexicans lodged the highest number of claims in 2020, and were in the top three countries from 2016 to 2021. This closely follows previous trends. The requirement for a visa was imposed by the Harper government in 2009 after Mexico became the single largest country of asylum seekers in Canada, with below-average acceptance rates (see Yeates 2018). While recognition rates for Mexican

Table 12.3 | Top twenty-five countries of origin and yearly totals of irregular arrivals in Canada

	2017		2018	
1	Haiti	5,845	Nigeria	7,645
2	Nigeria	3,730	Colombia	1,075
3	USA	1,305	USA	1,040
4	Turkey	540	DR Congo	690
5	Eritrea	450	Pakistan	635
6	Syria	435	Haiti	595
7	Yemen	415	Turkey	580
8	Brazil	280	Sudan	440
9	Sudan	245	Angola	420
10	Djibouti	225	Bangladesh	285
11	Burundi	220	Burundi	270
12	Pakistan	215	Eritrea	270
13	Colombia	205	Venezuela	245
14	Chad	190	Sri Lanka	245
15	Angola	180	Syria	240
16	Azerbaijan	165	Yemen	235
17	DR Congo	165	Chad	225
18	PA (WB & Gaza)	150	Stateless	215
19	Egypt	100	Egypt	200
20	El Salvador	90	PA (WB & Gaza)	195
21	Venezuela	90	Ethiopia	160
22	Libya	45	Zimbabwe	150
23	Bangladesh	40	El Salvador	145
24	Ethiopia	40	Rwanda	130
25	Iraq	40	Libya	125
Totals	(Apr–Dec)	15,405	(Jan–Dec)	16,455

Source: Data transmitted to author by Immigration, Refugees, and Citizenship Canada.

Table 12.3 | *continued*

	2019		2020	
1	Nigeria	2,915	Haiti	395
2	Colombia	1,470	Nigeria	320
3	DR Congo	995	Colombia	320
4	Pakistan	980	Pakistan	255
5	Haiti	865	Angola	155
6	USA	855	DR Congo	140
7	Sudan	715	Sudan	135
8	Angola	700	USA	125
9	Turkey	425	Sri Lanka	75
10	Venezeula	405	Venezuela	65
11	Yemen	320	Afghanistan	60
12	Burundi	280	Turkey	55
13	Egypt	280	Yemen	55
14	Rwanda	280	Ethiopia	50
15	Sri Lanka	275	Rwanda	45
16	Stateless	235	Brazil	45
17	Libya	230	Zimbabwe	45
18	Bangladesh	220	Burundi	40
19	Chad	205	Nicaragua	35
20	Brazil	190	Liberia	35
21	Zimbabwe	185	Stateless	30
22	Nicaragua	175	PA (WB & Gaza)	30
23	PA (WB & Gaza)	155	South Africa	30
24	Ethiopia	150	Eritrea	25
25	El Salvador	135	Cameroon	25
Totals	(Jan–Dec)	13,640	(Jan–Mar)	2590

asylum seekers have increased modestly since 2016 from 35 per cent to 38 per cent in 2021, so have the number of claimants abandoning or withdrawing claims.

While Mexican claims skew statistics from LAC, so do similar trends in recognition rates and abandoned claims from some states for sub-Saharan Africa, particularly from Nigeria. Regardless of these nuances, the major observation is that Canada resettles far more refugees from other regions with large numbers of asylum seekers, particularly from Africa and the Middle East. LAC is the major outlier, despite its geographical proximity with Canada and deep impacts on migration dynamics in North America, particularly asylum flows through Mexico and to the United States (see Odgers-Ortiz and Olivas in this volume).

As described by Banerjee in this volume, since 2016, Canada has seen a significant increase in cross-border asylum seekers from the US. While Canada felt relatively significant domestic impacts from the flow – particularly RSD backlogs, major governmental expenditures, stress on municipal reception capacities, and intergovernmental burden-shifting – its impacts on Canada's role in hemispheric migration governance are significantly under-studied. The first major cohort of arrivals were US-resident Haitians, who feared losing their Temporary Protected Status under the Trump administration, and who were spurred to move though misleading social media posts about Canada's asylum policies (see Noël 2017; Smith 2022; Stevenson 2017).

Mainstream media attention quickly popularized new asylum dynamics, and routes to Canada became more transnational with a wider array of source countries. Internal government estimates suggest that roughly 40 per cent of those who arrived in Canada were US residents, and the remaining 60 per cent had transited through the US with the intention of claiming asylum in Canada. While those who had or were able to obtain visas flew directly to the US, by late 2018, a significant number, predominantly from sub-Saharan Africa, were flying to South America to join the long, overland route via Mexico, the US, and eventually to Canada. Asylum seekers from the Western hemisphere were well-represented, as is evidenced by the top twenty-five source countries per year (table 12.3).

EXPLAINING CANADA'S STATUS-SEEKING GLOBALLY, AND INTEREST-SEEKING REGIONALLY

To summarize my observations, while Canada is weakly enmeshed in regional migration governance frameworks, it has increasingly acted as a policy and norms entrepreneur around responsibility-sharing for refugee resettlement. It is economically dependent on extractive relationships with the LAC region through mining and TFWs. It all but ignores resettlement from the region, and instead focuses on financial and political support for regional response mechanisms, and reacts to increased asylum flows from it with policies to contain refugees in the region or repel them from its border. We can thus witness a trade-off between its economic interests and perceived role in the international community.

Canada is often portrayed as a middle power with outsized influence earned through its participation in multilateral institutions and norm and policy entrepreneurship. Status-seeking is a core state activity, and small and middle powers rely on status more so that greater powers in order to build moral authority in the international system – particularly in their own regions (Volgy et al. 2017). As Wohlforth et al. (2017, 535) argue, "Small and middle powers may thus play the status game by involvement in areas that have traditionally been the hallmark of great power status: international peace and security." For several decades, but even more so since the Liberal government came to power in late 2015, Canada's status-seeking foreign policy has become evermore entwined with its immigration policies and humanitarianism, including international resettlement (Smith 2020). Its resettlement cannot be attributed solely to utilitarian purposes for status-seeking, given historical commitments to responsibility-sharing by governments from across the political spectrum. As Hashimoto (2018, 167) describes, decision-making based on identity and norms suggests that "states accept refugees via the resettlement route because it is an appropriate, ethical, and virtuous thing to do, regardless of eventual consequences or expected outcomes." But normatively-motivated and geostrategic international behaviour are not mutually exclusive, particularly if disaggregated by regions.

Canada's status-seeking and normative commitments are belied by the absence of engagement with resettlement from the LAC region. While its commitment to resettlement writ large can be ascribed to a genuine commitment to humanitarianism, it does not explain why Canada all but ignores resettlement from LAC states. Selection criteria for regions of origin thus require an interest-based explanation. Comparative analysis shows that international refugee resettlement to the US, for example, is often largely determined by geopolitical interests. Analyzing the overbearing preference for resettling Iraqi refugees versus Afghans, Micinski (2018) argues that US resettlement policy was used as a foreign policy tool for relations with refugee-producing countries and their neighbours which act not only as host countries for the bulk of displaced people but are also crucial strategic allies. Micinski found that the US resettles fewer refugees from host countries with a high degree of willingness to host long-term refugee populations. For example, the US focused on local integration rather than resettlement for millions of displaced Afghans in Pakistan because it was strategically useful for the US to keep Afghans in the region. It also resettled large numbers of Iraqi refugees from Jordan, while ignoring resettlement of the same populations from its strategic rivals Syria or Iran.

More broadly, refugee resettlement has been conceptualized as a form of *humanitarian governance*, in which states and international organizations act on humanitarian principles, and as a means of control (Garnier, Sandvik, and Jubilut 2018). In effect, selection of those who are most worthy is an exercise in power relationships – which is not necessarily mutually exclusive with normative behaviour. In effect, while Canada selects resettled refugees primarily on the basis of vulnerability, it also selects regions from which to resettle based on political motivations. Indeed, liberal states increasingly predicate resettlement on successful migration controls and the notion that refugees should patiently wait in the global queue rather than seek asylum through mixed migration routes: for example, in Australia's "Pacific Solution" or the UK government's controversial plans to deport asylum seekers to Rwanda for RSD.

In the case of Europe, resettlement is often only considered as a broad policy response to displacement when spontaneous asylum claims are successfully "managed" by externalized controls and pushbacks (Fitzgerald 2019; Hashimoto 2018). Evidence suggests a similar strategic rationale is at play in terms of Canada's selection criteria. As described above, Canada prioritizes geographically distant regions of origin while ignoring Latin America, from which an increasing number of asylum seekers arrive in Canada, as described in table 12.3. To reiterate, Canada pushed for the STCA with the US to explicitly keep asylum seekers from LAC states from arriving in Canada. It is the only geographically contiguous region which generates significant displacement, and Canada's relationships with Mexico, the US, and host states are entirely geared toward containing migrants away from its borders (see Smith n.d.). Seeking to limit large-scale asylum migration to Canada also means forestalling subsequent irregular migration from among broader social networks – which is well-documented in other regions (see Crawley and Hagen-Zanker 2018; McAuliffe 2017).

Even in the case of increased resettlement, mounting evidence suggests that liberal states select not solely on the basis of need, but on refugees' potential economic contributions (de Boer and Zieck 2020).While Canada largely resettles refugees on the basis of vulnerability in its GAR stream (see Cameron and Labman in this volume), its reliance on TFWs for its agricultural sector illustrates a clear preference for selecting based on specific and strictly delineated labour profiles. Its dependence on extracting a specific type of labour means tightly controlling immigration from the LAC region in order to select migrants who will remain in a temporary state, and who are not eligible for permanent residency, since they would then enjoy labour mobility and rights, and likely not opt to work in one of Canada's most precarious and underpaid sectors. The evidence suggests that Canada seeks to contain displaced people within the region, and select only temporary migrants on whom it has become dependent for food security.

Finally, the relationship between geostrategic interests and regional selection criteria requires a deeper conceptual understanding, since Canada has little global impact in terms of its foreign military action, which generates refugees or alliances to guarantee global power projection. However, refugee selection is often driven by what Bose (2022) calls the "primacy of national immigration interests over international migration policy." Put otherwise, domestic strategic interests often trump international norms and status-seeking. To use some recent examples, domestic political calculations drove Canada's selection of Syrian refugees since the Trudeau government bound its election promises with resettling Syrian refugees (Gilmour 2018), and later sought to boost its domestic popularity by extending visa-free travel access for Ukrainian refugees. Likewise, domestic interest groups have historically and still exercise significant sway over Canada's overall refugee selection (see Cameron 2021). But Canada's extractive interests militate against recognizing LAC as a region requiring large-scale resettlement. Canada's resource sector has significant influence on its foreign policy in the region. Its long-term relationships with often-oppressive governments in order to secure and maintain mining concessions means Canada is reluctant to label governments with the types of persecution or inability to protect citizens, which are the necessary grounds for resettlement.

CONCLUSIONS AND REFLECTIONS

Canada's middle power status in international relations depends largely on its normative power, humanitarianism, and engagement with multilateral institutions. Its role in migration governance in its own hemisphere, however, illustrates how that status-seeking behaviour coexists with geostrategic logics that often come at the expense of its well-established commitments to international refugee resettlement. Its focus on the Americas is to keep displaced people in their region of origin. Indeed, Canada's statement to the 2018 formal consultation on the GCR stated that "Canada believes we <u>all</u> share in responsibility to help ensure asylum for those who have fled their homes, provide them with opportunities to use their skills and capacities to build a better future, and support the countries and communities that host them" (with bolding and underlining included in the original document, as the only such emphasis added).[8] This chapter explains the absence of resettlement and the focus on containment by arguing that Canada's responsibility-sharing commitments are regionally selective when weighed against domestic economic interests and extractive foreign policy.

This chapter also draws out significant tensions for the prospects of more institutionalized regionalization of migration governance in North America given that Canada displays a preference for maintaining strict controls over immigration. Its role in North American migration governance is focused on facilitating narrow, high-skilled migration, maintaining and expanding TFW schemes from Latin America, support for keeping displaced people in the LAC region, and partnering with the US in order to limit asylum migration.

Indeed, partnerships to limit asylum seekers from entering Canada from the US is perhaps its main policy priority within North America. At the time of writing, the Supreme Court of Canada was preparing to hear arguments around the constitutionality of the Canada-US STCA, given its role in returning asylum seekers to arbitrary and punitive detention and chain refoulement (see Coen in this volume on the US breach of norms in the global refugee regime). The federal government argues that the STCA is an effective tool for responsibility-sharing. As mentioned earlier, in March 2023, the Trudeau government effectively extended the STCA to the entirety of the border in agreement with the Biden administration. As part of that agreement, it promised to resettle up to 15,000 people annually from the region via complementary pathways to offset or, more accurately, forestall irregular migration. At the time of writing, though, the implementation of those commitments was yet to be seen. Perhaps more importantly from a domestic perspective, the purpose of the STCA is to insulate Canada from the types of large-scale irregular migration flows that emboldened anti-immigrant populism in other liberal democracies (see Donnelly 2017; Stockemer 2016).

NOTES

1 See the Migrant Rights Network's 2020 "Status for All" campaign: https://migrantrights.ca/status-for-all/.

2 See USMCA Chapter 16, (10 December 2019): https://www.international.gc.ca/trade-commerce/assets/pdfs/agreements-accords/cusma-aceum/r-cusma-16.pdf.

3 MERCOSUR member states: Argentina, Brazil, Paraguay, Uruguay, and Venezuela; associate states: Bolivia, Chile, Colombia, Ecuador, Guyana, Peru, and Surinam.

4 See full text of US-Canada Safe Third Country Agreement (STCA) (5 December 2002): https://www.canada.ca/en/immigration-refugees-citizenship/corporate/mandate/policies-operational-instructions-agreements/agreements/safe-third-country-agreement/final-text.html.

5 EU models for linking relief, rehabilitation, and development have been around for decades, and UNHCR personnel have been probing at the disjunction since at least 2001. See Crisp (2001).

6 See "Canada" under "Cooperating Actors" in *MIRPS: Comprehensive Regional Protection and Solutions Framework*, available at: http://www.globalcrrf.org/wp-content/uploads/2018/05/MIRPS-english-version.pdf.

7 For up-to-date statistics see the R4V website at: https://r4v.info/es/situations/platform.

8 "Canadian Government Intervention for the final round of the Formal Consultations on the Global Compact on Refugees," Geneva, 3–4 July. https://www.unhcr.org/events/conferences/5b4f3b887/statement-canada-sixth-formal-consultation.html.

REFERENCES

Amnesty International. 2019. "Americas 2019." *Amnesty International Yearly Report 2019*. https://www.amnesty.org/en/countries/americas/report-americas/. Accessed 1 June 2023.

Awad, Ibrahim. 2017. "The Multiple Levels of Governance of International Migration: Understanding Disparities and Disorders." *American Journal of International Law (AJIL Unbound)* 11: 153–8. https://doi.org/10.1017/aju.2017.36.

Bade, Klaus J. 2003. *Migration in European History*. Malden, MA: Blackwell Publishing.

Beaumont, Hilary. 2020. "Coronavirus Sheds Light on Canada's Poor Treatment of Migrant Workers." *Guardian*, 20 July 2020. https://www.theguardian.com/world/2020/jul/20/canada-migrant-farm-workers-oronavirus. Accessed 1 June 2023.

Betts, Alexander. 2010. "The Refugee Regime Complex." *Refugee Studies Quarterly* 29 (1): 12–37.

– 2011. *Protection by Persuasion: International Cooperation in the Refugee Regime*. Ithaca, NY: Cornell University Press.

Betts, Alexander, and Lena Kainz. 2017. "The History of Global Migration Governance." *Refugee Studies Working Paper* no. 112. Oxford University. https://www.rsc.ox.ac.uk/publications/the-history-of-global-migration-governance/@@download/file. Accessed 1 June 2023.

Binford, Arthur Leigh. 2017. "Assessing Temporary Foreign Worker Programs Through the Prism of Canada's Seasonal Agricultural Worker Program: Can They be Transformed or Should They be Eliminated?" *Dialectic Anthropology* 43 (4): 347–66.

Binks-Collier, Max. 2020. "Evicting Lote Ocho." *The Intercept*, 26 September 2020. https://theintercept.com/2020/09/26/hudbay-skyecanada-mining-guatemala/. Accessed 1 June 2023.

Birn, Anne-Emanuelle, Leah Shipton, and Ted Schrecker. 2018. "Canadian Mining and Ill Health in Latin America: A Call to Action." *Canadian Journal of Public Health* 109 (5–6): 786–90.

Blackwood, Elizabeth, and Veronicka Stewart. 2012. "CIDA and the Mining Sector: Extractive Industries as an Overseas Development Strategy." In *Struggling for Effectiveness: CIDA and Canadian Foreign Aid*, edited by Stephen Brown, 217–45. Montreal: McGill-Queen's University Press.

Blanchfield, Mike. 2019. "UN Urges Canada to Take More Vulnerable Central America Migrants from Mexico." CBC *News*, 26 May 2019. https://www.cbc.ca/news/politics/un-urges-canada-to-take-more-vulnerable-central-american-migrants-from-mexico-1.5150446. Accessed 1 June 2023.

Bose, Pablo S. 2022. "The Shifting Landscape of International Resettlement: Canada, the US and Syrian Refugees." *Geopolitics* 27 (2): 375–401.

Brown, Stephen. 2016. "The Instrumentalization of Foreign Aid under the Harper Government." *Studies in Political Economy* 97 (1): 18–36.

Budworth, Marie-Hélène, Andrew Rose, and Sara Mann. 2017. *Report on the Seasonal Agricultural Worker Program*. Inter-American Institute for Cooperation on Agriculture. https://repositorio.iica.int/bitstream/handle/11324/2679/BVE17038753i.pdf;jsessionid=B34893176B387BA8453F751EFB3A68B7?sequence=1. Accessed 1 June 2023.

Cameron, Geoffrey. 2021. *Send Them Here: Religion, Politics, and Refugee Resettlement in North America*. Montreal: McGill-Queen's University Press.

Cantor, David James, Luisa Feline Freier, and Jean-Pierre Gauci, eds. 2015. *A Liberal Tide? Immigration and Asylum Law & Policy in Latin America*. London: Institute for Latin American Studies.

Carens, Joseph. 2008. "Live-in Domestics, Seasonal Workers, and Others Hard to Locate on the Map of Democracy." *Journal of Political Philosophy* 16 (4): 419–45.

Castles, Stephen. 2006. "Guestworkers in Europe: A Resurrection?" *International Migration Review* 40 (4): 741–66.

Castles, Stephen, and Derya Ozkul. 2014. "Circular Migration: Triple Win, or a New Label for Temporary Migration?" in *Global and Asian Perspectives on International Migration*, edited by Graziano Battistella, 27–49. Switzerland: Springer International Publishing.

CCIC (Canadian Council for International Cooperation). 2018. "Brief: Assessment of Budget 2018." Ottawa: Canadian Council for International Cooperation. https://ccic.ca/wp-content/uploads/bsk-pdf-manager/2018/05/EN-Budget-2018-Analysis-Final-Clean.pdf. Accessed 1 June 2023.

Chaves-González, Diego, and Carlos Echeverría-Estrada. 2020. "Venezuelan Migrants and Refugees in Latin America and the Caribbean: A Regional Profile." Washington, DC: Migration Policy Institute and International Organization for Migration. https://www.migrationpolicy.org/research/venezuelans-latin-america-caribbean-regional-profile. Accessed 1 June 2023.

Chioda, Laura. 2017. *Stop the Violence in Latin America: A Look at Prevention from Cradle to Adulthood.* Latin American Development Forum, Washington, DC: World Bank Group. https://openknowledge.worldbank.org/handle/10986/25920. Accessed 1 June 2023.

Consterdine, Erica, and Sahizer Samuk. 2018. "Temporary Migration Programmes: The Cause or Antidote of Migrant Worker Exploitation in UK Agriculture?" *Journal of International Migration and Integration* 19 (4): 1005–20.

Crawley, Heaven, and Jessica Hagen-Zanker. 2018. "Deciding Where to Go: Policies, People, and Perceptions Shaping Destination Preferences." *International Migration* 57 (1): 20–35.

Crisp, Jeff. 2001. "Mind the Gap! UNHCR, Humanitarian Assistance, and the Development Process." *International Migration Review* 35 (1): 168–91.

Czaika, Mathias, and Mogens Hobolth. 2016. "Do Restrictive Asylum and Visa Policies Increase Irregular Migration into Europe?" *European Union Politics* 17 (3): 345–65.

Devictor, Xavier. 2017. *Forcibly Displaced: Toward a Development Approach Supporting Refugees, the Internally Displaced, and their Hosts.* Washington, DC: The World Bank.

de Boer, Tom, and Marjoleine Zieck. 2020. "The Legal Abyss of Discretion in the Resettlement of Refugees: Cherry-Picking and the Lack of Due Process in the EU." *International Journal of Refugee Law* 32 (1): 54–85.

Donnelly, Michael. 2017. "Canadian Exceptionalism: Are We Good or are We Lucky? A Survey of Canadian Attitudes in Comparative Perspective." McGill Institute for the Study of Canada. https://www.scribd.com/document/338667559/Canadian-Exceptionalism-Are-We-Good-Or-Are-We-Lucky-Michael-Donnelly#from_embed. Accessed 1 June 2023.

Dowd, Rebecca, and Jane McAdam. 2017. "International Cooperation and Responsibility-Sharing to Protect Refugees: What, Why, and How?" *International and Comparative Law Quarterly* 66 (4): 863–92.

Duina, Francesco. 2016. "North America and the Transatlantic Area." in *The Oxford Handbook of Comparative Regionalism*, edited Tanja A. Börzel and Thomas Risse, 133–53. Oxford, UK: Oxford University Press.

Falconer, Robert. 2020a. "Family Farmers to Foreign Fieldhands: Consolidation of Canadian Agriculture and the Temporary Foreign Worker Program." *SPP Briefing Paper* 13 (21): 1–28. University of Calgary School of Public Policy and the Simpson Centre for Agriculture and Food Innovation and Public Policy. https://www.policyschool.ca/wp-content/uploads/2020/08/Family-Farmers-Falconer.pdf. Accessed 1 June 2023.

– 2020b. "Grown Locally, Harvested Globally: The Role of Temporary ForeignWorkers in Canadian Agriculture." *SPP Communiqué* 13 (17): 1–21. University of Calgary School of Public Policy and the Simpson Centre for Agriculture and Food Innovation and Public Policy. https://www.policyschool.ca/wp-content/uploads/2020/07/Grown-Locally-Falconer.pdf. Accessed 1 June 2023.

Finnemore, Martha, and Katherine Sikkink. 1998. "International Norm Dynamics and Political Change." *International Organization* 52 (4): 887–917.

Fitzgerald, David Scott. 2019. *Refuge Beyond Reach: How Rich Democracies Repel Asylum Seekers*. New York: Oxford University Press.

Freedom House. 2020. *Freedom in the World 2020: A Leaderless Struggle for Democracy*. https://freedomhouse.org/sites/default/files/2020-02/FIW_2020_REPORT_BOOKLET_Final.pdf. Accessed 1 June 2023.

Freier, Luisa Feline, and Nicolas Parent. 2019. "The Regional Response to the Venezuelan Exodus." *Current History* 118 (805): 56–61.

Fudge, Judy. 2012. "Precarious Migrant Status and Precarious Employment: The Paradox of International Rights for Migrant Workers." *Comparative Labour Law & Policy Journal* 34 (1): 95–132.

Garcia, Maria Christina. 2006. "Canada: A Northern Refuge for Central Americans." *Migration Information Source*. Washington, DC: Migration Policy Institute. https://www.migrationpolicy.org/article/canada-northern-refuge-central-americans. Accessed 1 June 2023.

Garcia, Mercedes. 2016. *Canadian Mining: Still Controversial in Central America – The Case of Honduras*. Council on Hemispheric Affairs. https://www.coha.org/canadian-mining-still-controversial-in-central-america-the-case-of-honduras/. Accessed 1 June 2023.

Garnier, Adèle, Kristin Bergtora Sandvik, and Liliana Lyra Jubilut. 2018. "Refugee Resettlement as Humanitarian Governance: Power Dynamics" in *Refugee Resettlement: Power, Politics, and Humanitarian Governance*, edited by Adèle Garnier, Liliana Lyra Jubilut, and Kristin Bergtora Sandvik, 1–28. New York: Berghahn Books.

Gilmour, Julie F. 2018. "The Trudeau Government, Refugee Policy, and Echoes of the Past." In *Justin Trudeau and Canadian Foreign Policy*, edited by Norman Hillmer and Philippe Lagassé, 233–46. New York: Palgrave Macmillan.

Global Witness. 2019. *Enemies of the State? How Governments and Business Silence Land and Environmental Defenders.* Global Witness. https://www.globalwitness.org/en/campaigns/environmental-activists/enemigos-del-estado/. Accessed 1 June 2023.

Golash-Boza, Tanya Maria. 2015. *Deported: Immigrant Policing, Disposable Labor and Global Capitalism.* New York: New York University Press.

Gottwald, Martin. 2014. "Burden Sharing and Refugee Protection." In *The Oxford Handbook of Refugee and Forced Migration Studies*, edited by Elena Fiddian-Qasmiyeh, Gil Loescher, Katy Long, and Nando Sigona, 525–38. New York: Oxford University Press.

Government of Canada. 2020. "CIMM – Additional Information – International Relations." https://www.canada.ca/en/immigration-refugees-citizenship/corporate/transparency/committees/march-12-2020/additional-information-international-relations.html. Accessed 1 June 2023.

Greenhill, Kelly M. 2010. Weapons of Mass Migration: Forced Displacement, Coercion, and Foreign Policy. Ithaca, NY: Cornell University Press.

– 2016. "Open Arms Behind Barred Doors: Fear, Hypocrisy and Policy Schizophrenia in the European Migration Crisis: European Migration Crisis." *European Law Journal* 22 (3): 317–32.

Grigera, Juan. 2017. "Extractivism and Citizenship." *In Handbook of South American Governance*, edited by Pia Riggirozzi and Christopher Wylde, 348–56. London: Routledge.

Grinspun, Ricardo, and Jennifer Mills. 2015. "Canada, Extractivism, and Hemispheric Relations." In *Beyond Free Trade: Alternative Approaches to Trade, Politics, and Power*, edited by Kate Ervine and Gavin Fridell, 133–51. London: Palgrave Macmillan.

Guild, Elspeth. 2017. "Questioning Temporary Migration Schemes in the EU." In *Pathways Toward Legal Migration into the EU: Reappraising Concepts, Trajectories, and Policies*, edited by Sergio Carrera, Andrew Geddes, Elspeth Guild, and Marco Stefan, 42–8. Brussels: Centre for European Policy Studies. https://www.ceps.eu/wp-content/uploads/2017/09/PathwaysLegalMigration_0.pdf. Accessed 1 June 2023.

Hansen, Randall, Jobst Koehler, and Jeannette Money, eds. 2011. *Migration, Nation States, and International Cooperation.* New York: Routledge.

Hashimoto, Naoko. 2018. "Refugee Resettlement as an Alternative to Asylum." *Refugee Survey Quarterly* 37 (2): 162–86.

Haslam, Paul Alexander, Nasser Ary Tanimoune, and Zarlasht N. Razeq. 2018. "Do Canadian Mining Firms Behave Worse than Other Companies? Quantitative Evidence from Latin America." *Canadian Journal of Political Science* 51 (3): 521–51.

Hollifield, James F. 2004. "The Emerging Migration State." *International Migration Review* 38 (3): 885–912.

Hollifield, James F., and Tom K. Wong. 2022. "The Politics of International Migration," in *Migration Theory: Talking Across Disciplines*, edited by Caroline B. Brettell and James F. Hollifield. New York: Routledge.

Imai, Shin, Leah Gardner, and Sarah Weiberger. 2017. "The 'Canada Brand': Violence and Canadian Mining Companies in Latin America." *Osgoode Legal Studies Research Paper* No. 17/2017. https://papers.ssrn.com/sol3/papers.cfm?abstract_id=2886584. Accessed 1 June 2023.

Joppke, Christian. 2003. "Immigration Challenges to the Nation State." In *Challenges to the Nation State: Immigration in Western Europe and the United States*, edited by Christian Joppke, 5–48. Oxford: Oxford University Press.

Katzenstein, Peter, ed. 1996. *The Culture of National Security: Norms and Identity in World Politics*. New York: Columbia University Press.

Kimber, Stephen, and John Kirk. 2019. "Selective Indignation: Why the Trudeau Government Needs to Reassess its Relationships in Latin America." CBC *News*, 23 November 2019. https://www.cbc.ca/news/opinion/opinion-canada-foreign-policy-latin-america-1.5369302. Accessed 1 June 2023.

Labman, Shauna. 2019. *Crossing Law's Borders: Canada's Refugee Resettlement Program*. Vancouver: UBC Press.

Lavenex, Sandra, Terri E. Givens, Flavia Jurje, and Ross Buchanan. 2016. "Regional Migration Governance." In *The Oxford Handbook of Comparative Regionalism*, edited by Tanja A. Börzel and Thomas Risse, 475–85. New York: Oxford University Press.

Lavenex, Sandra. 2019. "Regional Migration Governance: Building Block of Global Initiatives?" *Journal of Ethnic and Migration Studies* 45 (8): 1275–93.

Loescher, Gil, Alexander Betts, and James Milner. 2008. *The United Nations High Commissioner for Refugees: The Politics and Practice of Refugee Protection into the Twenty-first Century*. New York: Routledge.

Macdonald, Laura. 2019. "Canadian Development Assistance to Latin America." In A Samaritan State Revisited: Historical Perspective in Canadian Foreign Aid, edited by Greg Donaghy and David Webster, 273–92. Calgary: University of Calgary Press.

Malit, Froilan T., and Gerasimos Tsourapas. 2021. "Weapons of the Weak? South–South Migration and Power Politics in the Philippines–GCC Corridor." *Global Studies Quarterly* 1 (3): 1–11.

Martin, Philip. 2015. "Guest or Temporary Foreign Worker Programs." In Handbook of the Economics of International Migration, edited by Barry R. Chiswick and Paul W. Miller, 717–74. London: Elsevier.

Martin, Susan, and Sanjula Weerasinghe. 2017. "Global Migration Governance: Existing Architecture and Recent Developments." In *IOM World Migration Report 2018*. Geneva: International Organization for Migration. https://publications.iom.int/books/world-migration-report-2018-chapter-5-global-migration-governance-existing-architecture-and. Accessed 1 June 2023.

McAuliffe, Marie. 2017. "Seeking the Views of Irregular Migrants: Decision Making, Drivers, and Migration Journeys." In *A Long Way to Go: Irregular Migration Patterns, Processes, Drivers and Decision-Making*, edited by Marie McAuliffe and Khalid Koser, 103–39. Acton, Australia: Australian National University.

McKenna, Peter. 2018. "Canada and Latin America: 150 Years Later." *Canadian Foreign Policy Journal* 24 (1): 18–38.

Micinski, Nicholas. 2018. "Refugee Policy as Foreign Policy: Iraqi and Afghan Refugee Resettlements to the US." *Refugee Survey Quarterly* 37 (3): 253–78.

Moch, Leslie Page. 2003. *Moving Europeans: Migration in Western Europe since 1650*. 2nd ed. Bloomington, IN: Indiana University Press.

Moore, Jen, and Manuel Perez Rocha. 2019. "Extraction Casino: Mining Companies Gambling with Latin American Lives and Sovereignty through Supranational Arbitration." Mining Watch Canada, Institute for Policy Studies, and Center for International Environmental Law. https://miningwatch.ca/sites/default/files/isds_report_final_0.pdf. Accessed 1 June 2023.

Muggah, Robert, and Katherine Aguirre Tobón. 2018. "Citizen Security in Latin America: Facts and Figures." Strategic Paper no. 33. Igarapé Institute. https://igarape.org.br/wp-content/uploads/2018/04/Citizen-Security-in-Latin-America-Facts-and-Figures.pdf. Accessed 1 June 2023.

Noël, Brigitte. 2017. "Dubious YouTube Videos May be Driving Haitians to Emigrate to Quebec." *VICE News*, 18 August 2017. https://www.vice.com/en/article/bjdp5z/dubious-youtube-videos-may-be-driving-haitians-to-emigrate-to-quebec. Accessed 1 June 2023.

Norwegian Refugee Council. 2017. "Comprehensive Refugee Response Framework – Honduras and El Salvador: Less Promises, More Solutions." Norwegian Refugee Council.

OAS (Organization of American States). 2015. *Indigenous Peoples, Afro-Descendant Communities, and Natural Resources: Human Rights Protection in the Context of Extraction, Exploitation, and Development Activities*. Inter-American Commission on Human Rights. http://www.oas.org/en/iachr/reports/pdfs/ExtractiveIndustries2016.pdf.

OECD (Organisation for Economic Co-operation and Development). 2018. *OECD Development Co-Operation Peer Reviews: Canada 2018*. Paris:

OECD Publishing. https://doi.org/10.1787/9789264303560-en. Accessed 1 June 2023.

Porter, Catherine. 2020. "Virus Hits Foreign Farmhands, Challenging Canada's Self-Image." *New York Times*, 11 October 2020. https://www.nytimes.com/2020/10/11/international-home/virus-hits-foreign-farmhands-challenging-canadians-self-image.html. Accessed 1 June 2023.

Radford, Jynnah, and Phillip Connor. 2019. "Canada Now Leads the World in Refugee Resettlement, Surpassing the US." *Fact Tank: News in the Numbers*. Pew Research Centre. https://www.pewresearch.org/fact-tank/2019/06/19/canada-now-leads-the-world-in-refugee-resettlement-surpassing-the-u-s/. Accessed 1 June 2023.

Ruhs, Martin. 2013. *The Price of Rights: Regulating International Labour Migration*. Princeton, NJ: Princeton University Press.

Ruhs, Martin, and Philip Martin. 2008. "Numbers vs. Rights: Trade-Offs and Guest Worker Programs." *International Migration Review* 42 (1): 249–65.

Salehyan, Idean, and Kirstian Gleditsch. 2006. "Refugees and the Spread of Civil War." *International Organization* 60 (2): 335–66.

Selee, Andrew, and Jessica Bolter. 2020. *An Uneven Welcome: Latin American and Caribbean Responses to Venezuelan and Nicaraguan Migration*. Washington, DC: Migration Policy Institute. https://www.migrationpolicy.org/research/latam-caribbean-responses-venezuelan-nicaraguan-migration. Accessed 1 June 2023.

Shamsie, Yasmine, and Ricardo Grinspun. 2010. "Missed Opportunity: Canada's Re-Engagement with Latin America and the Caribbean." *Canadian Journal of Latin American and Caribbean Studies* 35 (69): 171–99.

Silverman, Stephanie, and Amrita Hari. 2016. "Troubling the Fields: Choice, Consent, and Coercion of Canada's Seasonal Agricultural Workers." *International Migration* 54 (5): 91–104.

Smith, Craig Damian. 2020. "A Model for the World? Policy Transfer Theory and Challenges to 'Exporting' Private Sponsorship to Europe." In *Stranger to Neighbours: Private Refugee Sponsorship in Canada and Beyond*, edited by Shauna Labman and Geoffrey Cameron, 286–302. Montreal and Kingston: McGill-Queen's University Press.

– 2022. "Policy Change, Threat Perception, and Mobility Catalysts: The Trump Administration as Driver of Asylum Migration to Canada." *International Migration Review* (October): 1–32. https://doi.org/10.1177/01979183221112418.

– n.d. "Power Politics and the Refugee Compact in Central America: Host States, Containment, and the Absence of International Resettlement." *Journal of Immigrant and Refugee Studies* (forthcoming).

Stevenson, Verity. 2017. "Misleading Social Media Messages Entice Haitian Asylum Seekers to Come to Canada." CBC *News*, 5 August 2017. https://www.cbc.ca/news/canada/montreal/misleading-information-haitian-asylum-seekers-1.4235565. Accessed 1 June 2023.

Stockemer, Daniel. 2016. "Structural Data on Immigration or Immigration Perceptions: What Accounts for the Electoral Success of the Radical Right in Europe?" *Journal of Common Market Studies* 54 (4): 999–1016.

Thielemann, Eiko. 2018. "Why Refugee Burden-Sharing Initiatives Fail: Public Goods, Free-Riding and Symbolic Solidarity in the EU." *Journal of Common Market Studies* 56 (1): 63–82.

Triandafyllidou, Anna, Laura Bartolini, and Caterina Francesca Guidi. 2019. *Exploring the Links between Enhancing Regular Pathways and Discouraging Irregular Migration: A discussion paper to inform future policy deliberations*. Geneva: International Organization for Migration. https://publications.iom.int/system/files/pdf/exploring_the_links_2019.pdf. Accessed 1 June 2023.

Triandafyllidou, Anna, and Lucia Nalbandian. 2020. "Can the COVID-19 Crisis be an Opportunity for Canada's Migrant Farmworkers?" *Open Democracy*, 5 August 2020. https://www.opendemocracy.net/en/pandemic-border/can-the-covid-19-crisis-be-an-opportunity-for-canadas-migrant-farmworkers/. Accessed 1 June 2023.

Tsourapas, Gerasimos. 2018. "Labor Migrants as Political Leverage: Migration Interdependence and Coercion in the Mediterranean." *International Studies Quarterly* 62 (2): 383–95.

UFCW (United Food and Commercial Workers Union Canada). 2020. *The Status of Migrant Farm Workers in Canada, 2020. Special Report: Marking Three Decades of Advocacy on Behalf of Canada's Most Exploited Workforce*. UFCW Canada and the Agricultural Workers Alliance. http://www.ufcw.ca/templates/ufcwcanada/images/awa/publications/UFCW-Canada-Status-of-Migrant-Workers-Report-2020.pdf. Accessed 1 June 2023.

– 2018. *Evaluation of Effectiveness of the Protection Transfer Arrangement in Central America*. UNHCR. https://www.unhcr.org/research/evalreports/5c7e63064/evaluation-effectiveness-protection-transfer-arrangement-central-america.html. Accessed 1 June 2023.

– 2020. *North of Central America Situation as of July 2020*. UNHCR. https://reporting.unhcr.org/sites/default/files/North%20of%20Central%20America%20Situation%20Funding%20Update%2009%20July%202020.pdf. Accessed 1 June 2023.

– 2021. *Global Appeal 2021 Update - Regional Summaries: The Americas*. UNHCR. https://reporting.unhcr.org/files/ga2021/pdf/Chapter_Americas.pdf. Accessed 1 June 2023.

– 2022. "Venezuela Situation." UNHCR. https://www.unhcr.org/en-us/venezuela-emergency.html. Accessed 1 June 2023.

van Selm, Joanne. 2018. "The Strategic Use of Resettlement: Enhancing Solutions for Greater Protection?" In *Refugee Resettlement: Power, Politics, and Humanitarian Governance*, edited by Adèle Garnier, Liliana Lyra Jubilut, and Kristin Bergtora Sandvik, 31–45. New York: Berghahn Books.

Volgy, Thomas J., Paul Bezerra, Jacob Cramer, and J. Patrick Rhamey. 2017. "The Case for Comparative Regional Analysis in International Politics." *International Studies Review* 19 (3): 452–80.

Wells, Don, Janet McLaughlin, André Lin, and Aaraón Díaz Mendiburo. 2014. "Sustaining Precarious Transnational Families: The Significance of Remittances from Canada's Seasonal Agricultural Workers Program." *Just Labour* 22 (Autumn): 143–67.

Wohlforth, William C., Benjamin de Carvalho, Halvard Leira, and Iver B. Neumann. 2017. "Moral Authority and Status in International Relations: Good Sates and the Social Dimension of Status Seeking." *Review of International Studies* 44 (3): 1–21.

Working Group on Mining and Human Rights in Latin America. 2014. *The Impact of Canadian Mining in Latin American and Canada's Responsibility*. Report submitted to the Inter-American Commission on Human Rights. http://www.dplf.org/sites/default/files/report_canadian_mining_executive_summary.pdf. Accessed 1 June 2023.

World Bank. 2019. *Leveraging Economic Migration for Development: A Briefing for the World Bank Board*. Washington, DC: World Bank. https://www.worldbank.org/en/topic/labormarkets/brief/migration-and-remittances. Accessed 1 June 2023.

Wright, Chris F., Dimitria Groutsis, and Diane van den Boek. 2017. "Employer-Sponsored Temporary Labour Migration Schemes in Australia, Canada, and Sweden: Enhancing Efficiency, Compromising Fairness?" *Journal of Ethnic and Migration Studies* 43 (11): 1854–72.

Yeates, Neil. 2018. "Report of the Independent Review of the Immigration and Refugee Board: A Systems Management Approach to Asylum." Government of Canada. https://www.canada.ca/en/immigration-refugees-citizenship/corporate/publications-manuals/report-independent-review-immigration-and-refugee-board.html. Accessed 1 June 2023.

Zimmerman, Susan E. 2009. "Irregular Secondary Movements to Europe: Seeking Asylum beyond Refuge." *Journal of Refugee Studies* 22 (1): 74–96.

Zoetweij-Turhan, Margarite Helena. 2017. "The Seasonal Workers Directive: '… but some are more equal than others.'" *European Labour Law Journal* 8 (1): 28–44.

13

Development Aid as Migration Control: Comparing Migration Management Aid in Central America and Africa

Ana Martín Gil, Nicholas R. Micinski, and Kelsey P. Norman

From 2007 to 2019, states of the Global North spent almost USD 130 billion on development aid to manage migration from developing countries, which increased from USD 5 billion to USD 18 billion annually over that period. Global North states increasingly leverage development aid as a means of preventing out-migration from the Global South. This chapter conceptualizes migration management aid as an emerging subcategory of foreign aid that purports to address the "root causes" of migration through economic development and democracy promotion, but which also aims to minimize both regular and irregular migration from countries of origin and transit (Norman and Micinski 2022). We include funding from Global North donor countries, as well as aid directed through international organizations, such as the United Nations High Commissioner for Refugees (UNHCR) and the International Organization for Migration (IOM), which ultimately attempts to control, regulate, and manage migration.

Specifically, this chapter compares the strategic use of development aid to control migration from two Global South regions: Mexico/Central America and Africa. In 2015, the EU created the EUR 5 billion European Union Emergency Trust Fund for Africa (EUTF), dedicated to addressing the root causes of migration and reducing irregular movement across North and sub-Saharan Africa. Similarly, President Biden proposed USD 4 billion in aid in 2021 to address the root causes of migration in Central America. However, both the US and EU have a long history of leveraging aid and conditionality to attempt to manage migration. Further, neither of these regional attempts to control migration through the provision of development aid can be disconnected from broader histories of colonialism and imperialism enacted by both the US and the EU toward Central America and Africa, respectively. Discourses of state incapacity and failure have been used to justify intervention for decades – whether in the form of military presence, direct rule, or conditional development aid – and migration management aid builds on such legacies by intrinsically linking the issues of migration and security (Adamson 2006; Weiner 1992). Since 11 September 2001 as well as after the bombings in Madrid in 2004 and in London in 2005, the migration-security nexus has been further solidified, further justifying development activities that focus on securing borders, increasing surveillance mechanisms and intervening in the domestic political and economic systems of Global South states in the name of migration prevention (Deridder, Pelckmans, and Ward 2020).

Through a historical comparison of recent decades of migration management aid and an analysis of the project-level data of the Organisation for Economic Co-operation and Development (OECD; 2007–19), we show how this form of aid distributed by the US toward Mexico and Central America and by the EU toward Africa utilized similar logics of intervention that failed to account for theories of migration and empirical lessons that help understand how migration and development are not substitutes for one another, or the lived experiences of migrants. Instead, migration management aid externalizes or projects migration policies from the Global North to the Global South. While this is done in the name of addressing the root causes of migration and promoting development, it fails to change the structural drivers of migration within regional corridors.

DEVELOPMENT AID AND THE ROOT CAUSES OF MIGRATION

The emphasis by US and EU officials on the root causes of migration over the last several decades is based on the assumption that most people emigrate because of poverty or the lack of economic opportunities. For example, in 2006, the European Commission (2006, 5) asserted that, "The prime challenge is to tackle the main push factors for migration: poverty and lack of employment opportunities. The EU must recognise that creating jobs in developing countries could significantly reduce migratory pressure from Africa." Similarly, in the US after the upswing of unaccompanied minors travelling from Central American countries to the US border in 2014, President Obama declared that "we have to do more to address the root causes of the problem, and that includes poverty and violence in Central America" (The White House 2014c). More recently, the Biden administration highlighted that "poverty and economic inequality, pervasive crime and corruption, and political leaders' drift toward authoritarian rule [in Central America] have stunted economic growth and diverted critical resources from healthcare and education, robbing citizens of hope and spurring migration" (The White House 2021e, 5). For both the US and the EU, the resulting policy prescription was to fund development aid in order to grow the economies of migrant-producing countries and thus reduce poverty, hoping to remove a "root cause" of emigration.

While seemingly common sense, most economists and migration scholars do not find empirical support for these ideas because policymakers overlook two key concepts: the migration transition and wage differentials. The migration transition describes the inverse U relationship between economic development and emigration – studies show that as per-capita GDP grows in lower-income countries, emigration actually increases until the GDP reaches about USD 11,389, at which point emigration begins to decrease (Berthélemy, Beuran, and Maurel 2009).[1] Scholars explain that as economies improve, people have more resources to emigrate; it is not until a country reaches an upper-middle-income level that development could reduce emigration (Clemens 2014; Telli 2014). As such, because economic and human development increases people's capabilities and aspirations, development tends to coincide with an increase, rather than a decrease, in emigration in the short to medium term (de Haas 2007).

Of course, people *do* move for employment, but a key pull factor is wage differentials, and not poverty, between labour markets in the Global North and Global South. For example, an individual might attempt to relocate because they can be paid around USD 12 per hour in San Diego instead of USD 3 per hour in Tijuana – simply crossing the US border increases Mexican-born workers' wages by 4.15 times (Aguayo-Téllez and Rivera-Mendoza 2011). But to address wage differentials as a root cause of migration, development aid would need to reduce inequality and fundamentally restructure the global economy. Migration-development aid (M-D aid), as proposed, lacks the scale, ambition, and political will for addressing the economic push and pull factors for emigration.

Nevertheless, policymakers in North America and Europe promote a root causes narrative in the hopes that development aid will solve their migration problems. This is partly because the message is politically appealing in liberal democratic states. Leaders can promote strategies that claim to be in the best interests of would-be migrants, helping them to avoid the perils of dangerous irregular migration routes, which is more politically palatable than promoting repressive border policies. It is also less of a domestic political challenge to externalize the issue of migration and attempt to stem migration at its source, rather than reform the immigration and asylum systems of liberal democratic states. Another complicating factor is that international organizations, including UNHCR and IOM, are highly reliant on project-based funding, thus creating a vested interest in root causes narratives and the assertion that development projects have the potential to prevent future migration. Migration scholars have critiqued the root causes discourse by documenting the complex and often layered reasons for migration decisions, including conflict, persecution, climate change, familial and social networks, and educational opportunities (Carling 2017; Carling and Talleraas 2016; Kugiel et al. 2020). However, development aid rarely targets these factors for migration.

Over the last twenty years, migration and development have become increasingly institutionalized within the UN system. Peter Sutherland was appointed in 2006 as the UN Special Representative on International Migration and Development and coordinated the first High-level Dialogue on International Migration and Development. Following the dialogue, the Global Forum on Migration and Development (GFMD) was created outside of the UN system because the member states could not agree to discuss the contentious issue of migration (Lebon-McGregor 2020). The GFMD focused on the positive contributions of migrants to development through remittances and investments. Later, migration was integrated into the UN Sustainable Development Goals (SDGs) in Target 10.7: "facilitate orderly, safe, and responsible migration and mobility of people, including through implementation of planned and well-managed migration policies." The 2016 NY Declaration for Refugees and Migrants and the 2018 Global Compacts further institutionalized migration within the UN development system. For example, the Global Compact for Safe, Orderly, and Regular Migration (GCM) recommends that states "minimize the adverse drivers and structural factors that compel people to leave their country of origin"[2] and the Global Compact on Refugees (GCR) emphasizes the importance of development aid to refugee hosting communities (Micinski 2021, 112–13). Both compacts recommend capacity building and call for aid and technology transfers to migrant-sending states in the Global South.

Despite the mainstreaming of migration and development in the US, the EU, and the UN policy spheres, migration management aid does not have purely altruistic motives. Migration management aid is part of wider portfolios of foreign aid and diplomatic strategies used to externalize migration policies by incentivizing or coercing states in the Global South into closing their borders and limiting mobility to the Global North. In the next section, we describe how the US and EU leveraged foreign aid to restrict migration from Central America and Africa. In both regions, large development aid packages were conditionally linked to readmission agreements, reform of domestic migration policies, and cooperation on security and counterdrug operations.

BACKGROUND AND CONTEXT

The United States and Mexico/Central America

US administrations have used different formulas for providing foreign aid to Mexico and Central American countries over the last several decades. The US has transitioned from foreign aid and technical assistance linked to geopolitical issues – such as addressing the spread of communism or countering narcotics – to the more recent M-D aid approach, similar to that of the EU. The US-Mexico migration partnership goes back to the twentieth century, when the Bracero Program[3] was established and the North American Free Trade Agreement (NAFTA)[4] was signed. In terms of migration prevention, the partnership materialized in 1989, when the US Immigration and Naturalization Service (INS) began cooperating with Mexico to decrease the number of migrants from Central America transiting through Mexican territory (Frelick, Kysel, and Podkul 2016). While bilateral migration relations between the US and Mexico have changed over time, most have the common theme of externalizing migration control; i.e., the US provides financial assistance to Mexico under the condition of controlling Central American migration across the border with Guatemala.

Direct aid to Central America started in the 1980s with the US providing USD 12.8 billion in aid to Central American governments – 43 per cent of which went to El Salvador to fight leftist insurgencies. While the broader goal was to combat Soviet influence in the region, deterring migration was also part of the strategy, as revealed by President Reagan's declarations during a public address: "Concerns about the prospect of hundreds of thousands of refugees fleeing Communist oppression to seek entry into our country are well-founded" (The Ronald Reagan Presidential Library and Museum 1984).

With the dissolution of the Soviet Union and the abating of civil conflicts in Central America, US aid declined in the mid-1990s (Meyer and Martin 2021; Meyer and Sullivan 2012). But in the late 1990s, US foreign aid to the region began to increase again and remained high through 2010, as a result of increased spending on humanitarian and development assistance. This was mainly due to Hurricane Mitch in 1998, which led the US to provide extensive humanitarian and reconstruction assistance to Central America (Meyer and Martin 2021). Despite the general decline in aid to Central America during the 2000s, Honduras, Nicaragua, and El Salvador were awarded Millennium Challenge Corporation (MCC) compacts in 2005 and 2006 (Brown 2019). The MCC compacts are "five-year agreements through which the United States provides grants to partner countries to support programs to reduce poverty through economic growth" (Millennium Challenge Corporation 2022a). For example, the MCC supported the Guatemalan government with USD 20 million for improved education and USD 5.8 million to prevent tax evasion and corruption (Millennium Challenge Corporation 2022b).

Mexico has historically received large amounts of counterdrug assistance from the United States, although these amounts were limited between the mid-1980s and mid-2000s (Seelke and Klein 2022). The same kind of assistance to Central America did not start until the end of the George W. Bush administration in an effort to address violence and crime in the region (Meyer 2019). The Mérida Initiative was created in October 2007 and established a package of US counter-narcotics and anti-crime assistance for Central America and Mexico (Seelke 2009). The original goals of the Mérida Initiative were to: "1) break the power and impunity of criminal organizations; 2) assist the Mexican and Central American governments in strengthening border, air, and maritime controls; 3) improve the capacity of justice systems in the region; and, 4) curtail gang activity in Mexico and Central America and diminish the demand for drugs in the region" (Seelke 2009, 2). During its initial phase, the Mérida Initiative largely focused on counter-narcotics and border security, but both directly restricted the movement of people. For instance, in order to reduce violence and crime, the US provided funding for inspection equipment and canine units to interdict trafficked drugs and arms, but also people (Seelke 2009; Seelke and Finklea 2017).

In 2010, the Obama administration decided to reformulate the Central America portion of Mérida and created the Central America Regional Security Initiative (CARSI). CARSI funds activities to support US and Central American security objectives – from providing training, technical assistance, and equipment to end organized crime and intercept narcotics to capacity building of Central American law enforcement and justice sectors (Meyer and Sullivan 2012). In 2011, the Obama administration expanded the framework of the Mérida Initiative and divided it into four pillars of security assistance, one of them being the creation of a "21st century border" to reduce the number of irregular migrants and goods from reaching the US border. Under this pillar, USD 130 million were allocated to training and equipment for the modernization and securitization of Mexico's borders, half of which was allocated to the Mexican southern border with Guatemala. As part of the initiative, Mexico's migration control databases were upgraded – under the condition that the information would be shared with the US (FitzGerald 2019; Seelke 2021). Funds were provided to Mexico to "develop an automated, interagency biometrics system to help agencies collect, store, and share information on criminals and migrants" (Seelke and Finklea 2017, 15). The ultimate purpose was to "track all persons entering and exiting Mexico, via air, land and sea" and "enable appropriate information sharing" with US agencies such as the Department of Homeland Security (DHS) (quoted in FitzGerald 2019).

Around 2014, the US started taking more significant steps to manage migration coming from Northern Triangle countries – namely, Guatemala, Salvador, and Honduras (Cheatham 2021). While migrants arriving to the US had traditionally originated from Mexico, that started to change around 2012, when migration from Central America accelerated, and peaked in 2014. The demographics of arrivals shifted from Mexican male migrants seeking work in the US to Central American families and children looking for safety (Meissner 2020). For instance, since 2012, most of the unaccompanied minors apprehended at the US-Mexico border came from Central American countries rather than Mexico (Meyer and Seelke 2015). To address the situation, the Obama administration implemented several aid programs in the region. The administration provided USD 40 million for a five-year US Agency for International Development (USAID) program in Guatemala with the purpose of "reduc[ing] the risk factors for youth involvement in gangs and address[ing] factors driving migration to the United States" (The White House 2014a). Another USD 25 million USAID program was funded in El Salvador to prevent crime and violence, offering "services to at-risk youth who are susceptible to gang recruitment and potential migration" (The White House 2014a). In response, the Northern Triangle governments enacted policies to bolster the US strategy to deter migration. The three countries launched several awareness campaigns in 2014, warning citizens of the dangers of undertaking the journey to the US and discouraging irregular migration (The White House 2014b).

To respond to the increase of unaccompanied Central American minors seeking asylum at the US border, the US government deployed Operation Coyote in 2014, aimed at reducing the number of irregular migrants from the Northern Triangle. Within the framework of this operation, investigators from DHS were sent to Mexico and Central America to provide intelligence and support efforts against human trafficking and smuggling (Frelick, Kysel, and Podkul 2016). Bilateral cooperation was further strengthened the same year, when the Mexican government launched Programa Frontera Sur (Southern Border Program). This program created the Office of Coordination for Comprehensive Migration Assistance at the Southern Border, within the Mexican Ministry of the Interior, to coordinate migration and border management, and deployed federal officials to the Mexican southern border. To support this program, the US government provided training for Mexican agents, scanning units, and paid for canine patrols and mobile migration control posts (FitzGerald 2019; Frelick, Kysel, and Podkul 2016;).

After the upswing in migration from Central America, the Obama administration also launched the US Strategy for Engagement in Central America in 2014, primarily addressed toward El Salvador, Guatemala, and Honduras (Meyer 2019). Its purpose was to stimulate economic prosperity, bolster governance, and increase security in the region, as the US government considered that increased migration was a result of the inability to find solutions to these challenges (Obama White House 2022). It is important to note that US aid to El Salvador, Guatemala, and Honduras provided within the framework of this strategy has been subject to certain conditions since 2016.[5] For example, in 2018, it was stipulated that 25 per cent of the assistance would be withheld until the Secretary of State certified that "each government was informing its citizens of the dangers of the journey to the southwest border of the United States" and "cooperating with US government agencies and other governments in the region to facilitate the return, repatriation, and reintegration of illegal migrants arriving at the southwest border of the United States who do not qualify for asylum, consistent with international law" (Meyer 2019, 14–15).

During his time in office, President Trump left the Strategy for Engagement in Central America in place, but the amount of foreign assistance requested from Congress for the Northern Triangle significantly decreased – from USD 507 million in 2016 to USD 181 million in 2019 (US Department of State and USAID 2021). In response to the spike in Central American asylum seekers coming to the US in caravans, Trump threatened to withdraw foreign aid to Northern Triangle countries. In March 2019, foreign aid to Guatemala, El Salvador, and Honduras was finally suspended under the premise that these countries were not taking concrete actions to address the arrival of irregular migrants and asylum seekers, or in Trump's words, "Mexico is doing nothing to help stop the flow of illegal immigrants to our country. They are all talk and no action. Likewise, Honduras, Guatemala and El Salvador have taken our money for years, and do nothing" (Lind 2019). The funds were withheld for over a year while the US negotiated several agreements and arrangements with Central American countries to curb migration (Meyer 2021). Throughout 2019, the US signed Asylum Cooperative Agreements (ACAs), also known as safe third country agreements, with Guatemala, El Salvador, and Honduras.[6] These agreements were another way of externalizing migration control, as they allowed the US to send asylum seekers back to countries they transited through on their way to the US without giving them the chance to apply for asylum.

Although a third country agreement between the US and Mexico never came to fruition, both countries signed the US-Mexico Joint Declaration in June 2019. With this agreement, Mexico committed to deploy its National Guard throughout Mexico, particularly to its southern border, to prevent migrants coming from the Northern Triangle from transiting through Mexico and reaching the US (for a related discussion of these dynamics, see Ferris and Matheson in this volume). Mexico also agreed to accept further returns of non-Mexican asylum seekers as part of the Migrant Protection Protocols (MPP) – a program implemented in January 2019 which returns migrants crossing the border irregularly to Mexico while they wait for their asylum claims to be assessed (Ruiz Soto 2020).

More recently, the Biden administration has shown its commitment to scaling up US assistance programs in the region and strengthening cooperation with Mexico.[7] On 2 February 2021, President Biden signed an executive order with the purpose of creating a Comprehensive Regional Framework "to address the causes of migration, to manage migration throughout North and Central America, and to provide safe and orderly processing of asylum seekers at the United States border" ("Exec. Order No. 14010, 86 Fed. Reg. 8267" 2021). The executive order tasked government officials with the creation of the United States Strategy for Addressing the Root Causes of Migration (the Root Causes Strategy) and the United States Strategy for Collaboratively Managing Migration in the Region (the Collaborative Management Strategy). The Collaborative Management Strategy was released in July 2021 as the "first US government strategy focused on strengthening cooperative efforts to manage safe, orderly, and humane migration in North and Central America" (The White House 2021a). It called for "a surge of humanitarian assistance to alleviate conditions in the region; messaging campaigns to deter irregular migration; support for partner governments' efforts to manage their borders, provide protection to vulnerable populations, and reintegrate returned migrants; and expanded access to legal migration and protection pathways in the United States and third countries" (Meyer 2022, 2). While the outcomes of this strategy remain to be seen, this exemplifies an important consolidation of the migration-development framework in the US context.

Whereas the Collaborative Management Strategy addresses short-term migration management policies, the Root Causes Strategy – also published in July 2021 – focuses on long-term socioeconomic, security, and governance issues (Meyer 2022). The strategy revolves around five pillars: combating corruption and strengthening the rule of law, promoting the respect for human rights, fighting organized crime and trafficking networks, reducing inequality and addressing economic insecurity, and combating sexual and domestic violence (The White House 2021b). In November 2021, USAID announced a USD 300 million initiative under the Root Causes Strategy "to empower local organizations in El Salvador, Guatemala, and Honduras to address the drivers of irregular migration to the United States" (USAID 2021). The initiative includes multiple programs geared toward bolstering economic growth, combating corruption, improving governance, and advancing human rights.

The European Union and Africa

In contrast to the US, M-D aid became a popular tool for EU policymakers as early as the 1980s because of its role in the externalization of EU migration policies. When the European Union created the Schengen area – an internal zone of free movement among EU member states – in 1985, it took steps to seal itself off from non-EU migration via externalization, which is the process by which the EU transfers its preferred policies to neighbouring states (Lavenex 2008; Lavenex and Schimmelfennig 2009). The concept is closely associated with "Fortress Europe" – referring to Europe's efforts to close off both regular and irregular migration routes – because it outsources or offloads responsibility for migration management to countries outside of the Schengen area in order to increase the internal security of the EU. The EU has pursued externalization through three primary strategies: accession negotiations, readmission agreements, and M-D aid.

As part of the accession process, neighbouring countries that wished to join the EU and Schengen area have been required to align their migration policies with the EU, particularly related to fighting irregular migration and human trafficking (Boswell 2007). The EU negotiated stabilization and association agreements by laying out the required reforms, but candidate states could not negotiate opt-outs for the Schengen zone, as that would require a rewriting of all Schengen policies (Grabbe 2000). EU accession conditionality was effective: throughout the EU's eastern enlargement, conditionality was applied to require the Czech Republic, Latvia, Lithuania, Estonia, Hungary, Poland, Slovakia, and Slovenia to pass the EU *acquis* on immigration, eventually leading to their admission to the EU (Mitsilegas 2002).

In an early version of M-D aid, funding was available via the PHARE (Pologne-Hongrie Actions pour la Reconversion Économique) and TACIS (Technical Assistance to the Commonwealth of Independent States) programs to support the adoption of stronger border control measures and systems for managing asylum for Central and Eastern European candidate countries and to the New Independent States (the eleven members of the Commonwealth of Independent States and Georgia). Assistance under PHARE was wide-ranging, beginning with humanitarian assistance and emergency aid to technical assistance for economic and social restructuring, and finally to assistance with specific harmonization requirements in order to facilitate accession (Matthews 1994). In the field of migration, "The bulk of the EU's aid provision – as with the demands in the Accession Partnership – [was] concerned with reinforcing controls on the candidates' frontiers, which [became] the new external borders of the enlarged Union" (Lavenex and Uçarer 2002).

In contrast, funding under TACIS was never meant to encourage or facilitate accession; rather, assistance was meant to support "individual states to develop effectively functioning market economies based on private ownership and initiative, and to encourage the development of pluralistic democratic societies" (European Commission 1992). Europe continues to utilize this type of "conditionality-lite" assistance in its EU Neighbourhood Policy with countries that are unlikely to ever become accession candidates (Sasse 2008). The 2007–13 European Neighbourhood and Partnership Instrument (ENPI) awarded EUR 13.4 billion in aid, while the 2014–20 European Neighbourhood Instrument (ENI) channelled EUR 15.4 billion in aid for sixteen countries in the region.[8] The ENPI and ENI both use conditionality through "incentive-based" rewards in which more reforms were rewarded with more aid (European Commission 2014).

The second approach to externalization was through the proliferation of readmission agreements, whereby third countries accept the deportation of their nationals – and sometimes the nationals of other countries – from the EU. In 2005, the EU agreed to the Global Approach to Migration (GAM) and again in 2011 the Global Approach to Migration and Mobility (GAMM), both of which laid out a common European approach to cooperating with other states on migration policies. The EU used policy instruments such as migration profiles, migration missions, cooperation platforms on migration and development, and mobility partnerships to initiate dialogue with migrant-sending and transit states (Cardwell 2013). The goal of these dialogues was to increase cooperation on controlling irregular migration and, ultimately, to sign readmission agreements. The readmission agreements often detail fast-track deportation processes and arrangements for regular communication and cooperation between the EU and other governments' officials. The first mobility partnerships were signed with Moldova (2008), Cape Verde (2008), Georgia (2009), Armenia (2011), Morocco (2013), Azerbaijan (2013), Jordan (2014), and Tunisia (2014). Scholars have questioned the overall impact of mobility partnerships and their implementation because of their focus on security of the EU over the interests of non-EU states (Menz 2011; Norman 2020; Reslow 2015; Reslow and Vink 2015).

The third approach to externalization has been through M-D aid, often linked to the reform of migration policies. The French government helped to pioneer the concept of M-D aid through its "co-development" policies[9] in the 1980s, in which France would cooperate to help migrants play a larger role in the development of their countries of origin. The early policies in the 1980s included training programs for Algerian migrants living in France who would agree to return to Algeria after their training was complete. These programs later began to support migrants before they arrived in France by sponsoring temporary training programs with the requirement of returning home to use their newly acquired skills (Magoni 2004). In the 1990s, the concept of M-D aid was picked up across Europe, and politicians began to advocate for development aid as a substitute for migration (de Haas 2007). In 1994, the then prime minister Rasmussen of Denmark proclaimed, "if you don't help the third world ... then you will have these poor people in our society" (quoted in de Haas 2007), and that same year the European ministers for development cooperation requested that the European Commission investigate the use of development aid to reduce migration to Europe.

This thinking continued into the next decade. The French government established the Consultation on Migration in 2000 with Mali with annual meetings between ministries on the co-management of migration and the return of Malians from France. France also established several funding schemes, one of which funded a nongovernmental organization (NGO) to create a handbook titled "Going Home and Doing Business" ["Se réinstaller et entreprendre au pays"] (Magoni 2004, 8). While some EU actors feared the development agenda and budgets would be coopted by security actors, Lavenex and Kunz (2008) argue that the frames "migration and security" and "migration and development" are not mutually exclusive and are often combined. The EU further embraced the framing of the M-D nexus as a response to increased international debate and the high-profile incidents of migrants scaling the fences between Morocco and the Spanish cities of Ceuta and Melilla in 2005. While many Europeans have become numb to violent skirmishes between European border guards and migrants today, the European public was shocked by images of Spanish and Moroccan authorities abusing migrants in Ceuta and Melilla in 2005. Just months later, the European Commission responded with proposals focused on closer cooperation with African governments through migration and development (European Commission 2005). The IOM and the International Labour Organization (ILO) began programs around migration and development including the Return of Talent Program and conferences on remittances in addition to increased debate at the World

Bank and the Global Commission on International Migration (Lavenex and Kunz 2008, 446–7). By 2006, at the EU-Africa Summit, governments signed the Joint Africa-EU Declaration on Migration and Development and in 2007 launched the "Africa-EU partnership on migration, mobility and employment."

However, it was not until 2015 that M-D aid moved to the centre of the EU's externalization strategy. In early August of that year, the UNHCR announced that 250,000 migrants had arrived in Europe by sea: 124,000 in Greece and 98,000 in Italy. By the end of the year, approximately one million individuals arrived in Europe by sea – three to four times more than in 2014 – the majority (about 800,000) of whom arrived in Greece, rather than Italy (Holland 2015). In response, the EU hosted the Valletta Summit on Migration in November 2015 and created the EUTF worth approximately EUR 5 billion to fund projects that address the root causes of migration. The purpose of the EUTF was to "contribute to better migration management as well as address the root causes of destabilisation, forced displacement and irregular migration, in particular by promoting resilience, economic and equal opportunities, security and development and addressing human rights' abuses" (European Commission 2015). Building on the EUTF, the European Commission launched a new Migration Partnership Framework in 2016 that directly connects migration to the EU's foreign policy goals and the externalization of EU migration policies (European Commission 2016). The Migration Partnership Framework seeks to engage countries of origin in dialogue with the goal of signing compacts on issues as broad as energy, security, development aid, migration, and digital policy. The framework is another part of the process of externalization that leverages large amounts of M-Daid through the EUTF.

With the EUTF, M-D aid has moved from the background of externalization – behind the accession process and readmission agreements – to the foreground. This is partly a response to criticisms that externalization prioritized the EU's security over the well-being of African nationals. In this way, M-Daid was used to compensate, at least at face value, for the EU's harsh migration policies with supposedly generous development aid. Despite the EU's shift in rhetoric, it is unclear if the EUTF, and M-D aid more generally, is actually funding development, or funding security projects that restrict migration under the guise of development aid (Micinski and Norman 2021).

Funding for European migration management aid is often channelled or negotiated through interior ministries, which supervise the budgets of border forces, immigration and asylum agencies, police departments, and security agencies. These aid schemes can be used to purchase new border and surveillance technologies and train border officers, in addition to funding biometric identification, civil registration, and police databases. For example, in Burkina Faso, the EUTF provided EUR 49 million to the government aimed to decrease migration by improving security and "strengthening the presence of the State in the Sahel region" (EUTF 2018b). The funding is intended to build "police stations, border police stations, regional judicial police services, republican security companies, territorial gendarmerie brigade, mobile gendarmerie barracks, group command posts and companies of gendarmerie" in the Sahel (EUTF 2018b). The security funding was packaged together with funding to improve basic social services such as increasing the number of drinking wells, health clinics, and ambulances. The danger is that funding security forces not only impacts migrants or would-be migrants, but can have spillover effects for citizens as well.

This dynamic is also evident through EUTF funds that aim to improve civil registration systems, which increase the capacity of recipient states to surveil communities, which can later be used for stronger taxation compliance and military conscription. Civil registration is typically paired with biometric databases that use fingerprints or iris scans to link individuals with their government files. In Côte d'Ivoire, the EU put EUR 30 million toward a biometric identity system that aims to register all citizens of the country, but the database will also be used by the EU to "facilitate the identification of people who are really of Ivorian nationality [in the EU] and organize their return more easily" (EUTF 2018a). The EU funded EUR 55 million in Morocco, EUR 28 million in Senegal, and EUR 5 million in Cape Verde and Guinea-Bissau to build similar biometric registration systems (EUTF 2018a). Migration management aid is used to develop and implement other technologies, including remote sensing and GIS (geographic information systems) technology for monitoring crops, police information exchanges, systems for detecting document fraud, and radar. Yet the flipside to increasing registration and monitoring is that the resulting surveillance of economic or political activities could be utilized by an authoritarian state to repress citizens via enhanced monitoring and tracking.

The EUTF officially ended in December 2021, but its aims were adopted into a new funding program called the "Neighbourhood Development and International Cooperation Instrument" (NDICI). With a budget line of EUR 79.5 billion, the NDICI will become the EU's "main tool to contribute to eradicating poverty and promoting sustainable development, prosperity, peace and stability" (European Commission 2022).

EMPIRICAL EVIDENCE

To further contrast the use of migration management aid in these two regions, we assess how development aid was spent on migration management in Central America and Africa over the last two decades. To do so, we utilized a dataset of official development aid (n = 1,639,266) using OECD project-level data from 2007–19. We created an indicator for migration management aid (MMaid) using a keyword search of project titles and their short and long descriptions. A grant was classified as migration management aid if the metadata had at least one of the following keywords: migrant, immigration, refuge, border, asylum, asylee, internally displaced person (IDP), remit, or diaspora. The MMaid subset returned a total of 51,429 grants, amounting to more than USD 129.7 billion in official development aid used for migration management during 2007–19. The following two case studies – one selected from each region – illustrate the types of projects that are included in our dataset.

CASE STUDY 1: YOUTH WORKFORCE DEVELOPMENT IN EL SALVADOR

"Bridges to Employment" was a five-year project (2015–20) funded by USAID aimed to improve El Salvador's workforce development system. It sought to integrate youth living in municipalities with high crime rates into the workforce, as USAID views unemployment as a major driver of irregular migration from the region (USAID 2019). USAID worked with job training institutions and Salvadorian youth aged between 16 and 29 years to improve their employability within high-growth sectors in the country. In addition to vocational training centres, partners for this project included the Ministry of Education, Ministry of Labour, National Youth Institute, municipal governments, and civil society organizations (CSOs). The project also encouraged companies to modify corporate policies and practices in order to support youth and other vulnerable groups. For example, Rotary Club member companies in El Salvador provided job opportunities for participating youth. The project also promoted youth policies related to education, health, civic participation, and employment, at both the national and municipal levels, and responded to the specific needs of youth – including youth with disabilities – in each community (USAID 2019).

CASE STUDY 2: AID FOR ETHIOPIAN DROUGHT-INDUCED FOOD INSECURITY

Ethiopian Drought-Induced Food Insecurity Relief is supported by EU funding, the Swedish International Development Agency (SIDA) partnered with the World Food Programme (WFP), Farm Africa, and Mercy Corps to provide aid to Ethiopia for a four-year project (2017–21), entitled "From Humanitarian Assistance to Resilience" (Openaid 2022). The project invested in disaster risk reduction as a result of recent droughts in Ethiopia that impacted 10 million people. SIDA contributed USD 9,145,868 (WFP 2018). This money was spent on improving irrigation resources, drought response systems, and market development in the region. Among the beneficiaries of the project were Somalian refugees in the Dollo Ado woreda (district) who suffered livestock losses of 37 per cent during each severe drought (Farm Africa 2022). As a result of the funding, Abdi Abdulahi, a member of one of the cooperatives created by Farm Africa and Mercy Corps, said he "was able to buy food for [his] extended family as they couldn't afford it due to the severe drought we faced this year" (Farm Africa 2020). The project illustrates how funders view the intersection of migration, climate change, and food insecurity in the region.

This is, of course, a rough approximation of migration management aid. It is possible that the keyword search sometimes includes grants that are only tangentially related to migration. For example, the words "refugee" or "migrant" could be included in a list of beneficiaries, rather than the main purpose of the grant. However, it is also possible our approximation is an underestimate, as grants aimed at controlling and minimizing migration via development may not explicitly state this goal in a project description. In 2018, the OECD Development Assistance Committee (DAC) established a new purpose code for the "Facilitation of orderly, safe, regular and responsible migration and mobility," defined as funding for states to manage migration, including border controls, labour migration, asylum, refugees and other displaced people, and voluntary return and reintegration. In 2018 and 2019, the DAC reported a total of USD 748 million (882 grants) as migration management aid. However, we argue that this total is almost certainly an underestimate because the DAC definition explicitly excludes grants targeting the "root causes of forced displacement and irregular migration."[10] Working toward a clearer definition and a means of

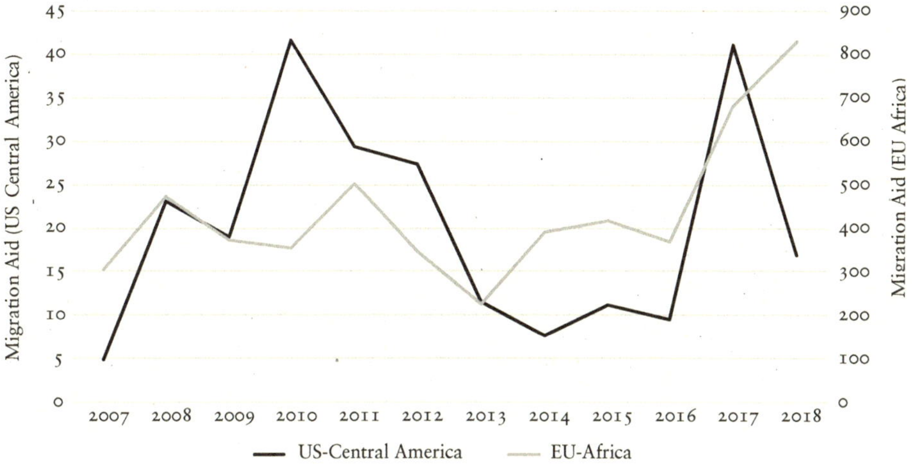

Figure 13.1 | EU and US migration management aid (2007–19)

Note: Figures are in million USD.

characterizing migration management aid, this chapter uses a broad definition and selection criteria in order to identify all development aid directed at controlling, regulating, and managing migration because – as identified in the previous section – policymakers in the US and EU directly connect aid to the supposed "root causes" of migration.

Overall, migration management aid has increased from USD 5.2 billion in 2007 to USD 18.4 billion in 2019. In 2007–19, we estimate that the US allocated USD 243.2 million in North and Central America on migration management, while the EU spent USD 5.9 billion in Africa. Figure 13.1 illustrates the changes in migration management funding by year. The EU's migration management aid to Africa followed the overall trend, increasing from USD 305 million in 2007 to USD 665 million in 2019. The peak in 2017 is explained by initial disbursements of EUTF funding across the continent, as well as other migration-related deals that proliferated in the wake of the 2015 refugee "crisis." However, the US's migration management aid to Central America varied considerably: aid peaked in 2010 at USD 42 million, but dropped drastically in the following years until rising again to USD 40 million in 2017. The spike in 2010 was due to two grants (totalling more than USD 11 million) to Mexico to strengthen and promote cooperation

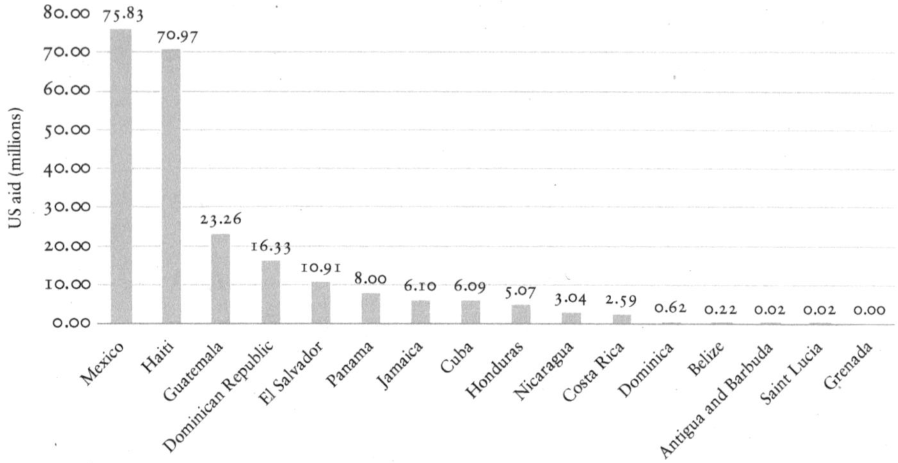

Figure 13.2 | Top recipient countries for aid by the US to Central America (2007–19)

Note: Figures are in million USD.

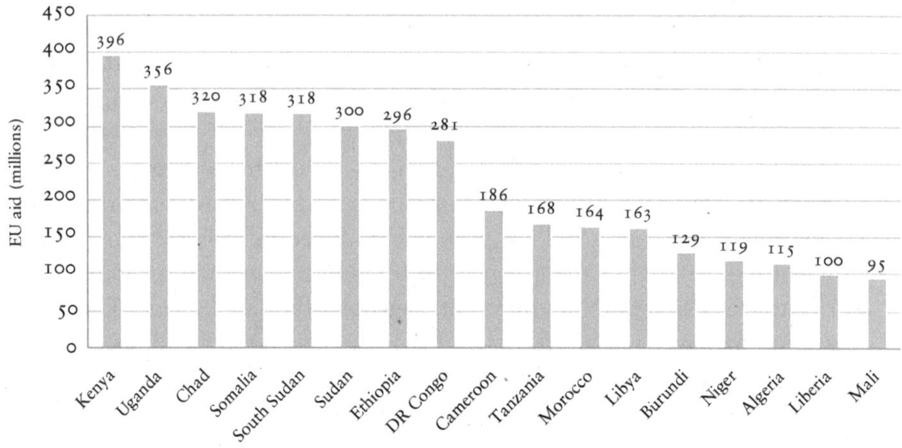

Figure 13.3 | Top recipient countries for aid by the EU to Africa (2007–19)

Note: Figures are in million USD.

among state legislative and executive branch institutions in Mexico and the US, particularly border legislation, and to build the capacity of the civil and criminal justice sector, including border security and police. Three relief assistance grants for Haiti in response to the 2010 earthquake (totalling more than USD 9 million) also contributed to the spike. The project that received the largest funding (close to USD 5 million) was implemented by the IOM to provide "support to communities hosting displaced Haitians in border areas and return assistance to Haitian earthquake victims in the [Dominican Republic]" (IOM 2010). The spike in 2017 was due to several grants of around USD 2 and USD 3 million each. The largest grant, financed by the Bureau of Population, Refugees, and Migration (PRM), was allocated to the Mesoamerica Regional Migration Program, implemented by the IOM to strengthen capacities for the protection and assistance of vulnerable migrants in the Northern Triangle, Costa Rica, Mexico, Nicaragua, and Panama.[11] Another grant was allocated to Cuba for the Migrant Support Program and three additional grants went to Haiti for relief coordination and support services.

We also examined disbursements of migration management aid by country in each region (figures 13.2 and 13.3). Unsurprisingly given its population, proximity to the US, and strategic importance, Mexico was the top recipient (31 per cent) of US migration management aid. Following this, Haiti received 29 per cent of US migration aid to the region from 2007 to 2019, and Guatemala received 9.5 per cent. The largest grants allocated to Guatemala had the purpose of improving the capacity and developing an effective and accountable justice system, in line with the US strategy to bolster governance in Central America. The Dominican Republic received 6.7 per cent of US aid, whereas other countries in Central America each received less than 5 per cent of the US allocation.

Kenya was the largest recipient of EU migration aid in Africa (see figure 13.3). The largest grants (USD 40.8 and USD 19.2 million) were from France and Germany, respectively, to provide food assistance to refugees in Kenya and increase the supply of drinking water in Nairobi, presumably to reduce the lack of food and water as a push factor. The EU provided significant investments (USD 28.7 million) in roads and infrastructure at the Kenya-Uganda border. Other grants went to direct food aid to refugees in the Dadaab camp, in addition to initiatives for self-reliance and economic integration in host communities. Interestingly, "frontline" countries geographically closer to the EU were not likely to receive more funding. Morocco, Algeria, and even Libya received less than 3 per cent each of the EU's disbursements. Overall, EU migration management funding has been fairly evenly distributed across African countries.

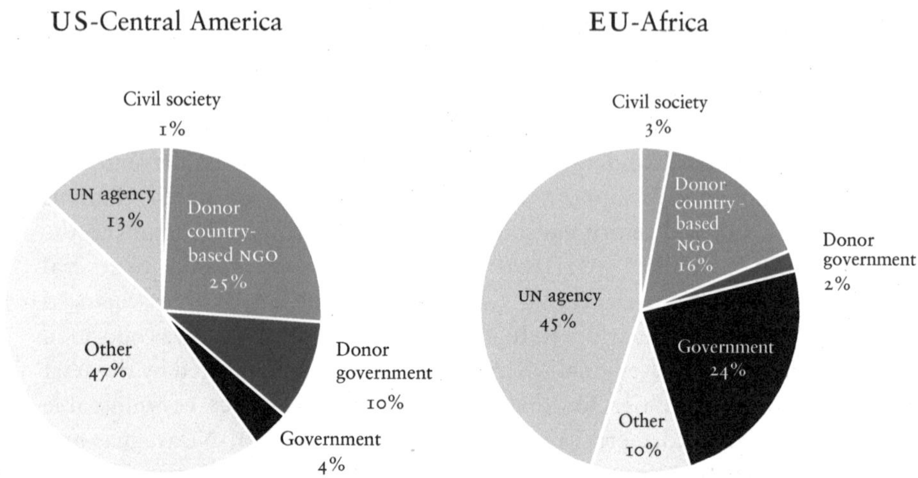

Figure 13.4 | Implementing partners of the US in Central America and the EU in Africa

We also compared the implementing partners utilized by the EU and the US (figure 13.4). One difference was that the EU relied heavily on UN agencies as implementing partners for migration management projects (45 per cent), followed by recipient governments that directly received 24 per cent of grants. The US relied less on UN agencies (13 per cent) and less on recipient governments (4 per cent). Instead, the US funnelled money to country-based donor NGOs (25 per cent) and an assortment of other categories such as consulting firms, private sector institutions, private-public partnerships, research institutes, and universities. The "other" category for US aid also included several projects focusing on justice systems in recipient countries that tended to distribute aid to private consulting firms which in turn funded actors including police, border security officials, prosecutors, forensics experts, judges, court personnel, public defenders, corrections personnel, private bar institutions, law schools, and legal professional associations. Another difference was that the US relied on its own government agencies to implement some projects (10 per cent), while only 2 per cent of EU grants went to EU agencies or EU member state governments for implementation.

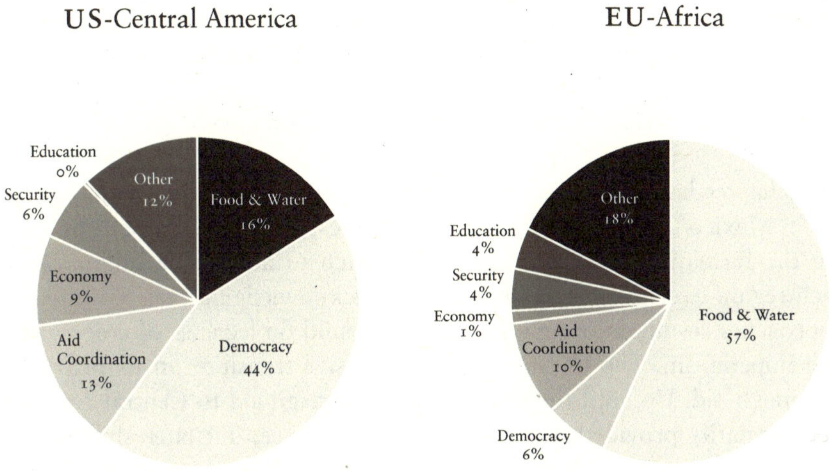

Figure 13.5 | Purposes of aid: US in Central America and EU in Africa

Finally, we examined the broad sectors that migration management aid purported to impact in each region (figure 13.5). For the EU's migration management funding to Africa, the vast majority of aid (57 per cent) went to direct material assistance (e.g., food and water). A much smaller proportion (less than 10 per cent in each category) was utilized for democracy promotion, economic development, and security. In contrast, the US allocated its largest percentage of migration aid (44 per cent) to democracy-related projects in Central America, in line with the narrative of addressing poor governance and corruption in the region. The US spent significantly less on food aid (16 per cent) and very little on education (0.3 per cent). Notably, the US invested USD 21.6 million (9 per cent) of its migration aid in economic development in Central America, while the EU only invested USD 77.3 million (1 per cent) of its migration aid in economic development.

Nonetheless, we should be skeptical of these categories, which may obscure the true nature and impact of aid on the ground. For example, if improving the provision of water to refugees also involves improving host state infrastructure, there may be tangible impacts for the economy or security of a host country not accounted for by the "food and water" category.

In addition, our dataset only includes official development aid related to migration management. Both the US and EU provided significant military and other foreign aid that is not reported in the OECD-DAC data.

DISCUSSION AND CONCLUSION

This chapter has compared the US and EU's use of migration management aid in Mexico/Central America and Africa, respectively. We began by tracing the formation of a root causes approach to addressing migration in each region over the last several decades, acknowledging that more recent approaches to migration management aid build on legacies of colonialism and imperialism. The US showed a progressive transition in its provision of foreign aid. Up until the mid-1990s, US foreign aid to Central America was primarily provided to prevent Soviet influence, but later shifted to a humanitarian and development tool that was partly aimed at preventing migration, especially after Hurricane Mitch in 1998. In the mid-2000s, much of US foreign assistance began to focus on counter-narcotics and anti-drug trafficking, conflating border security with the smuggling of both drugs and people, thereby linking foreign assistance with migration prevention. Finally, in 2014 under the Obama administration, the US started providing aid with the explicit goal of curbing migration, a strategy replicated and amplified under both the Trump and Biden administrations.

In the EU, France helped to pioneer the concept of migration-development aid through its co-development policies with former colonial countries. In the 1990s, the EU developed migration-development initiatives as part of its broader externalization efforts, especially through programs targeting candidate countries in Eastern Europe and the newly independent countries of the former Soviet Union. Later, in the mid-2000s and especially following the high-profile case of sub-Saharan African migrants scaling the fences dividing Morocco from Melilla and Ceuta, the EU doubled down on its border externalization efforts, including through the use of migration management aid. However, it was not until 2015 that M-Daid moved from the background to the foreground of externalization efforts with the EUTF for Africa.

Similarities in migration management between the EU and the US go beyond development aid (see Geddes in this volume for a related discussion). Both countries have used third-country cooperation as an externalization tool to deter migrants from leaving their home countries. A clear parallel can be established between the EU-Turkey deal and the ACA signed between the US and Guatemala during the Trump administration,[12] as both intended to return asylum seekers to another state that they transited. Both "safe third country" agreements were met with grave criticism as conditions for refugees in Turkey and violence in Guatemala called into question whether either of those countries could be considered safe. Although not considered a safe third country agreement, the EU-Turkey deal also bears resemblance to the MPP, commonly referred to as the Remain in Mexico program. Under the MPP, asylum seekers who crossed the border without authorization or who were undocumented could be forcibly returned to Mexico until their immigration court hearing. Similarly, anyone who arrived on the Greek islands irregularly from Turkey could be returned.

Making development aid to countries in Africa and Central America subject to conditionality is another strategy used by both the EU and the US. Those conditions included preventing migrants from leaving their home countries and reaching the Global North, subjecting countries of origin to accepting migrant returns, ramping up security and deploying military troops to apprehend migrants, or conducting advertising campaigns informing of the dangers of migratory journeys to deter migrants from leaving. In the US, 25 per cent of development aid to El Salvador, Guatemala, and Honduras in 2018 could not be obligated until those countries proved that they were improving their border security, which included preventing irregular migration, conducting awareness campaigns to halt outward migration, and collaborating on the return, repatriation, and reintegration of irregular migrants arriving at the southern US border.

In the EU, conditionality was part and parcel of Europe's externalization strategy since its inception. Migration partnerships and dialogues with third countries in Eastern Europe, the Balkans, and across North Africa often make trade deals or EU visa access contingent on border control and security efforts in order to prevent irregular migration toward Europe. However, a key difference is that Europe tends to rely on positive conditionality, whereas the US uses negative conditionality or the threat of punishment. For example, the EU incentivized Turkey to prevent irregular migration through the improvement of border controls and the construction of detention centres using the carrot of eventual EU accession. In contrast, the US has been more likely to threaten to cut off development aid to Mexico or Central American countries if they failed to adequately prevent irregular migration.

A final similarity identified in our analysis is the importance of critical moments in instigating a push for development aid as a "solution" to migration. In the EU context this occurred in 2005 with the highly-circulated footage of sub-Saharan African migrants scaling the fences between Morocco and Melilla in Spain. Similar calls were made for increasing development aid after the large increase in arrivals of asylum seekers in 2015 during Europe's refugee "crisis." In the US context, the increase of asylum seeker arrivals beginning in 2012 and peaking in 2014 spurred the Obama administration to work toward a number of development agreements with Central American countries in order to stem migration. Interestingly, in both the 2015 EU case and the 2014 US case, the change in demographics of those arriving – from mostly individual young men to families – coupled with the images of children's bodies washed ashore in the Mediterranean and children detained in cages in the US, pressured leaders to push for development aid as a "kinder, gentler" solution to preventing migration. In the context of families arriving and seeking asylum, development aid may appear more politically palatable than outright border control, even if in reality these strategies are implemented simultaneously.

NOTES

1 Note: this figure has been adjusted for inflation to US dollars in 2021.

2 GCM, Objective 2.

3 The Bracero Program was the first official labour program for temporary Mexican workers in the US, created in 1942 to address the labour shortage during World War II (see Library of Congress 2022).

4 Proponents of NAFTA in the US argued that the agreement would benefit Mexico's economy and create higher levels of employment which, in turn, would decrease "unwanted" migration and "keep Mexicans in Mexico" (see Jiménez Godinez 2013).

5 Imposing conditions on financial aid is a technique that goes back to the Clinton administration. In 1995, the US offered a loan to Mexico to prevent the collapse of the peso and "an increase in the flow of illegal immigrants across our borders" (see FitzGerald 2019).

6 Only the agreement with Guatemala was actually implemented during a short period of time. Under this agreement, non-Guatemalan migrants that had transited through Guatemala would be returned to that country under the premise that they could have applied for protection in Guatemala (see Meyer 2021).

7 Relations between the US and Mexico became strained during the Trump presidency but have improved since President Biden came to power. Biden and López Obrador (Mexican president) have expressed their commitment to work together in addressing the root causes of regional migration, improving migration management, and developing legal pathways for migration. In November 2021, both countries announced a joint investment in Central America that will address the root causes of migration and increase small farmers' incomes (see The White House 2021c and 2021d).

8 The sixteen countries the EU considers in their neighborhood are Armenia, Azerbaijan, Algeria, Belarus, Egypt, Georgia, Israel, Jordan, Lebanon, Libya, Morocco, Palestine, Syria, Tunisia, Moldova, and Ukraine.

9 Co-development is an abbreviation of "cooperation for development."

10 Authors' calculation based on the DAC-CRS purpose code (15190) for "Facilitation of orderly, safe, regular and responsible migration and mobility."

11 This program has been expanded over the years and is currently operating in Caribbean countries as well under four lines of work: migration management; regional, bilateral and local cooperation and dialogue on migration; emergencies and migration crises; and communication processes about regular migration, risks of irregular migration and alternatives to it (see IOM 2018 and IOM 2022).

12 ACAs with Honduras and El Salvador were also signed but never implemented.

REFERENCES

Adamson, Fiona. 2006. "Crossing Borders: International Migration and National Security." *International Security* 31 (1): 165–99.

Aguayo-Téllez, Ernesto, and Christian I. Rivera-Mendoza. 2011. "Migration from Mexico to the United States: Wage Benefits of Crossing the Border and Going to the US Interior." *Politics & Policy* 39 (1): 119–40. https://doi.org/10.1111/j.1747-1346.2010.00285.x.

Berthélemy, Jean Claude, Monica Beuran, and Mathilde Maurel. 2009. "Aid and Migration: Substitutes or Complements?" *World Development* 37 (10): 1589–99.

Boswell, Christina. 2007. "Theorizing Migration Policy: Is There a Third Way?" *International Migration Review* 41 (1): 75–100.

Brown, Nick M. 2019. "Millennium Challenge Corporation: Overview and Issues." CRS Report RL32427. Washington, DC: Congressional Research Service. https://sgp.fas.org/crs/row/RL32427.pdf. Accessed 11 September 2023.

Cardwell, Paul James. 2013. "New Modes of Governance in the External Dimension of EU Migration Policy." *International Migration* 51 (6): 54–66.

Carling, Jørgen. 2017. "How Does Migration Arise?" International Organization for Migration (IOM).

Carling, Jørgen, and Cathrine Talleraas. 2016. "Root Causes and Drivers of Migration." Oslo: Peace Research Institute Oslo.

Cheatham, Amelia. 2021. "Central America's Turbulent Northern Triangle." Council on Foreign Relations. 1 July 2021. https://www.cfr.org/

backgrounder/central-americas-turbulent-northern-triangle. Accessed 11 September 2023.
Clemens, Michael A. 2014. "Does Development Reduce Migration?" DP No. 8592. Institute for the Study of Labor.
de Haas, Hein. 2007. "Turning the Tide? Why Development Will Not Stop Migration." *Development and Change* 38 (5): 819–41.
Deridder, Marie, Lotte Pelckmans, and Emilia Ward. 2020. "Reversing the Gaze: West Africa Performing the EU Migration-Development-Security Nexus: Introduction." *Anthropologie & Développement* 51 (December): 9–32.
European Commission. 1992. "EC Technical Assistance to the Commonwealth of Independent States and Georgia: The TACIS Programme." https://ec.europa.eu/commission/presscorner/detail/en/MEMO_92_54. Accessed 11 September 2023.
– 2005. "Migration and Development: Some Concrete Orientations." Document no. COM(2005) 390 final.
– 2006. "The Global Approach to Migration One Year On: Towards a Comprehensive European Migration Policy." https://eurlex.europa.eu/LexUriServ/LexUriServ.do?uri=COM:2006:0735:FIN:EN:PDF. Accessed 11 September 2023.
– 2014. "European Neighbourhood and Partnership Instrument 2007-2013 Overview of Activities and Results." https://ec.europa.eu/europeaid/sites/devco/files/overview_of_enpi_results_2007-2013_en_0.pdf. Accessed 3 June 2022.
– 2015. "Agreement Establishing the European Union Emergency Trust Fund for Stability and Addressing the Root Causes of Irregular Migration and Displaced Persons in Africa, and Its Internal Rules."
– 2016. "Commission announces New Migration Partnership Framework: reinforced cooperation with third countries to better manage migration." http://europa.eu/rapid/press-release_IP-16-2072_en.htm. Accessed 11 September 2023.
– 2022. "Global Europe: Neighbourhood, Development and International Cooperation Instrument." https://ec.europa.eu/info/funding-tenders/find-funding/eu-funding-programmes/global-europe-neighbourhood-development-and-international-cooperation-instrument_en. Accessed 11 September 2023.
EUTF (European Union Emergency Trust Fund for Africa). 2018a. "Contrat de Réforme Sectorielle / Appui à La Réforme de l'état Civil En Côte d'Ivoire." European Commission. https://ec.europa.eu/trustfundforafrica/sites/euetfa/files/t05-eutf-sah-ci-01.pdf. Accessed 3 June 2022.
– 2018b. "CTR - Appui Budgétaire Pour La Mise En Œuvre Du Programme d'Urgence Sahel Du Burkina Faso." European Commission. https://eutf.akvoapp.org/en/project/7023/#report. Accessed 11 September 2023.

"Exec. Order No. 14010, 86 Fed. Reg. 8267." 2021. https://www.federalregister.gov/documents/2021/02/05/2021-02561/creating-a-comprehensive-regional-framework-to-address-the-causes-of-migration-to-manage-migration. Accessed 11 September 2023.

Farm Africa. 2020. "Irrigation Cooperatives are Bringing Communities Together to Combat Climate Extremes." 10 August 2020. https://www.farmafrica.org/latest/news/post/954-irrigation-cooperatives-are-bringing-communities-together-to-combat-climate-extremes. Accessed 11 September 2023.

– 2022. "Livelihoods for Refugee and Host Communities." https://www.farmafrica.org/ethiopia/livelihoods-for-refugee-and-host-communities. Accessed 11 September 2023.

FitzGerald, David. 2019. *Refuge beyond Reach: How Rich Democracies Repel Asylum Seekers*. New York, NY: Oxford University Press.

Frelick, Bill, Ian M. Kysel, and Jennifer Podkul. 2016. "The Impact of Externalization of Migration Controls on the Rights of Asylum Seekers and Other Migrants." *Journal on Migration and Human Security* 4 (4): 190–220. https://doi.org/10.1177/233150241600400402.

Grabbe, Heather. 2000. "The Sharp Edges of Europe: Extending Schengen Easterwards." *International Affairs* 76 (3): 519–36.

Holland, Hereward. 2015. "Over One Million Sea Arrivals Reach Europe in 2015." UNHCR. http://www.unhcr.org/afr/news/latest/2015/12/5683d0b56/million-sea-arrivals-reach-europe-2015.html. Accessed 11 September 2023.

IOM (International Organization for Migration). 2010. "IOM Assists Haitian Migrants Displaced by the 12 January Earthquake." International Organization for Migration. 26 April 2010. https://www.iom.int/news/iom-assists-haitian-migrants-displaced-12-january-earthquake. Accessed 11 September 2023.

– 2018. "Taking Sendai Forward: IOM Progress Report on Disaster Risk Reduction and Resilience 2018." https://reliefweb.int/report/world/taking-sendai-forward-iom-progress-report-disaster-risk-reduction-and-resilience-2018. Accessed 11 September 2023.

Jiménez Godinez, Miguel Ángel. 2013. "Legal Migration and Free Trade in NAFTA Era: Beyond Migration Rhetoric." *The Wilson Center*. https://www.wilsoncenter.org/sites/default/files/media/documents/publication/Legal_Migration_Miguel_Angel_Jimenez1.pdf. Accessed 11 September 2023.

Kugiel, Patryk, Henriette U Erstad, Morten Bøås, and Jolanta Szymańska. 2020. "Can Aid Solve the Root Causes of Migration? A Framework for Future Research on the Development-Migration Nexus." No. 1 (176). *The Polish Institute of International Affairs*.

Lavenex, Sandra. 2008. "Beyond Conditionality: International Institutions in Postcommunist Europe after Enlargement." *Journal of European Public Policy* 15 (6): 938–55.

Lavenex, Sandra, and Rahel Kunz. 2008. "The Migration–Development Nexus in EU External Relations." *Journal of European Integration* 30 (3): 439–57.

Lavenex, Sandra, and Frank Schimmelfennig. 2009. "EU Rules Beyond EU Borders: Theorizing External Governance in European Politics." *Journal of European Public Policy* 16 (6): 791–812.

Lavenex, Sandra, and Emek M. Uçarer, eds. 2002. *Migration and the Externalities of European Integration*. Lanham, MD: Lexington Books.

Lebon-McGregor, Elaine. 2020. "A History of Global Migration Governance: Challenging Linearity." *IMI Working Paper Series* 167 (September): 1–35.

Library of Congress. 2022. "1942: Bracero Program." Research guide. 2022. https://guides.loc.gov/latinx-civil-rights/bracero-program. Accessed 11 September 2023.

Lind, Dara. 2019. "Foreign Aid to Central America Is in Limbo Because Officials Are Afraid of Trump." Vox, 28 March 2019. https://www.vox.com/2019/3/28/18283941/trump-border-guatemala-mexico-foreign-aid. Accessed 11 September 2023.

Magoni, Raphaële. 2004. "International Migration and Relations with Third Countries: France." Brussels: Migration Policy Group.

Matthews, R.N. Clive. 1994. "European Union: The Way Forward - Country Report: Ethiopia: Dossier: PHARE-TACIS: EU Cooperation with Its Eastern Neighbours." The Courier N° 145.

Meissner, Doris. 2020. "Rethinking the US-Mexico Border Immigration Enforcement System: A Policy Road Map." Washington, DC: Migration Policy Institute. https://www.migrationpolicy.org/sites/default/files/publications/rethinking-enforcement-roadmap_final.pdf. Accessed 11 September 2023.

Menz, Georg. 2011. "Stopping, Shaping and Moulding Europe: Two-Level Games, Non-State Actors and the Europeanization of Migration Policies." *Journal of Common Market Studies* 49 (2): 437–62.

Meyer, Peter J. 2019. "US Strategy for Engagement in Central America: Policy Issues for Congress." CRS Report R44812. Washington, DC: Congressional Research Service. https://sgp.fas.org/crs/row/R44812.pdf. Accessed 11 September 2023.

– 2021. "US Strategy for Engagement in Central America: An Overview." Congressional Research Service. https://sgp.fas.org/crs/row/IF10371.pdf. Accessed 11 September 2023.

– 2022. "Central American Migration: Root Causes and US Policy." Washington, DC: Congressional Research Service. https://sgp.fas.org/crs/row/IF11151.pdf. Accessed 11 September 2023.

Meyer, Peter J., and Rachel L. Martin. 2021. "US Foreign Assistance to Latin America and the Caribbean: FY2021 Appropriations." CRS Report R46514. Washington, DC: Congressional Research Service. https://sgp.fas.org/crs/row/R46514.pdf. Accessed 11 September 2023.

Meyer, Peter J., and Clare Ribando Seelke. 2015. "Central America Regional Security Initiative: Background and Policy Issues for Congress." CRS Report R41731. Washington, DC: Congressional Research Service. https://sgp.fas.org/crs/row/R41731.pdf. Accessed 11 September 2023.

Meyer, Peter J., and Mark P. Sullivan. 2012. "US Foreign Assistance to Latin America and the Caribbean: Recent Trends and FY2013 Appropriations." CRS Report R42582. Washington, DC: Congressional Research Service. https://sgp.fas.org/crs/row/R42582.pdf. Accessed 11 September 2023.

Micinski, Nicholas R. 2021. *UN Global Compacts: Governing Migrants and Refugees*. New York: Routledge.

Micinski, Nicholas, and Kelsey Norman. 2021. "Aid, Migration and Authoritarianism: A Qualitative Analysis of Migration Management Aid and Governance in Recipient Countries." American Political Science Association (APSA) Presentation.

Millennium Challenge Corporation. 2022a. "Page: Our Impact." Millennium Challenge Corporation. 2022. https://www.mcc.gov/our-impact. Accessed 11 September 2023.

– 2022b. "Threshold Program: Guatemala Threshold Program." Millennium Challenge Corporation. 2022. https://www.mcc.gov/where-we-work/program/guatemala-threshold-program. Accessed 11 September 2023.

Mitsilegas, Valsamis. 2002. "The Implementation of the EU Acquis on Illegal Immigration by the Candidate Countries of Central and Eastern Europe: Challenges and Contradictions." *Journal of Ethnic and Migration Studies* 28 (4): 665–82. https://doi.org/10.1080/13691830210000032254.

Norman, Kelsey P. 2020. *Reluctant Reception: Refugees, Migration and Governance in the Middle East and North Africa*. Cambridge: Cambridge University Press.

Norman, Kelsey P., and Nicholas R. Micinski. 2022. "The European Union's Migration Management Aid: Developing Democracies or Supporting Authoritarianism?" *International Migration*: 1–15. https://doi.org/10.1111/imig.13075.

Obama White House. 2022. "US Strategy for Engagement in Central America." https://obamawhitehouse.archives.gov/sites/default/files/docs/central_america_strategy.pdf. Accessed 11 September 2023.

Openaid. 2022. "WFP | 2017-2021: From Humanitarian Assistance to Resilience." https://openaid.se/en/activities/SE-0-SE-6-11423A0102-ETH-74020. Accessed 11 September 2023.

Reslow, Natasja. 2015. "EU 'Mobility' Partnerships: An Initial Assessment of Implementation Dynamics." *Politics and Governance* 3 (2): 117–28.

Reslow, Natasja, and Maarten Vink. 2015. "Three-Level Games in EU External Migration Policy: Negotiating Mobility Partnerships in West Africa." *Journal of Common Market Studies* 53 (4): 857–74.

Ruiz Soto, Ariel G. 2020. "One Year after the US-Mexico Agreement: Reshaping Mexico's Migration Policies." Washington, DC: *Migration Policy Institute*. https://www.migrationpolicy.org/sites/default/files/publications/OneYearAfterUS-MexAgreement-EN-FINAL.pdf. Accessed 11 September 2023.

Sasse, Gwendolyn. 2008. "The European Neighbourhood Policy: Conditionality Revisited for the EU's Eastern Neighbours." *Europe-Asia Studies* 60 (2): 295–316.

Seelke, Clare Ribando. 2009. "Merida Initiative for Mexico and Central America: Funding and Policy Issues." CRS Report R40135. Washington, DC: Congressional Research Service. https://sgp.fas.org/crs/row/R40135.pdf. Accessed 11 September 2023.

– 2021. "Mexico: Evolution of the Mérida Initiative, FY2008-FY2022." Congressional Research Service. https://sgp.fas.org/crs/row/IF10578.pdf. Accessed 11 September 2023.

Seelke, Clare Ribando, and Kristin Finklea. 2017. "US-Mexican Security Cooperation: The Merida Initiative and Beyond." CRS Report R41349. Washington, DC: Congressional Research Service.

Seelke, Clare Ribando, and Joshua Klein. 2022. "Mexico: Background and US Relations." CRS Report R42917. Washington, DC: Congressional Research Service. https://sgp.fas.org/crs/row/R42917.pdf. Accessed 11 September 2023.

Telli, Henry. 2014. "Less Poverty, More Emigration: Understanding Migrant Flows from Developing Countries." *Migration and Development* 3 (1): 54–72. https://doi.org/10.1080/21632324.2013.831584.

The Ronald Reagan Presidential Library and Museum. 1984. "Address to the Nation on United States Policy in Central America." Ronald Reagan. 9 May, 1984. https://www.reaganlibrary.gov/archives/speech/address-nation-united-states-policy-central-america. Accessed 11 September 2023.

The White House. 2014a. "FACT SHEET: Unaccompanied Children from Central America." The White House President Barack Obama. 20 June 2014. https://obamawhitehouse.archives.gov/the-press-office/

2014/06/20/fact-sheet-unaccompanied-children-central-america. Accessed 11 September 2023.

– 2014b. "The Obama Administration's Government-Wide Response to Influx of Central American Migrants at the Southwest Border." The White House President Barack Obama. 1 August 2014. https://obamawhitehouse.archives.gov/the-press-office/2014/08/01/obama-administration-s-government-wide-response-influx-central-american-. Accessed 11 September 2023.

– 2014c. "Remarks by President Obama After Meeting with Central American Presidents." Whitehouse.Gov. 25 July 2014. https://obamawhitehouse.archives.gov/the-press-office/2014/07/25/remarks-president-obama-after-meeting-central-american-presidents. Accessed 11 September 2023.

– 2021a. "FACT SHEET: The Collaborative Migration Management Strategy." The White House. 29 July 2021. https://www.whitehouse.gov/briefing-room/statements-releases/2021/07/29/fact-sheet-the-collaborative-migration-management-strategy/. Accessed 11 September 2023.

– 2021b. "FACT SHEET: Strategy to Address the Root Causes of Migration in Central America." The White House. 29 July 2021. https://www.whitehouse.gov/briefing-room/statements-releases/2021/07/29/fact-sheet-strategy-to-address-the-root-causes-of-migration-in-central-america. Accessed 11 September 2023.

– 2021c. "Readout of President Biden's Meeting with President Andrés Manuel López Obrador of Mexico." The White House. 19 November 2021. https://www.whitehouse.gov/briefing-room/statements-releases/2021/11/19/readout-of-president-bidens-meeting-with-president-andres-manuel-lopez-obrador-of-mexico/. Accessed 11 September 2023.

– 2021d. "US-Mexico Joint Declaration." The White House. 1 March 2021. https://www.whitehouse.gov/briefing-room/statements-releases/2021/03/01/u-s-mexico-joint-declaration/. Accessed 11 September 2023.

– 2021e. "US Strategy to Address the Root Causes of Migration in Central America." https://www.whitehouse.gov/wp-content/uploads/2021/07/Root-Causes-Strategy.pdf. Accessed 11 September 2023.

US Department of State and USAID (US Agency for International Development). 2021. "Map of Foreign Assistance Worldwide." 2021. https://foreignassistance.gov/. Accessed 11 September 2023.

USAID (US Agency for International Development). 2019. "USAID Bridges to Employment." 10 July 2019. https://www.usaid.gov/documents/1862/usaid-bridges-employment. Accessed 11 September 2023.

– 2021. "USAID Announces Centroamérica Local Initiative to Empower Local Partners in El Salvador, Guatemala, and Honduras | Press Release | US

Agency for International Development." 4 November 2021. https://www.usaid.gov/news-information/press-releases/nov-4-2021-usaid-announces-centroamerica-local-initiative-empower-local. Accessed 11 September 2023.

Weiner, Myron. 1992. "Security, Stability, and International Migration." *International Security* 17 (3): 91–126.

World Food Programme. 2018. "Sweden Provides Critical Assistance for WFP Resilience Operations in Ethiopia." 19 February 2018. https://www.wfp.org/news/sweden-provides-critical-assistance-wfp-resilience-operations-ethiopia. Accessed 11 September 2023.

14

Smart Borders and the Diffusion of Travellers' Screening Programs in North America and Europe

Ruben Zaiotti

Since the turn of the millennium, North American and European governments have introduced sweeping policy measures to regulate cross-border movements of people.[1] This policy activism derives from the fact that countries on both sides of the Atlantic are (or, in some cases, such as Mexico and Greece, have recently become) major destinations of global migratory flows (Cornelius 2018; Düvell, Molodikova, and Collyer 2014). North American and European policymakers have sought to control these flows by encouraging regulated and "desirable" cross-border mobility including tourists, business people, high-skilled migrants, while at the same time limiting unregulated and "unwanted" movements of populations, including low-skilled migrants, asylum seekers, terrorists, and transnational criminals (Helbling and Kalkum 2018). The increased emphasis on the "filtering" purpose of border controls has raised challenges for policymakers across the Atlantic. The number of individuals arriving at points of entry in North America and Europe has steadily increased since 2000, especially at airports (McAuliffe and Triandafyllidou 2021, 35).[2] The nationality and profiles of inbound travellers have also become more diversified, leading to more complex travel documentation requirements (McAuliffe and Triandafyllidou 2021, 89, 109). At the same time, security-related events that have affected the two regions over the last twenty years – from the terrorist attacks in the US on 11 September 2001 (also called the 9/11 attacks) to those on European soil in the mid-2010s and, more recently, the phenomenon of "returning foreign fighters"[3] – have cemented into the policymakers' minds the need to tighten border security at ports of entry (Anderson 2018).

The competing requirements of travel facilitation and security have pushed North American and European governments to formulate new policy solutions in the border control domain. The most far-reaching policy innovation has come from the application of digital technologies to collect and analyze border data, coupled with the adoption of management techniques borrowed from the security realm such as risk analysis (Ajana 2015; Leese, Noori, and Scheel 2022; see Koslowski and Leckey, and Banerjee in this volume for a discussion on Canada-US border controls). This development is reflected in the array of "smart" instruments introduced or upgraded in this period to increase the reliability and efficiency of border control (Ajana 2013; Everuss 2021; Kenk et al. 2013). These devices are deployed for the collection and sharing of travellers' information (e.g., large databases), verification of identity (e.g., biometric scanners), and detection of suspicious movements (e.g., drones, sensors, and satellite tracking systems).

Various screening programs to collect personal information about inbound and outbound travellers underpin the growing role of data-gathering in managing international travel. These programs include Passenger Name Record (PNR), Advance Passenger Information (API), Electronic System for Travel Authorization (ESTA), and Entry-Exit Systems (EES). Although not formally visas, these programs serve similar purposes of screening travellers before crossing a border.[4] North American and European governments were early adopters of these programs. The United States introduced PNR in 2001 in the aftermath of the terrorist attacks of 9/11. Canada and the EU adopted an API system in 2002 and 2004, respectively, and PNR in 2003 and 2012. The EU has also proposed a version of ESTA (European Travel Information and Authorization System or ETIAS) in 2016 and an EES in 2017 (Alegre, Jeandesboz, and Vavoula 2017; Napieralski 2019), although, at the time of writing, both programs are not yet operational, pending the meeting of technical and legal requirements. North American governments and their European counterparts also reached agreements on the sharing of passengers' data. The EU signed bilateral PNR agreements with the US (in 2004, revised in 2011) and Canada (in 2014).

The adoption of similar smart border policy instruments by North America and European countries, and their active collaboration in this domain, suggests a process of policy convergence has been taking place since the new millennium. Transatlantic policy convergence is not a novelty; indeed, over the years, North American and European governments have introduced analogous policies in a wide range of domains, including internal security (Anagnostakis 2017). The fact that there has been a move toward convergence in the border control domain is nonetheless surprising. After all, North

American and European states have different traditions, styles, and priorities in this policy field. The most contentious issue has to do with the issue of data protection and privacy, as these programs involve the collection of citizens' personal information (Cole and Fabbrini 2016; Lowe 2016). European policymakers have been particularly vocal in raising their concerns. A good case in point is the heated debate over the American version of PNR, an initiative that some European policymakers have been critical of (Byrne 2012; Huijboom and Bodea 2015; Tukdi 2008). These disputes have involved legal and ethical issues defining border control as a policy field. They have also demonstrated how North American and European policymakers remain skeptical of following each other's methods and policies. These differences have periodically surfaced in transatlantic discussions over the issue of the handling of travellers' data and have affected cooperation between the two sides (Farrell and Newman 2019; Tzanou 2018). These contrasting perspectives have also spurred legal challenges, which have led to the suspension of bilateral agreements involving smart border measures. This was the fate of the US-EU and Canada-EU PNR agreements, which the European Court of Justice struck down in 2006 and 2017, respectively (Tambou 2018).

In light of these tensions and challenges, the fact that both sides would adopt, or even just propose to adopt, similar smart border policies and continue to cooperate over them is thus a startling development. How was a transatlantic convergence in the border control field possible, given existing differences between the two sides and skepticism over the value of the adopted policy measures?

In order to address this question, this chapter proposes an argument based on the concept of "practical learning." From this perspective, the convergence of smart border policies between Europe and North America is the result of the spreading of border control *practices* – conceptualized as "embodied, materially mediated arrays of human activity centrally organized around shared practical understandings" (Schatzki, Cetina, and von Savigny 2001, 2) – by American and European policymakers across the Atlantic. In turn, this diffusion depends on the acquisition on the part of policymakers of the *know-how* necessary to formulate and implement new policies, or what in this chapter is defined as practical learning.[5] The argument draws from the insights of practice theory (Reckwitz 2002) and sociological works on expertise and expert performance (Ericsson, Krampe, and Tesch-Romer 1993). How practical learning takes place in formal settings and in everyday life is at the core of these approaches. For this reason, this body of literature provides promising new perspectives on the mechanisms that lead to policy convergence. One of the implications of a practice-based argument to explain the present case is that by considering it a type of practice, border control should not be treated as an objective entity, fact, or condition (that of controlling the flow of people and goods across borders). Instead, it is a social process involving actual policymakers and practitioners formulating policies aimed at protecting a defined territory and learning from each other's activities. Policy convergence in this field can thus be conceptualized as the outcome of the diffusion of border control practices, and not just external material factors or power dynamics between rational actors.

The chapter is organized as follows: the first section outlines a practice-oriented theoretical framework to study policy convergence. In the second section, this analytical framework is applied to an empirical case of policy convergence; namely, the process that led to the adoption of similar travellers' screening programs across the Atlantic. In the concluding section, the chapter explores how the proposed argument can be deployed to understand the spread of smart border policies beyond North America and Europe.

ACCOUNTING FOR THE TRANSATLANTIC POLICY CONVERGENCE OVER SMART BORDERS: AN ANALYTICAL FRAMEWORK

The premise of a practice-oriented account applied to the case of policy convergence over smart border measures is that, at any given time, a particular constellation of policy practices shapes the border control field in Europe and North America. The recent transatlantic policy convergence thus stems from a concomitant transformation of these very practices. The mechanism through which this process occurs is *practical learning*. Practical learning is not just the collection and storage of new information by an agent (Holzinger and Knill 2005, 786). Instead, it is the acquisition of the skills and capacity to perform a new task. Practices, in fact, require a certain level of competence that not all agents possess as part of their "innate" talent, but which can be improved over time.[6] The ultimate outcome of this process of skill acquisition is the achievement of expertise (Ericsson 1996). Experts are those individuals who master a particular practice, who perform it "naturally," in an effortless fashion (Ericsson 1996). If the practice is collective (i.e., as part of a group or team), an expert performance implies a high degree of coordination and coherence among the participants.

How is this expertise achieved? The key factor contributing to skill acquisition is a practice's repeated performance over time (Ericsson 1996). Repeated performance is not relevant only in the reproduction of particular practices, but also in the acquisition of new ones. When carried out in a systematic manner, this activity takes the form of *deliberate practice* (Ericsson, Krampe, and Tesch-Romer 1993). Deliberate practice is a type of training exercise that involves a well-defined task with an appropriate difficulty level for that particular individual, informative feedback, and opportunities for repetition and correction of errors (Ericsson, Krampe, and Tesch-Romer 1993; Janelle and Hillman 2003, 27–8). Through deliberate practice, an actor can then learn a new skill by "practising it" over time.

In world politics, deliberate practice can take the form of repeated interactions among policymakers in the international arena. In these interactions, policymakers negotiate or discuss matters of common concern that require some kind of resolution or compromise. The most common of these engagements are treaty negotiations and bilateral or multilateral "dialogues" among policy officials representing countries or international organizations. International negotiations take the form of repeated interactions and verbal exchanges among participants based on a combination of bargaining and problem-solving (Starkey, Boyer, and Wilkenfeld 2005). In dialogues, participants repeatedly interact with each other, but, unlike in negotiations, their primary goal is to share best practices and inform each other about future plans (Krizsán and Zentai 2003). Dialogues are, therefore, typically less conflictual than negotiations. Examples of negotiations include the series of bilateral interactions that led to the signing of the respective US-EU and Canada-EU PNR agreements. Instances of international dialogues are the various transatlantic forums created as part of US-EU anti-terrorism cooperation (Funk and Trauner 2016). Both types of international engagements generally take place in ad hoc forums, whose degree of institutionalization varies. International negotiations tend to occur within formalized contexts, while dialogues are more informal. Crucially, for the present purposes, both types of forums offer the training ground where policymakers can perform a particular practice. Negotiations, in fact, typically require various rounds of interaction before they are settled, while dialogues involve various exchanges and open-ended channels of communication.

Training is aimed at getting better at a particular practice. The rule of thumb is that the more deliberate practice is performed, the better are the results (Ericsson, Krampe, and Tesch-Romer 1993; Proctor and Kim-Phuong 2006, 266). The existence of an institutional setting where these exercises can take place is an essential supporting factor in the successful acquisition of new skills, for it provides a proper spatial and temporal context for conducting deliberate practice. The outcome of systematic training is not, however, consistently successful. Indeed, it is a trial-and-error exercise, especially if the practice is new and there is no well-established example to follow. The performance studies literature concurs, however, that while "not all practice makes perfect ... perfect practice makes perfect" (Janelle and Hillman 2003, 27–8).

The mechanism through which new skills are acquired or refined through deliberate practice can take different forms, depending on the type of relationship between the "student" and the "teacher." The most common mechanism is "learning by imitation" (Byrne and Russon 1998; Offerman and Sonnemans 1998). Learning by imitation occurs when an agent with limited experience or expertise (a "novice" or "apprentice") mimics existing practices performed by somebody already established in the field (i.e., a master, an expert). A master can teach an apprentice new skills or improve her or his performance by mentoring or coaching her or him into the new practice. Mentoring and coaching involve providing advice and strategy in training, as well as encouragement and monitoring of progress. The apprentice can also learn by just working side by side with the master and observing her or him in action.[7] Since there is no direct interaction in this case, the master is not explicitly *teaching* the apprentice but *leading by example* (Lave 1988). Learning by imitation can also occur as a result of competition when an agent imitates the best moves of skilled competitors. In all these scenarios (learning by imitation, by example, or through competition), the transfer and acquisition of new skills are typically not automatic and (at least in the short term) immediately acknowledged by the agent involved. Whether an agent has actually learned a new skill can be determined by their actual ability to perform the new practice.

The types of interactions in world politics mentioned earlier, namely negotiations and dialogues, can be considered arenas where participants learn each other's "ways of doing things." This is particularly true during negotiations when participants interact and have the opportunity to closely monitor and possibly mimic each other's actions. The same can also be said of dialogues. Dialogues in the international arena, in fact, involve some form of exchange – exchange that is not just verbal, but also physical, as participants interact with each other face to face.

To summarize, practical learning depends on a series of conditions: the amount of deliberate practice agents can perform, the degree of institutionalization of the stage where training takes place, and the existence of relevant experts who can lead by example. The more these conditions are present in a given context, the more likely will the practical learning be successful. If practical learning is indeed successful, and a hitherto novice acquires new skills in a given field, then we can say that a practice has spread. As the following sections attest, this process of practical learning and spreading is what has characterized the border control field in Europe and North America in recent years.

PRACTICAL LEARNING AND POLICY DIFFUSION ACROSS THE ATLANTIC: THE CASE OF TRAVELLERS' SCREENING PROGRAMS

North American and European governments have been a reciprocal source of inspiration for smart border control measures introduced since the turn of the millennium. This phenomenon is particularly evident in the case of travellers' data screening programs, and PNR in particular. The American and European versions of PNR are similar in terms of name, content, and objectives. As in the European model, the US model requires that passengers travelling by airplane submit several items of personal data to the air carrier. The air carrier then must provide the authorities with electronic access to this information. The influence of the US on the European PNR is apparent if we consider its main purpose. The initiative's original goal was, in fact, to create a tool in the fight against terrorism, which the US championed since 2001.[8] The EU already had legislation regarding the tracking of suspect travellers,[9] but its sole purpose was to control against illegal immigration, not preventing and combating terrorist offences. European officials have tried to dispel the notion that the European PNR is a carbon copy of the US version. Tellingly, during a debate between the European Council and Parliament over this initiative, the French interior minister claimed that it was "different from the PNR signed with the United States."[10] In practice, however, these differences are either minimal or merely semantic.

The correspondences between smart border initiatives formulated in Europe and North America are not accidental. These policies' content and underlying assumptions have, in fact, spread between the two regions thanks to the growth in transatlantic cooperation in this field in the last twenty years. Before 9/11, border control was rarely on the agenda of North American-European relations. This policy domain has become more central in the politically charged and security-focused environment that characterizes the new millennium (Anagnostakis 2017). Issues such as pre-travel screening, data exchange, and, more generally, anti-terrorism have been a fixture of transatlantic meetings between, on the one hand, the US and Canadian governments and, on the other, individual European governments and the European Commission.

Because of the importance of the issues at stake – i.e., security, but also exchanges of people and goods – there has been intense pressure on both sides to cooperate in the fight against international terrorism and irregular migration, and to avoid possible externalities in this area. Over the years, however, US actions have been a recurrent source of tension in transatlantic relations. The US PNR is a typical example of this state of affairs, as it led to an acrimonious and lengthy debate between the US and Europe over the means to accommodate US priorities within European sensibilities. Despite its negative reverberations on the transatlantic partnership, this clash played a crucial part in the spreading of practices between the two sides. Indeed, during the bilateral disputes characterizing this period, some of the key conditions for successful practical learning were established, from sustained interaction between policymakers, to the growing formalization of institutional forums where these negotiations take place, to the repetition of these interactions over time. The following paragraphs analyze these three conditions in turn, showing how the PNR represented a case of transatlantic policy diffusion.

The first condition to be addressed is interaction. The dispute over the PNR was sparked in the immediate aftermath of 9/11. The US Congress passed the Aviation and Transportation Security Act, which requires that airlines with US-bound international flights electronically submit specific data to the authorities. These requirements, however, raised concerns regarding their compatibility with EU law, in particular, with regard to data protection. The awareness of the potential for conflict convinced the two sides to figure out ways to avoid confrontation and to engage in proactive cooperation to achieve common goals.

The need for greater transatlantic engagement has led European and North American governments to establish a dense network of cooperative arrangements between them and the sending and transit countries of migration around the world. This growing formalization of transatlantic cooperation is the second condition for successful practical learning. The encounters between European and North American policymakers (be it in the form of negotiations or dialogues) over the PNR issue took place in newly created bilateral forums dealing with migration and internal security issues. These discussions were primarily held within the framework of the broader EU-North America partnership. As previously noted, until 9/11, border control was not a central topic in bilateral discussions. The growth in political relevance and the number of issues on the agenda pushed the two sides to reorganize this cooperation. Special forums were set up with a different degree of formality and responsibilities (Buonanno, Nugent, and Cuglesan 2015, 99–102). The most relevant in the migration and border control field has been the EU-US Justice and Home Affairs ministerial meetings and senior officials' meetings, which have been held on a regular basis since 2001; the Policy Dialogue on Transport and Border Security (PDTBS), which was established in 2004; and, since 2021, the US-EU Migration Platform. In these forums, European and American senior officials have exchanged best practices and laid out the basic outlines of the solutions of disputes, basing their activities on the work undertaken in specialized working groups (e.g., Visa Working Group, Data Privacy Group) and referring the most hotly contested political issues to the yearly EU-US leaders' summits.

The intensification of transatlantic cooperation on migration and internal security matters has intensified and expanded to areas such as intelligence and data gathering (Anderson 2018). In 2015 the US signed two agreements with EUROPOL (the EU's law enforcement agency) concerning the sharing of information on irregular migration and foreign fighters' travel. Border-related issues, including the PNR, have regularly appeared on the agenda of the bilateral meetings between officials from both sides of the Atlantic. In joint statements issued after these meetings, the two sides have "reiterated their mutual commitment to exchange Passenger Name Record (and to) continue to work together in a constructive way on the findings and recommendations of the joint evaluation of the PNR Agreement."[11] They have also regularly informed each other of recent developments affecting their border policies. For instance, at the height of the "refugee crisis," a time when Europe was under pressure due to the sudden growth in migratory flows in and around the continent, EU officials shared migration information with their American colleagues. In turn, the US delegation communicated to its European counterparts about operational measures it has taken concerning border security and cooperation with third countries on issues of return and readmission.[12]

US-EU bilateral meetings involving matters of border control have regularly taken place throughout the Bush and Obama administrations (typically twice a year). Although less frequent and structured, these encounters also continued during the Trump presidency. As part of the Biden administration's efforts toward greater transatlantic engagement, bilateral meetings have resumed their twice-a-year schedule. Despite the tension that has periodically characterized transatlantic relations over issues of border control, the participants agree that this cooperation has yielded "impressive results" (Peterson et al. 2005, 13), which, over the years, has led to a greater institutionalization of the transatlantic partnership (Tzanou 2018). These results included not only the solution of existing disagreements but also the ongoing "exchange(s) of views on recent developments of their respective migration and asylum policies."[13] The recent discussions on how to ease the transatlantic travel restrictions imposed at the height of the COVID-19 pandemic are an example of this enduring spirit of collaboration. This ongoing engagement has thus provided the institutional context for an educational process in which both sides have learned directly from each other's experiences. Crucially, these dynamics have continued despite the crisis of contemporary transatlantic relations (Riddervold and Newsome 2018).

One of the implications of the formalization and regularization of transatlantic cooperation on border-related matters is that a network of policymakers and experts has emerged. On the US side, the actors involved are mostly officials from the Department of Homeland Security (DHS), and, to a lesser extent, the departments of state and justice. On the European side, the participants are typically from the Commission's directorates of Migration and Home Affairs and External Relations, representatives from the ministries of Interior and Justice of the European Union's rotating presidencies, and EU agencies (EUROPOL, EUROJUST, EU Counter-Terrorism Coordinator office). The members of this nascent transatlantic border-control policy-community have interacted with each other regularly, either directly through personal contact or indirectly through their belonging to the same policy network. Having "all people in a room," in turn, was crucial in facilitating negotiations.[14] In this network, some actors are new to the international scene, such as DHS and the European Commission (in terms of the home affairs portfolio), or old actors with new roles, such as the ministries of the Interior in European member states. These "novices" have brought new ideas and styles to negotiating. DHS, for example, as a "new kid on the block" in the international arena, has been particularly active with its European partners and adopted "a very combative negotiating style" in transatlantic relations.[15]

The dynamics between members of this policy-community are also relevant for the third condition necessary for successful practical learning; namely, iterated interactions among policymakers. Indeed, the dispute over PNR has dragged on for years and, to date, is not fully settled. Moreover, the trajectory of the negotiations between the US authorities and their European counterparts over this issue has not been linear, with phases of disagreement and tension followed by instances of compromise and progress. It is during this difficult gestation, however, that the spreading of practices occurred. Data privacy has been the main bone of contention in the PNR negotiations. North America and Europe have different visions (mirrored in different legal systems and traditions) on this subject. As noted earlier, PNR has relevant implications for issues of privacy since it entails the handling of sensitive information about private citizens. Initially, neither of the two sides was willing to compromise on this matter. To overcome the stalemate, in late 2001, the European Commission started negotiations with the US authorities to find a solution to the dispute. The initial agreement that the two sides reached (May 2004, US-EU

PNR agreement), however, was annulled by a ruling of the European Court of Justice. The European Commission and the US DHS, therefore, had to draft a new legal text, which they eventually signed in July 2007. Even this new arrangement, however, raised concerns among European policymakers, especially in the European Parliament. The main issues of contention were the amount of data to be shared, the length of time the data would be kept, and the lack of adequate recourse for EU citizens. The EU and US reopened the negotiations with a view to revise the 2007 text and address the EU Parliament's concerns. A new agreement was eventually signed in 2011.

During these lengthy negotiations, European policymakers have had the opportunity to learn from their North American partners about the proposed smart border policies and to build the practical knowledge necessary to implement them on their own. While publicly denying it due to political sensibilities, in private conversations, European officials acknowledge the US as an indirect source of inspiration for their initiatives and that they have been "following developments and trends in the US" in drafting smart border proposals.[16] The United States Visitor Status Indicator Technology (US-VISIT), for instance, is one of the existing EES that European policymakers assessed in order to find "key lessons and possible best practices."[17] The European proposal for an ESTA is also based on a North American model.[18] Although even more reluctantly than their transatlantic colleagues, US officials as well recognize the role of the European Union in informing US policy. A good case in point is the DHS decision to introduce a Traveler Redress Inquiry Program (TRIP) to respond to complaints about US authorities' passenger screening and to render the program available to both US and non-US citizens – a move which was partly influenced by EU stance on this issue. The issue of data privacy was taken up again in September 2015 with the signing of the EU-US Umbrella Agreement. This document provides a new regulatory framework to protect personal data exchanged for law enforcement purposes across the Atlantic. This arrangement formalizes the right of EU citizens to enjoy the same judicial redress rights as US citizens in case of privacy breaches. The importance of this arrangement to build transatlantic trust was highlighted by the then president of the European Commission, Juncker: "The United States must ... guarantee that all EU citizens have the right to enforce data protection rights in US courts, whether or not they reside on US soil. Removing such discrimination will be essential for restoring trust in transatlantic relations."[19]

These examples show that the ongoing transatlantic interactions between North American and European policymakers, together with the growing formalization of transatlantic forums dealing with issues of border control, have paved the way for the spreading of practices between the two regions and the undertaking by both sides of policy initiatives whose key features echo those introduced by their colleagues across the ocean.

CONCLUSION: FROM TRANSATLANTIC TO GLOBAL SMART BORDERS

The growing reliance on new technologies to manage the cross-border movement of populations has been one of the most notable developments characterizing the border control policy field in the last two decades. North American and European countries have been at the forefront of this policy trend. Governments across the Atlantic have introduced an array of "smart" border measures aimed at screening travellers crossing international borders. This chapter argued that the adoption of similar border control policies in North America and Europe is the result of an ongoing process of policy diffusion that has facilitated the transfer of policy ideas across the Atlantic. The mechanism driving this policy diffusion is based on the acquisition on the part of policymakers of relevant practical policy knowledge that is then applied to the development of new policy initiatives. This practical learning is successful when policymakers are put in a position to interact with each other on a regular basis, an institutional framework that facilitates the exchange of ideas is present, and mentors who can provide policy guidance are available. The chapter has shown how, in the last two decades, these conditions have been present in the policy context constituting the relations between North American and European policymakers, leading to policy convergence in the border control field. The dynamics characterizing this process are technocratic. Indeed, the spread of border control practices has occurred behind closed doors and involved unelected career bureaucrats shielded from public scrutiny. This state of affairs does not mean, however, that the process of transatlantic policy diffusion is apolitical. Arguably, the very attempt to depoliticize border security by shielding it from public scrutiny (a move which might not necessarily be the stated objective of those involved but one which these very policymakers are helping to reproduce through their actions) can, in fact, be read as a political manoeuvre to prevent potential domestic and international criticism (Trauttmansdorf 2017). The political nature of travellers' screening programs is also highlighted by the opposition they face from civil society and in the courts. The use of digital technology in mobility control indeed raises serious ethical and legal questions (Brower 2016; Leese, Noori, and Scheel 2022). The "filtering" effects of travellers' programs are overwhelming felt by citizens from non-Western countries, including those who are seeking protection as refugees. These programs are also rife with biases, human errors, and technical glitches, which can turn cross-border travel into a lottery. The unfair nature of these practices is magnified by the fact that states have delegated their implementation to private entities such as airline carriers (Rodenhäuser 2014). As a result, the level of accountability and opportunity for legal recourse for malpractices are limited. Data privacy is another major issue of concern. Rules about the storing and sharing of information about migrants are often opaque, inconsistent, and weakly enforced, particularly when exchanges between foreign governments are involved (Hayes 2017). It is not surprising, therefore, that litigation involving these programs has increased over time in national and international courts.

Considering the adoption of smart border policies across the Atlantic as an instance of policy diffusion through practical learning has implications for the future of these policies at the global level. Some of the initiatives spearheaded by the North American and European governments have, in fact, started to spread beyond the transatlantic arena. One case in point is the adoption by non-Western countries of passenger screening systems similar to the US and EU PNR, for example, Russia (Enerstvedt 2014). Some of the border control initiatives formulated by the North American and European governments have also been inserted into other international or regional forums' agendas and informed the development of global standards in this domain (Taplin 2021). Since the mid-2000s the PNR program has been a topic of discussion in meetings of the G7 – the international forum bringing together leaders of the world's most industrialized countries. The G7 has also called for the development of guidelines and best practices to improve the security of travel documents, including the use of biometrics. Inspired by the G7's actions, in 2010 the International Civil Aviation Organization (ICAO) drafted a document outlining guidelines that countries should follow in introducing and managing passengers' data.[20] In 2017, ICAO, in collaboration with other leading international organizations – the World Customs Organization (WCO) and the International Air Transportation Agency (IATA) – also issued the Passenger Data Umbrella Document, a text that offers guidelines for sources and systems for passenger-related information.[21] As for developments between Europe and North America, the trend toward policy convergence with regards to smart borders at global level raises some relevant questions about how this development is taking place. These developments can be read as the latest example of the North American and European governments projecting their agenda on other countries based on their interests as major destinations of migratory flows and their concerns about security (Givens, Busch, and Bersin 2018). A promising line of inquiry would be to assess whether practical learning is involved in the ongoing globalization of smart border measures, as has been the case for policy diffusion across the Atlantic. Some of the conditions for such learning are already in place. The European and North American governments, for instance, seem particularly eager to play the role of teachers of new policies to the rest of the world. Moreover, the number of international forums where policymakers can interact and exchange best border control practices is growing, as the involvement of international organizations such as the ICAO, IATA, and WCO attest. The task of this new research agenda will therefore be to establish whether transatlantic practices and the policy actors behind them are indeed responsible for the spread of externalized border control practices worldwide.

NOTES

1 It should be noted that, in the European context, border control matters are a shared responsibility between national governments and the European Union (EU). As a regional organization, the EU has, over time, acquired greater competences in this domain, especially since the late 1990s. EU institutions such as the European Commission (the Union's executive agency) and the European Parliament and Council of the European Union (the Union's main legislative bodies) have become primary policy actors in this domain, including in matters of international relations. The EU has also created a common free travel area across the continent ("Schengen area") and members of this arrangement share rules regarding crossing Europe's external borders (Zaiotti 2011).

2 This upward trend has been momentarily interrupted as a result of the global travel restrictions imposed at the height of the COVID-19 pandemic (Hale et al. 2021). At the time of writing, most of these restrictions have been lifted and international travel is returning to pre-pandemic levels (UNWTO 2022).

3 Returning foreign fighters are holders of North American or European passports who have fought abroad on behalf of entities that North American and European authorities considered terrorist organizations (e.g., Islamic State of Iraq and the Levant, or ISIL). Because of their status, these individuals can return to their country of nationality without requiring a visa and therefore are considered a security threat.

4 The PNR system was developed by the airlines for commercial purposes; nevertheless, due to security reasons (e.g., fight against terrorism), some countries require airlines to provide them with some data prior to the passenger's entry into the country (e.g., USA, Canada, Australia, and New Zealand). The API system is also implemented by airlines, but, in contrast

to PNR, it is on behalf of governments. The EES is a database for storing personal data of foreign nationals crossing international borders (Han, McGauran, and Nelen 2017).

5 On the use of the concept of "practical learning" to study transatlantic policy convergence, see Zaiotti (2012). The present chapter builds upon this work, elaborating its theoretical and empirical analysis and applying it to the case of smart border policies.

6 On "skill acquisition" in expert performance studies, see Proctor and Kim-Phuong (2006).

7 On the role of "observational learning" as part of practical learning, see Janelle and Hillman (2003, 42); Starkes et al. (1996).

8 European Commission, *Accompanying document to the Proposal for a Council Framework Decision on the use of Passenger Name Record (PNR) for law enforcement purposes—Impact Assessment*, SEC(2007) 1453, 6 November 2007.

9 "Council Directive 2004/82/EC of 29 April 2004 on the obligation of carriers to communicate passenger data." *Official Journal of the European Union*, L 261, 06/08/2004, p. 24.

10 Agence Europe. "EU/JHA: French Presidency repeats benefits of 'European PNR.'" 3 December 2008.

11 "Joint U.S.-EU Statement following the U.S.-EU Justice and Home Affairs Ministerial Meeting," 16 December 2021. https://www.dhs.gov/news/2021/12/16/joint-us-eu-statement-following-us-eu-justice-and-home-affairs-ministerial-meeting. Similar wording is present in other joint statements issued after meetings organized during the Obama and Trump administrations.

12 See, for instance, Outcome of proceedings of the EU-US Justice and Home Affairs Senior Officials Meeting (Rovinj, 5–6 March 2020). Available at https://www.statewatch.org/media/documents/news/2020/apr/eu-council-eu-usa-senior-officials-minutes-7083-20.pdf.

13 "Joint U.S.-EU Statement following the U.S.-EU Justice and Home Affairs Ministerial Meeting," 16 December 2021. https://www.dhs.gov/news/2021/12/16/joint-us-eu-statement-following-us-eu-justice-and-home-affairs-ministerial-meeting.

14 US DHS official, interview with author, Washington, January 2009.

15 US State Department official, interview with author, January 2009.

16 Outcome of Proceedings, EU–US informal JHA (Justice and Home Affairs) senior-level meeting (22–23 January 2007, Berlin), 5655/07, Brussels, 26 January 2007, p. 63.

17 European Commission, "Preparing the next steps in Border Management in the European Union - Impact Assessment", Commission Staff Working

Document, COM(2008) 69 final; SEC(2008) 154, p. 62. See also European Commission, *Communication from the Commission to the European Parliament and the Council. Stronger and Smarter Information Systems for Borders and Security*, COM(2016) 205 final.

18 European Commission, "Communication the possibility of introducing an EU ESTA – Roadmap" (2011). This document refers to the ESTA's US version as a term of reference to determine the system's applicability to Europe (p. 3). The proposal for a European version of ESTA was eventually adopted in 2018. See Regulation (EC). (2018). Regulation (EU) 2018/1240 of the European Parliament and of the Council of 12 September 2018 establishing a European Travel Information and Authorisation System (ETIAS) and amending Regulations (EU) No 1077/2011, (EU) No 515/2014, (EU) 2016/399, (EU) 2016/1624 and (EU) 2017/2226. In *OJ L 236* (pp. 1–71).

19 Cited in https://ec.europa.eu/commission/presscorner/detail/it/MEMO_15_5612; emphasis as per original.

20 ICAO, "Guidelines on Passenger Name Record (PNR) Data," Doc 9944, 2010. https://www.icao.int/Security/FAL/ANNEX9/Documents/9944_cons_en.pdf.

21 ICAO, WCO, IATA, "Management Summary on Passenger-related Information ('Umbrella Document')," July 2017. Available at: https://www.iata.org/contentassets/18a5fdb2dc144d619a8c10dc1472ae80/umbrella_document_v2_july2017.pdf.

REFERENCES

Ajana, Btihaj. 2013. "Asylum, Identity Management and Biometric Control." *Journal of Refugee Studies* 26 (4): 576–95.

– 2015. "Augmented Borders: Big Data and the Ethics of Immigration Control." *Journal of Information, Communication and Ethics in Society* 13 (1): 58–78.

Alegre, Susie, Julien Jeandesboz, and Niovi Vavoula. 2017. *European Travel Information and Authorisation System (ETIAS): Border Management Fundamental Rights and Data Protection*. Study for the LIBE Committee. Brussels: European Parliament - Directorate General for Internal Matters.

Anagnostakis, Dimitrios. 2017. *EU–US Cooperation on Internal Security: Building a Transatlantic Regime*. London and New York: Routledge.

Anderson, Jeffrey J. 2018. "Rancor and Resilience in the Atlantic Political Order: The Obama Years." *Journal of European Integration* 40 (5): 621–36.

Buonanno, Laurie, Neill Nugent, and Natalia Cuglesan. 2015. "Transatlantic Governance." In *The New and Changing Transatlanticism: Politics and*

Policy Perspectives, edited by Laurie Buonanno, Natalia Cuglesan, and Keith Henderson, 85–108. Abingdon: Routledge.

Byrne, Andrew. 2012. *Building the Transatlantic Area of Freedom, Security and Justice: The Case of the Passenger Name Record Agreements*. Istituto Affari Internazionali.

Byrne, Richard W., and Anne E. Russon. 1998. "Learning by Imitation: A Hierarchical Approach." *Brain and Behavioral Science* 21 (5): 667–721.

Cole, David, and Federico Fabbrini. 2016. "Bridging the Transatlantic Divide? The United States, the European Union, and the Protection of Privacy Across Borders." *International Journal of Constitutional Law* 14 (1): 220–37.

Cornelius, Wayne. 2018. *Mexico: From Country of Mass Emigration to Transit State*. Inter-American Development Bank. http://dx.doi.org/10.18235/0001415.

Düvell, Frank, Irina Molodikova, and Michael Collyer. 2014. *Transit Migration in Europe*. Amsterdam: Amsterdam University Press.

Enerstvedt, Olga M. 2014. "Russian PNR System: Data Protection Issues and Global Prospects." *Computer Law & Security Review* 30 (1): 25–40.

Ericsson, K. Anders. 1996. "The Acquisition of Expert Performance: An Introduction to some of the Issues." In *The Road the Excellence: The Acquisition of Expert Performance in the Arts and Sciences, Sports and Games*, edited by K. Anders Ericsson, 1–50. Mahwah, New Jersey: Lawrence Erlbaum Associates Publishers.

Ericsson, K. Anders, Ralf Th. Krampe, and Clemens Tesch-Romer. 1993. "The Role of Deliberate Practice in the Acquisition of Expert Performance." *Psychological Review* 100 (3): 363–406.

Everuss, Louis. 2021. "AI, Smart Borders and Migration." In *The Routledge Social Science Handbook of AI*, edited by Anthony Elliott, 339–56. London: Routledge.

Farrell, Henry, and Abraham L. Newman. 2019. *Of Privacy and Power: The Transatlantic Struggle over Freedom and Security*. Princeton, NJ: Princeton University Press.

Funk, Marco, and Florian Trauner. 2016. "Transatlantic Counter-Terrorism Cooperation." *European Union Institute for Security Studies Alerts* 15: 1–2.https://doi.org/10.2815/398052.

Givens, Austen D., Nathan E. Busch, and Alan D. Bersin. 2018. "Going Global: The International Dimensions of US Homeland Security Policy." *Journal of Strategic Security* 11 (3): 1–34.

Hale, Thomas, Noam Angrist, Rafael Goldszmidt, Beatriz Kira, Anna Petherick, Toby Phillips, Samuel Webster et al. 2021. "A Global Panel Database of Pandemic Policies (Oxford COVID-19 Government Response Tracker)." *Nature Human Behaviour* 5 (4): 529–38.

Han, Chang R., Rachel McGauran, and Hans Nelen. 2017. "API and PNR Data in use for Border Control Authorities." *Security Journal* 30 (4): 1045–63.

Hayes, Ben. 2017. "Migration and Data Protection: Doing No Harm in an Age of Mass Displacement, Mass Surveillance and 'Big Data.'" *International Review of the Red Cross* 99 (904): 179–209. https://doi.org/ doi:10.1017/S1816383117000637.

Helbling, Marc, and Dorina Kalkum. 2018. "Migration Policy Trends in OECD Countries." *Journal of European Public Policy* 25 (12): 1779–97.

Holzinger, Katharina, and Christoph Knill. 2005. "Causes and Conditions of Cross-national Policy Convergence." *Journal of European Public Policy* 12 (5): 775–96.

Huijboom, Noor, and Gabriela Bodea. 2015. "Understanding the Political PNR Debate in Europe: A Discourse Analytical Perspective." *European Politics and Society* 16 (2): 241–55.

Janelle, Christopher M., and Charles H. Hillman. 2003. "Expert Performance in Sport: Current perspectives and Critical Issues." In *Expert Performance in Sports: Advances in research on Sport Expertise*, edited by Janet L. Stakes and K. Anders Ericsson, 19–48. Champagne, IL: Human Kinetics.

Kenk, Vildana Sulic, Janez Križaj, Vitomir Štruc, and Simon Dobrišek. 2013. "Smart Surveillance Technologies in Border Control." *European Journal of Law and Technology* 4 (2): 1–12.

Krizsán, Andrea, and Violetta Zentai, eds. 2003. *Reshaping Globalization: Multilateral Dialogues and New Policy Initiatives*. Budapest: Central European University Press.

Lave, Jean. 1988. *Cognition in Practice: Mind, Mathematics, and Culture in Everyday Life*. Cambridge: Cambridge University Press.

Leese, Mathias, Simon Noori, and Stephen Scheel. 2022. "Data Matters: The Politics and Practices of Digital Border and Migration Management." *Geopolitics* 27 (1): 5–25.

Lowe, David. 2016. "The European Union's Passenger Name Record Data Directive 2016/681: Is It Fit for Purpose?" *International Criminal Law Review* 16 (5): 856–84.

McAuliffe, Marie, and Anna Triandafyllidou, eds. 2021. *World Migration Report 2022*. Geneva: International Organization for Migration.

Napieralski, Antoni. 2019. "Collecting Data at EU Smart Borders: Data Protection Challenges of the New Entry/Exit System." *Juridikum* (2): 199–209.

Offerman, Theo, and Joep Sonnemans. 1998. "Learning by Experience and Learning by Imitating Successful Others." *Journal of Economic Behavior and Organization* 34 (4): 55–75.

Peterson, John. 2018. "Structure, Agency and Transatlantic Relations in the Trump Era." *Journal of European Integration* 40 (5): 637–52.

Peterson, John, Richard Doherty, Michaël van Custem, Helen Wallace, Rachel Epstein, Fran Burwell, Mark A. Pollack, Joseph P. Quinlan, and Alasdair Young. 2005. *Review of the Framework for Relations Between the European Union and the United States. An Independent Study. Final Report.* 2004/S 83-070340. Brussels: European Commission.

Proctor, Robert W., and Kim-Phuong L.V. 2006. "Laboratory Studies of Training, Skill Acquisition, and Retention of Performance." In *The Cambridge Handbook of Expertise and Expert Performance*, edited by K. Anders Ericsson, Neil Charness, Paul J. Feltovich, and Robert R. Hoffmann, 265–86. Cambridge: Cambridge University Press.

Reckwitz, Andreas. 2002. "Toward a Theory of Social Practices: A Development in Culturalist Theorizing." *European Journal of Social Theory* 5 (2): 243–63.

Riddervold, Marianne, and Akasemi Newsome. 2018. "Transatlantic Relations in Times of Uncertainty: Crises and EU-US Relations." *Journal of European Integration* 40 (5): 505–21.

Rodenhäuser, Tilman. 2014. "Another Brick in the Wall: Carrier Sanctions and the Privatization of Immigration Control." *International Journal of Refugee Law* 26 (2): 223–47.

Schatzki, Theodore R., Karin K. Cetina, and Eike von Savigny, eds. 2001. *The Practice Turn in Contemporary Theory.* London: Routledge.

Starkes, Janet L., Janice M. Deakin, Fran Allard, Nicola J. Hodges, and April Hayes. 1996. "Deliberate Practice: What is it Anyway?" In *The Road the Excellence: The Acquisition of Expert Performance in the Arts and Sciences, Sports and Games*, edited by K. Anders Ericsson, 81–106. Mahwah, New Jersey: Lawrence Erlbaum Associates Publishers.

Starkey, Brigid, Mark A. Boyer, and Jonathan Wilkenfeld. 2005. *Negotiating a Complex World: An Introduction to International Negotiation.* 2nd ed. Lanham, MD: Rowman & Littlefield Publishers.

Tambou, Olivia. 2018. "Opinion 1/15 on the EU-Canada Passenger Name Record (PNR) Agreement: PNR Agreements Need to Be Compatible with EU Fundamental Rights." *European Foreign Affairs Review* 23 (2): 187–202. https://doi.org/10.54648/eerr2018020.

Taplin, Kailey. 2021. "South Africa's PNR Regime: Privacy and Data Protection." *Computer Law & Security Review* 40: 105524.

Trauttmansdorf, Paul. 2017. "The Politics of Digital Borders." In Border Politics: Defining Spaces of Governance and Forms of Transgressions, edited by Cengiz Günay and Nina Witjes, 107–26. Cham: Springer International Publishing.

Tukdi, Irfan. 2008. "Transatlantic Turbulence: The Passenger Name Record Conflict." *Houston Law Review* 45 (2): 587–620.

Tzanou, Maria. 2018. "The EU–US Data Privacy and Counterterrorism Agreements: What Lessons for Transatlantic Institutionalisation?" In *Institutionalisation Beyond the Nation State*, edited by Elaine Fahey, 55–74. Cham: Springer International.

UNWTO (United Nations World Tourism Organization). 2022. *World Tourism Barometer*. 20 (3) (May 2022).

Zaiotti, Ruben. 2011. *Cultures of Border Control: Schengen and the Evolution of European Frontiers*. Chicago: University of Chicago Press.

– 2012. "Practising Homeland Security Across the Atlantic: Practical Learning and Policy Convergence in Europe and North America." *European Security* 21 (3): 328–46.

15

Repertoires of Migration Governance in Europe and North America

Andrew Geddes

This chapter identifies and analyzes migration governance repertoires and their regional effects in Europe and North America. It draws on interviews with elite actors, conducted between 2014 and 2018 in the EU, Mexico, the United States, and Canada. While contexts between North America and Europe differ significantly, it is argued that a key effect in both regions arises from representations of the "normality" of migration and how these representations shape the responses to intermittent "crises." Elite actors in both Europe and the US, in particular, represent the potential for large-scale and potentially uncontrolled migration flows as a situation of "normality" with the potential, as they see it – whether it be real or imagined – for large-scale and potentially uncontrollable migration flows. These representations then shape responses to intermittent "crises" and drive parallel policies of deterrence. This was brought into stark relief by the Russian invasion of Ukraine and the displacement of more than 8 million Ukrainians by March 2023. This mass displacement has elicited a powerful and protective response across Europe for displaced Ukrainians – understood as Europeans – while the drive to deter non-European migration and refugee flows has continued.

The chapter's focus is on European and North American regionalism for two main reasons – albeit with the key caveat that they exemplify very different types of regional integration, specifically in terms of migration governance. The first reason, is that both regions – or key countries within them – have experienced significant immigration and the experience of the receiving states has played a powerful role in shaping regionalism. The second is the experience of relatively high levels of politicization around migration issues, albeit unevenly distributed across time and countries. In Europe, migration has been a high-salience political issue, with significant evidence of polarization. Similar patterns have been evident in the US too, with important effects on Mexico and migration policy and politics there.

To return to the caveat, a key difference is, of course, the extent of regional integration. This ranges from deep integration in Europe with free movement for EU citizens, plus the development of common responses to asylum and irregular migration for non-EU migrants. The EU also has a supranational institutional structure with legislative, judicial, and executive authority that is separate from the member states. In contrast, North American regionalism contains hardly any reference to migration and mobility, is strictly intergovernmental, and has a very limited – indeed barely existent – institutional framework. Thus, the point of comparison developed in this chapter's analysis is of elite perceptions of migration issues, which reveals key similarities between the drivers of migration governance within what, in many ways, are two very different regions.

The chapter first specifies what is meant by the terms regional, regionalism, and regionalization before paying attention to underlying concepts that inform the idea of migration governance repertoires. The chapter then uses empirical material from Europe and North America to explore their effects. This means that the chapter's focus is on governance processes, or, put another way, on opening the "black box" of migration governance to understand more about how elite actors perceive the challenges that they face. Focusing on these elite understandings or representations does not mean that international migration is something that occurs entirely in the minds of elite decision-makers. Rather, the research recognizes that international migration occurs because of powerful structural changes in social and natural systems, but that "migration governance occurs in the shadow of considerable uncertainty where facts, values and beliefs elide" (Geddes 2021, 1).

Perceptions and their effects are central to the analysis that follows. There are seminal works in the study of international relations that explore the causes and effects of perceptions and misperceptions, most notably Jervis's (2017) study of US-Soviet relations during the Cold War. Jervis (2008, 294) also argued that "to understand international behaviours we need to look inside the 'black box' of the state, and indeed to study the goals, beliefs and perceptions of the decision-makers." Actions emerge from distinct organizational contexts and the performance of roles, which means that they are "embedded in an organizational context, repeated over time and space, constituted by knowledge about the exploitation of potential force, and articulated as part of a complex set of other social performances, which may require learning and training" (Adler and Pouliot 2011, 7). Taking these insights into account in the context of approaching migration governance requires attending to the factors that shape and condition the perceptions of elite actors, and by extension, the political space that they understand themselves to be acting within.

Representations of migration – its causes, effects, and risks and uncertainties associated with it – have powerful effects on what is done and not done about migration. For an issue such as international migration, which is highly diverse and where facts and values combine in the shadow of uncertainty, it seems unlikely that perceptions are either wholly accurate or entirely inaccurate. It is also the case that a misperception or a partial perception if powerfully held – or held by the powerful – has significant real-world effects. These can be labelled "governance effects" that are themselves constitutive of international migration. What is meant by "constitutive" is that (mis)perceptions, (mis)representations, and (mis)judgments of what is going on "out there" – for example, of why people are migrating and the effects of migration – can shape or inform subsequent actions. Understood like this, international migration is not simply an exogenous shock to governance systems. Rather, it is manifestly the case that these systems of representation and repertoires play a powerful role in defining and shaping international migration.

REGIONAL GOVERNANCE

A distinction can be made between *regionalism* through the establishment of organizations that may or may not have competence for aspects of migration and *regionalization* that can be understood as broader social and economic processes that go beyond formal regionalism. While there are important differences between Europe and North America in the form and scope of regional integration, there is some convergence in terms of border management and security. Andreas (1998, 591) argues that a complex and paradoxical dynamic is at play as boundaries between developed and less developed countries, the expansion of cross-border economic activity, and the decline of geopolitical tensions are paralleled by a rapid expansion of border policing and rising tensions over prohibited cross-border flows. This is evident along the US-Mexico border and along the EU's external borders. Andreas goes on to note that: "These borders are increasingly protected and monitored, not to deter armies or impose tariffs on trade, but to confront a perceived invasion of "undesirables," particularly illegal immigrants, drug traffickers, and other clandestine transnational actors".

A wider point that emerges is the role played by borders in defining migration and migrants. It is crucial to note that some forms or types of migration have been defined as problematic and as subject to control and regulation, while others such as EU citizens with a right to free movement within the Union still pass relatively unheeded and tend not to be observed as a political problem. The term "migrants" then applies to particular groups of people whose arrival is defined as a threat to be deterred. A direct consequence of this has been the irregularization and criminalization of migration for these excluded groups, as well as pushing those who persist toward evermore dangerous routes.

Migration governance is always, everywhere, and necessarily an organizational process. This means that organizations – and actors within them – must address two basic questions: "what's going on out there" and, having come up with an answer to the first question, "what should we do next?" By addressing these questions, migration governance organizations shape the context in which they operate, meaning that migration governance is not an ex post response to migration flows; rather, migration governance systems actively shape international migration as a social and political issue through their categorizations based on judgments and misjudgments, perceptions and misperceptions, and inclusions and omissions.

Governance is generally seen as "a signifier of change," which could mean change in the meaning, processes, conditions, or methods of governing (Levi-Faur 2012). This chapter draws upon the dual meaning of governance identified by Pierre (2000) with two linked elements: the conceptual representation of change in underlying systems and processes, and efforts to manage or steer the effects of these changes. This is highly relevant for migration governance because migration itself is epiphenomenal, implying that the potential for, as well as limits to, the agency of migrants are necessarily shaped by changes in underlying social and natural systems. These changes in underlying systems are primarily economic and political, which can enable migration – the most obvious cases being the effects of relative inequalities between states or of conflict within or between states. These potential drivers and the extent to which they enable or constrain migrant agency are then influenced by social factors, particularly the operation and effects of migrant networks, the sociodemographic characteristics of migrants and would-be migrants (e.g., age, gender, ethnicity), and the effects of environmental/climate change. In turn, elite governance actors, with varying degrees of power and influence, try to make sense of what, for them, could be troubling issues that combine uncertainty and risk. Or, put more colloquially, they must address two questions: "what's going on 'out there?'" and "what should we do next?" Conversely, deciding what to do depends on understanding what's happening. Links between reasoning and actions – and justifications for those actions – are integral to the operation and effects of migration governance systems and thus shape and constrain perceptions of available repertoires.

The idea of a migration governance repertoire borrows from the sociologist Charles Tilly, whose work extensively documented the dynamics of political mobilization and protest. Tilly (1986, 4) understood a "repertoire" as being the ways in which individuals or groups make claims of different kinds on other individuals or groups. A repertoire of migration governance builds upon the idea of "narratives" as knowledge claims about migration. Narratives, as Boswell, Geddes, and Scholten (2011, 4) observe, contain "the factual beliefs espoused by policymakers and others engaged in policy debates." The idea of a repertoire goes beyond the notion of narratives to identify four other factors:

- *Social* content involves interorganizational relationships that can lie behind the representation of facts arising from interactions where positions are justified and challenged.
- *Affective* content involves responses to migration at a more emotional level as well as an emotional attachment to ideas and positions.
- *Performative* element arises when it is important to be seen to do *something* even if it is sometimes largely symbolic. Symbols are important because, as Edelman (1985, 1) observes they can "sustain and develop" individuals or "warp" them. These two need not be mutually exclusive: individuals can be sustained and developed by warped beliefs. Symbolic politics should not be seen as empty gestures because they can have powerful effects. Building walls as a migration control tool is a good example. Performance also plays a deeper and more embedded role in what have been called "international practices" that are "socially meaningful patterns of action which, in being performed more or less competently, simultaneously embody, act out, and possibly reify background knowledge and discourse in and on the material world" (Adler and Pouliot 2011, 6).
- *Ongoing* repertoires are considered so, because they do not have a beginning and an end. This means that, through their actions and inactions, actors both shape and are shaped by the environment in which they operate while, through interactions, they learn more about their own identities and about their accounts of the world (Thurlow and Helms Mills 2009).

Migration governance repertoires contain ways of knowing, ways of deciding, and ways of acting or behaving that can "stabilize" migration governance systems. Migration governance is replete with categories that can be normatively questionable but stabilize the field, at least from the perspective of elite policy actors. Destabilizing components then tend to be interpreted in the context of underlying representations within existing repertoires. In Europe, for example, mass Ukrainian displacement has led to a powerfully protective response to a displacement defined as European while reinforcing dynamics of externalization for non-Europeans who may be fleeing similar effects of conflict.

To support the analysis in this chapter, 220 interviews were conducted by the author and his research team between 2014 and 2018 with elite actors (defined by occupational role) in thirteen EU member states, with key actors at EU level in the EU institutions, and in the US, Mexico, and Canada. Interviews did not focus on organizational role or things that could be gleaned from a website or policy documents, but, instead, they tried to understand more about underlying representations and their effects. Interviewees were asked to identify what they saw as the key drivers of international migration and the extent to which they thought that these might change in the future. They were also asked to identify key risks and uncertainties and how their organizations dealt with them. They were also asked about their own sources of information and how significant events or experiences had affected their understanding of international migration.

EUROPEAN REGIONALISM

This section analyses the deeper regionalism in the European Union, while also highlighting the persistent influence of elite perceptions of the potential for uncontrollable or irregular migration flows, which has been a key driver of migration policy in Europe and, as will be seen in the next section, in North America too.

The analytical focus is on developments after 2015, although there are longer-standing patterns of cooperation and integration upon which these build. In September 2020, the European Commission published a *New* Pact on Migration and Asylum (CEC 2020, emphasis added). This followed on from the Global Approach to Migration of 2007, the Global Approach to Migration and Mobility of 2011, and the European Agenda on Migration of 2015 (CEC 2011, 2015). The use of the word "new" signalled very clearly an attempt to break with previous approaches that were seen to have failed, most notably, to deliver a common EU approach to the events after 2015, which are labelled as the "refugee crisis." An immediate question is how "new" is the pact? Does it break with previous approaches or are there significant continuities? A related question is: to what extent was the pact a response to a crisis after 2015 that changed the path of European and EU migration governance?

The new pact was an attempt by the European Commission to draw a line under the failed response to the post-2015 refugee crisis. Two elements of failure were particularly relevant. The first was the effective collapse of the Dublin system, put in place in the early 1990s to allocate responsibility among member states for asylum applications. The idea that an asylum application would be made in the first EU country in which an asylum seeker arrived remained central to the EU's attempt to develop a Common European Asylum System until 2015. In August 2015, however, German Chancellor Angela Merkel announced that the German authorities would suspend the Dublin procedure for Syrians fleeing the civil war in that country ("*wir schaffen das*," ["we can do this,"] as Merkel put it). Around 890,000 asylum applicants from Syria arrived in Germany that year. In September 2015, EU member states agreed to a scheme for relocation of asylum applicants away from those countries of first arrival that were under pressure from high numbers of arrivals, particularly Greece and Italy. By October of that year, Germany was reimposing controls by, for example, tightening the border with Austria and also declaring Albania, Kosovo, and Montenegro as safe countries, meaning that asylum applications lodged in Germany by people who had moved across those countries would not be assessed. The so-called Balkan route was also tightened when Slovenia, Croatia, Serbia, and Macedonia effectively closed their borders to migrants.

The second element of failure occurred when, in September 2015, a scheme for relocation of up to 160,000 asylum applicants from Greece and Italy to other member states was agreed by the EU member states, but never fully implemented. Governments that had high numbers of arrivals, particularly Greece and Italy, were strong advocates of solidarity via the relocation of asylum seekers across the EU. Particularly vociferous opposition to relocation came from the Visegrád group, comprising the Czech Republic, Hungary, Poland, and Slovakia, who effectively refused to accept relocated asylum applicants. In April 2020, the Court of Justice ruled that the Czech Republic, Poland, and Hungary had failed to implement their treaty obligations by refusing to accept any relocated asylum applicants, but, even after this negative decision, the Hungarian interior minister, Judit Varga, was able to tweet that the "EU compulsory relocation system of migrants is dead and today's CJEU judgement won't change that. It must be lonesome in the saddle since the horse died" (Zalan 2020).

The new pact tried to breathe life into the "horse." This was done by proposing a system of "flexible" solidarity that would not require the mandatory relocation of asylum seekers between member states. Member states could either choose to accept relocated asylum seekers or, if they refused, they would be able to "sponsor" the return/expulsion of failed asylum applicants from other member states or provide funding for migration policies in countries of origin and transit. The task for the Commission was to turn the ideas in the pact into legislation, which will be difficult given the divisions between member states. The context for this was redefined in 2022 by the full-scale Russian invasion of Ukraine and mass displacement. Within days of the invasion, the EU agreed to invoke – for the first time – the Temporary Protection Directive (TPD) that grants protection to Ukrainians fleeing the conflict for up to three years and allows them to move freely within the EU and access services such as housing, health care, and education. Significantly, the TPD had been within the EU legal framework since 2001 without ever being invoked, despite significant waves of migration by people seeking protection – most notably from Syria after 2015. The EU "internalized" its response to Ukrainian migration via the TPD while continuing to "externalize" its response to non-European migrants and refugees.

We now trace the origins of this situation to show how they are grounded in underlying understandings of the normality of migration, by which is meant scope for large-scale or uncontrollable flows. This also provides a point of comparison with North America where similar perceptions in the US as the regional hegemon have influenced policy development, albeit as has already been noted, in an entirely different regional setting. The basis for these shared perceptions was identified at the end of 2014 when we asked an interviewee from an EU agency to reflect on the causes and effects of migration and he responded: "Yesterday at this meeting of the US and the Commission and others ... [they] were repeatedly mentioning that this will be the new normal. These 250,000–280,000 irregular migrants a year, that's basically what we have to count on in the foreseeable future. Nothing will change in this regard. I tend to agree, because as long as things are going the way they are going on in North Africa, sub-Saharan African countries, Afghanistan, Iraq, what have you, I don't see an end unfortunately to that" (Interview, EU agency official, Brussels, December 2014).

Whether accurate or not, this view is based on a representation of the effects on migration of changes in the underlying drivers of migration held by elite actors in Europe and the United States; in this case, the effects of conflict. It provides an anchor against which assessments or judgments are made. The view was shaped by interactions between EU and US officials. Whether this is understood as being an "old" or a "new" challenge, the key word is "normal,". This is because of the way that representations of the perceived normality of migration shape judgments. Interestingly, in terms of the use of language, the European Commission in June 2016 proposed a new framework for working in partnership on migration with non-EU countries and also used the phrase "new normal" with reference to potential migration pressures. The Commission made a clear link between the framing of the issue (as external migratory pressure) and a set of proposed remedies: "External migratory pressure is the 'new normal' both for the EU and for partner countries. This requires a more coordinated, systematic and structured approach to maximize the synergies and leverages of the Union's internal and external policies" (CEC 2016).

The point is that such representations are not necessarily new. An effect of the end of the Cold War was to generate concern about the potential for large-scale migration flows to Western Europe from the former Soviet Union and its then satellite states in Central Europe. In the following section, we see their long-standing resonance in the United States too. In Europe, during the 1990s, Germany was Europe's key destination country. Around 1.1 million ethnic German *Aussiedler* (ethnic Germans not resident in Germany) moved to Germany from Central and Eastern Europe and from the former Soviet bloc. As ethnic Germans, they had a right to return under Germany's Basic Law, although restrictions were later imposed. The break-up of the former Yugoslavia also led to increased flows of asylum seekers, again with Germany as a preferred destination. Just over 1.5 million asylum seekers moved to Germany between 1989 and 1994. Framed by the idea of a migration crisis, the German government sought to "export" the crisis to the EU level (Henson and Malhan 1995). One practical example of this was the development of the idea of "safe third countries." Neighbouring countries to Germany in Central and Eastern Europe with the incentive of EU membership were incorporated within the EU framework for migration controls via their designation as "safe third countries" to which asylum applicants could be returned if they had passed through them on their way to an EU member state (Lavenex 1999; see Banerjee in this volume for related discussion).

The Dublin Convention of 1992 was particularly important because it established the principle that asylum seekers should make their application in the member states in which they arrived and not be able to move on to another member state. The convention began as an agreement in international law, but the subsequent Dublin regulation became a key legal instrument within what is now known as the Common European Asylum System.

By the end of the 1990s, the EU was beginning to elaborate measures on migration and asylum. At the time, these took the form of intergovernmental cooperation that required consensus and left only a limited role for EU institutions. The member states were also thinking collectively about the causes and effects of migration and this was having important effects on actions. The EU migration policy field has become much more densely populated since, but it was national interior ministries that set the direction of EU cooperation on migration and asylum in the 1980s and 1990s (Guiraudon 2000). It has been difficult ever since to deviate from the course that was set and the associated repertoire (Trauner and Servent 2016). Underlying knowledge of the causes and effects of migration emerged and was consolidated during this period and become embedded at EU level and associated with the idea that there was a major challenge – both real and latent – posed by large-scale flows to the external borders of EU member states.

Concern about large-scale flows enacted a "sensible environment" – by which is meant that it made sense to the actors concerned – and that centred on representations of the causes and effects of migration that not only appeared plausible to key governance actors but also motivated actions. A repertoire of migration governance was developed that shaped both the know-how and also expectations about roles held by key actors in European migration governance systems. This repertoire, as in other regions, involved narrative claims, but was social, affective, performative, and has been ongoing with effects clearly visible in the 2020s. Even by the early 1990s we can see the emergent shape of the EU "policy core," with a focus on stemming those flows defined as "unwanted" by member state policies. The 1990s were crucial years because they had a powerful and enduring effect on what key governance actors knew how to do and also their expectations about their role. We see similar dynamics in the US too in relation to "deterrence," discussed ahead.

The normality of EU cooperation on migration and asylum, as it developed after the 1990s, has been shaped by responses to intermittent crises that have centred on concern about real or potential migration flows and their controllability. This can then lead to confirmation bias, where such information is favoured that supports views that are already held. This quote from an Austrian government official when reflecting on conversations with Dutch colleagues helps to illustrate this point about the influence of past events on current representations: "I didn't have the feeling that there was really a new discussion … what we are discussing, what we consider as new ideas, they've already been discussing that in the early nineties" (Interview, interior ministry official, Vienna, January 2018).

Similarly, an official from the German Interior Ministry put it like this: "We also feel kind of, yes, confirmed in the certain premises we always made. Unfortunately, sometimes not the right conclusions were drawn from the actual knowledge which was available here at the level of experts so that this enormous influx could take place in the dimension we have seen" (Interview, interior ministry official, Berlin, March 2018).

This quote exemplifies the importance of looking back not only to provide a frame of reference but also to provide confirmation of an account of the causes and effects of migration.

Crises and the ways in which they are defined and understood are necessarily set against representations of the underlying causes and effects of migration, or put another way, the normality of migration. As an example, consider this first paragraph of a 2017 statement from a European Commission document evaluating delivery of the European Agenda on Migration (CEC 2017, 2):

> In the last two years, Europe experienced the largest number of arrivals of refugees and migrants since the end of the Second World War. The Syrian crisis played an important part in generating this record number, as did conflicts, instability and poverty in many parts of the world. Migration, asylum and border management systems were put under huge pressure. The Union and its Member States were not sufficiently prepared to respond effectively. The scale of the crisis had a powerful impact across the EU. The integrity of both the Common European Asylum System and of the Schengen area of free movement for European citizens was put into question.

This statement provides a representation of the reasons why people move to the EU and of EU actions. It refers to a lack of preparedness, high pressures on migration systems, and challenges to the integrity of these systems. Migration itself is represented as an act of desperation, driven by poverty, conflict, and instability. It is true that those who entered the EU by boat, crossing the Mediterranean Sea, were fleeing desperate circumstances and were exposed to many dangers. But most migrants to Europe do not enter by boat across the Mediterranean; they enter via regular channels for employment, or to join family, or to study, motivated by hope, love, aspiration, and ambition (Eurostat 2018). The point is that this kind of representation – of migration as an act of desperation – plays into longer-standing concerns about large-scale migration to the EU. In this sense, the "crisis" also represented powerful ideas about the causes and effects of migration. The practical effect is that a perception of what is normal about migration then enables certain actors and agendas to mobilize and to stake claims to resources that aim to stem or deter flows.

In 2015, during Europe's so-called refugee crisis, the number of people entering the EU via Mediterranean routes peaked at just over one million, of which around 450,000 originated from Syria. Greece, with around 830,000 people arriving in 2015, became a visual and political focus for the crisis, with hundreds of thousands of people then moving on in seemingly haphazard ways through Central Europe toward Germany, which was the preferred destination for many migrants. As flows across the Mediterranean increased in 2015 and into 2016, urgent measures were put in place by EU governments to try to reduce the numbers of arrivals and also to stop onward movement within the EU. An effect of this was the reimposition of border controls within the Schengen area. Efforts were made by the EU to get non-EU member states such as Turkey to stop people moving to the EU or, if they did get to Europe, to return them to the countries they moved from. An EU-Turkey agreement of March 2016 contributed to major reductions in numbers of people moving across what was called the "eastern Mediterranean" route from Turkey to Greece (Alpes et al. 2017).

The dynamics of the crisis between 2015 and 2019 also shifted in ways linked to EU policy interventions. Following the EU-Turkey statement of April 2016, the numbers of migrants moving along the "eastern Mediterranean" route from Turkey to Greece fell from 176,000 in 2016 to 35,000 in 2017. The statement provided for the return of all irregularly arriving Syrian nationals from Greek Islands to Turkey; a mechanism for one vulnerable Syrian to move to the EU for every Syrian returned to Turkey; a EUR 6-billion facility for refugees in Turkey; and designation of Turkey as a "safe third country" to allow the return of asylum applicants from the EU who had passed through Turkey (Council of the EU 2016). After the EU-Turkey statement came into effect and crossings via the eastern Mediterranean fell, the main point of arrival for Mediterranean crossings became Italy, where a total of 300,000 people arrived in 2016 and 2017, although this number fell back sharply to 23,000 in 2018 and to just under 11,500 in 2019 after Italy reached agreement with the Libyan authorities to prevent departures (Caponio and Cappiali 2018).

At the official level, the focus was directed almost entirely to the data on numbers of arrivals, who would arrive on almost a daily basis during 2015 and 2016. A European Commission official conveyed the immediacy: "When the numbers are up, we are under pressure. When the numbers are down, we are less under pressure. The effect of this immediacy was, in effect, a crisis bias that distracts from longer-term thinking … The debate is completely biased by the crisis" (European Commission official, Brussels, November 2017). This does not mean that there are not efforts to think beyond crises, but these too are framed by representations of the normality of migration, particularly concerns about the persistent pressure of large-scale flows. What did change as a result of the crisis was the level of politicization of migration, as the issue became salient across the EU, had important effects on election outcomes, and caused increased polarization within the political systems.

NORTH AMERICAN REGIONALISM

We now compare Europe with North America where, without strong formal regionalism, a regional effect is evident not only in policies and practices associated with borders and migration, but also in the underlying perceptions of the causes and effects of migration and in the social expectations about the roles that are held by key migration governance actors. This regional effect in North America does not mean that there is a shared understanding between Canada, Mexico, and the US; rather, it entails the effects on migration governance of particularly influential understandings. The resultant repertoire of migration governance powerfully centers on, and is driven by, understandings of the causes and effects of migration to the United States, in particular on the perceived role of "pull" factors exerted by the US economy and society and on deterrence measures that have developed to prevent migration. While the focus on border security itself was not new, the 11 September 2001 (or 9/11) terror attacks had transformative effects on regional security. Policies and approaches to immigration in the United States have been informed by particular understandings of the causes and effects of migration that have been shaped by the idea that the US economy and society exert a powerful pull for migrants. A negative politicization of immigration has informed the development of deterrence-based approaches since at least the 1980s. While there were no migration provisions in the North American Free Trade Agreement (NAFTA) or its successor, there has been cooperation on border issues that have been defined by security concerns and that have had important implications for migration governance. Regional migration governance has also been punctuated by intermittent crises, particularly in the US, but these have tended to affirm rather than shift the underlying understandings. The Trump presidency was an extreme manifestation of a hardline anti-immigration and anti-immigrant agenda, but elements of its approach are consistent with a longer-standing focus on border security and deterrence.

Perceptions of the causes and effects of migration play an important role. This can also include perceptions of how migrants perceive their own migration, as this official from the US Citizenship and Immigration Services (USCIS) put it when referring to his view of the factors that motivated migrant decision-making: "But the perception that now is the time to send your child out to get into the United States because the United States will accept these individuals, there is a lot of different instances of that perception. And, individuals sending their children and putting them in harm's way in order to take advantage of what they perceive is a policy that will allow their children to come in. That happens all the time" (Interview, USCIS official, Washington, DC, June 2015).

The idea of US openness is seen as being taken advantage of by migrants and as having an effect on decisions by families to send children to the US. If this is what officials think is happening "out there" then such a perspective would suggest that it could be necessary to try to deter such behaviours. Experiences of past events can also play a powerful role in shaping judgment which can combine with the effects of uncertainty, as was put to us by an official from the US Department for Homeland Security (DHS): "I think the more I've been in government the more I realize that senior officials ... are constantly making decisions with imperfect information. All they can do is rely on their experience and their judgement, in an environment that is inherently uncertain and unpredictable, to be able to make the best decision that they can, at the time, with the information they have" (Interview, DHS official, Washington, DC, June 2015).

The reference here is not only to limits on information, but also to how experience and judgment shape decision-making. Looking back to past experiences – as well as its limits – was captured by a Canadian government official who said: "There's a large focus on evidence-based policymaking, which makes a lot of sense, but I find in a way is backward looking by definition. You're measuring what has happened before and deciding what to do next based on how things were working" (Interview, Citizenship and Immigration Canada official, Ottawa, March 2016). Political direction is clearly important as this State Department official noted when comparing the Obama and Trump administrations: "Let's say there was a greater level of specificity and direction for particular policies because the incoming [Trump] administration had clearly given a lot of thought to this and had very, I would say, very solid ideas about what they wanted to pursue" (Interview, State Department official, Washington, DC, September 2018).

These quotes highlight: the importance of know-how, but also its contingency; how past experiences – particularly those judged successful – can anchor assessment of current challenges; how decision-makers may have to balance competing priorities; and the effects of changes in political leadership.

Expectations of role can also play a part, particularly of how wider public expectations are understood. An interviewee from US Customs and Border Patrol (CBP) in July 2015 put it like this: "The 9/11 experience for us has been monumental in how the public sees the work ... [and] ... the American public, in our case, wanted to have answers on and wanted to see metrics and cared more about what we did" (Interview, CBP official, Washington, DC, July 2015).

This sense of the issues becoming a preoccupation for all Americans who want "answers" has powerful effects on the migration governance repertoire in the US and its regional effects on Canada and Mexico. The 9/11 terror attacks had powerful structuring consequences on what governance actors in the US thought they should be doing. For a Mexican government official, this repatterning of migration dynamics fed directly into concern about how the US and to a lesser extent Canada perceive Mexico: "Mexico has the responsibility to keep working with the United States and Canada as partners. We need to accomplish and rescue some of these trilateral and regional initiatives in relation to migration that we were working on. Right now, the United States looks at Mexico as the problem and not as part of the solution, which we are" (Interview, Mexican government official, Mexico City, July 2017).

Such quotes are not meant to validate particular understandings of roles and expectations, but to show how actors in influential positions interpret and respond to signals and cues from their environment. It is certainly the case that 9/11 was a compelling signal for the US, with powerful effects on regional security and migration governance. Trump's election in 2016 simultaneously destabilized regional relationships while also heightening their importance.

In Mexico, there has been a major reshaping of migration dynamics from being a country of emigration to a much more complex situation of immigration, emigration, transit migration, and return, but, as always, powerfully influenced by the United States. Mexico's border with the US is a major international border of inequality across which there are intensive linkages (Selee 2018). Since the 2000s, Mexico has transitioned from being primarily a sending country, with most migrants moving to the US, to a much more complex situation with emigration from and immigration to Mexico as well as increasing numbers of Mexican returnees from the US. More recently, a heightened focus on border security, as well as transit migration, has emerged, particularly by men, women, and children from Central American countries, with many demonstrating protection needs.

The US policy focus increasingly shifted to the border with Mexico and the emergence of what Rosenblum (2011) refers to as "prevention through deterrence" – which became a mantra that developed during the Clinton administration after 1993, underpinned regional cooperation within NAFTA after 1994, and has persisted through into the approaches of the Biden administration. Prevention through deterrence makes attempted border crossings costlier and riskier. These were not "unintended consequences" as they were the specific intention of the prevention through deterrence approach (Cornelius 2001, 667). Higher costs also meant that migrants from Mexico in the US were unwilling to return to Mexico because the costs of getting back to the US were so high. It was also thought that forcing people into more dangerous routes would be a deterrent effect, which, again, was intentional and not an unintended consequence (Sanchez 2016).

There was skepticism expressed about the merits of a deterrence-based approach. Andreas (1998, 593) saw it as having more of a symbolic value that was: "less to do with actual deterrence and more to do with managing the image of the border and coping with the deepening contradictions of economic integration," while Gilbert (2009, 29) argued that: "deterrence as control and security risk management comes to legitimize the endless demand for wall technologies separating the USA and Mexico." Nevertheless, deterrence remains a central component of the "sensible environment" that informs US responses and that has a regional effect, as was put to us in 2015 by an official with US CBP: "We've really gotten very good at protecting large pieces of border that were previously unprotected or unaffective [sic] in our response. People always ask, "Well, is it the economy or is it what you guys do?" The economy is a big driver. If there is opportunity here, people are going to come, but also if they're caught and sent back, they stop coming. The economics don't work for them. You can only make a couple of attempts" (Interview, CBP official, Washington, DC, July 2015). This statement clearly expresses a view on the economic "pull" exerted by the US but also the perceived power of deterrence if people are apprehended and sent back to Mexico.

There was also a more insidious effect because, to make another attempt at entry, and to be re-apprehended, was considered as illegal entry and a criminal offence. This perception is consistent with the direction of US policy established in the 1980s and that developed further after 1996 in the Illegal Immigration Reform and Immigrant Responsibility Act (IIRIA) that increased enforcement efforts, but was also significant in that it marked a shift in the terms of domestic political debate away from the economic contributions of migrants toward a more pronounced focus on what were seen as migrants' use and abuse of public benefits and also the idea that the border was porous (Freeman and Birrell 2001). In terms of their place in the migration governance repertoire, perceptions of welfare abuse by migrants and the idea that the border is porous have been key drivers of US actions.

The end result is a particular kind of regional effect. In September 2018, a US State Department official captured quite succinctly the key characteristics of North American regional migration governance, or, to be more precise, its absence: "We're happy to say regionalism but in a very kind of not quite ad hoc but a looser sort of way. Happy to coordinate, happy to talk, happy to have standing structures to do it but there is no kind of coercion about it. That's something we would never accept, and I don't think most other governments in the region would either" (Interview, US State Department official, Washington, DC, September 2018). While there is no formalized regional migration governance, there is a North American migration governance repertoire that has a clear regional effect. As has been documented earlier, this stems primarily from developments in US immigration politics that focus on border security and prevention of migration through what are understood as deterrence measures, including detention.

A regional effect is evident through what Hadj Abdou (2019, 146) calls a "double bilateralism" linking Canada and Mexico with the US. This is clearly not a vehicle for supranational integration, but functions "as a tool to protect the interests of nation states in a globalized world." While the USA dominates regional interactions, the effects on both Canada and Mexico have been powerful. Canadians have a privileged travel relationship with the US, but the price for this has been the integration of Canada into US border security measures and preoccupations (See Koslowski and Leckey in this volume). Mexico was very much in the eye of the storm during the Trump presidency with inhumane and brutalizing border control and detention measures as well as efforts to keep Central American migrants in Mexico. The COVID-19 pandemic was used as cover for measures introduced under Title 42 of the 1944 Public Health Act to stop the spread of communicable diseases, but also to reinforce existing measures to prevent border crossing from Mexico. Plans to repeal Title 42 by the Biden administration became part of a highly charged political context reflecting both politicization and polarization in the run-up to the 2022 midterm elections. Being in power, the Biden administration maintained Title 42 provisions until May 2023 even as the pandemic's effect waned.

To bring the two sections together, in North America and Europe, intermittent crises have both shaped and been shaped by international migration. The US reaction to the 9/11 terror attacks had particularly powerful effects and reshaped regional security, but, in doing so, drew from already established components of a migration governance repertoire. There were intermittent migration and border crises before the 9/11 attacks. When evaluating events, governance actors often refer back to past experiences or to the experiences of others, because, as already shown throughout this chapter, meaning is given to events through interactions with others. When asked about risks and uncertainties, this interviewee from US CBP highlighted that current events are not necessarily new: "It's that way. It's always been like that; it's been like that since the 1990s. Having read and been able to talk to other people who had already been part of the federal government in the 1990s, they all told me the same thing: that it's cyclical" (Interview,

CBP official, Washington, DC, June 2015). When assessing child migration in 2014 and 2015, this official from the US State Department referred back to experiences in the 1990s with migration from Cuba during the Clinton administration and the so-called wet foot, dry foot policy: "Any Cuban we interdicted would be brought to the US and once they got to US soil they were 'legal'… That, again, showed to me that where migrants had a sense that their chances of success actually getting to the US were high, they would do something illegal or something dangerous. So that, too, showed me that we have to make clear that the chances of success are not high and we have to demonstrate that in the policy choices we make" (Interview, State Department official, Washington, DC, June 2015).

Intermittent crises have been shaped by underlying understandings of the "normality" of migration that, since the 1990s, have focused on the porousness of borders, the powerful pull factor exerted by the US economy and society, and the subsequent need to deter migrants.

CONCLUSION

While there are profound differences in the form and scope of regional cooperation on migration in Europe and North America this chapter has argued that focusing on elite perceptions and representations allows for the identification of points of convergence. To develop this point, the chapter understood governance as possessing a dual meaning as the conceptual representation of change in underlying social and natural systems and then efforts to manage or steer these changes as understood. This definition of governance highlights the importance of understandings and representations of migration held by elite actors in Europe and North America. It was argued that these can be understood as illustrative of migration governance repertoires that contribute to the creation of "sensible environments" that make sense to the actors involved and provide a basis to proceed without necessarily proving accurate. It was argued that in Europe and in North America, albeit powerfully driven by the USA, an understanding of the normality of migration has developed that centers on concern or fear of large-scale and potentially uncontrollable migration flows that have then informed policies of deterrence. These have become relatively stable components of migration governance repertoires in Europe and North America and have been stubbornly resistant to change with effects on the content of migration policymaking, on relations between states in the regional organizations, and on states that neighbour the European and North American regions.

NOTE

The research upon which these findings are based was funded by the European Research Council through the award of an Advanced Investigator Grant for the project Prospects for International Migration Governance (MIGPROSP) 2014–19. Thanks to the editors and Dr Kelsey Norman for their helpful comments and suggestions.

REFERENCES

Adler, Emanuel, and Vincent Pouliot. 2011. *International Practices*. Cambridge: Cambridge University Press.

Alpes, Maybritt Jill, Sevda Tunaboylu, Orcun Ulusoy, and Saima Hassan. 2017. "Post-Deportation Risks under the EU-Turkey Statement: What Happens after Readmission to Turkey?" Policy Brief 2017/30. Florence: Migration Policy Centre. https://doi.org/10.2870/132639.

Andreas, Peter. 1998. "The Escalation of U.S. Immigration Control in the Post-NAFTA Era." *Political Science Quarterly* 113 (4): 591–615. https://doi.org/10.2307/2658246.

Boswell, Christina, Andrew Geddes, and Peter Scholten. 2011. "The Role of Narratives in Migration Policy-Making: A Research Framework." *The British Journal of Politics & International Relations* 13 (January): 1–11. https://doi.org/10.1111/j.1467-856X.2010.00435.x.

Caponio, Tiziana, and Teresa Cappiali. 2018. "Italian Migration Policies in Times of Crisis: The Policy Gap Reconsidered." *South European Society and Politics* 23 (1): 115–32. https://doi.org/10.1080/13608746.2018.1435351.

CEC (Commission of the European Communities). 2011. "Communication from the Commission to the European Parliament, the Council, the European Economic and Social Committee and the Committee of the Regions. The Global Approach to Migration and Mobility." COM(2011) 743. Brussels: CEC.

– 2015. "Communication from the Commission to the European Parliament, the Council, the European Economic and Social Committee and the Committee of the Regions. A European Agenda on Migration." COM(2015) 240 final. Brussels: CEC.

– 2016. "On Establishing a New Partnership Framework with Third Countries under the European Agenda on Migration." COM(2016) 385 final. Strasbourg: CEC.

– 2017. "On the Delivery of the European Agenda on Migration." COM(2017) 558 final. Brussels: CEC.

– 2020. "A New Pact on Migration and Asylum." Brussels: CEC.

Cornelius, Wayne A. 2001. "Death at the Border: Efficacy and Unintended Consequences of US Immigration Control Policy." *Population and Development Review* 27 (4): 661–85. https://doi.org/10.1111/j.1728-4457.2001.00661.x.

Council of the European Union. 2016. "EU-Turkey Statement." Press Release 144/16.

Edelman, Murray Jacob. 1985. *The Symbolic Uses of Politics*. University of Illinois Press.

Eurostat. 2018. "Residence Permits - Statistics on First Permits Issued During the Year." Eurostat. https://ec.europa.eu/eurostat/statistics-explained/index.php?title=Residence_permits_-_statistics_on_first_permits_issued_during_the_year&oldid=507019. Accessed 14 April 2023.

Freeman, Gary P., and Bob Birrell. 2001. "Divergent Paths of Immigration Politics in the United States and Australia." *Population and Development Review* 27 (3): 525–51. https://doi.org/10.1111/j.1728-4457.2001.00525.x.

Geddes, Andrew. 2021. *Governing Migration Beyond the State*. Oxford: Oxford University Press.

Gilbert, Liette. 2009. "Immigration as Local Politics: Re-Bordering Immigration and Multiculturalism through Deterrence and Incapacitation." *International Journal of Urban and Regional Research* 33 (1): 26–42. https://doi.org/10.1111/j.1468-2427.2009.00838.x.

Guiraudon, Virginie. 2000. "European Integration and Migration Policy: Vertical Policy-Making as Venue Shopping." *Journal of Common Market Studies* 38 (2): 251–71. https://doi.org/10.1111/1468-5965.00219.

Hadj Abdou, Leila. 2019. "North America: Weak Regionalism, Strong Borders." In *The Dynamics of Regional Migration Governance*, edited by Andrew Geddes, Marcia Vera Espinoza, Leila Hadj Abdou, and Leiza Brumat, 146–65. Cheltenham: Edward Elgar.

Henson, Penny, and Nisha Malhan. 1995. "Endeavours to Export a Migration Crisis: Policy Making and Europeanisation in the German Migration Dilemma." *German Politics* 4 (3): 128–44. https://doi.org/10.1080/09644009508404417.

Jervis, Robert. 2008. "Signaling and Perception: Drawing Inferences and Projecting Images." In *Political Psychology*, edited by Kristin Monroe, 293–312. London: Lawrence Erlbaum.

– 2017. *Perception and Misperception in International Politics*. Princeton, NJ: Princeton University Press.

Lavenex, Sandra. 1999. *Safe Third Countries: Extending the EU Asylum and Immigration Policies to Central and Eastern Europe*. Budapest: Central European University Press.

Levi-Faur, David. 2012. "From 'Big Government' to 'Big Governance'?" In *The Oxford Handbook of Governance*, edited by David Levi-Faur, 3–18. Oxford: Oxford University Press.

Pierre, Jon, ed. 2000. *Debating Governance: Authority, Steering, and Democracy*. Oxford: Oxford University Press.

Rosenblum, Marc. 2011. "Obstacles and Opportunities for Regional Cooperation: The U.S.-Mexico Case." Washington, DC: Migration Policy Institute.

Sanchez, Gabriella. 2016. "Women's Participation in the Facilitation of Human Smuggling: The Case of the US Southwest." *Geopolitics* 21 (2): 387–406. https://doi.org/10.1080/14650045.2016.1140645.

Selee, Andrew. 2018. *Vanishing Frontiers: The Forces Driving Mexico and the United States Together*. New York: Hachette.

Thurlow, Amy, and Jean Helms Mills. 2009. "Change, Talk and Sensemaking." *Journal of Organizational Change Management* 22 (5): 459–79. https://doi.org/10.1108/09534810910983442.

Tilly, Charles. 1986. *The Contentious French: Four Centuries of Popular Struggle*. Cambridge, MA: Belknap.

Trauner, Florian, and Ariadna Servent. 2016. "The Communitarization of the Area of Freedom, Security and Justice: Why Institutional Change Does Not Translate into Policy Change." *JCMS: Journal of Common Market Studies* 54 (6): 1417–32. https://doi.org/10.1111/jcms.12397.

Zalan, Esther. 2020. "Court: Three Countries Broke EU Law on Migrant Relocation." *EU Observer*, 2 April 2020.

AFTERWORD

Human Mobility Needs Strategic Planning: Moving Beyond Populist and Exploitative Immigration Policies

François Crépeau

Migration is a part of humanity's DNA. We humans are constantly on the move, for all sorts of reasons. All countries are lands of mobility, being at the same time, in various proportions, countries of emigration, transit, and immigration. They all face multiple challenges: demographic shifts, such as an aging population or an inactive youth; economic challenges, such as a need for innovation, informal economic sectors, or labour shortages; social challenges, such as ensuring pensions and social protection; etc.

One key to meeting these needs is the relative free movement of people. States have managed this during the rural exodus that occurred historically in Europe and North America and is now occurring throughout the Global South. Regional free-movement zones, such as Europe's Schengen Area or South America's MERCOSUR (Mercado Común del Sur [Southern Common Market]), have shown this can be implemented in an interstate context, with significant positive outcomes for people, economies, and security. The long-term objective should therefore be regulated, conditional free movement for most non-citizens. To achieve this goal, multiple changes – both in terms of policy and in perspective – are required.

This volume shows how important migration and mobility policies in North America are, both from the point of view of migrants moving within and to the region, and from the perspective of the dire consequences of existing migration control policies for too many migrants.

Contemporary North America both grew and thrived thanks to migration, yet it still often treats most migrants as simple factors of production and equates the mobility of people with the mobility of goods, services, and capital. The refusal to build a full free-movement-of-persons section into successive free trade agreements (except for a minute number of businesspeople) is telling of the glaring absence of strategic vision that North American politicians have demonstrated on the issue over several decades.

The insistence on "border security" since 9/11 has transformed many migrants into objects of systematic suspicion and trumped most other considerations that could have pushed for a more rational migration governance – one that would bank on the migrants' agency and capacity to survive and thrive. Indeed, several chapters of this volume have shown how resourceful migrants can be when responding to the challenges they face. Their agency is too often discounted or considered a threat, thus considerably reducing the contributions they could make to their host society.

Other chapters have shown how states try to govern human mobility through myriad of single-issue-focused international agreements, such as bilateral temporary labour migration agreements or safe third country agreements, thus disregarding the multifaceted nature of migration and the adaptability of human nature. Creating multiple categories, each with their limited obligations, rights, and entitlements, produces a regulatory entanglement – one which enriches lawyers through migrants with high social and economic capital, while trapping those migrants who lack these resources in an often incomprehensible and arbitrary bureaucratic maze.

Many chapters highlight the human and financial cost for migrants of externalized border controls, and the hijacking of international development funds to finance what often amount to outsourced migration controls. They show that such strategies are counterproductive in that they create and subsidize criminal and exploitative underground markets. Finally, some chapters illustrate the volatility of migration governance policies, which are systematically reactive to the latest political pressure, brought about by any negative incident involving migrants at the border or within communities.

By way of reflecting on and bringing these strands together, let us draw some inferences from the emergence, over the past two decades, of a real international discussion around global migration governance. The following paragraphs are this author's thoughts after a four-decade research career on migration policies and a six-year mandate as the United Nations Special Rapporteur on the Human Rights of Migrants.

The reader will draw from this volume the understanding that many current migration policies aiming at containing migration will not succeed at their narrow-minded objectives and that their negative consequences for migrants cannot be termed "unintended consequences" anymore. States will repeat the same strategic mistakes until they realize that migrants need to be "governed" as human beings, not simply "managed" as goods, services, or capital. This will mean implementing the principle at the root of all human rights, Immanuel Kant's categorical imperative: "Act in such a way that you treat humanity, whether in your own person or in the person of any other, never merely as a means to an end, but always at the same time as an end."

At some point in the future, states will have to recognize that closing their borders to low-wage labour migration after the oil shocks of the '70s and '80s was a disaster, of which they are still prisoners. Closing borders is rarely an appropriate answer to external events, as was shown during the COVID-19 pandemic, when the World Health Organization (WHO) repeatedly warned states against imposing such measures. Blocking low-wage labour migration when millions of employers are willing to hire them creates, sustains, and subsidizes exploitative labour markets where these migrants are victims at the hands of many actors: employers, recruiters, smugglers, moneylenders, landlords, and others. Clandestinity and marginality generate criminal exploitation. If the state does not take charge of the mobility market, other actors will. This was the case of alcohol and tobacco smuggling and is still mostly the case for drug smuggling.

In this sense, migrant smuggling is entirely policy induced. The prohibition policies of receiving states are largely responsible for the violence and criminality that develops in this underground mobility business. At the same time, states themselves not only generate the conditions for irregularity by tightly limiting cross-border mobility, but do so in full knowledge that their domestic economies often depend on the presence of all migrants – documented or not – to function. We must recognize that crossing a border without papers or forgetting to renew a work or residence permit are not crimes, but simple administrative offences of little political or security importance, which regularization of status should remove and whose sanction should be limited at most to a fine. Policies of "zero tolerance" should be replaced by policies of risk minimization and crime reduction. Devoting obscene amounts of money in border closures is not a productive investment. Increased public spending on restrictive immigration controls has not resulted in reduced migration, but has undoubtedly generated vast criminal underground markets and exacted an enormous human cost that has been borne most directly by migrants.

Let us explore why we are currently at such an impasse. Globalization has led to the relocation of manufacturing sectors to benefit from lower labour costs in low-income countries. For the non-delocalizable economic sectors – agriculture, construction, mining, hospitality, fisheries, domestic care, and services – we have relocated working conditions from low-income countries to more advanced economies. These transformations have come to define today's global political economy, in the North as in the South.

The combination of repressive migration policies and a lack of enforcement of labour rights for migrant workers has led to precarity for these workers, based on the fear of being sent back empty-handed to the country of origin. This socially constructed precarity has allowed a considerable reduction in the cost of labour in these sectors – an indirect subsidy generated by state-enforced measures. This precarity is today structural and constitutes a conscious strategy for the reduction of the cost of labour, everywhere in the countries receiving immigration, North and South. We have thus recreated a *lumpenproletariat*, in the niche previously occupied by the nineteenth century industrial workers, the indentured labourers of the British Empire, and the slaves of other regimes.

On the one hand, repressive policies against undocumented migrants have targeted these workers, not their employers. Yet it is precisely the pull factor of the job offers that attracts migrants. They would not come if there were no jobs for them. On the other hand, states have developed single-employer temporary legal migration programs that all too often create the same precarity: kafala in the Middle East, sponsorship in Canada or Australia, "closed" work permits, etc. The combination of migration policies that induce fear of deportation and practices of non-application of labour law results in the creation of lawless zones in which migrants are exploited without being able to protest. Despite all the agency they demonstrate to survive and support their families, the fear of dismissal and deportation prevents them from mobilizing, publicly protesting, suing in complaint mechanisms or the courts, or unionizing.

No marginalized group has ever had its rights handed to it by the majority on a silver platter: workers, women, Indigenous peoples, the LGBTQIA+ community, minorities, detainees, and many others have had to fight publicly for the recognition of their rights. Migrants do not have the right to vote and therefore do not count in the context of public debate. Unlike citizens, they can neither reward nor punish politicians. The political class is free to say whatever is politically useful against them, since the electorate is not enlightened about the relevant issues as there is no inclusion and effective participation of migrants themselves in the public debate. We cannot even blame most politicians: warts and all, electoral democracies are the best political system ever invented and politicians – even the best ones – are spurred by electoral pressure.

Migration policies are thus made by non-migrants (elected politicians) for non-migrants (the electorate), just as policies toward women have long been made by committees of men. That is, those setting government agendas do not know what they are talking about, and migration policies are reduced to an electoral issue, being too often based on populist prejudices, myths, fantasies, and fears that are conveyed in the public debate, without contradiction, for lack of opposition. This is particularly evident in the prominent role the "security fantasy" plays in discussions of migration, where migrants are increasingly framed as a pernicious – if not existential – threat.

Yet another policy framework is possible and the 2018 Global Compact for Safe, Orderly, and Regular Migration (GCM) outlines how this may be realized. This pact is the first truly universal instrument on migration. It was negotiated by states: 152 United Nations General Assembly member states approved it. A soft law instrument, it creates a conceptual framework, a long-term game plan, for the coming decades. We should not expect major results in the short term. This is especially the case as it often suggests the opposite of what most states are doing today. But this gap between the principles and values it articulates and contemporary state practice should not be taken to undermine its importance.

Consider the Universal Declaration of Human Rights of 1948, a similarly nonbinding instrument which, for the first time, articulated the principles and values of human rights at the global level. It took eighteen years to adopt the two international covenants: the International Covenant on Civil and Political Rights and the International Covenant on Economic, Social and Cultural Rights, then another eighteen years for the Convention against Torture, then twenty-two years for the Convention on Enforced Disappearances, to take only these examples of how today's international human rights regime came into being. One hopes that the GCM will gradually engender a culture of migrants' rights, just as the Universal Declaration created a culture of human rights.

The central recommendation of the GCM is to "facilitate" mobility. In the negotiated English version, this term appears sixty-two times! Realizing this recommendation will be the greatest challenge for all of those who care about migrants' rights in the years to come.

In unpacking how its recommendations ought to be realized, the GCM proposes twenty-three objectives. Most of them aim at integrating migrants, decriminalizing their activities, and respecting their rights. Here are a few of the states' political commitments: to enhance availability and flexibility of pathways for regular migration; to facilitate family reunification; to facilitate fair and ethical recruitment and safeguard conditions that ensure decent work; to facilitate changes of employer and modification of conditions or length of stay, without unnecessary red tape, and without fear of arbitrary deportation; to facilitate regularization of status; to include migrants in crisis preparedness, emergency response, and evacuation measures; to save lives; to use immigration detention only as a measure of last resort and work toward alternatives; to provide access to basic services for migrants, regardless of their migration status, including by instituting "firewalls" between public agencies; to empower migrants and societies to realize full inclusion and social cohesion; to eliminate all forms of discrimination and promote evidence-based public discourse to shape perceptions of migration; and to invest in skills development and facilitate mutual recognition of skills, qualifications, and competences, at all skill levels.

We must therefore aim for a normally regulated labour market that allows migrants to come and look for work, provides equal protection for the rights of all workers, regardless of their migration status, and gives all migrant workers a voice in negotiating their working conditions. However, these goals cannot be achieved overnight. Forty years of cheap labour practices in non-delocalizable sectors cannot be erased instantaneously, or else entire economic sectors will collapse under the weight of increased labour costs. These sectors will require a longer transition, with investments to support them during this modernization process, as has been done for other industries.

Unfortunately, there is no long-term strategic planning for human mobility in any country. Our governments plan strategically for twenty, thirty, or fifty years in all other areas of governance: infrastructure, urban development, transport, energy, food security, health, education, environment, etc. In contrast, migration policies are almost always reactive to current events: "we need IT workers now," "we need to stop illegal aliens now," etc. Such changes thus depend on the mood of the mobilizable electorate. For the most part, the constituency that is most vocal on migration issues is essentially made up of citizens who oppose immigration – an electorate courted by all politicians, left and right. Most citizens have other priorities when elections come around.

However, as the GCM invites us to do, we will have to think about human mobility in the long term. To do so, we will have to ask ourselves collectively some difficult questions. What population do we want to have on these planned horizons, in terms of numbers for geopolitical reasons, but also in terms of skills for economic reasons? How should we account for the loss of creativity of an aging population, as well as a growing need for care work? How can we ensure the maintenance of the standard of living and compensate for the differences in wealth? How to better manage social diversity in all its components: age, gender, ethnicity, religion, etc.? How should we respond to migration emergencies, caused by violence or the environment?

This kind of debate requires the participation of all those affected by these issues. All ministries, all social actors, all institutions, all citizens. This is what the GCM calls "whole-of-government" and "whole-of-society" approaches. In particular, we need to hear from migrants themselves – whatever their status – to bring their lived experience to the debate, as a reality check. Migrants also need a #MeToo movement – in the sense of a broader societal reckoning with perspectives and experiences that have remained marginalized and ignored for far too long. A key condition for enabling this debate is to reduce the constructed precarity of migrants and to ensure their empowerment, to bring migrants out of the margins and give them "papers" and a regularized status, to recognize the legitimacy of their "voice," to provide them with the means to express themselves and to participate in public debates, without the fear of deportation.

As I have suggested above, today's migrant workers correspond exactly to the industrial workers of the nineteenth century whose collective efforts invented trade unions and brought about the much-needed reform of labour law. Together with other actors – nongovernmental organizations (NGOs), lawyers, social workers, health care workers, educators – unions could powerfully carry the voice of migrant workers.

From this concern to hear the "voice" of migrants, we will have to develop a strategic plan extending over one or more decades, with precise benchmarks, and foresee the necessary investments to reach these goals. Important components of this agenda should include: progressively apply labour laws to all migrant workers in all sectors; strengthen the mission of labour inspectorates and public officials responsible for monitoring working conditions; sanction exploitative employers; offer more and more work permits to foreigners who request them; not discourage unionization, but actively enable migrant worker organization; regularize most undocumented workers; reform the temporary worker recruitment industry; combat negative stereotypes; facilitate access to permanent residence and nationality. These objectives should of course be developed with the input and participation of those most directly affected by them, especially migrants themselves.

A thoughtful and collective approach will achieve several goals: meet the demographic needs of many countries; gradually increase the economic and social contribution of migrants; ease pressures on asylum systems by facilitating refugees' access to immigration mechanisms; diminish the power of criminal networks by reducing precarity; increase the border control capacity; and reduce anti-immigration sentiments across societies.

Human mobility will not abate. Growing inequality and environmental challenges will increase migration pressure. Closing borders is and will remain a costly and ineffective response. To get out of the repressive spiral, we must accept that governing mobility is not about prohibiting it. It means legalizing, regulating, and taxing it. It means investing in a governance infrastructure that accelerates the response to the many needs we confront across our societies by relying on the ingenuity of migrants themselves and that offers them pathways to integration, for the benefit of all. This transition must take place in the context of regional and international cooperation. No state can liberalize mobility alone. The role of free-movement areas such as the EU, MERCOSUR, Economic Community of West African States (ECOWAS), Southern African Development Community (SADC), and the African Union will be decisive as models of what needs to be done on a global scale.

Facilitating mobility means progressively making it simpler, safer, faster, and cheaper, for both migrants and host societies.

Contributors

KIRAN BANERJEE is associate professor of political science and Canada Research Chair in Forced Migration Governance and Refugee Protection at Dalhousie University. His current research addresses global migration governance with a focus on the role of international institutions and domestic political actors in responding to forced displacement. Before joining Dalhousie University, he was a faculty member in the Department of Political Studies at the University of Saskatchewan.

GEOFFREY CAMERON is assistant professor in the Department of Political Science at McMaster University. He is the author of *Send Them Here: Religion, Politics, and Refugee Resettlement in North America* (McGill-Queen's University Press, 2021) and co-editor of *Strangers to Neighbours: Refugee Sponsorship in Context* (McGill-Queen's University Press, 2020) with Shauna Labman.

ALISE COEN is associate professor of political science and chair of the Public and Environmental Affairs Unit at the University of Wisconsin Green Bay. Her research focuses on global governance, refugees, human rights, and US foreign policy. Her articles have appeared in *International Relations, Ethics & International Affairs, Politics & Religion*, and *The International Journal of Human Rights*. Her book, *Reconfiguring Refugees: The U.S. Retreat from Responsibility-Sharing*, is forthcoming with New York University Press.

FRANÇOIS CRÉPEAU is professor and Hans & Tamar Oppenheimer Chair in Public International Law at the Faculty of Law of McGill University, as well as the director of the McGill Centre for Human Rights and Legal Pluralism. He was the United Nations Special Rapporteur on the Human Rights of Migrants from 2011 to 2017. He has given many presentations and keynotes, published numerous articles, and written, edited, or co-edited ten books. In addition to this, he is a member of several editorial boards: *Journal of Refugee Studies*, *International Journal of Refugee Law*, *Refuge*, *Droits fondamentaux*, *European Journal of Human Rights*, *Inter Gentes – McGill Journal of International Law & Legal Pluralism*.

BRUNO DUPEYRON is professor at the Johnson-Shoyama Graduate School of Public Policy, University of Regina Campus. His major research interests are border and immigration issues, using political sociology and comparative perspectives.

ELIZABETH FERRIS is a research professor at the Institute for the Study of International Migration at Georgetown University. Previously she worked at the World Council of Churches in Geneva, the Brookings Institution, and several nongovernmental organizations (NGOs) and universities. She has published extensively on refugee and migration issues. Her latest book, *Refugees, Migration and Global Governance: Negotiating the Global Compacts* (with Katharine Donato) was published by Routledge in 2019.

JOSEPH GARCEA was a full professor in the Department of Political Studies at the University of Saskatchewan, where he taught courses on politics, public policy, public management, local and regional governance, and diversity management. His research agenda included a variety of projects related to Canadian immigration, settlement, integration and citizenship policies and programs. Joseph tragically passed in November of 2020.

ANDREW GEDDES is professor of migration studies and director of the Migration Policy Centre at the European University Institute, Florence, Italy. His most recent book, *Governing Migration Beyond the State: Europe, North America, South America and Southeast Asia in a Global Context*, was published by Oxford University Press in 2021.

ISABEL GIL-EVERAERT is a postdoctoral research fellow at El Colegio de México. She holds a PhD in sociology from the Graduate Center of the City University of New York (CUNY) and an MA in humanities and social thought from New York University (NYU). Her main research interests are international migration, refugees and asylum seekers, inequality, gender, and qualitative research methods. Her work has been published in the *Journal of Ethnic and Migration Studies*, the *Journal on Migration and Human Security*, and *Metropolitics*.

REY KOSLOWSKI is professor of political science, University at Albany, State University of New York (SUNY). He has published extensively on international migration and world politics including on topics such as human mobility and state formation, dual nationality, European Union citizenship, human smuggling, border control technologies, diasporic politics, and global mobility regimes.

SHAUNA LABMAN is executive director of Global College and associate professor of human rights, University of Winnipeg. She is the author of *Crossing Law's Border: Canada's Refugee Resettlement Program* (UBC Press, 2019) and co-editor of *Strangers to Neighbours: Refugee Sponsorship in Context* (McGill-Queen's University Press, 2020) with Geoffrey Cameron.

GEOFF LECKEY holds a BA and MA in modern languages from St Catharine's College, University of Cambridge. He is a former career civil servant in the Canadian federal government where, as a practitioner and policymaker, he has over thirty years of experience in developing and leading key programs in complex national and international environments.

ANA MARTÍN GIL is the research manager of the Edward P. Djerejian Center for the Middle East at Rice University's Baker Institute. Her research interests include human rights and sustainability, as well as refugee rights and migration management with a focus on the Middle East and North Africa (MENA) region and Central America. She is a graduate of Rice University's Master of Global Affairs program.

LEA MATHESON is currently working on a PhD at the Balsillie School of International Affairs, Wilfrid Laurier University. Previously she served for over fifteen years with the International Organization for Migration (IOM), including as deputy permanent observer in New York and senior humanitarian policy adviser at the IOM headquarters in Geneva.

NICHOLAS R. MICINSKI is Libra Assistant Professor of Political Science and International Affairs at the University of Maine. His research focuses on global governance, particularly how states and international organizations respond to refugees, migration, climate change, and peacebuilding. His most recent book, *Delegating Responsibility: International Cooperation on Migration in the European Union*, was published by University of Michigan Press in 2022.

KELSEY P. NORMAN is a fellow at the Edward P. Djerejian Center for the Middle East at Rice University's Baker Institute and director of the Women's Rights, Human Rights and Refugees program. Her research focuses on refugee and migration issues in the Middle East and globally, as well as women's rights, human rights, comparative political institutions, international relations, and Middle East and North African politics. Her book, *Reluctant Reception: Refugees, Migration, and Governance in the Middle East and North Africa*, was published by Cambridge University Press in 2021.

OLGA ODGERS-ORTIZ is a sociologist whose principal research interests are in the crossroads of migration, religion, and health, focusing on the experience of migrants trapped in mobility in the US-Mexico border. Recently she has been principal investigator for research on a range of interventions provided by the Evangelical Rehabilitation Centers for Drug Addicts in Baja California Border Region (Conacyt) and co-investigator (with Thomas Csordas) for the project *Tracing Mobility and Care Trajectories: Migrants and Asylum Seekers' Experiences at the US-Mexico border* (PIMSA).

OLGA OLIVAS-HERNÁNDEZ is an anthropologist with research expertise in the US-Mexico border region. Some of the research areas she has explored are new spiritualities, mental health and migration, substance use/abuse, as well as treatment and healing systems in different cultural contexts. She has a PhD in social sciences with an emphasis in social anthropology from CIESAS Occidente, Mexico. Recent research projects include: embodiment and subjectivity in religious treatments for drug abuse; life trajectories and substance abuse among Mexican migrants at the US-Mexico Border; and cultural perceptions of emotional wellbeing and patterns of help-seeking in Tijuana, Mexico. Currently, she is researching health and migration trajectories among asylum seekers stranded in mobility in Northern Mexico.

LUICY PEDROZA is a professor at the Center for International Studies (CEI) at El Colegio de México. She holds a doctorate in political science from the University of Bremen (summa cum laude). Her research focuses on migration policies from a comparative perspective, citizenship and migration, transnationalism in Europe, Asia, Latin-America and the Caribbean. Her recent publications include the co-edited volumes *Revising the Integration-Citizenship Nexus in Europe* (Springer, 2023) and *The Intersection of* Foreign *Policy and Migration Policy in Mexico Today* (El Colegio de México, 2021), the monograph *Citizenship Beyond Nationality: Immigrants' Right to Vote Across the World* (University of Pennsylvania

Press, 2019), and articles in *Democratization, Global Policy, International Migration*, and the *Journal of Ethnic and Migration Studies*, among other journals. She is a co-coordinator of Standing Committee on Migration, Citizenship and Political Participation of the IMISCOE international network of migration researchers.

SCOTT PRUYSERS is associate professor in the Department of Political Science at Dalhousie University. His research considers how political parties organize and operate as well as how party members and ordinary citizens interact with party and electoral politics.

ELOY RIVAS-SÁNCHEZ is assistant professor of sociology in the Faculty of Humanities and Social Sciences at Athabasca University. His research interrogates how ideologies, social structures, and institutional practices affect the lives and well-being of vulnerable populations, and how those affected enact agency to overcome domination, disrespect, and dehumanization.

TOBIAS GERHARD SCHMINKE is a PhD candidate in the Department of Political Science at Dalhousie University. His research focuses on party systems, political parties, and voting behaviour.

CRAIG DAMIAN SMITH is the cofounder and executive director of Pairity, an organization applying data-driven solutions to support refugee resettlement and measure the impacts of community sponsorship programs. He is also a research affiliate at York University's Centre for Refugee Studies, where he researches asylum and irregular migration trends. He was previously senior research associate at the Canada Excellence Research Chair in Migration and Integration Program at Toronto Metropolitan University and associate director of the Global Migration Lab at the Munk School of Global Affairs and Public Policy at the University of Toronto.

ZACK TAYLOR is associate professor of political science and public administration at Western University. He specializes in urban political economy and Canadian and comparative politics and policymaking, with an empirical focus on historical and contemporary multilevel governance of cities. Taylor also pursues parallel interests in municipal campaigns and elections, local public finance, and political geography.

TRIADAFILOS TRIADAFILOPOULOS is associate professor of political science at the University of Toronto. He teaches courses in public policy at the University of Toronto Scarborough and the Munk School of Global Affairs and Public Policy, and conducts research in the areas of immigration and citizenship policy in Europe and North America.

RUBEN ZAIOTTI is associate professor in the Department of Political Science, Dalhousie University, as well as director of the Dalhousie Jean Monnet European Union Centre of Excellence and Jean Monnet Chair in Public Diplomacy. He is the author of *Cultures of Border Control: Schengen and the Evolution of European Frontiers* (2011), editor of the collected volume *Externalizing Migration Management: Europe, North America and the Spread of 'Remote Control' Practices* (2016) and other publications in leading peer-reviewed journals.

Index

Page numbers in **bold** indicate tables, while page numbers in *italics* indicate figures.